Leo Braudy
The Frenzy of Renown

Leo Braudy has written extensively on British and American literature, film criticism, and cultural history. His comments on contemporary cultural events and persons have appeared in newspapers, magazines, radio, and on television. Among other awards, he has received a Guggenheim as well as a National Endowment for the Humanities Senior Scholar Fellowship. Now the Bing Professor of English at the University of Southern California, he has previously taught at Yale, Columbia, and Johns Hopkins Universities.

THE FRENZY
OF RENOWN
Fame & Its History

Leo Braudy

VINTAGE BOOKS

A Division of Random House, Inc.

New York

Grateful acknowledgment is made to the following for permission to reprint previously published material: *Harvard University Press:* Excerpts from poems #3, #290,
#303, and poems #288 and #441 from *The Poems of Emily Dickinson*, edited by
Thomas H. Johnson (Cambridge, Mass.: The Belknap Press of Harvard University
Press), copyright © 1951, 1955, 1979, 1983 by the President and Fellows of Harvard
College. Reprinted by permission of the publishers and the Trustees of Amherst Col-
lege. *Harvard University Press* and *Little, Brown and Company:* Poem #544, and ex-
cerpts from poems #567 and #709 from *The Poems of Emily Dickinson*, edited by
Thomas H. Johnson (Cambridge, Mass.: The Belknap Press of Harvard University
Press), copyright © 1951, 1955, 1979, 1983 by the President and Fellows of Harvard
College; and from *The Complete Poems of Emily Dickinson*, edited by Thomas H.
Johnson (Boston: Little, Brown and Company), copyright 1929 by Martha Dickinson
Bianchi, copyright renewed 1957, 1963 by Mary L. Hampson. Reprinted by permis-
sion of Harvard University Press and the Trustees of Amherst College and Little,
Brown and Company. *Little, Brown and Company:* Excerpt from poem #789 and
poem #1354 from *The Complete Poems of Emily Dickinson*, edited by Thomas H.
Johnson, copyright 1929 by Martha Dickinson Bianchi, copyright renewed 1957, 1963
by Mary L. Hampson. Reprinted by permission of Little, Brown and Company.

Library of Congress Cataloging-in-Publication Data
Braudy, Leo.
The frenzy of renown : fame & its history / Leo Braudy.
p. cm.
Originally published: New York :
Oxford University Press, 1986.
Includes bibliographical references and index.
ISBN 978-0-679-77630-7
1. Fame. I. Title.
BJ1470.5.B73   1997
306.4—dc21   97-5434
CIP

Random House Web address: http://www.randomhouse.com

Printed in the United States of America
10   9   8   7

For Dorothy,
Never finished, always complete

Preface

We live in a society bound together by the talk of fame. But it is the argument of this book that fame has a past as well as a present. We did not invent fame. It has a history that has decisively shaped our understanding of what it means. To document this history thoroughly would require the work of at least a lifetime, since everything preserved for us from the past can in some sense be considered a message that perpetuates someone's fame. My goal instead has been to map the major routes and important byways of this constant theme in the history of Western society. Such a mapping must cross the boundaries of many different specialized areas of knowledge. I have therefore tried to respect the current state of learning, without becoming too minutely involved in the swarms of controversy that preoccupy those with far greater expertise in such matters than I possess— or to which I aspire. Readers more deeply acquainted with some of these issues will notice that I do take sides in many long-standing discussions, for example, the degree of premeditation in the career of Julius Caesar, the order of composition of the Gospels, and the influence of Dante's *Divine Comedy* on Chaucer's *The House of Fame*. But, more often than not, I am led to such interpretations by my own developing argument about the changing nature of fame. My interests therefore give me an angle on these intriguing issues when I arrive at them. But I have not shaped the book in accordance with a preliminary study of them.

In order that the work be finished, if not completed, I have had to be ruthless in my inclusions and rely on advice and counsel to justify my omissions. Books like this, which attempt to sketch the evolution of a basic cultural theme, cannot be written without the immense aid of the vast and sophisticated historical scholarship that has developed over the last two hundred years. To accomplish even this much, I have had to call on the knowledge of specialists in a wide variety of fields and disciplines, both through their written work and through the greater courtesy of personal comments and suggestions. As Edward Gibbon writes in *The Decline and Fall of the Roman Empire*:

> . . . in the contemplation of a minute and remote object, I am not ashamed to borrow the aid of the strongest glasses (vol. 4, chap. 47, 106 n. 1).

I owe a considerable debt both to these writers, whom I identify in my notes and bibliographic entries, as well as to the many colleagues and friends who helped me find my way through such a voluminous literature.

The references at the end of this book indicate those works from which I have quoted or to which I had alluded, as well as those secondary works that I have found particularly helpful. I am grateful also for the opportunities I have had over the years to present some of these ideas in lectures at many universities. The National Endowment for the Humanities and the John Simon Guggenheim Memorial Foundation funded some of my early research, and I would also like to thank *Raritan Review* for publishing an earlier version of the section on Jesus.

I first began thinking about the ideas behind this book more than ten years ago in New York City, where faces and names are pressed upon you at every moment. I wrote it in Baltimore—a more quiet and reclusive place, whose distance from the rush of ambition engendered its share of detachment. I complete the final revision in Los Angeles—where the flocking to fame coexists atmospherically with a sense of being on the border of an eruptive nature that cares little for human aspiration. All three cities contributed their own special ambiance to the work, but friends and colleagues contributed more tangible goods. The enthusiasm of Erwin Glikes, first at Harper & Row and later at Simon & Schuster, helped me to cast the book into its early shapes. Bill Sisler at Oxford University Press drew on his own high energy and enthusiasm to bring it to publication. Faced with the task of editing the copy, Andy Yockers and Henry Krawitz have responded with a ferocious and fruitful attention to both its details and its whole, as have Margery Schwartz, who closely and thoroughly read the proofs, and Nick Humez, who brought both his care and his expertise to the making of the index. In the years this book has taken, my agent, Maxine Groffsky, has similarly contributed more than anyone could expect in the way of support and patience.

Hardly anyone to whom I spoke while researching and writing this book failed to contribute to it in some way. For their special help I would like to thank the following people in particular, among the many who supplied references, shared ideas, asked intriguing questions, and read sections of the manuscript: John Baldwin, William Cain, Jerome Christensen, Diskin Clay, Jane Cody, Vincent Crapanzano, Elizabeth Ferriter, Stanley Fish, David Fitzgerald, George Fitzgerald, Harris Friedberg, Allen Grossman, Susan Hartt, Jeffrey Henderson, Sandra Hindman, Peter Kafer, Herbert Kessler, Jane Kramer, Jerome McGann, Jay Martin, Dan Menaker, Raoul Middleman, Stephen Orgel, Annabel Patterson, Lee Patterson, Richard Poirier, John Pollini, Naomi Rand, Paula Rome, Stuart Rome, Frank Romer, David St. John, Elaine Scarry, Gordon Stewart, Jane Tompkins, Steve Weisman, Fred White, and Jonathan Yardley. Beth Blum, Jeffrey Burbank, Sonia Maasik, and Frank Donoghue helped track down often elusive facts for me. Nadja Awad helped collect the illustrations from a wide variety of sources, a task made immeasurably easier by the courtesy and knowledge of the curatorial staffs at the many museums and repositories, among whom I would like to mention Victor Ingrassia of the University of Southern California Art Library, Alan Jutzi and Susan Naulty of the Huntington Library, Cheryl Robertson of the Henry Francis du Pont Winterthur Museum, Wendy Wick Reaves and Will Stapp of the National Portrait Gallery, Cathy Lorber of Numismatic Fine Arts, and Rick Bucci of the Mark Twain Project. At crucial points in its genesis, the manuscript was quickly and expertly typed by Elizabeth Carroll at The Johns Hopkins University and Yvette Soto at the University of Southern California.

Finally, I dedicate this book to my wife, Dorothy, without whose insight and clarity it would never have achieved whatever coherence and point it has. Although I began the work when both my parents were alive and vigorous, neither has lived to see its completion. But their loss impresses on me still more the feeling that writing this book has nurtured: In the heart of aspiration is the desire for recognition by those whose approval is unconditional and therefore need never be sought, but also can never be assumed.

Contents

I

THE URGE
TO BE UNIQUE

Introduction

Man, out of man, will make himselfe a frame,
Seekes outward helpe, and borrowes that of Fame.
—FULKE GREVILLE,
An Inquisition Upon Fame and Honour

"What is honor?" asked Falstaff and answered "a word." With such an understanding of the way the name, look, and gesture of honor were becoming more important than the thing itself, he would hardly be surprised by our own preoccupation with the democratic descendant of honor, fame. What is honor? What is fame? A name? A face? The "it" in "making it"? Every day, from every corner of the world, faces and names pour into our eyes and ears. If we read, if we see, if we hear, we cannot escape the flood of human images that, desired or not, forces itself upon us. Some few last for a lifetime and beyond, most for no longer than it takes to scratch their initials on the walls of our attention. And yet all this effort, substantial as much as trivial, is done in the name of what is called fame.

"How many times do I have to kill before I get a name in the paper or some national attention?" complained a murderer in a letter to the Wichita police. Only with his sixth killing, he continued, had he begun to get his due in publicity (AP, 12 February 1978). In a cursory reading of any daily newspaper, it is easy to find similar stories that illustrate the various insanities to which individuals have been driven by the lust for recognition. Who knows whether the urge to fame drove this man to murder or his murderous nature found the language of fame-seeking a comfortable 'normality' to wrap around himself? But it is clear that, particularly since World War Two, the increasing number and sophistication of the ways information is brought to us have enormously expanded the ways of being known. In the process the concept of fame has been grotesquely distended, and the line between public achievement and private pathology grown dimmer as the claims grow more bizarre.

In great part the history of fame is the history of the changing ways by which individuals have sought to bring themselves to the attention of others and, not incidentally, have thereby gained power over them. But few self-assertions, especially those staged in public, are ever wholly original. From the beginning fame has required publicity. Alexander the Great ostentatiously imitated Achilles among other gods and heroes; Julius Caesar mourned that he had not done as much as Alexander; and murderer said he was moved by the same force that drove Jack Ripper. Each learned about his chosen precursor through some medium of communication. Whatever political or social or psychological factors influence the desire to be famous, they are enhanced by and feed upon the available means of reproducing the image. In the past that medium was usually literature, theater, or public monuments. With the Renaissance came painting and engraved portraits, and the modern age has added photography, radio, movies, and television. As each new medium of fame appears, the human image it conveys is intensified and the number of individuals celebrated expands. Shadowed by such powerfully evocative images, the daily reality of someone who is not famous in those terms often seems inadequate. Not long ago the *New York Times* ran a story about the problems of ranching in Wyoming. After recounting the adventurous life of one rancher, the impressed big-city reporter asked him to describe himself. "Well," said the rancher, stroking one leathery cheek, "I suppose you could say I'm one of those Marlboro Men."

Up through the Middle Ages clothes were a costume denoting one's place in a strict, though complex, social hierarchy in which individual nature was staged against the backdrop of inherited form. Chaucer may give a wonderfully precise portrait of his Monk, but all those details find their meaning primarily in the context of the Monk's social role. With the Renaissance, however, comes a fascination with creating one's own costume. In the terminology of the anthropologist Edward Hall, the media are "extensions" of the man, ways of increasing the scope of the senses. But in the history of fame the more elaborate extensions of human images often hinder self-awareness instead of expanding it. Our sense of wholeness is as fragmented by the media we use as it is by the media hurled at us. By now, in a society so suffused with images, the tricks and gestures of the surface have become easily detachable from whatever substance they once signified. Fame shades imperceptibly into fashion, while fashion, in its turn, spawns and then discards an infinite parade of superficial distinctions. In a world of crew cuts and good grooming, beards and long hair may imply antiestablishment politics. Soon enough, however, they adorn Ku Klux Klan members, college professors, and plumbers. Similarly, impressionists and mimics, who build careers by becoming a succession of specifically recognizable others, could hardly have existed before radio. And who can measure with precision the congealed role playing encouraged in each of us by the invention of the telephone?

Now that there are so many ways for names and faces to appear in public, the meaning of that appearance seems less and less personal. When each occupation, neighborhood, or club has its own events, publications, and T-shirts, fame also carries with it a comfortable element of familiarity. The fame of others, their distinguishing marks, becomes a common coin of human exchange—code words more forceful (and easier to express) than mutual political or religious beliefs for establishing intimacy. Similarly, the self-exposing and self-asserting gestures we learn from the famous become licensed for our own use. As we have a collage vision fostered by the rapidly escalating demands on our attention, so we have collage personalities made up of fragments of public people who are, in turn, made from fragments themselves—polished, denatured, simplified. In old documentaries the people being interviewed often regard the camera with wary hostility. It was an intrusion into their privacy and sense of self. Now, of course, it can be considered an enhancement. The passerby on the street naturally smiles broadly, gives an opinion, and even calls the interviewer by his or her first name. Armed by their vocational belief in publicity (more virtuously referred to as "the public's right to know"), television reporters never hesitate to ask a grieving parent, "How does it feel to lose a child?" The most personal tragedy will be soothed, for the audience if not for the individual, when the mourner can be assured a spot on the "11 O'Clock News."

Through the technology of image reproduction and information reproduction, our relation to the increasing number of faces we see every day becomes more and more transitory, and "famous" seems as devalued a term as "tragic." If these are famous, we may wonder, then what is fame? They certainly don't seem as permanent as the famous of the past, those names that echo in our minds—Alexander, Caesar, Cleopatra, Jesus, Mohammed, Joan of Arc, Shakespeare. But fame gives and fame takes away. In part it celebrates uniqueness, and in part it requires that uniqueness be exemplary and reproducible. What special individuals pioneered, many can imitate. Religion and morality may counsel that subordination of the self is the only way to both personal peace and social justice. But every newspaper constantly brings the message of assertion, without which, it is said, personal security is impossible. The choice seems absolute: Everything (and everyone) that fails to progress is doomed to decay. What only kings could accomplish in the past is now available to aspirants of more modest means. The impact of the face of Alexander the Great on a coin where only those of gods and mythical heroes had been before becomes thinned out in a million fleeting images on the evening news, images that reach a larger audience than Alexander could touch in his lifetime— or for long after.

Societies always generate a number of people willing and eager to live at least part of their lives in the public eye. The larger, more heterogeneous, and democratic a society is, the more such public people there will be aiming for the security of such a secular eternity. In a society committed to progress, the seeking of fame, the climbing of the ladder of renown, expresses something essential in that society's nature. Even the more grotesque forms of ostentation are connected to normal desires to be known for one's talents or for oneself. Entertainers and politicians, who court public appreciation (and possible disapproval) on a grand scale, cannot be considered normal members of their society. But they are certainly extensions of what is normal, extensions of everyone's culturally fostered desire to be given his or her due.

Between the ideal (and safely dead) figures of the past and the infinite compromises and corruptions of the present appear the figures of contemporary fame—aspiring to a condition of achievement and recognition independent of the normal pressures of age and imperfection. Like a dim remembrance of unfallen purity, the dream of fame promises a place where private dreams of recognition triumphantly appear in public. Fame allows the aspirant to stand out of the crowd, but with the crowd's approval; in its turn, the audience picks out its own dear individuality in the qualities of its heroes. Famous people glow, it's often said, and it's a glow that comes from the number of times we have seen the images of their faces, now superimposed on the living flesh before us—not a radiation of divinity but the feverish effect of repeated impacts of a face upon our eyes. The ease with which we allow ourselves to be absorbed by such images, the desires to be that way ourselves, confirms that the essential lure of the famous is that they are somehow more real than we and that our insubstantial physical reality needs that immortal substance for support. Where the infinite reproductions of the faces of the famous mediate between us and whatever they have actually done, the urge to public fame has little necessary connection to the urge to recognition for worthy actions. Its goal becomes a state of being. In compensation for the erosions of life and death, the new media of the nineteenth and twentieth centuries thus create the modern dream of fame as a vision of wholeness, an effort to move outside the blare of publicity by using it for oneself, to be an object of attention rather than one of the mob of attention payers.

Not everyone can be famous. But much of our daily experience tells us that we should if we possibly can, because it is the best, perhaps the only, way *to be*. Fifteen hundred years ago, St. Augustine, turning his face against Roman public life, argued that the emptiness that comes from living exclusively in the eye of others could be filled with God. But even he wrestled with the desire to be praised openly for his denial of worldly values. In the present, more secular dilemma, a competitive world of job seeking and visible achievement implies that only some will be filled by fame, while the rest must be satisfied with lesser degrees of emptiness. In compensation we have the fame of others—people we might have been if fate or even choice had not deprived us. The great of the past are, of course, already complete: dead as bodies, undying as images. And when death takes the idols of the present away, they too will be translated to the highest realms of fame—forever untouched by the innumerable irritations that plague the fan.

In the heart of the fan and the famous alike, fame is a quiet place where one is free to be what one really is, one's true, unchanging essence. To be famous, goes the myth, is to rest in solitude, but without aloneness: like Achilles in his tent, sulking at Agamemnon's affront to his heroic nature, while the Greeks wonder if he will rejoin the battle; like Lindbergh in *The Spirit of St. Louis,* flying over the Atlantic, while the world waits for him to land. In this dream the will is finally free, untrammeled by social forms, the expectations of others, or the pressure of the past—bounded if at all only by the confines of nature.

The dream of fame in Western society has been inseparable from the ideal of personal freedom. As the world grows more complex, fame promises a liberation from powerless anonymity. In search of modern fame, we often enter a world of obvious fiction, in which all blemishes are smoothed and all wounds healed. It is the social version of a love that absolves the loved one of fault, restoring integrity and wholeness. Those whose fame depends least on anything specific are, in an image-conscious world, the most likely to be emulated. To be famous for yourself, for what you are without talent or premeditation, means you have come into your rightful inheritance. To be compared to Farrah Fawcett required only hair. In the face of fragmenting social demands, fame creates its own etiquette, allowing the famous to be themselves in a way no one else can afford to be, and to be accepted into a mystic community of other famous people, a psychic city of mutual respect for each other's individual nature. The celebration of true fame as a personal justification that allows the famous to relax in the company of those equally secure and complete runs through all fan magazines, gossip columns, and even the more soberly intended "personality" magazines that began appearing in the late 1970s. I remember one inept candid shot whose main point was to show Jacqueline Kennedy and Elizabeth Taylor in the same room together because, the caption noted with an air of disbelief, these women, whose faces had appeared on innumerable magazine covers, had somehow never met.

The roots of the urge to find the place of fame were particularly fertilized in the eighteenth century when a new-minted industrial age set the scene for individuals to make their way relatively unhampered by the traditions and restrictions of the past. But at the same time new standards for achievement had to be defined. Fame and success therefore became much more important than they had been in a time when the orders of society and the realms of the spirit were more fixed. From the eighteenth century to now, two variations of the same story indicate the close relation of the desire for fame to the uncertainty of personal identity. In one the hero's true and noble nature is discovered beneath his socially insignificant surface; in the other his truly despicable nature is discovered beneath his socially superficial manners. Whether the story is that of the prince in disguise or of Jekyll and Hyde, it dramatizes the gap between what a person is to society and what he is to himself. In the past, said Samuel Johnson in the eighteenth century, "man was of a piece." But the new age brought anxieties that only success could allay, when the struggling individual would be gathered into the realm of security and justification that he thought awaited him at the top of the ladder. Without a Napoleon, who rose from obscurity, there could be no one with a Napoleon complex, mad for a recognition that had been denied him.

In contemporary America, a country born seemingly without a past, the desire to be unprecedented—the old dream of fame in European history—

has become a national obsession, the only way out of increasingly complex political and economic dependence on others. Of course, the escape is illusory. But I am not talking about fame as an extreme *expression* of individuality so much as fame as the *appearance* of individuality, the more and more baroque costumes people assume in order to distinguish themselves in a more crowded, corporate, and collective world. As *The Guinness Book of Records* demonstrates, everything humans can do has been turned into something that humans can compete to do, with someone, whose name one hopes will not be misspelled, coming out on top, at least until the next edition. Fueled by such expectations, we look at the past and wonder why great men and women were ignored, when perhaps the society in which they lived did not value individual personal recognition the way we do; Achilles or Jesus could do the job for them. In the midst of the present frenzy, some passages in the past history of fame seem like calm retreats, worlds in which (it seems) satisfaction for accomplishment was secondary to accomplishment itself, in which doing was not totally superseded by telling what had been done, and in which the appreciation by a few, or even self-appreciation, was sufficient, without the need for an ever-expanding, perpetually unsatisfying audience.

But such Golden Ages of true worth and justified fame never existed. And in any case we would never have heard of them, since to trumpet one's disdain for fame, as we shall see, necessarily follows in the tracks of fame itself. Nor can the answer (if answer could be given) to the search for recognition be found in the nostalgia for a more compartmentalized and hierarchical society, where, as in present-day Russia and China or in medieval Europe, we would be satisfied with a few famous who appear in public to represent all. America poses the problem of self-importance in a constantly changing democratic society. In these terms a famous person has to be a socially acceptable individualist, different enough to be interesting, yet similar enough not to be threatening or destructive. Thus the urge to fame intensifies the basic conflict between society and individualism, and the paradoxes of fame come from the effort to balance thinking about oneself with the obligations of belonging to a society. That these paradoxes are becoming more obvious is due to the effort of both American and European culture to maintain a public rhetoric of individualism that offsets an increasingly pervasive web of institutional and corporate relations.

In the urge to find a better, more perfect self, the possibility of uncovering a worse, more misshapen one hangs like a threatening cloud. Lurking behind every chance to be made whole by fame is the axman of further dismemberment. Fame promises a freedom from worry about the opinions of others, only to trap the aspirer inside an even larger audience. Every beggar knows how to exploit the mingled contempt and obligation engendered in the person for the moment onstage. We applaud our heroes, and we condemn them. The speed with which a president can change from an authority to a scapegoat cannot help but reflect the styles of other public

icon Contrast

performers—the comedians who alternately insult and flatter the
ences, and the singers who are as contemptuous offstage as they are
tive and pleading onstage. Whatever the field, in public life fame is
tract between the audience and the aspirant, a contract that the fame
seeker often knows less about than do those who are asked to be his appreciators. As Clark Gable remarked to David Niven on hearing of the
mysterious death of the actress Thelma Todd:

> We all have a contract with the public—in us they see themselves or
> what they would like to be. . . . They love to put us on a pedestal
> and worship us. . . . But *they've* read the small print, and most of *us*
> haven't. . . . So, when we get knocked off by gangsters, like Thelma
> did, or get hooked on booze or dope or . . . just get sold . . . the
> public feels satisfied. Yeah, it's a good idea to read that small print
> (Niven, 22).

Gable's opinion of the implicit contract between public person and audience may be excessively gloomy. But his basic insight remains: Modern
fame is always compounded of the audience's aspirations and its despair,
its need to admire and to find a scapegoat for that need. To dismiss the
circus of contemporary notoriety with pat versions of Daniel Boorstin's
phrase, 'a celebrity is someone who is famous for being famous,' too easily
allows us to ignore the importance of even celebrity in shaping the values
of our society, not always for the worse.[1] Moralists from the classical Stoics down to the present have made great reputations for books denouncing
the desire to be recognized. In our own time, when preachers evangelize
about inner, spiritual truths, they do it on television.

We have become immensely sensitive to the subject of fame. Since the
late 1960s, its hazards have become obligatory fare in every celebrity interview. But that sensitivity has not yet brought very much understanding.
Julius Caesar, for example, would hardly be a phenomenon today, in a
world that has seen varieties of Caesarism as diverse as Napoleon, Hitler,
and Douglas MacArthur. But in the first century B.C., Caesar created a career as military politician that left a pattern for ages to come. To ask how
he and others—warriors, politicians, spiritual leaders, artists—were able to
make such an impact on the minds of men (and historians) can allow us
to take the measure of how our own minds were created and what has dictated our individual desires for achievement. The urge to fame occupies
that strange and vitally important area where matters of the spirit and matters of the flesh meet. It has therefore to be understood or at least approached both in its history and in its immediacy, as a reaction to society
we share with each other as well as with people long dead—a reaction that
has changed along with society itself.

1. This is a frequent misquotation. In fact, Boorstin's formulation is *"The celebrity
is a person who is well-known for his well-knownness"* (57). See his chapter on
"The Human Pseudo-event" in *The Image*. As the subtitle (*What Happened to the
American Dream*) suggests, Boorstin's book is a witty diatribe against the way media
culture has alienated Americans from true values. My own argument questions his
assumption that, say, heroism and its expression can ever really be fully separated.

*   *   *

See, I never did want to be a big mucky-star. At the Vendome they said, "You're going over so big—you get up on stage to play your solos and we'll give you more money." I thought it was stupid and I wouldn't do it. They said, "Look at what it'll mean to you." I didn't see what it'd mean. Finally they just put a light on me in the pit. If I'd gotten up there on the stage, people would say, "Shoot, he just wants to be a star, an individual," and even your own musicians you're playing with, you wouldn't get that same warmth. See, I tried to have fun as long as I could, but they wouldn't keep it that way. . . . You know you don't have no fun at all if you get too famous. . . . [T]he main thing is to live for that audience, live for the public.

—Louis Armstrong

The process of fame seemed much simpler and the special nature of the famous much easier to appreciate in the ages before the present crush of people awaiting their turn before the camera, in a time when the aspiration to fame implied imitating a hero's actions instead of smoking his brand of cigarettes. Or at least the terms of the competition were clearer, and the contenders ideal figures, not the locusts of today. But our involvement with the famous, as well as our dismemberment and absorption of them into our own natures, is hardly an invention of the twentieth century. Nor is it an indication of contemporary decadence or of our unseemly preoccupation with ourselves. The history of fame is also the history of the shifting definition of achievement in a social world, achievement often defined by the eyes of others, but just as often by their ostentatious absence. Both the extreme gestures and the high-minded denunciations of the urge for fame spring from the ambiguous heritage of a Western society devoted, on the one hand, to Roman and classical ideals of public service, civic virtue, and national glory and, on the other, to Judeo-Christian ideals of humbleness, modesty, spirituality, and private virtue. "Read the lives of great men" advised the principal of my father's Philadelphia high school to the graduates of 1921, echoing a preoccupation with the example of past heroes that is hardly distinctly American, yet has been given a distinctive intensity by America's historical myth of the new man in the new country. Jean Paul Sartre once remarked that American society was like a skyscraper (the Empire State or the Chrysler Building, he meant, not one of the Kleenex boxes of the 1960s): exactly the same floor to floor, until the top, where individuality with all its curlicues and baroque elaborations could flourish. But Sartre—to shift his architecture slightly—forgot to observe that for every Levittown of uniformity there are neighborhoods of the defiantly unzoned and hodgepodge. And within every Levittown grows the need to be different, nurtured on the outside appearance of sameness. In Europe individualism has been generally considered antisocial, while in America it seems encouraged by society, although subject to society's often-hidden terms. Every American therefore draws in each breath simultaneous urges to conformity and distinction. No other country, in the midst of creating a modern state, has so defiantly evolved so many institutionalized differences, so many ways of being outside. No other country so enforces the character-wrenching need to be assertive but polite, prideful but humble, unique but familiar, the great star and the kid next door. To the extent that we are all stars, waiting to be discovered, no one is very surprised to discover that stardom and shyness, public assertion and private withdrawal, are the twin offspring of the desire for fame and recognition.

Whether outside or inside, one always needs credentials, even if one has to issue them oneself. In this book I am attempting to explore the general and historical nature of fame, but for the last few pages—with their talk of the "contract" between performer and audience and their assertion of what "we" feel about fame and what fame does to "us"—I have become uneasy with the pose of objectivity that steals into language whenever one attempts to generalize. Before going on, then, I want to say something about the way I became personally aware of the mingled strands of individual assertion and social approval in the urge to fame, and how the book, with all its intended historical sweep, grew out of my personal situation.

Growing up in America, I had dimly realized that my own impulses toward achievement, which if written out would appear logically contradictory, yet within me gripped on all sides with perverse strength. I wanted to be the best, yet noted for my humility. I wanted to be individual and distinct, somewhat of a recluse, yet be praised and applauded when I appeared and did my stuff. The more I was aware of these paradoxical urges, the less they seemed understandable. Whenever one was uppermost, the other would appear with a dark, beckoning hand to lead it astray. When in the late 1960s it became fashionable for celebrities to complain about the burdens of their fame on television talk shows, I could bask in the feeling that my personal confusions were mirrored by those of many famous names.

These otherwise common musings were painfully focused in the fall of 1971, when I discovered in the accumulated summer mail the manuscript of a book my first wife had written about the breakup of our marriage. My first reaction was a twinge of pleasure. I had known she was going to write it, and I welcomed the possibility. These, after all, were the 1970s, the confessional years. Although, of course, my own divorce was special, yet divorce was an important social problem and mine therefore carried within it the impress of larger cultural forces. Like a fragment of DNA, with its own set of the genetic code, it might be a key to what was going on between men and women all over the country. Not only was my ex-wife doing something socially useful, it would help her career as well. And how could I stand in the way of that? I was sure she would make many mistakes. But then we could appear on a talk show to argue the whole thing out. In some sense such a book was the culmination of all the reasons why we had come to New York in the first place, she as a journalist, I as an English teacher. We had been nurtured on the central importance of literary fame and New York as the place to get it. To be in New York, still more to arrive in New York, was to compete for the spotlight. I had already believed that writing in the public eye—reviews, articles, books—was one of the highest forms of cultural achievement. To be put in a book oneself was the necessary next step.

Virtually without knowing it, I had crossed the line between an urge to fame for specific achievement and a desire for public recognition that would be protective and justifying in itself. Reading the manuscript, however, threw cold water on my cheery anticipation of the warming attention the book would bring: I was totally unprepared to discover what it means to be a character in someone else's scenario. I thought the book was self-absorbed and self-deceptive, a narcissistic act pretending to be a social act, a transparent bid for fame and power in the guise of a baring of the heart that concealed much more than it exposed. Any value that it might have was entirely in the areas of encouragement and support: 'You're doing well,' it said to the reader. 'I've had a much harder life, and yet I've written a famous book.'

As time went on, my own complicity in what my ex-wife had done became more obvious. Since I had to sign a release for the book and was not willing to resist its publication, I had a lawyer draw up a list of changes I wanted, to obscure incidents involving my second wife, to change the name of our cat, and to try as much as possible to reduce the harm to innocent bystanders. But I could hardly bring myself to ask her to change anything that had to do with me, no matter how inaccurate I thought it was. It was a penance for my own complicity. I was beginning to realize that the heart of what it meant to "go public" was to be entrapped by the gaze of others, to be reduced by their definitions, and to be forced into shapes unforeseen in the innocent aspirations to the golden world of fame. Until now, I had some small sense of the problems and the paradoxes. But I didn't think they applied to me. And so I would stand in the stocks and be pelted by the crowd on whom I had forced my presence.

It's hard to sustain even such a marginal martyrdom when no one is looking. Without severe cost, I had been privileged for a moment to stand outside the apparatus of modern fame and observe myself as a tiny element in its vast operation. Perhaps my own piece of the puzzle, because it had contained so many of the same paradoxes, might also hold some of the clues. To gain the freedom that such understanding could bring, I began working in two different but allied directions—collecting examples of the baroquely warping effect the pursuit of fame was having on individual lives in the present, while examining the history of fame and the famous in the past.

The contemporary examples were easy enough to find and soon filled a fat folder: the person who wrote to *Time* magazine, "on behalf of myself and the 650 million people in India," to give thanks that the 1979 Nobel Peace Prize was given to Mother Teresa; the man who buzzed the United Nations to force his publishers to give him more publicity for his new book; the innumerable "political" actions by those who were convinced that the road to power lay through the publicizing of themselves and, secondarily, their cause; the rock-and-roll band whose members had plastic surgery in order to look like more famous (and usually dead) rock stars—to cite only a few. In such examples fame had collapsed almost entirely into self-regard, and the ancient belief that fame was the crown of achievement had been replaced by the conviction that it was the only thing worthwhile at all. Part of the ideology of the late 1960s had involved an assertion of the necessary entanglement of personal fulfillment and political well-being—the twentieth-century version of life, liberty, and the pursuit of happiness. But, as the next decade wore on, the cynicism about public life became even more acute and was complemented by a turn toward private satisfactions. In this vacuum the pursuit of fame, with its special formula of private justification through public acclaim, came to define the pursuit of happiness.

But, as I looked into the past, I discovered that the standards of modern fame had been in the process of refashioning for the last hundred years. Shakespeare in the sixteenth century was still suspicious enough about immediate fame to consider only fame after death as truly substantial. Fulke Greville, writing his *Inquisition Upon Fame and Honour* a few years later, characterizes the search for personal fame as an effort for men to find a "frame" beyond themselves that should be equivalent to religious and civic virtue. A more modern note appears in the middle of the seventeenth century in Thomas Hobbes's theory of the secular state, *Leviathan*. "In the nature of man," says Hobbes, "we find three principall causes of quarrell. First, Competition; Secondly, Diffidence; Thirdly, Glory." The first two describe actions undertaken for gain or for defense, the third for reputation. In his cool way Hobbes turns classical honor into modern fame by removing any justification beyond an inner demand to be appreciated. In competition and diffidence men act for tangible reasons, but in pursuit of glory it is "for trifles, as a word, a smile, a different opinion, and any other signe of undervalue, either direct in their Persons or by reflexion in their Kindred, their Friends, their Nation, their Profession, or their Name" (185).

With the beginning of the Industrial Revolution new political and economic factors further encouraged the transformation of the classic idea of personal honor—the unprecedented growth of urban population, the expansion of literacy, the introduction of cheap methods of printing and engraving, the extension of the political franchise, and the revolutionary overthrow of monarchical authority. In this world acting and self-promotion abounded. The proliferation of new modes of communication, the breakdown of hierarchy, and the careers now open to talents made it easier to author oneself. Ben Franklin dressed up in animal skins at the French court to mime the native American to the aristocrats; his face quickly appeared on fans, perfume bottles, and a hundred other items of fashion. Laurence Sterne, the author of *Tristram Shandy* (1760–1767) and the first English author who can be called a celebrity, said that he wrote "not to be *fed,* but to be *famous"* (90). Denis Diderot, the *philosophe* and compiler of the French *Encyclopédie,* carried on a long correspondence with the sculptor Étienne Falconet in which they debated the question of whether fame in one's lifetime or fame after death was preferable. Falconet chose immediate fame, Diderot looked to posterity. Appropriately enough, Falconet published the correspondence, while many of the works for which Diderot is now most famous did not appear until after his death. But, whether the choice was now or later, the eighteenth century seemed particularly preoccupied with the question of fame in the modern sense—as a way of defining oneself, making oneself known, beyond the limitations of class and family. Economic, social, and political revolution had produced so many new ways of naming oneself that what had been an urge in few, in many became a frenzy, a "frenzy of renown," as Matthew G. Lewis's novel *The Monk* (1796) calls it. Almost fifty years before, Samuel Johnson, in his poem "The Vanity of Human Wishes," had called it "the fever of renown." But "frenzy" predicted more of the future desperation, and the imagistic passage from sickness to madness promised little chance of a permanent cure.

* * *

It was a great party. A lot of names were there.
—DON RICKLES on "The Tonight Show"

Names inundate us in the present. And names flow from the past as well, sometimes accompanied with only a few half-remembered facts, coming and going in our minds like the transient names in the news. In this world of incessant information, we know so much about the people of the past, more than they usually knew about each other, that many names familiar to us may have been virtually unknown, except to a small group, for years after their death. One side effect of our possession of so much information is that we create fame retrospectively. People are aghast with the cosmic ironies when they read about the death of Socrates or the crucifixion of Christ. Didn't the Greeks and Romans know whom they were dealing with? But at the time of their deaths neither of these men had the stature that has retrospectively shone on them, singling them out, and making them famous posthumously. Fame is carried first by words and later also by images, and both Socrates and Jesus required men to transmit their messages and in the process create their fame. Socrates may have been famous to those who read Plato, but from the fourth century B.C. to the fifteenth century A.D., few either could or had the chance to read Plato. John Lennon of the Beatles caused a scandal by saying that his band was more famous than Jesus. As far as immediate fame goes, he was right. But the outcry over Lennon's remark is instructive because it implies that fame is by definition a positive category: If Jesus is the greatest man, he must also be the most famous. Some scholars similarly have argued for years that Shakespeare couldn't have written his plays because he wasn't smart enough or experienced enough—or famous enough—and so have assigned his plays to a variety of men with, they say, demonstrably greater learning and social status.

To understand the place of fame in our culture, I want to see its relation to a history of Western ideas of what an individual is. In older cultures, where few had either the resources or the inclination, the phenomenon might be seen in isolation and therefore a little more exactly. The careers of men like Alexander the Great and Julius Caesar became standards against which monarchs were measured for centuries. A different sort of model for fame was extracted from the lives of Socrates and Jesus, from Horace, from Dante, from Shakespeare. Yet to loosely call all these "famous," as we do, obscures the most interesting questions about the relation of the fame of the past to the fame of the present. To understand why some are remembered with more force than others, we need to investigate the process by which fame becomes a matter of premeditation, a result of media management as much as of achievement, as well as how the great of the past behaved in such a way as to project larger-than-life images of themselves that would last longer than any specific action. Gazing back from a world in which the production and multiplication of images is in the hands of many, we might wonder what it meant to be famous when the means of communication were slow and the methods primitive. Then we might be on the way to framing an answer to the question I was always asked when I first told people about this project: Was Julius Caesar (or Jesus) famous?—as if we had invented the category.

Fame is made up of four elements: a person and an accomplishment, their immediate publicity, and what posterity has thought about them ever since. The difficulty in writing about the great figures of the past is that in every age they have been reinterpreted to demonstrate the new relevance of their greatness. The continued interest in the most famous is similar to our continued fascination with a great work of art or an important historical moment: The ability to reinterpret them fills them with constantly renewed meaning, even though that meaning might be very different from what they meant a hundred or a thousand years before. Such people are vehicles of cultural memory and cohesion. They allow us to identify what's present with what's past. By preserving their names, we create a self-conscious grammar of feeling and action that allows us to connect where we have been as a society and where we are going. How they and their supporters ensured that they would be remembered is therefore a crucial part of the story of their fame. The style may be ostentatious or reticent, assertive or evasive, but it is always conscious of the audience who must be lured into remembering. Even those, like Stoics and Christians, who philosophically reject the classical idea of fame, still substitute their own models of renown and personal realization to stand as examples for the future.

This book deals with large movements in the attitudes individuals have had toward themselves, toward other people, toward institutions, and toward society at large. These attitudes are focused by the concept of fame, which sits at the crossroads of the familiar and the unprecedented, where personal psychology, social context, and historical tradition meet. Although I deal almost exclusively with western European culture and all those who have been brought into its orbit and absorbed (and transmuted) that way of perceiving the world, at the heart of the book is a theory of the effect of historical change on what has usually been called, with some overtone of invariability, human nature. I realize that calling attention to the fact that the desire for fame has a history (or to say that any emotion has a history apart from the personal expression) threatens to undermine that very independence and originality we associate with "true" fame. But knowing the historical roots of what otherwise seem to be purely personal urges is the first step to surmounting them. Are emotions innate? Developmental psychologists have charted the ages at which a child has the capacity for different emotions. But such charts rarely distinguish between having the capacity for an emotion and actually expressing it. They gloss over the fact that emotions have to be expressible in the terms that observers can read, that is, the terms that their culture has decided are appropriate. If for some reason a child has learned to repress anger or transmute it, will an observer then decide that it does not yet have the capacity for anger?

"You can't change human nature," we constantly say and hear. But every culture also determines its own guidelines for how emotion can and ought to be expressed, and these vary from age to age—even as they retain the common thread of connection to what that culture defines as human nature and the essence of human character. Understanding of ourselves and our cultural assumptions often comes, as Edward Hall has pointed out, when we realize that what we considered to be innate is actually only frequent or habitual. Ambition and the desire for fame are special cases of the need to understand the relation of emotion to its time-bound expression. Even more than anger or envy, they are the prime social emotions—especially in America, where the assimilation of so many groups and traditions have forced us to focus on what we hold in common.

The path to either changing or transcending history—let alone making one's tiny mark—must lie through history. Now, when so many gestures of fame are clearly known and easily manipulated, we have the impression that it is almost entirely our own creation. But if we think about the past at all, we think especially about its inhabitants who tried to announce themselves to the future. Beyond the self-serving statements, the inscriptions, the flattering portraits, I am looking for a style of self-serving and how it changes with the centuries. By focusing on some of the most famous individuals of the last twenty-five hundred years, I do not imply that their wills have shaped history, nor do I want to argue the greater importance of impersonal causes. I am less interested in the tactics of great battles or in economic development or in political structures than in the way such general and impersonal patterns meet in the nexus of individual desires to be famous—unique—extraordinary—and thereby to put one's mark on time.

Navigating the history of fame as it flows through a variety of political, religious, and artistic histories, my argument does not seek to substitute a new totalist view for the old, but to see familiar phenomena in new arrays. This book contains no Great Man or Great Woman theory of history. It is instead a quest for the ancestors we have chosen for ourselves and those who chose themselves for us, an effort to understand what is general in the history of individual nature in Western culture by observing those examples who tried to stand out on their own and those who stand out for our eyes as well. Their shape in our backward glance, just as the shape negotiated between themselves and their audiences, can never be the sole result of an individual will, but only of individual wills and cultural inclinations modifying each other. Too often historians think they are writing histories of politics or literature when they are in fact writing histories of political or literary fame. Just as often they believe that their proper role is to excavate whatever was invisible to the people who lived in the past. But here, instead of delving into hidden causes, I want to ask what was meant by the obvious, the explicit attempts to impose oneself upon the imaginations of others. In the pages that follow appear a gallery of emblematic figures. Different ones will resonate for different readers, but through them all one can read a psychic biography of what it means to be public in Western culture. The history I shall map in the following pages traces the inheritance we all share, wittingly or unwittingly, from those figures: the shards of individual nature embedded in our own. It proceeds in both art and daily life, within the heart and in the public square, in concepts of the good society and in visions of eternity.

Such a project must be accomplished in language, for language, visual as well as verbal, carries the message of the past to the present and beyond. Falstaff therefore begs the question when he says that *honor* is merely a word, because *honor,* like *fame,* is also a word that invokes the special ability of words to carry the human image beyond its immediate expression. The sensitivity to what language can do is crucial to the creation of fame. For reasons that we shall see, the words of fame that have come down to us are primarily Roman: *fama* (with a Greek ancestor), *rumor, ambitio, celebritas.* Even in Rome the terms could be positive or negative. "Famous" (*famosus*) is derogatory, "egregious" (*egregius*) is complementary. But *fama* itself is appropriately ambiguous. From early on its contradictions were an essential part of the nature of fame—a subject about which everyone has something to say.

In search of these patterns, I have cast this book in five main sections. The first part deals with fame as the effort to be unprecedented, taking its lead from two twentieth-century figures, Charles A. Lindbergh and Ernest Hemingway, and then moves back to the very beginnings of fame to discuss Alexander the Great. The second part focuses on Rome—a whole society animated by the urge for fame, whose definition of achievement was almost entirely oriented toward public behavior. The third part begins to tell the other side of the history of fame, in which not public and political but private and spiritual values are stressed, particularly in the direct challenge Christianity makes to Roman ideas about what makes a person worthy and his name last. In the fourth part I explore the effort—particularly since the Renaissance, but with many classical ancestors—to name the artist, the writer, and the wise man as the judges of true fame and the mediators between public show and private inwardness. The fifth part examines the evolution of modern fame amid the collapse of monarchy and the rise of an intricate web of national and international communications. Although the progression is roughly chronological, the organization is thematic, for time and the evolution of human societies have their effect most clearly on the arena available for personal distinction, just as the modes of communication available in a period indelibly mark what is communicated.

Often the most memorable formulations of the problem of fame have been those generated by the experience of performers and the contemplation of philosophers and writers. Nominally, they are at opposite ends of a continuum of professions stretching from the most public to the most private. Yet, perhaps for that reason, they seem equally sensitive to fame's paradoxes, acutely aware of the necessary role the audience plays in the completion of their actions and their writings. As Clark Gable would say, they read the small print of the contract between anyone who seeks an audience that finally finds him. The ignorance of what fame means and what it can bring may itself be a hallmark of our period. Only with the modern frenzy of renown have so many appeared with little or no comprehension of the contract of eyes and attention by which the audience and the fame seeker balance their desires. I therefore turn first to two men in whose careers the urge for publicity and the urge for privacy had a characteristically modern clash and commerce—Charles A. Lindbergh and Ernest Hemingway.

Above It All:
Lindbergh and Hemingway

From its beginnings fame has promised many a solitary eminence the chance to be separated from the crowds but watched by them, while one's own gaze looks toward the sky. In sculpture the head of Alexander the Great twists to one side and his eyes are fixed beyond the limited horizon of the person who looks at his representation. Above it all, that's what Charles Lindbergh also seemed to be: above the political tangles that World War One had hardly sorted out; above the forced gaiety of the Jazz Age; above the scramble for place and position; and on his flight even above bodily functions themselves. He was the Lone Eagle, the emissary to old Europe of American purity and innocence. A hero without tarnish, he rode the vogue for aviators that captured the imagination of the postwar world. In the breakdown of the old system of international aristocracy, fliers became aristocrats of the air, emblems of man's ability to take a new perspective, make sense of the disheveled terrain, and transcend its muck and blood.

As the pilot became the prime hero of the uncertain years between World War One and World War Two, Charles Lindbergh became the prime pilot by the simple expedient of his own single-mindedness. Just as there were great kings before Alexander and great soldier-politicians before Julius Caesar, so there were great pilots before Lindbergh. Although he did have the backing of several St. Louis businessmen and a press agent, who had been assigned (by a bet-hedging airplane-engine company) to follow several pilots around, most of Lindbergh's competitors had much more financial support and certainly much larger operations. Some, like Admiral Richard Byrd, who (reputedly) had flown over the North Pole, were already more famous. But, like anyone who achieves such absolute fame, Lindbergh's own temperament meshed so invisibly and so tightly with the heroic conception of the flier that it seemed as if fate had reached out, placed him aboard *The Spirit of St. Louis,* and sent them both across the Atlantic to the cheering crowds that awaited in France.

Fate always seems more rigid when we look backward. In fact Lindbergh had prepared long and well for the flight. His romantic conception of himself as a flier immeasurably enhanced not only his success, but also the meaning of what he had done:

> The first solo flight is one of the events in a pilot's life which forever remains impressed on his memory. It is the culmination of difficult hours of instruction, hard weeks of training and often years of anticipation. To be absolutely alone for the first time in the cockpit of a plane hundreds of feet above the ground is an experience never to be forgotten (43).

So writes Lindbergh in *We,* the book that appeared a little over two months after he flew the Atlantic in May of 1927. Who are "we"? Lindbergh and his plane, a pair as linked in the popular imagination as mind and body, "a flying pronoun" in the phrase of Fitzhugh Green, the writer hired to chronicle Lindbergh's heroic reception after the great flight. Throughout *We* and *The Spirit of St. Louis* (the autobiography Lindbergh wrote in 1953) recurs the image of a solitary pilot high in the air, in touch with a power beyond what he knows in normal life, sublimely irradiated by its presence until the depressing moment when he knows he must return to the ground. Unlike, say, the Wright brothers, whose sense of publicity was directed toward their creation of an unparalleled technical achievement, Lindbergh turned flying into a symbolic aspiration—the social mobility of a Horatio Alger hero now become social transcendence. The prize he competed for did not stipulate how many people flew from New York to Paris, only that it be done nonstop. It was Lindbergh's personal choice to go it alone, and the isolation and solitude he endured captured the imagination of the world as much as did the flight itself. Through the skies of Virgil's *Aeneid* flies Fama, spreading rumors false and true around the Roman world. In the Renaissance Virgil's literary image is pictorially revived and unambiguously associated with the hero astride a winged horse, soaring to fame, God, posterity—or all three. But while that Renaissance hero was often an artist or a poet, Lindbergh's soaring aloneness allowed a general participation in the mystical communion of "we": to celebrate the hero who seemed to care only for the purity of his action. As Fitzhugh Green told a waiting public:

> Caesar was glum when he came back from Gaul; Napoleon grim; Paul Jones defiant; Peary blunt; Roosevelt abrupt; Dewey deferential; Wilson brooding; Pershing imposing. Lindbergh was none of these. He was a plain citizen dressed in the garments of any everyday man (226).

Green neglects to mention that Lindbergh himself wanted to wear his colonel's uniform, but his press agent insisted on the plain suit. Like so many of those on whom the mantle of fame has unexpectedly dropped, Lindbergh had not yet realized what it was about his flight that had captured the imagination of the world. But he was learning quickly. The politicians, military leaders, and royalty who pressed forward to pose next to him were all trying to shore up their own uncertain power by associating themselves with this new source of authority, this newly anointed hero. Unbeholding, it seemed, to any organization or group, the Lone Eagle was an American, pure and simple, who had symbolically connected the United States and Europe at a time when political tensions were threatening to drive them apart. High in the air, cut off from communication, Lindbergh became a magnet for swirls of words and images. When he returned to earth, crowds pressed into his aura to receive the benediction of his presence as if he were some kind of secular priest. For those who already had status, he represented a spiritual legitimacy. For those still struggling, his achievement promised that their aspirations might have substance as well. Simple and unaffected, he had made the self-conscious decision to do something great, and he had succeeded. Nineteenth-century America was not dead. Lindbergh, like Horatio Alger's heroes, showed that merit without aspiration, without vision, was impotent. When the flight was over, Lindbergh's picture was everywhere, like Ben Franklin's when he arrived as ambassador to France, and the U.S. Post Office put his face on a stamp, the first to honor a living human being.

Franklin knew that the image of American rusticity needed a little exaggeration to get the attention of the Europeans—a goatskin hat and coat would increase the emblematic impact. And in his own way Lindbergh was not as innocent as he seemed. Despite Green's sonorous praise for "the absence of self-acclaim, the refusal to become commercialized" (278), Lindbergh had signed contracts with Mobil Oil, Vacuum Oil, AC Sparkplugs, and Wright Aeronautical even before he took off from New York. Yet he carefully steered away from any commercial connection that might undermine the moral image in which he believed as much as did his audience. With fame his associates began to be not fliers, but men from the world of finance and government. It is difficult not to conclude that the bargain was reciprocal: He was joining the elite to which he felt he naturally belonged; they were accepting a hero whose achievement confirmed their own most adventurous conceptions of themselves. Luckily enough, he was as conservative as they came. He had done it alone, and so his politics similarly emphasized the purity of the solitary quest as well as the necessary purity of the community that supported it. As the Greeks knew, heroes are often unsuited for civil life. Whatever the sincerity of Lindbergh's beliefs, in the context of the 1930s and 1940s they easily shaded toward fascism.

It hardly seems possible now that Americans or any other people would give the kind of credit to the views of an outstanding adventurer that was routinely accorded the political and economic opinions of Charles Lindbergh. We might admire the first man on the moon or the first person to jog from pole to pole, but that sense of being first and only is now the province of *The Guinness Book of Records* rather than of the diplomatic pouches of nations. Yet Lindbergh, as the godfather of all subsequent solitary adventurers and as the spokesperson for the expansion of air power in a world increasingly subject to war jitters, could make his presence known with little effort. As the example of Hitler and Mussolini in Europe made clear, the transcendent and daring leader satisfied many hungers that politics as usual could not. It is intriguing to wonder how much of Hitler's own imagery owes at least a passing debt to Lindbergh: the solitary plane winging toward the welcoming crowds (in Leni Riefenstahl's film *Triumph of the Will*), the leader's face smiling down from the skies, the massive Nazi eagle crowning the stadium.

But for all of Lindbergh's interest in political issues, he hardly seemed interested in becoming a political leader. Throughout *We* Lindbergh emphasizes the coolness of fliers, their self-contained ability to handle any emergency, their lack of interest in any reward but flying itself. Like medieval knights, with planes instead of armor, they carry on their hero's code: battling not monsters but the elements themselves, constantly searching for new challenges to keep their lances from getting rusty. The mobs that greeted his first performance on the public stage elevated him to a realm beyond electoral politics, although it was a realm that many competing for political power were eager to exploit. Encouraged by his new advisers, Lindbergh also was ready to draw on the special feeling millions had for him because of what he did and the way he did it. But, back on earth, he could not foresee the results of what he said and was often puzzled when many of his early supporters turned away from him. His frequently voiced belief that "alien blood" should be kept out of America was racist, they said. His conviction that German air power was so superior that it would defeat any other nation was called isolationist and pro-Nazi. Yet all these "ideas" are of a piece with the personality that attracted his early acclaim.

As his public career in the 1930s indicates, Lindbergh believed himself to be above national boundaries as an individual in the same way that the enthusiasm for his flight seemed, for the moment, to transcend the chaos of earthbound politics. As a young man, he had drawn up a long list of "character factors" and each day graded himself on the extent to which he had measured up. That self-contained purity, that integrity, that willingness to push himself constantly toward perfection was part of his appeal, and giving credit to "we" purged any taint of personal ambition by sharing public acclaim with the embryonic aeronautical industry.

Soon enough, however, he realized that people were fascinated by the foolish details of what he considered to be his private nature—his taste in clothes and food, his family background, his interest in marriage. It was then that he tried to withdraw the presence that he had at first been so eager to give the public. The new realization was hardly naive. Lindbergh was neither the first nor the last to discover that the urge to succeed in public carried unforeseen obligations, even torments. Lindbergh's suffering was to be more obvious and perhaps more emblematic than most. Two years after his flight, he married Anne Morrow, daughter of Dwight Morrow, diplomat and banker. Almost three years later their infant son was kidnapped from his crib and, after an anguishing several weeks, was discovered murdered about a mile from the house.

The publicity furor surrounding the kidnapping of the Lindbergh baby and the subsequent trial of the accused kidnapper Bruno Richard Hauptmann was only one, although no doubt the most elaborate, of the sensational murder trials that preoccupied newspaper and magazine readers in the 1920s and 1930s, because it also allowed another opportunity to look into the lives of the Lone Eagle and his family. Curiosity seekers mobbed the small town in New Jersey near which the Lindberghs had their estate and where the trial was held. As the supreme American hero of the moment, Lindbergh was the center of swirls of vicariousness. Like pilgrims seeking relics, the tourists snatched chunks of stone and wood and whatever else they could pick up from the area. The flight across the Atlantic had been the epic triumph. The trial was at once tragedy and farce. Instead of ambassadors and presidents, this time it was reporters and entertainers who pressed into the Lindbergh aura. One imposter strung Lindbergh along for weeks with the hope that his criminal contacts would locate the child. When faced with the news that the body had been found, he confessed that he had made the whole thing up to "become famous" (Mosley, 164).

With the kidnaping and murder of his child, then, Charles Lindbergh becomes a striking example of the essential paradox of fame in the twentieth century: the desire for transcendence through personal glory that leads not to freedom but to a new and more secure entrapment. Fame, according to Virgil, might fly. But gossip could bring the famous down to earth. The public that had praised him as the Lone Eagle was the same public that now threatened to destroy his privacy forever. And it would not be stretching the symbolic meaning of events too much to suggest that his own combination of self-exposure and reticence expressed a vulnerable ignorance of the fine print of fame that the kidnapper sought to profit by. "Who stole the Lindbergh baby?" went a song of the period, "Was it you? was it you? was it you? / After he crossed the ocean wide, was that the way to show our pride? / Was it you? was it you? was it you?"

Lindbergh may have believed in and been motivated by an abstract definition of glorious achievement. But the way he determined to gain that glory for himself was conditioned both by what his world considered to be achievement and by the way that world bestowed honor. He might have seemed above the petty celebrities of the café society of the 1920s, where gangsters, entertainers, and the rich mingled to compare notes on what it meant to be written about in the papers. But his exploits fed the same hunger to discover new objects of attention, new sensations, new people. After the trial he turned more and more toward his special combination of airplanes and politics, arguing for an increase in American military and commercial aeronautical development at the same time that he kept generally away from practical political action. No wonder that the antagonism between Lindbergh and Franklin Roosevelt was so great. In Lindbergh's version of the fame mythology, the purity of the hero ought to be reflected by the purity of his audience. The politics of coalition had no place in Lindbergh's visionary fatalism. His image of almost inaccessible integrity and Roosevelt's of democratic directness seemed doomed to meet head on.

Only a powerful new technology, Lindbergh thought, could save America from the forces eroding her resolve. Although he spoke long and often for the America First Committee in favor of keeping the country out of any European war, Lindbergh still considered himself to be a bridge between America and Europe, an umpire who could settle the disputes of nations purely through his own prestige—even to the extent of trying to promote a Franco-German alliance on the model of an airplane with a French body and a German engine. It was not that he didn't want publicity. He wanted it on his own terms. As someone quite familiar with the egos of pilots, Hermann Goering assured Lindbergh that there would be no crowds and undue publicity during Lindbergh's tour of the Nazi aircraft industry in the late 1930s. The assurance was hardly necessary since Lindbergh supplied his own audience: On his return to the United States, he testified at length about the futility of war with Germany and the need to reach an accommodation with Hitler. In fact he had swallowed a myth of German preparedness and power cooked up with him in mind. Once again, the beneficiaries of his aura had managed to understand the world and Lindbergh better than he could himself. His only excuse was his solitary self-sufficiency, the unwillingness to believe that he could be lied to, especially by Goering, who was, after all, a fellow airman and one equally concerned with national and personal purity. To his early audiences, Lindbergh had seemed like a shooting star, an individual unexplainable by any precedent but himself, the benevolent version of a Nietzschean superman. But his search for a world without intrusion, in which all motives and ideals were unalloyed, required an audience. Once committed to public gaze, he discovered that it was difficult to control where and when that gaze chose to shine, and he became as tied in the public mind as any movie star or politician to what he had done most recently. Lindbergh was the Phaëton who dared to drive the chariot of the Sun and came back unscathed and smiling. But this Phaëton had to grow up as well and watch the idea of himself that had fueled his first triumph become the impulse for his rejection.

After the beginning of World War Two, Lindbergh virtually retired from public life in the face of increasing denunciations by the Roosevelt administration and the loss of his isolationist constituency. By the early 1950s, memories had mellowed enough for his autobiography *The Spirit of St. Louis* to be a best-seller. But in his occasional political writings, he showed a loss of faith in democracy that may have been a surprise only to him. His fame was based on his isolation, and his political perspective developed from the basic premise of being above it all, seeing the terrain in a way that no one on earth could. The sense of separateness he cultivated in his temperament is equally the portion of the political dictator and the religious martyr. Lindbergh, however, was inclined to be neither one, despite his sympathy with their characteristic temperaments. He was instead a famous man, for a time the most famous in the world, but one who never quite understood how he himself had been an accomplice in the injuries fame had done to him. By instinct, talent, temperament, and timing Lindbergh established a fame for himself that mediated a fame of the spirit with the new material horizons of science and technology. Yet he believed his own publicity a little too much and acted as if he were as self-sufficient as he was being given credit for. In some sense the U.S. Space Program, with its insistence on the *team* of astronauts and technicians—all heroes together—speaks directly to the disastrous political fortunes of the Lone Eagle. Alexander the Great, whose career stands as precedent for all the aspiringly unprecedented heroes who followed him, understood the paradoxical need to aspire beyond anyone else while paying tribute both to one's ancestors in fame and to the audience that recognizes one's uniqueness. But Lindbergh thought he had done his part with the tickertape parades and could thereafter relax into seclusion and security. In nothing that he writes is there the barest indication of any awareness that his fame was other than deserved and that attacks on his later actions and politics were motivated by anything but envy of his natural gifts.

Forever the believer in will and action, Lindbergh in his last years devoted himself to the cause of ecology and the preservation of nature from the encroachment of the technological civilization to which he had given such a push forward. In the name of the purity of nature and the protection of primitive tribes, he could lend his fame much more effectively than he had in the past and be the savior from the clouds where it counted. To deflect the assertion of the transatlantic flight, he had evolved the displacement of "we," man and plane, battling the elements together. By the end of his life, he had left the "civilized" world behind entirely and found a different kind of pride from being accepted into tribes threatened by an onrushing industrial technology. Perhaps that noble marginality had been his essential motivation all along, and fame a mistaken detour.

*   *   *

Ernest Hemingway could almost be considered Lindbergh's wiser older brother. Born like Lindbergh in the small-town northern Midwest, Hemingway also first achieved fame in France, and his fame, like Lindbergh's, was at least publicly that of the new young American—strong, bold, without pretension, a cold draught of nature to shock the complacencies of both Europe and his own country. Lindbergh said that "we" had flown the Atlantic, and Hemingway also purged the older shapes of ego from his writing to create a spare, direct style that spoke of action, feeling, and the hard edges of things rather than their fretful nuances.

As a writer very aware of the literary traditions he was opposing and the literature he was trying to create, Hemingway would seem to have had many more resources than did Lindbergh to understand the phenomenon of fame and its questionable relation to the actual shape of his career and his ability. Yet he found it equally puzzling and was never able to make the "separate peace" with the world that he so often recommended in his novels. His characters were often in quest of a cleansing adventure that would involve action, combat, and a stretching of the self beyond the comfortable limits of its civilization. Short of death, however, his heroes could rarely compete with the array of wounds, breaks, and bruises that year by year accumulated on Hemingway's own body. In the quest, nature, his own and that of the animals he hunted, had to be fought and subdued. Only when he was feeling poorly in body could he write, said Hemingway, because writing was an act of the head. Thus the optimal style—"grace under pressure" he liked to call it—purified words into transcendent immediacy. The connection between Hemingway's ideals for his writing and his ideals for himself were therefore explicitly announced to his audience: the man and his work, as much a "we" as Lindbergh and his plane. Although he often complained about his own celebrity—"I do not give a damn for either fame or fortune" (*Letters,* 705)—and resented intrusions into his personal life, the public image of the rough-and-tumble "Papa" with a 30.06 on his shoulder clearly invoked the force and directness of his style. Like Lindbergh's effort to be above it all, Hemingway's ideal literary self involved a kind of sainthood, at once demanded by the audience of modern fame and yet virtually impossible for any human being to maintain. *Winner Take Nothing* he called one of his collections of short stories, a title that tries to bridge the contradictions: no rewards or honor, no fame or fortune—but still the winner.

In *Across the River and into the Trees,* written after World War Two, Hemingway makes his most elaborate attempt to untangle his public and his private identities. The hero, Colonel Cantwell, is closer to Hemingway in general biographical detail than is any previous "Hemingway hero." Yet it is the contrasts that are most telling. The Colonel is hardly famous. He dwells constantly on the past, especially on World War One and his initiation into manhood with his first battle wound. He scorns Eisenhower, Montgomery, and all the "soldier politicians" created by journalism with its demand for the "Big Picture" and its inability to understand real individual lives. They are all out to make a name for themselves, he tells his young mistress, like his first wife, who "had more ambition than Napoleon and about the talent of the average High School Valedictorian" (212).

What does this sour Colonel, wracked with the pains of his life as a soldier, have to do with the genial Hemingway beaming from the covers of national magazines all through the 1950s—the hero as American writer, Huckleberry Finn in a grizzled beard? In essence the Colonel is Hemingway's ideal image of himself—not the famous author, but the soldier, the hunter, the lover, the man of nature, the private person. Like Shakespeare's Marc Antony, who tells Cleopatra that if she wants he will leave the world of public fame and live "as a private man in Athens," Hemingway's Colonel Cantwell embodies an effort to imagine a life of privacy that is for the famous what fame is for the aspirant: the place where integrity and wholeness of being can finally flourish. The difficulty for both Marc Antony and Hemingway, as it was for Lindbergh, is that they want to relinquish their fame only partially. As the Colonel's mistress says to him, "I love to have people see us, but I don't want to see anybody" (267). The glow of being observed and appreciated by others cannot be given up. But it will also not be repaid. To exchange even glance for glance implies that there is a debt. Better that the audience only sit in silent appreciation. To acknowledge their existence erodes the purity of the heroic gesture and turns it into mere theater.

It has been estimated that in the medieval world the average person saw one hundred other people in the course of a lifetime. A contemporary city dweller, or anyone with a television set, can see that many in an hour. One effect of this ever-expanding crowd of other people before our eyes has been the blossoming of more contenders for symbolic singularity. Often, they are not interested in other people at all, except to gather them into an audience for their self-sufficiency. Whether antisocial or nonsocial or unsocialized, they all share or think they share the inability to be alone or be themselves unless there is someone there to appreciate them. Such an audience supplies the loving regard that makes them whole, removes them from isolation, and places them in the mainstream. When such temperaments go public to an audience beyond those who know them personally, the prime gift they can give is support and solace for the feelings of aloneness and inadequacy in those who flock to them.

The most usual mistake of the famous in our era is to think that the language of fame can be used without one being used by it: to be seen but not to have to see. I might call this the Lindbergh syndrome—to achieve fame because you fulfill the desires of an audience for a hero and then to deny that the audience or the times have anything to do with your fame. You deserve it only for your pure self, which you will dispense in increasingly tiny droplets to the faithful. As Greta Garbo once remarked, when asked why she remained a comparative recluse even at the height of her celebrity, "People take energy from me, and I want it for pictures" (Walker, 104). To see and not be seen is to be in the audience; to be seen and not to see, but to feel trapped by the gaze of others, is to be onstage. Every day in the gossip columns one entertainer or another complains of invasion of privacy. Usually, it is only the most famous who do this, for they are the ones who, after living their lives in public and appealing to the audience to award them the success they now enjoy must have the crowning glory of being famous only for what they give in the comparatively short time they are onstage—for no such person wants to be thought of merely as a performer in bondage to the audience.

In the ancient world the desire for fame is a desire to make an impact on time, to be remembered. But when heads are stuffed with names of old radio comedians, baseball players, and swing musicians, what is time and what is memory and what is fame? Hemingway's Colonel, a fictional character, could say that he didn't really care. But Hemingway himself, a real person who had allowed himself to be fictionalized as the Great American Writer, had to care, even while he created heroes committed to codes of personal honor independent of any audience or set of worldly values.

Whenever a writer creates a hero whose nature is like his own, whenever the energy of an art comes from an autobiographical and confessional impulse, the themes of fame and death are closely related. In a secular civilization fame and the approval of posterity replace belief in an afterlife; physical death may come, but psychic life will remain in the work. Like Lindbergh in his later years, Hemingway sought a sanction for his public exposure in a fealty to nature. The more famous he became, the less sure he was that his public image supplied an identity with which he could be comfortable.

Goethe once said that the hero of his novel *The Sorrows of Young Werther* (1774) had committed suicide so that the author wouldn't have to. But Werther was also ushering in a world in which the urge to self-destructiveness was becoming a mark of sensitivity. Hemingway's suicide, almost two hundred years later, may indicate that such complacent trust in the artist's creative ability to transmute his most destructive feelings was even less possible in the glare of publicity. The media-soaked years after World War Two spawned a whole tribe of artistic suicides, many of whom had discovered how hard it was to retain their personal integrity, when interest in their work played a weak second to fascination with their private lives and whether they would be able to repeat their past performances. In such a fragmentation of self and public image, suicide is the final act of cohesion, the final good faith, in a world where the false and the true are hard to tell apart. The more public, the more famous the person, the more sacramental and ritualistic the act. In the face of an audience that can neither be controlled nor catered to with any satisfaction, the only alternatives seem to be withdrawal, resignation, or a glorious death that forever fixes one in the posture of heroic assertion. Only then might the unprecedented singularity to which one aspires be maintained. But amidst the constant crowds and incessant gazes of the present, few such singularities of assertion or evasion are really possible. Centuries ago, however, the first aspirants to fame had the power to control their audiences and their imagery, as well as the ambition to be perceived as unique. Of them, the one who most defined the nature of fame for his inheritors and who therefore deserves to be known as the first famous person was Alexander III of Macedonia, later called "the Great."

The Longing of Alexander

. . . [W]hen a man compoundeth the image of his own person, with the image of the actions of an other man; as when, a man imagins himselfe a *Hercules,* or an *Alexander,* (which happeneth often to them that are much taken with reading of Romants) it is a compound imagination, and properly but a Fiction of the mind. . . . The *vainglory* which consisteth in the feigning or supposing of abilities in our selves, which we know are not, is most incident to young men, and nourished by the Histories, or Fictions of Gallant Persons; and is corrected often times by Age, and Employment.

—THOMAS HOBBES, *Leviathan*

In the beginnings, as we can decipher them from the tumbled temples and the half-eroded inscriptions, fame meant a grandeur almost totally separate from ordinary human nature. In Egypt particularly evolved the extraordinary exaltation of a single man, the pharaoh, the ultimate ruler whose giant image gazed down at his subjects through the centuries. In their tombs, like those of the earliest emperors of China, were the objects and images of their power, including the bones of servants and the statues of retainers—testimony to the future of the greatness that once was. In civilizations with a god-king, especially those that used a written language primarily for religious, astronomical, and mercantile computation, rulers often took the same name as their predecessor because the role of leader was much more important than the individual who occupied it. He became greater not by asserting his personal characteristics but by fitting into the eternal role as fully as possible. For king or general, priest or artist, the preexisting name shored up the weak and kept in check the strong.

But the true history of fame begins, not with the grandly repeated names of Egypt or Persia or China or Yucatán, but with a self-naming that steps out of the bounds of dynasty, beyond even the stature of the Egyptian god-king, and into a status simultaneously unique and yet suffused with the atmosphere of human possibility. Like so many other aspects of Western culture, such a fame receives its first clear definition in the Greece of the fifth and fourth centuries B.C. For many centuries there had been established traditions of celebrating the heroes of the past by shrines and cults. But with the rise of Athens as the center of Greek culture came the casting of the oral epics of the *Iliad* and the *Odyssey* into written form, followed by the grand fifth-century flowering of drama and philosophy, when the scattered images of the heroic drew together into a prolonged cultural mediation on the meaning of heroism. We do not know who Homer was or where and when he lived, although it was certainly hundreds of years after the events and people he depicts. But his works (if indeed he wrote both the *Iliad* and the *Odyssey*) embody the importance to the Greeks of the pursuit of an honor that will allow a man to live beyond death, as Hector says in the *Iliad*, "immortal, ageless all my days, and reverenced like Athena and Apollo" (198).[1] Such honor, which can be achieved only in war, frees its possessor from human time. Thus although the greatest heroes lived in ages long before the present, their memory remains. Set in a war the Greeks won, the *Iliad* is yet in great part a lament for a lost civilization of great men and women composed for the descendants of those who had destroyed them, assimilated them, or driven them out—as if an American of European descent would in the twenty-third century write an epic celebrating the heroic world of the American Indians. True heroism is ever receding. Even in the *Iliad* the ancient Nestor speaks of the great men who *used* to be around, so diminished does he consider heroism to be in the present.

The Greek word "hero" in Homer's works generally means "gentleman" or "noble," and his concept of heroism accordingly contains a strong element of class status and class obligation. But since only the future can know if the hero has achieved perfect glory, the present too often judges stature by material possessions, especially the booty captured in war. The plot of the *Iliad* therefore begins when Agamemnon, the military leader of the Greek expedition against Troy, uses the power of his position to force Achilles to give up the prize that his personal honor demands. As Aristotle would later imply in his *Politics*, the actions and temperament necessary for heroic fame may be opposed to those that make a good citizen. For most of the *Iliad*, Achilles sits passively in his tent, disdaining a glory that has been polluted by the greed of Agamemnon. Through this heroic conflict, Homer explores the division between the hero's loyalty to a social order and his aspiration to an honor sanctioned only by his ancestors and the gods. Achilles is capable of transcending the values of his society by a vision of the absolute honor beyond even life itself. But he also wants it to be clear that he is the greatest hero of the Greeks. If Agamemnon cannot accommodate Achilles' need for personal honor, then Achilles, until the death of his best friend Patroclus, will submit neither to Agamemnon's will nor to the social goal of winning the war against the Trojans.

Clearly, such choices, embedded in their greatest poem of war, were vexing to Homeric and post-Homeric society. The *Odyssey*, through its emphasis on the testing of Odysseus not in battle but in travel and adven-

---

1. As Bruno Snell points out in *The Discovery of Mind*, the Homeric phrase "imperishable fame" (*kleos afthiton*) agrees with Indo-European poetic diction and is thus both a conceptual and linguistic inheritance from one of the roots of the world language system (164).

ture, turns away from the two time-honored places of heroic assertion—where one was born and where one fights—to explore instead the possibility that heroism may flourish better outside the preordained world of social hierarchy and military rituals. The values of the *Odyssey* are instead values of movement, and even at the end of the poem, Odysseus is destined to leave for yet another adventure. In the *Odyssey*, when Odysseus is a leader and has an official troop of men with him, he generally gets them and himself into trouble. Only by the end of the poem, after he has wandered back to his home disguised as a beggar, has he been through enough alone to win his wife and his house back from the brash young suitors who had collected there. As the terms of the poem imply, even though heroic action often has a social dimension, its roots are best anchored by a private, even a domestic, sense of self. Odysseus, who is caught in the framework of Agamemnon's power and Homer's story, not only navigates through his world disguised and alone, but also himself tells a good deal of the story of the *Odyssey* to an eager audience.

In the *Iliad* competing warriors bellowed their own names and the names of their fathers and grandfathers. In the *Odyssey* this penchant for heroic publicity is explicitly criticized, for Odysseus has discovered that the echo of one's name in the world is not always a soothing sound. In Book IX, alone and virtually naked, he has been thrown by the sea on the shores of Phaiakia. Nausikaä, the king's daughter, has found him and brought him to her father's court where, after hearing a minstrel sing of Odysseus at Troy, he decides to reveal himself and tell his own story of what happened since. First, he tells them his name and then briefly recounts his voyages until he arrived at the land of the Cyclopes, a race of giants with one eye, who live isolated from each other in caves. Exploring the island, he and his men come on a Cyclops who captures and begins eating them two at a time. Recovering from his shock, Odysseus devises a plan. First, he offers the Cyclops wine and, when asked his name, gives a word close to the Greek for "nobody." After the Cyclops is drunk and falls asleep, Odysseus puts out his one eye with a flaming and sharpened stake of olive wood. Raging, the Cyclops calls to his neighbors that "nobody" has injured him. They leave and, says Odysseus, "I was filled with laughter / to see how like a charm the name deceived them" (169). Escaping the cave with his men, Odysseus boards his ship. But although the Cyclops is hurling huge rocks at the sound of his voice and his men warn him against taunting the monster, Odysseus cannot resist shouting his real name across the water:

> Kyklops,
> if ever mortal man inquire
> how you were put to shame and blinded, tell him
> Odysseus, raider of cities, took your eye:
> Laertes' son, whose home's on Ithaka! (172)[2]

2. Similarly, the lure of the song of the Sirens (*Odyssey*, XII) is their flattery of Odysseus as the hero of Troy: "the temptation is to know your ultimate reputation

Whereupon the Cyclops, whose name we have already learned is Polyphemus, calls upon the god of the sea, Poseidon, to prevent Odysseus from reaching home again until many years have passed and all his companions are gone. In effect Odysseus's need to brag of his exploits, to tell his name to the Cyclops, has forced him into the twenty-years' wandering that makes up the *Odyssey*. And returning his name to him, with a prayer that Poseidon bring him despair and pain is the Cyclops Polyphemus, whose name in Greek means "many fames"—for Odysseus, at least one too many.

The Homeric analysis of the place of heroic assertion in a world more complex than that of the battlefield stands directly behind the career of the man the Romans called "Alexander the Great." For the worldwide scale of his grappling with the problem of fame and his constant awareness of the relation between accomplishment and publicity, Alexander deserves to be called the first famous person. Nothing was ever enough for him. Like Achilles, he wanted fame through battle and conquest. But like Odysseus, he was constantly on the move, impelled by an urge to see and do more than any Macedonian or Greek ever had before. In an ancient world where so many rulers were amassing wealth and land, defeating armies, and killing enemies, Alexander remained in the world's imagination, not just for the quantity of his achievements, but for what was immaterial about them, the unspecifiable spiritual greed that constantly seeks new challenges. To many of his early historians his urges were almost mystical, welling from his inmost being. Arrian, a Roman military governor who wrote five hundred years later but is still our best general source for Alexander's career, called the urge *pothos* (longing), one of the Greek terms for sexual desire. Whenever Alexander does what Arrian cannot explain, he says it is due to his longing—to cross a river, to climb a mountain, to see the wagon of Midas at Gordium. *Pothos* is a cause of action that is entirely within Alexander, an endless desire to strive with no specific goal. In his short life of thirty-three years, Alexander constantly posed, fulfilled, and then went far beyond a series of new roles and new challenges until he himself was the only standard by which he could be measured. At the head of his army, his eyes forever on the horizon, he stood self-sufficient but never self-satisfied.[3] Unlike the time- and role-bound rulers of the more ancient civilizations, who believed that their greatest achievement was to come into accord with the rhythms of dynastic history, he sought to be beyond time, to be superior to calendars, in essence to be remembered not for his place in an eternal descent but for himself.

To reshape the nature of fame in a society as hierarchical as Alexander's, one must first step away from stability. Plutarch among others re-

---

before you are dead" (Vermeule, 203). In effect this has already happened to Odysseus when, in the court of Alkinoös, a minstrel sings the Troy story and Odysseus secretly weeps. When this happens a second time and his weeping is noticed by the king, the stage is set for the revelation of his name and the telling of his story.

3. For the connection of *pothos* with *eros* rather than with mere desire (*himeros*), see Vermeule, 145–78.

counts the story that when Alexander was in Corinth, long before he started his war against Persia, he went to visit the philosopher Diogenes and found him sitting under a tree. Leaving his military escort, Alexander went up to Diogenes and asked what he could do for him. Stay out of the way, Diogenes said, you're blocking the sun. The soldiers were horrified, expecting an outburst of Alexander's already famous anger. But Alexander just laughed and remarked that if he were not Alexander, he would like to be Diogenes. The visionary ruler and the philosophic recluse were equal in their desire for what was absent, equal in their separation from society, and therefore equal in their fame. The story recalls as well another favorite account of an incident in the youth of Alexander, when he tamed the great horse Bucephalus by turning its face toward the sun so it wouldn't be frightened of his shadow. One could either bask in the sun or become its rival. If Alexander could not stay out of the sun, he might strive instead to become the sun to others. All his visual representations take something from the iconography of Helios, the sun god. Like Diogenes, the philosopher who rejected the corruption of human society to live outside of it, Alexander was bent on defying any order that he had not created himself.

Many of Alexander's actions, particularly in his early career, seem to spring from a feeling of tenuous legitimacy that he transforms into a drive for superhuman achievement. Born in 356 B.C., Alexander grew up under the protection of his mother Olympias, a passionate worshiper of Dionysus, who in later years even committed murder to further her son's interests. Philip, Alexander's father, had made himself king of Macedonia at twenty-three, three years before Alexander's birth. As a hostage in Thebes some years before, Philip had acquired both a respect for Greek culture and a desire to make it his own. Thus a succession of tutors for the young Alexander significantly included Aristotle who, although he had already made a reputation in Athens, was born hardly thirty miles away from the Macedonian royal city of Pella. While Alexander grew up, Philip unified Macedonia internally and modernized the army beyond any in the ancient world. Forging a series of military alliances and capturing several crucial gold mines that allowed him to mint coins rivaled in value only by those from Athens, Philip began to extend his influence into Greece. Finally, in the summer of 338, with the important help of a cavalry charge led by the eighteen-year-old Alexander, he defeated a coalition of Greek city-states at Chaeronea and started to lay the groundwork for an attack against the Persian Empire, which had almost defeated Greece more than a hundred years earlier and was still a subversive force in Greek politics. But before Philip's plans could get much further than preliminary organization, he was murdered during the wedding of his daughter, a wedding that featured the appearance of Philip's image as the thirteenth among the twelve Olympian gods.

Aristotle thought that the murder of Philip was purely a private matter. But although it has never been proved that Alexander had anything to do with it, there is some reason to suspect the hand of Olympias. Two years before, Philip had taken another wife, Cleopatra, the niece of one of his generals, whereupon both Olympias and Alexander went into exile. Alexander was soon recalled to the court, but Olympias stayed behind in her native Epirus. Whatever the facts of Philip's assassination, a year or so later, when Alexander was away, Olympias had both Cleopatra and her infant son murdered. In this haze of intrigue Alexander moved swiftly to justify his inheritance, putting down a revolt in Thessaly and taking over Philip's leadership of the war against Persia. Of all Greece, only the Thebans resisted his rule, forming an army with the help of Persian bribes while Alexander was battling tribes to the north. Alexander speedily returned and, with some Greek allies, razed Thebes to the ground, divided its territory among the loyal states, and sold most of its men, women, and children as slaves. There would be no more armed resistance from within Greece until after his death. His home base now secure, in the spring of 334 B.C. Alexander crossed the Hellespont to invade the Persian Empire. Even in death, he would never return.

Since Agamemnon, a thousand years before, Alexander was the first Greek to lead an army against Asia. With self-conscious restaging, he went out of his way to lift anchor at Elaeus, the same place where, according to tradition, Agamemnon's fleet set sail to conquer Troy. Elaeus was not necessarily the best embarkation point, and the now-quiet town of Troy was hardly a strategic objective in the war against Persia. But the gesture meant something both to the army Alexander led and to Alexander himself. Not only would the Persian war be a revenge for Persian attacks against Greece, it would also justify the men of the present as heroic inheritors of Homeric grandeur. The Greeks of Alexander's day were hardly the Greeks of the *Iliad*. The families of most had vanished. But the royal house of Epirus still claimed Achilles as its ancestor, and, through Olympias, Alexander was considered his direct descendant. As war leader of all Greece, he therefore combined the blood of Achilles and the authority of Agamemnon, the hero and the leader. In contrast with the melancholic nostalgia of the *Iliad* for a lost race of heroes, Alexander's claim of connection with the past could make the present at least equal and perhaps superior to its greatness. Heavily conscious of his role as inheritor, Alexander at Elaeus also sacrificed at the tomb of the first Greek to be killed in the war with Troy. Landing on the other side, Alexander immediately went to the site of Troy, where he laid a wreath on the tomb of Achilles; he sent his lifelong friend Hephaestion to do the same at the grave of Patroclus, the friend of Achilles. Then, taking up a shield said to be that of Achilles, Alexander replaced it in the shrine with his own, which would be there for the edification of Roman tourists hundreds of years later. The Homeric holy war against the Persians had begun.[4]

---

4. According to Plutarch, Alexander also wanted to play the lyre of Achilles, perhaps as Achilles himself is playing it when, as Homer describes it, he receives Odysseus and others into his tent on their embassy to persuade him to return to the battle.

Xerxes, the Persian king who had launched the war against Greece more than a century before Alexander's birth, had called it revenge for the Trojan War. Within hardly a month of landing at Troy, Alexander had returned the favor, winning a major battle at the Granicus River and beginning a series of sieges that effectively liberated the predominantly Greek cities of Asia Minor from Persian sovereignty. But simple repayment for past injuries did not seem to be Alexander's goal. Within just over a year he had won another major victory, at Issus in the northeastern end of the Mediterranean, and extended his control over all of Asia Minor, inciting the Persian Empire to take enough notice to make a peace offer—which was quickly refused.

Between the battle of the Granicus and the battle of Issus, Alexander was in winter quarters at a city named Gordium, the capital of Phrygia, whose most celebrated ancient king was Midas of the golden touch. One day Alexander, who was always interested in the heroic legends of the lands he was passing through, went to the acropolis of Gordium to see the ancient wagon on which Midas had ridden when, otherwise unknown, he was designated king by an oracle. Midas's father had tied the yoke of the wagon to the pole by an intricate knot whose ends could not be seen, the Gordian knot. Like the Arthurian sword in the stone, it was a test that only the true king could pass: Whoever untied the knot would rule Persia. Riding on a crest of military success, Alexander was equal to the symbolic challenge as well. Either by slashing it apart with his sword or (depending on the story) pulling out the linchpin that held yoke and pole together, Alexander cut the Gordian knot. By stepping outside the traditional terms of the puzzle, Alexander had created a new solution. It was a scene that immediately became proverbial, propelling him once again beyond the usual triumphs of kings and conquerors into the realm of the imagination.

After Gordium and the victory at Issus, Alexander charged around the eastern end of the Mediterranean, accepting the submission of Phoenicia and conquering such fortress cities as Tyre and Gaza. Buoyed by these victories, he defeated Egypt easily and, hardly two years after leaving Greece, was crowned pharaoh at Memphis. To the political and military power Alexander was wresting from the great Persian Empire, he had added the Egyptian authority of the god-king. The next spring, after founding Alexandria, he cemented his new status by journeying to Siwah, an oracle in the middle of the Libyan desert noted throughout the Greek world for its truth telling. The oracle was dedicated to Ammon, a supreme god who, as Ra the sun god, was also father of the pharaohs and had been identified by the Greeks with Zeus. According to one account of Alexander's visit to Siwah, the head priest greeted him as the son of Ammon/Zeus; according to another, it was the priest's faulty Greek that made it seem such a greeting; according to a third, it was merely politically motivated flattery. In any case, after the greeting, Alexander had a private audience with the priest, although nothing of what passed between them has come down to us. Supposedly, Alexander wrote to his mother Olympias that he would tell her the oracle's secret message on his return to Greece. But, of course, he never did.[5]

Six hundred years later St. Augustine wrote that Alexander at Siwah had learned that the pagan gods were originally men. But surely Alexander's own exploits were teaching him that already. Later that same year he won the final battle over the Persian king, Darius; sacked the Persian capital of Persepolis; and set off for the East in pursuit of a fleeing Darius, whom he later found murdered by Persian officials in hopes of reward from the new conqueror. With Darius dead and Alexander's army in possession of all the richest and most powerful cities of the Persian Empire, it might seem that Alexander's mission was complete. But he was not out to conquer an empire but to conquer a world. Becoming pharaoh had added a crucial element of grandeur no Greek ruler had ever had. But the journey to Siwah emphasized Alexander's search for an unprecedented importance that belonged not to his power or his authority but to himself. Further and further toward the East he led his army, through present-day Iran and Afghanistan, north to Samarkand in Russia, and south to invade India. To commemorate his progress across Asia, he founded some eighteen cities named after himself as well as one named for his horse and another for his dog. It was an empire with a nomad king, and midway between the Aral Sea and the borders of China, he built Alexandria Eschate—Alexandria the Farthest, forty-five hundred miles from Macedonia.

Philip had also been a city builder, and Alexander had followed his father's example by founding Alexandropolis when he was about fifteen, during a military campaign. But the cities Alexander founded in the course of building his empire were less garrison towns than cultural beachheads. Like Achilles, he wanted to win the battles of personal honor and family prestige. Like Odysseus, he also wanted the submission of strange peoples in strange lands, where no Greek ever walked before. An Achilles in prowess and authority, he wanted also to be an Odysseus in movement and sensibility, a hero to be honored not because of his inheritance but because of himself. Unlike the Greeks, whose geographically mountainous and divided land set the stage for constant internal wrangling, unlike the Macedonians, whose domination was most secure over the plains but stopped uncomfortably at the foothills, Alexander considered the subduing of more and more geography as part of his achievement. Along the way he occasionally sent new information back to Aristotle to correct his former tutor's insular geopolitics. Three hundred years later, in the odd combination of competitiveness and respect that characterizes the Roman attitude toward Alexander, Livy writes that Alexander would never have conquered

---

5. The different versions are recounted in Plutarch's biography of Alexander, which was written not long before Arrian's. See any edition of the *Lives of the Noble Greeks and Romans*. It is most conveniently available in Ian Scott-Kilvert's Penguin translation, Plutarch, *The Age of Alexander* (1973), 283–84. (Scott-Kilvert's Penguin translations rearrange the "parallel lives" intended by Plutarch into a more chronological sequence.)

Italy because of Italy's mountains and forests. But if he had known of their existence, they would only have whetted his appetite. Plutarch recounts that a sculptor once suggested that Alexander commission him to carve Mt. Athos in northern Greece into his likeness. But Alexander replied that the Caucasus Mountains, the Tanaïs River, and the Caspian Sea would be monuments enough.

After his campaigns in India Alexander stops advancing toward the rising sun: practically because mutinies were developing among his weary soldiers and symbolically (perhaps) because a voyage down the Indus to the Arabian Sea had convinced him that he had finally reached the Great Ocean that surrounds the world. Marching back through the deserts of southern Pakistan and Iran while he sent his fleet through the Persian Gulf, Alexander returned to Persepolis and the other seats of Persian power. For the first time in his career a grand consolidation seemed to be in order, and the Persian model was infectious. He had long abandoned his early practice of appointing men from his own train to rule conquered areas and now generally kept the previous ruler as an underling. Similarly, he began to adopt *proskynesis,* the act of obeisance in Persian court ritual, and for a time maintained two separate courts, one Greek and one Persian. To the extent that he had a program for the nations he conquered, however, it was far more cultural than political. What has been called his "policy of fusion" aimed to bring Greeks, Macedonians, and Persians together into one grand culture whose presiding genius was Greek, nowhere more spectacularly than in the mass marriages celebrated between ten thousand Macedonian men and ten thousand Persian women at Susa after Alexander's return from the East. Among the marriage celebrants at Susa was Alexander's close friend Hephaestion, who ten years before had joined him in the ritual tribute to Achilles and Patroclus at Troy. Not long after the Susa marriages, Hephaestion was dead and Alexander decreed for him honors and funeral games that easily surpassed those given for Patroclus by Achilles in the last book of the *Iliad.* Within the next year Alexander himself was dead of a fever, eleven years after he had set sail to conquer the Persian Empire in the name of Greece.

The Homeric Pattern

No wonder that Alexander carried the Iliad with him on his expeditions in a precious casket. The written word is the choicest of relics. It is something at once more intimate with us and more universal than any work of art. It is the work of art nearest to life itself.
—HENRY DAVID THOREAU, *Walden*

To the extent that Alexander sought fame for his own achievement rather than for his predetermined place in society, he could create Alexander the

Great from Alexander III of Macedonia by two means: achievements beyond those of the past and achievements unheard of in the past. In recounting his extraordinary career, it hardly seems useful to separate the Alexander he created from the Alexander he became to others, or even from the Alexander he was to himself. Such distinctions assume that inner nature is more "real" than the social self and that a "true" explanation of Alexander would root his actions in adolescent fantasies of power (although his were hardly fantasies) or his personal and family history. But since Alexander was so overwhelmingly successful by the standards of his society and many societies to come, it is worth asking how that success might have been constructed. Instead of separating Alexander into the strands of his mother's passion, his father's military talent, and his tutor's teachings, we might focus on how Alexander brought those influences together uniquely into himself. For Alexander, as for all who live a life in public, the crucial question is less who he *was* than who he was *like,* how he explained himself to his own times and therefore how he wanted to be seen. Only then might we know in part how he saw himself. Throughout his career his achievements are inextricably tied to the way he understood the actions and characters of the heroes and gods he admired and emulated. So intertwined are his actions with the publicity that surrounds and shapes them that Alexander becomes the first clear example of the great man whose desire to excel puts earthly opponents a lowly second to the challenges posed by the heroes of the past, by the gods, and finally by his own nature.

I have used the contrast between Achilles and Odysseus to define Alexander's goals because he himself consciously exploited a genealogy of heroic fame that stretched back to the heroes of the *Iliad* and the *Odyssey.* Plutarch called the *Iliad* and the *Odyssey* Alexander's "equipment," as essential to his triumphs as his soldiers and more conventional weapons. On all his campaigns, it is said, he carried with him a copy of the *Iliad* especially annotated for him by Aristotle, and it was Aristotle's nephew Callisthenes who calculated for Alexander that it was exactly a thousand years to the month between the attack on Troy sung by Homer and the one embarked on against Persia by Alexander. Certainly, many other ancient rulers claimed descent from such semihistorical, semimythological figures. But Alexander invoked them as precedents by which he could convince others of not only his debt, but also his difference. His friendship with Hephaestion, for example, may have been modeled on that of Achilles for Patroclus, but it surpassed its model in intensity and glory. With the career of Alexander, the urge to fame begins to rely less on inheritance than on the willingness to assert that one deserves it as a member of a psychological tribe, with more affinities between each other than with any actual blood relatives, ancestors, or descendants.

Alexander's "program" was for fame as well as for achievement, and he succeeded beyond previous aspirants in part because he was raised in a society that had become self-conscious of its own inherited values. As a natural synthesizer, constantly assimilating and organizing meaning for his own purposes, Alexander illustrates that the monarchical personality is always a premediated construction. The only difference is in the quality and understanding of the builder. Many of the stories about Alexander indicate his special talent for transforming himself into the stuff of symbol and myth, and in the Macedonian society of his youth he found ready materials in a pervasive standard of Homeric heroism more intense even than that of Greece. In fact Macedonian society of the fourth century was much closer than Greek society to the world of the *Iliad*—with its proud nobles, its king the first among equals, and its constant need for a military defense against marauding tribes. Yet Macedonia also had a strong royal tradition of supporting Greek culture. It was in Pella under King Archelaus, fifty years or more before the time of Alexander, that Euripides wrote *The Bacchae,* with its tale of the fatal combat between the rationalist city-ruler Pentheus and the inspired followers of Dionysus, ancestor of the Macedonian kings. Alexander, a great reader and quoter of Euripides (as were most educated Macedonians), hardly needed his mother's example as a Dionysiac to reject the example of this boy-king who had only reason and order to protect himself. The artistic culture of Macedonia, although often sneered at by the Greeks, was in Alexander's time a rich heritage. Even before Archelaus, the Macedonian kings of the fifth century B.C. had welcomed Greek artists and artisans, philosophers and thinkers, to their courts— often when they were in flight from their native cities for political reasons. Alexander I brought Pindar, Perdiccas II invited Hippocrates, and Archelaus had his palace decorated by Zeuxis and even extended an invitation to Socrates in the midst of his trial.

Alexander's Macedonian heritage therefore included both a warrior aristocracy that valued the social forms embodied in the *Iliad* as well as a sophisticated culture that was often the product of artists unhonored in their native cities. His friend and early historian Onesicritus, would call him a "philosopher in arms," and Plutarch praised him as the greatest of philosophers although he wrote nothing. But I want to stress the strongly "bookish" way Alexander viewed himself and his world—a bookishness that was for him inseparable from realization in action. The honoring of the unknown soldier, invented by the British after World War One, depends on a modern army and a mass society. For the Greeks there is no such thing as an anonymous hero. Words and writing preserve the greatness of the past, and once that greatness has been described, it can be surpassed. The poems that celebrate fame and honor are handbooks of heroism for the future. To act historically, to make a figure in history, one must first stand apart and decide what history is. "Bookish" in our time implies a retreat from the world. But books for Alexander helped codify a world whose standards he first perfected and later transcended. Born in the middle of the fourth century B.C., Alexander is the true inheritor of fifth-century Greek literature—the drama of Aeschylus, Sophocles, and Euripides; the history of Herodotus and Thucydides; the newly written-down *Iliad* and *Odyssey*—because he understands how it allows a stepping back from mythology and the tales of heroes and thereby a new consciousness of how those stories might be reenacted and improved. Not long before, the Olympian family of twelve supreme gods had coalesced from the innumerable local gods and goddesses of Greece. Taking advantage of this new ecumenism of Greek religion, Alexander made himself the heir of almost all of its most outstanding figures.

In the restless search for achievement that took him beyond the boundaries of the known world, Alexander was also pressing beyond the traditional definitions of royal character. As familiar to Alexander as the works of Homer and the dramatists were the prescriptions for the good ruler in the writings of philosophers like Plato and his own teacher Aristotle. But until the biographies of Alexander that began to appear shortly after his death, there were few efforts to recount a king's life—or the life of any man. Power was not quite reason enough, unless an individual—like Cyrus in Xenophon's *Cyropaedia* or Pericles ın Thucydides' *History of the Peloponnesian War*—might help define the ideal of the good leader. But the interest in Alexander is as much an interest in the mystery of his personality as it is an effort to detail his political and military abilities. Aristotle in the *Politics* had allowed a supreme leader to exist only if the *arete* (the perfectly expressed virtue) of that leader is the summation of all the individual *arete* of the community. Thus the *arete* of the great individual is inclusive and absorptive, a kind of ultimate in nonprofessionalism. But the self-deception of rulers was also a major theme in fifth-century drama: If, like Oedipus or Pentheus, you don't know who you are, the trappings of public power will fall from you and you will end in disgrace or death. With such tutors of ideal and failure, Alexander realized the need to control the way he is perceived, making himself into someone to be talked about, interpreted, puzzled over, so that the mystery of his meaning would be as endless as his empire.

The tragedy of Oedipus is his unawareness of his ancestors, even his father and mother. But Alexander constantly manipulates his heroic background, even to the extent of superseding his parents with their famous forebears. By birth Alexander could call not only on Achilles as an ancestor, but also on Dionysus, Perseus, and Hercules—all heroic adventurers in whom the line between god and man was uncertainly drawn. The great dramatists of the fifth century had filled Greek places with their history and myths, not as vaguely remembered stories but as immediate, dramatic, and coherent events. Hercules especially was an attractive forebear (and one also emphasized by Philip), since he was the prime example in Greek mythology of the human being who by his own efforts became like a god.[6] Hercules was a man of action, a transcendent strongman whose twelve labors—in Greek *athloi*—placed him beyond the early attacks by Greek

---

6. According to myths reflected in Sophocles's *Trachiniae* (and later moralized by Isocrates), after the human body of Hercules was burned in the funeral pyre on Mt. Ida, his divine part ascended to heaven.

writers on the honors athletes received as opposed to thinkers. *Athloi* was also the word for the contests at the Olympian and Pythian games in which all the cities of Greece participated. The poet Pindar, a Theban of the previous century, had risen to fame on the basis of his poems in celebration of the winners. In a world where the calendar was usually determined by local priests or civic officials, the games represented the only division of time that was recognized across Greece, and in his odes Pindar celebrated the athletic hero by situating him in a national and familial mythology that was firmly anchored in the geography of a specific time and place.

When Thebes rebelled shortly after Alexander ascended the throne, he quickly destroyed the city and sold its citizens into slavery, exempting only the house and the descendants of Pindar. The action was telling, for Thebes was not only where his father Philip had been held hostage as a teenager, it was also the traditional birthplace of Hercules, not incidentally the founder of the Macedonian royal family. Thus Alexander combines cultural and military conquest by honoring the writer, the celebrator of heroes, while defeating the mythic protector of the rebellious city and progenitor of his own royal line. Alexander later restores the temple of Artemis, built long before by Croesus, and rebuilds the crumbling tomb of Cyrus the Great, honoring the great figures of the recent past. But the mythic gods and heroes are another matter. Alexander's relationship to these forerunners is like that of the *Odyssey* to the *Iliad,* the traveling Odysseus to the static Achilles. Turning away from an identity supplied by social order, Alexander opportunistically forges his name in a self-consciously staged combat with the past. Even much later, during his campaigns in India, when he hears of a citadel on an enormous rock that even Hercules could not conquer, he immediately lays siege to it and is the first to get to the top. In his respect for Pindar and his effort to supersede Hercules, Alexander defines this early moment of his public career in analogy to the situation of the competing athlete: Beyond your prowess, beyond your talent, can you also bear being looked at, praised if you win, but ignored or execrated if you lose? On his coins the features of Hercules and Helios gradually grow to resemble Alexander's—with his touseled hair, distracted gaze, and head slightly cocked to hear something more. Shortly after his death, Ptolemy I—Alexander's general and founder of a dynasty of Greek-speaking Egyptian rulers that ended three centuries later with Cleopatra—issued coins showing the head of Alexander, crowned with the skin of the Nemean lion, trophy of the first labor of Hercules. They were among the first coins to depict realistically an actual human being.[7]

---

7. Athletes were probably the earliest heroes to be praised formally by their contemporaries. The Olympic and other periodic sport competitions in ancient Greece furnished a chance to see the traits of a warrior's individual valor displayed before an audience, with a proper subordination to rules that are the equivalent of an internalized personal virtue. The games in this sense spiritualize war, and the athlete is a transcendent warrior.

In the *Odyssey,* Odysseus is most often likened to Hercules. But Alexander may also have been attracted to the Odysseus whom Homer compares three times to a poet. The final stage in Alexander's creation of his legend will involve becoming his own audience, combining both Pindar and those he praises. In contrast with the Platonic inclination to judge all by a philosophically determined ideal, Alexander's career displays a conviction that literature and story, the human record of the past, contain the basic standards against which behavior and character should be measured. The same historical consciousness sets Alexander against Aristotle's more practical ethics as well. Praise and blame, the monitors of Aristotelian behavior, are hardly appropriate ways to judge the hero who exists not in the context of a present society so much as in the timeless community of others like himself. Arrian, Alexander's Romanized Greek historian, recounts that Alexander at the grave of Achilles lamented that he himself had no Homer to celebrate his memory. This loss Arrian says he will supply with his book. But despite Arrian's bold claims to rescue Alexander from unjustified oblivion some five hundred years after he lived, in actuality there were at least six accounts of Alexander written by contemporaries as well as many later works. In order to present himself as the transcendent hero, Alexander clearly knew that he not only had to act heroically, but also had to make sure his actions were set properly into the records of time. To such awareness of the sanction of history, Pindar and Hercules may stand as godparents, for only recently had a universal calendar been generally accepted in Greece. Before, such local models as the succession of Spartan kings or Argive priestesses had been used. But by the time of Alexander the prime model had become the years of the Olympic games, and a crucial member of Alexander's Persian expedition was Aristotle's nephew Callisthenes, previously known for helping his uncle compile an authentic list of the winners of the Pythian games, now Alexander's official historian.

Empires have risen through the military and political ability of powerful kings only to vanish, leaving behind crumbling monuments and the dust of a few anecdotes. But Alexander's urge was for cultural and imaginative domination as well. Callisthenes' specific audience was the people of the Greek city-states, whom Alexander hoped to convince that he was the legitimate heir of the Iliadic heroes and the true standard-bearer of Greek culture. Accordingly, Callisthenes' particular role as historian-press agent was to note the indications of divine favor shown to Alexander in his quest and to underline the parallels between Alexander's actions and those of past (especially Homeric) heroes. With the first great victories in Asia Minor, Alexander also began to employ visual artists to depict him (and three hundred years later Horace would complain that Alexander had much better taste in visual artists than in poets). Of the artists, only Apelles the painter, Lysippus the sculptor, and Pyrgoteles the gem carver were allowed to depict Alexander from life; the others had to be contented with imitating their patterns.[8] By bringing the deeds of the Homeric heroes to life, Alexander gains a power over the minds of men as much as over their bodies, their land, or their gold. Plutarch praises Alexander highly for his support of the arts, while Arrian's Alexander is preeminently the great tactician and military strategist. But both appreciate Alexander's awareness of himself as an actor, a performer in public, who required art and language to preserve what he had done.

Kings have always been performers, but Alexander introduces the possibility that the king might be his own playwright and stage manager as well. Ancient historians concentrate so much on the battles fought by the great men of the past because there the premeditated will is clear. Only in their anecdotal reporting of strange episodes in the hero's life do they touch on why he has been remembered when so many great generals have been forgotten. Through his strategic abilities, his unparalleled development of siege machinery, and the decisive quality of the army he inherited from Philip, Alexander simultaneously helped to undermine the self-approval of the fighting soldier—so important to the Homeric conception of personal honor in war—even as he gave that sense of honor back by lavishly rewarding the heroic acts of individuals and units. He himself was the source of honor in his followers, their human intermediary with the standards of the heroic world. As all our sources attest, Alexander, unlike the Persian Great King and the Egyptian pharaoh, could maintain a closeness to his soldiers and companions—eating, drinking, being wounded—even while he was being worshiped elsewhere as a god or a god-hero. Absorbing precedents as rapidly as he absorbed land, Alexander therefore remains the earliest example of that paradoxical fame in which the spiritual authority of the hero is yet a model for a support of ordinary human nature.

Beyond the Horizon

Through the medium of the publicist-historian Callisthenes, Alexander had broadcast the story of his triumphs in terms that were understandable to a Greek world brought up on Homer. But in the next phase of his career that analogy is superseded. Previously, Alexander could be considered a hero who accomplishes things that anyone could do if they had only the opportunity, the power, the foresight, and the daring; afterward he becomes the hero who escapes even such grand categories in his con-

---

8. Renaissance painters were especially attracted to a story that Alexander had magnanimously given up his mistress Campaspe to Apelles, who had fallen in love with her while doing her portrait. None of the earliest sources contain the story, but it clearly appealed to the newly self-conscious Renaissance painters as a paradigm of the relationship between the great painter and the great patron.

stant urge to do things impossible, outsized, and unprecedented. In this new phase of his career, which begins after the first swift defeats of the Persian forces, Alexander's cutting of the Gordian knot is an emblematic incident. By refusing to untie the Gordian knot and slashing it apart instead (the most dramatic possibility), Alexander presents himself as someone free from the endless puzzles posed to men by the past. Unlike Oedipus, who has the wit to figure out the answer to the riddle of the sphinx but does not understand his own history, Alexander creates a new history for himself. Instead of unweaving the intricate knot, he swiftly and decisively makes its intricacy irrelevant to his solution. Alexander knew that cutting the Gordian knot would fulfill a prophecy of a conqueror come to Persia. But the act shows how Alexander both used and stepped beyond mere prophecy, first acquiescing in the usual ways of determining whom the gods favor, then creating his own portents. From the evidence of the story of the Gordian knot, as from so many other actions, we glimpse in Alexander a man who had an incredible sensitivity to the symbolic possibilities of his own personality. If there is premeditation in Alexander's construction of himself, it is not that of intrigue and plot. He defined boundaries in order to go beyond them, cutting the Gordian knot of past expectations of how problems should be solved and kings behave.

The victories after Gordium and the submission of Egypt to Alexander's power confirmed his assurance. Receiving the title of pharaoh had an important impact on Alexander's idea of his fame, just as triumphant visits to Egypt would later strongly affect Julius and Augustus Caesar, Marc Antony, and Napoleon. The Persians had created the first real world empire. But of all the rulers of the Middle East, the pharaohs had most elaborately and self-consciously kept the records of their dynasties and promulgated a national cult of their adoration. No more would Alexander's triumphs be sufficiently described in terms of the athletic labors of Hercules, the contests celebrated by Pindar, or even the martial prowess of the heroes of the *Iliad*. The fame of the athlete or of the soldier can be by extension a celebration as well of human nature, even that of the man drinking beer while he watches football on television. But in Egypt Alexander passes beyond the stages of athletic and military fame as celebrated by Pindar and Homer to enter a realm in which fame comes, not from the way one extends human nature, but from the way one goes beyond human nature—the realm of the man-god.

After being named pharaoh and founding Alexandria in the Nile Delta, the journey to the celebrated oracle of Siwah seems an almost compulsory next step for Alexander. Arrian notes that there was a tradition that the oracle had been consulted by both Hercules and Perseus, whom the Greeks considered to be the progenitor of the Persians, half of whose empire Alexander now controlled. As I've mentioned, we don't know with any accuracy what happened at Siwah. But the uncharacteristic secrecy of Alexander's meeting with the priest may itself be part of the publicity. Plutarch, like other later opponents of the Roman emperor cult, tries to exonerate Alexander from the charge of actually believing that he was the son of a god by saying that the assertion was made purely for policy, "to keep other men under obedience by the opinion conceived of his godhead" (North translation, 1286). But it is hardly necessary to make such a distinction. Not only does the ambiguity preserve the suggestion of divinity (always a vexed question for the historians of Alexander), but it also clearly implies Alexander's new effort to appear totally uncaused and uncreated by any earthly will but his own. Unlike the Homeric heroes, who went into battle as laden with their genealogy as with their armor, Alexander sought a self-motivation that could be sanctioned only by a direct relation to the gods. Previously, during his campaigns in Asia Minor, he had accepted his adoption by Ada, queen of Caria, in order to affirm his power over a nation otherwise uninterested in Greek politics or culture. Through the Siwah oracle's connection with the most high gods of Greece and Egypt, he had put himself up for adoption again, in a much more decisive way. The standards of the *Iliad* and the *Odyssey,* where gods intervened in the affairs of men, had been left behind for the possibility that god and man might meet on earth, in the person of Alexander.

After Siwah the atmosphere of Alexander's fame contains the new element of aloneness, his separation from mere mortals. More and more he saw in himself the intersection and mediation of disparate heroic, mythological, and national traditions. Conversely, if he could mediate those traditions, rule those territories, and be the living expression of those gods and heroes, then his own nature was coherent. Many later historians have denied that Alexander was a self-conscious Hellenizer. But he certainly made Greece and especially Greek literature the touchstone of value for an entire world, even to the extent that caused the historian Jacob Burckhardt to remark that if Alexander had not existed, we wouldn't know or care about the Greeks. Much as he had defined himself and his mission in accordance with the standards of Greek culture, so did he have to replicate that culture as he marched forward, in order that his achievement could be properly appreciated. But if the Greek polis now existed for him at all, it was not a geographical or a historical city, but a psychic one. In the Libyan desert Alexander's only competitor was the sun, until the oracle revealed how the sun—as Zeus, Ammon, or Ra—was his father. The journey toward the East and India is therefore also a journey toward the sun, as Alexander virtually established the tradition of a ruler's identification with the sun (perhaps once again superseding Odysseus, who had only stolen the Sun's cattle). Four hundred years later, in an effort to claim for themselves a large chunk of Alexander's former empire, Antony and Cleopatra would name their twin children Alexander Helios and Cleopatra Selene, Alexander the Sun and Cleopatra the Moon. As we shall see, by then the gesture had become a hollow repetition. But, for Alexander it was the necessary next phase in his sense of himself and the perception of himself he wished to give others. Lysippus, his official sculptor, blamed Apelles, the official painter, for now depicting Alexander with a thunderbolt in his hand rather than a spear. But the secret of Siwah made such a change in iconography almost compulsory.

Until Siwah, Alexander was self-consciously fitting himself into a tradition that in the process he was helping to define. After the oracle, and especially after the defeat and death of Darius, he begins to forge a tradition of his own, consciously or unconsciously dispensing with all who in any way might lay claim to having caused him to come into being. In the eyes of his ancient historians, his career falls into two parts. The second, although more triumphant, is marked with greater personal excesses, elaborate anecdotes about his drinking (a Macedonian tribute to Dionysus unappreciated by sober historians), and his frequent uncontrollable rages, which Plutarch calls the worst of passions because they are antisocial. In fact it does seem that a social control Alexander exercised over himself earlier in his career has, at least selectively, disappeared. Whether the oracle of Siwah confirmed his belief that the most high gods of Greece and Egypt were his real, his spiritual, or his symbolic fathers, no one can tell. But almost immediately following on the final defeat of the Persian forces and the discovery that Darius had been murdered, Alexander, through premeditation or chance or accident, rids himself of several crucial earthly rivals and progenitors: by the execution of Philotas, head of his elite corps of Companions; the execution of Parmenio, father of Philotas and head general of Alexander's army; the accidental murder of his cavalry commander Cleitus, who had saved his life at the battle of Granicus and whose sister had been his wet nurse; and finally the arrest and execution of Callisthenes, his historian and propagandist.

The pattern seems clear. In one way or another all four had asserted that they were either rivals to Alexander, antagonists of his new view of empire, or creators of his success. Two of the men, Parmenio and Cleitus, were his father's age and had been party to Philip's plans for the revenge attack on Persia. The two others, Philotas and Callisthenes, were closer to Alexander's age, yet loyal to his past preceptors. In addition all four were extremely hostile to Alexander's increasing effort to bring Macedonia and Persia together culturally as well as militarily. Cleitus especially had denounced Alexander's adoption of a modified Persian court dress and his new practice of maintaining two courts, Macedonian and Persian. Philotas had bragged that all of Alexander's military victories were due to him. Parmenio could easily have been thought to have encouraged his son's claim and in any case had been Philip's general as well. Cleitus, whom Alexander killed in a fit of drunken rage he deeply regretted, had the difficult honor of having saved Alexander's life and boasted of it; he also accused Alexander of having turned his back on his Greek and Macedonian heritage to enforce the "servile" ways of Persians toward their king.

Finally, after these military and political rivals, Callisthenes, the man of words, was accused of treason in his turn. The propagandist of Alexander's heroic grandeur, Callisthenes was also a nay-sayer to his divinity and had refused to perform the new court ritual of *proskynesis*. In the way of unreflective teachers, he was cut down by a power he helped to create. Appropriately enough, he was accused of instigating an assassination plot among Alexander's young pages, who were his pupils. Thus begins that conflict between rulers and writers that will become even more intense at Rome: the sharp and easily crossed distinction between the writers who support the great man and those who attack him; the king-politician's well-founded suspicion that all writers, whether now friends or enemies, believe that their work is innately superior to the conquering of lands and peoples. Some four hundred years later, the example of Callisthenes echoes ominously in the writings of the philosopher-politician Seneca. Once tutor to Nero and virtual coruler of the empire, Seneca had been forced into retirement, and soon was to commit suicide for complicity in a plot to assassinate the emperor:

> The murder of Callisthenes is the ever-lasting crime of Alexander, which no virtue, no success in war, will redeem. . . . Whenever it is said, "He conquered everything all the way to the Ocean and even made an attack on the Ocean itself with ships unknown to that water; and he extended his empire from a corner of Thrace to the farthest boundaries of the East," it will be said: "But he killed Callisthenes." Although he went beyond all the achievements in antiquity of generals and kings, of the things which he did nothing will be as great as his crime (193–95).

We have two traditions of what happened to Callisthenes: one that he was executed immediately; the other that he was carried around by the army in a cage until he died, fat and worm-ridden. Whatever its historical accuracy, it is the carnival-show revenge that accords symbolically with Alexander's new sense of himself. In the long battle between philosophers and politicians, his farcical exhibition of Callisthenes has the blooming mockery of a man who had decided to become his own historian. The Greek world of agonistic, one-on-one achievement—achievement through emulation and competition—was now irrelevant to his constantly recharted horizons and his constant movement beyond each succeeding set of limits. Instead of affording him a place to rest, each achievement impelled Alexander forward. Only a mutiny in his own army finally forced him to turn back. Callisthenes had compared Alexander's triumphs with those of myth and legend. But after surpassing Dionysus in India, Alexander was writing a history without analogy or parallel, his unending desire to assimilate the whole world to himself thwarted only by rebellions within. Fitting each newfound image of heroic power into the mosaic of his nature, Alexander made the past work for him, proclaiming by his career that those who would last through time would only be those who refused to be bound by time. He had been to Athens perhaps only once. But through Callisthenes he sent reports of his triumphs back to an Athens that was born from his own definition of its meaning rather than from the sordid realities of fourth-century Greek politics. A few years after the death of Callisthenes and only a year before his own death at thirty-three, Alexander asked for and received the status of a god in Athens. But on his deathbed, according to stories put out among his troops, he expressed a wish to be buried at Siwah.

The Heritage of Alexander

. . . [T]he noblest deeds do not always show men's virtues and vices, but oftentimes a light occasion, a word, or some sport makes men's natural dispositions and manners appear more plain than the famous battles won wherein are slain ten thousand men, or the great armies or cities won by siege and assault.   —PLUTARCH, "Alexander"

Alexander, like many of the surpassingly famous through history, was an individual who challenged basic assumptions about the way individuals intersect with their times and their societies. As the greatest figures often do, Alexander had appeared at a crucial juncture in history, when older definitions of both public and private behavior were breaking down. Somehow he had managed to synthesize elements of character and action that then and later struck many as a tissue of disparities and contradictions. In the course of his career he became simultaneously more abstract (as the Persian Great King) and more individual (as the unprecedented Alexander). Newly spun fantasies about his life still had tremendous popularity into the Middle Ages, when some authors postulated that he was at once god and demon. Even now historians continue to ask the ancient questions about his character: How could he build cities and yet murder a friend in a fit of anger, conquer the world's greatest empire and yet get drunk with his companions, assert that he was the son of a god and yet be wounded and even joke about the inconsistency?

Talent, of course, had much to do with Alexander's victories. But it was a talent thrust forward by an enormous desire to achieve and an endless longing to fulfill itself. His policies of resettlement, the founding of cities, the separation of civic from military power, and cultural fusion between Greeks, Macedonians, and Persians under the aegis of Greek language and culture created a new definition of what it meant to rule. In his wake Greek culture flowed daily, even permeating areas, such as Cappodocia in the center of the old Persian Empire, where Greek politics and arms had not.

Alexander's material achievements were unparalleled. But what supplied the inner force for those achievements as well as for the legend of Alexander was his special attitude toward himself. At the extreme eastern limit of his conquests, Alexander raised an altar to the twelve members of the Olympian family. Sometime before this, in yet another example of his unceasing exercises in comparative mythology, he had decided that by occupying and passing beyond the city of Nysa, he had now superseded Dionysus ("the god from Nysa") and the city's traditional founder. In this double inheritance of divinity—the official Olympians and the outsider Dionysus—may be some clue to the kind of renown he sought. In the Greek tradition Zeus was the head of the Olympian family and thereby the ruler of the heavens and the earth as well.

As W. K. C. Guthrie and others have pointed out, the Greeks viewed Zeus as somewhat on the order of the universal god of the monotheists, a supreme heavenly power who could potentially be likened to a supreme power on earth. But to this divine political power Alexander added the more personal politics of Dionysus, whose divinity enters into the worshiper. In the Olympian ritual, the god is *worshiped,* while in the Dionysian, the god (in his animal form) is *consumed.* Thus there are two Alexanders. In the later iconography of his sculptured image—a flowing mane of hair, head twisted toward the left, eyes turned toward the sky—Alexander resembles an enraptured Dionysiac or an inspired poet. But in his conquests and his empire, he inclines more to Zeus and the other sun gods, who stand at the top of all earthly and divine hierarchies, furnishing the pattern for divine rule in Western Europe from the Romans down to the Stuarts of England and the Bourbons of France.

In his time Alexander was alone. But that void of competitors was destined to become more crowded, if only because his career was now available as a guide. Whether their goals were to conquer the world through arms, through art, or through spirit, in some sense he had first shown the way. After his death, his myth, like his empire, was dispersed in a myriad of directions. From his generals arose a new generation of hero/god/kings, the Successors, who fought for shares in the sprawling empire. Of these, the most successful was Ptolemy of Egypt. With Alexander as his preceptor, he seems to have learned best how to gather to himself the traditions of another culture. Appropriately enough, it was Ptolemy who diverted the funeral cortege of Alexander on its way to Macedonia and brought it instead to Alexandria, where it could be viewed in uncorrupted conditions three centuries later: first by Julius Caesar after his defeat of Pompey at the battle of Pharsalus; and then by Caesar's heir, Octavian (later Augustus), after his defeat of Antony and Cleopatra. Like Alexander, Ptolemy put himself up for adoption, and his later policies of encouraging science, agriculture, and learning in Egypt imply that as Alexander's general he had also learned the lessons of cultural commingling along with those of military and political conquest. Ruling with Alexander's mythic sanction, Ptolemy also became one of his earliest historians and laid the groundwork for the great library of Alexandria, the center of Greek learning and intellectual activity for the whole Mediterranean world. And the hero-emulating Alexander may have been pleased with the irony that Zenodotos, the first head of the great Library of Alexandria, published a

Homeric glossary, collated manuscripts of the *Iliad* and the *Odyssey,* and, in tribute to the Greek alphabet, divided the two poems for the first time into the twenty-four books by which we now know them.

Alexander's example seems to have had a strong influence on political and national aspirations as well. In one of the most striking cases, Chandragupta, an Indian prince who had visited Alexander's camp on the Hydaspes, went on to found the Mauryan dynasty. His grandson Asoka extended the rule of this first great Indian empire to nearly all of India and Afghanistan. After his conquests, he renounced violence and converted to Buddhism. In the great expansion of religious building that followed, monumental column sculpture began to appear in a religion previously marked by an antagonism or indifference to representational imagery. Buddha himself would not be depicted for some centuries to come. But it is intriguing to note that one prime source of that later visual imagery is Gandhāra, a center of Buddhist studies in what is now northern Pakistan, which was ruled by Greek generals until the first century A.D. On the heads of these Buddhas is a characteristic topknot that some have traced from Indian precedents and others from the Macedonian war helmet, while their faces definitely resemble those of Apollo or Hermes. Thus although the image itself has predominantly Indian roots, the urge to such imagery owes some debt to the forces set into motion by Alexander. As Heinrich Zimmer writes, "the concept of the Buddha [was imbued] with the strong personal character of a victorious spiritual individual. . . . The cosmic savior was humanized in the manner of a semidivine Greek hero" (I, 345).[9]

Who could say that the career of Alexander did not have a philosophical effect as well? On the news of his death, Aristotle fled from Athens and died a year later. Not long after, another philosopher came to Athens: Zeno, the founder of Stoicism—a philosophy that would find its largest audience among the Romans who accepted Augustus's empire. So too returned to Greece a member of Alexander's train in Asia named Pyrrho, who founded the school of sceptical philosophy that asserted no knowledge was definite. But perhaps most intriguing of all the intellectual fallout from the career of Alexander was the work of Euhemerus, who served under Cassander, a longtime antagonist of Alexander.

9. In the early ages of Buddhism, before the introduction of Buddhist representational imagery, the *stūpa* or burial mound was one of the sole places for acts of veneration. Alexander commemorated the death of Bucephalus in Gandhāra by founding the town of Bucephala along the Hydaspes, and in nearby Rawalpindi there is an ancient *stūpa* locally venerated as the tomb of Bucephalus (Bamm, 55).

In Greece itself, as fifth-century dramatic literature had brought the myths into a more direct relationship with their audience, so portraiture in the same period was also becoming much more realistic. Even when it was idealized, it was based on living models rather than on traditional rules for the appearance of a god. The extent to which Alexander's actual features appeared on coins in his lifetime is arguable. But his example was influential, and it soon became common for local rulers in various parts of his former empire to impress some version of their faces on their money. Alexander's impact on Buddhist conceptions of authority, while still debated, are at least more uplifting, for his iconography introduces the possibility that visualization might enhance rather than diminish greatness.

After Alexander's death Cassander had asserted his rule over Greece by murdering Alexander's wife, his son, and his mother Olympias. Euhemerus, however, may have understood the lesson of Alexander's career better than the man who thought he could extinguish the fame of Alexander with his own. His most influential work, known to us only through fragments and an epitome by Eusebius, is a philosophical novel in which Euhemerus travels to an imaginary island where he learns from inscriptions that the gods—especially the high gods Uranus, Cronus, and Zeus—were in fact human kings about whom myths and stories collected. The idea had been around before, but never so forcefully presented, and it caught men's imaginations. Hardly a century after Alexander's death, Ennius, the first great Roman writer, wrote his own version of Euhemerus's novel, including the Roman Jupiter as well among the gods who had been kings.

With the establishment of the Ptolemaic dynasty and the Library of Alexandria, something of the institutional had come into the boundary-bursting world of Alexander's achievements. In the West it is Alexander-Zeus rather than Alexander-Dionysus who boasts the most descendants. At Rome his ever-expansive *pothos* and his dream of cultural fusion appear as a thirst for domination, ultimately transformed into a consolidation of administrative and military power under one supreme ruler, the Roman emperor. Alexander could still build in empty spaces. But by three centuries later the world was already getting more populated and the opportunities for uniqueness more restricted. What happens when there turns out to be too many Alexanders? In the fame society of Rome, as well as in the Renaissance, men were particularly intrigued by a late-blooming anecdote in which a young man named Herostratus, on the day of Alexander's birth, burns down the Temple of Diana at Ephesus so that he can be as famous as the newborn king's son: If the goal was only fame, then any extreme act, even violence and destruction, might do. Or, as the Renaissance writers often phrased it, we know the name Herostratus, but the names of the temple's architects are lost.

II

THE DESTINY
OF ROME

Public Men and the Fall
of the Roman Republic

> Public esteem is the nurse of the arts and all men are fired to application by fame, whilst those pursuits which meet with general disapproval always lie neglected. —CICERO, *Tusculan Disputations*

Once a vocabulary is created, once a group of gestures is made, they can be reproduced and refined by others. Yet few of Alexander's immediate Successors, with the exception of the Ptolemies, actually made his methods work for them. But his memory lay heavily on the Romans, a society that was especially susceptible to the destructive energies his example could unleash. About one hundred years after Alexander's death in 323 B.C., Hannibal invoked him as a forerunner of his own war against Rome. In the first century B.C., the last century of the Roman Republic, Mithridates, a king from Asia Minor who affected the dress and even the hairstyle of Alexander, fought three long and drawn-out wars against Rome until his defeat by Pompey who, as we shall see, also considered himself a second Alexander. Some fifty years later, early in the reign of Augustus, the historian Livy goes out of his way to attack those (unnamed persons) who believe that Alexander could have conquered Italy if he had lived. Certainly, says Livy, he could not have defeated the great Roman generals or outthought the wisdom of the Roman Senate. His greatness was attained in ten years only because of good fortune and despite a passionate nature. How could that compare with Roman virtue and eight hundred years of Roman military experience? No doubt his difficulties with the Roman landscape would have been similar to those found by Hannibal (with his elephants inspired by Alexander's in India) two hundred years later. Roman weapons are much better, Livy continues, the Roman battle line is more effective, Romans build better military works, can stand more fatigue and hardship, have stronger spirits, and would even have fought shoulder to shoulder with the Carthaginians against Alexander and his 'mongrel' army of Macedonians, Greeks, and Persians.

The competitive tone in Livy's account is unmistakable. As we shall see, much of it is colored by strong memories of Augustus's conflict with Marc Antony, who had styled himself an inheritor of Alexander's empire. But it is still remarkable that three hundred years or so after Alexander's conquests a Roman historian is moved to defend his country hypothetically against his power.[1] As usual, the terms in which the competition is posed are instructive, for they indicate the distinction between the official Roman definition of fame and that signified in the career of Alexander. His danger would have been greater, writes Livy, "inasmuch as the Macedonians would have had but a single Alexander . . . while there would have been many Romans who were a match for Alexander, whether for glory or for the greatness of their deeds, of whom each one would have lived and died as his own fate commanded, without endangering the State" (235–37). The Roman state, therefore, is the proper context for individual Roman glory. Without Rome, without the frame of the *res publica* (the public thing), individual assertion, especially on the grand scale of Alexander, is only the eruption of extraordinary fortune, a freak of nature, not a truth of history.

The lure of Rome as an idea is crucial to understanding the race for fame in the last century of the Roman Republic. Unlike the fame of Alexander, which was a heightened and elaborated version of the fame of the ruler, Roman fame was fashioned within a city—a city that had only recently emerged as the great power in the Mediterranean after defeating its archrival Carthage and the massed city-states of Greece, a city celebrated by its poets as the inheritor of Troy, a city that would give its name to an empire. Alexander sought to create one cultural world from Pella to Alexandria Eschate, and his policies were resisted by many Greeks and Macedonians. But Roman military and political expansion was always to the greater glory of Rome. Personal honor (*dignitas*) and national glory were linked, and all moved inexorably toward the absolute. Fame at Rome was defined by action in public for the good or ostensible good of the state. Privacy was suspect, especially when it detracted from an individual's public usefulness. In such a theatrical conception of life, when seeing someone from the outside constitutes the most accurate and authentic perspective, the offstage is the obscene. The Roman public man is a performer and a whole tradition of storytelling about early Roman history emphasized the virtue of symbolic acts in defense of the essential nature of Rome. Our own uncertainties about the morality of public behavior and the personalities of public people will arise in great part from the Judeo-Christian attack against Roman standards of public glory. But in the last century of the Republic such responses have hardly yet come into general currency.

The writing of history is always an effort to give time a shape through words, and the audience for historians is therefore often those classes and individuals who identify that meaning with their own interests and sharpen their wills on its edge. The emulation with Alexander first inspired rulers and those who sought absolute military and political power. But Rome

1. In fact, fourth-century Rome, hardly the same world power she later became, sent emissaries of submission and friendship to Alexander of Epirus, Alexander's brother-in-law, whom they supported in his invasion of Italy.

would infect the world with the desire for personal recognition. No wonder that the names of her great men still echo down to us after two thousand years. It takes some excavation to contemplate and interpret the Greek words for achievement in public. *Philotimia* (love of honor) and *doxa* (good opinion, praise) are hardly part of our everyday vocabulary. But the Latin words—*fama, ambitio, celebritas*—are still current, not only in English, but in many European languages as well.

In a world where to be from a great city was the most honored form of identity, a man in public was a man from a city. Since Rome was the greatest city, Rome produced the greatest men. Roman fame is therefore to a great extent urban fame, the fame that can be achieved in the *urbs,* the city whose resources for the propaganda and publicity of names and personal styles attracts the energies of aspiring men. Livy's defensive remarks about Alexander are written at the end of the first century B.C., about twenty years after Julius Caesar and his rival Pompey had helped plunge Rome into a civil war from which Caesar emerged victorious, only to be assassinated himself five years later. But Livy's view of the relative importance of Alexander and the Romans has been conditioned by a new perception of history first formulated by the Greek historian Polybius. Polybius was a hostage taken in the final defeat of Greece by Rome, and the message of his world history was Roman destiny—the divine providence that allowed Rome to build a materially and a morally superior empire—the special relation of Rome to time. Greece had been defeated, Carthage had been destroyed, and historians like Polybius would make the Roman aristocracy even more self-conscious of its historical mission. Alexander's regret that he had no Homer to sing of his exploits would be small assertion indeed compared to that of the Romans, who took the lesson Greek historians taught them of their inevitable greatness and imposed it on the rest of the world.

It is satisfying to be assured of a manifest destiny, but for the individual Roman the prophecy hardly induced passivity. Rome may be the agent of divine providence, went the message, but every true Roman must strive to make himself worthy of his place in the Roman order. In the hothouse atmosphere of the last century of the Republic, brought about both by important changes in the structure of Roman politics and by the looming examples of Alexander and Hannibal, the Roman urge to fame and distinction encouraged individuals who, in their turn, raised the social temperature with their outsized doings. Armed with their destiny, Romans constantly referred all political arguments to its final standard. Within the city, combat and competition between rival factions determined whose definition of that destiny would triumph. But to the world outside Rome, the city itself remained paramount, worshiped as early as the beginning of the second century B.C. in a Smyrna temple dedicated to the Deified City of Rome. From Rome down to its inheritors in Paris, London, and New York, visual fame has been what D. R. Shackleton Bailey in his book on Cicero calls "a metropolitan commodity" (14–15). In about the middle of the first century B.C., a certain Demetrius the Magnesian (a friend of Cicero's publisher, Atticus) wrote a book called *On Persons of the Same Name* and later another called *On Towns of the Same Name*. Both almost comically indicate the new difficulties in making one's mark in an increasingly large world. At the time of Alexander perhaps there was little need to go beyond a name, a place, and, for the great, a bit of genealogy (father and grandfather at most) to let people know who you were. But Demetrius seems to have designed his book as a guide to a world that was getting too large for the old methods of identification and naming. If people were designated by the first name and town, like Demetrius the Magnesian, what in an increasingly populated world would distinguish him from other Demetriuses born in other Magnesias?

When all distinction comes from public action, the stakes of fame get higher, the actions more grandiose, and the players look for theaters larger than the normal round of public office. When the state is the prime place where honor can be achieved, each new leap to glory helps heighten the conflict between individual and national glory—until one gives way, and the arena is either transformed or destroyed. In accordance with the prime importance of Rome and Roman history for determining the meaning of Roman behavior, Livy's history is *ab urbe condita,* "from the founding of the city," and the collective entity called Rome is its hero. In fact the origins of Rome are dim. But in the traditions summarized by Livy, the Republic was founded in the sixth century B.C. after a popular uprising against the king, Tarquin the Proud, that occurred when Lucretia, a Roman matron, committed suicide after revealing to her husband that she had been raped by Tarquin's son. With Tarquin's defeat the monarch was replaced by two annually elected leaders, the consuls. The first were Lucretia's husband and Junius Brutus, who led the revolt. With the shift in the nature of Roman government, a shift in the naming of Roman time occurred as well: The years were no longer defined by their place in the reign of a ruler or ruling dynasty, but by the names of the men who held the consulship for that term. By the end of the fourth century Roman public officials had begun to publish a calendar of important public events called the *Fasti,* which gave a chronological framework to the collection of myths, anecdotes, and fragmentary records that then constituted the Roman past. Like the invention of elaboration of such stories as the rape of Lucretia, the *Fasti* forcibly reminded every Roman citizen of a history imbedded in everyday life.[2]

Even before Polybius, then, the Roman view of history emphasized that the scope of public action in the present was always determined by the great events of the past. Naturally, if one could trace one's name or family back into legend, the pressure of competition and emulation was even

2. A hostile interpretation of the Lucretia story is the springboard for St. Augustine's attack on Roman concepts of public virtue in *The City of God* in the fourth century A.D. Augustine considers Lucretia's suicide to be a prime example of the general Roman urge to be virtuous primarily in the eyes of others.

stronger. At the end of the Republic, for example, the conspirator Brutus feels a compulsion to act against the rule of Caesar that comes as much from the example of Junius Brutus as it does from his political principles. Living in a country that prides itself on honoring individual merit irrespective of family ties, we might think such echoes are coincidental and anyone who takes them seriously is either superstitious or deluded. But the political history of Rome was clearly written in the genealogies of its great families for all to see. *Nobilis* in Latin originally means someone who is *known*. The upper class, the political class, was therefore by definition a class whose families were known for their public adherence to the public good, as that good had been defined by law and custom from the earliest days of the city. They were a class history had made extremely sensitive to their visibility in the state. In all Roman noble houses were displayed *imagines* (wax masks)—first idealized, later realistic—of ancestors who had held the chief offices in Rome reserved for those of aristocratic privilege. These masks were also worn (usually by actors) during funeral processions in order to celebrate not only the noble who had died, but also his illustrious ancestors (*illustris* [in the light]) for their service to the Republic, the public thing.[3]

The family was the basic Roman legal unit and the power of the father supreme within the family. Roman public genealogy was therefore in essence a continuity of paternal name and power, and intermarriage between great families an acknowledged mode of political aspiration, especially when, as happened so often in the first century B.C., war had severely pruned the crop of eligible noblemen. Not only did the Roman noble inherit family prestige, he also received the benefits of a system of obligations and responsibilities that bound him to other men and other families—called his clients (*clientelae*), for whom one of his ancestors had done a favor that established a time-honored relationship. Nobles swept through Rome with their clients who, among other requirements, were expected to furnish political support and even stand attendance at the noble's breakfast. The greatest nobles counted not just fellow Romans but even foreign rulers and whole cities or countries among their clients, in consequence of a battle won or a loan given at some crucial time. Like the Capulets and the Montagues fifteen hundred years later, the Roman nobles of the Republic inherited enemies as well as friends, but, unlike Romeo and Juliet, they rarely considered love to be an admirable motive for either public or private behavior.

Fame for public action was so important to the Romans, as it was to

3. In the domestic display of masks, lines painted on the wall indicated the family ties. As Pliny the Elder remarks in his description of the funeral practice, "always when some member of [the family] passed away the entire company of his house that had ever existed was present" (265). Brutus's special self-consciousness of the meaning of his ancestry is further indicated some ten years before the assassination of Caesar. Then, while he serves as one of the official Roman "moneyers," he has a coin minted with Junius Brutus on one side and C. Servilius Ahala on the other—both ancestors and both celebrated deliverers of their country from tyranny.

the Homeric Greeks, because in a religion without a developed concept of the afterlife it was the only way to live beyond death. But in contrast to the Greek warriors who sought glory for the manner of their deaths, the Romans more often focused on the way the death was celebrated. The greater the man, the more elaborate the tomb. The Latin word for large tomb, *mausoleum,* memorializes a ruler of Asia Minor a few years before Alexander, who is remembered not for his successful independence from Persian power but for the immense building he created to house his corpse. Similarly, after a life devoted to Rome, the aristocrat would make the largest assertion of his name in death and his tomb would be engraved with his face, his honors, and his ancestors.

This emphasis on fame at the point of death had its extreme model in the funeral practices of the pharaohs. The pyramids and burial chambers so lavishly decorated and supplied with food, furniture, and servants, facilitated the journey of the buried monarch toward another world, which is less the afterlife than the future. In the tombs were also innumerable messages about who this king was and what his accomplishments had been, who were his ancestors and who might be his descendants. The Egyptian attitude toward public identity can therefore be divided into two linked areas: possessions and publicity. The pyramids and colossal statues, the many temples, were all reminders to the living of the greatness that had once been on earth. The world after death for the pharaohs is therefore a forerunner of our own idea of posterity. It's hard to say that the method was not effective. King Tutankhamen, a very minor king by historical standards, yet amassed enough treasure for his tomb that in today's world he is viewed with wonder. The prestige of his possessions, his gold and jewels, lends him a celebrity that his achievements do not. Law contains a concept termed *personalty,* which means the individual as defined by his possessions. King Tut and his many rivals in the realms of wealth and profusion, while they may not have very much character, thus have a lot of personalty. The late nineteenth century in America was probably the last time in world history that such monument building by individual wealth could be done without irony. Now, after the abortive effort of Adolf Hitler and Albert Speer to restore the grandiosity of the Egyptian leader cult, it is primarily corporations who have the money or the nerve to create such gilded letters to the future about themselves, so that what they were—how much wealth they controlled—might not be forgotten.

The traditions of Roman public behavior were, like those of the Egyptians, expressed through the connected power of genealogy and money, with the difference that at Rome both were expressions of the privileges of a ruling elite rather than those of a monarch. The face was already negotiable in Roman society. One of the most effective ways of adding material power to its cultural power was by military victories. Generals were allowed to take their own share of the tribute conquered peoples paid to the Roman state. They could also directly sell the service of their armies to foreign rulers who wanted their kingdoms back or secured. For those aspirants to fame and power who belonged either to a newly noble family (like Pompey) or to one that had decayed (like Caesar), a clientele built up through military prowess furnished wealth enough to win elections at home. After his wars in Africa and the East, Pompey gave his soldiers gifts amounting to millions of dollars. By the time Caesar returned from his campaigns against Gaul, it was said that he had become even wealthier than Pompey. And Crassus, the third member of their unofficial "triumvirate" of rulers, was quoted as saying that no man could be considered wealthy who could not buy (outfit and support) a legion—six thousand men.

Such millionaire soldier-politicians were a symptom of the disease they sought to cure. So long as there was a balance of ambition within the Roman upper class and so long as the Roman people were content to allow that upper class to define the essence of Rome, then public virtue and personal ambition could be held in balance by the stately procession through public offices that the Romans called the *cursus honorum* (racetrack of honors).[4] The burden of the past was heavy at Rome—the example of great ancestors, the elaborate structure of law and administrative precedent, the social pressure of customary usage (*mos maiorum*). To our minds all these traditional structures might imply standards of social behavior that absorbed the individual. But because of the Roman upperclass tradition of self-display, they had a strong personal aspect as well. On the one hand, the upper-class tradition of state service implied the subordination of an individual's desires to the good of the state: Without Rome there is no *integritas* and no *dignitas*. But, on the other hand, the constant public self-presentation of the Roman upper class, their preoccupation with theater, ritual, and the restaging of history, indicates the ease with which men on either side of a crucial political issue could believe that they alone represented the true Rome. Similarly, from one point of view, the Roman Republic determined all social behavior through a vast fabric of laws. But from another, law itself was incomplete without the adversary situation of the law courts, where men made their reputations and came to political prominence (as did Cicero) by their ability to defend or (less often) prosecute on a raised platform in the Roman Forum, where every passerby could appreciate their performances. Thus, when Greek historians began writing of Roman destiny, and Roman victories seemed to make that destiny a fact, many Romans were encouraged to be more

4. Although the Latin *cursus* remains most obviously in the English *course,* it shares a more intriguing metaphorical relation with *career:* Both are words that first applied to horse races and later to the stages of professional development. Although *career* in its racing sense appears early in English, its modern meaning dates only to the early nineteenth century and even then primarily refers to a working life that contains striking moments. In the course of the nineteenth century, as professions and occupations begin to codify their internal standards and entrance requirements, *career* gradually comes to mean whatever work (above a certain level) one does, with the general suggestion that an improvement in status always continues.

self-conscious about their place in history and the most avid aspirants for fame searched for new ways to make time move more quickly.

Time, money, law—to win at Rome, it seems, one had to put a personal stamp on the traditional structure of things. What must it be like for the ambitious to live in a society where the years are called by the names of those who held a certain office—no matter what they achieved in that office?[5] Through an overwhelming sense of its own destiny, Rome by the first century B.C. had become a country that had stumbled its way into an empire that it could not control. It therefore sought a new kind of leader, one who could maintain that destiny and protect the city from internal dissension in the process. So long as a ruling class is self-confident, it can absorb such new forces without disruption. But when the class's image of itself and its values has been called into doubt, hairline inconsistencies develop into chasms. A respect for the past and defense of the status quo by many nobles therefore could go hand in hand with the efforts of others to reshape its legacy to meet new demands. Perhaps this will always be the situation when ruling classes fall out among themselves: Most members cling to their ancient privileges; some look for satisfaction to the future. Rome in the age of the Late Republic may not have been the first state in which personal ambitions undermined the politics that had nurtured them. But it offers an intriguing and influential model of several important ways the urge to personal fame and power can destructively collide with those political and national values that the new heroes believe themselves called on to preserve. In great part Augustus will create the Roman Empire to prevent such a collision from occurring again. But its ambiguous legacy is still with us.

How might I characterize the first rehearsals for the race for fame that would shape the political life of the last century of the Roman Republic? Perhaps the first group of Romans we might consider famous in the way later ages used the word were the Scipios, patrons of Greek culture and military heroes. Celebrated in Polybius's history as agents of Roman destiny, they absorbed the world into their names: Scipio *Africanus,* his brother Scipio *Asiaticus,* and his brother-in-law Aemilius Paulus *Macedonicus.* Of these, Scipio Africanus was the most flamboyant. Like his rival Hannibal (whom he finally defeated), Scipio was seized with a conviction that he was destined to be a world conquerer on the scale of Alexander. Depicted like Alexander with his head thrown back and long hair resembling the rays of the sun, Scipio even built a special addition to the public temple of Jupiter, where he could worship the king of the gods as the private god of his family. Despite the grand imagery, however, the fame of Scipio and his family still remained within the traditional circuit of noble ambition. Like Cincinnatus—the part-historical, part-legendary

5. In Greece, by comparison, the Olympiads were named after the person who won the sprint. In Athens, the years were named after the Archon Eponymous, not an elected official but one whose name was drawn by lot from the class with the greatest wealth.

Roman leader who left his farm, led the Romans to victory, and then returned to his plow—Scipio Africanus did not turn his military power into
political sway. Neither the times nor the customs were quite ready. A
century later Cicero, in exile, would consider the time of the Scipios to be
the last era in Roman history when personal fame and public service were
easily compatible.

Toward the end of the second century B.C., when the growing power of
other constituencies began to undermine the aristocratic control of Roman
politics, the brothers Tiberius and Gaius Gracchus launched a new force
in Roman politics, the *populares,* nobly born politicians who supported the
demands of the people against the privileges of the Senate. Occupying
offices that had for the most part been held by nonaristocrats, the Gracchi
established a program that forcefully attempted to open up the tight world
of Roman hereditary politics: free grain distribution for the Roman city
dwellers; land distribution for the increasing number of war veterans;
and the extension of Roman citizenship to neighboring tribes and cities
in Italy. At about the time another new force in politics arose—the rich
but unaristocratic equestrian class, originally the members of the cavalry
itself, but later those men who, through trade or banking, could afford
to outfit a troop of soldiers. When Gaius Gracchus helped give this class
control of the law courts, it emerged as a third factor, between the "people" and the hereditary nobility. From it would equally spring popular
figures like the general Marius and senatorial champions like Cicero.

Historians often spend many pages measuring the mix of political principle and personal ambition in the career of public figures. But the distinction is questionable, particularly in societies coming to new degrees of
national self-consciousness. *Ambitio* in Latin means to walk around, can-
vassing for votes. From the days of the Scipios and the Gracchi down to
the dictatorship of Julius Caesar, political programs and personal ambitions are aspects of each other, each candidate asserting or assuming his
interests with those of Rome. By widening the possession of political
power, the Gracchi might argue, they were helping to modernize a state
in transition from being the strongest one in Italy to being the greatest
power in the Mediterranean and western Europe. Their senatorial opponents, on the other hand, could with equal sincerity say that the Gracchi
had betrayed their class and country by going outside the accepted system
of political relationships and obligations. To prove their point, a group of
senators and their clients assassinated Tiberius Gracchus. Their leader was
a descendant of the Scipios, who feared that the popular programs of the
Gracchi would lead to a personal tyranny.

Politics always implies some relation between politician and electorate,
performer and audience. The murderous conflict of *ambitio* between the
Scipios and the Gracchi only highlights the growing conflict in Roman
society between those who accepted the traditional public modes of displaying their *dignitas* and those for whom that theater was archaic. In
this struggle the most crucial new constituency was the professional Roman

army, created by Marius at the end of the second century B.C. to defend Rome against the German tribes. Of crucial importance to later Roman politics was the fact that until the reign of Augustus, one hundred years later, the individual soldier was bound in loyalty not to the state but to his commanding general. Almost immediately another army under Sulla, one of Marius's former officers, arose to defend senatorial privilege. Appropriately enough for the history of fame, a crucial issue dividing Marius and Sulla was the leadership of the war against the Alexander-imitating Mithridates, who was taking advantage of Roman internal dissension to attack settlements in the East. In 86 B.C. a tribune gave the command to Marius. But Sulla marched into Rome with his army, killed the tribune, repealed the law, and took the command by force. Thus Sulla became the first Roman general to lead his army against the city itself while claiming to act in its defense. Five years later, after making a personal treaty with Mithridates, Sulla returned to Rome with his army, where he defeated the forces against him, massacred the Italians who had supported the government, abolished the power of the tribunes, and proscribed hundreds of his (mainly equestrian) opponents, murdering them and confiscating their property.

Sulla is a prime example of the professed defender of the state's most ancient traditions whose actions nevertheless undermine its most cherished political values. Marius had set the suffrage of the army against the traditional power of the senatorial party; Sulla turned that traditional power against Rome itself because it was in danger of being taken over by supporters of Marius. The message was clear: To the extent that there was a Rome made up of institutions and laws, the careers of Marius and Sulla indicated that those laws and institutions were primarily for normal situations. To the increasingly abnormal situations of the rapid expansion of Roman power, Marius and Sulla had added an army made up of landless men[6] who looked for security and advancement to charismatic military leaders who, in their turn, felt thereby licensed to decide what was in the best interests of Rome. The great men of the Late Republic would take the political stage in a Rome triumphing outside its borders even as it faced social and political conflicts within. But at the time of Marius and Sulla, the implications of new Roman political order were still unclear. Despite his brutality, Sulla, like so many earlier leaders, kept his personal aspirations within Roman traditions and retired from the dictatorship after a year. Julius Caesar, not yet twenty at the time, later frequently contrasted his own political programs with the vengefulness of Sulla's. But he also remarked that when Sulla resigned the dictatorship, he revealed that he didn't understand the basic vocabulary of politics.

The men in the armies of Marius and Sulla may have hungered for land; the Roman populace hungered for grain. But the business of Rome was not agriculture but war and honor. Unlike Athens or even the royal cities

6. Such men were called *proles*, the root of *proletarian*: Their only property is their children.

of Egypt or Persia, Rome therefore more resembled the modern capital city, which specializes in politics and communication, for which it demands compensation in food and money.[7] In such a city the need to climb a ladder of civic honors is more pressing than it was in the heroic past, when bravery in battle was sufficient to gain renown. But as cultural change begins to have more effect on human beings than does nature, as cities become a more common experience for those who seek fame and power than are farms and countryside, so new talents are forced into being, talents of self-promotion and communication as much as talents of action and leadership. Cincinnatus can no longer stay by his plow waiting to be asked to save the state. If he's at all interested in public service, he must let others know he's waiting. In our terms he has to become self-conscious about the way others see him, self-conscious in a way that primarily monarchs had been before. As the more perceptive Roman leaders began to realize, the essence of Roman sway was the chance the city offered outsiders to join its system of honors and obligations and become part of its destiny.

Yet at the center of Rome itself was a chaos of competing voices. In the ages of tribalism and primitive societies, the leader not only led the people, he represented them as well and might even be sacrificed for them if the need arose. But in the Rome of the last century B.C. the leadership of the senatorial class often seemed both practically and symbolically ineffective. The public men of that century stood at a crossroads where the nature of politics was shifting from its Greek city-state origins to its new setting in the national city of empire. The reforms of the Gracchi, the contentions between Marius and Sulla, mark attempts to create a new version of the old Roman virtues amid the practical problems of the present. But there was also a need for a new person who could unite conflicting traditions that were in danger of pulling Rome apart. The period of the Late Roman Republic has handed down to us more notable and lasting names than any previous period in world history, in part because the times both allowed and demanded the presence of men who could offer themselves as solutions to the combined symbolic and practical problems of the age. All of these men were explicitly animated by the desire for praise, all considered their personal advancement to be equivalent to the advancement of Rome, and all were impatient with the old shapes of both politics and fame. One of Sulla's reforms had been to make the *cursus honorum*—the official Roman pattern for a political career—more precise

7. By the end of the first century B.C. Italy had reached a population of about seven million, much too many to feed with its own resources. Most of the grain for the home population came from North Africa. It was a situation that required unceasing Roman command of the sea, and both Pompey and later his son Sextus Pompeius established reputations based on that command. In comparison, Greece at the time of Alexander contained about three million people and had a similarly insufficient agricultural base. Both Alexander's conquests and Roman expansion were therefore, in this sense, demographic safety valves. See McEredy and Jones, *World Population History*.

and limiting. But the prime result of his pains was the appearance of men who refused to be bound by the norm. Once the terms of the contest were set, many contestants showed up at the gate, and the most ambitious sought to create their own courses.

Pompey:
History and Histrionics

The Roman nobles who had used violence against the Gracchi assumed that those who sought solutions outside the traditional system were by definition traitors. But the whole Roman tradition of extraordinary powers awarded for special occasions—the granting of an *imperium,* the election of a dictator, the lavish display of a triumph—allowed the state the flexibility to call on individuals with special talents for war and politics to get it out of difficulties. A carefully marked step-by-step movement through the *cursus honorum* to the consulship might work properly in peacetime so long as there were many qualified candidates. But the civil war between Marius and Sulla, as well as Sulla's later executions of many of Marius's supporters, had helped create a situation in which the pool of available talent was low. With few candidates for normal advancement, the ambitious man had the opportunity to achieve outside the normal paths, by either doing more than anyone else or doing the same things earlier.

In Alexandrian fame, the aspirant seeks to be unprecedented, without context or cause, while in the fame that Roman society traditionally honored, the aspirant demonstrated that he was the perfect public expression of the values of his class, best of breed. Roman fame therefore tends to be political, impelled by the effort to master structure, while Alexandrian fame is more spiritual or aesthetic, fascinated by the unlimited, seeking to build in empty spaces. In the last century of the Roman Republic these two paradigms of public nature begin to clash. The ambitions of Marius and Sulla had been in line with those approved by the aristocratic class, to which Sulla belonged and to which (or to whose privileges) Marius aspired. Neither seemed very interested in a strictly personal power. For Sulla especially, the Cincinnatus model—do your job and then get back to the farm—remained forceful: After his dictatorship, he did return Rome to constitutional government. In the *Aeneid,* some fifty years later, Virgil optimistically writes that it is the destiny of Rome to impose peace, spare the humble, and defeat the proud (*superbos*). Pride, after all, made men think they were above the city (*super urbem*—the etymology is fanciful). But what if the city was in constant need of the prideful to ensure its own survival?

It is in the career of Pompey, whom Sulla allowed to add *magnus* (the

Great) to his name at the age of twenty-five, that the pressure of class and tradition most clearly becomes insufficient to curb the ambitions of those for whom fame consists precisely in breaking limits. Pompey was born in 106 B.C., the same year as Cicero and six years before Julius Caesar. All three were members of a generation ready to apply to their own careers the lessons of aspiration taught by Marius, Sulla, and the Gracchi. But before Caesar was twenty and Cicero had argued his first case, Pompey began his public career by mustering three legions of his own to help Sulla. Impressed by Pompey's victories, Sulla referred to Pompey as "the youthful butcher" (*adulescentulus carnifex*), publicly addressed him as *imperator* (then only the Roman word for general), and sent him to attack supporters of Marius in Sicily and Africa. On his successful return, Sulla, with some reluctance, awarded Pompey the unprecedented privilege (for a member of the equestrian class who had held no political office) of an official triumph. It was the beginning of a career in which Pompey became a specialist in gaining extraordinary commands and administrative power through his military skills and his precocious creation of a carefully assembled army of clients.

Plutarch points out that after his victories Pompey could have asked to be made a senator but sought a triumph instead because he was ambitious only for unusual honors. For him the city of Rome was as much a center of personal publicity as a political arena. An essential part of Roman political life was the holding of games, triumphs, and processions of all sorts to honor the living, the dead, but most of all, the victorious. Theatrical displays put on by the great to give the people a show were therefore an important aspect of the duties of the Roman politician. In the triumphs conquered kings might appear in tableaux illustrating their defeat, while prisoners of war would be forced to perform as gladiators in the arena. To indicate the importance of these public shows of victorious Roman order, the office of aedile, which carried with it responsibility for the public games, was the first office to confer full senatorial dignity on its holder, along with the *ius imaginis,* the right to have one's image perpetuated by one's family as a face to be remembered. Plutarch says that no Roman was ever so loved by the Roman people as was Pompey, and the details of Pompey's career included in Plutarch's *Lives* shows how avidly Pompey sought both the love and praise of his Roman audience. Like tickertape parades in New York in the 1920s and 1930s, fame in the Roman Republic was becoming the standard for the world, and Pompey placed himself on stage for all the Roman people. Later in his career Pompey even built his own theater at Rome—it seated forty thousand people. But he was only one of many Roman politicians who appreciated what could be learned from theater. Roscius, whose name became proverbial as the consummate actor, was knighted by Sulla and trained Cicero in oration. Marc Antony had numerous friendships with actors, and we shall see the importance of theater in the careers of Julius Caesar and his adopted nephew Augustus. A clear continuity in the interplay between theater and politics stretches from the theater of Pompey to Renaissance England down to the John F. Kennedy Center for the Performing Arts.

In the fame-oriented society of the Roman Republic it had become increasingly difficult to distinguish either achievement from the need to publicize achievement or the practical virtues of a leader from his symbolic virtues. The fatal line of Pompey's career illustrates how much his pretensions and aspirations blinded him even to his own abilities. A continuing motif, for example, is his identification with Alexander, which Sulla's award of *magnus* to Pompey's name only confirmed. Plutarch notes a physical resemblance between Pompey and statues of Alexander and reports that he was often called Alexander in his youth. No doubt many Roman youths were so flattered, as many Macedonian boys had been called Achilles. But Pompey clearly took the identification to heart. He wore what was supposed to be Alexander's cloak, put Alexander's emblem on his shield, and was portrayed with his head tossed in imitation of Alexander (and Scipio). Particularly after his defeat of the Alexander-imitating Mithridates, Pompey's contemporaries must have accepted his self-identification as latter-day Alexander more easily. Plutarch further records that during Pompey's campaigns in the East (and perhaps after reading Mithridates' diary), he not only subdued the Iberians, a Caucasian tribe Alexander had missed, but also fought against the Amazons—in clear rivalry with both the history and myth of his predecessor.

For all his desire to do unprecedented things, there is thus a definite strain of imitation and even unconscious subordination in Pompey's actions. As a kind of cowbird of fame, who hatches eggs that others have lain, he had aided Sulla in Sicily, took credit for completing Metellus's campaign against rebels in Spain, helped Crassus put down the Spartacus rebellion, and, finally, brought to an end the war against Mithridates that had been prosecuted by Lucullus. In each case, of course, he was more effective and more decisive than the man he had seconded. But the strong impression remains of someone standing on the shoulders of other, usually older, men, perhaps indicating the terms of the competition he had designed for himself—to be loved, so Plutarch says, as much as his father, Sulla's lieutenant, was hated. The only one of his accomplishments without this aura was his eradication of piracy in the eastern Mediterranean through the absolute power granted by an *imperium,* to which every senator but Caesar objected. But even there Pompey tried to make all honor his own, defending the Cretan pirates against another Roman, with an equally powerful *imperium,* who had previously been sent to battle them.

Pompey's awareness of the ways through the Roman course of distinction allowed him to proceed with extraordinary speed to honors that previously had taken men whole lifetimes to achieve. That the defeat of the pirates was his most unalloyed triumph metaphorically implies the basically piratic nature of his military fame. Gathering strength and money outside of Rome, muscling into the most profitable wars, Pompey became a state-sanctioned marauder, absorbing the tradition-bound accomplishments of others into his own. Lucullus, who had controlled areas and armies and had accomplished victories that rivaled Pompey's, yet could finally retire, giving up military and political power to become the lavish party giver and gourmet for which he is now best remembered. But Pompey, who defeated Mithridates after Lucullus failed, always pushed on, never quite satisfied, in search of a fame given only to those who never decided they had enough.

Yet even so, it is difficult to say that Pompey, like Marius or Sulla, ever thought consciously of absolute power for himself. Almost two thousand years of historians have yet to discover any consistency in his shifting political alliances—with traditional aristocrats, plebeians, equestrians, and a bewildering array of individuals down to the triumvirate with Crassus and Caesar—prompting the conclusion that he was constantly improvising, attuned at every moment only to what he thought would lead to his own greater glory. Psychic change often seems to lay the necessary groundwork for social change. If so, Pompey had the imperialist sensibility before there was an actual Roman Empire. Marauding outside the system, he still wanted to be acknowledged as an insider. Capitalizing on the framework laid down by others, he sought a kind of adoption, marrying first Sulla's stepdaughter and later Caesar's daughter, even though he had divorced his second wife supposedly for adultery with Caesar. In the early years of the empire, to call someone a Pompeian implied that he longed for the individual freedom of the Republic, and even while Pompey lived, Cicero could write about the virtues Pompey "represented." But Pompey himself primarily sought praise in whatever terms his society offered. Any politics beyond the equation of personal and public good might deplete the possible audience. Next to Pompey, Julius Caesar had principles and even a political program.

Can a state survive its great men? Pompey is a prime example of the talented individual who fails to realize that his efforts to achieve the highest honors of the system in fact threaten to destroy it. Those who watched him were hardly aware of the contradiction themselves because, after all, he was doing it for Rome. Those who dare to go beyond the bounds of a civilization are often politically very conservative. Although they may be too outsized for the state itself, they uphold a national idea more pure than anyone has who must deal with it from day to day. Our attitude toward the western hero—the various incarnations of John Wayne and Errol Flynn or Generals Custer, Patton, and MacArthur as themselves—contain threads of both trust and suspicion: trust for the purity of motives and allegiances; suspicion when it appears that the same purity will be an unrealistic response to practical situations. So too, I suspect, was the attitude in Rome toward Pompey. He was a mercenary cultivated at home, the flower of generations of young Romans who had been told stories of emblematic Roman behavior in times of crisis—Cato before Carthage, Regulus returning to be executed, Decius Mus jumping in the crevasse, Scaevola putting his hand in the fire, Lucretia committing suicide—tales of personal fame and national greatness crystalized in a moment of decision. They were not just stories about how members of a particular class behaved, but stories about the way Romans would like to be, so that future stories might be told about them.

As a newcomer to nobility and an out-of-towner as well, Pompey believed the myths of Rome and constantly pressed to go them at least one better. More than other Roman politician-generals, Pompey identified public life with theater, and he was so committed to his part that the alternative of Cincinnatian retirement was impossible. Breaking the Roman laws that specified when a public position could be held, he urged his time forward more and more rapidly. Like a Roman inscription so crammed with honors that it has become an almost indecipherable mass of abbreviations, Pompey's career is a triumph of accumulation, given nervous benediction by a Rome that hoped there was no distinction between his interests and her own. When Pompey demanded one triumph, two triumphs, or three triumphs; or the office of consul ten years before he could legally hold it; or extraordinary powers to defeat the pirates or the Spanish rebels or Mithridates, the possible fear that he would expand his limited power into perpetual rule was qualified by two prime considerations. The first was practical: He had shown that he had the ability to accomplish what he proposed and so his talents were necessary for the survival and defense of Rome. The second was situated somewhere between the spiritual and the political: Since Pompey's definition of his personal glory was so dependent on the Roman system of praise for public action, he might be expected to stay inside those parameters of judgment, whatever outsized demands he might make. Thus the career of Pompey indicates how the political and military expansion of Rome had helped foster a clear contradiction between the urge to fame and the needs of Rome, a contradiction that was hardly understood by either the Romans who looked for heroes or by the fame-seeking heroes themselves. For all the emulation with the great men of Republican Rome felt by the men who made the American Revolution some eighteen hundred years later, it was no doubt with Pompey's cautionary example in mind that George Washington resigned his command of the Continental Army and later accepted the presidency of the Society of the Cincinnati.

With such a historically self-conscious gesture, Washington implies that self-interest and national interest are rarely identical for too long. But Pompey, unlike say, Caesar, could hardly appreciate the distinction between himself and Rome. Like Alexander after Siwah, but with much less self-awareness, Pompey after the defeat of Mithridates characterized himself as the greatest conqueror of the age, proclaiming that while other men had had three triumphs, his were in Europe, Asia, and Africa—all three Scipios rolled into one. What Pompey could not understand was that, unlike Alexander, he was not the state itself, only one of its expressions. Preoccupied with older forms of triumph, he had little success in the political maneuverings in the Senate. Ironically, reports Plutarch, when the fleeing

Pompey sought help from the Egyptians after his defeat by Caesar in the battle of Pharsalus, they addressed him, as Sulla had forty years before, as "imperator." Lulled by the recognition of his stature, Pompey landed on their shores, whereupon they cut off his head and sent it to the victorious Caesar as a peace offering. Lost in his part despite his great abilities, Pompey was defeated by his Roman pride in the words of honor and praise, words that Cicero and Caesar knew far better how to use and manipulate. But he remains a prime example of the Roman love for the gestures of greatness, the theater of fame. That love would be extended into ludicrousness by a late emperor four hundred years later who called himself Magnus Maximus (The Greatest Great); and it was mocked by Shakespeare in *Love's Labor's Lost* when an amateur actor playing Pompey in a pageant of the Nine Worthies forgets his lines: "I Pompey am, Pompey surnamed the Big————."

Cicero: The "New Man"

Praise for the eloquence of Pompey, Caesar, and Antony pervades classical history writing. But with the exception of Caesar's *Gallic War* and *Civil War*, little of that eloquence has survived, in part because most Roman politician-generals considered the oration to be primarily an instrument of immediate policy rather than a claim on posterity. Much more than any other public figure of his time, it was Cicero who looked to a future that would celebrate him for the messages he was sending it, through his writing, about the true values of Roman tradition and his special ability to embody them. By publishing his orations, sometimes even when he had never actually delivered them, Cicero managed not only to preserve his own position for future generations (and an extended immediate audience), but also to characterize those of his antagonists (and to imply that there were only two positions from which right-thinking men could choose). Such a connection between writing, speaking, and thinking was natural to Cicero, and it indelibly marked all his attitudes, as it ensured his fame to later generations. As Ronald Syme remarks, "Posterity, generous in oblivion, regards with indulgence both the political orator who fomented civil war to save the Republic and the military adventurer Augustus who betrayed and proscribed his ally. The reason for such exceptional favour may be largely assigned to one thing—the influence of literature when studied in isolation from history" (4). What Augustus had learned from Cicero in the arts of literary management, as well as how Virgil, Horace, Ovid, and other writers fell in with his plans and attitudes, we shall soon see. Cicero is the self-prompting entrepreneur whose lengthened shadow stands behind every media politician. Augustus is the totalitarian emperor who will swallow him up and make his methods corporate policy.

Cicero's career of self-creation, his effort to become his own Callisthenes, is conditioned in great part by the fact that he is neither noble nor does he come from Rome. Born in 106 B.C. in Arpino, sixty miles southeast of Rome, Cicero is six years older than Marc Antony, who will be behind the order for his murder. As a member of the equestrian class of landowners, bankers, and merchants who was entering the aristocratic world of Roman politics, Cicero was a *novus homo,* a "new man." He would become the first to be elected consul since Marius himself, who in the bare coincidence of psychic geography had been born near Arpino just fifty years before.

It is an ideal still cherished in our own postromantic age that fame sought with premeditation is motivated not by the desire for a pure glory but by the darker urges of mere personal ambition. Even if we know, as in the show business "overnight success," that years of work preceded the crowning achievement, we often pretend that instant recognition is possible, perhaps because it is always in the interest of the fan to preserve the myth that someday recognition will come. Yet it is also striking how often the famous of the past prepared their way long in advance. Even when they clearly had the talent or even genius for whatever tasks they undertook, they also possessed not only the Alexandrian trait of making sure others knew what they had accomplished, but also what I might call the Ciceronian talent for planning their way. In a world of constantly shifting political and familial allegiances, Cicero, as an outsider, could not call upon either the interlocking system of family relations that was the heritage of nobles like Caesar nor the system of client obligations outside the boundaries of Rome that was the source of much of Pompey's power. But he did have a genius for social mapping and from his earliest days in Rome applied himself to meeting influential people, tracing their relations to each other and accurately estimating the specifics of their political and philosophical beliefs.

Whenever we consider how fame was gained and conferred in the past, we are examining the interplay between an individual and his society, the infinite reciprocity of psychology and politics. In the case of Cicero, the "new man" of the last century B.C., we can answer such questions with a particular richness since he not only wanted fame, but wrote about his desire incessantly: in his orations, in his philosophical writings, and in the private letters published by Tyro, his literary executor. As we have seen, those who aimed to succeed in the arena of Roman glory necessarily had to have both a tincture of the performer in their makeup and a sense of the Roman past. But unlike Pompey's past of heroic models, Cicero's was expressed in law and political forms, and in the Roman law courts he developed a reputation that challenged military definitions of greatness by replacing the general with the orator as the mainstay of the Roman Republic. In the courts, where speakers skilled in Roman laws and traditions argued in full view of an audience strolling by to pick up the best show, the young provincial quickly made himself known. "Let arms give way to the toga" became a favorite expression, suitable enough for one whose power was to come from the rhetorical and oratorical arts that previous soldiers and politicians had often hired others to supply for them.

Appropriately for Cicero's ambition, the orator was never paid, for that would place him in the nonnoble world of work. The most substantial reputations were made as a prosecuting magistrate in criminal cases, whom the Romans called an *actor,* the same word they used to designate a stage performer. (The divisions of a speech in the courts were referred to as the first and second acts, *actio prima* and *actio secunda.*) Plutarch says that Cicero learned techniques of delivery from Roscius the comedian and Aesop the tragedian, and his verbal sarcasm is constantly referred to by all the Roman historians. His voice may in fact have been feeble, but both his wit and his willingness to wound were legendary. In a world where faces were familiar and relations determined politics, personal attack could effectively destroy a reputation. Cicero's rise to fame and power was therefore predicted to a great extent on his ability to attack his enemies, flatter his friends, and magnify himself. It is remarkable in fact how often his orations rely on panegyric and invective and how little they engage what we would consider real political issues. Cicero's more ruminative works about politics, those that carried his name as philosopher into posterity, were in fact all written after he had entirely withdrawn from political life at the establishment of the triumvirate of Caesar, Pompey, and Crassus in 56 B.C.

"By his insatiable thirst of fame, he has lessened his character with succeeding ages," wrote John Dryden about Cicero in 1675, putting his own turn on a complaint that may have begun during Cicero's lifetime itself (268). Certainly, Plutarch's life of Cicero, written two hundred years after his death, is already speckled with sour remarks about Cicero's passion for glory, which, Plutarch says, constantly interfered with his intelligence and his will, making him an easy tool for Octavian's manipulation and generally compelling him to subordinate his beliefs to a desire to please an audience. As part of the format of the *Lives* Plutarch compares Cicero to Demosthenes as an orator-politician who trumpeted the divine heroism of his public service. The choice between the two is hard to make. Demosthenes may have taken bribes, says Plutarch, while Cicero was above such venality. But Cicero was much more infected by "an uncontrollable appetite for distinction," while Demosthenes was personally modest. Plutarch does allow some beneficial effect to Cicero's desire for fame: It made him superior to normal ambition, even to envy, and thus able to praise his contemporaries as well as the ancients. But his obsession with personal glory seemed hardly appropriate for someone who also recommended himself to future generations as a philosopher.

That Cicero was "intemperately fond of his own glory" (Plutarch) qualifies his achievements primarily for those who maintain an artificial separation between what Cicero considered to be inextricably entangled: the desire for fame in both politics and philosophy, serving the state while promoting himself to posterity. The paradox appears often in his writing, although the awareness of conflict rarely diverts his thirst for recognition.

He tells, for example, how he fell into a severe depression when it turned out that no one at Rome had heard anything about his accomplishments as a twenty-nine-year-old magistrate in Sicily. It was a disappointment that armed him for the future and made him acutely conscious of the need to publicize as well as achieve. Sometimes his methods didn't work, especially with the heavily courted Greeks. According to Plutarch, Pelops of Byzantium could not be persuaded to award Cicero "public honors" and, in a letter to his friend Atticus, Cicero complains that Posidonius, whom he hailed as the greatest living philosopher, had declined to write a history of Cicero's consulship (76).

Historians of Rome continue to debate whether the modern concept of political parties, with programs and general principles, can be applied to a state where the most vital principle was one's own *dignitas* and the most close-knit party was a collection of family and client obligations. To the extent that political principles first require a definition of goals and then a plan of implementation, the Rome of the Republic might be called prepolitical, with no consensus about what the state was or what might be done to improve it. Many commentators have complained about the inconsistency of Cicero's political alignments. But when tradition is at issue, the articulation of general political principles is often a weapon used by an emerging class against an established one. Cicero, the "new man," coming from a class without stable national power, thus makes an essential part of his program the effort to recall the senatorial aristocracy to the "true meaning" of Rome. His authority will come not from his origins but from himself. This strategy almost requires him to change his personal allegiances periodically to maintain his separation from the conventional system of political alliances and his connection with the values of the past. In his turn, then, he can confer value upon other selected outsiders, from either the traditional Roman classes or the other cities of Italy, who may have a similar insight into the nature of Rome and how to perpetuate her glory. Like Napoleon from Corsica or Charles de Gaulle from Lorraine, Cicero is the political leader from the geographical fringes of a country who argues therefore his greater self-consciousness of its most cherished values. His basic political identification is not with a particular group but with Rome itself. But he walks a narrow path between approving a system of honors that has rewarded him and criticizing it because, with that great exception, it has kept other such men out. His crowning achievement, the consulship, requires the support of the most conservative branch of the aristocratic party, which he gained by his aggressive fealty to the traditions of Roman greatness (as well as by the weakness of the other candidates).

Although fame is Cicero's personal preoccupation, it is also a national program, inextricably linked to his conception of Roman political virtue. A few years before winning the consulship, he had for the first time addressed the Roman people (rather than a law court) to argue that Pompey be given an *imperium* to fight against Mithridates. He speaks first of the personal "glory" of addressing the Roman people and ties it to the "glory" Rome has now lost through the victories of Mithridates, "that glory which has come down to you from your forefathers, great in everything but greatest of all in war." The Roman people, says Cicero, "have ever been, beyond all nations, seekers after glory and greedy of praise [*avidi laudis*]" (*Pro lege Manilia,* 19–21). Public men like Pompey act for the people, whose revenues have been threatened and lives destroyed by the conquests of Mithridates. Therefore, to regain the glory that has been lost, Pompey must have unlimited power in Bithynia, Pontus, and Armenia (roughly present-day Turkey, Iran, and Afghanistan) to prosecute the war.

Since most of Cicero's audience had no financial interests in Asia, it would seem that the killing of Roman citizens was his strongest argument. But here, as so often in his speeches, he connects the injury to Roman pride with a loss of money. That his arguments were effective (Pompey got the command) indicates how closely the Roman mind associated money with self-respect, from the soldier who desired a home and a plot of land for his services to the military politician amassing millions. Cicero's special turn on the general cultural theme is his insistence on the crucial need to preserve credit. Materially, he argues that the Roman economy itself will plunge with the loss of Asian fortunes, while metaphorically he ties financial credit to personal credit (both *fides* in Latin). Monetary obligation is linked to political obligation, belief in an individual's financial worth to belief in his worth as a person, that is, a Roman citizen.

For the "new man" who owed his rise to his oratorical and argumentative skills, his mouth and his mind, personal credit is an even more compelling concept than it might be to the hereditary aristocrat or the landless urban proletarian. Cicero's invocation of the combined need to gain glory and maintain credit reaches outside the specific boundaries of the city to embrace all those—especially merchants, businessmen, and tax farmers—who believed their personal efforts brought them success. Cicero might not have thought that property was a sacred right, but he did consider credit to have some of that religious tinge. His idea of glory takes us a small step beyond the fame that is totally determined by conquest and possessions and toward a realm where it is an accolade of the spirit. But affirmed by possessions such a fame still had to be, and so Cicero accumulated wealth and villas with as much rapacity as any more normally venal Roman politician.

As far as Cicero is concerned, then, fame is basically substantial. Pompey, he says, conquers by reputation as much as by prowess. Many historians have pointed out how much, temperamentally and intellectually, Cicero and Caesar have in common. Yet Cicero aligns politically with Pompey, whose self-creation accords more with his own. Since Caesar came from a minor aristocratic family, he did not markedly share Cicero's need to accumulate repetitions of his name in public as a psychic bank balance. As we shall see, Caesar's definition of his own fame was much more abstract: Although he used the money gathered from his conquests to ensure his power and reputation, he publicized his frugal private life. Such noblesse oblige disturbed Cicero. The enemies of Rome, he implies, would come from the nobles sunk in the sloth of hereditary power, untempered by the crucible of competition that produced men like himself and Pompey. With his orator's instinct for polarization, he argued that the political division between the *populares* and the *optimates* (or the *boni* [the good], as he called them) would tear Rome apart. The one man who might bind the factions together and save Rome is naturally enough the same man who has had the wit to see and define their divisions—Cicero.

In Cicero's year as consul, 63 B.C., three years after his speech for Pompey, the conspiracy of Catiline gives him the opportunity to achieve his prime political goal, the harmony of Roman classes, *concordia ordinum*. In response to Catiline's attempt to usurp power, patricians and knights, he seeks to bring *optimates, populares,* and people together in an alliance cemented by the execution of the accused. Throughout the four Catilinian orations runs a constantly invoked personification of Rome itself, to whose preservation all efforts should be bent. As he did in his speech supporting Pompey's *imperium,* he characterizes himself as the messenger who risks "unpopularity" to bring the people unwelcome news of affronts to "their" glory. He compares Pompey to the great Scipios, to Marius, and to other war leaders. Pompey, he says, wars for Rome outside Italy. But he, Cicero, wars for Rome within the city. And he hopes that there will be equal glory, if not now then in the future, for the man who has saved Rome from the enemies inside, as there has been for those who have protected her against the enemies without.

To Pompey, as to other Roman men of power, Cicero offered his services as philosophical and political partner, only to be rejected. They wanted supporters and advocates; he offered himself as teacher and guide, all the while implying the necessary subordination of military might to abstract thought. Cicero may have been a company man, but he wanted to run the company. Although he talked often of partnership and harmony, his championship of Pompey's *imperium* in Asia shows his commitment to the single savior who will knit together the conflicts of Rome. Within a year after his consulship Cicero writes to Pompey, disappointed that the great general, still abroad, has not congratulated him for saving the Republic from the conspiracy of Catiline. Invoking the relation of Scipio to an orator-philosopher of his day, Cicero goes on to offer himself as Pompey's "political ally and private friend—a not much lesser Laelius to a far greater Africanus" (*Letters to Friends,* 27). Pompey, for his part, was probably annoyed that Cicero took away his chance to sweep into Rome and save her from Catiline himself.

*   *   *

And what will history say of me a thousand years hence?
—CICERO to Atticus

Through the incessant self-praise of his orations, his invocations of posterity, and his cataloguing of the honors he has received, Cicero publicly reassures himself and his audience of the importance of what he has done, as if for fear they will forget, and down the ladder of success he will tumble, as quickly as he had risen. For his triumph against Catiline, he became the first Roman to be given the title "father of his country" (*pater patriae*), the similarity of the Latin words inviting a spiritual connection between the concepts. But above all, says Cicero, he wants to be remembered. A year or so after his consulship Cicero defends Archias, a Greek teacher-poet, against an attempt to take away his Roman citizenship. Such men, he argues, serve the state by celebrating generals and victories. We act in order to be remembered, and writing preserves the memory of our actions. Alexander, he remarks, took along many historians on his expeditions, and Pompey has similarly rewarded a certain Theophanes of Mytilene. The greatest men like praise; the poets give it. And even writers are not immune from the desire for fame for their writing of the famous:

> Why, upon the very books in which they bid us scorn ambition philosophers inscribe their names! The striving for praise is an universal factor in life, and the nobler a man is, the more susceptible is he to the sweets of glory (*Pro Archia, 35*).

He likes the sentiment so much that he repeats it several years later in the *Tusculan Disputations.*

In their intertwining of the striving for personal fame with service to the state, Cicero's orations exhibit no attitude that would be unfamiliar in the Renaissance, when the rediscovery of his speeches turned him into the favorite civic founding father of a new generation of political nationalists. Such striving in the name of the public good seemed particularly admirable to those who argued the superiority of secular institutions to the corruptions of the papacy. But the picture of Cicero that emerged from his private letters was less appealing. There, the noble aspirations for fame and glory appear as premeditated gestures rather than the instinctual outpouring of a great spirit. Yet, in this private writing, Cicero also spoke his personal desires uninflected by political judiciousness. If his orations inspired political theorists in the Renaissance to meditate on secular heroism, his letters, as publicized first by Petrarch, inspired the strivings for fame of a somewhat different group—the humanists, who attempted to establish a lineage of greatness unrelated to family, class, or nation, a brotherhood (with a few sisters) that stretched across the centuries, a family of the mind and spirit.

In Cicero's speeches the constant talk of fame and glory seems to be a compulsive articulation of what most nobles considered a class right unnecessary even to mention. But for the man whose public identity was built on his way with words, it appears like a homegrown portent, a personal talisman to guide him safely through the world he had determined to conquer. In the mapping of this world, as in so many of the activities of his life, Cicero's silent partner was a friend from school days, Titus Pomponius, later called Atticus, who, unlike Cicero, had chosen to turn away from Roman public life and live in Athens. Atticus was an equestrian with extensive ties to the nobility and vast personal wealth (primarily from banking). In Cicero's career he serves as both a material and spiritual mainstay. Not the least of his services was that of publisher, supplying money for the team of slaves who would make multiple copies of Cicero's speeches and writings for sale to the public. But Atticus was also the one person with whom Cicero unburdens himself of the weight of his public image. With Atticus he can complain without fear of repercussion; Atticus was a living, responding diary, who often advised but rarely if ever disapproved. As Cicero in later life tried to create a philosophical language for Latin to express Greek concepts, so Atticus lived inside him as a kind of Greek soul to which he might return for security and solace in his climb to the top. To Atticus, Cicero wrote more frankly and directly than he did to anyone else, including his younger brother Quintus, and it is from the letters to Atticus that some of the most damning evidence of Cicero's ambition has been generally culled. D. R. Shackleton Bailey cautions that "the letters that reveal him were never meant to become public property" (xii), as if we should therefore ignore them in our estimate of Cicero's character and achievement. But it is precisely the disparity between Cicero's public principles and his private ambitions that might reveal to us the nature of the Roman race for fame as displayed by one of its most distinguished participants. For Cicero's private nature is at least as much a construction as his public one. The orator and writer is usually a person for whom words do express a truth, if only a truth of language. To Atticus, Cicero could become a private person that complemented the one he had created in the law courts and on the rostrum. The intense desire to become the mediator of public harmony that fills Cicero's speeches in the middle 60s B.C. thus reflects his own tenuous balance between the desire for public recognition and the need for private support that animates the letters to Atticus.

The crisis years for Cicero's idea of himself occur after his consulship and the great achievement of thwarting the conspiracy of Catiline. He had reached the top of the ladder of Roman political success and had been given praise unprecedented—*pater patriae*—for defending the Republic. He had been named to every office possible, at the lowest legal age. Now, at forty-three, what could he do for an encore? The offices, the *cursus honorum,* had run out. But the ambition had not. Unable to absent himself from the fame arena of the city, he refuses the government of a province (a usual office for ex-consuls) and builds an enormously expensive mansion on the Palatine Hill in the heart of Rome. His occasional speeches become more and more filled with allusions to the central importance of the urge to fame as a motivation for public service. He begins an epic poem on his consulship. The pinnacle of Roman greatness had been achieved. But what did it mean? He never poses the question quite that way, but a letter to Atticus in 60 B.C., reflects his confusion:

> I must tell you that what I most badly need at the present time is a confidant—someone with whom I could share all that gives me anxiety, a wise, affectionate friend to whom I can talk without pretense or evasion or concealment. . . . My brilliant, worldly friendships may make a fine show in public, but at home they are barren things. My house is crammed of a morning, I go down to the Forum surrounded by droves of friends, but in all the multitude I cannot find one with whom I can pass an unguarded hope or fetch a private sigh (65–66).

Cicero was probably not the first to wake up at the top to realize that the hunger for recognition is rarely satisfied with any particular object or honor. In 60 B.C. he is clearly suffering from the consequences of his discovery of the hollowness of fame. So hungry does Cicero become for reassurance that until the end of his life—murdered at the orders of the second triumvirate of Octavian, Marc Antony, and Lepidus—he generally interprets praise of his principles as praise of himself. Similarly, he seizes the occasion of a law that seemed to attaint his actions against the Catilinarians to go noisily into exile, proving his importance to Rome by the ferocity of the opposition to him. Somewhere the distinction between his public and private nature had become tragically confused. At the end of 60 B.C. he writes to Atticus that he has been made an overture by Caesar that will ensure him peace and tranquility in his old age. "But I can't forget my finale in Book III," he says and then quotes the poem he has now finished *On My Consulship:*

> Meantime the paths which thou from earliest days did seek,
> Aye, and when Consul too, as mood and virtue bade,
> These hold, and foster still thy fame and good men's praises (84).

Fame and good men's praises—what resonant underlining: The speaker of the lines is supposed to be Calliope, the muse of epic poetry. In his letter to Atticus, Cicero decides against Caesar's offer by quoting his own poem in which, as Calliope, he tells himself to continue to earn fame and worthy praise. Inspire me to tell the deeds of heroes long dead, says Homer to his muse. But Cicero's muse fills its vessel to sing itself. Only Atticus, the accepting confidant, could have been the recipient of such a chorus of Cicero-praising Ciceros. Like Pompey and, as we shall see, unlike Julius Caesar, Cicero was a child of his culture, acting in accordance with its messages, but without the ability to hear much beyond them. Pompey took the Roman admiration for Hannibal, Alexander, and other heroic figures and expanded it into a personal model. Cicero took the Roman reverence for the past, the laws, and Rome itself and nominated himself its prime exponent and propagandist. But neither finally had any desire to create a future beyond one that would remember and thereby justify them personally. Their loyalty was to a system that their own careers proved was coming apart.

Caesar: Enter the Stage Manager

When conflicting groups and individuals can all represent themselves as firm supporters of the *res publica,* then the concept of the public good had begun to reveal its contradictions. Not that such contradictions need always be disastrous; they may also be part of a vital interplay of traditions, while an excessive uniformity could signify stagnation and tyranny. Some historians have argued that the period before the fall of the Republic was a time when private forces were turned against the state. They tend to ignore the fact that such actions were often taken sincerely in the name of Rome itself. Like England in the seventeenth century or France in the eighteenth century, Rome in the first century B.C. was passing from a class definition of the state (the nobles are Rome) to a nationalist definition (Rome is an idea). Ever since the Gracchi, the aristocratic ability to represent the true interests of Rome had been under attack, and politics increasingly focuses on the question of who might effectively personify the essence of Rome, unalloyed by the narrowness of class interests. Romans had often acknowledged the superior claim of those heroes who were called to rescue the city in its time of need. But in the first century B.C. there were many such, each with his individual measure of military, financial, and even moral power, and each claiming in some way to be a potential savior. When such powerful public men and groups fall out, civil war is usually the result, and, as in most civil wars, the battle is over who defines the nation—here especially not only "What is Rome?" but "Who is Rome?" as well.

The intertwined careers of Pompey, Cicero, and Julius Caesar define the moment when Roman reverence for public fame has obscured the issue of whether the society itself can survive. But among these "great men" Caesar occupies the unique position of being interested both in politics and in the structure of Roman law and power. Pompey accomplished many important victories, and the literary achievement of Cicero is even more lasting, although historians from Sallust on minimize the importance of the political role he played. But both of them, unlike Caesar, seemed to value the public act uncritically for its own sake, without regard to its effectiveness. One of the most frequent comments in the vast literature on Late Republican Rome mentions the lack of interest the heads of the optimate party, for example, had in the actual business of government. Roman leaders may have been efficient enough in the running of their armies and brilliant in strategy and tactics, especially against non-Roman opponents. But they followed the precedent of Marius and Sulla in taking the military model of order as the norm.

Caesar, however, understood that the Roman preoccupation with administrative procedure favored the power seeker who was also a good parliamentarian. Although his career begins much later and with much less initial energy than either Pompey's or Cicero's, he profited from and then passed beyond the examples of both the general and the orator. Coming from an otherwise undistinguished aristocratic family that claimed a lineage that went back to Venus and her son Aeneas, the founder of Rome, Caesar appreciated from the inside how Roman institutions were created for the man who knew how to present himself in public. Unlike either the Alexandrian general or the philosophic orator, Caesar could stand back from his public presentation and his assertion of symbolic leadership. Whether from nihilism or pragmatism, he was much less apt to mistake his lengthening shadow for himself.

One way of understanding Caesar's success is to realize with what clarity he was able to be his own audience. Claude Lévi-Strauss, the anthropologist, tells the story of the shaman who became more insecurely self-conscious each time he gave the members of his tribe a new demonstration of his powers: The approval of the audience served primarily to convince him of his inner unworthiness and the insubstantiality of his gestures. Pompey solved the difficulty by assuming the mantle of Alexander, while Cicero validated his public performance by appeals to his friend Atticus and to posterity. But Caesar, as politician, general, and literary man, was simultaneously able both to act and to know why he was acting. So many of the anecdotes handed down about him emphasize his explicit manipulation of his public image, especially his understanding of the need of the public person to make capital from his private life as well. When, for example, Clodius is accused of profaning the religious ceremonies that were being held by the women in Caesar's house, Caesar divorces his wife Pompeia because "Caesar's wife must be above suspicion." "Caesar" is thus a concept to Julius Caesar, a public version of himself, connected with yet different from his private nature, a separate self that he constantly reshapes and refines.[8]

Caesar was hardly immune from the Alexander-emulation that preoccupied so many of his contemporaries. A crucial event seems to have occurred when he was thirty-two and a magistrate in Spain. There, after

8. Clodius was another one of the ambitious young noble politicians of the Late Republic distinguished perhaps by a wider streak of obvious irreverence. Like his sister Clodia, the frequent subject of Catullus's poems, he changed the "aristocratic" spelling of his name (Claudius) to court popular favor. It is unknown why, beyond mere whim, he decided to dress in woman's clothes and infiltrate the annual ceremony in honor of the Bona Dea (Good Goddess). Although Caesar divorced Pompeia, he did not testify against Clodius at the trial for sacrilege. Clodius was acquitted by a bribed jury and continued his political activities. Several years later he was murdered by Milo, another aspiring politician, whose mob of armed supporters had frequently clashed with those of Clodius.

either seeing a statue of Alexander (according to Suetonius) or reading a history of Alexander's wars (according to Plutarch), he openly bemoaned that at an age when Alexander had done so much, he had done so little. If Caesar was in fact magistrate in Spain when this happened (or when he wanted others to think it happened), he was somewhat above the minimum age (thirty) decreed for that rank and so, unlike Pompey or Cicero, a fairly conventional follower of the *cursus honorum*. That Caesar could compare his accomplishments unfavorably to Alexander's may also have allowed him to see where his own genius might lead.

Caesar's taste for theater and symbolic staging appeared in full strength when he took up the next post of the *cursus honorum*, aedile, the public official in charge of public works, distribution of grain, and the public games. Suetonius devotes a good deal of his biography of Caesar to describing the unprecedented quality of Caesar's games and latei his triumphal marches. As aedile, he not only put on the usual games, but also produced lavish gladiatorial shows in honor of his father, who had been dead for twenty years and had made little figure in Roman political life. Displays of family loyalty had always been a feature of Caesar's public actions. At eighteen and a nephew by marriage to Marius, Caesar refused Sulla's order to divorce his wife Cornelia, the daughter of a consul who supported Marius; only with some difficulty was he pardoned for his resistance. Some years later, when he held the magistracy, Cornelia died and he married Pompeia, Sulla's granddaughter, but in the same year gave a funeral oration for his aunt, Marius's widow, in a ceremony that included the display of images of Marius, previously forbidden by Sulla. Through his own family relations, then, Caesar daringly presented himself as the common element in otherwise warring aspects of the Roman political psyche. During his term as aedile, he drew on the same acute sense of symbolism to restore to the Forum monuments to the victories of Marius that had been taken down by Sulla, and, like Alexander restoring the tomb of Cyrus the Great, he would later replace the statues in honor of Pompey and Sulla.

Two years after the aedileship, Caesar won his first important political battle against the old guard. Intriguingly enough, he was in pursuit of an office that at least on its face had little direct political or military importance—*pontifex maximus*, head of the state religion, an elective office usually held by men after they had been consuls. Caesar's support of a bill to return the office to election by the tribal assembly (a right taken away by Sulla) shows his clear understanding of the primitive religious roots of Roman political power. Part of his election campaign, it has been plausibly argued, was to present himself as a descendant of Iulus, son of Aeneas and the legendary founder of the Julian family, who had been *pontifex maximus* during the time of Aeneas. It was a lineage he had stressed as well in the funeral oration for his aunt. Leaving behind his undistinguished immediate ancestry, he emphasized instead the distant past, where his ancestors and the ancestors of Rome were the same. Pompey and others had taken the model of Alexander's conquest of bodies and land. But Caesar's temperament attuned him to the importance of Alexander's sway over minds. Through an office like *pontifex maximus,* Caesar could add the dimension of divine sanction to his actions in a way rarely exploited before. On coins he later issued during his time as dictator, the symbols of his pontificate appear prominently, underlining the relation between his political and his symbolic power. By cutting the Gordian knot, Alexander was creating his own portent. Plutarch, Suetonius, and other classical historians frequently note the importance of portents in the life of Caesar. But more telling for our purposes is the number of times they describe Caesar himself interpreting the portents, often in opposition to his soothsayers. That he disregarded the soothsayer who warned him to beware the Ides of March is less a mistake than yet another indication of the well-cultivated impression that his career was the constant concern of the gods.

Caesar's sensitivity to the symbolic meaning of situations gave him the perspective to see beyond those who were caught in its patterns. Cicero and most other public figures of the later Republic characterize its political conflicts in the terminology of the historian Polybius: a battle between the *optimates* who support aristocratic power and the *populares* who want to extend that power to the equestrians, the plebeians, and the other Latin and Italian peoples. But Caesar, while consistently supporting popular programs, presents himself as the unifier, the only way to dissolve this class polarization. In the so-called first triumvirate (which had no legal status) is is Caesar who brings together the otherwise opposed forces of Pompey, the general with his hordes of foreign clients, and Crassus, supposedly the richest man in Rome. Through his special perspective, his detachment, Caesar presents himself as the third term, the synthesizer, in an adversary situation otherwise at an impasse. Pompey and Cicero had both been leading actors in the Roman political theater. But Caesar was stage manager, producer, and director as well.

Suetonius records the slur that Casear was "every woman's husband and every man's wife" (*Twelve Caesars,* 32), and in its gossipy way the remark puts a sour turn to the perception of Caesar's synthesizing spirit. Such a strategy can be opportunistic and unprincipled. But opportunism can also be an enemy's word for a sensitivity to political reality. Certainly, the conflict between *optimates* and *populares,* like the legal system on which it was modeled, was offering few effective solutions to Roman problems. With Machiavelli's *The Prince* in mind, writers have too often searched for premeditation in the careers of those who have risen to supreme political power, and for centuries historians have argued the basic question of Caesar's career: "Was he at bottom driven by personal ambition or a desire to better the lot of his country?" (Peter Green, 105). But because all he did furthered his ambition, was all he did in order to further his ambition? Ambition and the urge to fame may in fact have little to do with material premeditation, which is either a part of every important decision or a poor long-run substitute for political instinct. Machiavelli may have taken Caesar as his model; he certainly attacks Cicero's argument that the state is a structure of laws and offices. But premeditation is a less accurate description of Caesar's efforts to achieve fame and power than improvisation coupled with his acute sense of how to make decisions that will win over enemies and consolidate supporters as much as possible. Machiavellianism is the power fantasy of the intellectual and the writer, who think that all is done by premeditation and foreknowledge. But the hero realizes that a sensitivity to situation can often succeed when the most carefully laid plans do not. It may be in the nature of those who achieve the greatest fame that they can do both, subsuming the standards of the past and showing their insufficiency, yet at the same time responding in a spontaneous and instinctive way to the crisis of the moment, doing naturally and immediately what is necessary.

Many of the historians and biographers of Caesar mention that he could have been a great orator if he had only kept up his interest. But the adversary position of the orator seems as alien to Caesar's temperament and style of fame as it is suitable to Cicero's. What marks Caesar is his appreciation for the intangible elements in fame and power. At the age of forty-two, with the unofficial compact between himself, Pompey, and Crassus just completed, Caesar embarked on the Gallic War, which was to last seven years (58–51 B.C.) and give him the military experience that put muscles on what he had learned in Roman politics. To that military power, however, Caesar typically added a self-conscious element—the writing each year of another book of the *Gallic War*. His goal was in part to assert a presence at Rome, even when he was not there. But beyond its propaganda value, the *Gallic War* shows Caesar's appreciation of the ways a literary perspective can be used to gain a power beyond what is achieved by money and military might. By becoming his own historian, he fashions an image of Caesar as the transcendentally effective creator of connection between events.

In light of the agreement he had recently concluded between himself, Pompey, and Crassus, it is intriguing that Caesar begins the *Gallic War* with the now famous phrase "All Gaul is divided into three parts," *partes* being the Roman word for political party as well. Caesar may be one of the parts, but he is also both the describer and definer of their relationship. The book is written in the third person, not the "I" of the orator, but "Caesar" the soldier whom Caesar the writer presents as he would like himself to be perceived—in the spare, plain style of the Roman soldier and good citizen doing his job, without the rhetorical or personal flourishes of the aristocratic oratorical tradition. Unlike Pompey's vaunting or Cicero's witty self-promotion, Caesar's language comes across as that of the self-confident aristocrat who can speak like a man of the people because he is without pretension. In contrast to Cicero's balanced sentences, the plainness of Caesar's language conveys the history of his duty to the state through a straightforward simplicity that aims to be trusted. Not only does his style embody his own directness and clarity, but it also serves to present him as a man with effective insight into the affairs of others, telling us the plans of the Gallic leaders, giving insights into their characters, discussing battle plans, interpreting portents, and constantly affirming the *Bona Fortuna* that complements his own abilities. The historians of Alexander, like many of the historians of antiquity, fix on the details of battles as the prime expression of human will against the chances of time and history, and therefore the best way to celebrate their heroes. But Caesar in the *Gallic War* exploits the symbolic use of geography and conquest as well—the expanding of the Roman Empire to the limits of the known world, the conquering of more nations and cities, the accumulation of more riches than ever before. These are the exploits of "Caesar," the great man as seen by his simple and direct other self, giving moral and literary force to the Marian precedent of the military commander with a loyal army.

Before Caesar, Suetonius tells us, no one making a report to the Senate had written in book form. Caesar was the first, as he was the first to write his war memoirs not as disconnected notes but as a narrative, a causal account of actions that implied logic beyond personal choice—where military strategy, the patterns of history, and the rhythms of Latin prose could meet. Even while seeming to serve the senatorial view of history, Caesar's writing allowed him to create a history of his own. After the triumvirate dissolved with the death of Pompey's wife (and Caesar's daughter) Julia in 54 B.C., the death of Crassus in the Parthian War (53 B.C.), and Pompey's refusal to enter into new family relations with Caesar in 51 B.C., Caesar published seven books of the *Gallic War* for all to read. It was a decisive crossing of some boundary between his private and his public self, presaging his later crossing of the Rubicon to invade Rome. Pompey may have been the most powerful, but Caesar would be unique. When the Senate orders him to lay down the generalship of his army, Caesar counters by suggesting that all holders of military commands (i.e., Pompey as well) should do so and become private citizens. His ability to envision this alternative and the rejection of it by Pompey and the Senate illustrates the difference between their styles of self-consciousness. In a striking description, without parallel in the life of Pompey, Plutarch describes Caesar before the Rubicon, arguing with himself about the proper action. This is the Caesar who understands the processes of symbolization in religious office and historical writing—the leader who carries within himself all possibilities along with the authority to decide which best and most decisively suits the occasion. Pompey, on the other hand, is a victim of his own desire for praise, an Agamemnon unwilling to miss the slightest morsel of men's attendance upon him. Pompey's soldiers fight for the glory of Pompey, but Caesar, like Alexander, inspires his soldiers with the desire to be praised themselves. No longer can the great man represent only the interests of a particular class. He must be able to excite a support that draws on aspirations shared by every Roman. Unhampered by the limiting arrogance of so many other Roman generals and politicians, Caesar is the great leader whose fame derives from what he enables others to do as much as from what he achieves himself. As the plain style of the *Gallic War* emphasizes, Caesar is the leader as highest common denominator for his followers, the embodiment of their own desire for glory.

When Caesar defies the Senate in 49 B.C. by taking his army across the Rubicon, he is reported to have said, *"Iacta alea est"* ("The dice are thrown"). But almost all our sources point out that he said it in Greek, not Latin, as befitted the occasion, a ceremony of himself in history. Similarly, Caesar's self-consciousness as a public man takes full advantage of the self-deceptions of his rivals. During the civil wars he constantly sues for peace and, in harsh contrast with Pompey's declaration that anyone not actively fighting on his side was a public enemy, he invokes a larger definition of what is Roman by a heavily publicized policy of clemency. In his later book on the civil wars, Caesar refers frequently to Pompey's jealousy of any equal, and in the war with Caesar he does seem like a throwback to an archaic age, finally sulking in his tent like Achilles, while Caesar's army, only half the size of his, wins the decisive battle of Pharsalus. Before the battle, says Plutarch, Pompey had dreamed of being applauded in his own theater. Knowing his opponent's romance with ostentation, Caesar had included in his battle strategy an order that his soldiers aim at the faces of Pompey's men, so that the young nobles, so confident of winning despite their lack of battle experience, might be routed by their own fear of disfigurement and deformity.

Caesar's ability to stand outside himself, to call himself "Caesar," helps explain his later unwillingness to be crowned king, since that would reduce what he had accomplished to traditional forms of authority. In the seventeenth-century, Oliver Cromwell, who became ruler of England after Charles I was defeated and executed, would also refuse the royal title, and Andrew Marvell interpreted that refusal in poetic terms that few men of Caesar's time could have understood:

> For to be *Cromwell* was a greater thing,
> Than ought below, or yet above a king.
> ("The First Anniversary," 225–26.)

By almost eighteen hundred years later, Caesar's style of self-creation was becoming a political act that undermined the whole structure of monarchical power. But in Caesar's own time, the only available models for the power he assumed were kingly, and the efforts of such belated Alexanders as Pompey to oppose him or Marc Antony to force the crown upon him only highlight his own lack of interest in those precedents. He would no doubt have found it appropriate that later generations made his name—Caesar, Kaiser, Tsar, Czar—into a synonym for ruler.

With our two-thousand-year-old knowledge of what the name of Caesar has come to mean, it comes as a shock to realize that he was a dictator for only two years. What a tiny lever to move the great weight of time! But in the short time before his assassination in 44 B.C., Caesar took his extraordinary political power and applied it with unprecedented force. Plutarch condemns both Caesar and Pompey for putting their own aspirations for glory before the good of their country. But for all Pompey's power, he didn't accomplish very much, while Caesar, whatever one may decide about his motives, did have things he wanted to do. Ordinarily, a dictator was named by the consuls as a supreme magistrate in a crisis, a military authority whose actions could be neither vetoed nor appealed during the usual six months of his term. Only Sulla had been dictator for a longer term before Caesar, and he had resigned. Caesar's ten-year appointment thus signifies both his own ascendency and the Roman belief that a wartime situation was now perpetual. But his actions as dictator went far beyond the war needs of Rome. Unlike Sulla, who used his dictatorial power primarily to consolidate military and financial sway, Caesar aimed at a psychic power as well. His sense of the symbolic value of his actions went along with a desire to expose aristocratic political power as essentially secretive behind its love of display. A new era in political affairs was announced when he decided to publish both the acts of the Senate and selected Roman statutes, thereby exposing the class-bound mysteries of the operations of state. But more lasting was his change in the nature of time.

Caesar's term as *pontifex maximus* illustrates his sensitivity to the need to rule men's minds as well as their bodies, especially in a world in which the traditional bounds of obligation and deference to a ruling class had broken down. One of the ritual obligations of the *pontifex maximus* was to drive a nail into a wall at the beginning of a year in order to mark the end of the old year. Taking this hint, Caesar in 46 B.C., reformed the Roman calendar to make the official year correspond more precisely to the natural year. The adjustment is oddly reminiscent of the way Caesar in the *Gallic War* detailed all the portents of nature that validated his own decisions. Pompey and Cicero may have wanted to make a mark in time. But Caesar would make time his own, by restoring it to a "naturalness" that he identified with his own destiny.

Politicians in the ancient world often had the power to make such adjustments in the calendar. But they acted primarily on an ad hoc and temporary basis. Caesar, on the other hand, changed the whole format of the Roman calendar, adapting the Egyptian solar calendar, adding two new months, and beginning the year in January (rather than March) because that was the month in which the consuls changed. Time had become both more natural and more political, more attuned to the rhythms of Rome. In order to make the details match, the year 46 B.C. had 445 days. The two new months were called Quintilis and Sextilis. Somewhat later their names would be changed to the Roman equivalents of our July (for Julius Caesar) and August (for Augustus). Caesar's new calendar would last for more than sixteen hundred years, until Gregory VII's revision by papal bull in 1582. (In England it lasted until 1754). Roman years were still referred to by the name of those who were consuls. But Caesar had defined the year, delivering himself from time in ironic invocation of the human-assisted form of birth referred to then and now as Caesarean.[9]

Caesar knew the power of literature and spent some time winning over Catullus, who had written satiric verses against him. But unlike the Cicero who wrote poems on his consulship and "his own times," Caesar could never have been satisfied by writing as an end in itself, even as a message to posterity. To place oneself in history, to create a name in time, becomes more possible when history is conceived as continuous and ever-expanding. Somewhat later, during the reign of Caesar's adopted son Augustus, is born a man whose birth would come to mark a new order of time, although it was not until the sixth century that the distinction between B.C. and A.D. comes into use. But it is striking how many of the most prominent figures of this period were concerned with reordering and redefining time. The reform of the calendar, while it may seem to be only a slight detail in the welter of Caesar's military and political actions, yet crystalizes his remarkable ability to go far beyond the fame competition of his contemporaries to perceive the context in which his achievements might have the largest meaning and sway. Rome as an empire has disappeared. But we still have July.[10]

Nearly one hundred years after the final battle between Caesar and Pompey, Lucan wrote his epic poem the *Pharsalia,* in which he imagines Caesar in the flush of his victory traveling to Troy to sacrifice at the tomb of Achilles, then proceeding to Alexandria to view the embalmed body of Alexander. Caesar himself, in the *Civil War,* mentions no such visits, perhaps because he no longer wants to publicize his debts to the past. But, even if the gesture seems to be a rote obeisance that Caesar's other actions indicate he had gone beyond, the effort of Lucan to make Caesar self-conscious of his Alexandrian and even Homeric predecessors at least accords with the way Caesar was later viewed. Thus it is ironic but appropriate that, in the Egyptian war following Pharsalus, the Great Library established by the Ptolemaic successors of Alexander should be burnt. Caesar after Pharsalus, by his liaison with Cleopatra, last of the Ptolemies, has both come into the Alexandrian heritage and, mirroring the tales of Alexander's liaison with the Queen of the Amazons, absorbed the Alexandrian legend. Once the last rival has been defeated, the great man moves beyond racial and national confines to mate with the great and mysterious

9. It is probable that Caesar anticipated naming a month after himself when he put the new calendar into effect. Important victory games were celebrated in his name during the month in 45 B.C., and his July birthday was declared a day of public sacrifice. Marc Antony proposed the name change, which was put into effect after Caesar's assassination over the protests of Cicero and the conspirators. See Weinstock, *Divus Julius.*

10. After his victory over Pompey, Caesar pardons the Pompeian supporter Varro and makes him head of a proposed public library, later ransacked after Caesar's assassination, when Varro was outlawed by Antony. In the peace after Antony's defeat by Augustus, Varro returns to his scholarly work, which includes a computation of the date of the founding of Rome (753 B.C., in our dating) that forms the basis for Livy's history.

forces at the edges of "civilization." But Caesar also knew that the imitation of literature and legend loses its force when one becomes more actor than playwright. Disentangling himself from Cleopatra and her mythic plans of empire, Caesar returned to Rome and the new substance of his power. After his assassination Antony and Cleopatra would try to replicate the Alexandrian world once again. But one wonders if Antony would have been so quick to fall in with Cleopatra's dreams if, like Caesar, he had been a writer.

Suetonius records the rumor that one of the reasons for the conspiracy against Caesar was his plan to move the seat of Roman government to Troy or Alexandria, and another his refusal to thank the senators properly enough for the honors bestowed on him. Whatever the details, the general implication seems accurate. Those sixty or so senators who joined in the conspiracy were animated by Caesar's defiance of what they believed to be the traditions of Rome. That they believed the threat he represented could be destroyed by murdering him is itself perhaps a left-handed tribute to his uniqueness. What they could not see was the way in which his sense of what Rome needed in its public men was a better solution than any they had to offer. Already in two years of his dictatorship, he had put his stamp on time itself. In the moment of his assassination, stabbed twenty-three times, yet, as Suetonius describes, with the self-consciousness that never left him, Caesar fell, arranging his toga so that even in death he would have control over his image. With remarkable speed, he had defined a way of being in public that his enemies could do little to change.

The Authority of Augustus

> Here is Caesar
> and all the line of Iulus that will come
> beneath the mighty curve of heaven. This,
> this is the man you heard so often promised—
> Augustus Caesar, son of a god, who will
> renew a golden age in Latium,
> in fields where Saturn once was king, and stretch
> his rule beyond the Garamantes and
> the Indians—a land beyond the paths
> of year and sun, beyond the constellations . . .
> Yet love of country will prevail
> and the boundless desire for praise. . . .
>
> —VIRGIL, *Aeneid*

In the career of Caesar's grandnephew and heir, Octavian, later called Augustus, the various strands of Republican fame, with its divisive urges toward personal aggrandizement and state service, are woven into a new, and for a good time, sustaining fabric. With symbolic premeditation, the assassins of Caesar had killed him at the foot of Pompey's statue. But there were other figures whose careers were potential rivals to his as models, especially Cicero, Marc Antony, and Cato. Of these, Cato, whom Cicero called one of the few men greater than his reputation, represented the view that public behavior is absolutely rooted in personal rectitude. His prime characteristic was his sureness, his uncompromisingly *apolitical* nature. After Pharsalus, he had committed suicide rather than be either captured or pardoned by Caesar, and so in some sense remained undefeated. Caesar's genius was to compromise and improvise, Cato's was to remain firm and unyielding, his suicide an emblem of his unwillingness to face a future in which his definition of virtue would have no part. In the later history of Rome he became the model not for the virtuous politicians but for the disdainers of politics and public life, who stand grandly above the flux, proclaiming their lack of ambition, while meaning only that they are not ambitious in the old sense.

Cato's image of personal austerity would be one Octavian absorbed for himself, just as he selected aspects of Caesar, Pompey, Cicero, and Antony either to imitate or attack. Yet the public man he worked so hard to create was by design singularly drab. After the meteors of the Republic, he would be the apostle of peace and calm, not the isolated hero but the state builder, the consolidator and administrator of Roman complexity.

All of the great men of the previous generation, even the austere Cato, were in different ways theatrical and emblematic. In such company Augustus would later seem notable only for his underplaying. Shakespeare, in his most jaundiced view of civic heroism, *Antony and Cleopatra,* seems mainly to sneer. At one point in the play Octavian comes to Egypt to offer Antony a peace settlement. The contrast between the two men, as generations of critics have pointed out, is between the grandeur of Antony and the cost accounting of Octavian, the outsized hero facing the soon-to-be-leader of a nation of imperial bookkeepers. The contrast owes little to Shakespeare's main source, Plutarch's life of Antony, but it does represent what at Shakespeare's distance seemed to be a distinction between the giant world of Antony and the petty, although politically more powerful, world of Octavian. Shakespeare's vision of the contrast between Antony and Octavian is Alexandrian, or, in more Elizabethan terms, it is Marlovian, preoccupied with heroes as out-of-scale people whose actions send shock waves through the world.

In both life and drama Octavian wins the conflict with Antony, although Shakespeare laments the grandeur that has irretrievably gone with the deaths of Antony and Cleopatra. To that extent *Antony and Cleopatra* is evidence of the Renaissance attitude toward Roman fame. Yet it also reflects Octavian's own historical presentation of himself as a contrast to Antony. In order to create a new Rome from the chaos of civil war, he creates an image of himself as the resolver of all conflict, the mediator between the Roman belief in legality, tradition, and order, on the one hand, and the Roman urge to distinction, individuality, and heroism, on the other. It is a paradox we are all familiar with, the paradox of an executive and imperial country that wants to foster both personal assertion and patriotism in its citizens while avoiding those extremes where assertion becomes independence and patriotism becomes repression. In Augustan terms this might be stated as the need to be neither Cato nor Antony, neither morally rigid nor heroically grand, neither too purely Roman nor too eastern and Alexandrian. Through the mediating figures of Caesar and Cicero, Augustus took on a little of both. More than any of them, he was a totally public man, and he began his career by remaking himself.

Augustus was born as Gaius Octavius in 63 B.C., during the consulship of Cicero and Antony, when the conspiracy of Catiline was thwarted and Cicero named *pater patriae.* His father, an equestrian "new man" and up-and-coming young politician married to Caesar's niece, had died when the young Octavius was about five. Without male heirs himself, Caesar took varying degrees of interest in his three grandnephews, but after the victory at Pharsalus directed his attention primarily at Octavius who, although somewhat sickly, showed an energy and determination to succeed that encouraged Caesar to believe that with training here might be a political as well as a personal heir.

Sooner than anyone expected, Octavius was put to the test. Caesar was assassinated and, on the opening of a will dated barely six months earlier, it was discovered that he had left Octavius three quarters of his estate and adopted him as his son. After some worry over his own safety from the assassins and strong opposition from his stepfather, Octavius accepted the inheritance and took the name *Gaius Julius Caesar* (although in this part of his career historians usually refer to him as Octavian for the "Octavianus" that legally but not in practice followed the name of his adoptive father). Two years later, when Caesar was deified, he added *divi Iulii filius* (son of the divine Julius) to his name. By that time, like Alexander, he had made himself his new father's son. Julius Caesar, like Philip, had shown the way, and their sons, both natural and adoptive, sought to revenge them, to implement their plans, and thereby to supersede them. Disliked and disregarded by Antony and the Caesarians, on one side, as well as by Cicero, Brutus, and the assassins on the other, Octavian managed in two short years to create a position of power and eminence for himself through his artful use of Caesar's fortune to win the support of the hungry urban populace and Caesar's name to win the support of his armies. In his own prescient way he enhanced his symbolic meaning as the mediating inheritor of Caesar until a consulship was forced for him against Cicero's opposition, and he proceeded to form a triumvirate with Antony and the millionaire Lepidus. Unlike the first "triumvirate" of Caesar, Pompey, and Crassus, this one was a legal entity, *tresviri rei publicae constituendae* (three men designated to organize the state), appointed for five years. Its prime actions were a series of legal murders and confiscations of property that purged the state of disruptive elements. In our eyes the most eminent victim was Cicero, who although not invited to join the conspiracy had hailed the assassination of Caesar and hoped to make common cause with Octavian against Antony. But even Octavian's habit of calling him "father" failed to save Cicero from Antony's revenge. The old orator was put on the list of the condemned, and after his death Antony had his head and arm nailed to the front of the raised platform in the Forum where Cicero had made his reputation.

It was a barbarous prelude to the much subtler methods of Augustus. But Antony was vengeful and Octavian was as yet only twenty years old, with something of Pompey's "teenage butcher" in his makeup. The proscriptions at home over, Octavian and Antony moved quickly against the assassins of Caesar who had fled Italy. The next year, at the battle of Philippi, the two most powerful, Brutus and Cassius, were defeated—Cassius in battle with Antony, Brutus in suicide when he heard of Cassius's defeat (even though his own army was beating Octavian's). After Philippi, Octavian went back to Italy and Antony went to the east, where he set up and took down local governments according to their support of the new order. Meanwhile, in Italy Octavian faced two challenges. First, he defeated the supporters of Antony in the brutal battle of Perusia, effectively killing off a chunk of Antony's backing in the upper classes. Then there was yet another enemy, Sextus Pompeius, Pompey's son with his own dreams of emulation and power, who commanded a fleet that was choking off the Roman grain supply. Octavian tried to conciliate Sextus Pompeius with a dynastic alliance but failed. But when Antony landed back in Italy, the strategy worked: Antony married Octavian's sister (as Octavian had sometime before married the daughter of Antony's third wife), and Sextus Pompeius was given Sicily, Sardinia, Corsica, and the Greek Peloponnesus. The record of these years, leading up to the battle of Actium in 31 B.C., where Octavian defeats Antony, is filled with enough political divisions, partial reconciliations, attacks, and underminings to fill many pages. For our purposes, the main events are Octavian's defeat of the truculent Sextus Pompeius, who had not been satisfied with the settlement; the award to Octavian of the personal sacrosanctity that was the privilege of tribunes; and the offer of the offices of *pontifex maximus,* which is prominently mentioned by Augustus later in his life as the priesthood "which my father had held." The retrospect is a significant one, for both personal sacrosanctity and the offer of the post of *pontifex maximus* marked Octavian's desire that the spiritual and religious honors of Rome be added to the military. It was a move, for which Caesar's career was a precedent, that Octavian would take to even greater levels of refinement. With the victory over Sextus Pompeius, Octavian also changed his official name from *Gaius Iulius divi filius Caesaris* to *Imperator Caesaris divi filius,* making part of his own name the title that the Senate had voted to Julius Caesar—a word that carried with it the aura of military triumph.

In contrast with the personal self-assertion that marked the heroes of the Late Republic, Octavian from early in his career thus worked to fashion himself into a symbolic leader whose name and nature subsumed all that was honorable within the state. With the deaths of Brutus and Cassius, there remained only one person who presented an active picture of the energies that led to the civil wars. Pompey was dead. Cato was dead. Caesar was dead. Cicero was dead. Whatever was owed to such father-patrons, their presence could no longer inhibit, only sanction, the central element in Octavian's politics: the identification of himself with Rome. Of the great men of the Republic, only Antony remained, and Antony, with his personal following, was to be the enemy. Once Antony was defeated, Octavian could begin to become Augustus.

In 37 B.C., the triumvirate of Octavian, Antony, and Lepidus was renewed for another five years, but within another year the defeat of Sextus Pompeius and the forced retirement of Lepidus left the field to the two who had always been the prime competitors. According to his temperament, each attempted to consolidate his position both by action and by propaganda, Antony concentrating on the east, Octavian staying at Rome. While Octavian wrapped himself in the traditional garb of Roman priestly authority, Antony and Cleopatra played on the religious forms of Egypt, with ceremonies announcing Antony as Dionysus-Osiris and Cleopatra as Aphrodite-Isis. While Agrippa, Octavian's chief general, was overhauling the Roman aqueduct system and ensuring a free-flowing grain supply, Antony was staging the "Donations," in which he recognized the legitimacy of Caesarion, Cleopatra's son by Caesar (a clear threat to Octavian), as well as the legitimacy of his twin children by Cleopatra (Alexander Helios and Cleopatra Selene), and allotted to them and to Cleopatra portions of the old Alexandrian empire.

Two years later, the conflict between Octavian and Antony reached its peak after months of mutual attack, including a strange and apologetic pamphlet by Antony called *On His Drunkenness*.[1] Octavian's legal power as a triumvir had lapsed. But he gathered support for himself from all of Italy, like that mustered for the exiled Cicero not too many years before. *Coniuratio Italiae,* it was called, "the alliance of Italy," and its special characteristic was an oath sworn to Octavian not as a public official but as the prime member of the family of Caesar. The two consuls, both supporters of Antony, left Rome along with one third of the Senators (three hundred or so). That summer Antony formally divorced Octavia, dissolving his family ties with Octavian, and the formal friendship they implied. But then came Octavian's master stroke: In the open Senate he read Antony's will, which he had seized from the Vestal Virgins, where it had been deposited. Among other things, it affirmed that Caesarion was the legitimate heir, gave large legacies to his children by Cleopatra, and ordered that wherever he died, his corpse should be buried in Alexandria— an echo of the rumors that Caesar had wanted to move the capitol to Alexandria in deference to Cleopatra's ambitions. Insensibly, Antony had taken upon himself a symbolic position as the consort of the Other. Even though he stood politically for a republican settlement, in the minds of the majority of Romans he had become alien. The declaration of war, which came quickly, was by Roman law declared against Cleopatra, not against Antony.

The brilliance of Octavian's defeat of Antony can hardly be found in the details of tactics and siegecraft so dear to the ancient historians. According to recent scholarship, the battle of Actium was not a decisive victory by any military measure. But whatever the truth of the details, the story of Cleopatra's withdrawal of her fleet and Antony's besotted pursuit decisively culminates the propaganda war that Octavian had been waging for years. In essence Octavian cast Antony as a renegade, a Roman who had been taken over by the wiles of the barbarian queen, turned into a drunkard, and inspired to un-Roman styles of greatness. Pompey, Caesar, and even Octavian himself may have kept the example of Alexander before them. But Antony actually attempted to restore the Alexandrian Empire, with himself and Cleopatra as divine king and queen at its head. Later historians have argued that in fact what Antony was doing was similar to what many Romans had done before. It was all right to put on the show of divine kingship in the East. That's what the locals expected. Just don't try it at Rome. But the prevalence of Octavian's interpretation of

1. Octavian's propaganda emphasized both Antony's sexual licentiousness and his excessive drinking. Both charges were not only directed against Antony's personal morality but also involved his associations with gods of excess like Dionysus.

events, even down to the present, shows that what may have been "normal" or at least precedented for victorious Roman generals in the eastern Mediterranean could easily be interpreted otherwise.

Ronald Syme, in *The Roman Revolution,* has detailed the importance of what he calls "the organization of opinion" to the ascendancy of Octavian. This molding of public perception was accomplished as much by Octavian's political actions as. by his literary patronage of such writers as Horace and Virgil. Like heroes of old, Pompey and Marc Antony were content to have writers merely sing their praises. But Octavian absorbed from both Caesar and Cicero a sensitivity to the ways a public man could collaborate with language to influence how events were perceived, not in the gross mode of the Stalinist rewriting of history, but by emphasis and above all by interpretation. In one of the Philippic orations against Antony that later cost him his head, Cicero quotes Antony to say that Octavian was "a boy . . . who owed everything to a name" (573), to which Octavian might have responded that Antony had too little appreciation for the importance of naming, the power of language.[2]

If we consider Antony's whole career rather than its flamboyant end, its shape is reminiscent of Cicero's. Antony was another great Roman who had achieved fame and then didn't know what to do next, until by chance or circumstance he found a partner, a co-conspirator, with whom fame might again regain its meaning and its immediacy. With Atticus, Cicero published books; with Cleopatra, Antony envisioned kingdoms. So far at least, in this story of men who aimed at supreme achievement, we find little account of the women who shared their lives, cementing the all-important family alliances. In the last years of the Republic there is a fascinating group of women, such as Antony's first wife, Fulvia, who married a succession of men, each violently killed in his turn, for whom war and warring politics was a profession. But the trappings of Roman public life were tailored for men, not women, and in accounts of heroes like Plutarch's *Lives* or Suetonius's *Lives of the Caesars* women symbolized a private life that only corrodes the male commitment to the world of public heroism: The good woman takes care of the domestic world; the bad woman either invades the masculine sphere or undermines her husband's (usually military) success by her unfaithfulness. As Roman matrons they had a special social role, attested to by innumerable stories of feminine virtue handed down from the early years of Rome. But if a woman moved outside the realm of the domestic, she threatened the Roman identification of masculinity and public display. In a world of sharply delineated gender roles, those who do not abide by the rules get a bad press. Because of his liaison with Cleopatra, Antony could no longer claim the

2. Cicero entitles his attacks against Antony "Philippics" in reference to Demosthenes' attacks on Philip of Macedon three hundred years before. In a less explicit way, Syme's book, published in 1938, owes much of its insight into Augustus's propaganda to the contemporary example of Hitler's, although the influence of that model may appear a little too strongly in his moral judgments of Augustus's methods.

self-sufficient virility of the hero and leader, and in his rule over the East he exemplified an ambition at state expense that was the downfall of the Republic. Many years later, in the final testament of his accomplishments, Octavian would refer to Antony only as "he with whom I waged war," and would proudly assert that he replaced all the Asian temple ornaments Antony had confiscated for his private use (30).

Octavian's propaganda therefore struck a sympathetic chord in Italy, especially when the "Donations" proved that a new dynasty was definitely in the making. According to Plutarch, Antony had several times offered to fight Octavian in single combat for the leadership of the Roman world. (No wonder Antony's popularity revives in the Renaissance!) But Octavian just as regularly refused. Perhaps more than he realized, Shakespeare the playwright resembles Octavian rather than Antony. Both are creators of order rather than masters of single combat, authorities behind the scene rather than vaunting heroes. Octavian gives the credit for winning the battle of Actium not to himself but to Rome, and the defeated enemy is not Antony but Cleopatra, whose effigy, with asps attached, is displayed in Octavian's triumph.[3]

From Octavian to Augustus

Plutarch, in the midst of a discussion of the Roman admiration for military achievement, points out that the only word for "virtue" in Latin (*virtus*) means *"manly valor:* thus the Romans made courage stand for virtue in all its aspects, although it denotes only one of them" (*Coriolanus,* 16). Octavian in contrast seeks to legitimize his rule by redefining that "virtue" in a civic and peaceful context. Rather than the monarch or even the emperor, he calls himself the *princeps,* the first citizen, and all his policies promote a myth of political inclusion rather than of personal competition. Ambition can, of course, still exist. But it must be judged by its contribution to the perpetuation of Rome, the only acceptable immortality. In his own career Octavian offers a model interweaving of personal ambition and state service by transforming himself from a military adventurer such as Pompey, Caesar, and Antony into the almost mystical embodiment of Roman stability and tradition called Augustus.

As virtually every historian of the period points out, Octavian was not a very good general. But, unlike later leaders (for example Napoleon) who

3. Horace's poem on the death of Cleopatra, however, embodies a crucial ambiguity. The bulk of it calls for celebration now that the lustful and drink-maddened queen no longer plots to ruin Rome and the empire. But when he comes to write of her suicide, he depicts it as a courageous act (shades of Cato?), done in private so that she would not be a display in someone else's triumph. With varying degrees of approval, in fact all three of the great poets of the reign of Augustus—Virgil, Horace, and Ovid—associate notable women with values opposed to male public assertion.

could never quite manage to sever their power from their military victories, Octavian simultaneously affirmed his heroic imagery while he underplayed those aspects of Roman character that were disruptive to a stable government. In 29 B.C. Octavian celebrated a triple triumph (the first ever, he noted later) for victories against tribes in the Balkans, against Cleopatra at Actium, and during the annexation of Egypt. After his military celebrity was confirmed in such an unmistakably grandiose way, he could then easily delegate military exploits to Agrippa while he himself turned to civic affairs. Once Antony has been defeated, for example, Octavian also accepts the Alexandrian analogy as a grace note for himself rather than a rival conception of leadership, visiting the sarcophagus of Alexander, placing a golden crown on its head, and scattering flowers on the body. At various times in his career, Augustus uses three seals for official papers: a sphinx, a head of Alexander, and (after 23 B.C.) a head of himself—and Suetonius repeats several "birth of the hero" stories obviously modeled on those about Alexander. In January of 27 B.C., he entered into his seventh consulship, a record equaled only by Marius, more than sixty years before. Then, having equaled Marius in the annals of Roman honor, Octavian abdicated the absolute power conferred on him by the Senate and announced that he had reestablished the Republic. As he said later, since he was now in possession of all things (*rerum omnium*), he transferred the Republic, the public thing, to the rule of the Senate. Whereupon he is given back virtually all the powers he had given up and awarded the name *Augustus,* a word whose associations bring together action (*augere* = increase, strengthen) and spiritual power (*augur* = prophet) in a sacred and political office whose sway extended to past, present, and future.

Some of Octavian's supporters thought "Romulus" would be a more appropriate new name for the refounder of Rome. But Octavian probably never shared that view. Not only were there too many royal associations with Romulus's name, but also the tradition that Romulus was murdered by Senators would have been an uncomfortable reminiscence of Julius Caesar's end. In any case the phase of Octavian's life was over in which he chose to be either in combat with any living man or the imitator of any predecessor. Livy uses the word *augustus* to refer to both Romulus and Hercules. To turn it into a name for a particular person identifies a quality, even a divinity, that underlays Roman history and has now been focused in a single human nature. Once an ambitious and aspiring man, Augustus had now become a national trait, a redefinition of virtue, a supreme possibility of the Roman spirit. After Octavian is named Augustus, the word *"imperator"* appears somewhat less frequently in official inscriptions and documents. As *princeps* rather than *imperator,* Augustus connected and sustained all that was Roman in past and present. According to Suetonius, he disliked the words of power, especially any word like *"dominus"* (lord) that implied an absolute power and was typically a title in the mouths of slaves. Adapting the lessons of Julius Caesar, Augustus had gained a freedom from the power of Roman language and tradition by constructing his own versions of them—always with amply trumpeted precedents from the honored past. In 8 B.C., twenty years after Octavian was named Augustus, his military command over the border provinces was reaffirmed for another ten years and the month Sextilis was renamed Augustus in his honor. Caesar had redefined the Roman perception of time. But Augustus had politically begun Roman time anew. Appropriately enough, Sextilis was not the month of his natural birth but the month of his first consulship at nineteen, the month of his victory of his entry into Alexandria—the month, that is, of his birth within the state.[4]

Depending on one's point of view, Octavian's claim to have reestablished the Republic was sincere or fraudulent. In fact it led to what has been called the Principate, in which Octavian (as Augustus) held supreme power without really saying so. In contrast with the grand assertions of the past, Octavian had introduced what might be called the knack of selective abdication, in which limited power is elaborately and ceremonially given up so that greater power might be gained. I have fallen into the use of "power" to refer to Octavian's sway over the Roman Empire both because it is the word we use and because to shy away from it might imply a naivete about the actual "power structure" of the empire. But he himself referred not to his power (*potestas*), a legal concept, but to his authority (*auctoritas*), a more abstract and spiritual concept, akin both conceptually and etymologically to *augustus* itself. As he says later in his political testament, after recounting the bestowal on him of the name Augustus: "After this time I stood before all in authority, although I had no more legal power than those who were my colleagues as magistrates" (36).

In place of the rampant individual ambition of the Late Republic, Augustus's emphasis on his authority rather than his power introduces a note that is at once both more personal and more abstract. Instead of being the best of the aristocracy, he presents himself as a leader for everyone, whose leadership has been both sanctioned and sanctified by the suffrage of the people. Although in the terms of political science, the permanent standing army created by Augustus replaced the old Roman oligarchical rule with

4. It is intriguing to contrast the calendars of different peoples and what they may have meant for their conception of the relation of chronological time to history and to nature. The Jews still begin their numbering of the years from the creation of the world by God, the Christians number forward and backward from the birth of Jesus, the Moslems from the flight of Mohammed to Mecca. The Romans, as we have seen, used the names of the elected consuls as well as the time A.U.C. (*ab urbe condita*).

But Augustus, like Caesar before him, sought a more immediate impact on the popular conception of time. Recent excavations have confirmed the existence of an enormous sundial constructed by Augustus on the Campus Martius, with an Egyptian obelisk at its center. On the day of Augustus's birth (September 23), it cast a shadow that directly intersected the Ara Pacis, built by the Senate in 9 B.C. to commemorate Augustus's safe return from Gaul and Spain. Thus the whole course of the year as well as the institution of a new age of peace and prosperity was defined by Augustan time in a way no Roman citizen could ignore. For details, see Buchner, *Die Sonnenuhr des Augustus,* and Pollini, *Augustan "Historical" Reliefs.*

a military monarchy, he had absorbed enough of the imagery of stoic self-abnegation to present himself not as much as monarch so much as the state's prime servant. In the nice formulation of the historians P. A. Brunt and J. M. Moore: "With *potestas* a man gives orders that must be obeyed, with *auctoritas* he makes suggestions that will be followed" (84).

Octavian gave way to Augustus, the adopted son to the civic godfather. *Pax* (Peace) appeared on his coins, and he set up statues to *Pax* and *Victoria* in Rome. Even Tacitus, in a sarcastic summary of Augustus's reign that is fully sensitive to the manipulation of names and images, pauses to admit that Augustus's great appeal was "the enjoyable gift of peace" (30). When in the past ill fortune had struck Rome and unprecedented individual ability was needed to set things right, the discretionary authority of the *imperium* had been given to the hero with special talents for special occasions. Julius Caesar tried to extend that discontinuity in Roman history into a new continuity, the perpetual dictatorship. Not satisfied with the obvious power of *imperium*, Augustus defined his leadership instead through *auctoritas*, a power of personality akin to what we call charisma, through which a person is at once individual and a glowing image of some purified form of human nature. In the process he stripped away the fame of the grandiose hero and replaced it with the civic virtue he considered suitable for the ruler of a vast empire.

In the sixteenth century an inscription was discovered on the walls of the temple of Rome and Augustus in Ankara, Turkey. There, Augustus, like Caesar in the *Gallic War* and *Civil War*, gives his authorized version of how he wished his actions and motivations to be known. This inscription is the *Res gestae Divi Augusti* (the things accomplished by the divine Augustus) that he ordered to be engraved on bronze tablets in front of his mausoleum at Rome, with copies like that at Ankara to appear in every major city of the empire.[5] Aside from a few obscene verses, the *Res gestae* is the only piece of Augustus's writing that remains (although Suetonius tantalizingly mentions among other works an unfinished *Reply to Brutus's "On Cato"*). Composed for the most part in the few years after he became *princeps,* it emphasizes what he valued most in his public identity.

So far I have drawn a few individual details from this fascinating testament. But Augustus's own arrangement, what he stresses and what he leaves out, conveys best the public figure he fashioned for his audience:

1–2.   His early career and defeat of the assassins of Caesar.

3–4.   His wars and military triumphs.

5–7.   The offices he held, both secular and religious.

8.   His reestablishment of a patrician class. His censuses of the Roman people. His revival of ancient practices.

5. *Gestae* is the word that sits parent to the medieval French word *gestes* which generally means accomplishments, but is used specifically to refer to what a knight does, that is, heroic deeds.

9–12.   Extraordinary honors granted him, including prayers for his health, the use of his name in a religious hymn, the personal sacrosanctity granted him as a tribune for life, the office of *pontifex maximus*, the consecrating of the altar of Fortuna Redux to him and naming of the day Augustalia in honor of his return to Rome in 19 B.C.

13.   The closing of the gate of the temple of Janus three times to signify that Rome was at peace.

14.   Honors given to his adopted sons, Gaius and Lucius Caesar.

15–18.   Money that he paid the Roman plebs and soldiers; land that he bought for soldier-colonists; assistance he gave to the public treasury from his own funds; grain that he bought for the people.

19–21.   Public buildings he built or restored, aqueducts and temples; gifts to temples from his war booty.

22–23.   Shows he produced for the people, including a naval battle.

24.   His restoration of ornaments to foreign temples that Antony had taken; his removal of all statues to himself set up during the war with Antony and dedication of the proceeds from them to Apollo.

25.   Ridding the sea of pirates, all Italy swearing allegiance to him; the senators who fought with him at Actium and their status.

26–30.   His victories and pacifications in the empire; annexation of Egypt; founding of colonies; defeat of new tribes.

31–33.   Tribute and embassies sent from foreign peoples and kings.

34.   The laying down of his power; named Augustus; other honors.

35.   Named father of his country, its inscription on his house and in Rome; his age seventy six at writing.

Two aspects stand out in this recounting: Augustus's claim to uniqueness as the new and unprecedented man; and his simultaneous claim to be the representative of the oldest and most deeply rooted Roman traditions. Augustus's respect for what Rome can award its leading citizens appears prominently as he recounts quantities and combinations of titles beyond what any Roman had ever received. Then, he speaks of specific honors given him that "no one before me" had ever received: from other Romans, whose vote to make him *pontifex maximus* was the largest ever recorded; from foreign kings, who had never before visited another Roman leader. Yet matched with the elaboration of distinction is a motif of almost formulaic refusal (*non recepi* [I did not accept] is the repeated phrase) of all power and offices "against the custom of our ancestors," including dictatorial power, which is nevertheless offered to him by the Senate and the people "in my presence and in my absence."

Thus Augustus characterizes himself as the pervasive mediator between the meaning of the Roman past and the demands of the Roman present. His personal achievements may be beyond those of any other Roman ("before this time," he sometimes anxiously adds). But they must be seen in the light of his refusal to go against tradition, even when the voices of both people and Senate implore him. The suffrage of the people is a paramount support of his legitimacy, therefore, except when they unknowingly seek to turn him against what has been established and honored by time. Like Cincinnatus, whose story is told in the first book of Livy's history of Rome, Augustus gives up his sole dependence on the immediate power of *imperium* once danger has passed. But instead of going back to his farm, Augustus will tend the state in peace as well as in war.

In Augustus's rebuilding of public Rome, we see a clear image of his urge to create a unique setting that simultaneously honors the past and "remakes" it for the present. In the restored stones and inscriptions, the public might read a renewed history of themselves, not as an aristocratic class but as a people. In the same way that Augustus edited the Sibylline books and burned those prophecies that seemed deviant or irrelevant, his conception of the physical symbolism of the city of Rome selected only those aspects of the past that he wanted to preserve as the precursors of the present. All the rest would be erased and the divisions of civil war healed in the state as he had healed them in himself. The Alexandrian Age of movement was over. The age of architecture and consolidation had begun. One strange detail remains in the *Res gestae*, as a further signal of how Augustus has transformed himself. Except for the usual Roman references to the names of consuls to designate years, there are very few proper names in the *Res gestae*. Even Gaius and Lucius Caesar are named only in conjunction with the consular designation they receive at fourteen. Lepidus is never named. Julius Caesar appears as "Divus Julius" or "my father." Pompey is the name of a theater that Augustus has restored "without inscribing my name." Agrippa is "my colleague." And Antony, as I have mentioned, is "he against whom I waged war." But in the midst of his recounting of the many building projects by which, as Suetonius says, he found Rome a city of bricks and left it a city of marble, Augustus mentions that he allowed the name of a previous builder to remain on one new structure he raised in its place. The name of the ancient builder, Augustus says, was Octavius.

To restore Rome, Augustus remade himself from the ferocious and ruthless Octavian into the serene and forgiving Augustus. Success always seems to legitimize the assertion that has succeeded and turns it into a possibility for future aspirants. But Augustus wanted to succeed in such a way that he would affirm the structure in which he succeeded instead of undermining it, as had the great men of the Late Republic. His personal success, therefore, had to be tied to and determined by the success of Rome. In the east he might allow cult worship of himself, in response to the political importance of ruler worship, especially for the Greeks of that time. But Augustus, Glenn W. Bowersock points out, eliminated "savior" and "founder" from honors a Roman magistrate might receive from his Greek city, although "benefactor" was allowed (117).[6] In general he allowed no

6. "The highest honour was worship, disclosing little about the religious life of the Hellenic peoples but much about their ways of diplomacy. . . . A man who had

temples to him that were not also temples to Rome—another example of the way he simultaneously qualified his personal fame and magnified his symbolic fame, at once proferring himself to the public even as he barricaded and baffled his personal nature.

A crucial part of Augustus's commitment to the continuity of Roman history, now restored after the years of civil war, was his effort to superintend public morals. Unlike the blazing names of the past, he enjoyed the endless details of administration, the infinite nuances of authority. After Actium he presented everything he did as legal, that is precedented, and the *Res gestae* tries to say that the Republic and its laws and customs were in fact always his main concern from his first appearance on the public stage. Through laws that he says the senate and the people wish him to promulgate, Augustus sought to reestablish the Roman family as a bulwark of traditional values. Even clothing carried a symbolic message, and Augustus passed laws that outlawed the new-style cloak and required the wearing of the toga (an otherwise old-fashioned garment) for special public occasions. In his own family he followed out his edicts by having his wife and daughters weave clothing in the old Roman way that he would then wear, presenting an image of unpretentious national values: Augustus and Livia versus the ghosts of Antony and Cleopatra still.

Unlike previous Roman heroes, who had replicated the heroes of the past, Augustus presided over a reinterpretation and renovation of past values that would regulate the present and help prepare for the future. Many of the decorations of public buildings in the time of Augustus featured children and many of the stricter moral laws Augustus passed emphasized the need for more children, especially of the patrician class. The civil wars had decimated the ranks of the upper classes. Augustus's moral legislation was therefore not only an attempt to mold manners in the present, but also to insure continuity for the future. Success required succession. Without male heirs himself, Augustus tried to follow Caesar's example. But first Marcellus (whom he married to his daughter Julia) died, then Agrippa (also married to Julia), then Lucius and Gaius Caesar (the children of Julia and Agrippa). The deaths occurred over a period of twenty-six years to be sure, but with enough palace intrigue for historians to speculate about conspiracy. Finally, Tiberius, Livia's son by her first husband, survived to rule after Augustus's death. Even to trace these relationships superficially requires an elaborate scampering over the genealogy charts. But Augustus was fascinated by the Roman system of family politics and used his authority as paterfamilias of the empire to force marriages to enhance family connections and thereby family continuity and power. Our own prejudices about marriage for love may no doubt find this cold-blooded. But if we understand the importance of the Roman family for Augustus's conception of the proper conduct of the state's authority,

received a cult in his lifetime might be honoured for generations to come, provided there was no offense to later kings or patrons" (Bowersock, *Augustus and the Greek World*, 12, 112).

we might see the pattern if not the justice of his actions. So much of the moral legislation he passed strengthened the already firm hand of the father in the Roman family as ruler of the household. As the empire unfolded, the Roman taste for defining family relations as national politics would be followed religiously.[7]

The Imagery of Augustus: Coinage and the Negotiable Face

Through his reestablishment of ancient religious rites, his revivals of ancient customs, his rebuilding of temples and public buildings, and his legal attempts to purify the Roman upper classes both morally and politically, Augustus affirmed an image of Rome on which his own status as leader and *princeps* was firmly based. Several aspects of his self-presentation are worth further comment for the influence they have had on fame seekers down to the present. Of these, perhaps the most intriguing is the literary renaissance over which he presided, which featured such writers as Virgil, Horace, and Livy and was remarkably concerned with the theme that Augustus had also made his own: the history and destiny of Rome. In these writers we see as well an elaborate and self-conscious treatment of the theme of fame—their own reflection of Augustus's second-generation self-consciousness in his political career. But the special turn that writing gives to the themes of fame and career—the shading by which authority becomes authorship—invokes instead fame in its spiritual guise. In the history of fame the writers of the Augustan period are therefore more notable for their affinities with the attack on Roman concepts of glory that lies at the roots of Christianity. For now, however, while it is still the political aspects of fame that is before us, let us consider two related areas of Augustan propaganda: first, the imagery of his coins; second, his promotion of particular gods as well as his own "genius" as appropriate objects of worship.

As many writers on the history of coinage have observed, the coins of antiquity (and I would say until the Renaissance) were the primary way in which news both of changes in government and shifts in ideology was brought to the man on the street. The face on a coin was the face of a leader. When the leader wanted to change his public imagery, he changed his coinage. Coins helped to legitimize power both by asserting the financial solidity of those who issued them and by furnishing a set of recognizable symbols for their authority. So clearly was coinage an instrument

7. Under the *lex Julia,* passed in 18 B.C., for example, a father might kill his adulterous daughter and her lover if they were caught in the act in either his or her husband's house; a husband did not have a similar right. Augustus's laws offering rewards for upper-class families with children and restricting the rights of the childless were overturned in A.D. 9 after much agitation. The laws on adultery stood and were made even more severe under the Christian emperors.

of Roman imperial policy that when Carausias, a naval commander in England, revolted against Rome in the third century A.D. and proclaimed himself emperor, he immediately set up the first mints in England to promulgate his image. (Appropriately enough, he was later assassinated by his finance minister.)

Once again, in the history of political fame, Philip and Alexander helped set the pattern. Capturing gold mines and minting coins were among the earliest steps in Philip's conquest of Greece, and his gold *staters* were in circulation for centuries afterward. Alexander, as he marched across Asia, established not only new cities, but also new minting centers to circulate those coins in which his own features gradually merged with those of Hercules, Ammon, and Dionysus. The perpetuation of his name and legend was no doubt aided immeasurably by the continued circulation of coins with his markings for years after his death, even by otherwise hostile countries. The example was infectious. But only those rulers most assertive about the divine sanction of their kingship put their own features on coins. In general, Asian and African rulers took more easily to the new display than European ones. The Ptolemies, partaking of the long-standing Egyptian tradition of divine kingship, were the most consistent, appearing on coins down to Cleopatra. The first portrait-from-life coin in Europe was that of Demetrius I of Macedonia, the son of one of Alexander's generals and a failed empire builder himself. With only a small literate (and potentially opposition) group to propagandize, writing clearly waits behind coinage and even oratory. The addition of explicit policy to image, and the need for writing to detail that policy, responds to the necessities of a later era.[8]

In republican Rome, the production of money was not the responsibility of a ruler, since there was none, but of a three-man board, the *tresviri monetales,* whose status intriguingly seems to be a precedent for the triumvirate of Caesar, Pompey, and Crassus. The similarity indicates the close relationship between politics and money in the Republic. Beginning in the middle of the second century B.C., the names and emblems of the individual moneyer issuing the coin began to appear, as a mark of its authenticity and to display both individual and family honor in the office. Reputation in the state therefore backed the value of the coins, and that reputation was affirmed first by the moneyer's name as it would later be by the ruler's image and slogans.

As we have already noted in the careers of men like Pompey and Cicero, a state office was often used as the vehicle of personal enlargement and honor. Although there is little evidence that any moneyer used the propaganda potential of coinage as a means to further political power, it obvi-

8. Another great center of realistic coin portraits that arose in the wake of Alexander's conquests was Bactria (roughly equivalent to Afghanistan). In Bactria particularly the ruling image so obviated the need for written propaganda that, as G. K. Jenkins remarks, these coins preserve "the names and portraits of an important line of kings most of whom are quite unknown to the meagre historical sources" (24).

ously helped. Generals were another matter. Like the moneyers, they were often given state bullion with which to pay off their soldiers. Thus, when they put themselves on those coins, the heroic effect was naturally enhanced by an especially grateful constituency. In the second century B.C. Flamininus, a rival of Scipio Africanus, commemorated his liberation of Greece from Macedonia by issuing a coin with his own features (as well as declaring himself a son of Aeneas in an inscription at Delphi). Similarly, Sulla, almost one hundred years later, commemorated his victories in the East with coins showing him on horseback or in a chariot, not quite full face. Pompey's head also appears on Eastern coins, but not in the West until after his death. In Rome itself, the imagery of coinage had been slowly changing from ancient heroes to past statesmen. When politics and generalship came together in the figure of Julius Caesar, it seems inevitable that in 45 B.C. the Senate voted him the honor of being the first living man to be portrayed on a Roman coin. With a taste for Caesar's imagery if not his politics, Brutus, a few years after the assassination of Caesar, issued a coin stamped with his own head. On the reverse was the cap of a freed man, flanked by two daggers.

In the years that followed, Antony issued portrait coins for payment to his legions. But in the war of monetary imagery Octavian was far more adroit. As C. H. V. Sutherland points out, coinage was an essential and early part of his ruling policy. Immediately after the battle of Actium and the defeat of Antony, Octavian set up new mints in the East and moved to regulate the Roman monetary system. By coins he introduced his designated successors and initiated a constant feature of later coinage: the semideifying of the imperial family. On coins also appeared what Ronald Syme has called the "catchwords" of the Augustan political settlement— *Libertatis p. r. vindex* (the victory of liberty for the Roman people), *Pietas* (loyalty, a Pompeian term taken over by Augustus), *Ob cives servatos* (on behalf of the rescued citizens), *Pax et Victoria* (peace and victory), *Aequitas augusti* (the fairness of Augustus), *Libertas augusti* (the liberty of Augustus)—whose daily repetition helped ensure that they would be embedded in men's minds.

Augustus's coinage policy had transformed the rare assertion of perpetual and godlike presence into a necessary part of any ruler's political sway. When we notice a special function of coinage later in European history, it will be as a footnote to Augustus. Unlike many of his imitators, however, Augustus always matched imagery with action, and in the *Res gestae* he allocates a good deal of space detailing how much of his own money he laid out on aqueducts, colonies, grain, soldiers' pay, and other benefits to the state. Authority is to power as honor is to wealth, and these numerous references to his expenditures testify to Augustus's desire that the Roman people believe he was worth the authority he in fact possessed. It is hard to overstate the role of money as the mortar of Roman politics. But in the hands of Augustus it more obviously takes on a metaphysical tinge that moves it beyond mere material wealth. Even though the distribution of money to the rich and corn to the poor was a recognized method for Roman politicians to get votes, and the exchange of money and gifts an important part of the bonds of friendship between politically allied families and individuals, money also carried with it the aroma of moral corruption, a corruption that the Roman historians with their strange precision dated from 212 B.C., when foreign conquests brought inordinate amounts of wealth into the previously frugal Republic. The expenditures of large sums of money on public building projects played a central part in the rises to power of Pompey, Caesar, Antony, and even Cicero. But in the hands of Augustus, money takes on a moral if not a metaphysical tinge. While he created an army that was loyal not to its general but to the state, he also, as the *Res gestae* attests, set up standards for the proper use of the spoils of war. One whole section details the building of the temple of Mars Ultor (the Avenger) and the Augustan Forum as well as a theater near the temple of Apollo and numerous gifts in the Capitol, the temples of Mars, Vesta, and Apollo—all "from booty." Unlike Antony, who took the spoils of war "for his own private use," the money and wealth Augustus accumulated was, he asserts, spent for the good of the state. It had ceased to be purely material and became instead the substantial expression of his *auctoritas,* the proof of his worth to Rome. Suetonius records that Augustus liked to give old coins as gifts. The domestic detail indicates his sensitivity to the metaphysic of money, at least in the way that a ruler can use it. Behind the coins of Rome lay Augustus, guaranteeing their material value by his political and spiritual authority.

Apollo and the Emperor's "Genius"

The psychic and material relationship between the leader and his audience that is embodied in Augustus's use of coinage appears as well as in his attitudes toward the gods and toward his own worship. Two elements are clear: the time-honored strategy of choosing appropriate protectors and associates; the characteristic Augustan displacement from the personal to the representative. In both modes Augustus had the short-lived but intense precedent of his adoptive father Caesar; and in both, as usual, he carried out the often bare suggestion of Caesar's methods with a flair for justifying the most unprecedented practice by founding it firmly in tradition and history. As in so many things, it was up to Augustus to stabilize the forces that Caesar had set into motion and to raise to another level of premeditation the Roman myths and tales he had used to enhance his position.

Many Roman individuals and families had particular gods and goddesses as their special patrons. Honor was paid to them usually on a private basis within the home. Such private versions of public religion changed dramatically in the Late Republic when an increasing number of public men called the gods not just their family protectors, but also their personal patrons and even their spiritual fathers. The extent to which an aspiring hero might call a god his forebear depended on his own conviction of destiny. The extent to which the relation would be accepted by others depended on their desire for the gods, who had previously supplied the groundwork and continuity of time, to take an active role in history through their designated heirs.

Quite early in his career, Octavian chose as his special protector not such gods of power and action as Jupiter (Scipio Africanus), or Venus (Julius Caesar), or Dionysus (Antony), or Neptune (Sextus Pompeius), nor even the god of his family, Mars. He chose instead the one god whose domain was the future—Apollo. Suetonius mentions a banquet in 40 B.C. to which all the guests came dressed as gods, Octavian playing Apollo. Such playacting foreshadows the gradual process by which Augustus made Apollo rather than Jupiter the central god of the Roman state. Apollo begins appearing on his coinage from 37 B.C. onward. After the battle of Actium, he dedicates a temple to Apollo, and in the *Res gestae* talks about restoring treasures to the temples of Mars the Avenger, Vesta, and Apollo. They are an intriguing trio of gods for the new Rome of Augustus: a war God who acts only in response to attack; a goddess of the hearth and home; and a god of the future, of prophecy, and of "august auguries." Vesta and Apollo have another typically Augustan relation in their power over fire, Vesta's hearth fire and Apollo's sun fire being brought together in Augustus's synthesis of Roman imperial power with Roman family virtue. For Augustus, Apollo is the god of civic peace, as Mars had been the god of civic war.[9]

Augustus certainly reaped the requisite amount of vanity from his identification with Apollo. Suetonius says that Augustus liked to believe his eyes shone with divine energy and could be flattered easily if someone who looked at him would turn away as if struck by a flash from the sun. (Shades of Alexander and Diogenes!) But more intriguing is the way association with a god allowed Augustus to displace attention from his own nature toward the impersonality or hyperpersonality of the ruler. Thus, he says in the *Res gestae,* when grateful citizens set up silver statues to him after the battle of Actium, he took them down and used the money realized to make offerings in gold at the temple of Apollo, in his own name and in the names of those who had honored him. Similarly displaced were the possibilities of worship for Augustus himself. Even in the East, Au-

9. Two centuries after Augustus it is a Greek priest of Apollo, Plutarch, who writes a series of Greek and Roman lives to test the limits that civility ought to place on individual assertion. Augustus's establishment of Apollo as the god of civilization as well as the god of prophecy and art strongly influences Plutarch's judgments and even the way his narratives unfold. It similarly stands behind Nietzsche's distinction between the Apollonian and the Dionysian temperaments in *The Birth of Tragedy* (1872).

gustus and Rome could officially only be worshiped together. But an exception was made for the worship of the Genius of Augustus.[10]

The changing definition of genius is a central element in the history of fame. With the worship of the Genius of Augustus we have arrived at an important turning point in its development. According to Roman religion, the *genius* was the spirit of a family or an individual, the link that connected the specific human beings to the forces of fate and the rhythms of time. Derived from the word for begetting and engendering, *Genius* was also connected with *gens* (family) and often represented by a phallic column akin to the Greek *herm,* in which a column was topped with a human head and featured a penis, but no other physical features.[11] In its nature, it has been argued, it resembled the Greek *daimon,* a kind of internal oracle (for Socrates a moral center) that could speak to the individual. Roman *genius* was a connection with powers outside one's temporal nature, although not, like the Egyptian *ka,* a guide to the afterlife. Unlike the modern concept of genius, which dates from the eighteenth century, it implied no special personal talent. Although the *genius* was originally a private and familial spirit, sacrifices to a Genius of Rome itself are recorded during the time of the Second Punic Wars and by the first century B.C. coins had been issued with the legend "Genius of the Roman people." Oaths were taken by Caesar's Genius in the last years of his life, and libations to the Genius of Augustus were decreed at all public and private banquets, although the actual cult of Augustus's Genius seems not to have materialized until after he became *pontifex maximus.* In his hands *genius* became a celebration of the point where the spirit of Rome, the spirit of the *princeps,* and the spirit of each person intertwined in a way that fostered the legitimacy of Augustus's rule.

Like an invocation of fate, *genius* could be used by the aspiring to deflect attention away from one's personal nature and toward one as a representative of the spirit of the people. Shortly after Julius Caesar's assassination, a comet appeared in the Roman sky for several nights. Augustus took that star as his own. Napoleon frequently referred to his star, as did Adolf Hitler and many other political leaders. It is a necessary image for a propaganda that emphasizes the leader not as himself but as the vehicle of a new national destiny. To trust in your genius, to follow your star, places the source and impetus for action in the world of the spirit. But unlike many later men with stars who were urged on by their genius, Augustus made it an essential part of his self-presentation to distinguish between the man and the fate that worked through him, between the fate that makes one great and the actions that bring that fate about. Among Suetonius's recounting of portents in the early life of Augustus

10. In municipal and private cults in the East, however, Augustus (and members of his family) could be worshiped directly.

11. As such symbolism indicates, the *genius* was masculine; the comparable spirit for women was called a *juno.* The *genius* is also frequently represented by a snake (e.g., the *genius loci*) or by a veiled figure, dressed in a toga and carrying a sacrificial dish and a cornucopia (e.g., the *genius* of the paterfamilias and of the *princeps*).

that presaged his greatness, he includes an anecdote that testifies to Augustus's double sense of being both in command as well as ruled by forces beyond him. While gathering forces for an assault on Rome to claim his legacy from Caesar, the young Octavian goes with Agrippa to consult an astrologer. First, the astrologer prophesies a great career for Agrippa. Then Octavian, disgruntled, has to be persuaded to tell his own birth date, whereupon the astrologer falls at his feet in abject worship. Relieved, says Suetonius, Octavian was from then on inspired by "a faith in the destiny awaiting him" (*Twelve Caesars,* 103).

Biography always dramatizes the past as the direct cause of the present, and the folklore of history battens on stories that end "and that boy is today. . . ." Certainly, the chaos of the civil wars inspired in many the belief that they were meant to rule primarily because they felt they ought to. But Octavian did survive. From one point of view, he may have invented himself. From another, probably his own, he did only what his fate led him to do, rising finally to the bronzed serenity of the *Res gestae.* It was a distinction that became the basis of his rule: not a military leader but first citizen, not in power but in authority, not me but my *genius.* Thus Augustus allowed only freedmen and slaves to worship his Genius at Rome, not citizens, perhaps because by worshiping his Genius, the noncitizens and the non-Roman were worshiping Rome itself. It somewhat reverses matters therefore to say that the worship of the emperor's Genius under Augustus's later rule and even more so under the Empire, was, as Lily Ross Taylor argues, "in veiled form a worship of the emperor himself" (151). In fact the emperor had already, through Augustus's reformation of the Roman political system, presented himself—and his family—as fleshly veils for the more substantial Genius of Rome. The loyalty of citizens and soldiers alike was therefore to Rome through Augustus, instead of the personal loyalties to great men that characterized the history that Augustus wished to put behind him. Julius Caesar's pioneering effort to apply to himself the sanction of as many Roman gods and traditions as possible had the ultimate result of setting him at the center of an array of fragments that only his personal authority held together. Augustus, by displacing interest from his individual nature to the traditions, gods, and civic qualities he embodied, sought to convince each individual Roman that the survival of Augustus ensured his own.

Every public person who successfully remains public protects himself by balancing an inner private world with the demands of the public audience. Caesar's array of divine authorities and personal publicity resembles a patchwork cloak that calls attention to the wearer; Augustus's resembles the simple Roman folk garments he promoted in his dress code. The panoply of the late Republic did not appeal to him, either personally or practically. The visual model of the orator arguing a case or the general leading an army gave way to the leader as first citizen and embodiment of the national spirit. Caesar was the great innovator, Augustus the great consolidator. As Octavian, he had resembled the flamboyant figures of the previous generation. But finally he had a different definition of the kind of theater in which he would appear—not the theater of individual oratory and personal style, but the theater of plot and order. Great ability had to be purged of the destructive ambition that had so often seemed to be its companion. Under Augustus's settlement, the old political and military function of the aristocracy disappeared, and patricians either withdrew from public life or became bureaucrats and administrators of a new stable empire that offered little of the old chances for extreme fame and greatness.

As the increasing complexity of the imperial bureaucracy changed the nature of individual assertion, so the concept of fame itself necessarily changed. Alexandrian achievements in the name of a lost heroic past were transformed into intricate competitions for an infinite gradation of honors and offices. With the defeat of Antony, the annexation of Egypt, and the pacification of the Eastern nations, Augustus had assimilated the Alexandrian Empire to Rome. In his own person he also mediated the energies of Caesar and Alexander, whom a writer of the second century A.D., commenting on the civil wars, would characterize as great men who, however intrepid, desired only to conquer and paid too little attention to prophecies.

In Augustus's eyes the great men of the past had too often been merely disruptive. Without the context of the state and the concept of civic virtue, heroes too easily became Herostratuses, aiming at fame for destroying what had been celebrated before them, raising themselves on the fragments of the past. Behind the Alexandrian assertion always lay the Herostratean potential. Yet one person was left out of the Augustan reordering of Rome: the emperor. Without Augustus's long experience in the ways of striving, later emperors often tried to justify their rule not by their authority but by their power and place at the top of the system. In the line of Roman emperors, the character types of absolute power appear in all their variety. Already with Caligula, just over twenty-five years after the death of Augustus, a Herostratus will be in office. Other emperors will evoke Hercules or Alexander as legitimating images for the power that so often was thrust upon them, or sought without knowing what it entailed. Two hundred years after the death of Augustus, the emperor Caracalla anoints himself with oil and runs around the tomb of Achilles at Troy—in imitation of Alexander. The political system continued; the imperial bureaucracy spread its myriad offices throughout the empire. But the imagery of politics had grown repetitive, stale, and unearned. In such a situation, the ruling ideology must suffer as well, and the political system becomes ripe for either transformation or destruction by the forces of a new purity.

Augustus's sense of the theater of public life was of a different sort. Leaving the stage of bold adventure to others, he became more the playwright than the actor, more the instrument of fate than the assaulter of the gods. The longevity of Augustus immeasurably solidified his accomplishments. By the time he died, at the age of seventy-six, few others could remember the great heroes of the Republic and what, if anything, they stood for. To all those who had been ready to die for Rome, Augustus's new structure furnished a context in which one could live, channeling the ambition that had led men to war into a public service festooned with ever more elaborate varieties of office and honor. Essential to his success was his own belief in the paradoxical mixture of assertion and subordination he himself represented, and his constant awareness of the way he appeared to others. Suetonius's account of his death indicates how deeply in him this urge ran:

> On the day that he died, Augustus frequently inquired whether rumors of his illness were causing any popular disturbance. He called for a mirror, and had his hair combed and his lower jaw, which had fallen from weakness, propped up. Presently, he summoned a group of friends and asked: "Have I played my part in the farce of life creditably enough?" adding the theatrical tag:
>
> > If I have pleased you, kindly signify
> > Appreciation with a warm goodbye.
>
> . . . Finally, he kissed his wife with: "Goodbye, Livia: never forget whose spouse you have been" and died almost at once.

No Shakespearian actor-king could have left the stage better.[12]

12. The phrase here translated (by Robert Graves) "farce of life" is in the Latin *mimum vitae* (mime of life). Margarete Bieber dates the invention of mime to the third century B.C. It was chiefly distinguished from previous theatrical tradition by its reliance on facial expression (rather than masks) and therefore marked a shift of emphasis from playwright to actor. Bieber also notes that a theatrical innovation at the time of Augustus was the pantomime, originally a solo performance done with gestures and facial expressions while a chorus or interpreter aside from the action supplied accompanying words or songs. It is necessary only to mention the general contrast between the Greek use of masks and ensemble playing and the Roman emphasis on the star-performer and typecasting for political analogies to spring to mind. The Christian hostility to acting, as we shall see, made the model of public performance the religious ritual rather than the play.

III

THE EMPTINESS
OF PUBLIC FAME

The Uneasy Truce:
Authority and Authorship

A way must be attempted, by which I too may
rise from earth and fly in victory on the lips of men.
I first, if life remains, will return to my country
leading the Muses with me from the Aonian peak . . .
In the midst I will have Caesar and he will possess the temple. . . .

—VIRGIL, *Georgics*, 29 B.C. (age 41)

I have built a monument more lasting than bronze
and higher than the royal palace of the Pyramids. . . .
I shall not totally die and a great part of me
will live beyond Death: I will keep growing, fresh
with the praise of posterity.

—HORACE, *Odes*, 23 B.C. (age 42)

And now I have built a work, which neither the anger
of Jove nor fire nor sword nor devouring time can
ever obliterate . . . in my better part I shall be carried
everlasting beyond the lofty stars . . . and wherever Roman
power extends over the conquered world, I will be
recited on the lips of men; and through all the ages,
if the prophecies of bards have truth, I shall live
in fame.

—OVID, *Metamorphoses*, A.D. 7 (age 50)

Deflecting resentment over his supremacy by identifying himself with the
genius of Rome, Octavian, the ruler as heroic adventurer, had metamorphosed into Augustus, the ruler as all-encompassing national symbol. In
the interest of state survival, he proceeded to enhance what was least
appealing about Rome—its rigid social and legal system, its imperialism,
its sense of its own absolute destiny—and diverted or dried up its tremendous reservoirs of individual energy and talent. Thus Rome became
the prime model for all the great states and empires that arose in her wake,
and Roman standards of public behavior and public fame became the
marks against which later aspirants would measure themselves. But at the
same time an alternate tradition of fame had taken strong roots even in

the heart of the empire. It was a tradition in some ways inextricably tangled with those of Roman public fame and in others unalterably opposed to it, a tradition that ranked the rewards of politics and military conquest below those of art, philosophy, and religion. Turning against the lavish visibility of Roman public glory, those who sought the fame of the spirit defined their power and their authority in less material and less quantifiable ways.

Of course, the most direct and most devastating challenge to Roman definitions of individual character, public action, and political value comes from Christianity. For the observer of the history of fame, what will be most striking in the years after the death of Augustus will be the reverberations of an event that occurs during his reign—an event that the connoisseur of coincidence might observe to have taken place not long before Augustus was proclaimed *pater patriae* in 2 B.C., the last and the most coveted of his honors. I refer, of course, to the birth of Jesus in an obscure corner of the eastern part of the empire, where Alexandrian precedents of the god-hero were still fresh. The teachings of Jesus, the Gospels that presented him to the world, embody a sharp contrast to all that the Roman public man believed about individual character and personal aspiration. They mark an epoch in the history of fame, for—to mention only one crucial element in the challenge—even now our own ideals still desperately attempt to mediate between Roman ostentation and Christian inwardness. With the reign of Constantine, three hundred years or so after Augustus, Christianity emerges from centuries of persecution into official favor, changing both Rome and itself in the process. Yet the groundwork for the later success of its ideas of human nature and social behavior—its attitude toward fame—was laid in the early years of the empire by Roman writers and philosophers who were uneasily accommodating themselves to the new imperial state.

Writing sometime after the deaths of Caesar and Cicero, Sallust remarks that, whereas fame is usually given to the public man, in chaotic times like these it is the private man, the writer and historian, who truly deserves it. The self-congratulation is obvious. But the distinction between two types of fame and therefore two versions of commitment to the values of Rome is crucial. It marks the growing independence of the writer's point of view and, as we shall see, looks down the ages to the more elaborate arguments for the special nature of the literary (and artistic) temperament that become so frequent from the Renaissance to the twentieth century. When literary men appeared in Greece as well as Rome, they were often the historians or poets who praised the soldiers and the politicians. They were necessary underlings in the rush toward fame and celebrity, propagandists who could lavishly present the hero to an audience, while they equally damned a rival. Those public men with greater imagination, like Alexander and Caesar, clearly perceived the importance of writing and its power to influence minds, while those more oriented toward panoply and spectacle, like Pompey and Antony, were content to have their praises sung without any special intervention. Yet all of those strivers after unique honors—with the important exception of Cicero—believed that the highest function of writing was to serve the fame of military and political men. Sallust's comment therefore invokes a new theme in the history of fame—the fame of the literary man.

Looking back on the past through both our prejudices and the surviving evidence, we are inclined to consider writers to be as important as political figures, if not more important. But, if we argue that Homer or Aeschylus or Sophocles or others of the Greek poets and playwrights were as famous as kings or generals, we mistake our own view of them for the view held by their own times, and even for the view they had of themselves. From the perspective of the present, they are more visible because they stand out of time. We forget that works now available in thousands of copies may spring from one or two ragged manuscripts discovered in the early Renaissance and that names familiar to anyone who has gone to college were once unheard for hundreds of years.

In Rome the competition was more direct, and it is the great writers of the reign of Augustus who establish the terms of fame through literature that will be repeated and varied through the centuries. Fame for them might even be called an ideological problem, a nexus of tangled motivations where their art and their politics half choke and half support each other. An important modern commonplace, self-consciously revived for us by the Renaissance, is yet clearly the legacy of the Roman literature of the reign of Augustus: Art, even officially promoted art, can last longer than politics. When the events and individuals it celebrates are swallowed up by time, the art still remains, to furnish ideals with which to judge the new events and new individuals of the future. Homer, with barely a reference to himself, celebrates the great men of the Greek past. So Horace praises Augustus, but also writes that his own poetry will last longer than even the Pyramids. Ultimately, he implies, the fame of Augustus depends on the quality of Horace's verse, and the quality of the verse rests on Horace's poetic authority. As later kings and emperors would take instruction from Caesar and Augustus on how to rule and how to present themselves as rulers, so writers would learn from Virgil and Horace how to write and how to comport themselves as writers. As the example of Antony might be shunned by aspiring politicians, so the career of Ovid, with its similarly subversive inclination to ease, sexual license, and other un-Roman values (underlined by his final banishment by Augustus) would stand as a mingled lure and caution.[1]

Augustus's awareness of the role of artistic and semireligious publicity in stabilizing his political settlement was more than matched by the eager inspiration with which poets and writers sat down to the task. Looking

---

1. This was not exile but *relegatio,* a technical legal term for a banishment in which the individual retained his property and voting privileges, but could not leave the place to which he was sent. Exile (*exsilium*), when used precisely, meant a self-banishment to avoid execution for a capital crime.

backward after generations of poets proclaiming their independence, we may find the relationship easy to mock. But more intriguing are the ways in which the great Augustan writers managed to celebrate both Rome and Augustus even while they carefully fashioned a special status and a unique perspective for themselves. Many of the poets of the Republic whose works are still remembered (like Lucretius and Catullus) were little concerned with public life except to criticize or satirize it. Cicero in the *Tusculan Disputations* (I, i–iv) mentions that the Greeks exceed the Romans only in learning and literature, because among the Greeks the oldest class (*genus*) of the learned is the poets. The Romans, he complains, welcomed the orator but generally took poetry too lightly, worthwhile only for praise or for a private pleasure shared at most by a circle of friends. Yet, even though he himself praises poets and men of learning, Cicero still seems a little apologetic: Since he has served his countrymen as politician and orator, perhaps it would be allowed that he can also serve by transmitting to them the Greek philosophy that had inspired his oratory from the first. Such attitudes of philosophical or lyrical detachment from public themes do persist in the poetry of Virgil, Horace, and Ovid. But they have become infused with a new awareness of the role of poetry in shaping public values.

The professional literary man is therefore to a great extent an Augustan phenomenon. What distinguishes the Augustan writers both from the writers of the Late Republic and even from the Greek writers to whom Cicero refers was their sense of themselves not only as a literary class, who had the *job* of writing, but also as a profession with a special ideology. Greek writers did not get paid as writers per se, but as teachers or authors who would declaim parts of their books to audiences for a fee, in hopes that the rich listeners would later pay to have the work copied by a slave. By the end of the fourth century B.C. the center of the ancient publishing and literary world had shifted to Alexandria, where Ptolemy's library offered employment for editors and grammarians as well. To Alexandria through both pagan and Christian centuries would come such authors as Theocritus, Euclid, Apollonius of Rhodes, Plotinus, Iamblichus, Clement, Origen, and Porphyry—drawn, as all writers are, to a literary center. But not until the empire is established does a publishing industry appear and books become products to be sold.[2]

Augustus's effort to identify his authority with the best traditions of

2. Cicero's unrequited desire that Posidonius write a monograph on his consulship indicates how thoroughly he believed that the *language* of fame was Greek. With a similar impulse to preserve true greatness through the ages, Francis Kynaston in the middle of the seventeenth century translates the first two books of Chaucer's *Troilus and Criseyde* into Latin. For the profession of authorship in the classical world, see Kenyon, *Books and Readers in Ancient Greece and Rome,* and Putnam, *Authors and Their Public in Ancient Times.* Fraser in *Ptolemaic Alexandria* includes a wealth of material about the establishment of the Alexandrian libraries and the growth of literary study.

Rome clearly harmonized with the interests of writers who drew their material from the Roman past—whether the form was the historical narrative of Livy, the pastorals and epic of Virgil, or the more personal and satiric poetry of Horace. Throughout the poetry of the Augustan period runs the hopeful image of the Golden Age, the age of peace and plenty, which Augustus has now revived. To emphasize further the public function of literature under his rule, Augustus founded two public libraries, among the earliest in Rome, one connected with the Temple of Apollo on the Palatine Hill (close to his house) and the other on the Campus Martius, perhaps connected with the Temple of Mars the Avenger. Each contained a collection of Greek or Roman authors housed in rooms decorated with busts and medallions of the great writers—the first hall of fame. In the earliest Roman public library, founded by Pollio the historian a few years before, only one living author was so honored, and Horace notes with some satisfaction that Augustus had included many.[3] In an age when there were no copyright laws and professional booksellers were only beginning to emerge, the institution of public libraries gave writers another source of support, connected with the religion and politics of the state rather than with the taste of the book-buying public. Editions were about five hundred copies, rarely one thousand—and Augustus's support of libraries certainly allowed a publisher, then as now, to anticipate at least breaking even.

Suetonius mentions that Augustus was willing to be the theme of a poet's work only if the writer was serious and of "highest standing."[4] He encouraged Livy, offered Horace a post as his private secretary (which was refused), was read several sections of the *Aeneid* as Virgil composed them, and countermanded Virgil's dying wish that the unfinished poem be burned. But Augustus's belief in the importance of attracting good writers to support his goals for Rome is most neatly symbolized by the fact that one of his earliest supporters of any consequence was Maecenas, a wealthy Etruscan who helped Augustus with both finances and negotiations and whose name has come to be proverbial for a patron of the arts. It was through the patronage of Maecenas that Virgil and Horace were brought to the attention of Augustus. His was not the only circle of artistic patronage in Augustan Rome. But two factors made his group unique: first, the quality of the writers that Maecenas chose to support; and second, the fact that Maecenas, although a trusted ambassador and negotiator for Augustus, never accepted the senatorial rank that could easily have been his, preferring to remain, as he had been born, an Etruscan knight. Maecenas and his circle thus represented less a group of literary men who

---

3. That single author was the scholarly editor, historian, and encyclopedist Varro. When Pollio founded his library, Varro was seventy-eight and the previous year had published an account of seven hundred famous Greeks and Romans along with their portraits. Before retiring from public life and founding his library, Pollio had been a supporter of Antony.

4. The word is *"praestantissimis"* (*Suetonius,* 258). Graves translates it as "reputable" (*Twelve Caesars,* 99). I've been somewhat more literal.

flocked to the victorious side than an alternate center of authority.[5] Although he refused public office, Maecenas, says Tacitus, was "a repository of imperial secrets" (131). When he died, his place was taken by the adopted son of the historian Sallust, who, like Maecenas, did not seek the ornaments of either military or civic fame but was content to retain the same secret power.

The patron connects the poet to financial and often to political power. By the eighteenth century, writers will often ferociously assert their independence of aristocratic patronage. But it is not surprising to read Horace, for example, luxuriating in the freedom given by the patronage of Maecenas to write as he pleases, without having to worry about the need to cater to an undiscriminating audience. Looking back through the periodic rapprochements between political and literary fame that are so concertedly revived in the Renaissance and imitated later, we can see how the Augustan age furnishes a fascinating model of mutual support. Horace, Virgil, and many of their fellow writers were, like Augustus, in reaction against the destructive individualism of the late Republic. Their answer, again like his, sought to make past values (as they defined them) into a framework for action: the measures of poetry, in Horace's image, applied to life. As Augustus in the *Res gestae* dwells on the number of his achievements and the amounts of money and grain he has given to the public, so he also seeks to be justified by the more than material numbers of poetic celebration. Suetonius notes that Augustus began writing his own autobiography, but stopped about the time of his wars in Spain (26 B.C.). The date seems significant. In 30 B.C. the second book of Horace's *Satires* had appeared, with an introductory poem on the problem of writing about Augustus, while in 29 B.C. his *Epodes* contain poems that fear the recurrence of civil war, look to a golden future, and celebrate the victories and achievements of Augustus at Actium and after. Also in 29 B.C. Virgil's *Georgics,* dedicated to Maecenas, were published, and in 26 B.C. Augustus writes from Spain to ask about progress on the *Aeneid.* With such writers making his career their theme, it is no wonder Augustus had little need to detail it any further himself.

Ironically or appropriately, the expansion of commercial publishing under the Principate and the empire therefore coincides with an effort, foreshadowed by Cicero, to bring a contemplative tradition of Greek philosophy and literature to bear on Roman public life. Writers emerged as a group somewhere between priests and politicians in their attitude toward public things. New sacred texts might be written in the present, just as a new Rome was, according to Augustus, rising from the chaos of the old. The special urgency of Augustus's involvement with literature cre-

5. The other major group makes an intriguing contrast. It gathered around Messala Corvinus, who had fought for Brutus and Cassius, then for Antony before coming over to Octavian. He was an active general and politician as well as a supporter of many writers, including Ovid, the lyric poet Tibullus, and for a time the young Horace, before Maecenas lured him away.

ated an environment in which perhaps for the first time (or the first time so self-consciously) writers could believe that public power *needed* their special blend of public mythology and private virtue. Cicero may have thought that literature should be a handmaiden to political greatness (as, for example, when he recommends himself to Pompey). But with Horace and Virgil literature becomes an alternate to the world of political action and public fame. Horace could not have written about the undying monument he is creating in his poetry without the counterexample of the more tangible (and therefore more fragile) public monuments that stood before his eyes. In the arena of such a conflict, the Jewish tradition of the importance of the word and the text would find strong allies. Literary fame would not be like the fame of the conqueror, or even the fame of the political consolidator, but one that reflected the fame of the wise, the private contemplator of time rather than its public master, a fame defined not by the things of the world but by its intangible ability to transcend them, the authority of its authorship.

Unlike the great writers of classical Greece, who were usually Athenians, the great Roman writers were often out-of-towners—Virgil from Mantua, Horace from Apulia, Ovid from central Italy.[6] They were rarely upper class, at most equestrian, and sometimes, like Horace (the son of an auctioneer and former slave) from even lower social groups. To a great extent, therefore, as outsiders to the traditional Roman social order, their perspective combined both idealization of Roman virtues and condemnation of Roman faults. In the careers of Virgil and Horace, as we shall see, the outsider has definitely moved inside. But the literary partnership with Roman public power is uneasy. It falls apart with Ovid and, except for the most tractable writers, hardly endures past the death of Augustus. In his refashioning of Roman culture, Augustus had sought to bring the best of the past to refresh the present. But once the ideal was stated, a falling off was inevitable. The anxiety about the judgment of the future that appears in the *Res gestae* surfaces as well in Augustus's late effort to write an attack on Cato, perhaps to defend his own practical politics against the already archetypal embodiment of absolute moral principle.[7] As even his most uncritical writers knew, the idealization of the past could easily become the standard by which the present was deficient, and all Augustus's antiquarian revivals potentially invoke images of degeneration as much as renewal. The difficulty Augustus had in finding a political successor was only one aspect of the problem. By his patronage of writers and his awareness of their importance, he gave them a place in the state they never quite had before. It was a social function for literature that was

6. Propertius came from Assisi; Catullus from Verona; Livy from Padua; Tacitus from northern Italy; Lucan, Martial, and Seneca from Spain; Statius from Naples. Of the major literary figures of the period, only Lucretius seems to have been a native Roman.

7. It is appealing to think that Augustus began this self-justification sometime after A.D. 8, the year that marks his removal of Ovid to the Black Sea.

explicitly patriotic but implicitly subversive. Working through ideals and myths rather than practical politics, writers like Virgil and Horace were establishing a cultural ideology for what Augustus was doing at the same time that they defined the standards by which his accomplishment ought to be measured. Central to their enterprise—the emblem of their belief in their own crucial importance to the state—is their preoccupation with the theme of fame.

Virgil: The Flight of Fama

> They sang to foretell that she would be illustrious
> in fame and fate, but to her people she portended a
> great war.
>
> —Virgil, *Aeneid*

Not many years after the assassination of Julius Caesar, in the midst of poems that celebrate an almost resolutely "inglorious" love of nature and a world outside the city's politics and its wars, Virgil had paid tribute to Octavian, the new leader whose actions he hopes will restore the Golden Age and make such a peaceful refuge possible: "Now is come the last age of the Sibyl's song; / The grand order of the centuries is born again" (*Eclogues,* 40 B.C., IV, 4–5). Ten years later, in the composition of the *Aeneid,* the poet of nature has turned into the bard of epic, and the preserver of peace into the heir of a line of Roman greatness that stretches down the ages from Aeneas, the ancestor of Julius Caesar. In the eighth book of the *Aeneid*, Venus, the mother of Aeneas, brings him weapons for his coming battle to ensure Roman settlement in Italy. Chief among them is a gigantic shield, modeled in poetic conception on the shield of Achilles in the *Iliad*. But whereas the shield of Achilles primarily depicts a pastoral world in contrast with the world of war that is the main action of the *Iliad,* the shield of Aeneas is covered by a prophetic vision of Roman history—down even to the Battle of Actium, where Octavian first defeats the "barbarous might" of Antony and his "(O shame!) Egyptian wife," and then celebrates his triple triumph.

> Such things Aeneas admires on the shield of Vulcan,
> The gift of his mother and, although ignorant of the deeds,
> he rejoices in the image, holding up on his shoulder
> the fame and fates of his descendants (VIII, 729–31).

The national war poem of the Greeks, the *Iliad,* is about the past, when men were greater than they are now. The national war poem of the Romans, the *Aeneid,* is about the ways the past has led to the present, celebrating a triumphant history that culminates in the figure of Augustus.

In its own way, then, the *Aeneid* is a handbook of heroic behavior, but a heroism much modified and shaped by the needs of what *will* happen: the Roman destiny that Aeneas, fleeing Troy in flames, has been born to realize. Ezra Pound recounts the story of a Latin teacher questioning a student about his opinions of the hero of the *Aeneid*. After several false starts, the teacher reminds the student that the hero was Aeneas. Hero? says the student, I thought he was the priest. True enough, for Aeneas is certainly not a vaunting Homeric hero or a striking individual on the model of the great men who rampaged about the countryside in the days of Virgil's youth. He is a hero of the new age, *pius Aeneas,* as Virgil often calls him, one who knows just what the proper obeisances and rituals should be, even though he sometimes forgets and sometimes is diverted. In Italy he finds his great opponent, Turnus, who calls himself another Achilles, the model of the archaic self-involved hero that Aeneas is not. In all the battles detailed in the *Aeneid,* the heroes who brag the most tend to be the ones who die the quickest. Aeneas instead is the hero as civic founder and pious citizen, who bows to the fates that drive him onward to his destiny and who subordinates his own desires to the commands of the gods. What need does Augustus have to write his own autobiography when in the *Aeneid* Virgil fashions a symbolic biography of the subduing of self to the state that is an essential part of Augustus's political and legislative message? Aeneas's final defeat of Turnus is a defeat as well of the disruptive heroism Turnus represents. In the first half of the *Aeneid,* Aeneas is lured by Dido, the Queen of Carthage, away from the trail of destiny and into love. But by the second half of the poem, he has few of the doubts and hesitations he showed before; he has proudly become an instrument of history.

Fame is therefore a crucial question for Virgil, because it is the place where personal desire confronts historic destiny. Cicero viewed fame as a kind of exalted reputation, an honor and glory known both to contemporaries and, he hopes, to the ages. But for Virgil fame is a messenger who tells the world of heroic events and heroic actors. If the way the message is presented cannot be controlled, then the fame itself is corrupt, and, if fame is subject to distortion, then why strive for it at all? In a crisis of fame, when so many are competing, the nature of true fame must be carefully defined. When many are free to put up statues to themselves and have poems published praising their virtues, art itself can be called into question.

In pursuit of a clear distinction between good fame and bad fame, Virgil creates a figure with a tremendous influence on writers and artists for centuries to come. Aeneas is walking in a field with Dido, who, because the stories of Aeneas's adventures have so moved her, has decided to break her vow never to marry. A storm comes up and they run into a cave for shelter, where, Virgil implies, she has her way with Aeneas.

> Then, swiftest of all evils, Fame runs
> straightway through Libya's mighty cities—Fame,

whose life is speed, whose going gives her force.
Timid and small at first, she soon lifts up
her body in the air. She stalks the ground:
her head is hidden in the clouds. Provoked
to anger at the gods, her mother Earth
gave birth to her, last come—they say—as sister
to Coeus and Enceladus; fast-footed
and lithe of wing, she is a terrifying
enormous monster with as many feathers
as she has sleepless eyes beneath each feather
(amazingly), as many sounding tongues
and mouths, and raises up as many ears.
Between the earth and skies she flies by night,
screeching across the darkness, and she never
closes her eyes in gentle sleep. By day
she sits as sentinel on some steep roof
or on high towers, frightening vast cities;
for she holds fast to falsehood and distortion
as often as to messages of truth.
Now she was glad. She filled the ears of all
with many tales. She sang of what was done
and what was fiction, chanting that Aeneas,
one born of Trojan blood, had come, that lovely
Dido has deigned to join herself to him,
that now in lust, forgetful of their kingdom,
they take long pleasure, fondling through the winter,
the slaves of squalid craving. Such reports
the filthy goddess scatters everywhere
upon the lips of men (IV, 173–95).

I have quoted Allen Mandelbaum's excellent translation of the passage, altering it only by changing back to "Fame" (*Fama*) what Mandelbaum, like most translators since the eighteenth century, calls "Rumor." Rumor is no doubt an appropriate English equivalent. Perhaps even Gossip might be the proper name for the deity. Although the monster *Fama* is essentially Virgil's own creation, he is inspired by the literary model of Eris in the *Iliad*—a goddess of wrath, anger, and fury, whom Homer uses to describe the growing ferocity and noise of the Trojan troops spoiling for battle with the Greeks, the tumult of mingled voices from men of different Asian countries. Like Eris, *Fama* rages and confuses. Sister to Coeus and Enceladus, two of the Titans who warred against the Olympian gods, she is a child of earth, not of heaven. Later in the *Aeneid* her description is echoed in Virgil's picture of Allecto, another female goddess, who stirs up war between the troops of Aeneas and the Latin peoples by maddening the Italian women and turning them into rioting followers of Dionysus, bent on the destruction of men and their plans.[8]

8. Virgil's creation of the goddess *Fama* from hints in Homer may also connect with his conception of Dido herself, whose character has been developed from some very sketchy materials in Virgil's sources. The word *dido* in Latin means "I broad-

Fama for Virgil is all the information that people receive, all the stories about the past and the present. *Fama est* (the story is) appears frequently as an interjection in his recountings of myths and legends within the *Aeneid,* as the poem gathers and coalesces the Roman past into an imaginative whole, casting history into the shape of epic, expelling rumors and half-truths, conferring honor on deserving actions and lives. At one extreme is the *Fama* that runs around the world to spread gossip with a thousand tongues about what Aeneas and Dido are doing in the cave; at the other is the *fama* that warriors properly seek, the *fama* validated and approved by the gods, the *fama* of (Augustus) Caesar "that ends only in the stars" (I, 287), the *fama* of becoming like Aeneas, "known by fame in the heavens above" (I, 379). While the frenzied fame fostered by women is attacked, the *Aeneid* celebrates another *fama,* which the gods control, the poets dispense, and men ought to strive for. The message from Jupiter that chastises Aeneas for his misguided love is brought by Mercury, a flying deliverer of true news as opposed to the eye- and tongue-bedecked *Fama.* Immediately Aeneas prepares to set sail for Italy without telling Dido. But she does hear; irreverent (*impia*) *Fama,* says Virgil, tells her what *pius Aeneas* would not.[9]

Retaining the original name of the goddess thus retains Virgil's desire to contemplate the proper ways of being known. *Fama* and *fatum,* fame and fate, both derive from the Latin for "speaking." But Virgil precisely distinguishes between the fame of earth, spoken by men, and the fame that comes from accepting the fate as spoken by the gods. Dido particularly invites a degraded fame because she is "ignorant of fate." A few lines before this passage, Virgil remarks that, by going into the cave with Aeneas, Dido showed that she wasn't moved by fame or good appearances anymore. In a sense the monstrous apparition that then carries the story of their secret moments across the world is her punishment for disregarding good fame. It represents what happens when the face one presents to the world is not premeditated, when public people disregard the gods and act as if they had only private goals. Women are the special agents of this impious turning away from the decrees of fate because they are so sus-

---

cast" or "I spread around," and in one of the few uses of the Latin *rumor* in the *Aeneid,* Virgil says that the rumor went around (*diditur rumor*) the camp of Aeneas that they were about to found the city of Rome.

9. That the purveyor of false and trivial fame is a monstrous female goddess and the great barrier to Aeneas's destiny is Dido's love underscores the extent to which true Roman fame is for Virgil essentially masculine. Christianity, in its opposition to Roman heroism and exclusively manly virtue, will allow women a somewhat larger scope for fame. A few centuries later St. Jerome could write to a woman who had publicly taken the veil as a virgin that, instead of being one man's wife, she would now be known to the entire Christian world. But the fame of women as public figures remains an anomaly in the history of fame at least until the growth of nationalist self-consciousness inspired in fifteenth-century France by Joan of Arc—who was executed for dressing like a man—and in sixteenth-century England by Elizabeth I—the "Virgin Queen" who never married.

ceptible to passion. By loving Aeneas, says Dido, she knows that she will lose the fame of being a good ruler, which was her only way to the stars.

In the career of founding Rome, Dido has no part, for true fame comes not from asserting one's own desires, but from giving up to the plan fate has in store. Jupiter, looking down on Dido and Aeneas, wonders why Aeneas would have turned aside to his private pleasures when there were worlds to conquer, empires to found, and a race to which to give his name. Both Dido and Aeneas, Jupiter thinks, are "forgetful of their better fame," and so he summons Mercury and sends him to remind Aeneas of his destiny, the good fame to which he should recommit himself rather than the ill fame, the gossip, into which he has fallen. Two words stand out in Jupiter's message to Aeneas, two words so important that Virgil has Mercury repeat the question that contains them almost verbatim a few lines further on. Why are you doing this? asks Jupiter. "If no glory of great things inflames you, or if you will not labor for your own praise . . . ," then think about what you owe to your son and the people of the future, the Romans to come. Glory and praise—these are the goals of the true hero, what distinguishes true fame from the rumor and gossip that attends the lapse from heroism.

Why should Aeneas have to be reminded by Mercury of these goals and the lure of this kind of fame? Because, Virgil suggests, the heroic urge, the urge to be famous, may not be a human instinct. It is something grander, something more akin to becoming like the gods (so long as one accomplishes it in accord with their orders), and therefore an urge from which one may often backslide, especially when the lure of private comfort and love are present. Aeneas must align himself instead with fate, steering by the stars rather than by his feelings. He is a hero who sacrifices himself to the grandeur of the future, a forerunner of later greatness who is only dimly conscious of why he must act as he does.

Between the gods and the hero stands the poet, interpreting their commands, explaining the nature of the history they rule, where *fama* and *fatum* connect and where they diverge. All stories begin in rumor. But it is the poet who refines the best into a truthful shape. Already in the first book of the *Aeneid,* Aeneas sees depicted on the walls of one of Dido's temples scenes from the Trojan war celebrating what in his own memory had occurred only a short time before, "now spread by fame through the whole world." At the comparable point in the *Odyssey,* Odysseus is washed up on a shore and brought back unrecognized to the court of the local king, where he weeps to hear a poet sing the tales of Troy. In the *Iliad* heroes resoundingly introduced themselves by telling of their genealogy. They were the spokesmen for their own fame. But unlike Achilles, who desires to be recognized for the hero he believes he is, Odysseus moves about in disguise, so bent on maintaining his own sense of himself that he reveals his identity only gradually and after much testing. In whatever time has elapsed between the *Iliad* and the *Odyssey,* "Homer" has discovered that even heroic fame can be a prison. Achilles must be recognized by all; Odysseus wants recognition only from his family and friends. It is part of Virgil's own later position in this evolution that Aeneas somehow wants both. But the need to found Rome must finally win out over the desire to stay in Carthage with Dido. By accepting the fate ordained by the gods, he accepts as well the pattern embodied in the poem itself, moving away from the dying civilization of Troy and toward the new civilization of Rome, the first of a new race rather than the last of an old.

The "vulgar fame," or fame of the masses, that appears when Dido and Aeneas go into the cave or when Aeneas sees the scenes on the wall, Virgil associates primarily with visual representation.[10] His distinction between true and false fame thus also emphasizes the moral ascendancy of one mode of communication over another. The basic precept, which becomes a central part of the idea of fame in Christianity, is the superiority of the ear to the eye, its receptivity to words rather than images. "In the beginning was the Word," says the Gospel of John, written about one hundred years after the *Aeneid*. But just as Virgil condemned the noisy words of *Fama*, so John knew the deceptive words that "itchy ears" hungered for. Only that special variety of words—those that are preserved on a page, in a poem—can transcend the frailties of human language and imagery. Of all artists, the writer does his best, according to Virgil, because he alone is a namer and rememberer of names. Already in his *Georgics* Virgil had emphasized his poetic role as a singer of geography, a perpetuator of the events and persons that speak in the names of streams, hills, and rocks. Because time continually erodes the memory of such people and events, the poet must preserve them in his verse and remind his audience of the link between poetic naming and the ever-present, ever-changing natural world. Similarly, in the *Aeneid* the poet stresses his role as a rememberer, mourning what is lost even as he shows how that loss fits into the greater goals of Roman power. Down in the land of the dead, Aeneas meets one of his men who had drowned accidentally and wants to be restored to the living. But Aeneas's companion, the Sibyl, tells the sailor to be calm. A tomb for him will be established and people will call the area by his name: "By these words his cares disappeared, and grief is driven from his unhappy heart; he rejoices in the land that bears his name" (VI, 383–84).

Without the poet, only the name would remain, if that. Augustus may politically deify Julius Caesar. Virgil will solidify that deification and the deification of all the heroes of the Roman past through the spiritual medium of his poetry. With such a power, the poet potentially rivals the hero. For all his adherence to god-approved fame, Aeneas does not gain much personally. He becomes the founder of the Roman race, the ancestor of

10. The meanings of *vulgus* in Latin generally refer to the widespread or common characteristics of something. *Vulgo* as a verb means to disseminate, to make generally available. A *vulgator* could therefore be either a dispenser of news or, with more sharpness, a teller of secrets.

Julius Caesar and Augustus. But he has lost some more tender part of himself in the process. Only Virgil really escapes the bind, recommending and approving the forces of destiny while dramatizing with sympathy what has to be left behind when destiny calls. Political and military men may walk unself-consciously in the ways of fate; but it is the poet who perceives its patterns. Virgil, unlike many later writers, never really talks of his own fame. Even in the *Aeneid* he is still the "inglorious" poet of nature, now contemplating a world of war. But it is precisely his authorial detachment and the insight it implies that allows him to award fame as he sees fit.

Explicitly and no doubt sincerely committed to Augustan values, Virgil yet reveals a striking ambivalence about the fame he affirms and the fame he disdains. The first follows the familiar Roman pattern of public service to the idea of Rome; the second, by contrast, feeds gluttonously on the hero's private life. But by making such a distinction, by creating the goddess *Fama* with her enormous and deluded audience to contrast with the knowing and wise audience that reads the *Aeneid,* Virgil places himself as the crucial intermediary between the hero and his public, between the patterns of the gods and the patterns of the poem. The *Aeneid* is thus a clear prelude to the ways later writers will first recommend themselves to rulers as a support for their fame, then assert themselves as the only means by which that fame can exist and be perpetuated.

Writing has always recommended itself as a preservative of the past, although Plato for one also believed that it corrupted memory by allowing a written crutch. But to writers the creation of a permanent history of human greatness has been a battle not only of memory against forgetfulness, but also of the god-appointed writer against the erosive forces of mere language—the language of the mouth and all the activities of the goddess *Fama.* Thus for Virgil as for the writers of the Old Testament, Bible stands against Babel, the Word against the chaos of words. The power of Rumor, with its multiplication of tongues and its relentless personalizing of all meaning must be opposed by the clear and inspired line of the pen, the rhythm of poetic meter, and the poem's overarching vision of general human truth. Virgil's distinction between true fame and false fame accords well with Augustus's own emphasis on authority rather than power, on state service rather than personal aggrandizement. The fame of the orator, who sways huge audiences, must give way to the more sheltered fame of the poet and prophet, whose work is ratified because it pleases the ruler, the supreme individual, rather than the multitudes of the city. When Virgil dies, he has just set out on a trip to Greece to examine the places he celebrates in his recently completed epic poem. Accompanying him is Augustus.

Horace: The Private Poet as Ideal Roman

> . . . and features are seen with no more truth, when moulded in
> statues of bronze, than are the manners and minds of famous heroes,
> when set forth in the poet's work.
>
> —HORACE, "Epistle to Augustus"

Although Augustus may have brought the new political settlement into
being, Virgil creates the poem in which that settlement is predicted; and
down through history his work will be both witness and affirmation of its
historical inevitability. Although from our perspective Virgil thus clearly
implies that the celebrating poet furnishes the crucial validation of Augustan values, he still explicitly supports the superior charisma and *auctoritas* of the political leader. It is in the poetry of Horace, who was
Virgil's almost exact contemporary, that poetic perspective is shown to
be uniquely separate and self-sufficient.

Horace is much less concerned with the past than is Virgil and hardly
interested at all in the process of heroic self-definition. One of his early
poems does allude to some of the same heroic genealogy that is so important to the *Aeneid*. But Horace's professed desire to praise Augustus
in these terms never amounts to much. A major theme of his poetry is in
fact the refusal to write epic poetry. As a nineteen-year-old student in
Athens, Horace had joined Brutus's army and was among the defeated
at Philippi. It was a time in arms he refers to at various places in his
poetry, as if to remind the reader of his military credentials even while
he creates a poetic world that specifically excludes military standards of
valor and virtue. The aspiration of political *ambitio* is suspect as well. The
race for public honors, says Horace, traps men, and the urge to glory and
praise ruins both the wellborn and the lowly. Those who desire the trappings of fame, who constantly change their desires from one goal to another, who lust to make more and more money, act from a sense of their
own emptiness: "Those who seek much, lack much." Instead, says Horace,
one should be wise enough to aspire only to what truly satisfies.

If Virgil's poetic methods reflect Augustus's synthesizing politics, Horace's new definition of the poet is more akin to Augustus's idea of himself
as a leader. In Virgil's work Augustus could see the evolving iconography
of his political destiny. But in Horace's he might find clues to a personal
poise created without benefit of an illustrious ancestry. Horace's poetry
emphasizes not the deeds of the hero, but his self-consciousness and his
private joys—traits that Aeneas tends to leave behind with Dido in Carthage. "What I was," he says in one poem, "I tell in a story."[11]

11. Both Horace and Virgil lost their patrimonies during the land confiscations in
41 B.C. by which Octavian rewarded his army. Later writers say that Virgil's family
lands were restored after intercession by friends. The evidence is inconclusive. No
such stories exist about Horace. But he was pardoned for his adherence to Brutus
and became a public official for a time until Maecenas's patronage and gift of a

Horace's father was a freedman, his grandfather a slave. But, he says, his father gave him an upper-class education, and therefore he remains free because he has the knowledge of the wellborn without their need to distinguish themselves publicly. *Fama* in Horace's early poems thus usually refers to social reputation, and especially to the sexual intrigues of those who don't want to lose public face. Similarly, in later poems, even when Horace is being more positive about public recognition, a world like *decus* ("prestige") carries with it an ironic edge for its similarity to the Latin word for decor—another implication that visible renown is a social creation that can easily slip into the superficiality of scrambling for public honors. In such a race the unknown (*ignotus*) Horace can stay personally untouched while others run toward ruin. Thus Horace in his own way echoes Virgil's attack on mere rumor and public whisperings, but with none of the epic poet's interest in adjudicating the types of fame. His father, he says, for example, was neither *claro* nor *praeclaro,* and that is for the best, for he wouldn't have wanted political, "illustrious" parents. His place is in his poetry, far from military or elective ambitions. Only stupid judges, he says, assess people by their genealogy. They are enslaved to fame, dazzled by titles and wax masks of ancestors, and therefore they give honors to the unworthy. In direct competition with the mutterings and images of that kind of fame is poetry. Its power is to make such waxen images live.

Throughout his poems, Horace plays on the various associations of the Latin word *liber,* which means not only "free" but also "book," as well as being the name of the Roman equivalent of Dionysus, the god of wine in whose honor the poet drinks and speaks with free inspiration. The freedom of movement of the poet (*libido*) therefore directly contrasts with the route the politically ambitious must travel to solicit votes. The only boundaries that the poet respects are the boundaries of nature and the boundaries of writing itself. Thus Horace celebrates Sylvanus, the country god, as "the guardian of boundaries." People who strive constantly to be greater, who are always dissatisfied with what they do, fail to understand the natural measure in all things that must be neither superseded nor undershot. The self-contained man, whether politician or poet, knows his limits and does what is right despite the demands of the crowd. Even though Maecenas has refused Augustus's offer to make him a member of the senatorial class, Horace (in a reversal of the Cicero-Atticus relationship) constantly cajoles him to be less concerned with public affairs and more involved in the pleasures of friendship. Throughout the poems, Horace's effort to turn Maecenas toward private life acts as a lightning rod for his own elaboration of its virtues, particularly its ability to meet the present directly, without anxiety for the future.

It is a clue to Augustus's own personality that the author of poems with

---

farm made him independent. Since Virgil died in 19 B.C. and Horace in 8 B.C., the period of their greatest influence on Augustus comes in the crucial years between the battle of Actium (31 B.C.) and Augustus's assumption of the position of *pontifex maximus* in 12 B.C.

such a distinctly wry, if not hostile, view of public life should have been commissioned to write the central choral poem for Augustus's celebration of the Century Games in 17 B.C., a festival supposed to be held once every hundred years. Two years after the death of Virgil, Horace had clearly become the national poet. But even in his "Song of the Century," the mood is more private, peaceful, and leisurely than public, martial, and dramatic. Through all the works leading up to this nominally public poem as well as in many that follow it, Horace has elaborated an implicit identification between the private poet in his country farm and the private man whose rule has saved Rome. The refusal to bow to the taste of crowds and the desire instead to teach the young to sing are the measures of Horace's originality; they reflect Augustus's hope for the future as well. As if to emphasize the private and poetic streak that he celebrates in Augustus, Horace in one poem even refers to himself as *princeps,* not in politics but in poetry, "the first of men who, powerful from a low beginning, led Aeolian [Greek] song into Italian measures." In another passage, he similarly uses the language of political and military leadership to talk about his poetry: "I was the first [*princeps*] to set free steps in an empty place. I put my foot where no one else had been. The leader [*dux*] who trusts himself rules the crowd."

Horace's enshrining of the private nature of the poet as an alternative to the showy temperaments of public life leads him to use not *poeta* as his most frequent word for poet but *vates,* a word that had meant "fortune-teller," "medium," or some other sort of low-level seer. Virgil had sometimes used *vates* to refer to a person with a visionary and prophetic understanding of history, in a way that may reflect Augustus's designation of Apollo as his chief god. But Horace makes the role his own and associates himself with Augustus as partaker in Apollo's power. Even in his private retreat, Horace is the "priest of the Muses," both shaper and renovator of Roman culture. In the quasi-public form of the *vates,* he addresses the equally garbed representation that is Augustus with a language magically infused with prophetic power, and therefore capable of organizing belief with a force at least equal to that of Augustus's laws and his authority. As Augustus has woven a new political fabric for the state, so Horace will weave a poetry within which the old Roman values will be restored to meaning. Apollo, he says in his last work, the fourth book of *Odes* (13 B.C.), gave him the inspiration, the art of song, and the name of a poet (*poeta* here). In this same poem he also uses his own name, saying that the children of the illustrious nobility will boast of having learned poetry "in the measures of the *vates* Horace." Military and political action may make things happen, but poetry ensures that they are remembered. Nothing is famous without being sung, writes Horace. Augustus may have restored the old ways for which the name of Rome was known and thereby spread its fame and empire from east to west. But Horace's poetry has accomplished the writer's task of celebrating that fame in time and thereby ensuring that it lasts. Without such poets, public men quickly turn to dust:

Many heroes lived before Agamemnon
but all are unwept and unknown,
weighed down by the long night,
because they lacked a sacred bard.[12]

The power to name, and have that naming last, is the power of the great writer. Both Horace and Virgil make crucial distinctions between themselves and previous poets: they are writers, members of a profession with a special importance to the state; they have powerful patrons and they frequently address those patrons about the crucial place of poetry at the heart of Roman culture. But Virgil's poet is clearly a loyal hand-maiden to political power, while Horace's meets his patron on more equal ground. Through their mingling of poetry, history, and mythology, Virgil and Horace helped create a literary atmosphere to support the actions Augustus was taking in public life. But, as Horace particularly foresaw, their works have survived more handsomely than his, and the new poetry Augustus as patron and inspirer helped bring into being has lived long beyond the circumstances of its engendering. With his sensitivity to the propagandizing effectiveness of literature, Augustus must have foreseen the future as well. As evidence, we have an edgily joshing letter he wrote to Horace, sometime after the publication of the *Epistles,* complaining that Horace wrote letters to everyone but him and wondering if he was left out because Horace was worried that association with Augustus would make Horace infamous to posterity. With his genius for self-display, Augustus understands that it is Horace, much more than Virgil (even in his pastoral phase), who has most powerfully developed the image of the poet as an outsider who dispenses fame, the one who truly understands the meaning of history and individual action in a way inaccessible to the prac-titioners of war and politics.[13]

Although in their own lifetimes Virgil and Horace were at peace with Augustus, their poetry contained the terms through which in later centuries timeless literature and temporal politics would battle over whose was the greater truth, whose the more lasting fame. Horace's emphasis on the poet's distance from the world of public affairs especially leads him to attack the Roman aristocratic traditions of family eminence and public display as essential characteristics of the aspiring man. When he uses the word "virtue," it has a personal, an internal tone that can strike even at the fame and integrity of the *Princeps* himself. Classical scholars argue over how exactly Augustus was invoked at Rome: Did people swear by his name, by his Genius, by his divine power? The evidence that Horace's poems furnish for this controversy is of an interestingly ambiguous sort.

12. Without hard proof of a direct connection, it is still intriguing to note that Horace (and perhaps Virgil as well) begin to use *vates* as a term for the poet in the wake of the Battle of Actium, when Octavian made his connection to Apollo explicit.

13. The word Augustus uses is *infamis,* a legal term for loss of Roman citizenship owing to condemnation in criminal or civil cases, the practice of disreputable oc-cupations, and so on.

According to the manuscripts we have, Horace may have referred to the "name" (*nomen*) of Augustus or to his "divine power" (*numen*). Surely, as a writer who so often invokes the closely akin powers of literary and religious language, he must have meant both. But we are certainly not to forget that it is Horace, the lowly born private poet, who does the naming. In another such intriguing wordplay, Horace echoes *ingenuus* (wellborn) with *ingenius* (individual, talented). Perhaps some may worship and others swear by the Genius of Augustus, but Horace reminds his readers that everyone has a *genius,*

> a companion who controls the birth-star,
> the god of human nature, mortal for each person,
> although changeable in face, white and black (*Epistles,* II, ii, 187–89).

In more public poems, like the *Odes,* Horace speaks in the quasi-public role of the *vates.* By asking to be addressed in the more personal form of the *Epistles,* Augustus has ventured onto Horace's home ground.

Horace may never have been aware that he was in competition with Augustus. But the values he celebrates in his poetry easily became the source of an opposition to political achievement rather than a friendly complement to it. Horace's insistence on himself as an outsider to the Roman inner circles, who preferred his country farm to city life and whose father had been a freedman, emphasized the greater clarity of his perspective than that of the traditional Roman ruling classes. The crucial challenge of literature to politics, implicit in the works of Horace, will be much clearer in those of Ovid, who uses the pose of the poetic outsider to strike an uncompromising (although perhaps unwitting) blow at the roots of the Roman commitment to public action and public achievement. In brief, this challenge is the championing of spiritual as opposed to material status, along with a ferocious insistence on the superiority of literary to visual art. In Horace's late-blooming "Epistle to Augustus," for example, he sets out to explain to Augustus the importance of supporting Latin literature, contemporary as well as ancient. Alexander the Great, says Horace, although he allowed only the greatest painter and the greatest sculptor to make his likeness, let his praises be sung by a very bad poet. Of course, Augustus is a much better judge of literature than that. But he should also know enough to prefer the complex messages of literature to the simple ones of visual representation. Bronze shows only the faces of the famous. Writing shows their mind and manners; it is an art attuned to invisible essences. Although the joys of the eye, in a stage play or painting, may move a viewer, they are finally "empty" compared to the nourishing joys of the ear, into which words flow. Sculpture, painting, even public inscriptions, as Horace writes in another poem, have nothing like the ability of poetry to convey true renown and defeat time. Without literature, the fame of the political man vanishes because it is essentially visual and theatrical. No matter how well Augustus has fashioned a powerful political image of himself, soon as he dies and another appears—even one he has personally selected—that image would begin to be effaced. Literary insight into the invisible truth of things may help support the public man. But it stands aloof from his methods. At the end of the "Epistle to Augustus" Horace turns away from the notes of epic celebration and refuses with a blush the ultimate accolade of a Roman public audience—to cast his face in wax and sell the reproductions in shops—the first century B.C. equivalent of Renaissance steel engravings, eighteenth-century busts, and twentieth-century posters.

Amor / Roma: Ovid and the Subversion of Political Fame

> . . . O highest ones, if you see the deeds of mortals,
> may I be remembered (nothing more does my tongue
> want to pray) and may I have my story told through long ages
> —what time you have taken from my life, give to my fame.
> —OVID, *Metamorphoses* [14]

Horace's emphasis both on the importance of private nature as a recommendation for fame and on the ability of the talented individual to understand the traditions and history of Rome better than had the aristocratic classes corresponds closely to Augustus's political goals. Thus Horatian lyric individualism as much as Virgilian national epic helped undermine the old system of political clients and replace it with a transcendent image of the Roman nation; and those later emperors who thought that ascendancy was achieved primarily through control of the army or of the senate tended to be somewhat less successful than those who followed the Augustan model of adding the talents of image making and self-consciousness to their more practical abilities.

Yet, as the example of Horace makes clear, from the very first the Augustan accord between literature and politics was potentially an unstable one. The troubles Augustus had designating a successor who would carry his family dynasty into the future contrast sharply with the nongenealogical dynasty of Horace and Virgil, who hardly needed to ensure their succession, since in each generation there would be those to nominate themselves proper heirs. With the death of Horace it is Ovid who takes his place as the prime Roman poet, and Ovid's poetic career inexorably brings him into a conflict with Augustus that results in his banishment to a small town on the shores of the Black Sea at the age of fifty. Not that Ovid in any clear way was politically opposed to Augustus or attacked him directly;

---

14. These words are said by Iphis, a young man who has been ignored by Anaxarete, with whom he has fallen in love. After this speech he hangs himself in her doorway.

scholars still argue over what exactly caused Augustus to act against the greatest poet of his day. But the general terms are clear. In the poems of Horace and Virgil, the poet and the public man stand together to celebrate the nation. But in the poems of Ovid the poet begins to assert himself as the true nation, to substitute cultural history for political and military history, and to contrast his Rome with the one that the politician-generals have brought into being. In the *Metamorphoses* particularly the Horatian turning away from public life has been transformed into a coherent and competitive set of values. Thus in both late antiquity and the Middle Ages Christian writers discover that Ovid can be interpreted through their own preoccupation with the problems of the self and the soul. The literary fame sought by Virgil and Horace is still primarily a fame conditioned by Roman traditions. Each of them in his will left the bulk of his estate to Augustus. But the fame that is also a crucial theme for Ovid is, despite his own protests, a fame that has moved away from Roman public values to prophesy instead the spiritual fame of the Christian saint, the chivalric fame of the medieval knight, and the combined fame of literary genius and psychic sensitivity embodied in a nineteenth-century figure like Byron.

Unlike Horace and Virgil, who have experienced social and political chaos and look fondly on Augustus's golden order, Ovid was born a year after Caesar's assassination and was enjoying "the peace of Augustus" before he was out of his teens. His father, a prominent member of the provincial equestrian aristocracy, had intended him for a public political career. But, after a few minor posts, Ovid turned to poetry full time. It would be easy to make too much of the symmetry of this rejection of his father's plans at the beginning of his career and the exile by Augustus at the end. But the analogies between the public man and the poet that preoccupied Virgil and Horace affect Ovid in quite a different way. From his first works Ovid is not the poet of epic grandeur or pastoral solitude but the poet of love, love between individuals and love in the energetic social world of contemporary Rome. In a sense he becomes a national poet whose works and even way of life are an implicit attack on most of the professed national values: His underlying theme is that not *Roma* but *amor* conquers all.

With such a view, we might expect that Ovid takes Dido's side of the argument rather than Aeneas's (and Virgil's). So he does, just as he supports or at least explores the complaints of many other notable women in his *Heroides*—a series of letters from each woman to her love, the first from Penelope to Ulysses. It is a point of view that in one way or another permeates all of Ovid's work, not just the interest in the ways of love and the ways of women, but also the awareness of the contrast between male and female ideas of what is valuable. In his earlier works a sense of parody and a city-dweller's arched eyebrow often determine the tone. But, as the later poems make clear, Ovid's attention to the special concerns of women leads to an appreciation of virtues of emotion and self-expression usually rejected by the trumpet calls of epic or the softer tones of Horatian male camaraderie. Most of the women in the *Heroides*, like Dido, have been betrayed by men who are consumed by another, usually god-given goal. Virgil has the sensitivity to impersonate Dido, but like Aeneas, he leaves her behind to complete the task of writing the poem. Ovid, in contrast, continues to explore the pain of his female characters, their vanities, and their losses. It is a very different idea of what a poet does than any sanctioned by Augustus, and in Ovid's greatest work, the *Metamorphoses*, it yields a very different view of human history and heroism.

The *Metamorphoses* is Ovid's epic. He begins writing it in about A.D. 2, and it is published in what he considered to be an unpolished form in A.D. 8, the year of his exile. If the *Aeneid* is its model, it is a strange epic, for its binding theme is not the Virgilian virtues of unflinching duty and piety, but an unceasing change that Ovid defines as the nature of history. As he has Pythagoras say in the final book of the poem:

> Time itself flows on in constant motion,
> just like a river. For neither the river nor the swift hour
> can stop its course; but, as wave is pushed by wave,
> and as each wave is pushed by and pushes the next,
> so time both flees and follows equally
> and is forever new . . . (Humphries, 371).

Even when the ascendancy of Rome is celebrated, it appears in a context of other great cities that are now powerless or destroyed. At the center of time stands not the Virgilian ruler of destiny and history but a different sort of poet, impresario of changes and master of shifting perspectives.

Although the poem seems to trace the evolution of civil society from a haphazardly entangled world of gods and humans, Ovid's final uniting of his own fame to the spread of Roman military and political power rings hollowly for the reader of the rest of the *Metamorphoses*. For Ovid the gradual advance of history is not military and political but personal, emotional, and artistic. Only when he reaches the verge of a collective human history in Book XII with the Trojan War do military matters enter into his narrative in any important way. Even there he stresses the origins of the war in the strife that began when the human Paris awarded the golden apple to Venus (who promised him the most beautiful wife), thus incurring the wrath of Juno (who promised power) and Minerva (who promised wisdom). And the major scenes of the war he describes are introduced by the story of a warrior who had once been a woman until changed by Neptune in return for his rape of her. From the early sections of the poem onward, power is represented by the male gods, particularly Jupiter, who can never resist a beautiful human woman or (to state the situation in Ovid's terms) can never resist the opportunity to show off their absolute power, their absolute difference from human beings, by indulging in casual and frequent rape. In the general pattern, a god disguises himself, usually as a normal man, and pursues a beautiful nymph, who escapes by turning into some part of nature—a tree, a flower, a stream. Like the people in the *Aeneid* whom Virgil believes should be consoled for their deaths by having their names attached to pieces of the countryside, the hapless nymphs of Ovid give their names forever to vegetable or animal forms: "Her hair was changed to leaves, her arms to branches, / her feet just now so swift were stuck in lazy roots, / her head was a treetop. Only her gleaming splendor remained" (I, 550–52). Thus Daphne changed into a laurel tree to evade Apollo. He tries to embrace her further but, says Ovid, even the wood shrinks, until he pledges to make the laurel his emblematic tree, the material for his lyre and quiver as well as the crown on his head and on those of Roman generals in triumphal processions.

Yet, unlike Virgil's name-bestowing progenitors, Ovid's metamorphosing women have hardly been rewarded. The unwelcome attentions of a god are escaped only by ceasing to be human. Without control over the way their looks affect the eye of a god, they retreat into immobility and nonhumanity, exchanging their uncertain human lives for the certainty of natural cycles, filling nature with thwarted potential. Their human beauty is an intolerable burden. Endlessly running away from their potential rapists, their only escape is to be able to run no more, to be fixed. The poles of Ovid's mythology are incessant motion and eternal stasis; nothing seems to exist in between. Perseus transports the head of Medusa to a battle and freezes into statues everyone who does not believe that her face has the power to do just that. In the midst of striking or warding off a blow, warriors are turned to stone, and animals forever chase each other across a field.

It does little justice to the complex and fascinating detail of Ovid's retelling of mythology to pick and pull at only a few of his innumerable stories. But the kinds of stories he tells indicate his crucial place in the history of fame. In direct contrast with Virgil's pageant of the necessary interplay of gods and humans in the fashioning of human history, Ovid depicts them as cruel and ferocious competitors. A frequent disguise of gods on earth is as the aged, under whose wrinkles and stooped forms the ageless god will be least suspected. Yet by fate or confusion these immortal monuments to the unchanging have become the standards against which human achievement is measured. Thus god-rapes in the *Metamorphoses* gradually evolve into stories in which human beings try to make inroads on godlike immortality. After the women who run from Jupiter come those who finally give in to him and become his favorites, even one that he turns into a constellation to help her escape the wrath of his wife Juno. ('Juno may consider you a whore. I'll make you a star.') But saddest of all these is the story of Semele. A disguised Juno persuades her to ask Jupiter to make love undisguised. Whereupon she is virtually burned to a crisp, the only surviving remnant the fertilized egg that will become Dionysus, who spends his gestation period sewn into Jupiter's thigh.

In later phases the competition becomes more direct and, appropriately enough, it focuses not on strength and sexuality so much as on artistic talent. Arachne, recounts Ovid in Book VI, is an accomplished weaver. But, like so many other such characters in the *Metamorphoses,* she is not content merely to be the best human weaver; she has to be better than the gods. Minerva, disguised as an old woman, warns her about her assertiveness. But Arachne persists until the outraged Minerva throws off her disguise and the contest begins. First, Minerva weaves a tapestry of the Olympian family of gods, including herself, placing in the four corners scenes from other ill-fated attempts of humans to compete with the gods. Meanwhile Arachne weaves together the many stories that portray the gods as devious schemers, interested primarily in sex. When both tapestries are done, neither Envy, who is judging, nor Minerva herself can find any fault with what Arachne has accomplished. But Minerva rips the tapestry apart anyhow and hits Arachne over the head with her loom until Arachne in despair hangs herself. Somewhat mollified, Minerva changes her into a spider, condemned to hang and weave forever.

In this story are contained all the elements of Ovid's other tales of those who dared to compete with the gods. Centuries later it will become a cautionary story for many painters of the Renaissance, who saw in it the fruitless combat between artists and rulers. Arachne is a Horace-like artist whose family and place of birth are both insignificant. Only her own talent and skill, says Ovid, give her "a memorable name" in the surrounding cities. In the weaving competition, Arachne does turn out to be as good as Minerva, and, to compound the lèse-majesté of her assertion against Minerva, she spins stories of the ways the gods willfully impose their power on human beings, while Minerva counters with a portrait of the gods in majesty. But Arachne's talent finally makes no difference. Minerva not only has the power. She wants the praise as well, specifically for being the source of whatever it is that is valuable in the skills of Arachne.

Minerva's anger is therefore directed specifically against Arachne's grandest assertion: her self-sufficiency. Arachne refuses even metaphorically to say her skill comes from the goddess, and when the disguised Minerva chides her for seeking fame beyond the share of mortals, she scorns the old woman's advice: "My own advice is enough for me." Her punishment is therefore to be turned even further toward herself, her talent doomed to fruitless and repetitive originality, spun out of her own belly. You may be able to create, Minerva in essence says to Arachne. But I can kill you, change you, make you less than human.

In the one incident in the *Aeneid* that presages the competitions of Ovid, the sea god Triton, jealous of the trumpeting ability of the Trojan Misenus, catches him by the sea one day and drowns him. With a mournful but stoic shrug Virgil accepts the verdict and affirms the absolute power of gods over humans. But Ovid, by focusing on characters more akin to artists and writers, gives his contests an ideological immediacy that cannot be resolved in cliches about human nature chafing against fate.[15] Arachne

15. In what may be an allusion to the Triton episode, Ovid refers to Minerva a few times as "Tritonia," one of her many names. In later depictions, figures derived

tells stories of the tyrannical behavior of gods that include many that Ovid has already told in the poem. The response of the injured deity is to freeze the human being into one gesture, repeated forever. But the response of Ovid, overseeing the weaving that creates the poem, is to tell another story, to flow onward, to reassert and to connect. If the gods do exist and are jealous of human accomplishment, the only glory, the only humanity, might be to continue to combat with them, to continue to indulge the human taste for change and flux—and storytelling.

An imperfect, changing human being who competes with a perfect, unchanging god aspires to an immortality somehow compounded of the imperfection and flux of human nature, its subjection to time. What is the difference between what Arachne fails to do and what Ovid, we assume, believes he succeeds in doing? Virgil at times clearly subordinates artistic power to temporal power. Horace turns away to create the poet as a prophetic isolated figure, greeting Augustus from his own special sphere. But Ovid implies that the poetic continuity with the past is more real than the political, just as the nation defined by poetry is the real nation, not the one that shows itself visibly forth in the trappings of earthly power. For Ovid, the prime language of public power is sculpture, power frozen in the round, above the viewer, imposing on him. Like the gods, rulers cannot be as complicated as poets because they are committed to an unchanging imagery of power, while poets are at home with the constantly changing and shifting, the true essence of human nature and history.

For such private authority to have much to do with public power inevitably stains it with the kind of ambitious absolutism that characterizes the urge for public fame. Ovid sympathizes with Arachne, because for all her self-sufficiency she cannot be self-satisfied. She must compete with the unrivaled; only then, she thinks, will she be truly content. Such a hunger for fame appears in all its nakedness in a story not about an artist who phrases her assertion in the terms of her art, but someone who asserts himself for no special reason at all—consumed by a desire not for the fame of doing, but for the fame of being. This insatiable aspirant is Erysichthon, a scorner of the gods who breaks into the sacred grove of Ceres, the goddess of earthly plenty and fertility, and chops down her largest tree. After an appeal by her priestesses for punishment, Ceres sends a messenger to Famine (*Fames*) to ask her help. (Since Ceres and Famine are totally opposed deities, they can't get near each other personally.) Famine agrees, flies through the air to the bedroom of Erysichthon, crawls inside of him, and fills his body with a hunger that can never be satisfied: "[W]hatever would satisfy cities / or a people, doesn't satisfy this one person" (VIII, 832–33). From then on Erysichthon eats and drinks incessantly, but without pleasure or fulfillment: "All food in him / is the cause of food, and the place within him / constantly becomes empty by eating" (VIII, 841–

from Virgil's *Fama* often carry the long-barreled trumpet used by royal heralds. Alexander Pope's early eighteenth-century reference to "Fame's posterior trumpet" sounds the death knell for any unselfconscious use of the imagery (*Dunciad,* IV, 71).

42). He runs through all his patrimony, buying more and more food until finally he even sells his daughter. Luckily, it turns out that his daughter can metamorphose herself and so he sells her again and again, sometimes as a bird, a cow, or a deer. But even her Protean masquerades don't help, and finally Erysichthon turns his ravenous hunger on his own body and consumes himself. Like the ambition of the public man, Erysichthon's assertion against Ceres, the goddess of earth and fertility, is empty of everything but the urge to destruction, to cut down anything that presumes to be taller than he is. Eternal emptiness is therefore his appropriate reward.

In the context of the many other combats with the gods in the *Metamorphoses,* the famine (*fames*) Erysichthon gets is the image of the fame (*fama*) he seeks. The verbal echo winds its way through the lines of Ovid's story to emphasize the emptiness of spirit that the urge for fame without content implies. It is a word play that will be made even more explicit in Christian writers like St. Augustine, who interpret the hunger as an emptiness longing to be filled, not with fame, but with God. Thus, within the heart of the pagan empire itself, Ovid supplies an important clue to the imagery of subsequent Christian attacks on Roman values. But his goals are somewhat different. There is no question of belief here, or of transforming the self into another kind of person, a better person, by conversion (as, for example, there is in Augustine's autobiographical *Confessions*). "Therefore be *perfect* [complete yourself] as your heavenly Father is *perfect,*" says Jesus in the Sermon on the Mount within twenty years after Ovid writes the *Metamorphoses*. But for Ovid that kind of perfection is like the perfection of statues. Human nature, in contrast, is constantly shifting; a true insight requires the ability to understand and encompass the flux, without reducing it to simplistic pattern. Thus, while Virgil creates the goddess *Fama* as a monstrous bird spreading gossip and rumor, Ovid's *Fama* is a goddess who rules over the world of *all* stories, both false and true:

There is a place at the world's center,
Triple boundary of land and sky and sea.
From here all things, no matter where they are, are visible;
Every word comes to these hollow ears.
Here Fame dwells, who has chosen her home high upon the mountain-top,
With countless entrances, a thousand openings,
And no door to close them. Day and night
The house stands open. It is entirely built of echoing bronze
Which repeats every word, redoubles all it hears;
There is no quiet, no silence anywhere inside.
Yet there is no clamor either, only the murmur
Of little voices, like the murmur
Of sea-waves heard far-off, or the last rumble
Of thunder when Jupiter smashes the clouds together. The halls
Are filled with shifting crowds, and everywhere

Rumors in thousands, lies mixed with truth,
While confused words fly about.
Some fill their idle ears
With talk, others go elsewhere to tell
The stories they have heard, and every story grows,
And each new author adds to what he has heard.
Here is Credulity, and reckless Error, vain Joy, and panicky Fear,
Sudden Sedition, and Whispers of uncertain authorship, while Fame herself
Sees all that happens in heaven, on sea and land,
And pries into the whole world for news (XII, 39–63).[16]

Ovid's goddess does not yet have the specialized crowds of petitioners seeking fame for themselves (or, infrequently, anonymity) that will be added in later versions of this scene by Chaucer (*The House of Fame*) and Pope (*The Temple of Fame*) among others. Yet her seat of power is obviously a court, whose cavernous halls echo with stories funneled in from the world outside. Unlike Virgil's monster, whose malevolent influence in the world must be countered by the true fame conferred by the poet, Ovid's goddess embodies the fame presided over by a royal patron, into whose precincts come the works of all authors, gossips, and rumormongers swirling together. In Chaucer's poem, almost thirteen hundred years later, the goddess Fame will be asked (with little result) to winnow the false from the true. But in her first incarnation in the *Metamorphoses* her actions are less important than both her regal character and the setting of her home at the very heart of all the intersecting forces of the world. The shifting nature of what she rules over bothers Ovid less than it does Virgil because Ovid's subject is the inescapable mingling of truth and fiction. Virgil's *Fama* appears briefly in the *Metamorphoses* as "talkative fame" (IX, 137), who grows larger by lying. But, unlike Virgil, Ovid does not try to sift the pure line of Roman destiny from the uncertain stories of the past. Instead he associates fame not with private reputation or public honor so much as with an ongoing tradition that has an integrity separate from the demands of military and political power. Virgil's *Fama* is a horrible female monster; Ovid's is a ruling female goddess, whose kingdom is the world, "unconfined fame, obligated to no one's orders" (XV, 853).

Read this way, the subversive quality of the *Metamorphoses* becomes clear, and it is appropriate that Pythagoras appears in the final book to offer an extended philosophical account of the central importance of change in the structure of both the universe and human affairs. It is an insight for which Ovid's own preoccupation with metamorphosis has pre-

16. Unlike Virgil's characterization of Fame, which occurs when Aeneas turns aside from his public "destiny" to court Dido, Ovid's is set at the beginning of his account of the Trojan War, thus undermining Virgil's distinction between the 'bad fame' of private gossip and the 'good fame' of epic praise. For a detailed account of Ovid's effort in this passage to subvert Virgilian ideas of *bona fama*, see Zumwalt, *"Fama Subversa."*

pared the way. The ability to change becomes the standard against which fixity, stability, and the armored personality is found deficient: Even his daughter's ability to change into anything he needs cannot help the unceasing hunger of Erysichthon to be the greatest. Thus, when Ovid ends the poem with a pious belief that his works will last "wherever Roman power extends over the conquered earth," it is hard to take him seriously. His fame, as he has just finished saying, is contained in the book, impervious even to Jupiter's wrath. Time, in which great empires have risen only to fall, will be escaped only by the art that understands its rhythms and its ceaseless change. Undermining the smug assertions of imperial destiny, the *Metamorphoses* celebrates instead a history that the poetic imagination has made its own. Virgil's need to link poetic authority with political power to gain the sanction of history has in Ovid's great work been attenuated to a final perfunctory reference to Roman power. In his earlier poems Ovid mocked the grand plans of war and battle by using them as metaphors for the strategies of love. By his later works the implicit competition had become much clearer, perhaps more clear to Augustus than to Ovid himself. At the time of his banishment, Ovid was not only finishing the *Metamorphoses,* but was also halfway through the *Fasti,* a poetic version of the Roman calendar that attempted to give a narrative account of the mythological and historical origins of all the Roman holidays. No wonder Augustus was inclined to consider Ovid a subversive force in the new imperial settlement. In the *Metamorphoses* Ovid pits the human authority of the artist against the inhuman power of the gods. In the *Fasti* he implies that it is only in literature that Roman history and religion can be truly explained.

Ovid's poetry written in exile implies that he himself was unaware of the real nature of his challenge. In fact those poems are filled with despairing references to fame and frequent repetitions of his own name, as if to preserve himself somehow from oblivion. But Augustus made no mistake. Ovid's work occupies the crucial intersection between the pagan objection to politics in favor of love and nature and the Christian objection to Rome in favor of the soul and God. In the twelfth century Ovid will be rediscovered by French poets and lovers seeking to create a world of love in contrast to the wars and politics that had overtaken medieval Christianity. Once again, literary patronage by women rather than by men will play a crucial role, and Ovid's stories of transformation will be given innumerable interpretations in the terminology of Christian love. In the Renaissance Virgil's bird *Fama* is reflected in countless illustrations. But Ovid's house of Fame will have more influence on writers, for the way it raises specifically literary questions about the nature of fame, who gives it and who gets it. With appropriate shyness Chaucer in his poem says he comes to the house of Fame not to gain fame himself but for "tidings of love." He finds instead a chaos of names and stories and some few statues of great writers, including Ovid, who upholds the fame of love. The hall was full of writers, says Chaucer,

Of them that write of old deeds
As many as there are rook's nests on a tree;
But it would be a confusing matter
If you wanted to hear all the deeds
That they wrote of, or what their names were
(*The House of Fame*, 1515–1519).

Caligula and Nero: The Monstrous Emperor and the Stoic Withdrawal

The entente between emperor and author that characterizes the early years of the reign of Augustus fragments with the banishment of Ovid and falls apart completely with the suicides of Seneca and Lucan, after a failed conspiracy against Nero. By then, barely fifty years later, the division of renown between Augustus and Horace has turned into a sharp and polemical war, on one side the writer-philosophers and on the other the emperor-performers.

For Augustus, public nature was always premeditated, each gesture tailored to the leader as point man on the road to national destiny. He was the performer who had to have the constant attention of his audience, for his political control was qualified only by his formulaic assertion of fealty to it as the source of his power. Yet, because he was the leader, he was always alone, playing himself sincerely because there was no room for any private nature that does not contribute to his public authority. After Augustus, the inheriting emperor had that same celebrity and power of position. But fame is best fought for, while celebrity is at worst conferred. What then is ambition to one who never had to struggle? Looking back almost one hundred years from the comparatively settled times of Hadrian and Trajan, Suetonius in *Lives of the Caesars* treats these later emperors as a strange collection of monsters known best for their baroque sexuality and flamboyant murders. In their careers the noble goal of unique public stature turns into an obsessive effort to see what outsized inhumanities will be enough to ratify their imperial status.

The only way a ruler without special political or military talents can recommend himself is by his arbitrariness, the mystery of his personality. When that mystery no longer exists, his pretense of absoluteness is in tatters. Romans were willing to give up supreme authority to Augustus because he had created a peaceful settlement after years of civil war. But for anyone without Augustus's administrative and political talents, all that was left of the position of emperor was its theater. Of the early emperors, Caligula and Nero particularly show the warped effects of a renown that they had little to do with bringing about. Unlike Augustus, who was manipulating public events for political purposes, their prime goal was to call attention to themselves. Both became emperor when very young—Caligula at twenty-five, Nero at seventeen—and neither had any recommendation beyond their genealogy. Both emphasized the element of performance in the role of the emperor and presented themselves as great artists, even entertainers, for whom approval had to be immediate.

In so many of the actions of both Caligula and Nero, Augustan values find their hideous mirror image: the theater stripped of substance, the ties of family turned into incest, the ostentatious moral probity become arbitrary violence and murder. When one's inheritance was absolute power, only the striking colors of art or crime could make one truly distinctive. Fittingly, both Caligula and Nero appropriated the panoply of Alexander without either his charisma or abilities. Crucial to both was the need to be known not only in Rome (that was their heritage) but also in Greece. Caligula in his usual rudimentary way stole Alexander's breastplate from Alexandria to wear as part of his costume as a triumphal general. Nero, with a little more substance, gave Greece freedom from taxes. But both similarly attempted to absorb Hellenistic and therefore ultimately Alexandrian concepts of divine monarchy into their own persons.

Obsessed with surpassing every precedent, Caligula was violently jealous of the fame of others: replacing heads on the statues of Greek gods with his own, allowing no statue or bust of a living person set up without his permission, and seeking to suppress the unduly competitive works of Homer, Virgil, and Livy. Deification after death had been established for Caesar and Augustus. Caligula, who believed that his mother had been born of an Egyptian-style divine incest between Augustus and Julia, set up an altar and priesthood to himself during his lifetime. By insisting that his horse be elected consul, he further mocked Augustan political rectitude and showed his superiority to the rituals of imperial ceremony that Augustus so loved by receiving ambassadors and conducting state business dressed sometimes in bathrobe and slippers and sometimes as a woman.[17] Just as Caligula made the theatrical gestures of rule the entire point of ruling, so the arbitrariness of his will constituted the prime test of his power, and he spent enormous amounts of money to accomplish projects whose only recommendation was that they were thought impossible. Says Suetonius: "Villas and country-houses were run up for him regardless of expense . . . [He] construct[ed] moles in deep water far out to sea, [drove] tunnels through exceptionally hard rocks, [raised] flat ground to the height of mountains, and [reduced] mountains to the level of plains; and all at immense speed, because he punished delay with death" (168).

---

17. Behavior that is informal or aberrant for most people can be used by the great man to illustrate his transcendence of the customs others must observe. Lyndon Johnson, for example, often held meetings while sitting on the toilet. Howard Hughes, in deathly fear of contamination by the mere presence of others, yet typically walked among his subordinates half-clothed and unkempt. What is naked or vulnerable behavior to the normal person can thus be another sort of armor to the man of power, imposing his will by demonstrating the irrelevance to him of normal standards of behavior and vulnerability.

The power of the performer is essentially a power over minds and feelings (especially his own) within the compass of the performing situation. But when the entirety of a reign or an administration is a performance, the spectators may lose the ability to disentangle what is real from what is not. Although it is common for a public performer to have stage fright, it means something more sinister when it is the fear of a politician or a ruler. Suetonius concludes that Caligula's strangest trait was his mixture of "over-confidence and extreme timorousness" (174). Similarly, before going on stage, Nero, who was much more interested than Caligula in praise as an actual performer, was always filled with anxiety about the talents of his adversaries and the standards of the judges. Augustus, Antony, and Caesar may have been heroes of politics and battle. Nero would be a hero of art. He entered singing and lyre-playing contests in Greece (even though the cities that held them routinely sent him the first prize anyhow), and he forced the untraditional introduction of a musical competition into the Olympic games. Like Caligula in competition with the gods and great men of the past, Nero also took the opportunity of winning various contests to tear down the statues of those who had won before. So winds on the despair of those who must follow in the footsteps of a grander age: Caligula's impossible projects are echoed in Nero's abortive effort to name a month after himself (Neroneus, equivalent to April) and to name Rome itself Neropolis.[18] When Nero prepared for war in Spain, he spent most of his time putting together a train of wagons to carry his theatrical equipment and dressing his concubines as Amazons. Before he committed suicide, he lamented to onlookers, "What an artist I am destroying" (*Suetonius,* 176).

Agrippina, Nero's mother, whom he succeeded in having murdered after several attempts, is reported by Suetonius to have prevented him from studying philosophy because it was contrary to the need of a ruler. But it was particularly during Nero's reign that a force contrary to imperial theatricalizing gathered new strength for its definition of fame and public service. Neatly enough, the most important representative of this view was the philosopher Seneca, Nero's tutor and virtual coregent (with the military leader Burrus) of the empire during Nero's minority. Seneca's descent was not from the imperial family but from the history of philosophy, where the philosopher, with his plain dress, beard, and austere life, was as recognizable a figure as an emperor or a public official. Seneca's philosophy was stoicism, a guide to behavior determined not by the state but by virtue and learning. Plutarch, some hundred years later, characterizes Stoics as irremediably hostile to the cult of imperial worship and general scorners of both princes and great men. But since the Hellenistic period, just after the death of Alexander, philosophers in general and Stoics in

18. Such pretentiousness was not confined only to the younger emperors of the Julian family. The bookish Claudius, who reigned between Caligula and Nero, succeeded in adding three new letters to the Latin alphabet. None have survived.

particular had shown a strong interest in monarchical government and produced many treatises with the general title of "On Kingship." One of their
martyred heroes, as we have seen, was Alexander's historian Callisthenes,
whose fate Seneca invokes in a scarcely veiled dig at Nero. If only the
mature Alexander had been as attentive to Callisthenes as the young
Alexander had been to Aristotle! Between the lines of such treatises glim-
mers the assumption that any ruler who listened to philosophical counsel
would be by definition worthy. At the fountainhead of such a tradition was
Socrates, who by the early empire had already become so proverbial for
his wisdom and particularly his self-control that Seneca invokes him constantly, usually as the only Greek in a line of Roman men of virtue embodied most recently by Cato. The emperor might be the greatest man
inside the Roman system. But he should bow to the philosopher who saw
into the eternal truths that controlled everything human, including Rome.
Virtue in this philosophical sense was more closely related to spiritual
truth than to public service, and by its nature tended to qualify if not
subvert the public ambition of the great men of the state. After Augustus
had undermined the political and military function of the old aristocracy,
they turned more and more toward the civic spirituality of stoicism, in
which the continuity of the state was confirmed not by allegiance to a
particular family but to an idea of Rome compounded of laws, institutions,
and, above all, virtuous men. Ceremonially and politically, Nero inherited
the mantle of the Augustan settlement. But the Stoics invoked a different
sanction for their action, more akin to the *auctoritas* that Augustus claimed
for himself.[19]

Stoicism under the early empire was to a great extent the creed of a
cultured class cut off from its traditional easy access to public power. But
with the ascendency of Seneca came the strong revival of the belief that
Greek philosophers should create the context within which rulers governed. Nero could act, but Seneca would write the plays. During the time
he served as Nero's minister and political advisor, Seneca amassed a huge
fortune that in our eyes might undermine the virtuous austerity of his
philosophical views. But Seneca's attacks were never on fame but on
ambition; if the state chose to reward virtue, all the better for the state.
After almost ten years as Nero's "guide," Seneca voluntarily retired. His
philosophical presence had not been enough to restrain the young emperor. A few years later Seneca was implicated in a conspiracy against
Nero and compelled to commit suicide. Most of the conspirators were
Stoics or had Stoic sympathies, including Seneca's nephew, the poet Lucan,
who had at first been a favorite of Nero's until he began to publish his

19. In "Stoicism and the Principate," P. A. Brunt argues that Stoics "had no
theoretical preference for any particular form of government, monarchical or Republican," and tended to accept "the ideas and practices current in their society"
(31, 32). For a thorough account of the relation between Seneca's philosophical and
his political views along with the latest effort to explain or explain away his relation
to Nero, see Griffin, *Seneca*. For an effort to separate the historical Nero from the
monster of gossip, see Warmington, *Nero*.

Frontispiece to Hendrik Goltzius's *Fame and History* (1586). This elaborate engraving of allegorical figures cavorting in ancient ruins is the last in a series depicting Roman heroes. A broken column and a stag shedding its antlers enhance the central images of decline and renewal. As Fama pirouettes atop a skull, she blows her horn. (Note the eyes on her wings.) Meanwhile a fruitful Ceres reads a book labeled "Historia" on a tomb bearing the Greek inscription "Undiminished Strength." Between her legs grows wheat, her emblematic creation. In her left hand she holds a phoenix rising from the ashes. In the poem beneath the engraving the shortness of human glory is lamented and then solaced by fame and posterity. *The Art Museum, Princeton University. Bequest of Junius S. Morgan*

2   3

(*Opposite & above*) Images of Alexander appear prominently in both sculpture and coinage, especially after his death, when his successors sought to assume his symbolic sanction for their own ambitions. (1) Head of Alexander with characteristic lion's mane hair and tilt toward the heavens. *Museum of Archaeology, Istanbul* (2) Silver tetradrachm of Lysimachus, early third century B.C. A diadem encircles Alexander's head, with the horns of Jupiter Ammon denoting his descent from the gods. *Numismatic Fine Arts, Beverly Hills* (3) Silver tetradrachm of Heliodes, the late second century B.C. ruler of Bactria. As Alexander moved across Asia, the model of his self-presentation was imitated by later rulers, whose very realistic images have often come down to us unaccompanied by any record of their deeds. *Numismatic Fine Arts, Beverly Hills*

(*Below*) However firmly fixed the image of Julius Caesar has become through later depictions, it has usually been verified primarily through coin images rather than sculpture. (1) Silver denarius of Caesar with the words "Perpetual Dictator" in Latin. Under the privilege granted Caesar by the Senate, he was the first Roman to have his portrait image on a coin in his lifetime. The wreath around his head may be the "golden crown" worn in triumph. *Numismatic Fine Arts, Beverly Hills* (2) Shortly after the assassination of Caesar, Brutus issues his own silver denarius. On one side is his face; on the other, shown here, is a liberty hat flanked by two daggers and the words "EID. MAR." (Ides of March). *Numismatic Fine Arts, Beverly Hills*

1   2

1

As befits his self-conscious implementation of Caesar's program of publicity, as well as the immense length of his reign, the images of Augustus are much easier to find and verify. (1) Augustus as a young man. *Henry Lillie Pierce Fund; courtesy, Museum of Fine Arts, Boston* (2) Augustus in the robes of the *pontifex maximus*, a post he assumed in 12 B.C. *Museo Nazionale Romano, Rome* (3) Coin of young Augustus, with his image and the words "Caesar Augustus" on one side; on the other is a representation of the comet or star that appeared in the sky after Caesar's assassination, with the words "Divus [Divine] Julius." *Numismatic Fine Arts, Beverly Hills*

2

3

Early images of Jesus include the Orphic poet who can descend into the underworld, the young warrior, the philosopher, and—with the official recognition of Christianity—the emperor of the universe. Here are two youthful examples depicted on elaborate sarcophagi. (1) A solid and chunky young man: the Good Shepherd. *Christian sarcophagus, Museo Laterano, Rome; Alinari/Art Resource*

1

(2) A more ethereal and wise young man: the ruler of the universe and dispenser of the law, treading upon an older-style, unruly god (representing the cosmos). *Sarcophagus of Junius Bassus, Vatican, Rome; Alinari/Art Resource*

2

Artists, Writers, and Patrons.
(1) William Caxton presents the *Recuyell of the Historyes of Troye*, his own translation of a medieval prose history of the Trojan War, to Margaret of York (c. 1475). The *Recuyell* was the first book printed in English, and this is also the first line engraving. *Henry E. Huntington Library*

1

(2) Botticelli, *Young Man with a Medal of Cosimo de' Medici* (1460s?). The medal embedded in the painting is made of gesso covered with gilt. Its original was probably struck when Cosimo was named *pater patriae* after his death in 1464. The contrast between the celebratory Roman profile of Cosimo and the complex emotions on the face of the young man who holds it defines a distinction not only between public and private character but also between the two different artistic views of how character ought to be remembered. *Uffizi Gallery, Florence; Alinari/Art Resource*

2

1

The Faces of Fame. In the Renaissance revamping of classical imagery, the figure of Fame undergoes many transformations as it becomes a more acceptable human urge. (1) An illustration of Petrarch's *Triumph of Fame* from a fifteenth-century manuscript. This goddess of fame, seated on the triumphal cart, is clearly a military figure, like Athena or Joan of Arc. Following her elephant-drawn throne are soldiers, statesmen, and wise men. *Walters Art Gallery, Baltimore* (2) A grotesque *Fama* from a 1544 edition of the *Aeneid*, covered with feathers and eyes, sowing rumors and untruth through the cities and palaces. *Virgil, Opera* (1544), *By permission of British Library*

2

3   4

(3) From Cesare Ripa's influential book of emblems titled *Iconologia*: Pure fame, depicted as Mercury, the messenger of the gods, leading (or perhaps reining in) Pegasus, the horse that carries great men to the skies. *Ripa, Iconologia (1630), Henry E. Huntington Library* (4) Also from the *Iconologia*: Rumor ready to let fly his arrows. *Ripa, Iconologia (1630), Henry E. Huntington Library* (5) Bernardo Strozzi's early seventeenth-century angelic and ladylike *Fama*, complete with two different-sized trumpets: the iconographic invention of celebrity? *Reproduced by courtesy of the Trustees, The National Gallery, London*

5

1

The Self-Conscious Artist: The Sanction of the Spiritual. (1) Rogier
van der Weyden, *St. Luke Painting the Virgin.* Luke, who was re-
puted to have painted a portrait of Mary, was considered the patron
saint of painters. Van der Weyden became master of the Tournai
Guild of St. Luke in 1432. Iconographically Luke and the artist become one in a kind of displaced self-portrait. Van der Weyden's
Luke, although in the process of making a metalpoint drawing,
seems to have momentarily turned aside from essentially religious
duties. In a later version Vasari painted a similar scene, with himself
as Luke seated at an easel, clearly a working painter. *Museum of Fine
Arts, Boston. Gift of Mr. and Mrs. Henry Lee Higginson, 1893*

2

(2) Michelangelo, *Deposition* designed for his tomb (c. 1550). Michelangelo depicts himself as the beggar Nicodemus standing behind the group of Jesus, Mary, and a holy woman. *Florence; Museo dell'Opera del Duomo*

1

The Self-Conscious Artist: The Body and Its Work. (1)
Albrecht Dürer had a medical complaint while traveling
and so wrote a letter to his doctor to show where it hurt.
The pointing finger is a frequent motif in Dürer's self-portraits. His bearded look and the place of the ailment are
reminiscent of Jesus and the Passion. *Kunsthalle, Bremen*
(2) Dürer, *Melencolia I*. Is this the first depiction of artist's
block? Or the first effort to make artist's block a subject of
art? Sporting *Fama*-like wings and an artistic wreath
around her head, Melencolia, surrounded by all her artistic and architectural equipment, still wonders what to do
next. Some have seen the image of a skull in the flat rock
on the left. Dürer created no *Melencolia II*, although the
graphic depiction of anxiety has many descendants. *Los
Angeles County Museum of Art, The Mr. and Mrs. Allan C.
Balch Collection*

2

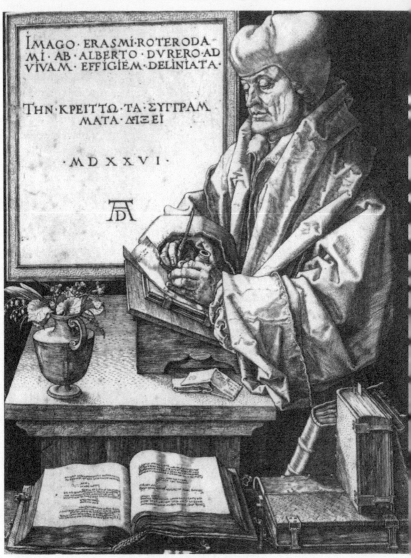

1

The Writer and Artist as a Public Person. (1) Dürer's engraving of Erasmus. The Latin records that this is an image of Erasmus drawn by Dürer from the life; the Greek conveys the pious hope that Erasmus's writings will point to the better way. Erasmus didn't appreciate the likeness, and it was never used as the frontispiece for which it seems designed. *Henry E. Huntington Library* (2) Frontispiece to the expanded 1568 edition of Vasari's *Lives of the Painters*. Note, at the top of the illustration in the center, the figure of Fame with triple trumpets, no doubt one each for painters, sculptors, and architects. *Henry E. Huntington Library*

LE
VITE DE' PIV ECCELLENTI
PITTORI, SCVLTORI, ET ARCHITETTORI,
Scritte, & di nuouo Ampliate da M.
GIORGIO VASARI PIT. ET ARCHIT. ARETINO.

HAC SOSPITE NVNQVAM HOS PERTISSE

VIROS, VICTOS AVT MORTE FATEBOR.

CO' RITRATTI LORO
Et con le nuoue vite dal 1550. insino al 1567
Con Tauole copiosissime De' nomi, Dell' opere,
E de' luoghi ou' elle sono.

IN FIORENZA APPRESSO I GIVNTI 1568.
Con Licenza, e Priuilegio.

The Artist as Maker. With the seventeenth century, the personal self-consciousness that characterizes northern European painting mingles with the cultural self-consciousness of southern European painting to produce works that treat the process of painting itself as a suitable theme. Rembrandt, *An Artist in His Studio* (late 1620s). Here the artist—perhaps Rembrandt himself—is neither shown working nor depicted as some notable personage from the past; he merely stands in front of the intimidating canvas. The door is closed, and inspiration or energy has not yet come upon him. *Courtesy, Museum of Fine Arts, Boston. Zoë Oliver Sherman Collection. Given in memory of Lillie Oliver Poor, 1938*

(*Opposite above*) Velázquez, *Las Meninas* (1656). The best spectators as well as the best subjects, the king and queen of Spain at whom the artist looks, are glimpsed in the mirror on the back wall. Above the mirror are paintings depicting the flaying of Marsyas and the transformation of Arachne into a spider, punishments meted out for their impiety in competing with the gods. *Prado, Madrid; Alinari/Art Resource*

Vermeer, *The Art of Painting* (1670s?). We are spectators behind the scenes while the artist paints Fame, or perhaps Clio, the muse of history, as a young girl posing with trumpet in hand—a guise very similar to that in Cesare Ripa's emblem of History. *Kunsthistoriches Museum, Vienna; Courtesy of Saskia Ltd., Cultural Documentation*

1

The Painting as Personal History. (1) Rowland Lockey's reworked version of Holbein's painting of the family of Sir Thomas More (1596). More and his family, originally painted by Holbein in the late 1520s, each stare off into an individual space, while the family of his grandson, Thomas More II (added by Lockey), look directly at the viewer. *National Portrait Gallery, London* (2) Portrait of Sir Henry Unton (c. 1596) commissioned by his wife after his death, in which all the important events of his life surround the main figure. Note Fame, with her trumpet, to the left of Unton and Death, with his hourglass, to the right. *National Portrait Gallery, London*

2

epic, *Pharsalia,* with its ferocious defense of republican virtue. Nero, as Tacitus says, "impeded his reputation by vetoing his publicity."

In opposition to the histrionics of Nero and the ranting of the heroes of his own plays, Seneca at his death proposed himself as the model of philosophical calm, while Lucan, the blood draining from his veins, recited his own verses on the similar death of a soldier.[20] Even though the deaths had been ordered by Nero, the calm accomplishment of that suicide was the ultimate act of moral reputation and a duty to Rome that existed beyond any individual emperor. When Seneca's wife Paulina said she would die with him, he agreed:

> "Solace in life was what I commended to you," he said. "But you prefer death and glory. I will not grudge your setting so fine an example. We can die with equal fortitude. But yours will be the nobler end" (Tacitus, 364).

The suicide that was ordered by the emperor would be turned into an emblem for posterity of resistance to imperial power. But, since Nero did not have any special grievance against Paulina, he ordered that her suicide attempt be thwarted by slaves, who tied up her wounds after she had lost consciousness. With what thoughts of lost transcendence did she awaken?[21]

Who can measure what role Seneca's philosophical commitment to the repression of strong feelings played in his pupil's later frenzied urge to be celebrated for his talents at performance? On the surface, there seems to be no sharper contrast than that between Seneca's stoic self-sufficiency and Nero's constant demand for adulation and approval. Seneca's letters, so much less revealing than Cicero's, illustrate how his ideology of control extended even into this area of seemingly relaxed amiability. But an age had passed since Cicero. Personal letters that might have originally been a private solace for the public man are transformed by Seneca into a

20. Lucan's career could easily furnish several more flourishes to the competition between stoic and imperial fame. In his middle twenties he published the first three books of the anti-Caesarian *Pharsalia,* which he boasted was written at an age when all Virgil had produced was a poem called "The Flea." Soon after, Nero, previously his friend and patron, barred him from public performance of his work—an act that Suetonius at least ascribes to the mutual jealousy between the two. Despite what "stoic" signifies then and now, the histrionic seems to have been a strong element in Lucan's personality as well as his poetry. Like so many artists and philosophers through the ages, he could never reconcile his desire for a fame possessed by only the greatest public men (like Alexander or Caesar) with his attack on virtually every act and aspect of character that helped bring it into being. Later writers took pleasure in repeating the story that Lucan during the conspiracy first praised the glories of killing tyrants; then, when found out, he turned in everyone involved, as well as his innocent mother. The *Pharsalia* itself remained unfinished at his death; he had made his way through the battle and the murder of Pompey, but never quite got to the suicide of Cato. Lucan died at twenty-six; Nero was twenty-eight.

21. So compelling were these examples of the general stoic view of suicide as a moral act that such early Church Fathers as Origen and Tertullian argued that the Crucifixion was a self-conscious suicide. The interpretation of Jesus as a suicide is revived along with the revival of stoicism in a seventeenth-century work like John Donne's *Biathanatos.*

means of creating an image of privacy and directness, to be published with propagandistic premeditation. Under their obvious differences, Nero and Seneca thus share the desire for an audience appropriate to their abilities. Until Nero removes Seneca from all public offices and later forces him to commit suicide, Seneca thinks that such a sufficient audience might be the young emperor. He discovers that it will actually be posterity.[22]

The story of Alexander and Diogenes neatly illustrates the fascination the classical world had for the competition between absolute monarch and detached philosopher. But the ones most attracted are those who write and thereby perpetuate the story. Stoicism attracted writers because, for all its emphasis on duty, its focus was not so much on the present audience as on the audience of the future, where justification and honor waited. Whatever he hoped to achieve in the present, Seneca in his writings practices the politics of posterity, always impractical because always ideal, an ethics of observation rather than an etiquette of being seen. As Horace and Ovid had hoped, control over language would last long after control over men and things had vanished.

The alternate definition of true fame that is embodied in the works of the Stoics lays the groundwork in Roman society for the acceptance of Christian ideas of virtue, character, and personal success in spite of a corrupt public world. Their vocal distrust of the urge to distinction in public life, their emphasis on duty to the patterns of history and virtue, and their paradoxical urge to a fame defined by turning away from recognition, are all in great part still with us, if only whenever we believe that anyone interested in public office is by definition not suited to it. As the empire expanded, the choice between the urge to rule and the urge to retire was a continual philosophical question. Plutarch especially brings a stoic focus to bear on the great public men of the past, combining a distaste for public affairs with an acknowledgment of their necessity. By lauding Alexander not as the great conqueror but as the philosopher in arms, he argues the possible integration of public and private virtues in the rulers of the present. At virtually the same time Arrian could devote his literary leisure (while a military governor) to creating a realistic Alexander in opposition to the hero of the romances. Arrian laments that Alexander had "no worthy chronicler to tell the world of his exploits" (67), while "nonentities" who had the fortune to be celebrated by great writers like Pindar live on. Despite his other accomplishments, it will be Arrian's own greatest claim to recognition:

> No matter who I am that make this claim. I need not declare my name—though it is by no means unheard of in the world; I need not specify my country and family or any official position I may have held. Rather let me say this: that this book of mine is, and has been

22. For some intriguing remarks on the place of public role playing in stoic belief, see Hans Jonas, *The Gnostic Religion*, and Brunt, "Stoicism and the Principate." In his *Meditations*, Marcus Aurelius, the stoic emperor, accuses the early Christian martyrs of an illegitimate self-dramatization.

from my youth, more precious than country and kin and public achievement—indeed, for me it *is* these things. And that is why I venture to claim the first place in Greek literature, since Alexander, about whom I write, held first place in the profession of arms (68).

His other major work is a compilation of the writings of the anti-imperial stoic philosopher Epictetus, who was, perhaps in Arrian's edition, the philosopher most admired by Marcus Aurelius, the emperor who neatly embodied stoic withdrawal and imperial rule in the same philosophical package, continually counseling himself that only death awaits even the grandest human action.

That Arrian, Plutarch, and Suetonius should all have flourished in the second century A.D. intriguingly marks that era as a time when literary men paused to look back and tried to explain the public reputations of the past—not as myth but as history. In a sense they are the true inheritors of the stoic opposition under Nero and, as Horace asserted, it is in their works to a great extent that the memory of the past is preserved. Roman emperors down to Constantine will still be interested in situating their public monuments in the Roman Forum, competing with each other to build the grandest edifices. But the new-found authority of Roman literature and the empires of the spirit envisioned by Roman stoicism foster a movement away from the visible sites of Rome to refound the temple of fame not in the political state but in the mind and the spirit.[23]

23. Another important figure in this second-century assessment and consolidation of past names and reputation is Pausanias, the travel writer who went all over Greece, describing in minute detail every building and site of importance with particular attention to the inscriptions and memorials of the great men and women of the past. In many cases the only place their honor is now preserved is in his *Guide to Greece.*

Christianity and
the Fame of the Spirit

It is far from honoring him who made us, to honor him whom we have made.

—MONTAIGNE, *Apology for Raymond Sebond*

In a contemplation of the history of fame and those names that still move us, the strikingly overlapping careers of Augustus and Jesus—the one carried out before the full public gaze, the other in relative obscurity—define a crucial contrast. Whether Stoic or emperor, writer or soldier, all prominent Romans believed that appearance in public was necessary to self-definition; the only question was how that public nature was used. But it would be the promise of Christianity to define an arena for individual nature well beyond the political. With its rise comes a direct critique of Roman public behavior: Render unto Caesar what is Caesar's and render unto God what is God's. In a recent essay on honesty in Roman politics, T. A. Dorey has remarked that "the aims of the leading Roman politicians of the Ciceronian age were inherently selfish, and were pursued without regard to the consequences for the rest of the community" (34). Conditioned by his cultural traditions, however, it would have been difficult for any Roman great man to understand what it would mean to separate his own private interests from those of Rome. With the advent of Christianity, "selfish" came to mean not a turning away from the nation but from God; self as opposed to soul. Augustus had transformed the more destructive aspects of the Roman ambition for public fame by making the state the only place where personal dignity could be conferred. At virtually the same historical moment, in the east of the empire, Jesus set the foundations of an alternative view of self in which personal dignity was conferred not in the service of Rome, but in the service of God, heaven, and the community of the faithful.

For early Christianity, public service is not the solution to the ills of private ambition, but a similarly deficient diversion from the true ends of human life: the contemplation and service of the Kingdom of God. In the history of fame, therefore, the Augustan political settlement and the Gospels constitute alternate definitions of the course of individual life, its choices and its goals. One tends toward the socializing of the desire for personal recognition, the other toward its spiritualizing. But each also contains a small form of the other: the stoic core of imperial state service; the multiplication of offices in the community of the faithful. By the time of the political revolutions of seventeenth-century England and eighteenth-century America and France, political and cultural beliefs akin to those of the Stoics buttressed the individual right, even obligation, to correct and reform civil society by an active infusion of moral spirit. To understand those modern revisions of the Roman concept of public service and public fame, we must now consider the challenge of Christianity, whose every idea of personality and virtue was first formulated as an explicit or an implicit attack on the Roman self, and whose attitude toward fame is revealed less in the many patterns of individual careers than in the beliefs about the true end of human nature as embodied in the life of one man—Jesus of Nazareth.

Jesus: The Publicity of Inner Worth

And after six days Jesus took with him Peter and James and John his brother, and led them up a high mountain apart. And he was transfigured before them, and his face shone like the sun, and his garments became white as light.   —MATTHEW, 17:1–2

His face shone on the mount, his fame in the world.
                                        —AUGUSTINE, *City of God*

When Jesus instructs his disciples to "render unto Caesar what is Caesar's and render unto God what is God's," he precisely separates the individual's obligations to the state from those to the world of religion and spirit. In contrast to the Roman absorption of foreign gods into their pantheon and foreign lands into their empire, Christianity elaborated the Jewish exclusionist view that there was only one truth about the inner nature of the world. The Gospel formulation of the separate realms of Caesar and God therefore seems both conservative, because it assumes no conflict will arise, and subversive, because its absolute distinction between the political and the spiritual leaves no question about which is superior. Augustus defined the emperor as *princeps,* first among equals, the common bond among all Romans, the human representative of the essence of social man. But Jesus, born in Augustus's reign, offered a justification beyond society, an affirmation of the divinity in all human beings.

In the careers of men like Julius Caesar and Augustus, we can often glimpse clear patterns of the urge to greatness, infused by a desire for fame, that is expressed as both Alexandrian personal longing and Augustan political ambition. Christianity, however, or at least the new form of Judaism preached by Jesus in the Gospels, changed the course of fame forever. Whatever variations Caesar, Augustus, and others had made on the Alexandrian model of the public hero, that energy and activity was still available primarily to those who had birth and power to begin with. The focus on Rome as the prime arena of fame ensured a limited participation in the contest. But Christianity was by definition open to all who believed. It created a new and universal hierarchy that was not, at least at the beginning, related to political or social orders or national institutions (including the tribal and nationalist God of the Jews). Christianity meant for the believer a new definition of time, a break with the past psychically even more than politically. The story of the rise of Christianity to earthly power under Constantine therefore involves first the assertion of a sphere of individual spiritual nature separate from the interests and coercions of the state, then the establishment of an idea of community apart from that of civil society, and, finally, a reintegration with the Roman Empire. In the course of three hundred years, terms would be given on both sides. Rendering to Caesar and rendering to God were no longer so distinct, especially for those with the ambition for public success. By the time of the Christian emperors, to be *both* Roman and Christian had become the preferred identity. If not a master of history, one could aspire to be more than a victim or a mere denizen.[1]

But the Jesus of the Gospels had made a clear distinction between the world of God and the world of Caesar. At a time when the public display of power was necessary to ratify its existence, the Jesus of the Gospels is a strangely wary figure, characterized from the earliest as evading any publicity for his messianic power. His fame is not a fame for action but a fame of being. In the very compressed first chapter of Mark, for example, Jesus is foretold, baptized by John, and begins to collect the small group of his disciples. Later, to the consternation of the onlookers, he exorcizes an "unclean spirit" from a man in the synagogue of Capernaum:

> And they were all amazed, so that they questioned among themselves, saying, "What is this? A new teaching? With authority he commands even the unclean spirits, and they obey him." And at once his fame [in Greek, "the hearing about him"] spread everywhere throughout all the surrounding region of Galilee. (Mark, 1:27–28)

Thus far Jesus acts very much like a crowd-pleasing orator and healer. But quickly enough he touches the pole of solitude, the loneliness that is the other side of Alexandrian charisma, praying "in a solitary place" until Simon and the rest come to remind him that "all men seek for thee" (1:37). Embarked anew on his public mission ("therefore have I come forth"), Jesus goes to preach in the next town, where he heals a leper,

1. The simultaneous continuity and break with the past is, of course, already present in the Gospel presentation of Jesus as the Messiah, the summary and realization of all past traditions. But the familiar division between B.C. and A.D., with its constant reminder that time has changed utterly, does not appear until the computations of Dionysius Exiguus in the sixth century.

with more success than he has in controlling the enthusiasm of his audience:

> And he sternly charged [the leper], and sent him away at once; And said to him, "See that you say nothing to any one; but go, show your-self to the priest, and offer for your cleansing what Moses com-manded, for a proof to the people." But he went out, and began to talk freely about it, and to spread the news, so that Jesus could no longer openly enter a town, but was out in the country: and people came to him from every quarter. (1:43–45)

In his typically direct way, Mark expresses in this first book the kernel of enigma in the career of Jesus that still preoccupies believers and theolo-gians. Commentators on the New Testament have called the reticence so clear in Mark and reflected with varying strength in the other Gospels the "messianic secret," devised by Mark to strengthen the resolve of a young church and its martyrs.[2] It is the "unclean spirits" who are forbidden to proclaim the power of Jesus' healing; only the pure, the martyrs ("wit-nesses" in Greek), should have that privilege. But such an interpretation ignores the extent to which Jesus in the Gospels—especially the synoptic Gospels of Matthew, Mark, and Luke—simultaneously performs public acts of healing even while he rejects the public acclaim that comes as a result of them. Multitudes follow him. But he constantly attempts to separate him-self from them for fear they will "throng him" (Mark, 3:9). In a sense part of the ratification of Jesus' messianic mission for the writers of the Gospels lies precisely in his refusal to assume the normal public preroga-tives of the prophetic healer. Mark preserves the exasperation of Jesus at the crowds much more bluntly than do the later Gospels:

> And he said to them, "Come away by yourselves to a lonely place, and rest a while." For many were coming and going, and they had no leisure even to eat. (6:31)

But the people surge after him nevertheless, as drawn as are the disciples to his dynamic evasion, the mystery of his assertive withdrawal:

> As he landed he saw a great throng, and he had compassion on them, because they were like sheep without a shepherd; and he began to teach them many things. (6:34)

Jesus' audience must be fed by his presence, which supplies them, either in teaching or, in the soon-to-follow incident of the miracle of the loaves and fishes, with the spiritual and physical sustenance they lack. Yet Jesus himself, while he gradually becomes more accustomed to the obligations of this larger audience, never quite feels as comfortable with them as he does

2. The debate over the order of composition in the Gospels does not bear on my argument here, although the development I see does incline me to agree with the tra-ditional view, recently challenged, that Mark was the First Gospel. But even the first must be an interpretation and presentation of what did or was thought to have hap-pened.

with the small circle of his immediate disciples. Almost at the heart of Mark's Gospel appears a deaf man with a speech impediment. Jesus takes him "aside from the multitude" and heals him:

> And his ears were opened, and his tongue was released, and he spoke plain.
> And he charged them to tell no one; but the more he charged them, the more zealously they proclaimed *it;*
> And they were astonished beyond measure, saying, "He has done all things well; he even makes the deaf hear and the dumb speak." (7:35–37)

Here is the paradox crystalized: The deaf will hear, and the mute will speak; but they should not speak of Jesus and what he did to open their mouths and ears. Similarly, in a passage that echoes throughout the synoptic Gospels, Jesus asks his disciples, "Who do men say that I am?" (Mark, 8:27; Matthew, 16:13; Luke, 9:18).[3] When they answer that some think him John the Baptist, some Elijah, and others another of the prophets, he asks, "But who do you say I am?" and Peter responds "the Christ [anointed of God]." Whereupon Jesus again charges the disciples not to tell anyone about it. In the different Gospels, there are slight variations in the phraseology of these repeated questions that underline their crucial role in the effort to understand the place of Jesus' personality in his message. But questions also indicate Jesus' own sensitivity to the problem of his audience—the relation between what he says he is and what others say he is. So too, before Pilate, he refuses to accept the title "King of the Jews" and instead turns the words back on Pilate and his accusers until, in the Gospel of John, Pilate himself becomes an accomplice in Jesus' sensitivity to naming and being named:

> The chief priests of the Jews then said to Pilate, "Do not write, 'The King of the Jews,' but 'This man said, I am King of the Jews.' "
> Pilate answered, "What I have written I have written." (John, 19:21–22)

Once again, we can read the Gospels as much for their indication of what the Gospel writers wanted to record as what Jesus might actually have said. Like Augustus's *Res gestae* or the histories of Alexander, the Gospels preserve the compounded angles of how both an individual and his admirers wish him to be remembered. But what is extraordinary about the man glimpsed through these stories is the capacity of his nature, as perceived by others, to accommodate such a variety of both dreams for the multitudes and interpretations by his more learned followers. The hesitancy with which Jesus accepts the multitudes as a proper audience reflects his apprehension that they will flock more to his person than to his message, more to his career than to his teaching. The Gospels are therefore

---

3. In the Gospel of John, where there is much less doubt about Jesus and his mission, a kindred passage occurs when similar questions are posed to John the Baptist.

essential to any wider purpose: They promulgate the fame of the Messiah at the same time that they emphasize its mystery and its secrets. Without the intermediary of fame—talking and hearing—the teaching will be lost with the death of the generation that heard it at its engendering. The often garbled telling of the immediate story, like the far-flying vulture *Fama* in Virgil's *Aeneid,* must therefore be supplanted by a good fame, a glorification, that arises from the evangelical retelling of the story of Jesus for a particular audience. Already by the middle of the second century, about one hundred years after the death of Jesus, the Four Gospels had been codified sufficiently for a continuous narrative to be fashioned from them. But by the fifth century, they had been separated again, their very divergences and the differences of perspective a testimony to the paradoxes of Jesus' perceived personality. Coincidentally enough, at about the same time that Christian theologians and teachers were beginning to reconcile the different accounts of the life of Jesus, the stoic emperor Marcus Aurelius in his *Meditations* repeatedly emphasized the transience of human striving for glory and the vanity of its celebration:

> See thou dower thyself with this present time. Those that yearn for after-fame [*hysterofemia*] do not realize that their successors are sure to be very much the same as the contemporaries whom they find such a burden, and no less mortal. What is it anyway to thee if there be this or that far-off echo of their voices, or if they have this or that opinion about thee? (viii, 44).

Yet Marcus Aurelius's disdain for "after-fame," with its ironic echo of the "coming fame" that Anchises foretells for Aeneas, has merely reversed the usual Roman public values. Through the figure of Jesus, the writers of the Gospels present a totally different perspective. Unlike the classical celebration of obviously distinguished men by obviously distinguished authors, the evangelists present themselves primarily as simple people, without the conventional marks of literary talent, who were yet able to appreciate the greatness of Jesus, when others did not, precisely because it was spiritual and private rather than ostentatious and public. As the Gospels repeatedly emphasize, it is the essence of Jesus and his message that neither can be appreciated by the normal (i.e., Roman) standards of physical and visual importance. Would you have recognized him, runs the implicit question to the readers of the Gospels, and can you recognize his message within yourself—without fanfare or spectacle?

As much as Horace or Ovid, Jesus and the writers of the Gospels had a strong faith in the ability of true language to outlast monuments as well as the frailties of the body. "Ephemeral all of them, the rememberer as well as the remembered," Marcus Aurelius reminded himself (iv, 35). But in the face of the classical absolute that individuals in history could be remembered or forgotten, Jesus added the historical and transcendent possibility that they could also be forgiven. The Gospels preserved the memory of such forgiveness. As early as Mark, Jesus tells the disciples that the woman who anointed him with costly oil will be remembered when the Gospel itself is retold to others (14:9). Thus, in the evolution of the Gospels, their own status as record is increasingly emphasized. They are both continuous with the Old Testament and a realization of it. Mark first begins to note Jesus' urge to fulfill what has already been written about the Messiah, and his self-conscious establishment of prophetic continuities will be displayed even more elaborately in Matthew, Luke, and John. Matthew begins his book with a genealogy that places Jesus in a line that goes back to David. Reversing and expanding Matthew's order, Luke begins with Jesus and looks back beyond David to Adam. Both passages recall the way Virgil situates Aeneas at the beginning of a genealogy that stretches from the heroes of Troy and the founders of the Julian family down to Augustus. In all three accounts to the uniqueness of the hero rests as much in his ability to inherit and fulfill the greatness of the past as in the uniqueness of his own nature:

> And beginning at Moses and all the prophets, he expounded unto them in all the scriptures the things concerning himself. (Luke, 24:27)

The telling and retelling of the career of Jesus by the Gospels therefore reflects his consuming interest to evade or subsume preexisting categories that might explain and thereby pigeonhole and limit his meaning. Like Alexander or Augustus, Jesus emphasizes that he both justifies and is justified by the great names of the past. But the ways in which he has been foretold increasingly place him less in direct descent from a nationalist past than into a universal human continuity that goes back to the first man. With the overwhelming presence of Rome and the classical model of prestige and public nature, it could hardly have been otherwise. The nature of Jesus is less that of the conqueror or politician than that of the teacher, the man who talks and is heard. The power of his presence cannot be truly conveyed by any visual detail or hardly by any action. It is reminiscent instead of another man of words celebrated and reinterpreted in a series of dialogues and stories—Socrates—who also aimed to draw out the hidden connections of reality in a language that he chose not to write down. The contemporary figures who most repelled Jesus are therefore those for whom ostentation of both piety and thought substituted for reality: the Pharisees who pray in the streets; the scribes and the grammarians who love to be noticed in public. Jesus expresses his authority instead through a reticent, almost anonymous, wisdom, couched in paradoxes and parables that entice the hearer and the reader into an act of interpretation and understanding. The contrast clearly invokes the pervasive Old Testament opposition between the Jews and their more powerful, more empire-minded, and more famous neighbors. There, the Jewish power is most often the power of the underdog, of David against Goliath and of the outcast son, Joseph, against his older brothers. Perhaps such will always be the banner of those who write books against worldly power. They assert the authority of wisdom and language, the force of the single prophet, against the arrayed might of empires.[4]

No wonder then that the Jesus of the Gospels spends so much time saying what he is not and so little affirming what he is. The authority by which he acts is neither the authority of Israel nor the authority of Rome. It may draw upon the visions of the prophets and the magic of the healers, but it cannot be explained by them. Nor can the concept of king, with its air of political and social hierarchy, suffice. Even the name of Christ is never accepted directly. Just as Jesus teaches that his followers must give up all their previous family ties to accept him, he also stands outside all such relationships, distant even from his own mother. Although his message is first preached to the Jews, it aims beyond the bounds of a national or tribal community to create a community of individuals bound together by spirit and belief rather than by politics. Blood family will be replaced by psychic family, dynastic continuity by the continuity of the faithful. Such a community is based, not on the Roman infinitude of public rank and distinction, but on the similarity of everyone in the eye of God.

To those around Jesus it is precisely that polemical lack of interest in the lineaments of public position that must constantly be tested:

> And they came and said to him, Teacher, we know that you are true, and care for no man; for you do not regard the position of men, but truly teach the way of God. Is it lawful to pay taxes to Caesar, or not? (Mark, 12:14)

Here is the familiar distinction in its original context: "Render to Caesar the things that are Caesar's, and to God the things that are God's" (12:17). The vehicle of instruction, it should be remembered, is a coin, which Jesus, appropriately enough, does not have but asks to be brought to him. On the coin, of course, is the image and inscription of the emperor, those emblems of authority used so effectively by Augustus and imitated by those who followed him. But whereas the materiality of Roman power and ostentation is reducible to a face on a coin, those who treat Jesus as a divine showman will never be able to discern the substance of what he keeps secret.

To the imperatives of Roman public behavior, the teachings of Jesus contrast a transcendental inwardness, a private devotion that links man and God without the intermediary of public institutions and that focuses not on this world but on the world to come. The controversies over the nature of Jesus that preoccupied so many of the early church theologians therefore reflect as well the essential Christian belief in the importance of

4. When Old Testament heroes achieve public stature, they, like so many distracted Greek and Roman heroes in the accounts of Plutarch, are in danger from the corruptions of complacency, leisure, and the distracting lures of women—David and Bathsheba, Solomon and Sheba, Ahab and Jezebel, down to Herod and Salome.

redefining human nature itself as part of the newly revealed truth. Jesus could not limit himself to the traditional roles of prophet, healer, king, even Messiah, because he brought a message of being as well as a message of belief. The full force of this message is revealed in the Gospel of John, which, more than the other Gospels, both expresses the importance of the way the message is conveyed to the world and most sharply contrasts the Roman style of heroic political assertion with that of Jesus. John's Jesus is not only the man who speaks truth and about whom words are heard around the world. He is the Word itself, the messenger through whom God speaks. The written gospel is therefore necessary to the creation of the church because Jesus cannot authenticate himself directly, but only as the bearer of God's truth:

> If I bear witness to myself, my testimony is not true. (John, 5:31)

The Gospel of John, then, has two functions for *its* audience. By speaking of Jesus, it allows him to avoid speaking of himself, for "he who speaks on his own authority seeks his own glory . . ." (7:18). And by turning Jesus into the Word, it resolves the conflict between the secret and the fame that vexed the earlier Gospels. The witness, the Word, the good news about Jesus becomes more substantial than the man himself, and perhaps even a more dependable way to truth for those whose eyes are clogged with the physical. Actions are certainly important in the present moment:

> But the testimony which I have is greater than that of John: for the works which the Father has granted me to accomplish, these very works which I am doing, bear me witness that the Father has sent me. (5:36)

The danger is still that the audience will stop at the actual figure of Jesus and not understand that God is the real prophet, healer, and miracle worker. It is a mistake that Jesus must continually guard against, even though it is impossible to prevent. After the miracle of the loaves and fishes in John, Jesus has a much more specific worry than the unpleasant attention of crowds:

> Perceiving then that they were about to come and take him by force to make him a king, Jesus withdrew again to the hills by himself. (John, 6:15)

But this withdrawal is not a retreat. It affirms instead that, just as God is the source of Jesus' authority, so God is his only sufficient audience. Those who believe but refuse to confess their belief love the praise of men rather than the praise of God (John, 12:43). So too, those whose belief must be extracted by miracles, says John, are hardly a worthy audience. Doubting Thomas, at the end of John, refuses to believe in the Resurrection until he can feel the stigmata and the wound in Jesus' side. Jesus appears and Thomas is convinced. But his belief is definitely of an inferior sort, for Jesus tells him "blessed are those who have not seen and yet believed," in other words, those who have not seen Jesus but yet have read or heard the Gospel of John.[5]

Paradox and parable press language to release the juices of its inner truth. For the figure who stands for such a new truth, the refusal to perform is a crucial element in his message, as much for himself as for his audience. The temptations in the wilderness particularly focus the evolving assertion by negation that underlies Jesus' teachings. If one is to love and be loved for a human nature owed to God, they imply, then the impulse to be praised for performance can only undermine the acceptance that God has already given. In Mark the temptations by Satan are very briefly referred to (1:13). In Matthew (4:1–11) they take a firm three-part form: turn a stone into bread; prove that God will send his angels to save you from injury and death; receive earthly power and glory in exchange for worshipping Satan. In Luke (4:1–13) the temptation to earthly glory moves up to second place, and in John, whose view of Jesus is more settled, the temptations do not appear at all. Like the crowds rushing to see the latest healing, Satan tempts Jesus to distinguish himself in miracle-working power. But Jesus refuses. Like Pilate, Satan tempts him to distinguish himself as an earthly king. But he refuses. In all three ways, Jesus refuses the Roman trap of distinguishing himself from an ordinary human being. Yet at the same time his career furnishes a pattern of grandeur from his refusals, a theater for his reticence. His seeming lack of premeditation is itself anti-Roman. Unlike Caesar or Pompey setting out to rival Alexander, Jesus seeks a different mode of being, whose only precedent may be the Old Testament God himself: "I am what I am." Because of these refusals, his greatness is more than the greatness of those who perform miracles, attain earthly power, and evade death. The only acceptable audience of such unwillingness to cater to an audience is the storytelling witness of the Gospels themselves.[6]

However institutionalized Christianity later becomes, the example of Jesus always contains a radical potential to sanction withdrawal from public life and its standards, to become an anti-institutional alternative to

5. The emphasis of Jesus and the evangelists on the meaning beyond the visible asserts an authority in contrast with that of temporal power and public triumph. John's view of the person of Jesus is the most visually abstract at the same time that he has the keenest political sense of the situation in which Jesus' message appears. As we shall see, this emphasis on the subordination of the visible representation to the invisible word creates difficulties when Christianity itself emerges as the official religion of the Roman Empire. Then the political and the spiritual leader must dispute for the same arena of action, while the writer, and later the artist, elaborate the claim to invisible authority.

6. Thus, in the parable of the talents (Matthew 25:14–30, similarly in Luke 19:11–28), merely hiding and preserving what has been given is not enough; one must be able to invest and enlarge it. The evasion of earthly power is therefore strengthened in the parable, which otherwise seems to attack the unwillingness to be tried. Similarly, the light that should not be hidden under a bushel is not the light of power but the light of divine truth. So Augustine later identifies the sun with the illumination of the knowledge of Christ rather than the absolute power perceived by Alexander and, for that matter, Constantine.

established orders of all sorts. No wonder that early Christianity appealed especially to those who had no place in the state's hierarchy because of their birth or social position. In a short time Christianity would become the inner truth of the empire, an alternative bureaucracy. Yet the rising influence of hermits and holy men, the establishment of monasteries, and the preoccupation with theology all underlined the potential for division within the Church itself. Such divisions underlay the competitions between power and spirit, the rhythmic interplay of hierarchy and democracy, that mark the history of the Church in the Middle Ages. Christians were in power, although many, like St. Augustine, would find it difficult to reconcile their belief with their public lives. The hair shirt that Thomas More wore beneath his robes as Henry VIII's chancellor symbolizes as well as any other biographical detail the uneasy commerce of private and public in the ages when Church and State were hardly so separable. Did More perhaps wear the shirt to mortify himself for his own desire, his own willingness, to serve earthly power, especially power so flamboyantly public as that of Henry VIII? If so, then his execution for thwarting Henry's desires to circumvent the Christian doctrine on divorce might have been expiation enough.

The impact of the career of Jesus was therefore felt particularly in those areas where individual nature and public nature threatened to conflict. The importance of private spirituality was transfused into all areas of life, even, finally, the political. We have yet to recover from the confusions that the absolute division between the things of Caesar and the things of God has sown. In times of disgust with public men, those who claim a spiritual sanction for their authority seem purer and less personally compromised. When Pope John Paul II visited the United States in 1979, he was hailed as a "true hero" by politicians and television reporters. In the absence of any knowledge about his personal nature, his position as pope gave him an absolute validation that every minor detail—patting a dog, kissing a child, singing a song—seemed to "humanize." Soon enough his pronouncements on Church doctrine revealed his actual beliefs. But even so, with the recording of his songs and the publication of his poems, he tried to maintain the less controversial image that had first attracted such a huge audience, restating in modern terms the desire for transcendent legitimacy that prompted Pope Alexander VI in the Renaissance to have his genealogy traced back to Osiris. So in the wake of Jesus, public men of all sorts develop a kind of guilty conscience about their desire for achievement in front of an audience. Marcus Aurelius may have countered such feelings with stoic belief in human insignificance. But stoicism was a philosophy of the privileged and wellborn. Christianity, through the example of Jesus, turned the effort to bring together public and private obligations, the fame for action and the fame for being, into a struggle no matter what one's origins or social position. More vexings of doctrine and struggles over meaning would come in the future. But the appeal of the Christian message to the individual, its emphasis on the self fashioned through mind and spirit, can be illustrated by the third-century Roman emperor who kept statues of Abraham, Christ, Orpheus, and Apollonius of Tyana in his private chapel; the Gnostic priest whose followers worshiped images of Homer, Pythagoras, Plato, Aristotle, Christ, and St. Paul (Dodds, *Pagan and Christian,* 107); and the Renaissance pope who sanctified and thereby saved so many monuments of Roman antiquity by topping them with statues of saints and martyrs famous for their humility.

Augustine's Confessions: The Glory of Dependence

I speak with the voice of the Church.
—AUGUSTINE, *Sermons*

The Gospel career of Jesus may seem to unfold in isolation. But Christianity necessarily defined itself in relation to Rome and Roman ideas of state, religion, and being—accepting, contradicting, compromising. The story has been told often and from many points of view. But here I want to pick out several aspects of the early history of Christianity that crucially influence the history of fame in our time: the appearance of such new or newly defined types of personal assertion as the saint, the monk, and the hermit; the changing attitude toward the physical and spiritual nature of Jesus Christ; and the stages by which Christianity became the official religion of the empire. The impact of such radical changes in the definition of the public personality is most clearly expressed in the works of the great theologian and writer St. Augustine, a young North African whose early career included a classical education as well as a personal search for religious truth that culminated in his conversion to Christianity through the influence of St. Ambrose in Milan. Augustine became the most influential polemicizer for Christianity in the early centuries of the Church and the theologian most preoccupied with creating a Christian philosophy that absorbed what was best in the classical tradition. At the same time, perhaps necessarily, he was also preoccupied with defining what was specifically Christian against the vast legacy of a Rome that still, less than a hundred years after the conversion of Constantine, might again become the agent of persecution. For the *cursus honorum* of the Roman civil service, he substitutes a course of Christian development, a spiritual journey. In both his *Confessions* (written in his thirties), where he virtually created the literary form of spiritual autobiography, as well as in the *City of God* (written in his seventies), the enormous work in which he contrasts the heavenly city of God with the worldly city of Rome, the issue of personal fame and what it means is central to his thought.[7]

A constant theme in the *Confessions* is Augustine's rejection of his early search for "ignominious glory" through the fame of his eloquence and his turning toward God, who contains all the goals of true aspiration. About halfway through the *Confessions,* Augustine is walking down a street, thinking about an oration that he is to make in praise of the emperor. Then he sees a drunken and carousing beggar. At first he disdains the emptiness of the beggar's self-involvement. But he quickly realizes that his own driven frenzy to succeed and be admired is equally empty, because he seeks only to please his audiences, not to teach them. Similarly, he says, he had come to Carthage, loving to be in love and to be seen by others to be in love. The pride of his career, he realizes, is to be an entertainer. As yet, he is unaware of his hunger for a love that is truly satisfying, the attention of God, which alone can fulfill the longing of the soul for glory.

The love of praise, says Augustine, seems to be virtuous because it excludes or inhibits other vices, principally the love of money. The sins of the flesh, the amassing of riches, the joys of vision that the theater and spectacle supply—all the temptations of the physical world seem easier to vanquish than the aspiration to renown and recognition. After all other temptations have been conquered, men's souls are still tried by "a furnace of human tongues." But every man, argues Augustine, must conquer this Roman pride in the physical and in personal assertion with a Christian glory that subordinates individual desire to divine will. Only through the love of God can man strip himself of the need for public praise and glory. Without God, he thinks only of himself, wondering what others will think of him. With God, he is fulfilled. "You gave me to myself," he says, and characterizes the conflict between the desires of the flesh and the desires of the spirit in his own life as "me myself against me myself." Christian virtue is the way to eternal life, while the desire for earthly reputation leads only to eternal death. Love of God is the way out of self-obsession because only God is complete, permanent, unchanging. He alone rules without pride.

Intriguingly enough, Christ plays little role in Augustine's theology, except as the Word. The primary relation in the *Confessions* is between Augustine and God, and the whole book is a conversation with God about the progress of Augustine's wanderings through error to enlightenment. Christ is less mediator than model, and every individual reenacts Christ's life in his own journey of faith.[8] Augustine, like Paul before him, uses his

7. Although there is no direct evidence, Augustine may have gotten more than a hint for the *Confessions* from *The Golden Ass* of his fellow North African, Apuleius. Augustine certainly knew Apuleius's more philosophical works. His story of the adventures of the man turned into an ass until he is rescued and becomes a priest of Isis offers a fascinating pagan parallel to the Christian journey of Augustine two centuries later. Especially intriguing is their similar disgust with theatrical spectacle and the display of public life.

8. In his book on the fourth century, *Pagan and Christian in an Age of Anxiety,* E. R. Dodds remarks that "The human qualities and human sacrifice of Jesus play

own experience to illustrate the workings of God on earth. But where the conversion of Paul was immediate and catastrophic—the flash of enlightenment on the road to Damascus—the way of Augustine is an evolution of understanding, so slow that, as he says, he spent nine years divided between the private Christian and the public-courting orator and rhetorician.

The Roman public career thus supplies for both Augustine and his readers a basic definition of achievement that Christian doctrine aims to supplant. True self-discovery comes when one rejects the approval of the world and seeks instead the greater glory of dependence on God. The deeds by which one reaches out for justification and praise from others may even be good deeds and the life a worthy life. But love of praise, he writes, collects votes for personal excellence like a beggar taking handouts. What Arrian had called Alexander's "longing," Augustine characterizes as the emptiness of all men searching for what will fill them. Because of his emphasis on the inner as opposed to the outer structure of personal identity, developed in the *Confessions* and his book on the persons of the Trinity, Augustine has been credited with being the first writer to elaborate the philosophical concept of a person.[9] Since E. R. Dodds has also pointed out that *ego* appears as a philosophical term in the writings of the third-century Neoplatonist philosopher Plotinus, an acknowledged influence on Augustine, it seems hardly worthwhile here to weigh rival claims. But it certainly deserves note that the question of what constitutes a person or an individual arises from the philosophical collision of Rome and Christianity. Augustine continually depicts heavenly glory in terms of earthly glory, in part because the *Confessions* illustrate his own turning from one to the other. But the desire for what he usually calls "human glory" is a hunger for the rewards of the world, by which it can never be filled. They satisfy the body, the visible self. But the rewards of God satisfy the soul, which Augustine, reflecting Plotinus, calls the real self. With his rhetorician's love of wordplay, Augustine, like Ovid, implicitly associates the hunger for food (*fames*, "famine") with the hunger for worldly *fama*, and he contrasts them both with the absolute nourishment given by God. The famine of fame hungers for what is insubstantial. The progress of the soul toward

---

singularly little part of the propaganda of this period; they were felt as an embarrassment in the face of pagan criticism" (119). The criticism focused on the amalgam of God and man in the nature of Jesus—a central issue for Christian theologians even after the establishment of the Christian Empire. Augustine particularly is less interested in the historical details of the career of Jesus and the Incarnation than he is in the Trinity and the relations between God, Christ, and the Holy Spirit. In the Old Testament his favorite texts are the praises of God in the Psalms and the exposition of creation and the beginning of things in Genesis.

9. In *Augustine on Personality*, Paul Henry, a Jesuit theologian, argues the novelty of Augustine's "analysis of the philosophical and psychological concepts of person and personality. . . . I very much doubt that any philosophy—left to its own devices—would have developed a concept of man or personality—except it be in the Western Christian world or in one influenced by Christianity" (2, 7). For a full discussion of these issues, see O'Connell, *Augustine's "Confessions"*: "[For Augustine] the real 'I' is a soul, fallen into a body, the resulting amalgam being a 'man' " (24).

God is a gradual process of understanding what it is one truly yearns for. Real appreciation, truly filling, truly satisfying, occurs only when the audience is God.[10]

Augustine's City of God: Pilgrims in the World

At the beginning of his life of Demosthenes, Plutarch, the stoic priest of Apollo, denies the saying that no one is happy who has not been born in a famous city. Virtue, says Plutarch, grows where it is rooted in a suitable mind and nature. Only in the mind can the qualities that make for true happiness be found. The city, the public context of such virtue, is therefore of only secondary importance. Plutarch's philosophical indirection barely veils his attack against the necessary centrality of Rome as the only place where renown and therefore achievement and honor are conferred. But for Augustine, writing some two centuries later, even those virtues that Plutarch shows are common to both the great Greeks and the great Romans are not worth praising. In his lifetime Rome has been subject to periodic attacks by barbarian tribes that culminated in the sack of Rome in A.D. 410. No longer could the myth of eternal Rome be supported. What had replaced it? And what had replaced its claim to being the exclusive theater of human glory? Constantine, by founding Constantinople in 323 as a Christian capital, had already set up an urban alternative to the arena of Roman glory. But the precedent of Constantine and later Christian emperors was not especially soothing to Augustine. They are praised in the *City of God,* but their example is less convincing than the contrast between the goals of Christianity and those of Rome. Paralleling sacred and profane history, Augustine points out that both Romulus and Cain murdered their brothers, and both were known to history as the founders of great cities.

In the *City of God,* begun shortly after Alaric's sack of Rome, Augustine attempts to remove the human city entirely as a focus of ambition—since, as he says, God is in no one place—and to replace it with a city not of this world. Absolute dependence on the approval of God thus compensates for the necessary and constant pilgrimage of the Christian on earth.

> He spurned an earthly throne and the pride of it. This interpretation of "the chair of pestilence" is a legitimate one, because scarcely a man is immune from love of power or desire for human glory, and pestilence

10. One of Augustine's analogies for the loss of God is the loss of the loved one *looking at you.* See Brown's *Augustine of Hippo* for an excellent discussion of the theme of praise in Augustine's works and the desire for God as a desire for completion.

implies a disease so widespread as to infect all or nearly all (*Psalms*, 21).

So Augustine begins his interpretation of Psalms by commenting on the enumeration that the first psalm makes of the ways a man might be blessed. But the man who seeks heavenly glory rather than earthly is not therefore to be silent, nor does he lack models by which to measure his own achievement. Like Seneca and the Stoics, Augustine invokes Socrates as a forerunner for the Christian philosopher, not only for his influence on Plato, but also for the example of his life—the wise man persecuted by the state. The example of Socrates is particularly pertinent to the *City of God* because his crime was the corruption of youth by undermining the pretensions of the state to be the only bestower of renown. In its place he substituted a state that arises not from the urge to political or military glory but from the search of mind for virtue and truth. For Augustine, the Ciceronian "new man" in the state was irrelevant. His goal instead was a new life apart from the state—a nonpolitical and nongenealogical ennobling of the individual soul through God's grace. The climactic event in the life of Christian individual was not the achievement of political or civic honors, but the moment of conversion, in which the old life was left behind and the converted achieved a oneness with God. In place of the Ciceronian and Augustan pride in being named *pater patriae* (father of his country), the career of Jesus illustrated the Christian ideal of the *servus servorum dei* (servant of the servants of God).[11]

The process that led toward conversion was a discovery of the true self within the public shell. If only God can confer credit on human action, there is no need to seek the approval of other men. In such terms the distinction between a Caesar and a Cato, although it exists (Augustine does think Cato is more virtuous than Caesar), hardly matters. Both seek to enlarge themselves in the eyes of some human audience. The array of offices Roman society makes available for aspirants, says Augustine, encourages the theatricalizing of human nature, even when one is nominally opposed to its values. Thus, corrupt or pure, all use the same vocabulary of external reputation to express their separate goals. The Stoics and their heroes must therefore especially be attacked, because their actions appear more virtuous and might lead the incautious into thinking that there are two Romes, a Rome of the spirit that is good and a Rome of aggression that is evil. Later in the *City of God* Augustine will argue that the virtue of the early Romans and their love of liberty led God to reward them with the beginnings of empire. But too quickly they became obsessed with a "lust for domination" and a hunger for praise and glory. In his opening chapters, then, sacred names like Lucretia and Cato are the object of his most ferocious sarcasm.

11. As St. Paul says of Jesus, "[he] made himself of no reputation, and took up him the form of a servant. . . ." Hadrian had already managed to amalgamate these two seemingly opposed concepts by styling himself *"servus servorum Romae,"* servant of the servants of the Roman people (Mackail, *Lesson of Rome*, 25).

The crucial issue is whether suicide, even that of a Lucretia or of a Cato, can ever be a virtuous action. Absolutely not, says Augustine. At best, suicide (the phrase in Latin is *mors voluntaria,* "wilful death") might be considered the act of those with greatness of soul, but not wisdom. After discussing those Christian women who committed suicide rather than be raped, tortured, or killed during the sack of Rome, Augustine moves to the example of Lucretia, the fabled Roman matron who committed suicide after being raped by one of the sons of King Tarquin the Proud. In the traditional Roman story her honorable death was the moral motive force for throwing out the tyrannical Roman kings and instituting the Republic. Her suicide is therefore at the root of Roman republican virtue and represents a nobility, a self-control, even to the willing of one's own death. But for Augustine, she is neither heroine nor model, but "a Roman woman, too eager for praise" (I, xviii–xix). The Christian women who were raped by the barbarians, he argues, were not truly violated. Chastity is a property of the soul, not of the body, and is retained even when the body is forced to yield, just as the body cannot remain pure if the soul is violated. But Lucretia has not even the misguided but sincere excuses of the Christian women at Rome. She commits suicide because she wants to make what is in her heart visible "to the eyes of men," so they don't think she had acquiesced. Her supposedly heroic and virtuous suicide, like Cato's, is therefore just another version of the overweening Roman commitment to the superiority of what can be seen, their need to be public in everything, and their identification of what is public with what is real. The words he uses to describe Lucretia and Cato are *praeclarissa* and *praedictus*—the most visible and the most talked about. A more suitable model for behavior would be Job or, among the Romans, Regulus, the general who, as a Carthaginian prisoner of war, first came back to tell the Romans not to give up the fight, then returned to Carthage to be executed. There, says Augustine, is true self-control and true integrity, from which theater has been purged. The stoic suicide, even though it may be cherished by the pagan opponents of imperial power, is just another species of Roman role playing to be contrasted sharply with the deaths of Christian martyrs and the faithful in general, who are not (or should not be) greedy for their own praise but committed instead to the growth of Christianity. In fact, he concludes, it was not because of personal endurance that Cato committed suicide but because of his inability to endure.[12]

Augustine's attitude toward the Roman desire for personal glory connects directly with his general subordination of body to spirit and external renown to internal integrity. Furthermore, it is cast polemically in terms of a distinction between the kind of individual rewards and individual charac-

---

12. Augustine may also be responding here to the attacks of Marcus Aurelius among others (*Meditations,* xi, 3) on "the futile but seductive exhibitionism" of the early Christian martyrs (Frend, *Early Church,* 13). Frend also discusses the ways in which Christian writers of the period frequently used the imagery of a contest for martyrdom, in which the confessors were athletes (20).

ters fostered by the world-state and those fostered by the world-religion. Like Christ being tempted by Satan in the desert, true goodness (as opposed to temporal greatness) is demonstrated not by any action, but by the *refusal to perform.* To the Roman definition of virtue as military and political action (with its root in *vir,* "heroic man"), Augustine opposed virtue as a characteristic of the soul.

Writing: The Alternate Empire

> I understand, said Glaucon: you mean this commonwealth we have been founding in the realm of discourse; for I think it nowhere exists on earth.
>
> No, [Socrates] replied; but perhaps there is a pattern set up in the heavens for one who desires to see it and, seeing it, to found one in himself. But whether it exists anywhere or ever will exist is no matter; for this is the only commonwealth in whose politics he can ever take part.
>
> —PLATO, *Republic*

Augustine's argument for the virtue that brings eternal life intriguingly resembles an artist's belief in the vindication by posterity. Virgil and Horace had implied that only poets knew who would get true fame rather than the rumors of popular notoriety. Their sentiments are echoed in the opening lines of the *City of God,* but with the voice of the theologian rather than that of the poet:

> Most glorious is the city of God both in this course of time, when she lives from faith wandering among infidels, and in that firmness of an eternal seat, which she now awaits with endurance.

"Most glorious is the city of God," and its glory will be sharpened and clarified by contrast with the now insubstantial glory of Rome, the city of man. In the image of the poet who confers true fame on his subject because he masters time, Augustine has envisioned a God who controls both time and the order of things, who should be worshiped not for what help he can be on earth, "but for a happy life, which can only be eternal." Roman history is thus not the only way to understand time. Instead there is a continuity beyond the families and classes of Rome and even beyond earthly history in which the city of God both includes and transcends the city of man.

The human tradition that most truly diverges from the Roman is the genealogy of wise men, prescient writers, and prophets who have now deposited their inheritance in a line of Christian bishops. When Aeneas was at Rome, says Augustine, Labdon was a judge in Israel, and when Romulus was king, the Seven Wise Men flourished in Greece. Whatever his distrust of the Roman effort to be first, Augustine, in his history of great men who did not wield political or military power, emphasizes priority in time. While he praises Socrates and Plato, he also insists that prophetic authority is older than philosophical authority: Moses lived before Orpheus; Abraham lived before Isis. But the evidence of both prophetic and philosophical tradition comes crucially through their writings. So too, the lasting virtue of Rome exists primarily in its writers, especially those whose values can be interpreted against or apart from those of the state and the civic religion. Virgil is important because he prophesied the coming of Christ, Cicero because he dealt with issues vital to Christian philosophy. The city of Rome might fall, but whatever inner truth that structure contained would be preserved for the ages by its writers.

The question of the proper uses of a literary language is crucial to Augustine because he, like so many other great writers of the early centuries of Christianity, was attempting to merge a classical education with Christian revelation, rather than merely leave one behind to embrace the other. Without wanting to reduce Christian doctrine to a collection of metaphors for the life of writing, one can still notice the influence of literary habits of mind, especially on men trained in the Latin classics and attuned to the assertions of Cicero, Horace, and others that they will live forever in their works. Christ for Augustine is the eloquence of God and therefore the source of a new and polemical use of language. Augustine's attack on the Roman concept of public fame is therefore interwoven with an attack on the Latin language of public fame as well. Since the true virtue and the true act of will is less in action than in resistance, less in visible worth than in personal integrity, the words themselves must be redefined.

Unlike the pagan religions, both Judaism and Christianity emphasize the written word as their prime connection to both God and history. In the early centuries of the Church, the revision, clarification, and translation of Scripture supplied a format for arguments between Christians and Jews and within Christianity itself about the true meaning of the word, once it has been given. This community of exegesis was founded on the existence of a common text, the Bible. Christ as the Word and Christ as the Divine Teacher were figures that iconographically intensified the preoccupation with the authority of interpretation. In the controversies over the nature of the Trinity that brought about the early Church councils, the importance of the Christian writer—the controversialist, the verbal witness—was clearly celebrated. By the fourth century the pagan consul Symmachus, who was Augustine's sponsor to Ambrose, knew the importance of literary ability to a young man's advancement in the world as well as did St. Jerome, Augustine's almost exact contemporary, who tells of a dream in which God accuses him of being not a Christian but a Ciceronian (*Letters,* XXII). At the end of the century, Jerome published a book called *Concerning Illustrious Men*—a chronicle of short notices of 135 Christian writers, based in format on Suetonius's account of the Latin poets—while pagan authors were offering the *Aeneid* in competition as a pagan Bible.[13]

In our own time, when so many books are public events that externalize and sensationalize virtually every aspect of private life, it may be difficult to recapture a state of mind that appreciated the personal and spiritual possibilities of literature. The Church itself had pioneered the parchment codex—the ancestor of the modern book—as a cheaper and handier alternative to the papyrus scroll and the vellum tablet. By the time of Augustine, the codex had become the dominant format. Passed from hand to hand, the book embodied the alternate empire, where authors and authority were both invisible, and words served to bring the Word to men. Since man's knowledge is incomplete, Scripture is open to a variety of interpretations. Yet none of them—like Augustine's many reinterpretations of the meaning of creation in Genesis or his fascinating series of metaphors for the Trinity— aims to contradict the other. They represent instead the various ways the divine message is perceived. It is an act of perception, a stepping away from the earthly blocks to divine knowledge, that the spiritual book particularly helps bring into being. The meaning of the spiritual may lie in realms to which language finally has no access. But language can still show the way beyond the mere names of things. At one point in the *Confessions,* Augustine makes much of the fact that Ambrose, his mentor, could read without moving his lips. So too, the clarity and simplicity of Scripture reached inside the reader, by way of the book, bypassing rhetorical gesture and external display. Love, says Augustine, is the connective force in the universe, and the love a writer has for his work is like the love of God for his own creation, and for himself in his creation. The proper use of language enables the Christian writer to emerge from mere self-obsession into an obsession with God. Instead of being an assertion of one's uniqueness, writing, properly understood, allows the writer to displace the urge for his own fame, instilled by pagan tradition, into an urge to glorify God.

But an essential part of the glorification of God was the celebration of those who followed their own paths to God's word. If the basis of conflict was the question of man's nature, how better to carry on the polemic than through biography? In periods of national expansion like the English nineteenth century, the outpouring of biography affirms a pattern of heroism through exemplary characters and careers. In the fourth century A.D., the lives of Stoics and saints similarly asserted a new way of being. Pagan and Christian both seemed hungry to contemplate the shape of a life unbeholding to what public Rome had defined as satisfaction. The ferment of being was extraordinary, and the search for precedent charged with passion. In tandem with the celebration of the first Christian emperors arrived the polemical focus on the solitary in the desert, struggling with the devils of

13. In fourth-century Rome, where Augustine went to make his fortune, Christians and pagans worked together and in opposition like members of competing political parties. A new young man of high intelligence could be a plum to either group (Bloch, "Pagan Revival").

selfhood. Eusebius, the close associate and biographer of the emperor Constantine, says in his history of the Church from the days of persecution to victory under Constantine that the first recorded Christian hermit was Narcissus. The name, he might have added, signified less the love of his own image than his combat with all the fleshly degradation that image implied. So, in his own effort to show how Christianity had brought pagan philosophy to fruition, Eusebius typically pruned away all the individualizing detail that rival pagan panegyrists were emphasizing in their heroes, and took time as well to attack a biography of the second-century pagan mystic and wandering teacher, Apollonius of Tyana, in which the writer claimed that Christ was just a pale reflection of the virtues possessed by Apollonius.

At about the time of Augustine's birth, a crucial step in the controversy was taken when St. Athanasius published his life of St. Antony, the archetypal desert saint, who recapitulated in painful detail Christ's temptation in the wilderness. Many historians have pointed out that Christian writers like Athanasius invented the saint's biography as a literary form. The pagan model for history was still political and military, although the lives of philosophers (written especially for followers) supplied a precedent. It is intriguing to note, however, that in the wake of the biography of St. Antony, a pagan counterattack in the form of similarly admiring lives of famous sophists had been mounted. In such an atmosphere of sharp argument over the spiritual and social basis of human nature—and with the attempt of the emperor Julian the Apostate (361–363) to restore the imperial status of paganism fresh in mind—Augustine necessarily searches outside the context of Rome not only for an alternate definition of personal nature, but for alternate heroes as well. Socrates is one such hero, as he will be through the ages, whenever the genealogy of the wise is preferred to that of the powerful. But Socrates has another virtue for the writer, like Augustine, who yet wishes to go beyond the conventions and traditions of language: Socrates never wrote a word. He lived his philosophy and he spoke it. For Augustine, in transit from the "lies" of Roman eloquence to the simple truth of the Christian Word, such a model is especially attractive. Similarly, in the *Confessions* an important moment occurs when Augustine hears for the first time of the life of the unlettered St. Antony.

A fellow African visits Augustine and, noticing a copy of the *Epistles of St. Paul*, begins to tell Augustine about Antony. First, he relates how he came to discover the existence of Antony. Accompanying the emperor to the chariot races at Trier, two of his friends happen into a little house, inhabited by Christians, where they find a book in which the life of Antony is told. Immediately upon reading the book, they are inspired to imitate the life of Antony. Discovered by two other friends, one of whom tells the story to Augustine, the two converts affirm their decision and immediately leave their imperial employment to go with God.

Augustine's friend approves what the converts have done, even though he does not follow them. Like Augustine himself, who has spent years creating a public career while maintaining his spiritual ties to Christianity, the friend does not feel compelled to make such an absolute step. But for Augustine the story reveals the face of his own corruption. Antony stands for a different life, opposed to the rewards of the traditional Roman career, yet coherently and movingly told in a book. What particularly amazes Augustine about Antony is that he should have lived so recently, "almost in our own times." And the converts phrase their embrace of Antony's model in terms with which Augustine enthusiastically sympathizes:

> What do we hope to gain by all the efforts we make? What are we looking for? What is our purpose in serving the State? Can we hope for anything better at court than to be the Emperor's friends? Even so, surely our position would be precarious and exposed to much danger? We shall meet it at every turn, only to reach another danger which is greater still. And how long is it before we reach it? But if I wish, I can become a friend of God at this very moment (167–68).

The goals of political and military ambition are both more perilous and more limited than the service of God. It is a key moment in Augustine's journey toward his final conversion, and it occurs through the discovery that Augustine's friend has made of the power of the book:

> After saying this he turned back to the book, labouring under the pain of the new life that was taking birth in him. He read on and in his heart, where you alone could see, a change was taking place. His mind was being stripped of the world.

Through the literary version of the life of St. Antony, the old world can be left behind and the new life begun. Neither a document nor an inscription, the book helps perpetuate instead the communal fellowship that first brought the good news of Christianity. In the midst of the world, such a book can make one realize the greater reward in being a friend of God than in being a friend of the emperor. Unlike the vain eloquence of the orator and the empty learning of the rhetorician, it connects its reader with a world of timeless truth.

The Augustinian sense of the individual as a voyager in the world and of the Christian in search of a home in heaven is thus imaged in the writer's relation to his work, whose goal is not to justify the state but to discover the soul, the true self. Augustine is both an introspective writer for whom reinterpretation of one's own past is a way to truth and a theologian who is fascinated by the question of human will and the analogies between classical and Christian literary traditions. His work explores the connections between the obligation of man to discover himself, the writer to express himself, and God to create from Himself. In their combination they revolutionize the Roman conception of what it means to be a person, let alone what it means to be an important person. Gathering strength from the Jewish preoccupation with the actual text of God's words and the special status given to those men who conveyed those words to the world, the

Christian writer could draw as well on the model of the Roman writer's special, private, perspective. Rather than a way to entertain and to win preferment on earth, mastery of the word would lay up honor in heaven. The Cicero of the Church Fathers is neither consul nor orator but philosopher, who, in the words composed outside of public office, defined philosophy as oration in exile—an attractive formulation for those making the transition from Roman to Christian audiences. As Augustine and others argued, there were two parallel histories, the sacred history that issued in Jesus and Christianity and the profane history that produced Rome. But with the privilege of establishing such traditions goes the privilege as well of deciding who belongs to them.[14]

The Self-sufficiency of the Holy Man

Apa Epiphanius was a Monophysite Coptic anchorite who took up residence in the portico and courtyard of the Eleventh Dynasty tomb of *Dagi* at Thebes in the dramatic half-century that preceded the Arab conquests. His fame became wide-spread and he was referred to as a saint in graffiti.

—LABEL on a case containing a collection of potsherd documents, Metropolitan Museum of Art, New York

In all his writings Augustine is preoccupied with defining the obligations and inner nature of the individual—in relation to God, to the community, and within the self. The discovery of a biography of St. Antony at the heart of the *Confessions* therefore validates and reflects the prime mode of expression. Weakened by the pagan word, the true self had become prey to the world's corruption. Strengthened by the Christian word, the soul would be cleansed, revealed, and made whole. In the *City of God* Augustine remarks that the secret Alexander heard at Siwah was that the gods were really men, kings who had done great works to benefit all humanity.[15] But the Christian god, he continues, is not material in any way. The indi-

14. For an acute and suggestive discussion of the importance of writing and creativity in Augustine's thought, see Garry Wills, "Radical Creativity." Wills calls the *City of God* "a kind of anti-*Aeneid*" (1023) and the *Confessions* "the soul's *Aeneid*" (1024). In the *Aeneid* the burden of history must be shouldered and its obligations fulfilled. In the *Confessions* the excavation of the sinful self of yesterday enables the purity of today. As Wills argues, remembering (especially the act of memory conveyed in words) brings the new self into being. To remember is to transcend. Man must love not the sinful self, but "the recoverable self of possibility" (1025).

15. Augustine says that a "certain Leo" was the priest who told Alexander, perhaps identifiable with Leon of Pella, a Macedonian who wrote a book on the Egyptian gods in the form of a letter from Alexander to Olympias.

vidual moves toward God as he moves away from an obsession with his own materiality. Thereby he nurtures the pure soul, the real self, that part of man most akin to God. For Augustine, introspection was an essential guide to truth. Once he had described the path of the individual soul toward enlightenment, it could become a highway with clearly marked road-signs for the less resolute, who until then had no map, only scattered notes and intuitions.

This was all well enough for a doctrine of spiritual discipline. But what of the operations and action of the individual in the world? If the Roman model of a public career with public honors is rejected for a journey of the soul, that wandering stranger in the world, can the individual live within a society at all? The question is a crucial one because in the century of Augustine's birth Christianity had become the state religion of the Roman Empire. With such official approval, after generations of mixed tolerance and persecution, the possibility of a new prosperity might be difficult to reconcile with Christian injunctions to poverty and austerity. And the conflict would be especially keen for those men of aspiring desires who sought, like Augustine, a fulfillment in this life in order to preach more effectively the greater fulfillment in the life to come. For all the inspiration of the story of Antony and for all the personal journey of the *Confessions,* it remains equally true that Augustine for much of his life was a hard-working bishop: taking care of his congregation, meeting visitors, and continually involved both in the business of his local community of Hippo and (through his books and letters) with the institutional life of the Church throughout the empire. Like the friend who tells him the story, Augustine hopes to nurture the Antonian side of his spirit even while he continues to participate in the world. He would be self-sufficient on earth because he was supported by heaven. Antony and Augustine thus present two prime varieties of the Christian "new man," the one resolutely disencumbering himself of everything that is urban and traditional, the other seeking a new synthesis. Antony's radical Christianity is fine, Augustine implies. But it is the biography that has made it truly effective. Otherwise, like the career of Christ without the Gospels, it would have existed only, if at all, either as rumors or as a dimly understood story.

As Augustine's preoccupation with Antony's "recent life" indicates, every new theory of human nature gathers strength from real examples who embody its otherwise abstract precepts. His polemical formulation of the Christian doctrine of the individual thus owes a clear debt to the appearance in the Roman world of several newly minted varieties of spiritual hero—the monk, the prophet, the hermit, the saint in the desert—all of whom stood outside the usual hierarchies of Church and State. Alexander, the ruler of Greece, seeks out Diogenes the unkempt philosopher and, for all his glory, feels an affinity with this man who has rejected that temporal power. Augustine contemplating Antony is therefore reminiscent of Alexander before Diogenes, a self-absorption shaped by literature and social order facing a self-absorption mindful only of its own torments and triumphs, irrespective of an audience.

Four types of Christian fame might be distinguished in the late days of pagan political power: the bishop who ruled his congregation, the theologian who wrote to clarify Scripture, the holy man who lived apart from the comforts of society, and the martyr whose death bore witness against civic order and for religious truth. Often more than one of these roles was filled by a single person. But the crucial distinction is in their social dimension: The bishop immediately affects his congregation and the theologian enters a larger community of discourse, while the holy man and the martyr crystalize eternal truths unbeholden to society and politics. Augustine, for one, divided the members of the Church into a small group that lived its beliefs every moment and a larger group for whom the smaller was its intermediary and intercessor with God.

The Christian message most subversive to the Roman view of life was the capacity of everyone to receive God's grace. Even philosophically inclined emperors like Marcus Aurelius and Julian the Apostate believed that Christianity was a threat to the existence of any well-run state. Christ had preached a spiritual metamorphosis that called on the individual to leave family and class behind and be connected only to God. But this all-but-explicit attack on the hierarchy of classes, this upending of social privilege by a vision of true reward and glory in heaven, suited as uneasily with Church hierarchy and discipline as it did with pagan civic virtue. Many Christians, their beliefs shaped by hostility to Rome, could easily conclude that there could be no civil society of any value at all. If the perfect society was in heaven, anything on earth might be a corrupt version of it. With the coming of secular power, the testimonies of the more celebrated saints and martyrs must somehow be assimilated and perhaps domesticated in a Church that was no longer persecuted or clandestine but a partner and mainstay in the stability of empire. In the struggle, the individual's search for fulfillment, so conditioned by Roman models, could be satisfied either by turning away from public employment and glory (as did the men who discovered Antony's biography) or (as Augustine did himself) by transfiguring the Roman public man into a different kind of authority. Many writers have characterized the fourth century as a time when Christians and pagans fought their final battles over which party would retain its hold over the imagination of the European world. Crucial to such a contest were men who could combine the sanction of tradition with the force of new beliefs. In fact the inner horizons of Christianity were beginning to attract men who in a previous age would have turned their energies toward achievement in the state. As Arnaldo Momigliano remarks,

> Christianity produced a new style of life, created new loyalties, gave people new ambitions and new satisfactions. . . . St. Ambrose, St. Jerome, Hilarius of Poitiers, St. Augustine in the West; Athanasius, John Chrysostom, Gregory of Nazianus, and Basil of Caesarea in the East; almost all born rulers, rulers of a type which, with the exception

of the scholarly emperor Julian, it was hard to find on the imperial throne.[16]

The most distinct mark of the separateness that brought spiritual power was a philosophical indifference to, an active scorn of, or a defiant struggle with the lures of the physical world. St. Antony alone in the desert became the spiritual father of a monastic movement that was often hardly so isolated from the paths of normal life. Personal asceticism, especially commitments to chastity and poverty, set off even the most influential Church dignitary from his imperial counterpart. In those cities or regions where the imperial order showed little or only a corrupt presence, the local bishop could highlight its deficiencies by his own spiritual integrity. The monk-bishop (like Augustine) was a living emblem of the need for personal purity (in imitation of that of Christ) for the good of the community as well as for the salvation of the individual. In the fourth century, and for some time later, a studious plainness, austerity, even studied unattractiveness in the Christian public figure polemically contrasted with the centuries of Roman pomp and display.[17]

The more extreme the austerity and asceticism of any figure, the more he or she could be considered an emblem of the essentially otherworldly emphasis of the Church. Hermits, anchorites, monks in the desert, holy men like *Apa* Epiphanius, scholar-administrators like Augustine and Ambrose, exemplified the concentration on the spiritual life that formed the bulk of the teachings of the early Church, and would later be invoked to justify its secular power. When safely dead, the more flamboyant warriors against the devil could easily become part of the calendar of saints. But while they were alive, they embodied a potentially antisocial element in Christianity that had been present from the first turning away from Roman standards. The gradual growth of an elaborate Church organization supplied a more cohesive framework for both individual piety and temporal power. But the tensions would continue between the apostles of order and the apostles of inspiration, those who met God through ritual and those who sought him out alone. Within the heart of the institutional Church resided the fragmented purity of the martyr church with its wanderers and outcasts. In the future such individual men and women might be comfortably absorbed into a calendar of saints and at least become local heroes. But in the present they represented a way of finding identity outside the social order, a way that was both part of the original Christian promise as well as subversive to the increasingly established position of the Church as an institution. In the decentralized organization that was the Church before

16. (*Paganism and Christianity*, 6, 9). "Pagan" itself is a word that begins to appear in the fifth century, designating those, especially from the countryside rather than from the cities, who still held to the old religion (*paganus*, "country dweller").

17. The "great Satan" of the secular world is not a rhetorical invention of present-day Islamic fundamentalists. For the hostility between Christians and the empire in this period, see, for example, "Regnum Caesaris Regnum Diaboli" in Cochrane, *Christianity and Classical Culture*, 114–75, and "Lord Caesar or Lord Christ?" in Frend, *Early Church*, 210–35.

it became the official religion of the Roman Empire, the bishop was an authority to his congregation. As the Church expanded, he became a new kind of public man in the life of the empire, whose power derived from his understanding of God's word. Even though the prime authority of the bishop of Rome, the pope, was not officially recognized until the eleventh century, as soon as Constantine abandoned Rome for Constantinople the potential existed for a Roman apostolic succession that by its nature would oppose the dynastic efforts of the emperors. Already, in congregations all around the Mediterranean, spiritual leaders asserted their allegiance to the new authority. "I speak with the voice of the church," writes Augustine or, since the Latin verb is passive, a double deference: "I am spoken by the voice by the church." It was a formula that could serve equally well to condemn Roman modes of public power and self-expression as well as to subdue the anxiety over seeking praise for spiritual virtue.

But in the eras of revolutionary fervor, spiritual politics is often accompanied by a ferocious puritanism about sexuality and money. Like the emperors who were at the top of the social scale, many holy men pushed themselves to some edge of human nature to demonstrate the uniqueness of their particular form of submission to God's will and message. For them, dependence on God allowed a self-sufficiency before the world along with varieties of self-assertion and even megalomania that would be unsupportable by the individual's authority alone. The bishop had transubstantiated the Roman public man; the hermit in the desert denied him any value at all. Peter Brown has pointed out that the depictions of the Christian saint descend from those of the classical man of letters.[18] For the genealogy of fame I am tracing here, the remark is especially apt if we remember the potentially subversive contrast between the classical man of letters and the Roman military politician. Christian criticism of Roman standards of public behavior had also licensed extreme states of being that justified themselves by Old Testament examples of the virtually anonymous, politically powerless, prophet who in times of trouble understands better than the king what is really happening. Such Jewish prophets, like the later Christian holy men, asserted their access to a different history, a different conception of the connections of the world, beyond the capacity of any ruler to perceive. Like the historians, philosophers, and poets of the classical world, they set themselves outside of public life in order to clarify the special insight of their traditions. The burgeoning of their numbers clearly implied how little trust could be placed in traditional public power. Their power was psychic rather than military, political, or economic, and their vows of poverty, their general asceticism, and the often strange paraphernalia of their mortifications (like the column-sitting St. Simeon

18. ". . . the Christian bishop with his open Bible, the inspired Evangelist crouched over his page, are direct descendants of the Late Antique portrait of the man of letters" (*Late Antiquity,* 32). Compare Henry Chadwick's characterization of Pope Damasus, whom Augustine knew at Rome, as a fusion of "the old Roman civic and imperial pride with Christianity" (*The Early Church,* 162).

Stylites) emphasized their purified indifference to the corruption of work-aday human nature.

In an increasingly decentralized world, where neither Rome nor the new capital of Constantinople exercised the old imaginative sway, the holy man linked his local audience to universal truth. On earth such men presented themselves as intermediaries between ordinary men and God, who recommended themselves by their detachment from all activity that seemed normal. Accordingly, their self-stylizations were more than a match for those of many emperors:

> The imperial ceremonial, which attracts the attention of most historians, was but an intermittent flickering compared with the lifetime's work of true professionals at self-definition. In a procession at Rome Constantius II [son of Constantine] stood bolt upright and refrained, for a few hours, from spitting: but Simeon Stylites stood without moving his feet for nights on end; and Macrius the Egyptian had not spat since he was baptized (Brown, "Holy Man," 93).

We might recall here Alcibiades' description in Plato's *Symposium* of Socrates standing stock still on the battlefield for twelve hours working out a philosophical problem. The physical restraint, the self-control, of this type of classical wise man finds its rocky realization in the purity and ostentatious piety of many of the early Christian saints. Like the most image-conscious emperors, the most successful holy men presented themselves as exemplary versions of the individual. The extent of their power was the extent to which their audience could appreciate them simultaneously as intermediaries with God and extensions of themselves. No doubt that in the early centuries of Christianity, as before and since, there were individuals who separated themselves from their fellows without a thought of gaining an audience for their denial. But the history of fame is a history of the changing nature of the audience and the performer. And the first seven centuries of Christianity furnish a rich repository of individuals whose commitment is to an order of merit, a glory, not defined by society. Through the ages such individuals continued to fascinate and inspire both those who had made some accommodation with the world and those, like the writers and theologians, who honed the edge of their own ambiguous marginality on the harsh lives of the self-designatedly different.

Willfully separated from the economic structure of the community by his poverty and socially separated by his chastity and austerity, the holy man was seen as the perfectly just arbiter of local disputes, sought out by supplicants from neighboring towns and cities for advice and council. In Syria, where monasticism was not as influential as the single holy man, crowds would travel miles and gather to hear his latest pronouncements. Untrammeled by the lures of the world, he could see into the heart of things. As Peter Brown remarks,

> He was thought of as a man who owed nothing to society. He fled women and bishops, not because he might have found the society of

either particularly agreeable, but because both threatened to rivet him
to a distinct place in society ("Holy Man," 92).

In his depiction of the holy man in antiquity, Brown insists particularly
on the deliberate inhumanness of the holy man's "self-created" personal
role. But, I would argue, the humanness the holy man both embodied and
by his pronouncements helped nurture was a humanness unbeholden to
society for its origins, even though in effect it could help to revitalize a
fragmented community. The holy man's rise to authority in the Late Roman Empire corresponded to the general shift in Christian doctrine away
from competition or separatism ("render unto Caesar . . . render unto
God") and toward complementarity and community. The spiritual. no
longer opposed to the world, instead became its internal truth. Unlike the
local imperial official or the local bishop, the holy man could connect
that truth directly to the supplicant. His only superior was God. In its
alienation from all social and religious hierarchy, the holy man's spiritual
power maintained Christianity's promise of salvation for every individual
soul, regardless of position on earth. The holy man in his austerity and
mortification may seem deliberately inhuman. But the human possibility he
stood for in the eyes of his clients was an ideal of holiness and wholeness
here on earth. When there is a market for such benefits, of course, there
are many charlatans, mediocre practitioners, as well as experts with a fame
well beyond their neighborhood. Already in the fourth century, Basil of
Caesarea has established a Rule for monks, namely,

> to give institutional form to the novitiate and the solemn profession,
> and to insist on obedience as a means of restraining the excess, the
> competitiveness, and the ostentation of histrionic individuals who
> were bringing the monastic movement into disrepute ("Holy Man,"
> 93).

We may imagine the desert saints wrestling alone with the demons that
threaten humankind, and we may envision the pious monastery far from
the bustle of cities. But their separation was actually much less absolute
than it seems in retrospect. The monastic Egyptian communities might act
as moral shock troops and invade a lapsing village. Despite C. P. Cavafy's
romantic belief that St. Simeon Stylites was "the only man who has dared
to be alone," the column-sitter had constant crowds of admirers. As Brown
points out, "the lonely cells of the recluses of Egypt have been revealed,
by the archaeologist, to have been well-furnished consulting rooms" (93).
With such precedents, it is not surprising to note how often in the history
of the Church we discover the seemingly shy recluse emerge from the
cloister or the cave to become the master of men. Such a career suits the
Church's own ideal opinion of itself as an otherworldly institution. And
when the self-sufficiency of the spiritual loner was buttressed and supported by the alternate society of the monastery, the talented aspirant
could easily challenge the skills of intrigue and manipulation developed by
those schooled in royal or imperial courts.

By the fourth century, the cult of saints and martyrs had spread around the Mediterranean. Like the coins commemorating the Bactrian kings that followed in the wake of Alexander's triumphs, the inscriptions and martyrologies placed the individual in history, making his or her act a universal statement rather than a whim of fortune or circumstances. To some extent the veneration might arise from the martyr's own witness through writing. But much more often the religious community itself retrospectively designated the person to be honored, even in the absence of any information beyond a name or an unearthed pile of bones. In North Africa especially, the desire for the relics of famous martyrs from afar was complemented by an urge to collect the memorials of local saints as well:

> People were not satisfied till every little church on a country estate, every little monastery in the mountains, and every chapel in the town, had a stone bearing a number of famous names (van der Meer, 481).[19]

In time, each locality, each region, and each nation would nominate its own saints to supply an invisible essence that justified its earthly importance. Commemorating the name of the dead saint, martyr, or holy man connected the average member of the congregation with the line of sacred history that the theologians contrasted with the profane history of the city of man. Down even to the present, in the recent revision of the calendar of saints, the impulse to establish an alternate definition of both time and community persists. As one annotator of the lives of saints remarks, "Men, women, and children, black, white, red, yellow, brown, clergy and laity, powerful and helpless, eloquent and tongue-tied—all are represented in this glorious company" (Delaney, 9). The public theater of spectacle and extravagance, so despised by Augustine, was turned into a theater of spiritual example. The labors of Hercules had long since been allegorized by Stoics and Neoplatonists as a story of the conquering of one's lower nature in the battle with demons. The acts of the martyrs, the mortifications of the holy saints, even the intellectual labors of those like Augustine himself, similarly recorded the fiery purgatory of the earthly part so that the true heroic self might ascend to heaven. In the second century Pausanias records the monuments and inscriptions of classical heroism in Greece. But by then the Olympic calendar of athletes was being replaced by the calendar of saints, and Pausanias may have been fighting a pagan rear-guard action. A more typical tourist experience is recorded in the fourth century by St. Silvia, from France, who visits a Good Friday service

19. Van der Meer's section on "The Cult of the Martyrs" in *Augustine the Bishop* contains many details about the development of veneration and Augustine's attitude toward it. He was mainly positive but ferociously read out those he considered to be "false" martyrs, that is, men and women who died for beliefs Augustine believed to be heretical. Augustine himself was made a saint quite soon after his death. Both van der Meer and Peter Brown compare the veneration of martyrs to the celebration of sports heroes. But some distinction should be made between those who seek bodily perfection and those for whom the life of the body is irrelevant.

in Jerusalem. There she discovers that the old custom of passing around the piece of the True Cross for pilgrims to kiss has been discontinued. Now the bishop and deacons hold it quite firmly as the faithful file past, because a previous worshiper had managed secretly to sink his teeth into it and thereby carry home a substantial souvenir (Grabar, 292).

Travel and tourism embody a fascination with environment, the special quality of places and things. Each visit to a different place is a kind of pilgrimage, and from the earliest times tourists and pilgrims have brought back objects to memorialize their less tangible experiences and feelings about places and people that hold them in psychic sway. From Alexander's grand gesture of exchanging the shield of Achilles at Troy for his own to the anonymous muncher of the True Cross, the decline is already apparent. We need hardly mention the crocheted potholders and monogrammed ashtrays of the present. But our own age has also added a dimension longed after by the pilgrims of the past but not yet within their total control: the photograph, which puts us in the picture and allows us to remember not just the place, but us in the place. The more fragile and distant the past, the more valuable becomes the memento. Like so many memories of the passage of time, it is also a talisman against death. Christianity, said the emperor Constantine, is "the struggle for deathlessness." Venerating the acts of past heroes can vitalize a movement still repressed in the present. Without excessive risk, it may also keep a successful movement mindful of a difficult past, with its honorable but no longer quite relevant precedents.[20]

The Genius of the Emperor / The Soul of the Christian

For the most part, the Christianity I have just described professed ideals so often apolitical, internal, and aware at most only of an immediate community, that it seems a model more suitable for revolutionaries than for anyone who must deal with the daily running of an empire. In fact, for the first few centuries of the Church, it was essentially underground and its spokesmen railed against Rome as the great Satan. Marcus Aurelius, the second-century "good" emperor and philosophical Stoic, whose *Meditations* are a striking portrait of the pagan inner life, nevertheless considered the Christians such a threat to the state that he approved the bloody per-

---

20. In addition to his belief in Jesus as the God of Battles and his assimilation of the vision of the Cross over the sun to pagan worship of Sol Invictus, Constantine personally believed that the Incarnation occurred "to remove the torment of death and proclaim the rewards of immortality" (Barnes, *Constantine and Eusebius*, 243). On Constantine's efforts to recast his family in terms of both Christian and pagan (Augustan) models, see Vogt, "Pagans and Christians in the Family of Constantine the Great."

secutions at Lyons. With such hostility so commonplace, what can we make of that strange hybrid, the Christian emperor? In terms of practical politics, the answers may be easy. But I would like to emphasize instead the effort to intertwine what I have characterized as two very different ways to be famous, the Roman and the Christian, in the public character of Constantine, the first Christian emperor. In many ways his effort to combine spiritual and political sanctions will be reflected through the Middle Ages into the Renaissance, down through Charles V, Louis XIV, Napoleon, and the twentieth-century dictators—until that time when the whole idea of a world-monarchy, Christian or otherwise, will have disappeared or utterly changed.

In the crude example of Constantius II not spitting during a ceremony, we see roughly portrayed the way in which a Roman emperor of the fourth century presented himself as the special and defining case of all premeditated social behavior, affirming the nation by both his political order and his symbolic personality. In fact he needed both, since the emperors who depended only on military support were usually as short-lived as those for whom the show was all. As the empire aged and subsequent emperors could count less and less on Augustan *auctoritas,* the elaborate panoply of the Hellenistic conception of the divine monarch (with its roots in the figure of Alexander the Great) furnished at least a ceremonial coherence for the empire. Other sanctions could include a revival of coin types from the earlier years of the empire (like Trajan's), a reenactment of Alexandrian tourism (like Caracalla's run around Troy), and an effort (also Alexandrian in source) like that of Aurelian to establish sun worship as the state religion. In the increasing depredations of the border tribes and nomads against the empire, not to mention revolt from within, an essential part of the emperor's job became the effort to unite in his person all those elements in popular history and mythology that promised victory and unity to the precarious present.

The standardizing and ritualizing of imperial self-importance had always been a traditional part of Roman policy. The difference between emperors lay only in the flair of the individual ruler and his court imagists. What on the individual level might seem to be insufferable self-deification, on the political level could in the right hands amount to an emotional justification of rule that would otherwise be tenuous, if it depended only on one's control of the army. Since Greeks and later even Jews and Christians had considered the success of Rome to be the evidence of divine approval, when the empire or the emperor was less successful, they might reasonably conclude that approval had been withdrawn. For three centuries the more symbol-sensitive emperors drew primarily on either Roman or Hellenistic ideas of the divinity appropriate to a king. The need for an emblem, an inspiration, was as strong as the need for a leader, an actual manager of men and institutions. Anyone with the skill and the shrewdness to achieve the position must have been faced with the moment of wondering what exactly he would do to affirm and establish his power. Up through the

Renaissance and beyond, history was considered an essential part of the education of princes. Perhaps that is why it was so often biographically oriented: One chose among models, or, if one were particularly ambitious, one combined models. It is tempting to envision Trajan and Hadrian (both employers of Suetonius) poring over the *Lives of the Caesars* for both cautionary and exemplary clues.

Destructively enough for their ultimate political interests, however, many emperors seemed intent on demanding an absolute fealty that was difficult to exact. It had been considered a mark of Caligula's insanity that he wanted to place a statue of himself in the Great Synagogue at Jerusalem. But by the end of the first century A.D. the emperor Domitian was insisting that all Roman citizens and subjects swear oaths by his *genius* as an assurance of their support for the empire. The Jews, who for a long while were the only subject people exempted from worshiping the emperor and his genius, had raised several revolts against Roman rule from the mid-first century to the mid-second century. Now, their rejection of the state religion could no longer be considered an innocuous cultural separatism but a potential treason. C. N. Cochrane points out that Domitian persecuted not only Jews and Christians but also pagan philosophers like Epictetus and Apollonius of Rhodes: ". . . Domitian's lust for self-importance entailed stricter control over acceptance of foreign religions by Roman citizens, especially when this might detract from respect to be paid to his own majesty" (215). With a certain grim appropriateness, the reign of Diocletian, just prior to Constantine's, saw the most savage persecution of Christians as well as the most extensive effort since Alexander to introduce Persian court ceremony and dress as well as *proskynesis*. In a related attempt to stabilize the always precarious dynastic situation, Diocletian also created four new offices, complete with resounding titles, to manage the increasingly fragmented empire—an Augustus and a Caesar for the East and a similar pair for the West. By Alexandrian ceremonial, a revival of Roman law, a reordering of administrative lines, and a purging of those he considered to be enemies of the state, he hoped to set the empire once again into the march of history. In 305 he retired because of poor health, but in the hopes that his innovations had managed to raise the imperial office away from factional dispute and dynastic degeneration.

Quickly enough, however, in a series of battles and power struggles, the new Augustuses and Caesars fell out. Diocletian had been the twenty-sixth emperor in a century and it seemed that the old struggles for supreme power were doomed to repeat themselves endlessly. But when a victor emerged, he added an entirely new element to the authority of the empire and that of the emperor. Constantine, the son of one of Diocletian's Caesars, emphasized in both his person and his propaganda that his prowess was due to his favoring of the God of the Christians. The story of Constantine's conversion and the subsequent change in the fortunes of Christianity within the empire can hardly be presented in detail here. But certain themes again shine forth strongly when these events are considered

in the light of the changing nature of public behavior and individual ambition. The question of Constantine's own motivation (beyond personal
belief) has never been definitively solved, nor is the personal quality of his
belief itself clear. But Constantine in some way connected his allegiance
to Christianity with his imperial aspirations for himself and his family. It is
this connection, seen against a background of Christian doctrinal hostility
to the Roman state, which brought intermittent persecutions and tolera-
tions by the authorities, that seems most unprecedented and intriguing.

Constantine himself was primarily a sun worshiper. At the Milvian
Bridge outside Rome he was said to have seen a vision of the cross over
the face of the sun. Constantine then went on to defeat his major rival in
battle and thereby become the Western emperor. The personal acceptance
of Christianity for Constantine was therefore inseparable from his recognition of its effectiveness in military terms. The Roman gods no longer
seemed to watch over the security and power of the empire. Some new
protection was necessary, and Christianity, which had for centuries been
reviled by devout pagans as the cause of all Roman weakness, might now
be considered in the twilight of Rome's power as the only guarantee of its
strength.

What happens when a religion that has concentrated on the private self
goes public and is invoked as a salvation for the state? Marcus Aurelius
could be both Stoic and emperor because of the stoic emphasis on social
duty. Emperor was a social role with as little or as much falseness as any
other. The individual could do nothing about the fate that time had thrust
upon him. But Constantine seems attracted to Christianity because it sanctioned his willfulness rather than his passive acceptance of the tides of
time. Christ was the god of history who would bring favor in the way that
the old Roman gods had supported the heroes of the Republic and the
early empire. In the vision at the Milvian Bridge, sacred and profane history came together. No longer would Church and Empire be at odds; in
the figure of Constantine they would become one.

The Roman emperor was the living symbol of Roman power and Roman
character. But in the reign of Constantine both the center of gravity and
the center of power in the empire shift away from Rome as a specific city
and become vested instead in the empire and the emperor himself. More
than any other event, Constantine's vision of the cross at the Milvian
Bridge marks the change that is concretely affirmed with his founding of
Constantinople where, as Eusebius boasts in his *Ecclesiastical History,* no
pagan worship had ever occurred. Not that Rome totally loses its significance as the city that ratifies true triumph. The barbarian invasions that
begin to plague Rome in the fourth and fifth centuries imply that at least
some aspiring military leaders believe that conquering Rome would make
their names memorable. But the imaginative pull of Rome as the spawning
ground for heroes had definitely begun to flag in a world more and more
resembling the decentralized and weakly urban society of the Middle Ages.
Diocletian, for example, had visited Rome for the first time only two years

before he abdicated. Walking through the Roman Forum today, one realizes that Constantine was in fact the last Roman emperor to have much enthusiasm for the monumental competition that had drained the mountains of their marble. He is still impressed enough with establishing himself at Rome to feature his entry into the city on some early coins; and he later revises and enlarges a basilica in the Forum begun by his defeated rival. The Romans themselves raised the Arch of Constantine to welcome the victor. But as every art historian of the period points out, the arch depends for its decorative work on marble cutters either crudely or energetically outside Roman traditions. Like the movement away from Rome by Constantine himself, the designs are the products not of the capital city but of the provinces. Soon enough Constantine turns toward establishing himself and his family as a new imperial dynasty, beyond Roman precedents.

The rarefied position of the emperor connected him with his heroic forebears, while the immediacy of holy men and women cultivated the spiritual possibility of all. Thus, for good measure, Constantine invoked Alexander as well as Christ as a predecessor and appeared with him on coins. They were a compatible pair because Constantine's god was Christ the warrior, god of battles. Almost one hundred years after the battle of the Milvian Bridge, Augustine's *City of God* attempts to reclaim and reclarify what is not secular and political about Christianity from its then official and established character. In the same way, although from the opposite point of view, Julian the Apostate, in a brief reign that followed those of Constantine and his two sons, tried to restore paganism and classical philosophy as the spiritual essences of the empire. But in the world of political power, Constantine's merging of Roman and Christian sanctions became the basic pattern of kingship down into the Middle Ages and beyond. So flourished as well the pattern of the monarch's disingenuous and ceremonial assertion: I humble myself only before God. (Otherwise, I do not humble myself at all.) The image of the sun, "the unconquered sun," as it is called in Constantinian ceremonial, stands at an intersection between paganism and Christianity. For Augustine the sun represented the knowledge brought by Christ. But in the Alexandrian dimension favored by Constantine, it signifies the presence and power of the all-sufficient leader.

In his brief stand against the tide of the Christian empire, Julian the Apostate revived the idea that Christianity was a religion inimical to the needs and spirit of Rome. In his dialogue *The Caesars,* Julian parades all the great emperors before the gods to argue who was best. His own sympathies are with Alexander, the progenitor and model of monarchical power and personal charisma. The archvillain is Constantine, Julian's uncle, who embraced the religion of the fraudulent magician Jesus. Julian presents himself instead as a philosopher with contempt for those men who claimed to be gods. Both emperors called on Alexander the Great as one of their forebears. But Julian's Alexander was the philosopher in arms celebrated by Plutarch, while Constantine's was the golden sun god. Julian reigned for three years, dying appropriately on an expedition against the

Persians from a lance in his side—hurled, some say, not by a Persian or a Roman but by a Christian. His mission had failed. Within less than a hundred years, only Christians were allowed to serve in the army, to ensure that God would look with favor on any battle Rome fought with its opponents.

Constantine's career as Christian emperor demonstrates the ease with which a spiritual and nonpolitical religion can be politicized when an absolute ruler adopts its definitions of the nature of the individual and the true meaning of history. The worship of emperors is a worship of their dynasty and therefore of the state, while the worship of holy men venerates a potential for spirituality possessed by everyone. But under Constantine the discovery of new relics and the inscribing of new saints assimilated the Christian belief in personal salvation to the political needs of the empire. Constantine's mother, Helena, did her part by visiting Jerusalem, founding churches on the appropriate New Testament sites and, it is said, discovering the True Cross. If the sanction of Roman tradition and genealogy was running thin, the patronage of saints, holy men, and theologians could give the imperial power new vitality and authenticity. For the individual, Christianity might mean a turning away from public life to contemplate the truths of the spirit and the soul. But for the public man Christianity connected his authority to that of God himself. The Hellenistic ceremony that had more and more become a normal part of the public attitude toward the emperor was easily tailored to a Christian belief in the ruler as God's representative on earth. As the realization of both Roman and Christian traditions, Constantine was at once the most unique and the most abstract person in his world. So the historian Ammianus Marcellinus describes the public appearance of Constantine as a kind of human statue unruffled by any particularized detail. The most famous person was the most pure and uncorrupted, embalmed above ground, like the corpse of Lenin in Moscow.

All aspirers to recognition have a sense of their audience and an interest in appealing to it. So much is almost redundantly true. But the greatest aspirants seem as well to have a final unwillingness to believe the approval of any particular audience, an inability to be reassured that drives them on to greater feats in search of their "true" audience. Turning away from any immediate applause, they look for an absolute sanction—God, the past, the people—that allows them to be totally self-willed. When their goals are personal and spiritual, such seekers of ultimate recognition can be saints or great thinkers. But when men with a desire for immediate reward and power assume the mantle of spiritual value for their actions, we often find some of history's most vile tyrants.

The distinction between what should be rendered unto Caesar and what unto God is dissolved by Constantine's adoption of Christian spiritual sanction for imperial policy together with his fostering of his own dynastic ambitions. In a society engaged in perpetual war, the continuity of the society can often be designated as feminine, since it is the men who go out to fight and die while the women maintain the stability and coherence of the laws and traditions for which they are supposedly fighting. Rome is a woman, Athens is a woman, and female gods are worshipped as the embodiment of the history and essence of the city. But this feminine continuity is overbalanced by the male urge to ensure perpetual rule and public importance. In the empire that urge appears especially in the reliance of the emperor on the army. The Julian family line of the Caesars disappears with Nero, but the male, army-supported imperial system remains and prevails, despite the efforts of a few emperors to bureaucratize power and thereby separate the civil from the military. Rome as a city may be feminine, but Rome as an empire is masculine. One might swear an oath by the emperor's Genius rather than by the emperor himself. But only men can have a genius, at least until the Middle Ages (Nitzsche, 3).

When Christianity becomes the official religion of the empire in the fourth century, it has also gone through a doctrinal and historical development that justifies its place in history through a male continuity stretching back to Jesus and the Apostles. (Mary as the mother of Jesus does not become important until some time later.) Each generation gains its authority through having been in the direct presence of the previous generation and, in a way reminiscent of the passing on of Roman imperial power, "adopted" by it. Eusebius, who wrote that Constantine had inherited God's promise to Abraham, composed his *Ecclesiastical History* primarily to give a documented shape to the links between the Old and New Testaments and to harmonize the genealogies of Christ found in the Gospels. Like the genealogies of gods and heroes commissioned and bragged about by Roman politicians, the history of saints and bishops furnished a continuous link for the faithful back to the progenitor himself, David or Aeneas, Jesus Christ or Julius Caesar.

Both Romans and Christians asserted that their traditions constituted the only true pattern of history. Their prime difference is that the Romans (like the Jews) often went through extraordinary contortions to make all the links part of one blood family, while the Christian theory of inheritance was much more spiritual and metaphoric: First, everyone was eligible for the revelation by his mere humanity; then, the task of carrying on the Church itself was in the possession of a much more strictly defined line of Church officials. It is striking that as more and more upper-class Romans converted to Christianity, the doctrines of apostolic succession and asceticism become increasingly the mark of the official and the orthodox. With the conversion of Constantine and the later institutionalization of Christianity within the empire, Roman imperial history and Christian apostolic continuity became virtually identified in their interests. In both, although mothers (like Constantine's or Augustine's) were often honored, women were generally excluded from the direct use of power. It was as difficult for women to be bishops as it had been for them to be heroes.

Christianity, which began as a religion of the private and spiritual life, in its march to official success had therefore quickly absorbed the patterns by which renown was celebrated in the classical world. The Roman general-politician gave way to the Christian bishop-politician. But the modes and strategies of Roman grandeur still dictated, by imitation or by contrast, the shapes of public assertion. Constantine may have converted his mother Helena to Christianity. But she also modeled her hairstyle on that of Livia, the wife of Augustus. More than seventeen centuries later northern Greek villagers dance barefoot over hot coals in honor of Saints Constantine and Helena. At that distance in time perhaps the aspects of emperor, desert ascetic, and the martyr of the faith are difficult to distinguish. As an Athenian sociologist has remarked about the village coal-walkers, "the only thing they all have in common is that at a certain moment they are seized with a lust for the fire" (Gage, I, 11).

When the spiritual definition of individual nature that was at the heart of Christianity was assimilated to the Hellenistic conception of the god-king, the emperor could place himself at the top of two separate hierarchies: the political and military hierarchy he controlled as emperor and the hierarchy of being he crowned as leader of the faith. In the West, Rome was the center of church organization; in the less-organized East Constantine took over the role of controlling both doctrine and hierarchy. Through the centuries Julius Caesar's interest in the office of *pontifex maximus* is reflected and reshaped in Constantine's interest in Church doctrinal controversies and his summoning of theologians and leaders to conferences at Nicaea (near Constantinople) to work out their differences.

Appropriately enough, the prime issues of these first Church councils is the nature of Christ (to what extent human and to what extent divine) and the relation of the members of the Trinity (to what extent subordinated and to what extent equal). Augustine would later argue that the most appropriate analogies for the Trinity were the various functions of one human mind. Constantine's early councils, in contrast, are much more preoccupied by such analogies as the nature of the emperor (to what extent human and to what extent divine) and the relations between Church and Empire (to what extent subordinated and to what extent equal). How could the imperial power assert itself in Church policies without a doctrine of spiritual subordination? Considering Constantine's desire to found an imperial dynasty, to celebrate the sanction of the Christian God for his triumphs, and to establish his personal authority as the sole ruler of the empire, it seems a foregone conclusion that his religious views would favor the superiority of God to Christ and minimize the Holy Spirit. Augustine's image of the Trinity as parts of a single mind illustrates his emphasis on introspection as the way to true belief. Political Christianity, on the other hand, often takes the form of Arianism, in which God specifically preexists Christ, and political authority thus gathers validation through a metaphor of ascending states of spiritual perfection. Even though the orthodoxy of the Church soon becomes the trinity of relations between God, Christ, and the Holy Spirit, rulers and military leaders would still tend toward the hierarchical in their Christianity as well as in their social politics. The "barbarians" who attacked the empire increasingly from the fourth century onward (until many were hired to guard against the attacks of newer tribes aiming to assert themselves), were usually Arian in their new-found Christianity. Like Constantine, Clovis, the leader of the tribe that would evolve into the French, was converted to a Christianity symbolized by Christ, the young captain and god of victorious battles.[21]

The propaganda of public fame usually rests its claims to be unprecedented in a firm foundation of tradition. Christianity had begun by offering membership in a new society unconfined by past loyalties—to family, to city, to state, or to previous gods. Yet by the time of its establishment as a central institution of the Roman Empire, it could turn in two directions: toward the spiritual expansion of the individual and toward the spiritual justification of the ends of whatever political leader could best use its imagery. Thus were sanctioned two very dissimilar attitudes toward public renown, recognition, and power: the one more internal, spiritual, and personal, which emphasized the individual relation with God; the other more external, hierarchical, and authoritative, which emphasized God's approval for whatever the ruler thought best.

These two faces of Christianity, personal and political, are imaged in the two Christs—Christ in the desert rejecting the temptations of the Devil, and Christ in majesty at the top of the temporal as well as the spiritual hierarchy. Julian the Apostate's rejection of Constantine's Christianity is thus also a rejection of Constantine's idea of the emperor. Appropriately enough, to match the two Christs, there seemed to be two Alexanders as well, the victorious general and the introspective but charismatic leader. In the imagery of the great, both Christ and Alexander could therefore be invoked either as unique human beings or as the fountains of institutional power. In these terms, the Christian emperors took on the mantle of a Christ who validated their own separation from their subjects, while Julian, the philosophic pagan, tried to humanize and demystify the emperor's person by such self-mocking devices as a dialogue that poked fun at his own straggly beard. In the power struggles of history, such self-awareness is rarely a mark of success; it belongs more to the realm of literature and art than to that of politics and military power. The double nature of Christ, like the double nature of Alexander, shows the human hankering for a leader who can be both exemplary and individual at the same time. Yet vulnerability is rarely appreciated in a leader, especially at those times of disruption and chaos when followers are looking for someone more controlled than themselves to order events. Who can be sure whether or not the imagery of self-control, the Constantinian statue, the saint standing on one foot, has anything to do with real self-control? But so long as leaders are viewed from a distance, the equation will be made.

"By this sign you will conquer," a voice is said to have told Constantine when he saw a vision of the cross athwart the sun before the battle of the

---

21. Antony emerges from the desert to support the anti-Arian party at Nicaea, which is led by Athanasius, the author of the biography of Antony read by Augustine.

Milvian Bridge. But the model of fame embodied in the figure of Jesus and affirmed by Christian doctrine was not one of the city and the center of things, but of the desert, the lonely places, the edge between matter and spirit. Fulfilling all prophecies, yet evading the grip of preexisting categories of public behavior, Jesus embodied a fame compounded of vulnerability, marginality, and powerlessness—a polemical denial of everything his audience had both admired and feared in the traditional imagery of public men and public institutions. For a Church now emerging into the glare of public approval and power, it would remain an ambiguous legacy.

IV

THE INTERCESSION
OF ART

The Imagery of Invisible Power

[Christ] is the image of the invisible God, the firstborn of every creature. . . . And he is the head of the body, the church: who is the beginning, the first born from the dead; that in all things he might have pre-eminence.

—*Epistle to the Colossians*

As we shall see, Christian imagery in the early years of the Church maintained its commitment to the superiority of invisible power. But what could be the public imagery of Christianity when in the fourth century it became the new state religion? In the history of the Christian Church that Eusebius wrote under Constantine, he praises the "fame" of the Church and its growth through persecution and martyrdom to its present high status: As far back as Tiberius, he says, even emperors had heard about it. But then the Church existed in private homes and other unostentatious places. Now, as befitted its new status, it began to move into public buidings, many especially constructed by Constantine and other high officials to absorb columns and building blocks from torn-down pagan temples. In the politically repressed martyr Church, the revelation of Christ was the great secret to be nurtured away from the glare and danger of worldly places. But with the establishment of Christianity as the state religion,[1] the Messiah from outside earthly history is rehoused in the form of an honored, powerful, and concrete public institution. How then could Jesus—with his vision of the invisible world to come, with his inclination to the greater significance of words rather than objects or images, and, most of all, with his scriptural unwillingness to be pinned down as healer, miracle worker, king, or even Christ—how could such a figure be depicted?

1. It has frequently been argued that all Constantine (emperor, 324–337) and Julian (emperor, 361–363) did legally was to declare freedom of choice in religion, although Constantine clearly favored Christianity and Julian tried to revive paganism. In this interpretation, Nicene Christianity became the "official" religion of the Roman Empire in 381 under Theodosius I (emperor of the East, 379–395; emperor of the West, 392–395), who then banned all forms of pagan religious practice in 391. For a detailed argument that Christianity was made "official" under Constantine, although he did not enforce all his prohibitions against pagan ritual practices, especially in the West, see Barnes, *Constantine and Eusebius,* especially 210–11.

The Face of Jesus

"Whose is this image (*eikon*) and superscription?" says Jesus in the Gospels, pointing at the coin with the face and name of the emperor to illustrate his distinction between the things of Caesar and the things of God. Such a distinction accorded well with the Old Testament injunction against graven images and idols and reflected the absence in Jewish areas, observed by Tacitus, of statues to either human or divine figures (*Histories*, 274).[2] In contrast with the emperors and rulers who carved and coated the world with their faces and their triumphs, the Jesus of the Gospels is the anointed teacher who uses the material world only to illustrate his spiritual messages and whose physical features are never specified at all. Thus the impact of the career of Jesus on Roman concepts of fame is clearly reflected in the changing ways Jesus himself was viewed by artists, whose conceptions drew as much from the attitudes of their patrons and audiences as from their own ideas. The transmutations of the face of Jesus through the history of Western art respond so directly to the changing pressures of religious doctrine, political circumstances, and artistic method that we might easily conclude that he had died not so that the uncertain might attain certainty but so that their uncertainty might yet be fruitful.

Visual imagery in early Christianity was of relatively little significance, when it existed at all. Only a few groups felt the necessity to have such images, and many early theologians, following Old Testament injunctions, considered them blasphemous encouragements to idolatry. The Gospel of John, with its identification of Jesus as Logos (Word), especially supported those for whom the central message of Jesus was a turning away from the material world and its rewards. The early Church thus emphasized individual witness within the community of the faithful and actively discouraged pictorial display—a practical necessity in the face of persecution as well as a theological principle. In such a context, for example, an inspirational visual object like the Shroud of Turin, with its supposed imprinted image of Jesus, would have no real meaning. Until the controversies between iconoclasts (image breakers) and iconodules (image worshipers) that arose some centuries later, no one would be interested in it. In some basic sense it could not have been seen even if it were authentic. Only after centuries of experiencing the varieties of faces and interpretations of Jesus, as well as a series of political upheavals and persecutions that turned on the question of the proper use of religious images, could an eye trace the figure with any assurance.

The essence of Jesus might at first have been his verbal message and his spiritual presence. But the pressure toward the evolution of some accompanying visual imagery mounted as the Church itself expanded. Repre-

---

2. Tacitus's remark appears in the midst of a violent attack on Jews and their cultural practices.

sentations of Jesus and his life began to make their appearance in places of worship, especially, as was the classical custom, when the faithful were buried and friends came periodically to pray and share a celebratory meal in the catacombs and cemeteries where the passage to another life was properly commemorated. As the number of pagan and Jewish converts increased, the bareness of the Christian place of worship began to be filled with images that drew upon their already established pictorial traditions and reproduced them with very few changes. Often the figure of Jesus himself was missing from such scenes, which featured instead Old and New Testament examples of God's intervention and deliverance: Shadrach, Meshach, and Abednego in the fiery furnace; the healing of the paralytic man; and the raising of Lazarus from the dead. The message of such scenes to the mourners was God's care for the faithful rather than the nature of the person who had brought God's message to man.

Both pagan and Jewish converts to Christianity had been accustomed to representational images as a frequent element in their previous religious experiences.[3] In their new religion they often looked for and helped create the same kind of ritual support. Throughout the history of fame, the new hero both imitates and supersedes the grandeur of the past by being garbed in its most striking attire—Alexander as Achilles, Augustus as Alexander, Charlemagne as Augustus, Napoleon III as Charlemagne. But because the early Church rejected worldly power, the Roman influence on the depiction of Christ comes not from the politics of the city or the power of the army but from the poetry of pastoral nature. In these first images on church or catacomb walls Jesus is a youth, an ephebe, a beautiful young man with a beardless face and golden hair, or an aristocratic countryman, sometimes sitting on the ground, more often standing with a lamb resting on his neck—the Good Shepherd. Similarly, he is elsewhere depicted as Orpheus, soothing the animals with his music, appealing through sound rather than sight, touching the inner life of his listeners. Even into the fourth century, when the newly official status of Christianity was accompanied by new images of Jesus, the beardless youth continues to appear, invoking through his poetic and literary associations the possibility of a deliverance that is allied with the eternal spirit of the countryside rather than the history-making activities of the city. Jews might understand such a figure as a variation on Moses—the Jew turned Egyptian aristocrat who gives up his status to lead his people to freedom. For Romans this Jesus carried as well the virtues of the pastoral retirement celebrated by Horace and Virgil.

Jesus as Orpheus, Jesus as the Good Shepherd, Jesus healing the sick— such images satisfied for a time the need of many early Christians for a

3. Although Judaism is generally considered to be a religion that avoids representational imagery, it has not always done so. The third-century synagogue excavated at Dura-Europos, for example, is lavishly decorated with Old Testament scenes, much more so than a nearby Christian church, which, however, had a more clandestine existence.

hero portrayable in terms of the heroes of the past, even though immeasurably superior to them. No historian of early Christian art has yet come up with a clear evolutionary development in the faces of Jesus; few have tried, and most have denied that it is possible. As Christians began to come from wealthier classes with more elaborate cultural traditions, other faces began to appear, especially a bearded Jesus with a high forehead, well-dressed in the style of a classical philosopher. Such an image corresponded to the Gospel emphasis on Jesus the teacher and also served as a visual analogue for the efforts by Christian theologians to demonstrate the intellectual respectability of the new religion through a genealogy for Jesus that went back not only to Moses and Adam, but also to Plato and Socrates. By the fourth century, scenes from Jesus' evangelical career became more common, although they generally depict moments related to rituals like baptism and the Eucharist. The cross now appears as both emblem and object. But scenes from the Passion and the Crucifixion are (from our point of view) conspicuously absent, as is any version of the Last Judgment. They would not be prominent for some time. To see Jesus teaching his Disciples and handing down the law fulfilled the promise of a new life to the faithful. The greater meaning later generations would discover in his death did not yet appeal to believers for whom he was the inaugurator of a new age.

The versions of Jesus I have sketched support private devotion to a figure whose transcendent nature has nothing to do with earthly status. With the toleration and then the establishment of Christianity as the official religion of the empire, new images appear—the warrior Christ of Constantine and the imperial Christ (or Christ in majesty) of the emperors who follow Julian the Apostate. If Jesus was worshiped by the emperor, how could he be any less powerful? The earthly triumph of his heavenly glory was to be expressed in images of earthly power, and the motifs nearest to hand were those that had traditionally been the privilege of the emperor himself. So the Jesus of the Gospels, whose prime impulse seems so often to be to escape mass adulation and fame, by the fourth century begins to be depicted with the greatest hyperbole and luxury available. A church now above ground and gaining strength had its new importance visually proclaimed by Constantine's program of building, not only in Rome, but also in Constantinople (called "the new Rome") and Jerusalem. In the interests of imperial power, the obeisance due to supreme authority on earth and in heaven was visually located in the image of Christ as lord and king. When Constantine built a church over the traditional site of Jesus' tomb and when Eusebius in his *Ecclesiastical History* boasted that the emperor Tiberius had heard of Jesus, the outsider who had preached a different definition of power and personal nature was garbed in the traditional robes of Roman celebrity. To the more intimate and occasional images of the early centuries of Christianity was added a new image of Jesus as a Hellenistic divine ruler. Like the emperor, he was distant from his subjects, and his now more exacting, measuring, and sometimes crueler face hung high above the heads of the faithful, inscribed on the inner domes of the newly lavish churches, surrounded by his disciples, saints, and bishops, like an earthly ruler in his court.[4]

From the intermingling of the Church's destiny with that of the empire arose the double significance of Jesus as a model. In one aspect the events of his life and his teachings shaped a story into which every one of the faithful might fit his or her own struggle. In another he represented an unparalleled supreme power to which only the person of the emperor offered any human analogy. Although the distinction is hardly rigid, to a certain extent the more personal Jesus was transmitted through literature, with its more intimate connection between reader and word, while the grand and isolated Christ was conveyed through painting and mosaic, an object of awe for a much larger audience, constructed through motifs and techniques that had previously been used primarily for Roman imperial art. As both Caesar and Augustus drew upon Roman traditions of divine patronage, Constantine positioned his own family at the center of a Christianized imperial iconography, assembling a political program from what had previously been scattered cultural details. Early Christian art had absorbed both classical and Jewish visual motifs to express its message. Imperial propaganda similarly helped fashion an image of Jesus that accorded with its own definitions of power and authority. When Julian forced the empire to sever its ties to Christianity for the three years of his short reign, he opposed this militant and authoritarian Jesus in the name of classical philosophy. But already at Rome, in the holy place that occupied the ground where St. Peter's now stands, Jesus was being worshiped in the manifestation of Helios the Sun god, across whose face Constantine had seen the cross. That the worship of Jesus at Rome was also in the process of replacing the cult of Aesculapius, the divine physician, only reaffirms the extraordinary ability of Christianity to maintain the double image of Jesus as both the embodiment of supreme power and the graceful savior of each individual.

The Cult of Saints and the Fame of Intercession

I have been emphasizing the absorption of imperial motifs in the depiction of Jesus and the related shift in the meaning of his life and career for both Christians and non-Christians. But the Christian attitude toward the visible world, as embodied in the New Testament and derived from the Old, had

4. Appropriately enough, the fourth century also witnesses the beginning of an imperial court that defines the center of the empire by its presence. Constantine may have built monuments in the Forum, but with the founding of Constantinople, the fifth-century establishment of Ravenna as an administrative center, and the churches and monuments built in Jerusalem, Rome has become only one of many stages for imperial power.

a strong effect on classical attitudes and imagery as well. The most striking result was the virtual disappearance of sculpture. As André Grabar remarks:

> The domain in which the triumph of Christianity is most conspicuous— if in a negative way—is that of sculpture in the round and, in particular, statuary. The new faith dealt the death blow to this form of art, hitherto preponderant throughout the Roman empire. No written records explain the reason for its abandonment, which was, however, so general and so abrupt that there must have been some sort of prohibition, probably an unwritten one (*Early Christian Art*, 268–69).

Elsewhere Grabar ascribes this lack of sculpture to the Christian belief that statuary verged on idolatry, certainly when it was in the round and perhaps also in relief. But neither fear of encouraging idolatry nor a lost series of edicts is really necessary to explain this fascinating example of the interplay between ideology and visual technique in the history of fame. Caesar staggering over to fall dead at the feet of the statue of Pompey embodies the Roman association between sculpture and permanence: The image of Pompey stands, even though he is dead—so may the image of Caesar. Even in life the emperor strove to look like a statue, impressing on his audience the eternity of his individual nature. The bas-relief of the imperial face on coins bound together Roman society and economy. The painting and the icon defined the face as a possible object of worship. But the statue associated the entire human body with the civic space of a public square. Instead of being privately venerated by the viewer, it must be approached as a monument, an embodiment of the power to impose oneself on others. Civic sculpture is primarily *there,* standing proudly in the viewer's path. Representational civic sculpture revives in the Renaissance and remains important through the nineteenth century in part, as we shall see, because of the simultaneous reassertion of the importance of the state, its leaders, and those artists who celebrate them. But from the triumph of Christianity through the Middle Ages rounded civic sculpture went into a definite decline. When churches began to include statues of the saints, they were firmly attached to the structure. What would it mean to be able to walk around God or Christ or one of the saints? They stand beyond perspective and beyond realistic depiction, just as they stand beyond the world of the senses in general. Thus if emperors were to take on semidivine status as God's representatives on earth, their imagery as well had to become more flattened and hieratic, emphasizing not the body but the face and its barely personal expression of God's will. As Christianity theologically focused on the world in heaven, so even on earth its adherents, whether priestly or political, were depicted as men and women in touch with divinity, gazing beyond the present into eternal life.

Yet those who had true spiritual fame were clearly different from those who availed themselves of its new worldly trappings. In the face of an increasingly institutionalized Church and a still strong empire that drew its authority from both its military power and its special relation to the King of Heaven, the role of the saints in helping Christianity to maintain its human relevance can hardly be overestimated. Between those oddly suitable contemporaries, Antony in the desert and Constantine in the capital, stood a church whose own values could easily range between the selfless and the self-serving. The evolving definition of the word *ecclesia* (Greek for church) offers an emblem of the conflict: At first it meant the entire body of the faithful; then it came to mean the building where worship was carried on; only by the twelfth century, when the power of the popes at Rome was definitely established, had it come to mean the hierarchy by which Christianity was perpetuated on earth.

Instead of affirming the absolute analogy between the hierarchies of earth and the hierarchies of heaven, the cult (*colere,* "to honor") of saints helped preserve the original Christian promise that the rich and powerful had less claim on human memory (and God's attention) than the virtuous and the rich in spirit. Like the earliest definition of the Church, the earliest definition of the saints was the entire body of the faithful. Grabar has pointed out that among the first specifically Christian motifs in early Christian art was the depiction of Jesus not alone, but among the apostles. Appropriately enough, the first of the followers of Jesus to be individuated pictorially was Paul, not, of course, one of the original apostles at all but the greatest publicist, organizer, and theologian of the early Church. Somewhat later, Peter (especially in the West) emerges from the otherwise indistinguishable group of twelve. By the second century many martyrs were also being celebrated, usually in their own localities as individuals who had died in imitation of the sacrifice of Jesus himself.

Because saints at death immediately entered the presence of God, they could be intercessors for the person who worshiped at their shrines. Like a powerful political figure whose influence could help someone with a suit at court, the saint was a divine patron who had a better chance of success with the omnipresent God than the local magnate might have with the distant emperor. Like Jesus, the saint obliterated the absolute distinction between life and death, earth and heaven. For those ignored or persecuted by the world, the venerated martyr promised that the last would be first, the rejected in the past become the only true heralds of the future. Each pilgrimage, each encounter with the relics or image of a saint, allowed the faithful for a moment at least to perceive the divine characteristics as a potential in themselves.

As essentially local and personal connections to God, the saints were a group of emblematic individuals through whom the faithful could also link themselves to a church otherwise growing toward an impersonal remoteness. Like Horace's Roman belief that for every person there was a particular star containing a genius that would watch over him throughout his life, the cults of the saints countered the daily experience of political and social hierarchy with the possibility of a direct route to the divine. The crucial difference was that the saint had once been human, not a god or an angel or a daimon or a genius. By the fourth century, with the gradual erosion of the ability of the classical gods and heroes to capture mass belief, some of the more effective trappings of pagan cult practices could be adapted to Christian use. The private commemoration of family and friends through funeral portraits added some more visual touches to the veneration of saints. The victory of Christ over death was thus extended into time by the religious image. As the Church itself emerged from its embattled underground status, saints began to be honored as much for the manner of their lives as the martyrdom of their deaths. Whether the saint was a victim of persecution like St. Polycarp (whose cult is usually considered the earliest) or a thinker and theologian like St. Augustine, rival churches often competed ferociously for the relics of their physical being, each bit of hair and bone a testimony to another human's conquest of death.[5] As the number of saints grew and the codification of their characteristics became more minute, the Church authorities began to insist on official approval of new saints in order to keep out spiritually pretentious suicides, confused heretics, and the occasional case of mistaken identity. But it was not until the twelfth century that canonization became the exclusive privilege of the popes and papal authorization was required for the institution of new cults, and not until the heart of the Counter-Reformation in the seventeenth century that the papacy took total control of all saintly cults. Despite official theories that sainthood could be an ideal but not a career, its institutionally subversive potential remained, and a strong part of the appeal of the new monastic movement was its promise of a kind of ready-made sainthood in life. With one aspect of Jesus co-opted as a support for empire, the saints kept vital that other Jesus, whose fame at the margins of the Roman world had so forcefully created an alternate definition of human nature.

Thus, like the emperor, whose image on his coins and on the walls of his courtrooms repeated and reinforced his psychic closeness to his subjects, the imperial Jesus of the church domes and the grand mosaics was complemented by the saintly Jesus of the icons, an immediate presence, depicted in a medium that was more intimate in scale and could be easily moved to wherever the worshiper desired. Icons depicting Jesus, Mary, the apostles, and various saints, along with statuettes and commemorative plaques, increasingly were for sale in places of pilgrimage—visual links to the divine. In the fourth century, when such images took a great leap in popularity, Eusebius wrote of seeing pictures of Jesus and the disciples for sale even in bazaars. Many Christians also took advantage of their newly acceptable status in the empire to wear clothes embroidered with Gospel scenes, perhaps in imitation of the elaborate new vestments Constantine

5. In the seventh century papal authority is redefined by Pope Gregory VII to come from the possession of the body of St. Peter, that is, his relics. Thus the connection to the past and its authority is authenticated by its tangible remnants, and the body of the Church (as opposed to that of the empire) kept whole by the participation of each individual church, through its saints and their relics, with the community of saints in heaven.

was introducing to Church ritual. With an above-ground Church, visible representation became more acceptable and theologians were beginning to make approving statements about the uses of pictorial art along the lines of Pope Gregory the Great's later remark that Christian images were "the poor man's Bible." By the fourth century the "good news" of language had acquired a strong competitor in the sacred image.

Icons and Iconoclasm

Then John, who had never beheld his own face, said to [Lycomedes] . . . "How can you persuade me that the portrait is like me?" And Lycomedes brought him a looking-glass, and when he had seen himself in the glass and gazed at the portrait, he said, "As the Lord Jesus Christ liveth, the portrait is like me; yet not like me, my child, but like my image in the flesh. . . . But do you be a good painter for me, Lycomedes. You have colours which he gives you through me, that is, Jesus, who paints us all (from life) for himself, who knows the shapes and forms and figures and dispositions and types of our souls.

—*Apocryphal Acts of John*

Although the evolving art of the icon was primarily spiritual in its attitude toward ultimate reality, the artists often sought to respect whatever traditional knowledge they had about the actual look of Jesus and other figures. Like the Trinitarians whose beliefs became the orthodoxy of the Church, the icon makers sought to fuse the historical reality of Jesus with his divine mission, linking the physically evasive Jesus of the Gospels to the eyes of each worshiper. Because the depiction of Jesus and the saints had to be cast in visual terms that the Christian convert already understood, however, the allusion to past, non-Christian imagery often upset the theologians. Early Christian writers, following the Old Testament injunction against graven images and idolatry, had especially prohibited portraits of holy figures. They were much more comfortable with narrative scenes or symbolic depictions, since these clearly were material for interpretation, aids to the impressing of the Christian message. Whether it be by a teacher or a preacher, interpretation required a controlling intermediary. But portrait images could be experienced directly and so were dangerously close to diverting the worshiper from the Person whom they represented.

By the sixth century the cult of images had brought about a situation in the Eastern empire wherein the images themselves were being worshiped. Just as Jesus and the saints began to have more and more miraculous stories collected around them, certain famous images were credited with protecting or at least distinguishing the cities they made their home. Because their origins were either lost or mysterious, they were called *acheiropoitai* (not made by human hands). Sometimes they were ascribed to a great progenitor, like the painting of Mary, a fragment of which is now in Rome, that was supposedly done from the life by Luke when he and Mary were in Troy. (Alexander and Apelles might have smiled.) The face of Apollo, often placed on the gates of private homes and cities to ward off evil, was replaced by the face of Jesus. Although the practice was considered vulgar, Neoplatonic Christians justified such actions by theorizing that only through images of the holy ones could earthbound men receive even an approximation of the divine. The exemplary and didactic use of images sanctioned by early writers had thus in a few hundred years passed over into the worshipful; the acceptance of the image as an aid to understanding had been transformed into the veneration of the image as a direct route to the divine reality. Just as Jesus the Teacher had metamorphosed into Jesus the King of Heaven, so the road to salvation could now be followed through the luminous eyes of a portrait, which, as an image of the divine, was analogous to the Incarnation itself.[6]

By the sixth and seventh centuries the cult of images had become so widespread that a reaction against it, sponsored by several of the Byzantine emperors, broke out in a wave of persecutions and destructions of holy objects usually referred to as the Iconoclast Controversy. The arguments were extensions of the more rarefied theological arguments over the human or divine nature of Jesus that had agitated so many Church councils. The more accurate an image was, argued the iconoclasts, the more blasphemous. Since it was probably even more blasphemous to create an inaccurate image, no image could be any good. Jesus should be unique and undefinable, like God himself, not the possession of every individual and church that could afford a reproduction. Placing images lower down on the walls of the church (as was happening in many places) only encouraged an impious familiarity. Although there is little direct evidence, the antagonists of the image may have also objected to the way in which the faces of patrons were beginning to appear along with divine figures in some religious art.

The iconoclast issue seems like a rarefied combination of religious and aesthetic considerations only if we forget for a moment the analogous modern question of socialist realism and the cult of the personality. In theory the split was between iconoclasts, who did not want to permit any visual analogies to holy or divine beings, and their opponents, for whom visual analogies were powerful and appropriate. Explicitly, then, the debate seemed to be over depictions of spiritual authority rather than of political authority. At a time when Church and State had become so recently allied, both the iconoclasts and iconodules did agree that they should continue to venerate the emperor's picture (the *lauraton*), versions of which were

6. In a particularly elaborate example of the new importance of tangible evidence of the divine, Ernst Kitzinger retells the fifth-century story of a miraculous picture that appeared in Uzala in North Africa whose subject was a recent miracle performed by the relics of St. Stephen. With only a dim tradition of actual artistic practice, the faithful, impressed that the source of the picture was a stranger to the area, concluded that they had been favored by a divinely wrought work ("Cult of Images," 113).

distributed on wood and canvas around the empire (not yet to post offices) to sanctify legal and judicial proceedings: Caesar could have his images. But for some emperors, the analogies were getting too close. Defenders of the religious image like Athanasius had argued that the relation of Christ to God was like the "co-equal" relation of the emperor's image to the emperor, "The image might well speak: 'I and the emperor are one, I am in him and he is in me'" (*Oratio contra Arianos*, II, quoted by Kantorowicz, *The King's Two Bodies*, 440). By extension, if the holy man's image conveyed an authority beyond the ruler's, whose sanction would prevail when they came into political conflict?

The Iconoclast Controversy carries within it the seeds of the final separation between the secular and the religious views of ultimate authority that comes with Henry VIII and the Protestant Reformation of the sixteenth century—again accompanied by a decisive wave of state-supported iconoclasm. In practice the first iconoclasts were supported by emperors tender about their own exclusive status and the success of their military and political rule. Iconoclasm becomes definitely political in the mid-eighth century. Shortly after the emperor Leo the Isaurian attacks the use of images, one of his officials is murdered by a Constantinople crowd outraged by the attempt to remove an image of Jesus. In response Leo issues an imperial decree banning all religious images, and for more than a century images are destroyed and image makers and worshipers persecuted. Leo's son, Constantine V, who has come down to us in history accompanied with the name Copronymus (roughly "whose name is shit"—a triumph for iconodule historiography?), calls a synod in 753 that forbade invocations to Mary and the saints as well as reaffirmed the ban on images. In 787 another council tries to make peace between the warring factions. But some twenty-five years later two successive emperors took up the iconoclast cudgels once again, until the next ruler put an end to the imperial crusade against images forever (at least as far as the Byzantine Empire was concerned).[7]

In the history of fame it is difficult not to see in the Iconoclast Controversy a ferocious attack against divine imagery arising from an imperial fear that the spiritual sanction so welcomed by Constantine and his successors was now threatening to erode their authority. The icon, simultaneously an effort to achieve historical accuracy and to create a link to the divine, associated the viewer with a kingdom of values independent of imperial order. Just as the cult of the saints, with its emphasis on locality, often turned the believer away from the center of imperial power (and toward what in future centuries became a new nationalism), so the holy

7. Curiously, the two rulers who did the most to thwart and divert the forces of iconoclasm (which had a certain momentum, especially among the army, once it got started) were both women—Irene and Theodora—who came to the throne after the deaths of their iconoclast husbands. In a grisly touch, Irene, who in 797 became the first woman to rule the empire, had her son's eyes gouged out—a traditional way of dealing with rivals in Byzantine dynastic politics, although particularly appropriate to the iconoclast issues.

icon eroded the need for any institutional structure, imperial or ecclesiastical, to mediate between the individual and God. Just before the beginnings of official iconoclasm, Justinian II had become the first emperor to put Christ enthroned on his coins (with himself piously standing as the servant of God on the other side). Render unto Caesar and render unto God were now just the opposite sides of the same coin. Threatened from without by the Arab invasions and from within by iconodules who promised a way to personal salvation independent of state control, the iconoclast emperors reasserted the ancient Roman monopoly over models of human nature. Some centuries after the imperial army had been purged of pagans in order to maintain its spiritual as well as military power against invaders, they sought to turn the attention of their subjects from heaven to earth by destroying their visual links to a world beyond power and politics.

Appropriately enough, the most consistent opponents of iconoclasm and the invariable targets of the worst persecutions were those Christians most clearly committed to an alternate definition of society on earth—the monks. In the face of Leo III's decrees, John Damascene, their main theorist and propagandist, argued that the Old Testament prohibition against graven images had been superseded by the Incarnation celebrated in the New Testament. The "render unto" passage was not, he said, a distinction between the worlds of denatured political image and integral Christian spirit, but an explicit approval for separate traditions of secular and religious portraiture. Divine images were not the same as what they depicted. But they were analogous enough that whatever honor or worship paid to them would pass directly to their prototypes. Images stood between the human and the divine: Christ could be depicted to the extent that he had been human, and the image was an appropriate object of devotion because it created a path between his humanity and his divinity. The human artist who depicted the divine therefore had a special obligation to be personally unblemished because his work was analogous—although, of course, on a lower level—to God's creation of man.

Little in John Damascene's argument could comfort those fearful that the alternate traditions of secular and religious portraiture were potentially competitive. Emperors might have their own images honored, it implied, but they should have no special role in the traditions of worship and doctrine that were the history of the Church. Their Jesus was still the Jesus of Constantine, the young warrior winning battles for the empire. The Jesus of the icons, with his calm gaze focused equally on the viewer and on eternity, too easily allowed that viewer to make a distinction between states of being that could only be to the detriment of the emperor and his court. The Islamic conquest of many of Christianity's holiest sites emphasized the underlying politics of the doctrinal dispute. John Damascene, as his name implies, wrote his defense of icons in Damascus, where he was a Christian monk whose father had been treasurer for the caliph. Imperial power therefore had no influence on him. Prohibiting graven images and human representation in their own religious art, the Moslems nevertheless seemed hospitable to icon worship among the Christians. Perhaps they didn't care. But the iconoclasts cared deeply about the political effects of imaging the divine, although their understanding of the power of images seems at best incomplete. Within imperial territory, for example, at the height of the controversy, some fervent iconoclasts caused verses written in praise of images to be burnt into their author's forehead. With the waning of the controversy and the effective defeat of the iconoclast movement, that man became a high church official in Nicaea, his face the living emblem of the failure of the iconoclasts to co-opt the power of images for themselves alone. With the death of the last iconoclast emperor, Christ enthroned returned to Byzantine coinage and remained there until the final defeat of the empire by the Turkish Moslems in 1453.

Charlemagne and the Unrestricted Image

Images of greatness gather their power from traditions of seeing. No matter how secular the principles of rulers, in countries of the iconic tradition like Russia, they can draw freely on its theory of the relation between image and person to reinforce their authority. The victory of the image makers over the image breakers in the ninth century assured the continuance of a tradition of sacred portraiture and image worship down to our own day. In the country that had the most complex tradition— Russia—it continues still, in the embalmed corpse of Lenin, the posters of Marx, and the small images of Stalin on Moscow taxicab windshields that embody the icon-lover's belief in the image's ability to transmit worship in one direction and spiritual power in the other.

In western Europe the image, the person depicted, as well as the artist who made the image played a somewhat different role in the establishment of present and future reputation. One pope had already refused to go along with the Byzantine attack on images and the next took the more active step of excommunicating all iconoclasts. The controversy over images thereupon became the prime theological issue over which the popes of Rome separated themselves from the political authority of the Eastern emperor at Constantinople. After a long period when Rome was hardly even a symbolic center for the empire, the popes of the eighth and ninth centuries took the opportunity of imperial iconoclasm to assert themselves as inheritors of the traditions of Roman greatness, which sprung equally from the policies of Augustus and the founding of the Church by Peter. With the military support of Pepin the Short, the father of Charlemagne, the papacy for the first time possessed a kingdom of its own, which included not only Rome but Ravenna, which had become the imperial capital in the West. The advent of Charlemagne himself, a dynamic ruler with his own aspirations to empire, immeasurably aided their case. Like Constantine, after whom he modeled himself, Charlemagne was deeply involved with theological issues. In the later eighth century, a few years before being crowned emperor but some time after he had begun the vigorous expansion of his kingdom, Charlemagne launched an attack against both the iconoclasts and the iconodules. Images, said his Synod of Frankfurt (794), could stir, teach, and adorn. But they had nothing to do with faith itself. The only objects effective in terms of faith were scripture, the cross, and the relics of saints, and they were objects of veneration rather than worship.[8] Thus in the West images never became official objects of worship, and so there was little need to control the details of their depiction or to regulate the artists employed to create them. Instead of the double tradition of secular and religious art that was the Eastern legacy of the Iconoclast Controversy, in the West there was a single mixed tradition in which the images of holy persons, because they had no fixed theological significance, could form part of a general artistic vision. Many of the Church Fathers had made analogies between artistic and divine creation, although the modern idea that the artist is an autonomous creator would not appear for centuries. But the position that Charlemagne's council took on images—or, rather, its refusal to take a position—sets the stage for a development of Western art in general and portraiture in particular that differed sharply from what occurred in the East. When neither political nor spiritual power solely controls the making of images, then the ability of art to mediate between those powers becomes a possibility.

The transcendental justification of the icon may have raised Eastern artists to a new status tinged by an access to the world of the spirit. But western European artists could be freer, like their rulers, to combine and invent traditions. In Byzantine painting, saints were often shown with naturalistic features but weightless, while those who were alive were solid and earthbound, with more geometric, deindividualized faces. In the West the split between transcendent and earthly person was never so visually codified. Spiritual justification, therefore, need not wait until the afterlife. Some glow of divinity might be possible to man while still on earth. The rise of a secular power clearly unbeholden to Church sanction and of artistic status totally unreliant on Church patronage waits upon the upheavals of Renaissance and Reformation. But in the history of fame its seeds are planted by Charlemagne's insistence on the subordination of the image to scripture, the cross, and relics as instruments of faith—and there-

8. Believing that the Second Council of Nicaea (787) "had enjoined an adoration of images equal to that due to the Holy Trinity," the Frankfurt Synod rejected what it took to be its distinction between *proskynesis* (veneration) and *latria* (worship), similar to the distinction between *doulia* (service) and *latria,* often invoked in discussions of religious images. The former can be paid to saints, while the latter is reserved for God. The Western attitude thus turned away from Eastern controversies over the link between image and transcendent reality.

fore the freedom of the image to become the instrument of a very different kind of belief.

In essence the West preserved the Roman connection between the portrait-image and the individual reality it depicted. Western Christian iconography in the Middle Ages was not an official code but a pictorial consensus, a diffused language of images—where variation and change were always possible through the talent of the artist or the intention of the patron. Depending on the occasion, for example, the face and figure of Jesus might be invoked either to support the Church against secular encroachment or a secular ruler against papal tyranny. The Western resistance to iconoclasm, which arose in part to serve the political ambitions of the papacy, therefore also kept alive the double image of Jesus—the fame of his power and the fame of his spirit—and the ability of artists as well as public men to have equal access to both.[9]

When we look back over the Middle Ages to note those individuals whose careers inflected the history of fame and gave it a different turn toward the future, our eyes are apt to be dimmed by the proliferation of names that pour at us out of the history books. So many have become famous in retrospect, picked out of the masses of popes and rulers because what they did was developed by the men of the future, often decades or centuries later, sometimes more quickly. For every Charlemagne or St. Francis of Assisi who immediately moved their audiences, there were innumerable others whose marks on time were deciphered only much later. As new situations arose, those who sought precedents for new actions rediscovered figures from the past and made them famous to serve the interests of the present. In a world of slow communication and brief lives, it is difficult to say that anyone is "famous" in the sense of having an immediate audience of the kind we have become used to since the eighteenth century. But such audiences do build up over the years, as certain figures gather around themselves layer upon layer of interpretation. In the Middle Ages particularly, when the urge for exclusively worldly glory was condemned throughout Christian Europe, it is difficult to hew anything like a straight line of development for the concept of fame. Only because we know what happened from the Renaissance to our own time, when the Christian focus on divine justification became supplanted by a justification of self on earth, can we see the medieval progenitors of those attitudes.

Unlike those modern aspirants to a fame without precedent, the most intriguing "famous" of the Middle Ages were always aware of their precedents, reaching into the past to establish a continuity in which they took prime place. The originality of neither writer nor ruler was in question. Older authors were searched, older works combined and recombined to create a history that justified the present. In the usually inert world of

9. See Kitzinger, *Art of Byzantium,* for a description of a twelfth-century royal chapel in Sicily that adopts Byzantine iconic faces and postures to depict the ruler, Roger II, as the ally of Christ against the pope.

medieval decentralization, many rulers appeared with the ambition to bring together disparate realms under their banners. Few lasted very long. It was a time of abrupt assertions and precipitous declines as secular power and papal authority clashed again and again. Often the most famous men to later generations were therefore those who defined the sharp edge of controversy between the power of the Church and the power of the king— Henry II and Thomas à Becket, Henry IV and Pope Gregory VII.

The most successful builder of a new empire in the Middle Ages was Charles the Great, more familiarly known in English and French as Charlemagne, the Latin form of calling on his name—"O you, Charles, the Great." Charlemagne also liked to be called "the athlete of God." But the Herculean and even Alexandrian analogies of the divinely favored hero are only part of his imagery, for he saw himself in a line of great kings, going back past Constantine to Augustus and David. His kingly person thus synthesized the Jewish, Christian, and Roman public man—an amalgam of governor and priest—like Augustus both *princeps* and *pontifex maximus* or like David both psalmist and king. Born in lands that Caesar conquered in the Gallic Wars, Charlemagne reasserted a Roman authority now combined with the sanction of Christianity. He considered himself the ruler of all the Christians of Europe, wherever they might be. As one of his early biographers says, God had destroyed the Romans, but in their place, to expand their heritage, he had raised up Charlemagne. Like many rulers in this tradition, he was not content just to have power, win battles, and expand territory. He sought some other, less tangible, sanction. In great part that sanction came from the Roman past. But it came as well from his connection with Christian faith, for he was king "by the grace of God"—a formula that had become popular not long before his reign. To sanction and propagandize his position as restorer of the Roman Empire in Europe, Charlemagne took marble from Rome and Ravenna to decorate his palace at Aachen, modeled his throne on Solomon's (with cavities in the sides for relics), and revived the ancient image of the youthful Christ to testify to his own rebeginning, for Aachen was to be the "second Rome." Imitating the manners and rituals of the early Roman courts, Charlemagne was in his turn imitated by kings like Offa of England, who returned from Charlemagne's court to issue Roman-style portrait coins of himself and his wife.[10] Charlemagne also maintained relations with the rulers of the Eastern empire in Constantinople, although a marriage between their children proposed by Empress Irene fell through, and he exchanged gifts with Harun al-Rashid, the Islamic caliph, who sent him an elephant.

In later controversies both the advocates of the pope and the advocates of the empire called upon the figure of Charlemagne for sanction. In fact,

10. Along with regulating weights and measures, one of Pepin's innovations was to introduce a new coinage that featured the king's name and monogram. The coinage of the previous dynasty had been in such disarray that Byzantine coins had become the standard for all transactions.

although Charlemagne was crowned emperor and named Caesar Augustus by the pope, Charlemagne kept his distance. The popes were making their own move to establish the continuity of the papacy as a vital line of political authority. But as far as the historical Charlemagne was concerned, God's sanction came to him as directly as it came to the popes, perhaps even more directly, and certainly not by their agency or their intercession. A few hundred years before, papal political theorists had begun to distinguish between the pope's authority and the emperor's power. But Charlemagne appreciated the need for both; in his view, no doubt, the coronation as emperor was at best an affirmation of what already existed. Through his decrees he regulated Church activities, fostered preaching in local dialects, and took a strong interest in music and liturgical reform. Clerical costume began to be modeled more and more on Roman dress—the tunic and toga. Carolingian theology, perhaps reflecting the concerns of Eastern monastic anti-iconoclasts like John Damascene, gave Mary, the mother of Jesus, an increasingly important position (including a major shrine at Aachen) and first discussed the views that would later coalesce into the doctrine of the Immaculate Conception. The emphasis seems appropriate, for Mary represented a link between man and God more clearly human than the Jesus whose varying portions of human and divine nature were constantly being debated. Thus, as Charlemagne brought together Roman conceptions of power with Christian conceptions of authority to create his empire, so the writers and theologians of his cathedral schools, by focusing on Mary, were preparing the way for a transformation of the classical conception of the muse into the mingled representation of earthly and divine love. Somewhat later, in the persons of Petrarch's Laura or Dante's Beatrice, she would inspire the writers of the early Renaissance and foster a new conception of authorship.[11]

Who Was Charlemagne?

Charlemagne's empire was essentially the work of one man and with his death it was already fragmented. But the fiction of its existence was maintained even into the early nineteenth century, and still exists in the concept of "Europe." Although Charlemagne and his father Pepin had helped establish papal political power, they came to represent for many a secular authority that often opposed it. True to his dual conception of himself as the priest-king, Charlemagne, in one of the common ironies of the history of fame, was available not only to sanction secular authority but papal as well. Later emperors considered him and therefore themselves

11. The theological preoccupation with Mary also tends to be linked with a positive attitude toward holy images, in which the artist reaches within and beyond himself to portray a conception that itself is divine. The monks, often the prime antagonists of the iconoclast emperors, were particularly devoted to the cult of Mary.

to be the heirs of the Caesars and the promulgators of a rule of secular law. The popes, on the other hand, considered him the protector of their freedom who had acknowledged that his power was the gift of the Church. As an emblematic figure, Charlemagne had come to be invoked as a spiritual overseer both for those who sought a world empire independent of Church approval and those for whom the Church was the world empire beyond all others.

As Charlemagne drew upon David, Augustus, Constantine, and Justinian as precedents, so he became a wellspring of combined religious and political justification in his turn. About two hundred years later Otto the Great of Germany was also crowned emperor by the pope, this time not at Rome but at Aachen, where he had reintroduced some of the rituals of Charlemagne's court. His grandson Otto III discovered Charlemagne's tomb in the propitious year 1000 and dreamed of a "renewal of the Roman Empire." By the eleventh century Charlemagne begins appearing in frescoes as a saint. His exchange of gifts with Harun al-Rashid metamorphoses by the Crusades into an actual pilgrimage to the Holy Land where the caliph names him ruler of Jerusalem. In the twelfth century, just prior to the Third Crusade, Frederick Barbarossa, in the midst of a conflict with the papacy, has Charlemagne canonized by his own antipope.[12]

Two lives of Charlemagne, one written by a member of his court, the other by a monk some seventy years after his death, illustrate the ways in which his legend and especially his double nature were elaborated. Einhard, a layman who spent more than twenty years in Charlemagne's service, models his life structurally on Suetonius's *Lives of the Caesars*. Like Arrian on Alexander, Einhard says that he writes so that the memory of what Charlemagne has done will not "sink into the shades of oblivion." As Charlemagne is in some sense a thirteenth disciple for Jesus, so in Einhard's biography, for those familiar with the *Lives* of Suetonius (which included any literate person of the time) would see him arrayed in a language that made him a thirteenth Caesar as well. But, unlike Suetonius, Einhard provides no salacious detail and little personal anecdote beyond those moments that fit easily into his depiction of Charlemagne's grand humanity. A perfect amalgam of Roman and Christian precedents built on Frankish soil, Einhard's Charlemagne is a finely sculptured, virtually impenetrable, public person.

At first glance the life of Charlemagne written by a monk usually identified as the poet Nottker the Stammerer is much more casual and anecdotal, and his Charlemagne is a rougher, folksier figure than the *princeps* celebrated by Einhard. Yet Nottker also deeply cares about the image of

12. The invocation of Charlemagne's sanction was not limited to the medieval period. Looking down the ages, we might note that among the treasures of Napoleon III, the last emperor of France, is a lavishly decorated reliquary, commissioned by Barbarossa, that contains Charlemagne's forearm. And Hitler, who boasted that he was the first person since Charlemagne to have such unlimited power, had his retreat at Berchtesgaden built with a direct view of the mountain under which Charlemagne had supposedly been buried (Speer, 199).

Charlemagne. He writes specifically for Charlemagne's great-grandson, Charles the Fat, and his view of Charlemagne is just as exemplary as Einhard's, although with somewhat different precedents. Both emphasize Charlemagne's symbolic descent from the great rulers of Rome. But, while Einhard places Charlemagne next in genealogical line from those celebrated by Suetonius, Nottker praises him as one who transcends Roman categories of leadership, not only because he has a Christian mission, but also because he has rekindled the spirit of the villages and the monasteries so often opposed to official Church rule. A good portion of Nottker's work is taken up with satiric stories about the grotesque activities of bishops, particularly their self-importance and their fame seeking. In this context Charlemagne's patronage of learning, which Einhard includes as only an important part of Charlemagne's program, becomes for Nottker the center of his general cultural significance. Einhard may pattern his work on Suetonius's. But Nottker alludes to a whole group of works, both classical and biblical, that situate Charlemagne at the confluence of literary as well as political and spiritual traditions. Einhard mentions with praise Charlemagne's relations with Harun al-Rashid. But Nottker elaborately recounts even more of Charlemagne's embassies to the East and his fame throughout the world. In the exchange between East and West fostered by Charlemagne, says Nottker, Virgil's phrase for an impossibility—that Parthians should drink from French rivers and Germans from the Tigris—has been superseded. Charlemagne is therefore not merely the latest figure in a line going back to Rome and the Old Testament kings. He includes and then goes beyond them to synthesize all secular and divine authority:

> It was said of him what has never been said of any other human being, that he excelled all other men in his knowledge of secular and divine literature, in the singing of both church and popular music, in the composition of poems and in their recitation, and above all in the sweet fullness of his voice and the inestimable pleasure which he gave when he spoke (Nottker, 131).

Such a conception of Charlemagne's qualities grows with a flourish from Nottker's own perspective as a literary monk. Unlike the grand public man of Einhard, his Charlemagne, like the later figures of Arthur and Alfred, is the subject of stories told by the people. Even more extensively than Einhard, Nottker indulges the writer's rhetorical humbleness, his difficulties when faced with the task of recording such greatness. But both Einhard and Nottker nevertheless emphasize the Horatian theme that it is through the writers that great men are remembered. If even Charlemagne must be recalled to his own descendants, what of the less great, who don't understand the need to engage the favor of writers and artists?[13]

That one figure could be called on to sanction such different purposes may be a tribute to the way Charlemagne consolidated his own authority

13. Nottker at one point quotes a few lines from Virgil's description of *Fama* to underline Charlemagne's lack of time for idle stories.

by gathering so many precedents into himself. Unlike many of those who later sought to assume the mantle of his power, Charlemagne helped create a legend for himself as a patron of learning. The monastic schools administered by his friend Alcuin admitted students solely on the basis of merit, rather than rank or wealth, and thus had a strong influence on later generations, especially, of course, on those who were writers. In early Christian art the figure of the sage, carrying a scroll, appears frequently. The sage was both teacher and preserver. He connected the past with the present, the finite with the eternal; and in the Middle Ages he began to supply his patrons with genealogies and chronicles that affirmed the greatness of the past as it was realized in the power of the present.

In the far-flung medieval world, where communication was slow and often difficult and diseases could lay waste entire regions, the competition for lasting power was thus most often carried on as a competition of written continuities—primarily the continuity of the Church versus the continuity of secular rule, dynasty, and, with increasing frequency, the continuity of law. Appropriately enough, the early Middle Ages also witnessed an enormous growth of forgeries in both secular and ecclesiastical chanceries, whose prime goal was to affirm the immemorial existence of an authority that Charlemagne had asserted by force of arms. Most famous of the forged documents was the Donation of Constantine, which purported to give to the papacy the imperial authority in the West. It is hardly necessary to question the sincerity of the holy forgers: They were merely supplying documentation for what they believed to be God's truth—and the clerks in Charlemagne's own chanceries were doing the same. What greater homage to the sufficiency of the word? Like those great rulers, whether monarchs or popes, who sought to pull together under their names cities, towns, nations, and regions that were otherwise perfectly content to go their own ways, the documents of the Middle Ages aimed to organize what was otherwise a discontinuous set of incidents in time and to fashion them into sanctions for worldly authority and power. Charlemagne's favorite book, it is said, was Augustine's *City of God*. But what Augustine had distinguished, Charlemagne set out to synthesize. Subverting Augustine's primary intention, Alcuin, Charlemagne's chief cultural consultant, said that his empire was the "practical manifestation" of Augustine's heavenly order.

What Augustine thought was outside time and the struggles for human glory could, through the name of Charlemagne, be invoked to give both history and human aspirations a tinge of the divine. The roots of that individual aspiration to glory that is usually associated with the Renaissance therefore lie deep in the Middle Ages and particularly in the person of Charlemagne, the first great medieval ruler. Charlemagne, even more than Augustus, was the initiator of an empire that could not really outlast his own connective presence. But the *idea* of Charlemagne remained vital through the Middle Ages and beyond because it summoned up an idea of European unity itself, connected with the unity of the Church but finally more all-embracing. Whatever the difference in view between Einhard as a member of Charlemagne's court and Nottker as a monk, they share a conception of the great public man as also a spiritual authority.

Medieval Kingship: The Spirit of Arms

The presence of the Church is so overwhelming in the European Middle Ages, so complete is its penetration into social and political life, that its explicit doctrines and dogmas are usually taken to be the measure of its practice. Unlike modern theorists, writers then had little interest in discussing the shape into which the state, the Church, or any institution cast the malleable earthly nature of man. They looked instead to what was invariable and eternal in human nature. As far as medieval theology was concerned, individuality was not an important issue. Life on earth was principally a preparation for the true glory to come, and the mingled human and divine status claimed in imitation of Charlemagne by strong rulers such as the Ottos and Frederick Barbarossa was hardly an option for anyone else.

In our world of image multiplication, it may be hard to appreciate this comparative lack of interest in what we like to think of as individuality. We—and our conception of history—search for different things: We note the anonymity of many medieval artists; we examine the few works that by any stretch of the imagination could be called autobiographical; we observe that few "great men" of the Middle Ages had careers that were not connected with the all-embracing institution of the Church—and we conclude that the Middle Ages were not interested in individuals. Nervously, we feel an itch to rush on to the Renaissance, past this world of monks and knights and peasants, when all ambition seemed to be subordinated to the demands of faith.

The conclusion is true enough, as far as it goes. The Middle Ages did not foster an individuality that we would recognize as such. Yet every student of medieval history knows how many acres of names—kings, popes, generals, monks, reformers, theologians, saints—must be surveyed. Often medieval history seems made up *only* of individuals, perfunctorily arranged in chronicles and genealogies with occasionally a few lines of commentary. The historian of fame despairs of focusing on a decisive moment, motif, or career, for such details, when they are available, are often distilled or obliterated by the medieval writer's effort to precast his subject into the mold of final judgment. In the lives of saints or monarchs, what we look for is often so different from what the authors want to supply: Instead of personal details and individuation, we are offered the triumphant fulfillment of precedent and pattern.

For the purposes of the history of fame, then, the struggle between kings and popes is less important to an understanding of the Middle Ages than the imagery in which the quarrel is cast and the concepts of character brandished by the opposing sides. For it is through the nature of kings that the Renaissance will contemplate a human character that can potentially be shared by many with neither kingly birth nor kingly power. In Shakespeare's kings, for example, we see dramatic conflicts—between individual and office, between private nature and public face—with which his entire audience can sympathize and even identify. From the contemplation of such human features writ large in the faces of kings, the aspirations of otherwise ordinary people took on definition. But such a tremendously important shift in the nature both of fame and human character must wait on several factors, not least the waning of religious influence over visual imagery, the invention of the printing press with its spread of words and images around the world, and the rise of a theater in which such personalities could become matter for both noble and commoner to contemplate.

Yet even in the more restricted imagery of the Middle Ages, when the gap between permanence and transience was impossibly wide, we may note a few familiar landmarks. I have already mentioned what seems to be an echo of Arrian on Alexander in Einhard's biography of Charlemagne. Similarly, while the influence of the image of Charlemagne is spreading through the eleventh to thirteenth centuries, Alexander is also appearing more and more as the hero of chivalric romance, an ideal courtly prince, a learned king who lacked only Christianity to make him perfect. Of course, there were still writers who took the Senecan line and condemned Alexander for murdering Callisthenes (and thereby true philosophy). But it is easy to see in their writings and those of other anti-Alexandrians a strongly pro-papal point of view that casts Alexander as a diabolical secular ruler interested only in his own ambition. When earthly aspiration, particularly in the service of ideals, becomes respectable once more, Alexander again comes into fashion. The enormous number of medieval versions of the Alexander story attest to the continuing hold he had over that part of the European imagination still fascinated by the example of the ruler who was committed to cultural expansion as much as to military and political conquest. The stories most often woven together were not taken from Arrian and the "hard" historians, but from what scholars have called "the Alexander romance." There the main figure is not Alexander the general but Alexander the Odysseyan traveler—who flies through the sky, explores underwater, and makes love to the Queen of the Amazons—or Alexander the possessor of hidden wisdom—who converses with the mystics of India and receives from Aristotle what all the ambitious rulers of the Middle Ages longed to have, the *secretum secretorum* (the secret of secrets), the definitive text on how to rule.[14]

14. Books on the medieval image of Alexander cited earlier in "The Longing of Alexander" are also relevant here, especially Cary, *The Medieval Alexander*. See also two recent translations of Alexander-romances: *Iskandarnamah: A Persian Medieval Alexander-Romance* and *The Romance of Alexander the Great by Pseudo-Callisthenes*.

It is hardly surprising to note that Alexander's literary and pictorial (mainly through woodcuts) vogue corresponds roughly to the height of the political influence of the memory of Charlemagne. They were both rulers who sought to put learning into action and whose theater was the world. As Charlemagne furnished a forebear for every strong medieval king who wanted to expand his realm and assert his authority over priestly appointments, so the Aristotle-Alexander relationship sanctioned the growing number of writers who were bent on giving counsel to secular rulers based on a philosophical and historical understanding of what kingship and individual authority and power really were.

The characters of kings, real and fictional, bore the weight of such attention because for most of the Middle Ages there was no settled concept of the state as an entity separate from the ruler who literally and figuratively embodied it. The word "political" itself was not in common use until the thirteenth century when the rediscovery of Aristotle by way of Islamic and Arabian philosophers reintroduced the definition of man as a "political animal." "Political" of course derives from "polis" (city). But the general experience of the Middle Ages, unlike that of the Renaissance and later, was not that of cities but of the countryside, with its castle-individualism and its village communities on the one hand, and its pervasive Christianity on the other. All over Europe these tiny islands of clustered peoples were tied together by the invisible bonds of the Church, whose regimen and rituals were familiar despite the gaps of geography. Until the reign of Charlemagne, it was almost exclusively the papacy that had in the West developed the arts of a far-flung administration. But Charlemagne's synthesis of the biblical priest-king with the Roman emperor had been carried out with a revival of Roman administrative structure and political forms as well. And in the seesaw between popes and monarchs that preoccupied the next several hundred years, the strength of a king and the shadow that he casts in history was almost always in direct proportion to his prowess as an administrator and expander of administrative institutions. With the notable exception of Richard the Lion-Hearted, who was a remarkable general and strategist, the great kings of the Middle Ages were less figures celebrated in their times for their military prowess than they would be later for their role in creating the foundations of the centralized national realms of the Renaissance and the modern idea of a sovereign state. The popes could claim a continuity of power stretching down from their possession of the body of St. Peter. What then was the continuity of early kings? In part, as Augustus had tried to establish, it was dynastic and genealogical—a line of blood in contrast to the spiritual line of election that created the papacy. Thus one reason for the enforcement of celibacy was to prevent Church power from becoming the possession of an earthly family.

But, emerging from Charlemagne's invocation of the double sanction of the empire and the Bible for his reign came a concept of the king as having two bodies—an earthly natural body and an eternal heavenly body. Combining God and Caesar where Jesus and Augustine distinguished them, medieval rulers gradually evolved a definition of their power that drew upon the terms of early debates on the nature of Christ—to what extent divine and to what extent human—to define the nature of kingship. In a sense what was happening was the Christianization of the pagan concept of the emperor's Genius, that greater than human expression of the emperor's nature, which at times could be worshiped when the individual himself could not be. Once anointed (*christus*), the king could claim to be Christ on earth. As the Church had become a kind of empire, so the Empire was reaching for the status of a church. With the early Crusades, the Church tried to harness some of the new energies and direct them toward a recapturing of the Holy Land and the actual geographical places of Christ's life. So went the spiritual sanction of the Crusades. But there was as well the legal and historical sanction of Charlemagne's supposed authority over the Holy Land given by Harun al-Rashid. Earthly glory in the service of a goal of the spirit was becoming increasingly tangled with the aggrandizement of territory and the capture of peoples and riches. The Crusades offered a new way to make an earthly name with heavenly approval. They mark the transition from a medieval world in which all individuals were part of the body of the faithful to a time when certain individuals began to stand out, not for their allegiance to God alone, but for the way they invoked the divine sanction in other arenas of glory. Charlemagne may have taken an interest in church councils and monastic schools. But it was Frederick Barbarossa who called his realm the Holy Roman Empire, set up his own pope in opposition to Rome, and conferred sainthood on Charlemagne.[15]

In the evolution of Western theological politics, the medieval ruler took on two prime aspects. As the vicar of God on earth, he claimed spiritual authority; as the giver of law, he connected his rule with precedents that stretched back through to the Roman Empire. The characters of kings thereby became a hothouse of speculation about the place of the divine and the human in individual nature because, when that individual happened to be a king, the distinction had profound legal implications. One aspect was out of time, the other definitely in time, and both met in the specific human person of the king. Thus, in their conflicts with the papacy, royal appeals to an authority beyond the individual were sanctioned by a continuing body of law and precedent to which the papacy—itself an earthly institution—was gradually forced to adhere. In practical terms the continuity of the kingdom, through families, had begun to supplant the spiritual continuity decreed by the popes.

So long as kings were under the authority of the Church, aspiration,

15. After Barbarossa's death by drowning during the Third Crusade, a myth was generated that he and his warriors would come alive when the empire was again in peril. This Barbarossa story was revived by Kaiser Wilhelm I and Bismarck to herald the proclamation of the German Empire in 1871.

the desire to be more than oneself, primarily took a spiritual form. Seneca had told Nero that, as emperor, he was the soul of the *res publica* and the *res publica* was, in its turn, his body. But such an abstract reciprocity between the monarch and the entire state was not quite to the liking of someone like Nero, who ached for personal and individual glorification as well. In the Renaissance, as we shall see, the Roman taste for a theatrical presentation of the ruler will be revived with all the earthly panoply that a reawakened and newly secular artistic world can give. But in the Middle Ages, the route of personal visual glorification was not the mode of the times. For Augustine (and, in general, the Middle Ages follow his lead) the true theater of action was not on earth but in heaven. In this sense the papacy, with its prior claim on spiritual imagery, would seem to be the invariable victor. But iconographically self-conscious monarchs could, as we have seen, adopt as their protector a Jesus opposed to papal tyranny, and the kind of secular divinity established by the legal doctrine of the king's two bodies opened a way to new authority on earth.

For most of the Middle Ages, when a king died, the papacy had decreed that Christ was the ruler until another was anointed (*Christus regnat*). But in the late thirteenth century, in both England and France, kings insisted on taking office by inheritance. Both of these successions—Philip III of France replacing (Saint) Louis IX and Edward I of England replacing Henry III—took place while the new king was on crusade and the old one at home dying; and these were in fact the last noteworthy crusades. The establishment of a firm national stage for kingly glory in England and France seemed to drain away the enthusiasm for papally sponsored heroic endeavors in the Holy Land. Until the establishment of such strong monarchies, rulers like Charlemagne and Otto the Great and Frederick II had kept the genealogy of a race of heroic kings alive. The political theologians of the Church might answer that such kings were unique and unique they should remain. But in realms like thirteenth-century England and France, with their established royal line, the religious consecration of a new dynasty was no longer necessary. Once history and precedent became important to both Church and Kingdom, once law was studied as a humanly devised and perpetuated structure of relationship between men and institutions, then Charlemagne's sense of inheritance became a possibility for more than just the occasional strong ruler. As Ernst Kantorowicz points out, the growth of a legal concept of kingship with simultaneous secular and spiritual validations turned the attention of increasing numbers of aspiring men away from the otherworldly goals of spirituality and toward a glory that could be recognized right now. Aspiring eyes began to be focused on earth rather than heaven. Not just kings but nobles of all sorts began tracing their genealogies back into the still lustrous realms of the past. The counts of Flanders looked to Charlemagne; the Normans, like Theodoric in late antiquity, traced their ancestors all the way back to Troy. With a similar urge, in thirteenth-century Sicily, the court of

Frederick II, who was called "the wonder of the world," took up the question of true nobility. It would be pursued further by Dante and, three hundred years later, be turned into a thorough Renaissance program by Castiglione in *The Courtier:* how one should embody and exhibit the best possible behavior, approved perhaps by God but exhibited to the world.

The Intermediary and His Audience

Francis of Assisi: Sainthood in the Streets

> . . . in comparison with Francis, what did Julius [Caesar] or what did Alexander do that is memorable? Julius conquered the enemy, Alexander the world, Francis both. And it was not only the world and the enemy that Francis conquered, but himself, victor and vanquished in the same battle.
>
> —Latin *Versified Legend of Saint Francis*, written at the court of Henry III of England (1232)

Through his two bodies, the medieval king could embrace both spiritual transcendence and earthly power. But usually there was only one king to a country and, as far as anyone else was concerned, there was little possibility of imitation. In the late Middle Ages, however, the world expanded. The Crusades opened up a thriving mercantile traffic across ancient boundaries. Population steeply rose from the eleventh to thirteenth centuries; towns and cities grew. Until about 1300 only the Church had anything like a far-flung diplomatic structure. After that more and more individual states began to recognize the existence of each other at the same time that they were beginning to assert their own unique historical existence. Instead of the distinctions of name and status being irrelevant to one's true nature, they became an integral part of it. Universities specializing in law, philosophy, theology, and medicine opened the door to the learned professions as well. New vocations flourished; new occupations were born. There was still a theological urge to ignore the specifics of human nature and contemplate instead the general spiritual nature to which all should aspire. But what one *did* was becoming a more crucial clue to what one *was*.

Throughout Europe individuals were responding to this new scope for acting significantly and visibly within time. The new attitude toward earthly renown was reflected in language as well. By the twelfth century, for example, the Latin words *locare* (to rent) and *laudare* (to praise) were both represented by the French word *louer*. The coincidence was part of a natural linguistic development. But it might also be considered a pun that bubbles from the depths of a culture to reveal its inner juices—like similar Greek words that link the concept of praise with getting one's due materially. Such a verbal overlap clearly points to fame in one's lifetime, the fame of military success and personal riches indicated by the tripods and shields the Homeric heroes collected with such vigor. But to this simple division between status in life and status in death, the double meaning of medieval French *louer* adds a cautionary nuance: To praise is to rent. As La Rochefoucauld will remark some centuries later, "we usually praise only to be praised" (*"on ne loue d'ordinaire que pour être loué"*). The person praised is the tenant of the praiser, who must give him his due, in return for the obligation conferred. Thus, with the dawning rebirth of a competition for civic and national honors, words themselves, at least in France, associate the praise of others not with a showering of gifts but with assuming control.

Once there is fame on earth, there is a potentially capricious audience to go along with it. The double meaning of *louer* suggests that in late medieval France not only has fame become a common currency of social interchange, but also there is only a limited amount, with some having so much that they rent portions to others who can muster little on their own. If we can peer into a society through one of its verbal quirks, *louer* allows us to see a situation of fame accumulation and dispersal affirmed by more conventional sorts of evidence about the growth of centralized monarchies, knightly orders, genealogical charts, and so on. The spiritual criterion of self-realization in the name of God is beginning to be complemented by more material means of making a name, in which praise can be a medium of social exchange and a level to social power. *Louer/laudare* goes back to *laus,* the word for the laurel wreath that crowned the winners of athletic contests. *Louer/locare* refers to *locus,* a physical place. Thus praise itself has been transformed from the spiritual aspirations of an Augustine into a function of social position, and thereby in the gift of the earthly power who grants the place and furnishes the entry into the arena of praise—the king who leads the state, the lawyer, the jurist, the historian who gives the nod of posterity to individual life and action. In the transnational rule of the papacy, the profession of Christian spirituality had shifted enough toward the administrative and the hierarchical that secular power could easily argue that its vision of order had at least equal justification. Reacting to the expanding system of trade that brought new prosperity to the cities and an increased freedom from feudal obligations to local landlords, the nascent political imagination of the Middle Ages contested the Church's claim to define exclusively the true nature of man's life either on earth or in heaven. One argument, as we have seen, rejected the Church's involvement in secular power; the other opposed its assumptions about spirituality and personal virtue.

The first may be called the legacy of Charlemagne, the second that of Francis of Assisi.

It is impossible to say whether new models for human behavior lead or reflect what is happening in an entire population. The influence of Francis on the nature of aspiration goes far beyond the new spiritual lives made possible by the institution of the mendicant order that bears his name. In a Church grown more worldly and more prosperous, he stands for a return to the Christ of the spirit who lives not in heaven, the hermitage, or the monastery, but pervades the city and the countryside, the earthly world.

For much of the Middle Ages the Church, through the monastic movement, had provided for those of spiritual and intellectual aspiration a sanctuary from the less hospitable world outside. But a few years before Francis was born, Pope Alexander III had ruled that monks could no longer study law or medicine because such study threatened the spiritual exclusivity of their calling. The old monkish calling of preserving culture through the copying of manuscripts and the dissemination of learning, with its ready potential to threaten the centralizing of authority in the papacy, was in effect threatened as well. There arose in its place a new professionalization of learning, beyond the cloister, in the urban universities as well as in the innumerable groups that famous masters collected about themselves in towns and cities across Europe. In contrast to the older tradition of a teacher essentially supported by the Church, the new masters demanded and received their fees directly. Ideally, went the old view, the man of wisdom should not be paid: Socrates was not paid, for pay would subordinate him. Similarly, in a world where all scholars were members of the clergy, it was assumed that learning was a gift of God and therefore should not be sold (although gifts were acceptable). But when the demand for masters became greater than their number and when the papacy, upset at the number of virtually illiterate priests, urged at least some study for all, the mercantile model of payment for services rendered became more compelling. The separation of the scholar and man of learning from dependence on the Church had begun. From the Gospels onward, Christ had been characterized as the Teacher. But by the end of the Middle Ages, he was getting strong competition. Even within the Church, a theologian like Thomas Aquinas drew on Aristotle to create a body of interlocking doctrinal thought that might compete with the propaganda of secular rulers. Outside the Church, the teacher even more obviously was forced to shed some of his quasi-spiritual trappings. He now had to please his audience, and their willingness to pay became the index of their satisfaction. As John Baldwin summarizes the late medieval situation,

> No longer belonging to the holy monk in rural isolation, learning had become the property of the urban master who produced his intellectual goods within the *atelier* of his school and sold them to his students at a price to compensate labor and skill (56).

Books as well changed their social and thereby their intellectual function. In the fourth century, the transformation of learning and the promulgation of the word was signaled by the replacement of the scroll by the codex. In the twelfth century, the shift from the lavishly illuminated book of the elite to the quickly produced and widely distributed school text conveniently presented to a new generation of students what had before been the preoccupation of isolated monastic scholars.

For Francis, however, whose life (1182?–1226) came virtually in between those of a "new" teacher like Abelard (1079–1142) and a grand systematizer like Aquinas (1225–1274), such hard-won knowledge was not the point of a Christian life at all. Throughout his writings, learned language, with its roots in time, is downplayed and even attacked in favor of the plain, direct language of personal revelation, the standards of physical nature, and the life of Christ. But, like those who were bringing learning out of the monasteries and into the cities, Francis was committed to a display of spiritual intensity in the world. Concluding that it was no longer possible to *be* the members of the primitive Church, as many monastic reform movements had already attempted, he aspired to be *like* them as much as contemporary life allowed. The retreat to the monastery did not respond to the new complexity and populousness of the world. It put spirituality into an artificial environment and therefore its triumphs were suspect. According to Francis, the truly spiritual person constantly subjects himself or herself to the world, because exemplary spirituality deserves as wide an audience as possible.

Francis therefore takes the necessary self-consciousness of a desire to become spiritual and, instead of stripping it away, forces it to work in his favor, to push him toward greater and greater sacrifice, precisely because he is so aware of his limits, his fears, and his desires for comfort and rest. Within a world of others, without the security of the monastery, he still seeks to release his nature from a self validated by the opinions of others, the necessary legacy of growing up in the heart of a bustling market town. Part of Charlemagne's contribution to the history of fame was to affirm the existence of a cultural continuity that surmounted local loyalties and could in time rival the Church's claim to an exclusive insight into the meaning of Christianity. Francis is similarly unbeholden to the hierarchies of church and regional authority. But he rejects both legal precedent and intellectual system as well. The original thrust of his teaching and his "rule" (rather than what it later became) separates the individual from all authorities other than that of Jesus, whose life was to be imitated, as well as from one's own nature, which was to be respectfully transcended. In the face of rulers who took for themselves the title of Christ on earth, Francis sought a Christ who might infuse with a spiritual ardor the lives of individuals otherwise corrupted by the demands of earthly show.

Francis's attack against learning and culture therefore does not support mindlessness so much as the ability of the mind to change the self, to step outside one's culture and upbringing and become other than what one's background determined. In Francis the urge was there from the start. "I shall be a great man," said the young Francis to a friend while he was imprisoned after a battle in which he, not yet a wandering man of religion but a young soldier, was captured by the enemy. In the terms of his time "a great man" was a knight, and Francis, who got his name (odd for the Middle Ages) from his mother's love for France, was filled with the stories of Charlemagne and Roland sung by the French troubadours. But the knights of his own time were hardly the knights of legend, heroic individuals embarked on quests that required both spiritual enlightenment and physical prowess. Many were instead mere hirelings or unpaid citizens of towns battling for property and trade privileges. Francis, like Don Quixote sometime later, sought instead to be a knight of the spirit. It is a mark of the distance between the impulses of the twelfth century and the seventeenth that Francis phrases his quest in terms of the identification with Christ, even unto the final appearance of the stigmata on his own body, while for Cervantes the quest of Don Quixote discovers the power of the literary imagination and ends with a celebration of the relation between character and author.

"No man in this world can possess you," Francis was later to say about Christ, "if he does not die to self." The essential elements in that death to self were for Francis the denial of all material possessions. As the young son of a wealthy cloth merchant, he had been a lavishly dressed town dandy. But he threw off the rich show of clothing and costume and appeared instead in rags. His bride, he said, was Lady Poverty. To reject possessions, to have no fixed home, to refuse to handle money were calls by Francis to turn away from the worldly power the Church had gained and regulate the self by the model of Jesus.

I must stress again how self-consciously Francis undertook his mission, if only because in our own day self-consciousness and premeditation are usually thought to undermine spiritual goals. Francis's love of nature—his preaching to the birds, his prayers to Brother Sun and Sister Moon—reflects the same self-conscious desire as his imitation of Christ's wandering poverty to remedy the blindnesses imposed by his privileged urban upbringing. Because it is our fashion to believe that upbringing "causes" personal psychology, it would be easy to conclude that Francis's youth as a merchant's son "caused" him to revolt against it and self-consciously become the poorest of the poor. But in fact one's upbringing and background are the inescapable imagery by which one lives life, no matter what shape it has. To be without such imagery is never to have been alive. Without the voices of individual lives, we might never know the power of the wordless attitudes that actually existed. Some patterns can sweep across centuries, like that linking doting mothers with sons who strived to be different from their immediate communities—Olympias telling Alexander tales of his Achillean heritage, Monica telling Augustine of the life of Jesus, and Mama de Bernadone filling the ears of the young Francis with stories of the knights of Arthur and Charlemagne. But even such intense family connections do not determine or explain behavior; they color it. Without the spark of synthesis that the individual personality gives them, they remain only stories told before a dying fire.

The impact of Francis was immediate. Attracting followers quickly from many noble families, he continued to use the richly embroidered imagery of chivalry and knighthood to describe what to the eye of his unsympathetic contemporaries was a singularly ragged and destitute way of life. To a world that he believed had strayed too far from the reality of Christ's life, he and his followers presented a daily reminder. In a sense Francis was the Crusades brought home. Instead of liberating the Holy Land, the places of Christ's birth and ministry, the Franciscan rule brought the meaning of that life out of the cloister, out of the hands of glory-seeking crusaders, and into the world of the towns. His fame would be a fame of the spirit, capitalizing on the theater of earthly life in order to deny it. With transcendental mockery he repeatedly courted personal martyrdom by trips to Syria, where he would try to preach to the troops of the Sultan just before they battled the Crusaders. He was overcome, he said, with a "thirst for martyrdom," to be a witness to God's truth, but to be a witness who himself was witnessed, an example to others. With no formal churchly vocation and armed only with his own sense of mission, he preached that absolute poverty of the flesh would lead to an enhancement of the spirit. When his father, who wasn't sure whether he was crazy or merely disobedient, accused him of stealing money to help build his church, the young Francis, already gaunt and threadbare, gave even those meager clothes to the rich cloth merchant and said that hereafter he would recognize only his father in heaven. It was a gesture worthy of the Jesus of the Gospels, but cast strikingly in the terms of the mercantile greed and ostentation that Francis continually mocked, just as he transmuted the show of knighthood into images of spirituality. In the Rule he promulgated in 1223, the rejection of any kind of ownership is crucial. The followers of Francis would have no class and they would have no fixed homes. They would be unburdened of money, property, learning, and any other comforts the world could offer so that they might more easily bring to the world the transcendent truth that both renewed its vigor and condemned its corruption.

For Francis, as for many others in his time, the religious doctrine on which everything else rested was the Incarnation: God had become man in Christ. But there was another side to the transformation, for man had also connected to God through Christ, and each man and (an important aspect of Francis's preaching) each woman might personally become *like* Christ in turn. Christ therefore was not merely unique. He was also exemplary. God may have become man only once in human history. But he thereby created a way for man to approach him, not as the top of a social hierarchy of power but as the top of a hierarchy of being. In the long view of the centuries, the personal model Francis furnished for the imitation of Christ corresponded to contemporary efforts to resolve a doctrinal dispute that had preoccupied theologians for more than a century. Within Francis's lifetime transubstantiation—the actual turning of the bread and wine of the sacraments into the body and blood of Christ—was proclaimed an authorized doctrine of the Church (1215). It was not a mystical event; it actually happened. There was a "real presence" on the altar. Unlike the warrior Christ of Constantine, the victor over death, the Christ of Francis was thus the suffering redeemer. And, in the wake of the religious ardor that Francis inspired, a new element was added to the depictions of the Crucifixion: The four nails became three, the feet were crossed, the face and body no longer serene and calm, but agonized and twisted—a picture of real human pain.

As we have seen, such a denial of the usual avenues of public recognition is potentially subversive and the views of Francis are no exception. Yet his dissatisfaction with the ways of being human that had been defined by his culture and even his Church never strayed into the political. A martyrdom for religious nationalism, which became more common in the sixteenth century, or even a martyrdom against secular power, like that of Thomas à Becket hardly ten years before Francis's birth, was not in his nature. He accepted the authority of the Church and so the Church accepted him, although I would like to have seen the expression on the face of Innocent III, that wily and learned statesman, when the ragged Francis appeared in his court. Other spiritual groups devoted to poverty had been worrying the papacy with their antihierarchical and even antiritual views. But Francis had no such disruptive assertions to make. He and his followers, he said, were "minstrels of God," not threats to priestly power. In Innocent's own campaign to reserve to the church the right to name bishops and to reject the appointments of secular rulers, the selfdenial and otherworldly piety embodied in the rule of Francis could be a welcome imprimatur of transcendental justification. So Innocent accepted the Franciscan order as he would later the sisterhood of Clare, who had joined Francis in the early years.

But the potential for subversion still remained. After Francis's death and his almost immediate canonization, the Church sponsored official biographies intended in part to stem the tide of Franciscan legend already gathering. Quickly enough, the Franciscans split into two factions, one (called the Spirituals) that wished to follow the rules Francis had laid down, the other (called the Conventuals) willing to compromise in the name of what had become an increasingly wealthy institution. Hardly ten years after Francis's death, the papacy began to crack down on those who imitated Francis too closely, and six Spirituals were burned at the stake for heresy in Lyon, where a thousand years before a community of Christians had been tortured and executed with the approval of Emperor Marcus Aurelius.

Like Abelard and other charismatic teachers, who transformed traditional theology in the previous century, Francis's life had a tremendous impact both immediately on those who became his own followers and later on men for whom the Franciscan rule of poverty was less important than the new sanction he had given the life of the individual spirit. Francis himself may have had an essentially quietistic politics, but to ignore politics is often itself an implicitly political act. The growing political issue of Francis's day was the relative power of the papacy and the secular ruler—never one of his considerations. But his example could, like that of Charlemagne or Jesus, be used by partisans of either view. Thus the official lives of Francis depicted him as a true son of the Church, while the popular legends preserved another Francis, one whose example nurtured those who sought a spiritual life separate from any institutional realms. By the nineteenth century, when Francis as a figure was revived and his works perceived anew in the heyday of European imperialism, he could be celebrated particularly by historians like Jules Michelet and cultural commentators like Matthew Arnold, for whom he was a figure beyond the concerns of nations. As we shall see, in the centuries that followed his death, his most important influence was not among the pilgrims who would come (and still come) to Assisi to steep themselves in the relics of his presence, only to return to the materialistic lives they briefly left behind. Instead it pervaded a new group of men who wished to distinguish themselves from both the institutional spirituality of the Church and the institutional legalism of the state to create an internationalism beyond nations, a transcendental internationalism of art and wisdom.

Dante: The Fame of Fame's Bestowing

> . . . tell him who you were; he can make amends,
> and will, by making bloom again your fame
> in the world above, where his return is sure.
>
> —DANTE, *Inferno*

> He . . . was wont, when weary of the vulgar herd, to withdraw into some solitary place, and there consider in his speculations what spirit moveth the heaven, whence cometh life to the animals that are on earth, what are the causes of things; or to rehearse some rare invention, or compose some poem, which shall make him though dead live by fame amongst the folk that are to come.
>
> —BOCCACCIO, *Life of Dante*

Christian society had begun in opposition to Roman standards of public praise, but quickly enough it had absorbed those standards and made them its own. By the end of the Middle Ages it had become an oppressive hierarchy whose infinite degrees and offices stifled individual desire without allowing it any truly spiritual outlet. The reforms of Francis took the time-honored step of a recommitment to religious purity, looking to a world of spirit and nature, in which men and women could stand as human beings before God, stripped of the emblems of their tangible status. Francis's innovation was to make that commitment before the eyes of the world—a theater to chastise those who had fallen away from its ideals. Dante's more literary and more history-conscious alternative was to revive Rome not as a model in rule but as a spiritual reality beneath the secular dross. The theater of Roman politics, condemned as empty show by Augustine, could in this new life be filled with a spiritual substance that went beyond institutional Christianity to justify the soarings of the human spirit. In a world where, as Garrett Mattingly has pointed out, those we call Europeans "had no common name for themselves except Christians" (16), Dante's fascination with reputation is a prelude as well to the heroic nationalisms of the Renaissance, where history would be searched and researched for the names of those forerunners whose actions could sanction the pride of the present. The Middle Ages emphasized that writing did not spring from individuals but from tradition by way of individuals. The assertion of a claim of originality would not come in full force until the eighteenth century. But already in the works of Dante we clearly see the beginning of the writer's and later the artist's preoccupation with balancing the claims of an inspiration that came from God and one that came, somehow, from inside the individual himself. Like the men of the Roman Republic and the early Empire, Dante, Petrarch, and Boccaccio, as well as painters and sculptors like Giotto, Ghiberti, Donatello, and Brunelleschi—to name only the most prominent—allied their artistic achievements to a fascination with the theme of earthly glory, its lure, and its transience.

In the model affirmed by the influence of Charlemagne, the writer and the artist had remained only the bearers of the ruler's fame in the present and the heralds of it to the future. Horace's grand assertion of the superior durability of poems to empires was rarely on the medieval mind. At best the writer drew his own fame from the fame of his subject, as Einhard's emphasis on his relation to Charlemagne echoes Arrian's claim to become famous because he has rescued the fame of Alexander from oblivion. Poignantly enough, Einhard's life of Charlemagne, as it has come down to us, has nothing in the text to tell us who wrote it; the name was supplied a few generations later by another writer to make sure that the fame of Einhard would not be lost in that of his great patron.

In the literature of Greece and Rome, while there are frequent metaphors for the act of writing drawn from other areas, there are few drawn from literature. Plato may write of the pen sowing seeds, but no one, for example, writes of the "book of life"; no one says "I see with my pen" or "my mind is like a blank page"—all common images from the Middle Ages (Curtius, 302–47). Similarly, Virgil, Horace, and Ovid rarely dwell on the *book* that contains their works or the pen and ink that writes them down, in part because their model and competition for the transmission of knowledge and insight was the public orator. Horace could style himself as a *princeps,* but it would hardly be a compliment to call Augustus a poet, and Nero's attempts to be an artist were an indication of his unsuitability to rule.

In contrast, with the basic model of the Bible in mind, writing in the Middle Ages could be a special occasion for the muted aspiration toward the infinite and the eternal. In a way hard to appreciate in the world after the printing press, the book after the rise of Christianity was a mystic space in which spiritual being could openly display itself. The Judeo-Christian God is, of course, himself a writer, one of the very few gods of antiquity to be so characterized. God had written the Ten Commandments and the Law as well as dictated the Bible to Moses. Jesus himself appears in early paintings, as I have mentioned, often in the guise of a Greek philosopher, holding a scroll. Without the written witness of Matthew, Mark, Luke, and John, the story of Christ's life and ministry could hardly have been appreciated as widely, and Paul kept in touch with congregations around the Mediterranean through letters that themselves became part (perhaps the oldest) of the New Testament.[1]

Such precedents were ready-made for any newly revived literary culture in the Middle Ages. They stood behind the cultural plans of Charlemagne, and they were increasingly invoked in the twelfth century when a European literary culture began to discover closer links with past writers than with present rulers. During the earlier Middle Ages poetry writing had essentially been schoolwork and poets were primarily scholars who learned and taught the ancient models, suiting them to more immediate purposes. Poetry was also a skill of courtiers, and the poetry of praise, when it did exist, was written in Latin to flatter the ruler-patron, who supported the poet with an official job at court, since to be paid for his poetry would turn him into a mere tradesman. It was thus possible to *become* a poet, that is, to learn the skills of writing poetry, but impossible to *be* a poet.[2]

But by the thirteenth century there comes a growing assertion that true authority belongs not to the secular or even the spiritual rulers so much as to those like Francis, Dominic, and the mendicant friars—who deny both the status and personal realization attainable in a hierarchy—and those like Dante, Chaucer, Petrarch, and Erasmus—who reach beyond the hierarchies of the present and align themselves with a literary and artistic tradition that serves but more often judges worldly power. The newly

1. The Gospel of John includes the story of the woman taken in adultery, where Jesus is described as writing on the ground while the Pharisees attempt to catch him in a violation of the law. According to scholars, this appears in only one Greek manuscript and was probably not part of the original text. Intriguingly enough, however, it has many word usages more typical of the synoptic Gospels, including the only mention of "scribes" in John. The contrast between Jesus writing in the dust and the false authority of the law unmediated by individual judgment ("He that is without sin among you, let him cast a stone at her") would be striking to any writer seeking to render the message of Jesus in more permanent form.

2. The medieval writer found his social justification in presenting his work to a patron, usually a ruler or a high Church official. See the illustrations to Sherman, *Portraits of Charles V of France.*

fashioned instrument of their authority would be the ability to decide who should be given any fame at all. The rise of literature written in vernacular tongues, exemplified in the works of Dante and Chaucer, have always been greeted as the origin of national cultures formed by the break away from the unified Latin culture of the Church. But we should be aware how much the national assertion involved in such literary moments also reflects a desire to determine what should and what should not be remembered, what is worthy and what unworthy of praise, and who is the person to bestow it. The writings of Dante especially foreshadow a host of later efforts to fuse the Christian emphasis on the afterlife with the classical urge for earthly fame and honor. Christ had promised a victory over death to Constantine and the Christian emperors. The gaze of posterity on the Christian poet might confer a similar or even superior victory. After the combats between popes and emperors, it is the writers who furnish a reconciliation of spiritual and political fame, through the celebration of Roman political and literary figures, mediated by the spiritual authority of the book. With consummate appropriateness, Dante—the first writer of the Middle Ages to write at length of himself and of the fame of his work, the poet most conscious of reputation and its meaning in the present and the future, the exile whom Ernest Hemingway seven hundred years later was to call (with self-exonerating glee) "the Florentine egotist" (*Islands,* 197)—constructs his greatest poem as a voyage into the lands beyond death: hell, purgatory, and heaven.[3]

The history of fame is a history of the shapes taken by individual desires for public expression, whether to the glory of God, of society, of self, or some combination of those audiences. The fame for individuality, like the growth of portraiture, awaits the coming of a new sense of character that grows out of the social experience of cities rather than from the equality of all souls in the universal Church. Although medieval chronicles and tapestries were crammed with names and faces, yet it was the emblematic patterns and the postures that were most important—the fame of the great ruler or the great churchman or the fame of particular saints, especially those with a relation to an individual because of birthday or occupation. From about the early fourteenth century on, the newly energized chivalric view of life, with its knightly code of honor, virtue, and bravery, also gave rise to a representation of emblematic heroes, sometimes drawn from the stories of the wars of Troy or Thebes, the exploits of the Arthurian knights, the varieties of the Alexander romance—or in the special form of depiction known in France as the *Neuf Preux* and in England as the Nine Worthies. Flourishing especially in wall paintings and tapestries, the roll call of the Nine Worthies varies, and the lordly patron may sometimes add himself or an ancestor as a tenth. But in general there are three Old Testament figures (Joshua, David, Judah

3. See also Hemingway's *Across the River and into the Trees,* in which Dante is frequently invoked to characterize the clash between writer and man, especially in contrast to the Dutch painters "whose names no one remembers" (191).

Maccabee), three classical (Hector, Alexander, and Caesar), and three medieval (Arthur, Charlemagne, and Godfrey of Bouillon, who fought in the First Crusade and sided with Emperor Henry IV in his battle with the papacy). Often women were added to the number, and equivalent groups of Nine Worthy Women also appear in two intriguingly different formats: one akin to the men in valor and political importance (including, for example, Zenobia, Hippolyta, Melanippe, Lampedo, Penthesilea, Tomyris, Teuta, Semiramis, Deipyle, and sometimes Joan of Arc) and one an unparalleled group of "good women" (including Lucretia, Veturia, Virginia, Esther, Judith, Jael, St. Helena, St. Brigid, and St. Elizabeth).[4]

In the career of Dante particularly, this emblematic fame that characterizes the Middle Ages is transformed into a fame that must be justified by a city: a fame of theater and role playing; of politics, art, and intrigue; of life stories and actions on earth. Nurtured on medieval spirituality, Dante's presentation of himself as the poet who preeminently awards fame furnishes a visionary core for the tremendous effort undertaken by the newly wealthy Florentines, from the thirteenth to the fifteenth centuries, to affirm the importance of themselves and their city by the construction of monuments, public buildings, and private homes, along with a patronage of the arts on a scale unrivaled since the days of Rome. Augustine considered the fame achievable in a city to be like famine, a hunger that could never be satisfied. But fame in the writings of Dante becomes a political and cultural force, specifically motivated by a Florentine civic pride that resented the incursions of the papacy. In later centuries, when it is fostered by patron-politicians like Lorenzo the Magnificent, it reinforces a cultural and political nationalism that can withstand, influence, and even gain control of the universal Church.

Secular aspiration requires a definition of the history within which one

4. Many of these figures are at best semihistorical and, although familiar to the Middle Ages, have virtually vanished from our own heroic stockroom. An interesting place to get some idea of how fame for women was defined is Boccaccio's *Concerning Famous Women* (*De Claris Mulieribus*), the first such book in a genre previously devoted entirely to men. Zenobia is the warrior queen of Palmyra; Hippolyta an early queen of the Amazons; Melanippe the consort of Poseidon; Lampedo a war leader of the Amazons; Penthesilea the leader of the Amazons in the Trojan war; Tomyris the queen of Scythia who defeated Cyrus the Great; Teuta the queen of Illyria in the battles with Rome; Semiramis the queen of Assyria and supposed founder of Babylon; and Deipyle the wife of one of the seven attackers of Thebes. In the equally unfixed list of "good women," Lucretia's rape and suicide helps create the Roman Republic; Veturia defends Rome from attack by her son Coriolanus; Virginia is murdered by her father to save her from slavery; Esther, the Jewish queen of Persia, protects her people; Judith and Jael kill enemy generals who have attacked the Jews; St. Helena is the mother of Constantine; St. Brigid is an important figure in Irish Church history; and St. Elizabeth of Hungary is renowned for her charity.

In accord with the effort of the formulators of the Nine Worthies to create an imagistic ideology of heroism for the knightly class, the period of its origin also witnesses the appearance of playing cards with their similarly metamorphosed chivalry. The depiction of the Worthies and Worthyesses remain a strong tradition across Europe until the seventeenth century. Playing cards have lasted a bit longer. Schroeder give a detailed treatment of the evolution of the nine male worthies and their female counterparts in *Der Topos der Nine Worthies*.

seeks fame. By the accidents of medieval politics, Florence, previously a minor town reputedly founded by the Romans, became the outstanding model for the newly independent cities of Italy, outside the direct authority of both empire and papacy and therefore the constant battleground of their interests. In the century of Dante's birth, Florence had undergone a rapid expansion of population, land, and influence unparalleled in Europe. By the time he was born, the Florentine gold piece (the "florin") was the standard of exchange throughout Europe and the Near East, exemplifying the international connections of Florentine commerce and industry as well as Florentine banking.[5] With due allowances for his own temperament, clearly something in the air of Florence itself encouraged the kind of self-assertion that prompted Dante at the age of eighteen (1283) to write a sonnet to Beatrice and send it to all the most notable poets in Florence, who just as remarkably (according to his own story and those of Boccaccio and others) immediately welcomed Dante into their company.[6] By the age of thirty Dante was enrolled in the Guild of Physicians and Specialists, a vague category that seems to have included those who dealt in spices and jewels as well as sellers of books. By thirty-five he became one of the six Priors who ruled the city under the new constitution and took his place in a reorganized Florentine politics that itself was only a few years old. Under the new constitution Florentine government was based on the representation of the city guilds (*arte*), those professional and craft organizations that regulated the nature of work, its sale and interchange. Thus the Florentine government constituted a decisive break with both the imperial feudal government of the secular rulers and the spiritual hierarchies of the Church. It was a government based not upon spiritual sanction or upon aristocratic tradition but upon local institutions that gave a shape to the individual career amid professional colleagues and professional precedents. But, two years after Dante became one of the civic leaders of Florence, a new party was in power, and he was banished for life.

Dante died in Ravenna after almost twenty years of political exile from

5. For the growth of Florence, see Goldthwaite, *Renaissance Florence*. The florin was first issued in 1252.

6. According to his own account in *La Vita nuova* (c. 1292), Dante first met Beatrice Portinari, the daughter of a wealthy Florentine, when they were both nine years old and his first look at her totally agitated his mind, body, and soul: "[F]rom that time on, Love governed my soul" (Musa, 4). He sees her again at eighteen and she greets him. Overcome, he returns to his room, sleeps, has a vision that seems to be of God and Beatrice together, whereupon he awakes and writes a sonnet "addressed to all of Love's faithful subjects" for their interpretations. The rest of *La Vita nuova* explores the meaning of his passion for Beatrice in its spiritual dimension, just as in *The Divine Comedy* it is Beatrice who allows Dante to pass beyond the barriers of death and guides him through Paradise. *La Vita nuova* seems to have been written about two years after Beatrice herself died. She had been married then for some years (before 1288) to a banker. Dante himself had been married also, perhaps as early as 1284 (at nineteen) to Gemma Donati, who bore him four children, did not go into exile with him in 1302, and is never mentioned in his works. Arranged marriages were frequent in the period, but at least in his writings Dante's love for Beatrice, like Petrarch's for Laura, is a way to self-transcendence, not romance.

Florence, still hoping that he would be asked to return. The celebrity that he had already achieved in the rest of his world was not as important to him as acceptance by his native city. When the laurel wreath of civic poetry was offered to him by the University of Bologna two years before his death, he refused, because it could not be conferred on him in the Florentine church where he had been baptized. Dante's constant effort to set his career within the context of the city of Florence harkens beyond the virtually cityless Middle Ages to the early centuries of the Roman Republic when fame meant nothing if it was not achieved at Rome. With a fully Christian view of the universe, Dante also desired not only the audience of God but also the audience of those earthly spirits who resided in his native city. As Beatrice promises him on the way to Paradise, there he will forever be "citizen of that Rome where Christ is Roman" (*Purgatorio,* xxxii, 102–3).

*   *   *

> He was very greedy of honor and glory, more so perhaps than beseems his fame and virtue. Yet, what life is so humble as not to be touched by the sweetness of glory?
>
> —BOCCACCIO, *Life of Dante*

Before his exile from Florence, Dante had held a high post in the city that was at the forefront of the revival of civic power and civic spirit on the Greek and Roman model. Accordingly, his greatest literary work, the *Commedia* (*Divine Comedy*), is not directly concerned with political events at all but with the journey of a man named Dante through the lands of the dead, where he ticks off their fates according to how they lived their lives on earth. In exile from the city that was the arena of his own early political and literary fame, Dante's poetic fame is thus dependent on knowing exactly what true fame is. He is the arbiter of all traditions—artistic, political, and military—and by his insight defines what the best and most true traditions of his own country and particularly his city are. Commentators have argued with great intricacy over Dante's religious and political beliefs, trying to disentangle a virtually impenetrable web of pro-imperial and antipapal politics. But in the history of fame, *The Divine Comedy* stands out for its constant preoccupation with adjudicating who deserves to be remembered, for what reason, and in what way. Like Augustine, Dante believes that writing supports memory and rescues worthy things from oblivion. But Dante also transforms Augustine's wary hostility to the Roman forms of public achievement into a fascination with reputation that links worldly action with the honors or punishment awaiting one in the afterlife. Rejecting Augustine's division between the city of God and the city of man, Dante attempts to synthesize spiritual with temporal fame in much the same way that his political views (particularly in his late treatise *On Monarchy*) emphasize a reconciliation of spiritual and temporal authority in the world. Instead of separating sacred from profane history, he argues that, by the occurrence of Christ's birth during the reign of Augustus, God gave secular rule directly to Rome. Thus a universal temporal monarchy should coexist with the papacy, each responsible for its own sphere. The cosmic compendium of Dante's great poem is therefore not like those of the medieval theologians, ending in Aquinas, who sought through Christian doctrine to ask and answer every possible question about the nature of man and the universe. Instead *The Divine Comedy* absorbs the specifics of daily history and earthly time into an overarching poetic and providential plan, casting individuals in stories told by the poet and assigning them to their proper places—as far as he is concerned—in hell, purgatory, and heaven.[7]

With our greater sensitivity to the writer as creator of his work, it is clear that Dante is the one who determines the merits and deserts of the shades who appear before us. But he himself phrases the poem as a divine revelation through which he is led, first by Virgil, then by Statius, and finally by Beatrice. The division corresponds to his sense of authorship as well. In his own time he is one of the few to give such importance to the writers of antiquity, presaging the revival of Roman culture that will become so common in the few hundred years after his death. But he also clearly supersedes their authority as much as he praises it. Virgil must return to hell and Statius remain in purgatory before Dante enters heaven. For all their wisdom, "great in fame, not yet in faith," pagan writers lack the Christian perspective, and so Dante must finally be instructed by Beatrice, the embodiment of God's love.

Dante's division of himself in *The Divine Comedy*, between the eager but inept student who is being shown the world of death and the poet who has created the poem, thus corresponds to the division in the late medieval mind itself between the humble individual learning at the feet of the great men of the past and the assertive individual who raises his own fame on their shoulders. There are certainly precedents for this method in other medieval poems, where the structure of a dream vision allowed the poet to be both the wide-eyed dreamer and the behind-the-scenes author. But it is Dante who first draws out its crucial implications for the definition of the poet, his audience, and the life of the poem. In the process the Augustinian conflict between humbleness and assertion becomes more and more intensified, and the contrast between Dante's journey and the spiritual quest of Augustine's *Confessions* seems both intended and appropriate. Augustine's story of his conversion and gradual movement toward God's truth appeals to those like himself searching for belief in an age of

7. Aquinas's *Summa theologica* becomes official Catholic doctrine only in the sixteenth-century response to the Reformation. It is worth noting how much the reputation of Aquinas may owe to Dante's celebration of him as the prime expositor of heaven in the *Paradiso* and to the scribes and printers who drew on Dante as a guide to what deserved remembrance and preservation even outside the churchly sphere. Aquinas is canonized in 1323, two years after the death of Dante.

competing religious and philosophical systems. Dante, writing at the end of a period marked more by uniformity than by contradiction, assumes belief in order to chart the world beyond. Augustine's autobiographical *Confessions* thus has the shape of a spiritual roadmap, while *The Divine Comedy* depicts a journey no one else could have made or will. Dante is not the believer who happens to have the gift of articulation and can therefore write of his experiences to others. He is clearly and constantly the poet, whose special nature has been rewarded with God's gift of this vision of divine order.

What constitutes true fame is thus a crucial issue throughout *The Divine Comedy*. In the *Inferno* the prime urge of the dead is to ensure that they are still remembered on earth because without reputation, whether good or bad, what does life on earth mean? When Dante asks their names, they invariably want to know who he is as well. Because he will be permitted to return to the world, he can "refresh" their fame (xiii, 53). In purgatory the souls are less earth-centered. There Dante meets Oderisi, a notably vain manuscript illuminator, who can now appreciate the work of others because death has released him from envy:

> O empty glory of all human power!
> How soon the green fades from the topmost bough,
> Unless the following season show no growth!
>
> Once Cimabue thought to hold the field
> as painter; Giotto now is all the rage,
> dimming the lustre of the other's fame.
>
> So, even one Guido takes from the other
> poetic glory; and, already born
> perhaps, is he who'll drive both from fame's nest.
>
> Your earthly fame [*romore*] is but a gust of wind
> that blows about, shifting this way and that,
> and as it changes quarter, changes name (*Purgatorio* xi, 91–102).

The passage is intriguing for the way it acknowledges the transitoriness that undermines the competition for human excellence at the same time that it seems to absolve Dante himself from the need to compete. Consider the terms in which the question has been raised. From an artistic world in which works were fashioned according to formats and motifs built up over the centuries, and the artist's name was known principally if he was a superior workman, we have moved to a world in which the "best" artist is a matter of argument and discussion and those considered the best are beginning to command a respect far beyond that given to craft and care. The older audience was primarily interested in the object created. A later audience has come into being that prides itself on knowing the names of the best practitioners, those who can transform the traditional materials and give them a stamp of the new, the individual, the "modern." Cimabue was the foremost painter of Dante's youth; Giotto lived to paint Dante's own portrait in a fresco on the walls of the Florentine Bargello.[8] Already there is a lively sense of the genealogy of art, as one artist supersedes another. Similarly, one school of poetry has superseded another and both will be superseded again, by an unknown poet.

This new awareness of simultaneous descent from the past and competition with the present allows Dante to step outside earthly time and into poetic history. Since the first notable Florentine poet who praised Dante's early work was Guido Cavalcanti, who had surpassed Guido Guinizzelli of Bologna, it is difficult not to see Dante himself as the poet who will go further than both of them and their schools. The situation is reminiscent of that moment in the *Aeneid* when Aeneas in hell, after being shown the panorama of Roman history, sees a shadowy youth who will bring it all to fruition, the young Augustus. But appropriately enough, the most comparable scene in *The Divine Comedy* does not foretell the coming of a great ruler, but of a great poet. Beginning in the lyric mode of Cavalcanti, Dante has fashioned a new synthesis of personal and spiritual cosmology from the love laments of the troubadours and the cosmological musings of the medieval theologians. Already in the early cantos of the *Inferno,* he makes himself a sixth of the great poets, along with Homer, Virgil, Horace, Ovid, and Lucan. But throughout the poem Dante's sense of literary self-importance is qualified by the weakness and hasty judgment of the character "Dante" within the poem. The combination of Christian humility and literary assertion is thus not a contradiction in Dante's work, but an important part of its basic content. When Oderisi says that Giotto, not Cimabue, now has the "cry," he stands in the circle of the proud, whose punishment in purgatory is to recite the Lord's Prayer continually, to remind themselves of who the true Creator and the true Audience is. Such reminders do not daunt Dante's aspiration for his work, because he seeks not earthly fame (*romore,* "noise")—like the "cry" that celebrates Giotto—but an eternal Virgilian renown for conferring true fame on deserving men.

To the renown he receives as the bestower of true fame, Dante adds the fame of the poet for having created the poem, a fame explicitly sanctioned in the *Paradiso*. There he meets his great-great-grandfather Caccia-

8. Or at least it has been attributed to Giotto. Although at our distance the difference between Giotto and his teacher Cimabue is best appreciated after some study, Dante's reference to Giotto in the *Commedia* is the fountainhead of a general fourteenth- and fifteenth-century effort to make Giotto the prime Italian famous artist, whose separation of painting from its previous "Greek" and less realistic mode parallels the new awareness of literature and the general reawakening of all the arts. Propagandists of Italian painting, like Vasari, linked him to both Dante and St. Francis. Yet despite his emblematic importance for writers and other painters, we know little for certain about his exact commissions and the stages of his career. His only undisputed work is in the Arena Chapel at Padua and the Santa Croce at Florence, which includes a series based on the life of St. Francis. About 1330, it is supposed, he went to Naples to paint a group of famous men for King Robert. But of that as well as of the *Vana gloria* he did in Milan for Azzone Visconti, nothing remains, and Giotto's role in the Francis paintings in the chapel at Assisi is much in doubt (Smart, *Assisi Problem*).

guida, who foretells his exile. Dante responds that he fears to write *The Divine Comedy* because he might be hounded for it in the present and condemned for it by posterity: "And if to truth I am a timid friend, / I fear to lose life amongst those / who shall call this time ancient" (*Paradiso*, xvii, 118–20). But Cacciaguida reassures him and orders him to write the poem—"make your whole vision manifest." Since Dante's poem will become both the cry that celebrates and the wind that demolishes the highest reputations, it has been ordained that he meet only famous people in the afterlife, for unknown examples have no impact on those who hear them.

No doubt the special circumstances of Dante's exile intensified the cultural and spiritual nationalism whose canon he creates. But he also lives at a moment in history when the writer is beginning to assert authority less for how thoroughly he possesses authoritative knowledge than for how he has superseded past authority. The theme of fame as it comes down into the Renaissance with Dante's patronage accentuates the seemingly contradictory elements of respect and supersession: The past is venerated, but it is also outdone. Thus fame appears in two aspects, as something transitory that only fools seek and as something permanent that is the reward of true greatness. The literary and artistic preoccupation with the theme of fame that stretches from Dante until the early years of the nineteenth century (when its nature changes decisively) can be described as a tug of war, partly sincere and partly rhetorical, between the classical ideal of overt praise and honor and the Christian ideal of spiritual aspiration and inner virtue. Both versions are already present in the Virgilian distinction between good fame and bad fame embodied in the *Aeneid,* which, along with Ovid's House of Fame in the *Metamorphoses,* becomes a favorite source for many later writers wrestling over the question of fame—in works by Petrarch, Boccaccio, and Chaucer down to such late-blooming versions as Pope's *The Temple of Fame* and sections of Byron's *Don Juan.* That writers are first and particularly drawn to the struggle indicates the central importance of the attitude toward language and verbal learning in the transition from the Middle Ages to the Renaissance. Words in general may be cries in the wind, but Christ himself was the Word of God, and the truly inspired poet could make cries and raise winds that might be substantial enough to smash or change the seemingly solid structures of the material world. Unlike earlier medieval writers, Dante therefore thinks continually about the appropriate audience for his work, both in the present and in posterity. His essential claim for *The Divine Comedy* is that it must be interpreted, for it is not the encyclopedic work that lays out information so much as it is the cosmic work whose truths will be revealed only after careful study. In a letter he wrote to a patron, Dante even outlines the various ways the poem should be read, in line with the methods that had been developed to read the Bible. Commentaries sprung up almost immediately. Two of the earliest were by sons of Dante, and, barely fifty years after Dante's death, a chair of Dante studies was established at Florence, whose first occupant was Boccaccio. In accord with Dante's own sense of fealty to a tradition of teachers, the continuities of the learned had been reestablished—but now in a realm of the secular spirit—fostered by literary study outside the confines of the Church.

Dante uses the double sanction of classical literature and Christian faith to fashion that special mingling of tradition and originality we call artistic. We know very little about the life and works of Cimabue, for example, and those of his paintings attested without doubt are comparatively few. He still works in a less assertive medieval tradition. Giotto, on the other hand, is much better known, not only to us, but to his own time, when he traveled all over Italy performing commissions on paintings, sculpture, and buildings. Dante himself in his exile took advantage of the new relations between the cities of Europe by acting as an occasional ambassador. As the connections originally forged by the Roman Empire were revived to serve a new politics, so artists of all sorts traveled to Florence and Rome to seek the enabling sanction of classical forms. To a great extent the history of fame is a history of explicitness, and Dante's forays into the question represent a new self-consciousness of fame as a problem, particularly for writers. In their different ways both Einhard and Nottker subordinated themselves to the "great man" who was the subject of their works. But Dante's decision to cast his great spiritual epic in terms of the names and careers of men and women who deserve to be remembered with honor or loathing makes a decisive break with the medieval use of a few emblematic figures. His double role as voyager through the afterlife and creator of the poem mimes his own implication in the history he attempts at once to celebrate, to judge, and to transcend. The awareness of classical precedents and the preoccupation with his debt to the line of Virgil and Statius keep him keenly aware of their own fascination with the theme of fame and in particular the distinctions, sometimes overt, sometimes more subtle, between the fame of the literary man and the fame of the public man he both celebrates and instructs. So in Dante's polemical works, particularly the Latin prose treatises *De Vulgare Eloquentia* (*On the Common Tongue*) and *De Monarchia,* he speaks as a writer conversant with the greatness of past literature and learning who is now addressing the great public men of his own world and giving them the benefit of his uniquely focused perspective.

As the repository of past literature, the writer is especially equipped to confer fame in the present because he knows the greats of the past. Given a special turn by the circumstances of Dante's life of exile, the literature of the past and the language of the present become a new country to which the writer now pays his allegiance, sometimes in addition to his own, sometimes opposed to it, and sometimes, as in *The Divine Comedy,* in the name of a purer, more ideal, country that might through the poet's ministrations return again. If this idea of the poet as a wandering member of a kingdom of literature not bound geographically or politically by the borders of his world is reminiscent of Augustine's concept of the Christian, the association is appropriate. By combining the journey of a soul with the exploration of a truth mediated by poets, Dante emphasizes the spiritual associations of the poetic enterprise as opposed to the aristocratic. As we have seen, it is a potential that is present with increasing clarity in the works of poets like Virgil, Horace, and Ovid. But Dante teases it out in all its complexity, supplying both writers and artists with a repository of imagery, connected to but separable from the codified religious motifs of medieval painting and literature.

Dante thus takes a crucial step in the redefinition of artistic fame by placing himself at the nexus of political, spiritual, and cultural history. *The Divine Comedy* begins, he says, when the stars are in the same position that they were when Love created the world. Like Augustine, Dante can make an implicit analogy between his own creation and God's without yet feeling as guilty or as competitive as will later artists and writers. But his way of dissolving the contradiction between the Roman urge to fame and the Christian awareness of its emptiness was to define the urge as an inspiration by God to an exemplary true fame, opposed to mere power, mere words, and mere public show. The dreamer, the man who has had the vision of eternity, must bring it back to tell it publicly for the delectation of those who could not make the same journey. To an extent, Dante's model, as he had been for St. Francis, was the evasive Jesus, who both performed and turned away from mere performance. Through their careers, Jesus' evasion of publicity was becoming a category of public action; and the writer's claim to bestow proper fame, a well-developed social role. *The Divine Comedy* complexly courts fame. But in other works Dante speaks of the inconveniences of fame, and anecdotes tell of the reactions of those who shied away from him because he had made the journey to hell as well as those, usually patrons or the worldly powerful, who tried to best him with practical jokes. Yet he continued to address himself to those who would be able to judge his works with the understanding they deserved. In his journey through the afterlife, protected, as he says, by God, he had begun to discover the audience that exists in the world.

Chaucer: The House of Fame

> Now pray I to them all that hearken this little treatise or read it,
> that if there be anything in it that pleases them, that they thank our
> Lord Jesus Christ for it, from whom proceeds all wit and all goodness.
> And if there be anything that displeases them, I pray them also that
> they ascribe it to my ignorance, and not to my will, that would full
> fain have said better if I had had knowing.
>
> —CHAUCER, *Retraction* to the *Canterbury Tales*

Dante had pioneered a synthesis between the classical and the Christian attitudes toward fame that allowed him to place his own journey toward transcendence at the center of his work. Born some twenty years after Dante's death, Geoffrey Chaucer (1340?–1400) is fully aware of Dante's method as well as those of the two other prominent seekers of literary fame—Petrarch (1304–1374) and Boccaccio (1313–1375)—whose careers overlapped his. In their different ways all three Italian writers attempt to reconcile the classical (especially Roman) idea that the urge for fame and glory is ultimately in the service of the highest value with the Christian objection that fame and even glory is the production of empty images and even emptier words. But whatever inspiration Chaucer had from their example, he contemplates some of the same issues with a much more jaundiced and mocking eye. He is intensely suspicious both of fame and the desire for it, even to the extent of undermining himself as an author in order that he not stand between the reader and the truth that his writing might be able to divulge. Chaucer stands to the development of English literature in the way Dante stands to Italian literature. But the literary aspiration that Dante (and later Petrarch and Boccaccio) exonerate through Ciceronian paradoxes seems to Chaucer to be the source of much more confusion and uncertainty. He barely disguises his feeling that Dante's humbleness is merely a pose, masking a poetic grandiosity and personal assertiveness that to Chaucer may be blasphemous, is certainly dangerous, but is continually fascinating. As we shall see, Chaucer's adherence to Christian and stoic ideas of the emptiness of worldly fame paradoxically yields an affirmation as strong as any of the three Italian aspirants. All four writers, by placing the literary man as an intercessor between the spiritual and temporal worlds, achieve a personal stature unparalleled in the usually subordinate position of literary art in the Middle Ages. All in their different ways sit as ancestors to the many styles of artistic self-consciousness to follow.

Like Dante, Chaucer appears as both character and poet in many of his works, including *The Canterbury Tales*. But Chaucer's attitude toward Dante's redefinition of the poet's scope and nature is at once more satirically secular and more medievally communal. Dante may be frequently a weak and imperceptive figure in *The Divine Comedy,* but Chaucer is usually a comic figure in his works, particularly in *The Canterbury Tales,* where he tells two of the least appealing tales. Where Dante in *The Divine Comedy* is led by his distinguished guides until he finally soars with Beatrice up to God, Chaucer tags along beside the pilgrims on the way to Canterbury, recording their stories while his "character" is often the butt of their jokes. Dante's world is that of the afterlife, where divine justice has meted out the appropriate rewards and punishments. Chaucer focuses instead on the journey of earthly life itself, with its diversions and uncertainties. Although both are fascinated by the varieties of human nature, it is Chaucer much more than Dante who allows his characters to tell their own stories, to justify or incriminate themselves. Whatever the personal appeal of his characters, Dante makes it clear that they belong in the circle of hell, purgatory, or heaven to which they have been assigned. But Chaucer's pilgrims are allowed to present themselves more fully and sometimes very differently from the way he has first introduced them.

Such distinctions, interesting enough as ways into understanding how the two greatest poets of the fourteenth century conceived their callings, come into sharp perspective when we realize that among Chaucer's earliest works, written when he was about forty, is an extended seriocomical poem on the nature of fame and writing entitled *The House of Fame.* Exuberantly intertwining matters that the Middle Ages had generally kept apart, *The House of Fame* sets Virgil and Ovid in the light of both Christian attitudes toward earthly fame and the new aspirations brought onto the literary stage by Dante and his inheritors. Dante in *The Divine Comedy* may live through, be torn by, and finally transcend the conflict between secular and spiritual fame. But Chaucer in *The House of Fame* examines the paradox with unflinching directness, even while slyly mocking Dante's high-minded anxiety about posterity. For the next hundred years it is the most influential of Chaucer's works, and, appropriately enough, it is the most original as well, the least indebted to preexisting sources, and the one that transforms the sources he does use with the greatest freedom.

In *The House of Fame,* Chaucer's presentation of himself has little of the assertion of the Italians. Often, it seems defined precisely against the aspiration of Dante or Petrarch or Boccaccio, with their learning, their aspiration to transcendent vision, and their linking of themselves across the ages with the great names of the classical past. Chaucer pays tribute to those names, but he does not aspire to be one of their number. While Dante sought his own fame through his bestowal of fame upon others, Chaucer is a social poet, whose theme is not the out-of-scale assertion but the domestic continuity, not the unique but the familiar, not love as a route to the infinite but love as a preoccupation of men and women.

As *The House of Fame* begins, Chaucer awakes in a temple of glass, built in honor of Venus and richly adorned with scenes from the *Aeneid:* Aeneas escaping Troy, the sojourn in the cave with Dido, the journey to the underworld, and the conquering of Italy. Amazed by the wonder of the images graven on the walls of the temple, Chaucer leaves the temple and finds himself in an empty desert with nothing to see at all for miles around until he looks toward the sun and sees an eagle flying there.

In the invocation to the second book, Chaucer calls on everyone who understands English to hear him and again says that his vision is more blessed than anyone, classical or biblical, has ever had. Thought alone made all he dreamed and shut it up in the "treasury . . . of my brain." The story continues with the eagle flying down to pick up Chaucer in its claws and carrying him off. Chaucer faints. The eagle, calling him by name, tells him to wake up and explains to his apprehensive passenger that Jupiter has decided to reward his service to Venus and Cupid in his writings by letting him go to the House of Fame. There he can learn new "tidings" of love to use in his poetry, which has otherwise been limited because he has learned of love only from books. The House of Fame collects all such news, explains the eagle, because all the sounds on earth come there in the shape of the person who said them. Then the eagle spots the House of Fame and drops Chaucer before the front gate.

The invocation to Apollo for aid in writing that begins the third book of *The House of Fame* recalls Dante's invocation to Apollo at the beginning of *Paradiso* for the ability to write of heaven. The House of Fame, like that in Ovid's *Metamorphoses,* sits high on a rock, at the intersection of earth, sea, and sky. But, as Chaucer looks more closely, he sees that the rock is made of ice, not of steel, and on its base are engraved the names of the famous. At the top of the rock there is a castle, filled with windows and surrounded by harpists and minstrels, from the great singers like Orpheus to the lowly pipers who entertain at village feasts—all who tell the stories of those who long for fame. Too many to recount, says Chaucer, more than the stars in heaven. Inside the great hall of the House of Fame, courtiers and court officials rush back and forth, arrayed in a variety of costumes emblazoned with noble insignia from Africa, Europe, and Asia. The hall itself, packed with people, is covered everywhere in a half foot of gold. On a dais sits Fame herself, who seems at once both tiny and tall, with as many eyes as birds have feathers and as many ears and tongues as beasts have hairs. Around her the Muses sing of Fame. On her shoulders stand Alexander and Hercules, and supporting her throne are seven pillars, each surmounted by a different figure: Josephus, Statius, Homer, Virgil, Ovid, Lucan, and Claudian. Around the throne surge petitioners, some seeking fame itself and some anonymity. But Fame dispenses her favors with total arbitrariness and instructs her herald Eolus, the god of wind, to blow from the trumpet named Slander or the trumpet named Praise as the whim takes her.

After telling a passerby that he is there not for fame but to seek tidings of love, Chaucer is led out of the House of Fame to another place, like a cage of wood, but sixty miles long, filled with holes, and constantly whirling—a house of story and rumor, filled with different versions of everything that happens in the world. Nearby, the eagle sits on a stone. Recalling Jupiter's desire that Chaucer receive new tidings of love, the eagle flies him in a window. In the house, filled with sailors and pilgrims and all sorts of wandering tale-tellers, Chaucer watches stories being told at top speed from one person to another, growing larger and larger until they fly out a window, sometimes colliding with contradictory tales to emerge mingled together. Hearing a great noise, he runs to the part of the hall where love-tidings are being told. A mob runs with him, half trampling and climbing all over each other. Finally, Chaucer sees a man he doesn't know,

> But he seemed for to be
> A man of great auctorily (2157–58)

—and there the poem abruptly ends.

I recount the plot of *The House of Fame* because, for the historian of fame, Chaucer's poem is a treasure trove of attitudes, situations, and details that display his simultaneous fascination with and repulsion from the concept of fame. Standing at a crux in the warring traditions of Roman and Christian fame, *The House of Fame* does attack certain kinds of fame and favor others. But its importance is larger than Chaucer's own attitude (itself very ambiguous), for it supplies a critical compilation of the thought of centuries. In every nuance, every allusion, and every reference, we can read the pressure the problem of fame has placed on Chaucer's sense of his own vocation as a writer, and in the poem's seemingly up-in-the-air and unfinished finale, we glimpse his own irresolute attitude toward the issue he has helped bring to a greater self-consciousness. Unlike earlier works, which considered fame in bits and pieces, *The House of Fame* is concerned less with literary fame or spiritual fame or heroic fame than with fame itself, and it thereby foretells a future where fame is not just one of the central themes of art and literature but, in many hands, the crucial question whose nature arrays all the rest.

Although Boccaccio plays some important allusive roles in *The House of Fame* and Petrarch's work influences Chaucer somewhat later in his career, it is especially against Dante and Dante's conception of both poem and poet that Chaucer's work seems directed. I say "seems" because Dante's actual name comes up in *The House of Fame* only once, as a writer (along with Claudian) to whom Chaucer directs anyone who wants to know more about hell. Yet throughout *The House of Fame* allusions to the *Divine Comedy,* particularly in the form of parodic or distorted translations, occur with enormous frequency.[9]

Not long before writing *The House of Fame,* Chaucer had made two, perhaps three, trips to Italy on government business, and we know certainly that he was in Florence sometime in 1373–74, just about the time that Boccaccio was inaugurating the lectures on Dante that the Florentine City Council had hired him to do. But the connection need not be made even so precisely. By the time Chaucer visited Italy an important shift in

9. Literary scholars have long debated the specifics of influence and allusion. Boccaccio, in a poem entitled *Amorosa visione,* had introduced an enthroned Goddess of the Glory of Worldly People with great men celebrated around her.

the iconography and recounting of fame had occurred. All over Italy rulers were commissioning artists to paint on the walls of their homes groups of famous men from the past. In some sense these decorations derived from the tradition of the Nine Worthies, but they were unbounded by the numerical minuteness of the medieval grouping and often even included an image of the patron himself or some contemporary he admired. Of these depictions perhaps the most interesting is the Room of Illustrious Men in the palace of Padua, which was based primarily on Petrarch's *De Viris illustribus* (a collection of mainly classical biographies), which the ruler of Padua had encouraged him to complete after years of sporadic work. The urge to enumerate and depict the great was sweeping across Italy, and audiences flocked to hear their names and read their stories.[10] It requires no minute tracing of specific sources and influences to realize the impact such an environment must have had on Chaucer, coming from a country still heavily involved in medieval conceptions of the limited importance of the individual, either in the world or *sub specie aeternitatis*. Comparing Chaucer to these writers who so often are his sources, we are as struck by his self-conscious handling of the theme of fame as much as by the ease with which they take it for granted. In the second canto of the *Inferno* Dante wonders why he has been chosen for the journey—"*I* am not Aeneas, I am not Paul, / neither I nor any man would think me worthy" (32–33). By the fourth canto, Homer, Virgil, Horace, Ovid, and Lucan welcome him as a sixth to their company, and the contrast with his previous humility causes hardly a ripple in the surface of the poem. But when Chaucer is carried aloft by the eagle, instead of humbly glorying in his new position, he is fearful of being arbitrarily chosen:

> I neither am Enoch, nor Elijah
> Nor Romulus, nor Ganymede (588–89).

While Dante's modesty rejects an association with the hero of the *Aeneid* and the institutional propagator of Christianity, Chaucer more fearfully (and mockingly) refuses to identify himself with those who are passively swept up to heaven by the highest God, not only as prophets or founders of great cities, but (with Chaucer's usual note of nervous parody) in a role as questionably subordinate as that of Ganymede:

> That was borne up, as men read,
> To heaven with don Jupiter,
> And made the gods' butler (590–92).

As a public servant and official in noble houses, he had already been on several diplomatic missions. But as a poet, he is generally not a participant but an observer. Dante is welcomed into the company of great poets in the *Inferno*. But when Chaucer comes to nominate his genealogy of great

10. The civic context of such celebration is emphasized in Filippo Villani's book on the lives of famous Florentines, *De origine civitatis Florentiae et eiusdem famosis civibus* (c. 1381). For Petrarch's role in inspiring the visual imagery of fame, see Mommsen, "Petrarch and the *Sala virorum illustrium*."

writers in *The House of Fame,* they appear as pillars supporting the throne of Fame, and he himself is more like an interested tourist than a claimant to be one of their number.

Dante's goal is to establish genealogies of great men in all areas of life. Placing himself in the ranks of the great classical poets confirms his whole conception of the poet's sublime authority to know and judge greatness. One crucial aspect of the contrast Chaucer makes between himself and Dante is his rejection of epic heroism as a theme, the epic hero as a subject, and the epic aspiration as the defining characteristic of the great writer. Down to the eighteenth century, poets of the largest aspiration will link their personal assertions to their attitudes toward the classical epic, sometimes through imitation, sometimes through attack, sometimes through translation. But whatever continual fascination Chaucer has with the classical authors, he has a definite prejudice against those values that he, like Ovid, considered to support imperial power. On the walls of the temple of Venus in the beginning of *The House of Fame,* he comes upon the scene in which Aeneas and Dido hide in the cave. What follows in the original, of course, is Virgil's elaborate description of *Fama.* But Chaucer at this point is not interested in *Fama;* he is interested in love. At first he says that he won't speak of what happened between Dido and Aeneas because it upsets him too much to write about it and because it would take too long to tell anyhow. But the story compels him onward, and he tells of Dido's total commitment of herself to Aeneas, making him "Her life, her love, her lust [desire], her lord" (258). She thinks he is a good man, "for he such seemed." Whereupon Chaucer breaks in to rail at Aeneas for his betrayal of this loving woman, even though she was deluded by the sight of him. Complaining of the way men use women to further their fame and then sacrifice them to it, Dido laments her treatment by Aeneas and prepares for her suicide. If you want to know any more about this sad story, continues Chaucer, read the *Aeneid* or Ovid's epistle from Dido in the *Heroides*—only two of the innumerable books about the falseness of men to women. Strikingly enough, in a work so filled with allusions and references to past literature, Dido's lament over Aeneas has no certain precedent: 'I dreamed this,' says Chaucer, 'I didn't get it from anyone else.' In contrast, he points out that Virgil excuses Aeneas's behavior by saying Mercury had told him he had to fulfill his destiny and found Rome ("as the book us tells"). A scene that begins by glorifying the *Aeneid* has thus spent half its space in complaints about the bad behavior of the epic hero. At the very outset of *The House of Fame,* Chaucer has associated fame directly and pejoratively with the epic assumption that male destiny necessitates the rejection and ill use of women. Later, around the throne of Fame, the Muses sing. Leading them is Calliope, the muse of epic poetry.

The contrast in *The House of Fame* is not merely between the mock-meek Chaucer and the grand poets of epic. Something more subversive is at work, undermining the belief that the epic vision is all-encompassing and asserting instead that it is only one among many, and a humanly deficient one at that. The eagle tells Chaucer that Jupiter has ordered that he be carried to the House of Fame so that his understanding of love and love-tidings be widened beyond books. Thus Chaucer's Jupiter, unlike Virgil's, is a high god more interested in the English poet of love than in the Roman poet of epic fame or the Italian poet of the spiritual quest. In the face of Dante's dependence on Virgil for guidance through the afterlife, Chaucer searches instead for news of love. According to the plan of *The Divine Comedy,* of course, Dante finally does go beyond the instruction of Virgil, and then Statius, to be directed through paradise by Beatrice, *his* embodiment of Divine Love. But here, too, Chaucer will implicitly criticize Dante's approach. After passing through purgatory, Dante is told by Virgil that his will is now free from sin and he may enter the Garden of Eden and the Earthly Paradise in preparation for his journey to heaven, "for which reason I crown and mitre you over yourself" (xxvii, 142). Then, at the beginning of *Paradiso,* Dante invokes Apollo and asks to be crowned from the sacred laurel tree, so that Apollo's powers of poetry and prophecy will enter into him enough to describe paradise. As in the moment of purification in purgatory, the imagery of the poetic and personal power is taken from that of worldly authority. Virgil in purgatory describes self-sufficiency as an ability to rule oneself like a king or a pontiff; Dante in paradise considers the laurel tree the appropriate crown "for the triumph of Caesar or of poet" (29). In Book III of *The House of Fame,* when Chaucer similarly invokes Apollo, he turns Dante's paean almost on its head. Although Chaucer calls Apollo "God of science and of light" (1092), he says specifically that he doesn't want "art poetical" (1094), only that Apollo make sure that his rhymes and meter are correct. If Apollo grants this, he says, he'll run and kiss the next laurel he sees—a parodic evocation not of the grand Augustan Apollo of Dante but the Ovidian Apollo, a god-rapist whom Daphne evaded only by being changed into a tree—Apollo, in other words, as merely another treacherous male. Chaucer therefore in effect rejects the high-flown support for poetic inspiration favored by Dante, and opposes even more strenuously Dante's association of poetic fame with that of the emperor and the pope.

Like the followers of John Wycliffe, who objected that the doctrine of purgatory was only a way to increase the temporal power of the Church, Chaucer mistrusts the urge to worldly status, for cleric or for poet. In *The Divine Comedy,* for example, Dante always treats the stars positively. Combining the light of knowledge with the light of heavenly power, they are a source of wisdom and inspiration suitable to his conception of his poetic mission. In his movement from hell to heaven, they are the place to which he wants to ascend. When he meets Justinian in the *Paradiso,* in the realm of those who on earth searched for fame and glory, Dante is inspired by the starry glow that comes from the emperor as he recounts the history of the great Romans. Other ambitions and other prides may be criticized in *The Divine Comedy,* but there is as well a starry pride celebrated in heaven, where those who were ambitious on earth are pleased to be recognized and even happier to tell about themselves and their deeds. In *The House of Fame,* by contrast, the stars are more dangerous. When Dante dreams in purgatory that an eagle has picked him up and taken him to the sphere of fire, the hope of transcendence overwhelms the reaction of fear. When Chaucer is borne away, he wonders instead what it all means: Is he going to die? Is Jupiter going to "stellify" him?[11] Not yet, says the eagle, and tells Chaucer his mission, in the course of which they fly near to the constellations (the sphere of fire), where others have been stellified by the gods. The eagle asks Chaucer if he'd like to know more about them or see them more closely. No, says Chaucer, I can read about them in books if I want, and, if we go too close, my eyes will be burnt out.

Rather than a poet akin to the secular or spiritual ruler, Chaucer is much more like the reader's representative at strange occurrences. 'Just think how disappointed you'd be if I didn't continue,' says Dante to the reader during Justinian's discourse. Chaucer's more usual comment is to cut things short: 'I won't include this because you can read it elsewhere and I don't have the time.' What he does have time to do is to describe in detail the celebrators of fame who stand outside the gates of the House of Fame, the great figures depicted within, and the various groups of petitioners who surge forward asking the goddess for the fame they desire. Nine groups appear. None are described in terms of their professions or their characters or their actions, just in terms of their desire for fame. The first want "good fame" for their works; Fame tells them no one will ever say a word about them. The second want fame for their nobility of spirit; Fame tells her trumpeter Eolus to blow on his horn of Slander for them. The third say they want fame because they deserve it; Fame promises them more than they want. The fourth don't want fame because they did what they did only to serve virtue; Fame agrees and tells them their works will be dead. The fifth also want to hide their works from fame because they acted only for God's love; you're crazy, says Fame, and signals Eolus to blow the golden clarion of Praise. The sixth never did anything but want to be as famous as those who achieve noble deeds and are beloved by women. They are not interested in women's bodies, they say, "sufficeth that we have the fame" (1762). Of course, says Fame. The seventh want the same as the sixth; she rages at them and awards them Slander. The eighth and ninth want fame for their wickedness; one Fame rejects, the other she grants.

It would not be Chaucerian to look for too minute a pattern in the different groups. Fame is fickle. Although real merit does often receive fame, it just as often does not. Fortune, whom Chaucer calls the sister of Fame, had in the course of the Middle Ages been Christianized into a goddess whose seeming arbitrariness was just a veil behind whose acts lay the clear pattern of God's will. But Fame in Chaucer's conception acts by no principles at all—except perhaps to be attracted particularly to those aspirants who worship her purely—with no real credentials or talents whatso-

11. "Stellify" means "make into a star." It becomes a popular poetic word after Chaucer, and the chances are that it is Chaucer's own coinage.

ever. In this sense Fame is like a totally secular God, a deity that inspires worship and attracts endless petitioners who have no idea of what she wants and are moved only by their own uncomfortable urges for her favor. It is through these petitioners that Chaucer most clearly modernizes Ovid's depiction of Fame's house, his prime inspiration. Unlike the classical *Fama,* Chaucer's Fame is clearly a medieval monarch. Therefore he can satirize the preoccupation with fame as well as the preoccupation with the nature of sovereignty, authority, and order that are at the heart of the Dante's effort to synthesize classical and Christian power in the figure of the poet.

Chaucer's own image of self-sufficiency is very different. As he watches the petitioners, a man comes up and asks his name and asks him if he has come to seek fame. In Pope's version, more than three hundred years later, the narrator hems and haws: 'Well, of course, young poets always want fame, but I know it's insubstantial and you have to go through pains for it, and I wouldn't want it at anyone's expense or if it's only "wretched Lust of Praise," ' and so on. Chaucer is altogether more brisk. He certainly hasn't come here for fame himself:

> It's enough for me, even if I were dead,
> That no person have my name in hand.
> I know myself best how I stand;
> For whatever I suffer, or whatever I think,
> I will myself all it drink—
> Certainly, for the most part,
> To the extent that I know my own art (1876–82).

In contrast to his earlier fascination, Chaucer now appears garbed in a stoic self-containment with which to withstand the fickleness of worldly fame. At about twenty-three the young Alexander Pope may feel compelled to revise this assertion of integrity into a more frank avowal of the writer's desire for fame. But by the time of *Essay on Man* (written when Pope is about forty-five) he has clearly imbibed some of its spirit:

> What's Fame? a fancy'd life in others breath,
> A thing beyond us, ev'n before our death. . . .
> All that we feel of it begins and ends
> In the small circle of our foes or friends. . . .
> All fame is foreign, but of true desert,
> Plays round the head, but comes not to the heart:
> One self-approving hour whole years out-weighs
> Of stupid starers, and of loud huzzahs (iv, 236–37, 241–42, 253–56).[12]

Yet, despite the contrast that Chaucer implies between himself and Dante, their attitudes are as linked as much as they differ. Each sets out

12. Before placing Chaucer and Pope too easily alongside each other in the history of fame, we should remember that (as Pope's lines themselves imply) Pope's attitudes themselves have been conditioned by living in a literary culture more different from Chaucer's than Chaucer's was from the Romans. In the time between has come the invention of the printing press, with the vast increase in literacy, dissemination of literary work, and therefore of literary fame that arrives in its wake.

to define the role of the writer through his intercession between the reader and the meaning ("sentence," Chaucer would say) the work is trying to convey, and each makes a definite break with medieval conceptions of literary fame and the literary act. The orderly afterlife that *The Divine Comedy* maps and interprets stands in strong contrast to the haphazard rushing world viewed by Chaucer from the air or standing in the reception hall of Fame. *The Divine Comedy,* as centuries of interpreters beginning with Dante have shown, is immensely organized both verbally and conceptually. *The House of Fame,* after systematically questioning all assertions of authoritative knowledge, presents itself as incomplete, and Dante's assertion of a poetic authority that transcends the ages is mocked by the abrupt end of Chaucer's poem with the appearance of the "man of great authority."

No authority perhaps, but still an author—and it is the distinction between authority and authorship that separates Dante from Chaucer just as it separated Virgil from Ovid. By taking on and then superseding the authority of Virgil, Dante makes himself authoritative. To expect glory, honor, and fame for his poetry is only to demand its due as a transcendent vision given to him by God. But Chaucer distrusts the whole business of visionary enlightenment and aspiration. The larger question of *The House of Fame*—with its endless round of competing authorities, aspirants for fame, and singers of the famous—is how any writer, anyone whose works look to a public audience, knows that, underneath it all, he is not writing merely for fame. 'Are you here for fame?' he is asked. 'No,' says Chaucer, who avoids giving his name (although we have heard it already from the eagle). 'I have come to hear love's tidings.' That is to say, my writing, which tells of love's tidings, is done for its own sake. Dante's blithe embrace of a particularly elevated sort of fame and glory is therefore countered by Chaucer's questioning of *all* such assertion, including his own.

*　　　*　　　*

I sought no homage from the race that write;
I kept, like Asian monarchs, from their sight.
　　　　　　—POPE, "Epistle to Dr. Arbuthnot"

In the *Retraction* that ends *The Canterbury Tales,* Chaucer asks forgiveness for all his works, including specifically *The House of Fame.* The only ones that Chaucer is willing to take credit for are his translation of Boethius "and other books of legends of saints, and homilies, and morality, and devotion" (*Works,* 265). Otherwise he asks Jesus and Mary that until he dies they send him grace "to bewail my guilts, and to study to the salvation of my soul." Thus Chaucer maintains a separation between the truths of religion and the truths of literature that Dante, for one, is bent on eliminating. Chaucer's pose of ignorance, his reference of learned matters to "great clerks," hides an extraordinary suspicion of the ability of language to achieve true knowledge. Books to Chaucer are a weight on perception and understanding; they warp more often than they guide. Dante's implicit claim that the structure of *The Divine Comedy* is really "out there" excites perhaps his greatest antagonism. Chaucer emphasizes instead that his dream in *The House of Fame* comes from his own head, the material of his brain, packed with books, as the eagle complains. The proper subject for writers is therefore not the eternal but the temporal, not the ultimate judgments on behavior but the pairings of lie and truth that are the invariable elements in everything human. Dante may be the learned poet, but Chaucer is the writing poet. And he is much more preoccupied than Dante with the difficulties of using language, with the proliferation of liars and the virtual impossibility of distinguishing them from those who tell the truth. Everywhere you go, says Chaucer, you'll find a crush of people trumpeting fame. But who is really worth it no one can tell. That Dante says he can tell is an indication of his self-delusion.

Dante might counter that it is the sublimity of his inspiration and the purity of his language that ensures the truth of his vision. Against this assertion of divine inspiration and favor, Chaucer sets his own integrity— "I know myself best how I stand." Perhaps it is the distinction between a writer in exile who writes for an ideal audience and a writer who often reads his compositions to a court, looking his audience in the face. Dante, like Petrarch, argues polemically for a separation between the emperor who rules the secular world and the pope who controls religion. As Petrarch emphasized, both should have their seats in Rome, the dual heartland of secular power and religious authority. Chaucer, the islanded Englishman, has no such polemical interests. In his public career he is diplomat and supervisor of customs, an intermediary between the rulers of his own country and those in other countries. The burning issue of pope versus emperor on which Italian writers focused so much of their own energy hardly exists for him. Dante and Petrarch, limiting the spheres of politics and religion, make literature a third term—an exalted *cultural* position that encompasses the conflict. By asserting control over time and posterity, they argue that the vision of the writer and poet is the crown of earthly glory; Chaucer, in contrast, finally rejects a secular hierarchy of fame-oriented value in favor of Christian submission.

Both the fame-seeking Italians and the fame-wary Englishman do gather strength from the Christian emphasis on the power of the word. But while Dante draws on its sanction to ratify his own literary ventures, Chaucer ultimately contrasts his language with the greater language of the Bible, to which he must defer. Dante asks us to interpret *The Divine Comedy* and see through its language to the truths it perceives; Chaucer in *Troilus and Criseyde,* written in the same period as *The House of Fame,* kisses the feet of the great Latin authors but worries that his own work will be misunderstood and misread because of the diversity of the English tongue and the ways of writing things down. The fame of being known is obviously transient. But the fame of writing vanishes along with the shifting of language itself. Thus time presses on Chaucer in all his works, particularly in *The House of Fame*. He seeks "tidings" of love, the little fragments of time-bound stories that themselves quickly vanish. He has committed himself to the flux of time rather than to the eternity of spiritual or epic vision. It is, he implies, all that human understanding can achieve. Perhaps it was possible in Greece and Rome to claim otherwise. But those days are gone. The best one can do is become Daedalus and fly out of the labyrinth one has constructed, ignoring the possibility that you are actually an Icarus in disguise, soaring too high, or a Phaëton, who grabs the reins of his father's chariot before he has either experience or control.

Dante also believes that he lives in the closing ages of the world, but he nominates himself as the last of the great line of writers whose visions can encompass the universe. Dante's work appears at a point in Italian history when a newly energetic urban culture allows it to be appreciated and understood with the attention it continually demands. Certainly, there had been a line of late medieval writers who attempted to synthesize knowledge before Dante. But he much more elaborately situates himself as the one who adjudicates the contribution of each person to the present. Dante initiates the obsessive Renaissance urge for individual fame—sometimes as a vehicle for the fame of locality, nation, or to the greater glory of God— but necessarily also a desire in itself. It was a possibility that fell on fertile ground, as the eagerness with which writers like Boccaccio and Petrarch took up Dante's cause illustrates. Boccaccio in his *Life of Dante* fully accepts the title of theologian for Dante and says that in fact poetry is theology; Petrarch similarly spends a good deal of his career showing how theology can be replaced with history and the values of medieval Christianity absorbed into the cultural values of a revived Roman literature. A new hierarchy was forming, a religion of learning. Chaucer in his *Retraction* rejects most of his works and accepts only those that are consonant with his desire to be saved and absolved of his guilts. Yet, of course, the books are not themselves destroyed: The works of literature and the retraction in the name of true religion go forth into the world together; and Chaucer's own career quickly becomes a model for other writers. Here is the paradox that will be elaborated much later, in Pope's sense of isolation as well as in the special sensitivity to feeling cultivated by the Romantics: The poet is in touch with the greatest general truths precisely *because* he is the grand eccentric, spiritual lightning rod, and alienated individual. The keynote of the Renaissance humanism to which Dante, Boccaccio, and Petrarch stand as godfathers is philology: the love of the word. Unlike Chaucer, they seek an absolution not from god but from posterity.

The Rediscovery of Posterity

About posterity: I only think about writing truly.
Posterity can take care of herself or fuck herself.
—ERNEST HEMINGWAY (1950)

Posterity can be rejected only after it has been taken seriously. Thus, when the refusal of posterity becomes a possible pose or belief of writers in our own time, it depends significantly on the courting of posterity, its rediscovery, during the Renaissance. To buttress his position, Chaucer resurrects the combined Christian and stoic attack against civic fame (and the literary fame that celebrates civic virtue) that is principally formulated for the Middle Ages by the sixth-century Roman consul and author Boethius. Formerly a trusted minister and favorite of Theodoric, the Ostrogothic king of Italy, Boethius in his early forties was accused of treason and executed. While in prison he wrote the *Consolation of Philosophy,* a series of dialogues, in prose and verse, between himself and Philosophy, a woman who chases away the Muses, whom he had thought were consoling, to replace them with a serenity and self-containment before the fate and accidents of an uncertain world. Boethius is in particular concerned with the vicissitudes of fortune. His account of Fortune's Wheel, which degrades the mighty and raises the lowly, is as much an influence on visual artists in the Middle Ages and the Renaissance as his ideas are on writers and, intriguingly enough, on monarchs: Alfred the Great, the first notable English king and an assiduous patron of learning, chose the *Consolation* as one of the four classical works he translated into Anglo-Saxon; Elizabeth I, the Renaissance monarch with the most self-awareness about the uncertainties of fame and fortune, did a translation herself when a teenager.

At just about the same time that he was writing *The House of Fame,* Chaucer was also reading and translating Boethius, primarily for his own use. Boethius is referred to by name in *The House of Fame* and Chaucer quotes one passage in which Thought, outfitted with the feather of Philosophy, flies into the air, leaving the earth far behind. But a more significant use of Boethius occurs when the eagle is carrying Chaucer through the air. High over the earth, "Jeffrey" watches everything grow smaller, until the earth itself is but a pinpoint. Alexander, he thinks, never flew so high, nor Daedalus and Icarus. Similarly, in Boethius's most extensive discussion of fame, Philosophy tells him that the earth is but a pinpoint in the heavens: How much smaller, she says to Boethius, is the inhabited part of the earth, and how much smaller still one's own country, the only place in which, because of the differences between languages and customs, fame means anything. Even in Cicero's time, Rome itself was unknown beyond the Caucasus Mountains. If Rome could be unknown, how can a Roman expect to be celebrated. Famous men have been forgotten because no authors wrote of them. But authors and their works perish in time as well. Can we expect to know the dead through words? Perhaps their names, but their bodies are gone. Following his source, Chaucer in his translation glosses this passage as implying a double death for every man: first of one's body, then of one's fame.

Chaucer's image of the perspective of the writer is that of the helpless passenger of the high-flying eagle, who soars above the villages, fields, and seas until the earth itself looks like a mere "prick," a small division on the clock of time. But the Italian view, as shown in Dante, Boccaccio, and Petrarch, is that of an elaborate pageant that they half discover and half create themselves—looking simultaneously back in time toward the great figures of the past and forward into posterity to glimpse the fame of themselves and their works. The English poet therefore sits godfather to a kind of poetic eccentricity, fully knowledgeable about the past yet essentially separate from its continuities, an observer rather than the latest in the long line of honor. The study of Chaucer leads us back into the rich literature of the Middle Ages. The study of Petrarch (like that of Dante) is meant to lead us back to the Romans and to fill us with appreciation for our guide. Boethius's stoic rejection of the urge to fame because of its irredeemably local and transitory nature is implicitly countered by Dante's emphasis on the simultaneous context of Florence and eternity for his greatest poem. After the urban decline of the Middle Ages, *The Divine Comedy* helps mark a renewal of fascination of the city as the place of true honor. Boccaccio, in his *Life of Dante,* emphasizes Dante's attachment to his city and his unwillingness to receive the crown of civic and artistic honors anywhere else. If you long for a glory that is equal to that of Athens and the other great cities of antiquity, Boccaccio exhorts the Florentines, bring back Dante's bones from Ravenna, where he died in exile. Restore him to a place of grandeur and nobility *within the city.* For—and here Boethius is directly contradicted—it is the great man who makes the city famous, particularly the great writer.

In his book *The Fates of Illustrious Men* (*De Casibus virorum illustrium*), which Chaucer drew on for his *Monk's Tale,* Boccaccio, with one section yet to finish, describes how he fell into a funk and wondered why he was doing this chore, chastising himself for building his own reputation on those of the dead. What good is fame anyhow, he wonders with Boethian melancholy. When the body is gone, that's the end. Whereupon Petrarch, whom he has admired for years, appears before him and tells him that renown is acquired only through virtue. Far from being irrelevant to life, it extends life and allows us to praise the great dead as if they were still alive. To praise others, like praising God, earns praise for oneself. So pull yourself together and finish the book: Hard work is the most important thing in life. Reinvigorated, Boccaccio goes back to his writing, praising Petrarch, "the most famous man of our time" (206) and, says Boccaccio, an incredibly hard worker. There is little Chaucerian worry here about the erosions of time; those wounds are to be remedied by earnest literary activity. Time can be restored, just as Petrarch and so many later scholars knitted back together the fragments of rediscovered classical texts in an act, we might say, of remembering. The great men would not be forgotten and the writers (and painters) who celebrated them would have their fame as well. By the end of the fourteenth century, the Florentine guild of judges and notaries commissioned a fresco depicting the four great Florentine poets: Dante, Petrarch, Boccaccio, and— Zenobio da Strada. The Italians in general and the Florentines in particular had learned and retaught the lesson that one could be celebrated for the quality of one's celebration. Perhaps in the case of Zenobio da Strada, the lesson did not take very well. But throughout Europe the poet was now to be celebrator of the great men of his own profession as well as those heroes of war and government who were his nominal subjects. Chaucer at the end of his life might retract all those works that most succeeding generations thought made his name live. But not long after his death John Lydgate, a literary follower, in the prologue to his own English version of Boccaccio's work, awarded Chaucer what in *The House of Fame* he shied away from. Chaucer, says Lydgate, is the lodestar of the English language, who refined and reformed it with his sweet colors, making it a possible vehicle for literature:

> Wherefore let us give him laude [praise] and glory
> And put his name with poets in memory (*Fall of Princes*, 279–80).[13]

Although Chaucer was probably most intricately aware of the complexities of fame, Dante, Boccaccio, and Petrarch put fame to work. 'Know yourself through your heroes' could be the motto of at least the Italian version of the Renaissance. The commerce in faces that begins sometime in the fourteenth century or so and gathers momentum with the invention of printing has no parallel in the Middle Ages. Even the look of powerful rulers then has less distinctiveness than any recently deceased young Roman of the fourth century. People were no doubt just as individual, just as diverse in their personal makeups in the Middle Ages as they were at any time in history. But the prevailing understanding of human nature dictated a lack of interest in those diversities and nuances. So much Greek and Roman biography and autobiography was lost in the Middle Ages, not through some willful attempt to erase the past but because the individual details of someone's life, what made him interesting or exemplary to Greeks and Romans, were less important to the monk copying ancient manuscripts than those timeless attributes that fit the pattern of a Christian soul. In the third century, Christian historians could still be interested in preserving lists of Olympic winners in order to link the saints

---

13. At the end of his long praise of Chaucer, Lydgate becomes nostalgic for the days when kings used to listen to poets and writers, as Caesar listened to Cicero: "And notwithstanding his conquest and renown, / Unto books he gave great attention / And had in story joy and great pleasure" (369–71).

of the new religion with the heroes of the past. By the high Middle Ages, biographies of classical figures were routinely left on the scriptorium floor. With notable exceptions like the lives of Charlemagne and, of course, the locally produced and consumed lives of various saints, biography essentially disappeared as a literary form. The individual shape of human life was not as interesting as its general pattern and, therefore, only a few were necessary. From St. Jerome in the fifth century down to the fourteenth century, there was little attempt to write the biographies of the new age. Jerome called his short lives of Christian writers *De Viris illustribus* (*On Illustrious Men*), and not quite a thousand years later Petrarch adopts the same title for a book of primarily Roman biographies that preoccupies him on and off for his whole life. Similarly, one of the prime projects of the Renaissance was the restoration of hundreds of "famous" figures to cultural consciousness, through the stories of the famous who acted and the manuscripts and celebration of the famous who had written. Quickly enough, other artists-painters, sculptors, and architects would be revived and celebrated in their turn. But the process begins with the writers, and a crucial implication in the appeal to posterity was their eagerness to celebrate the deserving of the past. Alexander restoring the tomb of Cyrus stands behind Dante's celebration of Virgil or, more ambiguously, Petrarch's lifelong writing of a finally unfinished epic poem in celebration of the career of Scipio Africanus.[14]

Petrarch is a prime example of the new fascination that writers have with the question of posterity and their own relation to its rewards. A man who spent his entire career within the Church, although not in any priestly or administrative position, Petrarch was never particularly interested in theology or doctrinal issues. Throughout his life, he moved peripatetically through France and Italy, stopping for a few years here and there. But his works and his letters constantly weave a fabric of European relations with friends, acquaintances, and sympathetic men of power that was couched primarily in terms of both a celebratory exploration of the classical world and an often openly unself-conscious desire for personal fame. Dante was forced into exile, but Petrarch made exile into an element in the new definition of the writers. Unlike the proud but needy Dante, who writes of the pain of constantly having to eat the bread and climb the stairs of others, Petrarch ensured that both his solitude and his wanderings were comfortable. Courted and coveted as a guest, he easily took up residence under the protection of whatever local secular or spiritual power appreciated his scholarly interests and commitments:

14. Until the nineteenth century, generalizations about human nature tended to be staked within a grid of analogies to the actions of prior figures, both classical and biblical. Their emblematic lives expressed psychology not through personal insight or introspection but through the recaptured forms of outsized, "famous" human beings who were visible and understandable versions of human behavior. When Freud defines the Oedipus complex, he continues the same tradition, even though he nominally seeks to define a psychology quite different from that embodied in a history of great men.

> Whatever its origin, I know that in men's minds, especially in superior minds, resides an innate longing to see new places, to keep changing one's home (*Letters,* 135; *Rerum familiarum,* 260).

Without a Church that still could confer benefices and livings on a man who was obviously celebrated and learned, as well as pious, Petrarch could not have survived. But it is also possible to call some of those who supported Petrarch his patrons. That system of political support for scholarship and art was just beginning to emerge from the medieval relation of lord and servant-retainer through the midwifery of a classical revival that Petrarch did much to promote. The new patronage would supply the cultural expertise that the rising politicians of the Renaissance needed to furnish a historical legitimacy they often lacked in their personal background. Soon rulers everywhere sought to hire artists to paint them and literary humanists to adorn their homes and libraries with the testaments of classical glory. Not that their celebrations were uncritical. When Petrarch was asked by the emperor Charles IV to inscribe the unfinished *De Viris illustribus* to him, Petrarch said he would do so when Charles had demonstrated that he had the personal spirit and achievements to be counted among those heroes instead of being the beneficiary of merely inherited power. Not all the men of learning who became part of courts all over Europe in the next few centuries would have the same scruples. But Petrarch's example of integrity contained the revived Horatian promise that the works of the learned would in fact last longer than the deeds of the politician and the military man. The custodians of the word might write and praise to eat, but the self-sufficiency of their art was part of their new faith. It would last through time and they with it.

Fame and renown, says Petrarch to Boccaccio in *The Fates of Illustrious Men,* are kind to the physically deformed because in posterity they become "handsome, illustrious, and revered" (205). Thus although the fame sought by Petrarch had visual implications in the depicting of the great men of the past (and Petrarch himself), in its way it was as disembodied and as rarefied as the spiritual commitment with which Augustine countered Roman public ostentation. Petrarch's country retreat and his cultivation of the bucolic virtues emphasized that the aspiration toward the new fame would be as immaterial as the journey of the soul toward God. The urge for literary and cultural fame could therefore be, as *The Divine Comedy* implied, a kind of spiritual autobiography, structured by its effort to achieve what was most pure and virtuous on earth. The self that sought fame was akin to the soul that aspired to union with God, defined not, however, by the order of spirit but by the recapitulation and restoration of history, in particular the history of Rome: "What else indeed is all history but the praise of Rome?" Petrarch asks in a late work (quoted by Mommsen, 115). God was still the prime audience. But he was beginning to have to share the privilege with others, on earth, to whom the writer was also directing his messages.

Petrarch thus reinstitutes for the Renaissance the impulse to historical reenactment that allows the individual simultaneously to invoke the great names of the past and propel himself toward the future. His biographies of great men and his constant use of classical parallels encouraged public men to self-conscious action by kindling their desire to make a figure in posterity. And he himself was spurred on as well. In his thirties, with many projects launched but few completed, Petrarch proposed himself as a candidate for coronation as supreme poet, a post that had been revived not long before in imitation of supposed Roman practices. This was the coronation that Dante refused because it could not be held at Florence, even though the University of Bologna volunteered. The University of Paris had invited Petrarch to be crowned there, but he infinitely preferred Rome. There, he believed, both emperor and pope ought to reign in their mutual realms, and so he too would reign there as the supreme poet and man of letters, by his presence reviving in Rome itself its paramount European importance; for "nowhere is Rome less known than in Rome" (Bishop, 63).

Petrarch's message was primarily designed for two classes of individuals—the writers who knew the lessons of the past and the rulers who were wise enough to listen to them. Alexander attending to the wisdom of Aristotle is a favorite theme of Renaissance painting and many a treatise is produced instructing the young rulers in all aspects of behavior. Similarly, the judges of Petrarch's claim to be supreme poet would not be fellow writers but first a learned monarch, Robert of Sicily, who would examine him (despite Robert's confessed lack of feeling for poetry), and then the Roman Senate. Clearly, Petrarch considered his status to be in the bestowal of civil power. But, once crowned with the wreath of the Caesars, he almost immediately retired to a home in southern France where he led a solitary life, filled with literary chores, but characterized (in his letters) as a retreat from worldly affairs. Status may have been conferred upon him by the City, but his response was that now he could leave the City behind. He had in a sense become his own place, just as the Latin language was a separate place for him as well, a ground on which he could converse with the great men of the past while he reserved Italian for his poems of introspection and his tribute to his muse, Laura. Thus Petrarch neatly claimed for himself the right of descent of the great poets of Rome and yet escaped from the theater of their triumphs to create one of his own in the French countryside of the Vaucluse, which he called his "transalpine Helicon." His literary assertion had been licensed by the forms and ceremonies of antiquity. Now he would achieve a European fame, not quite for his aloneness as for his place as a constantly moving focus of culture. Like St. Francis, who had brought holy behavior out of the hagiographies and the monasteries to brandish it firmly in the face of everyday life, Petrarch defined the scholar as a secular monk, living apart as a moral admonition and guide to the great actions of the world, while drawing on the classical past for his repository of moral principles and exempla. Throughout his life, he would recount the details of his day to sympathetic correspondents, as if to provide guidance for their own. Rumors of his death circulated constantly in his later years—a kind of left-handed tribute to the fascination with which people viewed him. And, like many harassed celebrities of today, Petrarch toward the end realized that his extraordinary status had also brought him unwanted fans and imitators who would press their poems on him as he traveled through their cities.

Petrarch's appeal to Robert of Sicily to approve his poetic status, like his later support of Cola di Rienzi's effort to set up a new Roman Republic, illustrates the ultimately secular implications of his literary career. By establishing a personal genealogical link to the classical world, Petrarch in effect had opened the way for others to make much more decisive breaks with the continuities established by the Church. Thinking of posterity, he argued, allowed one to move out of the annoyances, irritations, and compromises of the present and thereby be free to act nobly. The concept of posterity was therefore a moral concept, but one that was secular rather than religious in origin, even though in its disdain for the frailties of the body and in its constant eye on perfection it might be called a secular spirituality.

Despite the internationalism of his cultural connections, Petrarch was an ardent Italian, because Roman culture to him was Italy's great gift to Europe. His own awareness of the desire for fame therefore allowed him to make his tutelage in good fame a polemic for a renascent Italy. At first he thought of willing his own elaborate library to some religious institution for good keeping. But later in his life, he decided to try to make it the kernel of a public library in Venice. Thus, inexorably, the context of his own career, monastic in its origins, merged into Italian national culture. In an analogy rarely far from the minds of Renaissance writers, several cities in Greece had battled for the honor of being the birthplace of Homer. Saints had helped celebrate as well as protect local regions during late antiquity and the Middle Ages. But Dante's preoccupation with Italian places and Italian history hallowed the land and its great men another way. These were saints of culture, whose aura might be invoked even before they lay beneath the earth. Even Lorenzo the Magnificent, a hundred or so years later, could not persuade Ravenna to return the bones of Dante to Florence. But twice the city had attempted to make amends by inviting Petrarch to reside there, as did many other cities all over Italy. By the prime of Petrarch's life, the papal-imperial conflicts that kept Dante in exile were subsumed in the admiration of a figure who belonged to the whole country.

*   *   *

The kind of fame Dante and Petrarch approved was the contrary of a Boethian turning toward philosophy and a stoical acceptance of one's lot. Like Petrarch admonishing Boccaccio, Dante emphasized activity and the ability to make one's own fame as an act of will. As Virgil says to him in the Inferno, when Dante has rested too long:

> Come on, shake the covers of this sloth
> . . . for sitting softly cushioned,
> Or tucked in bed, is no way to win Fame;
> and without it man must waste his life away,
> leaving such traces of what he was on earth
> as smoke in wind and foam upon the water (xxiv, 46–51).

Such a fame, informed by spiritual insight, will live beyond death. As one of the characters in the *Paradiso* remarks of a fellow spirit, who was both poet and monk on earth,

> See if a man should make himself excell,
> so that another life should follow the first! (ix, 41–42).

Similarly, Petrarch's scale of values defines fame specifically as the victory over death. He may worry about his own desire for fame to the point of self-conscious paradox: "The fame we seek is but a breeze, smoke, a shadow: it is nothing" (*Rerum familiarum,* 21). But to the extent that it is a concept of fame held by the men of Rome, it is a windy, smoky, shadowy nothing that he will bring back to vibrant life.

Petrarch's attitude toward the great men of the Roman past, whether he criticizes or celebrates, is thus founded on his belief in the power of words to master time and penetrate eternity. When the works of the classical past are retrieved and their language properly understood, death itself can be defeated. Chaucer the social poet fears that words will warp and vanish in time. Petrarch the scholar-poet first elaborates the perception that they can be restored and preserved. Chaucer's words fly around the world with no one authoritative enough to disentangle the false from the true. But in the eyes of the word-loving philologists, words were not mere rumors or the report of fame but human products through which we might know a society and through which a society knew itself. What would Horace's "monument more lasting than bronze" have meant if the words in which it was raised could not be understood? Horace might have assumed that Latin would last forever, although he would have been puzzled to discover that it was the Catholic Church rather than the Roman Empire that had assured its legacy. But it took the hands of Petrarch and the Renaissance humanists to return Latin to the purity of its origins.

In such a project of retrieval, law was the crucial meeting place of language, history, and society. Following in the steps of Petrarch, Lorenzo Valla in the fifteenth century discovered through an analysis of its language that the Donation of Constantine, on which the papacy based its claim to political and military control of its territory, was in fact an early medieval forgery. Later critical scholarship supplied the arguments and precedents for a revamping of the legal tradition, at first to purify the law of what Valla called "barbarous" medieval accretions but gradually to understand the specific evolution of Roman law into the various national legal systems. To a great extent the wise men "famous" in the sixteenth century were historians and jurists, building their reputations on an analysis of legal texts whose polemical goal was to legitimize the national monarchy as a historical continuity more authentic than that of the papacy. With such a mission, the philologist could consider himself to be a secular priest of language, whose personal fame was linked to national glory. For someone like Guillaume Budé, called "the French Petrarch," who spent his life in the service of the French royal house, the equation was easy to make. But there were also those for whom the Petrarchan revelation of a spiritual but worldly fame required an independence of the emerging European system of nation-states, a fame that was more medieval in its international scope. The promise of such a wisdom, beyond national boundaries and unbeholding to national prejudices, would later shape the ambitions of such thinkers as Spinoza, Descartes, and Newton.

With the revival of classical learning, the writers especially had begun to construct a cultural history that could be an alternative to both the political and the religious history of Europe. Reaching back to the great names of the classical past, they created their own predecessors and established lines of connection often independent of papal or political dynasties, thereby creating themselves as members of a new international profession—the humanists—with standards and values that were potentially in conflict with both the traditional classes of society and the orders of the Church. If there was a basic combat, it was over what was truly central in human nature and human behavior and who could best serve as models of inspiration for being and action. As Petrarch had refused to dedicate his book on illustrious men to Charles IV until the emperor had clearly performed some virtuous action, so the humanists, even while they might nominally serve temporal power, reserved for themselves the ability to judge what was beneficial to mankind and therefore deserved praise, honor, and fame. Dante and Petrarch had considered themselves to be the last of a great line, while Chaucer turned away from his works and looked to heaven. But their examples were later invoked as forerunners of a new concept of culture and a new definition of achievement that by the sixteenth century was supplying actual and professed wise men of all sorts with an international stage for their work. For an otherwise isolated and embryonic literary culture of people scattered all over Europe, Petrarch became a beacon, an enabling figure whose renown and career released them to follow interests that before had seemed either outlandish or somehow wrong.

To this acceptance of himself as a symbolic figure, Petrarch contributed more than his share, although not always with full premeditation. In the revival of intellectual and cultural ideas, no less than in the revival of fashion, self-consciousness is always an element. As godfather to a great age of classical scholarship and antiquarian research yet to come, Petrarch constantly searched for manuscripts, exchanging letters with scholars and patrons all over Europe. He does not question the Church's authority in matters of the soul or spirit, for no direct attack is yet necessary or warranted. He searches instead for a history that will be authoritative for behavior and thought, affirming his own contemporaneity with the classical past by turning away from institutional preferment in the present. Prompted by his discovery of a manuscript of Cicero's letters, he writes letters himself to the great men of antiquity as if they were all contemporaries, praising them for their virtues and chastising them for their faults. Now, when the smallest library can easily obtain a translation of Cicero's letters, we might try to remember when Petrarch made the rediscovery of the past an adventurous search that could prompt him to deny Charlemagne the title of "great," because he didn't deserve to be ranked with Alexander and Pompey.

Books and writing allowed Petrarch to enter a company otherwise closed to him in his own world. Stepping outside the class-bound medieval world of kings, knights, and powerful churchmen, he fashions the love of antiquity into a shield for his own self-sufficiency, and his works are filled with a constant stream of self-description. In his *Secretum,* for example, Petrarch carries on a dialogue with Augustine about the divisions in himself between his desire for glory, his love of Jesus, and his fealty to Laura. Laura is a real but idealized woman (like Dante's Beatrice) who has inspired Petrarch's Italian love poems and thereby helped him out of the "common way." His love for Laura and his love of fame both divert him from the embrace of Jesus, he writes elsewhere:

> [A] sweet sharp thought, enthroned within my soul in difficult and delightful weight, oppresses my heart with desire and feeds it with hope; for the sake of kindly glorious fame, it does not feel when I freeze or when I flame, or if I am pale or thin; and if I kill it is reborn stronger than before. This thought has been growing with me day by day since I slept in swaddling clothes, and I fear that one tomb will enclose us both; for when my soul is naked of its members, this desire will not be able to come with it (*Rime sparse* 264, 55–67).

But in fact Petrarch's constant invocations of Laura as the appropriate object of his praise and the audience for his work are an integral part of his piety. They allow him (as Beatrice does Dante) to both seek and deny fame by celebrating another, "not caring about myself." His motivation for writing is therefore a kind of supreme love, and his desire that his own fame will last is made more acceptable by saying that he wishes it so that hers will as well:

> [F]or her love I put myself early to difficult undertakings; so that if I reach the port I desire, I hope through her to live a long time, when people will suppose I am dead (*Rime sparse* 119, 11–15).

In his *Africa* Petrarch trumpets that the poem will be famous in the last ages of the world. But his praise of Laura and his linking of her to his own ambivalent attitude toward fame announce a more modern preoccupation with the subject and audience of women rather than the heroic deeds of men. Petrarch's God, like Chaucer's and Dante's, is the embodiment of Creation and Love rather than the supporter of kings or even the justifier of saints and martyrs. For all their differences, the Italian shares with the English poet a stronger inclination for Dido than for Aeneas. Like Chaucer's Virgil, Petrarch's and Dante's is a Virgil read through Ovid, and all three say that Dido was killed by love (Dante, *Rima petrosa,* 626–27; Petrarch, *Rime sparse* 29, 82–85). Intriguingly, the main evidence that we have of the actual existence of Laura as more than a pretext for poetry is Petrarch's notation of her death on the flyleaf of his most treasured copy of Virgil. Ostentatiously presenting himself in writing to the world, he yet displaced that self-conscious artistic aspiration into praise of Laura, the pole of his emotional life, and praise of the classical authors, the poles of his intellectual life. Linking those seemingly contradictory impulses was the act of writing that served both God and history, the self-presentation that was acceptable because it lasted beyond the body.

From the twelfth-century rediscovery of Ovid into the Renaissance, a rising new audience of women for poetry enhances the possibility of a literary fame more closely related to love than to war. When God is defined as love and a force of creation, then the praise of individual but idealized women becomes a way for the poet to link his work to both the human and the divine. The relative importance of the themes of epic and love to these four writers is therefore an interesting index to the circumstances of their writing and their ideas of both poet and audience. In a suite of connected poems called *The Triumphs* (*I Trionfi*), written over the course of his literary life, Petrarch embodied all the paradoxes of the desire to achieve fame and glory that his simultaneous engagement with the classical past and the Christian present had fostered. As much as anything else he ever did, *The Triumphs* raised Petrarch from a poet and scholar into a European figure celebrated for grappling with some of the most pressing psychological questions that faced the new men and women of the Renaissance. Through innumerable civic processions, paintings, and tapestries, his formulations and images particularly appealed to aspiring public figures, down two hundred years and more, for example, to the translation encouraged by Henry VIII and published by Elizabeth I's official printer "with the privilege of the Queen's Majesty."[15] Each poem of *The Triumphs* corresponds to a stage in Petrarch's own life, as he himself moves from obscurity to celebrity. But the poetic movement seems instead toward the denial of worldly greatness. Each triumph is successive—Love over Chastity, Death over Love, Fame over Death, Time over Fame, Eternity over Time—as the inner plot reveals Petrarch's gradual realization of the true values that rule the universe. Like Chaucer in *The House of Fame,* he is essentially an observer, watching the great parade of the past and being told by others of the meaning of their bondage to

15. This first English translation of *I Trionfi,* entitled *Tryumphes of Fraunces Petrarcke,* was done by Henry Parker and published sometime after Parker's death in 1556. The modern translation is by Ernest Hatch Wilkins. For illustrations of some of the many visual representations of the poems, see Carandente, *I Trionfi nel primo rinascimento.*

the triumphant god. The model for the poems, as he stresses often, is the Roman triumph, with which the victorious general, often in the guise of Jupiter, was ceremoniously brought into the city. In the first, "The Triumph of Love," Petrarch watches Cupid being brought in on a triumphal chariot. In Cupid's train are the captives who have abjectly succumbed to his power, first Romans, then Greeks, Old Testament Hebrews, and, finally, the heroes and heroines of medieval romance: Lancelot and Guinevere, Tristram and Iseult. Finally, Laura appears, unique and indescribable, the maid who can take Love himself captive because she herself is rebellious and untamed. Petrarch's acknowledgment of his inability to describe Laura then leads to glimpses of poets enslaved to Love, including Dante to Beatrice. In the second poem, "The Triumph of Chastity," Laura's power over Love is explained by her purity, leading Petrarch to introduce another procession of the famous, this time those holy women whose chastity rescued them from Love. In their number, intriguingly, is Dido, who committed suicide, says Petrarch, not because of Aeneas, "as is the public cry," but to wipe out the shame to her dead husband.

These first two *Triumphs,* although later revised, were written in Petrarch's early years. With the death of Laura in 1348, however, he wrote again: first a "Triumph of Death" celebrating Laura, who had led him out of his common pursuits to follow something higher; then a "Triumph of Fame." Fame, he says, saves man from physical death and gives him another life. Many of her votaries are those of Love as well. Once again, the parade appears: a whole troop of Roman heroes, the Old Testament leaders, warrior women, and the warrior-leaders of the Middle Ages—Arthur, Godfrey of Bouillon, Saladin, and others, down to only two contemporaries: King Robert of Sicily and Cardinal Giovanni Colonna, one of Petrarch's earliest patrons. Further on, says Petrarch, he also sees a group of philosophers and wise men, headed by Plato and Aristotle, but in no particular order, the chronology intentionally jumbled. In the final two poems, written much later, Petrarch celebrates the "Triumph of Time," the racing sun that makes even fame obscure and sends it to a second death; and the "Triumph of Eternity," when there is no past or future, only the eternal present of God's heaven and the Day of Judgment.

Although Petrarch never completely coordinated the six poems into a final form, their relation is clearly marked by both their references to each other and their common preoccupations. Laura turns up throughout, reappearing finally at the end of "The Triumph of Eternity." Similarly, the otherwise abstract concepts of love, chastity, death, fame, time, and eternity are all given flesh by the great figures from the past that walk—sometimes proudly, sometimes laden with chains—in their triumphs. By placing fame in the midst of the group, Petrarch would seem to be qualifying its power, in an almost Chaucerian subordination to the greater authority first of earthly time and then of God's power over all. Petrarch's eternity, like Augustine's, does constitute a stillness, a static perfection, in which all earthly competition has been left behind. But, unlike Augustine, Petrarch does not quite make eternity the opposite of time, but rather a perfecting of time's inadequacy, just as heaven is a realization of earth. Similarly, the urge for fame is not transcended, but refined and perfected as part of the soul's preparation for heaven. Even in "Triumph of Time," the sun's urge to outspeed and therefore destroy earthly fame is thwarted by historians and poets:

> Chiefly of these the Sun was envious:
> For they, escaping from the common cage,
> Had mounted upward, into soaring flight (98).

"Great lengths of time" may be "poisonous to great names," but Petrarch also celebrates those who combat against time and carry those names into the future. In eternity, the place without history, fame does not vanish. If it is truly great, it is confirmed:

> The years no longer in their hands will hold
> The governance of fame: the glorious
> Will glorious be to all eternity (110).

In his *Triumphs,* Petrarch has transmuted the medieval and early Renaissance doubts about fame into an optimistic aspiration toward a fame unconfined by time, a true fame that eternity confirms instead of obliterating, a spiritual fame that is assertive rather than evasive. The chivalric family of the Nine Worthies was essentially a closed system. With their three heroes each from the classical, the Hebrew, and the medieval worlds, they coordinated three ages of human aspiration and implied the ranks were closed. But the heroic lists of Dante and Boccaccio and Petrarch, together with the eager proliferation of the images of past and sometimes present heroes on the walls of Italian palaces and mansions, announced a system of fame to which every individual might add himself by his own exertions. The sanctioning models were in the past, but the audience was posterity and the present. In such a contest, the notes of aspiration and humility must be mingled, for the supreme aspiration is to be considered not one of the great powers of the world, master of men and possessions, but one of the great authorities, master of language and thought—and master of self. Perhaps nothing in Petrarch's work marks his self-consciousness of these issues like the "Letter to Posterity" he wrote at forty-seven, a few years after Laura's death and ten years after his poetic coronation at Rome. The first lines are worth quoting in full:

> You may perhaps have heard something about me—although it is doubtful that my poor name may travel far in space and time. Still, you may by chance want to know what sort of man I was or what was the fate of my works, especially of those whose reputation may have persisted, or whose name you may have vaguely heard (*Letters,* 5).

The letter is incomplete, but its ambivalent attitudes are clear. Throughout, Petrarch both tells of the way he was celebrated and courted by the great and then confesses his inability to understand why they bothered:

"Nothing annoyed me more than display." He was always a private man, he says, who never sought recognition; it just came to him and he took only what he liked of it. As a young man he, like all young men, thought he deserved every honor he received. Now, he wonders why anyone bothered: "[T]hough I was a person of small account, I was of even less account in my own esteem" (6). Throughout, Petrarch tells us at some length and in some detail about his own lack of significance, just as in other places he tells of his desire to be recognized for his connection with timeless values. The tropes of ambivalence may be similar to those of Chaucer and other writers of the period. But the crucial difference is that Petrarch always has an eye on the way the future looks back; as he writes letters to the greats of the past, giving them his opinion of their works and lives, so he writes letters to the future, modestly, of course, doubtful that the future will care, but convinced that there will be a future to care and determined in all humility to make his claim.

Printing and Portraiture:
The Dissemination of the Unique

O *Printing!* how hast thou disturb'd the Peace of Mankind! that lead,
when moulded into Bullets, is not so mortal as when founded into
letters!

—ANDREW MARVELL, *The Rehearsal Transpros'd* (1672)

In "The Letter to Posterity" Petrarch details both his frugal habits and
dress and tells us what he looks like, aligning himself with a tradition of
high-minded poverty that reaches back to the early saints and contrasts
with the ostentatious display of learned courtiers and other urban intellectuals.[1] But the self-displaying reticence to which Petrarch aspires recalls
Augustine or Francis less than it anticipates figures like Dürer and Erasmus, in whom the urge toward fame must take into account such new
phenomena as the invention of printing and the changing relation of artist
and writer to ruler and patron. Even in the midst of his attack on ostentation, Petrarch in fact recognized the interplay of written and visual
depictions of greatness when he characterizes himself at the end of "The
Triumph of Love," looking at the great spirits confined by Love, "like one
beholding lengthy painted scenes." Petrarch's own musings on the subject
of true fame may have devalued theatrical display, but he also opens the
way for visual arraying of the heroes of past and present as well as (in
the *Triumphs*) a new pattern for royal ceremony and the flourishes of
theater.

Lady Philosophy had ejected the muses in Boethius's *Consolation of
Philosophy* so that the imprisoned intellectual could turn his mind away
from fame and the pursuit of worldly glory and think on eternity instead.
But art in the Renaissance took the spiritual capital it had collected
through centuries of subordination to religious subject matter and invested
it in the depiction of contemporary political power. Petrarch's celebration
of the great Roman figures as models for the enlightened strongmen of

1. As Hans Baron argues in "Franciscan Poverty," the lower social status of the
learned in the fourteenth century accorded with a part-stoic, part-Franciscan ideal of
the nobly poor wise man who possessed only his own wisdom and needed little more.
On the other hand, the celebrators of civic culture, with its dependence on a prince-
led court, argued that intellectual labor was demeaned by being paid for—leaving
low-born artists and writers little way to be both respected and financially secure.

fourteenth-century Italy expanded in the next few centuries into a whole artistic and intellectual profession, supplying cultural and historical forebears for the great individuals of the present. By the late fifteenth century few thought it worth objecting that Botticelli painted the wife of Lorenzo de' Medici and her children as if she were the Virgin Mary and they cherubs. But by the sixteenth century even such emblematic guises were used much less frequently. The subject was the individual face, painted neither in historical, mythological, or religious guise nor at the verge of the grave like a Roman funerary portrait, but taken directly in the midst of life. Sculpture had again begun to flourish. Lorenzo, called "the Magnificent" and untitled ruler of nominally democratic Florence, took Petrarch's *Triumphs* and turned into lavish public displays what had been originally created as a meditation on ways to transcend the rewards of the world. Within virtually the same generation, Henry VIII in England separated the English Church from Rome with a wave of iconoclastic destruction of innumerable religious buildings and images, even as he fostered the first vigorous growth of an English tradition of secular portraiture.[2]

It is a fairly recent idea, hardly more than two hundred years old, that artists constitute a permanent opposition to the public policies and politics of their countries. It is an even more recent idea that governments ought to tolerate and even support their opposition. In the Renaissance, as part of the general revival of classical culture, the arts of human representation join forces with politicians, leaders, and conquerors who wish to assert the sway of their image as an adjunct of their power. Not that the artists were reluctant, for it was through their own assertions of cultural importance that the powerful often got the idea. The result was an unprecedented propaganda of images for both patron and artist to trumpet their importance. The secular portrait may have been commissioned, but it absorbed both payment and materials into a statement of secular transcendence and fame akin to the spiritual accrual gained when a pious patron would be included in the crowd around Jesus on an altarpiece. No longer was the presence of holy figures necessary to legitimate the assertion. The eternity of their images now had to compete for attention in a world newly fascinated by the details of social self-presentation.

We are familiar enough with the ways photography, film, and television have defined the cultural significance of the individual face. But we should also remember that at virtually the same time portrait painting began to take a prime place in a world of art previously dominated by religious imagery, the influence of its focus on the individual face was expanded tremendously by the new technology of printing. Printing allowed the negotiable face, previously the possession of only the rich, to become a medium of more general cultural exchange. Images of the wise, the artistic, the

2. Lorenzo extensively promoted the works of Dante, Petrarch, and Boccaccio as part of his own political rule. He was helped immeasurably by the fact that these as well as his innumerable other cultural activities occurred in the context of the first widespread use of printing in Italy.

holy, and the powerful began to be published widely as examples of contemporary heroism, alongside freshly minted visual models for the ways one could act, dance, dress, or even preach with the proper gestures and body movement. With the more widespread use of engraving after the mid-sixteenth century, portraits and illustrations could be multiplied in even greater detail. Faces were appearing everywhere, in poses that in part alluded to Roman precedents but also helped create a new array of heroes for the present and the future.

Some historians, economists, and political scientists might dismiss the portrait as evidence of nothing more than the public man's growing taste for the more subtle or artistically respectable forms of flattery. But, as we have seen, there existed a historical interplay of status between artists and their patrons that dated from the classical world. Artists sought to celebrate, rulers searched for new and more compelling ways to proclaim their greatness, and the Roman past contained a whole vocabulary of self-assertion waiting to be drawn upon and developed. The *Res gestae* inscription of Augustus was rediscovered in the sixteenth century. But Augustus's effort to use the arts to buttress his authority had been excavated long before. Like those modern show-business films and biographies that simultaneously glamorize performers while recounting their desperate lives, publicizing the difficulties of fame implicitly sought to keep it a closed club. The Middle Ages were not yet over, and the shadow of the Boethian concept of Fortune's Wheel (which could raise the lowly, but mainly humbled the great) still hung over a world in which plagues and seemingly endless wars destroyed individuals and drained the energies of nations. But the belief that worldly fame was something for the lowly to stay away from and for the wellborn to approach only in watertight spiritual armor was clearly vanishing. Everyone who made a career in public—and the number of public professions was speedily increasing—was being made to realize how both art and printing could make him more symbolic, more essential, and more powerful. Whatever holy aura had attached to the image, whatever link with eternity was asserted by the book, was becoming accessible to all who cared to make their claim.

The articulation and ordering made possible by printing fostered a new cultural consistency as well. Classical and Christian symbols, mythographies, histories, and the Bible itself became more codified and therefore interpretable by a wide audience of readers who, for the first time in history, might assume that they were looking at exactly the same work as an individual thousands of miles away. Petrarch, Dante, Chaucer—whatever their different views of literary fame—could anticipate only a fairly limited audience, in its nature unchanged since the days when Atticus would hire extra Greek slaves to get out a few more copies of Cicero's latest oration. But with printing came the possibility of an audience limited only by the ability to buy the book and read it without the need to travel far distances to read rare manuscripts chained to a shelf. The old contrast between the good fame of the elite, whether spiritual or intellectual or political, versus the bad fame of common report carried by the tongues and ears of the vulgar crowd was shattered by the possibility of far-flung readers, organized by the easily reproducible book. Royalty especially grasped hold of the new engines of fame. Writers and artists, stagers of processions, architects of the new and transmuters of the old, worked with them in concert. Through a new self-consciousness of the past, rituals were relearned, hierarchies were reaffirmed. In the process, of course, envy between aspirants became more prevalent, and with envy came more aspiration—aided especially by the printing press and the copper engraving. The competition of images we blindly associate with the present had already by the sixteenth century begun in earnest. It was a new world of fame, in which visible and theatrical fame would become the standard, and public prominence a continual theme. One of its earliest manifestations came with the effort to maintain and restore a "true" image of the king.

Depicting the Royal Line

In the later Middle Ages rulers increasingly turned to writers who created for them elaborate genealogies, legitimizing their power by demonstrating the continuity of past and present, and defining the coherence of the kingdom as the historical continuity of the monarch's family. Thus, merely by being born, the ruler took the prime place in a fame corporation founded long before, stretching back to some outstanding and appropriate progenitor—Aeneas, Constantine, Charlemagne, or Arthur. In England, the island nation, where political evolution had especially favored an early centralization of authority over local magnates in a single monarch, the invocation of such enabling figures was especially prevalent. In earlier times, Arthur and his Round Table, for example, had furnished a judgment seat of ultimate knightly accomplishment for both England and France, a secular counterpoise to the religious orders.[3] But, even as Arthur was disappearing as a backdrop to French chivalry, his political importance in England continued to rise. In the fourteenth century Edward I cited Arthur to Pope Boniface VIII as the wellspring of English kings and thereby justification for his claims to Scotland. Arthurian chivalry was behind Edward III's institution of the Order of the Garter in 1348. Springing from Constantine and Charlemagne, Arthur was the great man, English style, who similarly bridged the worlds of piety, politics, and learning. After Henry Tudor defeated Richard III at Bosworth Field to become Henry VII, he helped establish his own legitimacy by invoking a Welsh ancestry to name his eldest son Arthur and then arraying around Arthur and his court a program of chivalric praise in imitation of that of the dukes of Burgundy

3. Some of the more lasting stories woven around the medieval kings, with their roots in tales of Alexander and others, are treated by Davis, *The Normans and Their Myths.*

that was written (substantially in French) by Bernard André, whom Henry had imported from Toulouse. The native tradition of royal praise as yet needed some foreign priming. Arthur appears frequently as one of the Nine Worthies in court festivities throughout the sixteenth century, and, at the end of the century, late in the reign of Elizabeth, Edmund Spenser embarks on his celebratory epic *The Faerie Queene* as a work of twelve books, each to represent one of the Aristotelian virtues and each realized in the "magnificence" that contains all those virtues—the figure of Arthur.[4]

As the legends and folktales that grew around figures like Charlemagne and Arthur indicate, they shared the ability of the saints of late antiquity to appeal to audiences who looked for heroes to ennoble the history and geography most familiar to them, as well as to rulers who wished to absorb that transfiguration into their own beings. In the reign of Henry VIII (Prince Arthur's younger brother), such enabling figures became useful precedents for a monarch who sought to assert his own national power against the international order of the papacy as well as for writers and artists for whom Rome was less a physical place than a realm of the spirit, now refounded in England. According to Polydore Vergil, an Italian humanist historian who at one time or another numbered both Henry VII and Henry VIII among his patrons, Constantine was "begotten of Helena in Brittaine" by Constantius, thus making the English kings the heirs of both Aeneas (through his great-grandson Brutus) and Constantine, the founder of Rome and the first Christian emperor:

> Albeit the imperie remained not long after in the stocke of Constantine (so sodaine is the fall of humaine treasures), neverthelesse the maiestie of the imperie coulde not perishe, sithe that even at this presente the kinges of Englonde, according to the usage of their aunciters [ancestors], doe weare the imperiall diademe as a gifte exhibited of Constantinus to his successors (98–99).[5]

The emphasis on genealogy and the sanction of great predecessors may also carry with it the implication that the effectiveness of a ruler in the present moment is less important than the way he embodies the authority

---

4. Spenser's poem remains unfinished by half, although Arthur still figures prominently in the court propaganda of the early years of the reign of James I (1603–1625). By the mid-seventeenth century, however, the relation between nationalism and individual heroism has changed enough that Milton decides to write *Paradise Lost* rather than an epic "Arthuriad" in celebration of English history. Several works with Arthur as a central figure come out in the 1690s, including an opera by John Dryden and Henry Purcell and two long poems, *Prince Arthur* and *King Arthur,* by Richard Blackmore. But Arthur as an inspiring character virtually disappears from English literature until Tennyson revives him in the age of high English imperialism some 150 years later (*Idylls of the King,* 1859).

5. This is an early translation from the original Latin work published in 1534. Polydore Vergil was one of the best historians of his time, but still took this old story at face value. It is true that Constantine was first proclaimed Augustus by his soldiers while in Britain. But his mother, Helena, was born in Bithynia and he on the lower Danube in Serbia. Henry VIII, however, was no doubt pleased with the affirmation of his independence.

of the past. In medieval terms especially, who the monarch was individually was less important than who he was genealogically. Time and family justified more than did personal nature, and all were *sub specie aeternitatis*. The royal portraiture of the Middle Ages, when it does exist and, more usually, when it doesn't, indicates how little it then seemed necessary to assert a visible difference between the faces of kings. Since there was essentially only one way to be a king, there was also essentially one official look, with small variations. By the end of the fifteenth century in England, however, the combined realization that there were different kinds of kingly power as well as different kinds of kingly imagery began to be recorded in an increasing amount of royal portraiture. The king's need to impose his image along with his power was becoming a more important aspect of his attitude toward kingship itself. Being a king may always have been a role, but it was beginning to be played with increasing self-consciousness.

In the Middle Ages, especially in such joint international ventures as the Crusades, the kings of Europe might subdue their personal desires to become the next Charlemagne and pay allegiance instead to the goals of the Church. But with the rise of the strong monarchies of England and France, the need to justify the nation through justifying the king became an accepted method of propaganda. In both countries the increasing imagery of national kingship paralleled a shift in the organization of the armies from noble commanders to professional captains. Soldiers became more motivated by national pride than by the urge to chivalric glory, or, more precisely, individual glory became more dependent on the context of king and nation than on the chivalric code. We tend to see Henry V through Shakespeare's depiction of him as the great English patriot-king, which is to a large extent true. But we should also note that in addition to giving rousing speeches Henry was also the patron of a whole group of both national and personal histories primarily aimed at establishing him both as a devout Christian prince and as an injured monarch whose rejected claims to the throne of France justified war. Like Joan of Arc, who began hearing voices just about the time he died, Henry V fused spiritual validation with national ambition. Her goal was to assert the legitimacy of a line of "pure" French kings in opposition to those French nobles allied with the English, while he expected the demonstrations of his personal piety and historical precedents would convince others of his legal right to rule France. She scorned learning, while he employed historians and writers. Yet both in effect made the nation rather than the Church the arbiter of continuity and authority, and both as a result stand in relation to their own countries as nationalist saints, able to be called upon by any faction who claims to have the good of the country at heart. Like Washington or Lincoln or, most recently, Franklin Roosevelt in America, their actual policies are irrelevant to their iconographic status. Joan in her armor, Henry V in his monkish tonsure, combine the piety of a national history sanctioned by God with a determination to defend that history through force of arms. Chivalry itself, and the chivalric image of Jesus as a Christian knight, was less and less the code of a particular noble class than a series of stories, metaphors, and images that evoked a national past that could be shared by many.

In Henry and Joan reappears the Jesus who supported the local and the individual against the power of the Church. Joan especially represents a new kind of nationalist charisma, drawing together elements of sainthood and military politics, Roman heroic action and Christian isolated glory. For the previous few hundred years the papacy had exercised a monopoly over the introduction of new saintly cults. Although Joan herself was exonerated twenty-five years after she was burnt at the stake, she was not made a saint until the twentieth century. But the new heroic aura that she exemplifies brought new centers of iconographic power and new cults into being. Kings had long since fallen out, chivalry was giving way to diplomacy, and soon Christianity itself would split apart. But in the history of fame Joan of Arc (a name she never used herself) sets the stage for Elizabeth I, who builds beautifully on her legacy. Part warrior and part saint, a figure as open to contradictory interpretations as Alexander, Charlemagne, or Jesus, Joan maintains her hold on the imaginations of the French through the centuries until she is forcefully revived in grandeur, first by Napoleon as the patron saint of the new French Empire, then by innumerable writers of the nineteenth and twentieth centuries fascinated by her fame and personality, and finally by Charles de Gaulle, who adopted the cross of Lorraine, her home region (and his), as the emblem of the Free French Army and later the Fifth Republic.[6]

Although Joan la Pucelle, "the Maid of Orleans," became a figure whose name, face, and story later inspired millions of her countrymen, little certain is actually known about how she looked and the most authentic of her words come from her testimony in her trial for heresy. Henry V, with his livelier interest in the uses of visual and verbal art, sought a quite different effect on his audience. According to Roy Strong (*Tudor,* I, 261), Richard II was "without doubt" the first English king to sit for a portrait from life, and the moody self-centeredness of Shakespeare's Richard II may reflect the actual king's inability to fashion an authority that matched his expectations. But with Henry V, I would say, first clearly appears the interest in personalizing the monarch as a method of strengthening royal power. The portraits of Henry V, says Strong, "seem definitely to be depicting a person as against an image"—or, I might amend, an image that for political reasons looks more like a person (by our standards). The

6. Joan of Arc's brief but crowded public career has been the subject of constant attention over the centuries. Recent scholarship is agreeably brought together in Gies, *Joan of Arc,* while a more speculative work about Joan in terms of the contemporary cultural patterns on which her imagery drew and the persistence of that image down to the present is Warner's *Joan of Arc.* For the chivalric background, against which Joan's saintliness defined itself as much as did that of Francis of Assisi some two centuries before, see Painter, *French Chivalry.* On Joan's trial, see Barrett, ed., *The Trial of Jeanne d'Arc,* and Lightbody, *The Judgements of Joan.*

politics of such imagery is aimed particularly at establishing a royal authority where there might be a question about the claims to power. Like the Medici, then coming to power in Florence, the English kings were learning that cultural patronage and promotion could help affirm political power in the interests of a stronger, more self-conscious nation. Decades before the introduction of printing, Henry sponsored works of history, genealogy, and biography, adorned by woodcuts of kingly heads, that asserted his legitimate right to France. His example was powerful. Henry VIII sponsored an English translation of a Latin life of Henry V written by "Tito Livio." During the reign of Elizabeth, two English histories commissioned by Henry V were lavishly republished by Matthew Parker, antiquarian and archbishop of Canterbury, along with an even older life of Alfred the Great. Only a few years before, Elizabeth had been excommunicated by the pope. But, as these polemical volumes indicate, she had learned the lesson first taught by Henry V very well. Books and pictures were the way to men's minds. The editions were extraordinarily ornate, and the Alfred particularly boasted an intricate frontispiece celebrating the monarch astride the geographical world, surrounded by emblems of all humanistic knowledge; the names of great thinkers, geographers, and mathematicians; and, at his feet, Mercury—messenger of the gods, bringer of the news, the herald of good fame to Aeneas and his descendants.

What should a king look like? How should a king behave? Perhaps for the first time since the Christian bishops of late antiquity were attacking the Roman definition of the public man, such questions were open for speculation. In the fifteenth and sixteenth centuries all over Europe—in books, paintings, and triumphal processions—actual and aspiring royalty were remembering or inventing their direct descent from many different sorts of noble dead. They crowded into the ranks of Petrarchan triumphs, sponsored intricate self-celebrating displays, and associated themselves with a variety of gods and demigods from classical mythology, the most popular of which was probably Hercules—the original man become god, who had gained added intellectual luster by being reinterpreted as a saint of stoic virtue as well as an indomitable athlete.

It may be a rule of thumb in periods of political unrest that the weaker the historical claim to power, the more elaborate will be its imagery. But imagery has a history as well, and the most innovative often draws on past associations amalgamated and reminted. Thus in the light of the difficulties Elizabeth was facing with the papacy and all of Catholic Europe, Parker's seemingly remote and scholarly project takes on quite immediate political dimensions: to present a handsome and tradition-sanctioned justification of both the legitimacy of English rule and the relation of historiography to statecraft by affirming the confluence of the two great lines of English monarchy—the Saxon Alfred and the Norman Henry V—in Elizabeth. That this affirmation of the legitimacy of secular power appears under the sponsorship of the archbishop of Canterbury underlines the shift of English allegiance from pope to monarch quite clearly.[7] Henry VII, father of Henry VIII and grandfather of Elizabeth I, came to the English throne in 1485 with the shakiest claim in some time. Throughout his reign he had to face claimants to the throne who said they were either Edward V or his younger brother the Duke of York, both supposedly murdered in the Tower by Richard III or his henchmen. Along with its new self-consciousness about the characters of kings and its innovations in royal propaganda, the age is also marked by imposters, both fraudulent and sincere: some claiming to be lost or strayed kings; some saying they were Joan of Arc, miraculously snatched from the flames (and authenticated by her own brothers). The more sincerely convinced had to be defeated in battle or at law; the less self-possessed might be bought off with money or court jobs. But in an age more and more aware of the extent to which kingship was a self-presentation, the pressure of imposture was always there. To buttress his own uncertain background, Henry VII, with the aid of the Italian humanist writers and visual artists he attracted to his court, became a great experimenter with iconography, aiming at an audience whom he could sway by images as much as arguments. Richard III still wears the malevolent character tailored for him by Henry's campaign against his memory. Like Augustus in the *Res gestae,* Henry's own court historian, Bernard André, praised his patron more for his coinage and diplomacy than for his military prowess, and in that coinage from 1485 to 1509 can be traced an increasing movement away from the traditional bland stiffness of the monarchical face and toward a more realistic, more individual, depiction. Individual talent and inheritance would both be stressed at once: Like so many later monarchs, Henry VII implied that he was both self-made and historically justified. Even more than Henry V, he made England the arena of his legitimacy, drawing upon traditions of portraiture being pioneered in Medici Florence. Among the images of Henry VII that have come down to us is an extraordinary painted and gilded terra-cotta bust made by Pietro Torrigiano, a Florentine sculptor. Henry was less lucky with his painted portraits, however. When one in the new realistic mode was sent to Margaret of Austria, a prospective wife, she turned him down abruptly. Perhaps he didn't look enough like a king.

In the disruptive successions that characterized the sixteenth century in England, royal portraiture became a crucial mode of establishing legitimate continuity. The king's position as God's vicar on earth was directly connected to his personal status as a special member of a special family. In such a context only a very self-confident patron could afford to let his painter experiment freely with imagery and techniques. New but somehow familiar patterns had to be established, which simultaneously celebrated the monarch as both necessary ruler and glorious individual.

7. As befits a man of words, Parker was also a little behind the times in the subtlety of his visual imagery. The role of kingship was in his eyes still more important than the figure of the king, and so, for example, he used the face of Alfred from one book for that of Richard, Duke of Normandy, in another.

Sixteenth-century political power—whether that of Henry VIII, the Holy Roman Emperor Charles V, the French monarch Francis I, or the Medici Pope Leo X (son of Lorenzo the Magnificent)—thus employed writers and artists of all sorts to help justify itself and its acts. Francis I was pleased to be called "the father of the Muses." Charles V, in his grant of nobility to Titian, compared their relationship to that between Alexander the Great and Apelles. An ideology of image was taking shape based on the newly self-aware notion that rulers had audiences as well as subjects.[8]

Charles V and Titian are only the most familiar examples of the general Renaissance invocation of the Alexander-Apelles model for the patron-artist relationship. By creating images of Alexander indulgently giving his mistress Campaspe to Apelles, or of Augustus listening to the *Aeneid* being read to him by Virgil, artists showed their patrons how art should be appreciated by truly great men. In an act of energetic complicity, the artist/writer created a heroic mold into which the statesman/king/politician wished to fit himself, or, if you prefer, the public man, consumed by his desire to reenact past greatness, specifically commissioned his celebrator first to imitate and then to invent heroic poses for him. Depending on patron, artist, and social setting, any combination of events was possible. In England, for example, Henry VIII's political attack on holy faces set the stage for the development of a secular iconography and potentially a secular sainthood—first of monarchs and heroes and then of artists themselves. Henry's forbidding face, Francis's more genial looks, and Charles's studied alternation of grandeur and informality are all aspects of the general trend. Although we might like to trace the authoritative look of Henry

8. Apelles supposedly fell in love with Campaspe while painting her as Aphrodite for Alexander. Botticelli's *Birth of Venus* is based on the verses in which Angelo Poliziano, the inseparable companion of Lorenzo de' Medici, reconstructs all the references to Apelles' painting in classical literature. Botticelli also painted an attempted reconstruction of Apelles' *Calumny*, which Leon Battista Alberti had revived in his treatise *On Painting* from the ancient description by Lucian. Paintings and drawings based on Botticelli, Alberti, Lucian, and other sources, both literary and artistic, are frequent from the fifteenth through the eighteenth centuries. In the original story, Apelles is falsely accused by another artist of a plot against the Ptolemaic ruler of Egypt. He is found guilty and condemned to death. But then justice prevails. He is released and executes a painting whose subject is the danger of calumny, slander, and false witness to the political order. Historically the scene is implausible, since it would be difficult for Apelles to be both the favorite painter of Alexander and the supposed conspirator against Ptolemy IV Philopater about a hundred years later. But its complex themes obviously appealed to Renaissance artists: first, that great artists were not a political threat to rulers; second, that great artists were often misjudged both politically and aesthetically by ignorant authorities; and third, that the more widespread fame of artists was accompanied by an increasingly explicit envy and competition. In addition to Botticelli, Mantegna did a drawing (later owned by Rembrandt), Dürer did an elaborate version of the motif to decorate the Nuremberg Rathaus, and drawings and paintings were done as well by Peter Brueghel, Raphael, Zuccaro, and others. See Alberti, *On Painting*, and Cast, *Calumny of Apelles*. The popularity of the Alexander-Apelles theme in the sixteenth century might be compared with that of the Pygmalion theme in the nineteenth century: the artist given his beloved model by his magnanimous great-man patron versus the artist whose own work comes to life, superseding that of the model.

to his effort to emerge from the shadow of his father and the easy smirk of Francis with his own more secure sense of his power, such psychological equations are finally less interesting than the efforts of both to live more in the public eye than monarchs had before.

Although, because of Hans Holbein, our mental image of Henry VIII is the strongest of any English monarch except Elizabeth and perhaps Charles II, he was comparatively a slow learner in such matters. He even kept the image of his father, Henry VII, on his own coins for the first seventeen years of his reign (1509–1526). Yet he was to become a central figure in an age when monarchs were becoming more explicitly concerned with how they appeared both to their own subjects and to the world. Without concluding that the English Reformation was slyly plotted by Henry to rid himself of the iconographic competition, it still seems possible to say that the nationalism he represented was itself ready to be extricated from the universal embrace of the Church to spawn a line of its own. Henry, it is said, first grew a beard in imitation of Francis I, perhaps because Francis seemed to look and act more like a real king, and, intriguingly enough, Henry's emergence as a "strong" king follows upon Francis I's capture by Charles V in the battle of Pavia (1525). In the royal context of emulative imagery, Henry would soon produce a few innovations of his own. Henry VII had used the propaganda of history and visual imagery to help establish his legitimate relation to the past. Henry VIII, especially through an extraordinary number of portraits of his son, the future Edward VI (born 1537), similarly sought to ensure the future.[9]

* * *

> There is no evidence that Elizabeth had much taste for painting; but she loved pictures of herself.
> —GEORGE VERTUE, *Anecdotes of Painting*

The monarch most attuned to the possibilities of visual representation and therefore the strongest influence on its expansion in the late sixteenth century was Elizabeth I. We are all aware of the tremendous impact she had both on the history of her own time and on the consciousness of a host of writers and visual artists who celebrated her as Gloriana and Eliza, the embodiment of England. But the particular nature of Elizabeth's self-consciousness might also be gauged by the contrast between her image as queen and that of her predecessor and half sister Mary Tudor, who has come down to us as "Bloody Mary." In fact we have quite a lot of evidence about Mary's physical appearance and comparatively very little about Elizabeth's. Yet in our collective mind's eye Elizabeth bulks very

9. It is tempting to picture the gradual conditioning of Henry's view of himself and his kingship through his emulous contention not only with the royal rivals, Francis I and Charles V, but also with commoners of such different ambitions as his successive lord chancellors, Cardinal Thomas Wolsey and Sir Thomas More, and the chief of his new administrative elite, Thomas Cromwell.

large, while Mary is easily subordinated to the mixed drink that bears her nickname.

The contrast between the portraits of Mary and Elizabeth is a contrast between royal images made because it is the prevailing style and royal images made to achieve particular political effects. Elizabeth's own efforts are directly in line with both Henry's ban on religious sculpture and painting (1538) and his debasement of the coinage (1544) as well as with her half brother Edward VI's order to destroy all existing examples of religious imagery (1548). All these actions confirmed their belief that the monarch was the prime creator of all real as well as all symbolic value and could lower it or raise it as he or she chose. In most of the physical descriptions of Mary, she comes off badly to our image-drenched eyes, in part because her observers seem to identify display with insincerity and indifference to religious belief: "She has no eyebrows, she is a perfect saint and dresses very badly," reports the Venetian ambassador (Strong, *Tudor,* I, 211). Yet it takes no subtle reading to note the ambivalence in such a report. Mary's idea of majesty, however spiritually justified, did not quite impress even her Catholic foreign supporters. Elizabeth, on the other hand, from the early years of her reign (1558–1603), consciously propagated an image of personal majesty, perhaps at first because, like Henry VII, she had to overwhelm doubts of her legitimacy. Unlike Mary, she wants to live up to being a ruler instead of merely filling a preexisting role.[10]

Perhaps another Mary influenced her as well. In 1561 Mary, Queen of Scots, then briefly queen of France, initiated an exchange of portraits with Elizabeth, but it took the reluctant Elizabeth six years to fulfill her part of the bargain. In the meantime, in 1563, five years after she came to the throne, a Draft Proclamation sought both to set up proper patterns to be followed in depicting Elizabeth as well as to destroy all debased images in order to procure the "naturall representation of hir Majesties person, favor, or grace" and create a "perfect patron [pattern] and example" for others to follow (*Tudor,* I, 5). The proclamation was never officially put into effect, although the portraits of Elizabeth that exist are clearly modeled on the style the draft calls for. Perhaps the memories of past iconoclasm were too immediate to risk this new official purge. Perhaps Elizabeth or others thought that popular and unlicensed depictions of the queen would ultimately provide more help than harm. Defaming caricatures of the new Protestant monarch were already circulating on the Continent. In response or in anticipation, a virtual cult of Elizabeth's image, drawing in great part on the iconography of the Virgin Mary, sprung up in England. Just

10. As the daughter of Henry VIII's second wife, Anne Boleyn, Elizabeth was declared illegitimate in 1536 shortly before the execution of Anne on charges of adultery and incest. But Henry's will put her as well as her half sister Mary (daughter of Catherine of Aragon, Henry's first wife) back into the succession behind their half brother Edward (son of Jane Seymour, wife number three). When Elizabeth became queen, Henry II, king of France, still considered her illegitimate and supported the claim of Mary, Queen of Scots, next in line after Elizabeth, and his own daughter-in-law.

as Titian and Charles V in some basic sense worked together on the imperial image, there is reason to believe that Elizabeth's imagery also helped explain herself to herself. She became a consummate performer of the role of the monarch, fully aware of what precedents she absorbed and what she discarded. At Hampton Court, for example, are a series of six tapestries she commissioned based on the Dido and Aeneas story in the *Aeneid*. For a literary monarch, well skilled in the imagery of power, the queen of Carthage could be both a justifying forebear and a cautionary example.

What, we might wonder, was inferior about the portraits that Elizabeth wished to suppress? Likeness does not seem to be really the issue. Rather it may have been an insufficiently majestic setting for the portrait, some undermining of her desire to present an image of unchanging value. Only modern taste causes us both to differentiate between realism and flattery in portraits and to try to match past portraits with written testimony about the sitter's features. Living in a constant spray of human images, we have been schooled in or have osmotically absorbed so many ways of interpreting faces that we can barely appreciate how primitive were the means available to a Renaissance audience, just emerging from centuries in which it was the contours of the soul rather than those of the face that received the most attention. By the late eighteenth century books on physiognomy begin to appear, suggesting that the vogue for interpreting faces had finally reached a wider public. But it is notable how little of such interpretation is a concern in the Renaissance. When Machiavelli analyzes the character of a prince and how to serve him, he defines the prince's nature according to his social role rather than the intermingling of individual psychology and public presentation that more attracts our interest. When individuality is only beginning to be a social value, its status as a pictorial value must be rudimentary as well. The intentions expressed in the Draft Proclamation indicate that the young Elizabeth, beset with political and iconographic threats to her legitimacy, sought to enforce a compact with those who were entrusted with the creation of her image, recognizing the power of art at the same time that she wanted to control its ability to present her in ways she might not approve. The proper intercessor must be chosen and the opportunities for intercession appropriately restricted. Roy Strong estimates that only three truly distinct portraits of Elizabeth exist—with innumerable copies and adaptations—and he points out that only one drawing of her was known to have been made in her presence. She represented England; and a variety of poses, moods, or times of life would have been detrimental to the iconic effect she wished to achieve.

Elizabeth, however, was hardly alone in her understanding of the usages of visual representation. Throughout the sixteenth century the book and the picture were becoming ways to a renown and a power that could just as easily threaten royal prestige as celebrate it. Courtiers eager for royal favor might adopt and expand the same motifs, while aristocratic aspirants to some portion of the royal aura could employ the same painters and sculptors. If imagery was power, others might use it as well as or better than the monarch. Hans Holbein had already painted portraits of such noted humanists as Thomas More and Erasmus when More introduced him to Henry VIII, who virtually made him the official court painter. With such an atmosphere of official display, it seems hardly coincidental that the poet courtier Earl of Surrey, born in the reign of Henry VIII, who bragged of his descent from Edward I and was finally executed on a fraudulent charge of treason under Edward VI, also "sat for his portrait more times within the short span of his life than any other Tudor courtier" (Strong, *Icon,* 307); or that the family of the poet Sir Thomas Wyatt (whose son would be executed for treason under Bloody Mary) were patrons of Holbein; or that John Rastell, author of *The Pastime of People,* the first sequential portrait gallery of English kings from Aeneas on down, was a brother-in-law and close friend of More, Henry VIII's lord chancellor. Henry's disestablishment of the Catholic Church and his confiscations of Church treasures and land helped create whole new dynasties of the wealthy. With these new-found riches and with the example of Henry's own assertion, patronage could flourish. Everyone with the money and a bit of vision might become his or her own work of art, appropriately highlighted and framed.

Once the power to impose by portraiture is learned—the grand Henry VIII of Holbein looking down on artist and viewer alike—it is difficult to restrict. The glory of being depicted, the fame of imitating the greats of the past, could not remain a royal preserve for long, especially for young men in a hurry to be famous. Galeazzo Sforza took Nero as his model, and so his three assassins followed the pattern by assassinating him in the name of liberty. For every Caesar there was a potential Brutus, intent on immortality himself. When Anthony Babington was brought into a conspiracy to murder Elizabeth and bring Mary, Queen of Scots, to the throne, he quickly commissioned portraits of himself and his co-conspirators so that posterity would know whom to thank (Neale, 271).[11]

Yet, while printing and the reproduction of images was expanding the audience for display far beyond a monarch's immediate court, centuries of Christian attack on the spiritual weakness of the eye must engender a fear of its inquisitiveness as well, its ability to open the way to violation. Art may make you last, but art may also make you more vulnerable, too accessible to the eyes of others. For a long time, therefore, the paintings of important figures embody distance as well as exposure. The image of the king is before us, say, but we see him at his window: Look, but don't touch; approach, but stay out of my space. As figures of grandeur they exist in a place the viewer could never inhabit. Henry and

11. In 1537 Lorenzino de' Medici, the great-grandson of Lorenzo, murdered his cousin Alessandro de' Medici, hereditary ruler of Florence, and proclaimed himself to be a reborn Brutus. In what may have been a gesture of sympathy for both the act and Lorenzino's own sense of his historical mission, Michelangelo in 1540 completed a bust of Brutus. See Linda Murray, *Michelangelo.*

later Elizabeth are especially sensitive to the problem, but Edward VI and Mary Tudor were hardly immune. Throughout the century, for example, the laws of treason are refined and elaborated, especially those that cover injury to the king's reputation, as opposed to his person. In sixteenth-century Europe, men could be boiled alive for counterfeiting, that is, reproducing the king's image by their own authority and for their own gain. In England under Henry VIII such "imagining" was high treason and forgery trials occasions for government propaganda. Henry VIII may have at first been lax about his coinage. But when Cardinal Wolsey minted a groat—while entitled to mint only half a groat—the case for lèse-majesté was symbolically clear, and Wolsey's fall inevitable.[12]

Henry VIII's use of Holbein to fashion a formidable royal image of himself thus lays the groundwork for a future when visual access to kings is not so easily controlled. Like coinage, royal portraiture enforces the royal presence when the monarch is not around. But, to complete the equation, when the monarch is present, the ceremony of royalty must at least match the portraiture in glamor and visual complexity. The increasing taste for miniature painting in the later sixteenth century indicates how portraiture has made viewers increasingly acute about the meaning of *both* public and private visual representation. These portable images embody a more private, more intimate, and more sentimental relation between the viewer and the subject. Instead of being part of a hall of ancestors or a tribute to the monarch, they verge on the one-to-one relation of reader to poem or to novel. No wonder perhaps that in the miniatures appear some of the first English self-portraits of artists themselves.

Styles of Artistic Assertion

The first great care of one who seeks to obtain eminence in painting is to acquire the fame and renown of the ancients.
—LEON BATTISTA ALBERTI, *On Painting*

A critical view of politics and political men is often complemented by a blandly "aesthetic" appreciation of their artistic celebrators. But in a cultural atmosphere conducive to individual assertion, if we do not explore how artistic subject matter and style intertwine with the necessities of career and commission, then art remains barred from the history that it so often sought to shape. Perhaps this is where both artists and their patrons would like to keep it. But fame and its publicity, however much it pretends to be transcendent, is itself a historically influenced concept,

12. See Brooke, *English Coins,* 173–77. For the political context of the attack against Wolsey, see Elton, *Reform and Reformation.* Between 1352 and 1485 less than ten treason statutes were passed; between 1485 and 1603 there were sixty-eight (Bellamy, *Tudor Law of Treason*).

and artists were not long immune from its sway. After the late medieval reawakening of fame, the interests of artists and rulers often combine to create the proper way of seeing what ought to be seen. As nobles and monarchs had earlier commissioned family trees and chronicle histories, so, with the rise of portraiture and a new fascination with Roman greatness, they directed the creation of visual genealogies as well. History was no longer irrelevant to human goals. It could be seen, presented, and thereby controlled.

The competition between artists and monarchs sensitive both to the newly revived imagery and the new media in which it could be expressed would not break out until somewhat later, when, as is usual in the history of fame, the celebrators began taking credit for creating as well as enhancing their subjects. But in the beginnings, the two groups were generally allied, and the patron-monarch had the upper hand. Strong rulers like Elizabeth at first tried to control artistic self-assertion in the name of a "true" image. But such visual dictation was much more successful in the Eastern empire, where the icon still retained its quasi-divine status and the artist was the tractable handmaiden of its creation. In Russia, for example, not long before Elizabeth's Draft Proclamation, a church council, responding to several questions posed by the monarch, insisted on personal purity for all painters who made icons as well as stringent regulations for the entire craft. Wandering icon painters ought to be outlawed, they said, and bad icons should be destroyed. Appropriately enough, the ruler asked to implement these suggestions was Ivan IV, known as "the Terrible," who only a few years before had become the first Russian ruler to be officially crowned Caesar, Tsar. But in the West there were few traditions that could similarly keep artistic insight firmly subordinate to institutional decisions about what constituted the look of holiness. The Russian Church council readily answered Ivan's queries and readily expected him to follow its suggestions for keeping the guild free of the unworthy.[13] The most prolific and original Western painters, however, served a newly aware national state with motifs often both implicitly and explicitly opposed to those of the institutional Church. The more aspiring the artist, the more potential ambivalence over being only a publicist for nonartistic fame, even on the best of terms. In Botticelli's painting of a portrait of a young man holding a medal of Cosimo de' Medici that is actually embedded in the painting, we see the palpable shadow of some ironic tension between the realistically painted young man and the golden classical profile of Cosimo. Why choose between the young man and Cosimo, we seem to be asked. Choose instead the artist, who by profession is so finely attuned to their mutual desire to have their faces last through time.

13. See Gerhard, *The World of Icons*, 176–81. This Great Moscow Council of 1551, among other actions, affirmed the use of traditional motifs as well as the need of icon painters to maintain a moral personal life as a prerequisite for their trade and petitioned the tsar to outlaw the free lance lay icon painters who were cutting into the official craft's market.

When we look back on the artists of the past, we tend to give them all equal status. No matter what the conditions of their work and employment, no matter what they thought of themselves or were thought of by their audience, we clothe them equally in the robes of "artist" and discuss them as if their most crucial connections were with other artists, in their own time and through history, by means of shared motifs and formal concerns. But we must remember that artists themselves helped create the concept of a history of art in a largely successful attempt to give themselves a fame first akin, then similar, and finally superior to the status of public figures whose fame was dependent on their wielding of political and military sway. They began as cooperative employees, and they gradually became rivals, first serving the desire of their patrons to make a deeper mark in history, then raising themselves out of history and into the timeless realm of "art."

In general, "art" and its cognates derive from Greek and Latin words meaning what is joined, properly fit together, and so on. Such an etymological history is reflected in the medieval Latin word for a joiner or carpenter (*ars*) and the Italian word for a guild (*arte*), referring equally to the union of craftsmen and to the "hands on" nature of their occupations. The effort to reserve "art" and especially "artist" for a more rarefied sense of making is comparable to our current urge to distinguish fame from celebrity. Similarly, Renaissance artists and their celebrators argued that the immediate tangibility of craft could not have any lasting value unless it was enveloped in the eternity of artistic theory and ideas. This honorific use of the word "artist" derives from the medieval Latin for a student of the liberal arts, that system of knowledge that every educated man should know and from which the visual arts had been excluded. Thus when they made their move for status, it was defined by what writers had always possessed—a special relation to all knowledge and history rather than a journeyman-like mastery of the techniques of one's craft. By the sixteenth century when painters in particular were being employed with greater and greater frequency to emblazon the images of monarchical power, they began calling themselves artists with the kind of assertion and implication we associate with artists of our own time—something between profession (with its mysteries of craft and talent) and calling (with its tinge of spirituality and transcendence). In 1563, the year of Elizabeth's Draft Proclamation, several Florentine painters, sculptors, and architects, under the leadership of Vasari, founded the Accademia del Disegno, the first step toward receiving (in 1571) the exemption of such "artists" from the requirement of guild membership. In celebration they mounted a lavish funeral service for their most famous member and published a description entitled *Obsequies of the Divine Michelangelo Buonarotti*. As Rudolf and Margot Wittkower point out, the death of Michelangelo, who had expressly asked to be buried in Florence rather than Rome, was "a unique opportunity" to publicize two ideas: "[f]irst, that men of genius should rank next to, if not above, the highest civil and ecclesiastical dignitaries;

secondly, that the Academy of Design—the first proper academy of art ever established—was the legitimate representative of a rising new type of artist," whose genius was independent of his country and his family (Guinti, 42).[14]

From antiquity onward, the importance of writers to the process of gaining fame, and their potential competition with their patrons or subjects, has been apparent. But with the Renaissance we enter a period when both being visible and creating standards of visibility is what one thinks of when we say "fame." The pattern-portraits and engravings of the Renaissance bring fame out of its previously restricted and elite world and into the gaze of an immensely wider audience. A courtier's loyalty to Elizabeth might be cemented by a portrait of her on the wall, confirming a more immediate relation than that with a stained-glass saint high in a cathedral window. But the loyalty of an entire nation becomes a possible goal when that portrait can be reproduced in books. As sainthood had been a link between the ordinary person and God, so both visual artists and writers had become the intermediaries between the greats of the past and those of the present, administering their fame for an ever-increasing audience of posterity. In doing so they began to achieve their own renown as the keys that opened the door of shuttered time. After centuries of being subordinate to the framework of Church and State, they were becoming a third force, with its own traditions, its own great men, and its own canon of great works. The fame of writers, as we have seen, was more often an alternative to the fame of public men. But the fame of artists becomes a direct rival. Unlike the writers, whose sense of fame was influenced by the spiritual values of inner life and public evasion, the artists and the public men competed in similar terms of visual display. Writers learned soon enough to emulate their methods. But I think even now we can say that the greatest aspirations of writers is to be beyond the categories of social hierarchy, while artists—like Michelangelo, who sought a patent of nobility, or Velásquez, who refused pay so that he might be eligible to join a noble military order—define their ambitions by the heights of earthly status.

It would be hard to be precise about the stages by which the painter first moved away from the position of artisan-employee, then became animated with the possibility of being assimilated to his patron's class, and finally began to realize the ability to create a new class of his own. Unlike the artists of the East, who still worked in a tradition in which the holy object conferred status on its creator, the medieval European painters and sculptors were essentially wage earners who worked for hire in shops, traveled around the countryside drumming up trade, and exhibited their wares at local fairs alongside other craftsmen. The supposed anonymity

14. The *Oxford English Dictionary* points out that the modern use of "art" to refer especially to painting, engraving, and sculpture does not appear in any English dictionary before 1880, even though "artist"=painter is used from the eighteenth century on. "Arty" appears soon after.

of medieval artists is part of a genial nineteenth-century myth about a golden age before commercial ambitiousness ruined art. Artists have signed works and their names have been known ever since art reached beyond the local village to a market where someone might admire the work but not know where to get his own version of it. A signature on a piece of Greek pottery, for example, where so many of the names of the earliest artists are found, was part publicity and part contract, displaying the patron's taste in his purchase from so renowned a master and guaranteeing the work by the master's own name. On a grander level, the names of architects sometimes found on Egyptian monuments or Gothic churches similarly allied the maker with the artifact while still maintaining the subordinate relation of artist to his God and his patron. From our point of view, every Greek artist painting the gods on a krater and every Egyptian celebrator of the pharaoh in stone was adding a nuance to the visual terminology of divinity. But until the fourteenth and fifteenth centuries, artists were workmen, no matter how elevated. The more severe patron might even argue that, since the painting was contracted for and the painter paid, why should he sign it at all? And the medieval focus away from the rewards of the world toward heavenly glory might reinforce the point.[15]

Two important factors come into the new assertions of artistic status that characterize the Renaissance and influence our view of art and artists to this day. One is the invention of movable-type printing, which allowed the dissemination of reproductions of the artist's work to audiences far beyond his usual sphere; the other, closely related, is the greater mobility of the artist himself. No longer necessarily bound to the guild of his native or adopted town, if he dared and had the talent, he could travel to gather inspiration from other artists and art works, to seek out new patrons, and to become a member of an international class called "artists." For the artists, signatures became calling cards. For the patron, the signature made the painting a more valuable possession, and the most prestige-sensitive rulers began to collect artists as well. The pilgrimage to Italy and to Rome became an important part of the education of any artist of aspiration, the dip into the world of opulent classical forms, the anointing at the font of visual and plastic art. To non-Italian artists, the change in status could be a revelation. As Dürer wrote to a friend in Nuremberg while on a trip to Venice in his mid-thirties (1506), "Here I am a gentleman, at home I am a parasite" (Panofsky, 9).[16] Interlocking families of painters, engravers, and printers grew up that rivaled both the dynasties of kings and the economic monopolies of the guilds. Such powerful and often closely associated artists as Titian, Rubens, Teniers, and Van Dyck were creating

15. In contrast with the new assertion of artistic signature in the later fifteenth and sixteenth centuries, compare the cautious balance of Giovanni di Paolo in 1427, signing (and dating) an altarpiece portrait of the Virgin Mary, while surrounding it with a halo that reads, *"Hic* [sic] *qui te pinxit protege virgo virum"* ("Virgin, protect the man who paints you").

16. See also Wittkower, *Saturn,* 36. The phrase occurs in a letter to Dürer's friend and patron Willibald Pirckheimer.

through their patrons and connections a new market for artists among the temporally powerful, who might see in the grand painter a sensibility similar to their own and fully attuned to their purposes.

As individual patrons gradually replaced the Church as the main sponsor of visual art—a process given a tremendous push forward by the Protestant Reformation—artists of aspiration began to separate themselves from the late medieval structure of craft guilds and establish themselves as "masters" who contracted separately with their patrons outside guild regulations and control. The medieval concept of the "masterpiece" as the final test of skill before an apprentice is allowed into a guild—of painters, watchmakers, or whatever—remains in fashion for some time. But, although talk of "original genius" does not become current until late in the seventeenth century, "masterpiece" by the sixteenth century is already beginning to mean a great work in the history of human endeavor rather than a union term for the test of professional credentials. Our own view of the importance of art gathers strength in the eighteenth century when the histories of the various arts were beginning to be written, the great names listed, and the important national and stylistic schools defined. But this intellectual formulation takes place after two hundred years of cultural change in which the social position of all artists was in ferment.[17]

In Protestant Europe, especially after the frequent officially supported outbreaks of iconoclasm, painters sought employment outside the Church, and the most ready clients were those who had politically benefited from the overthrow of religious images.[18] Sculptors and architects often gain these secular commissions before painters and begin to explore new subject matter. But it is in the history of attitudes toward portraiture that the artist's new sense of himself and his profession can be most clearly traced—in his relation to the faces of his patrons, his friends, his family, and himself. In the beginning we might be told, 'This is a portrait of Henry VIII'; somewhat later, 'This is a portrait of Henry VIII by Hans Holbein,' perhaps because we would like to hire Holbein to do our portrait. Still later, we might want to know that it was Holbein who painted Henry VIII, because we believe that any cultured person should recognize the work of an artist so outstanding that he was hired by Henry. Up to this point the appreciation of Holbein is confined to a small group of potential patrons and appreciators. The crucial step still lacking in the evolution of artistic status comes when not only art, but also art history, achieve distinctive intellectual importance, and the subject portrayed has become

17. The first works to be generally called masterpieces are buildings, the marvels of the ancient world and then the modern (i.e., sixteenth-century) efforts to match them. For an intricate consideration of the changing nature of the "masterpiece," see Walter Cahn, *Masterpieces*.

18. John Phillips points out that, ironically or appropriately, many of the most enthusiastic iconoclasts in England were the painters and sculptors who had made the images (*Reformation of Images*). For a consideration of the European Protestant artist's dilemma in the age of resurgent iconoclasm, see also Wittkower, *Saturn*, 25–31.

totally subordinated to the portrayer: 'This is a portrait of Henry VIII by Holbein' changes to 'This is a portrait by Holbein of Henry VIII.' At first, the artist is a celebrator of the ruler. Now, it is the artist who is independent, while his patron or employer is primarily an event in the artist's career, and the significance of the painting, once a function of its subject, has become the fact that Holbein painted it. In this new status the artist's career must be perceived as an unfolding whole, a view first popularized in 1550 when Vasari published his *Lives of the Most Eminent Painters, Sculptors, and Architects*. Vasari's project had begun as an account of Paolo Giovio's collection of paintings of illustrious men, but it quickly gathered its own momentum as a series of artistic lives, each exemplifying a somewhat different personal style and career. Determining attributions when no signatures or other records were available, noting whenever painters included themselves in their paintings, Vasari permitted himself to be puzzled at the naivete of those early Italian painters whose names were lost for their lack of desire for fame. In his second edition (1568) he included portraits of the artists as well, and later he painted his own as St. Luke painting the Virgin Mary.[19]

Two artistic motifs especially favored in the Renaissance play out the drama of the changing status of the artist: Perseus rescuing Andromeda; and Jesus' descent from the cross aided by Nicodemus and Joseph of Arimathea. In the first, which has its roots in the medieval moralized versions of Ovid, Pegasus the winged horse flies through the air with Perseus poised on its back, ready to save Andromeda. In the original story Perseus defeats two monsters—the Medusa (from whose blood sprung Pegasus) and an anonymous sea monster threatening Andromeda—while it is Bellerophon, in yet another story, who rides Pegasus. Conflating the sources by putting Perseus in the saddle allows a hero (rather than a rash youth) to ride the winged horse, which, according to mythological interpreters, signified the good fame that carries heroes to heaven. The Medusa, of course, changes everyone who meets her gaze to stone. Perseus defeats her by polishing his shield so that he can see her face in a mirror that also reflects his own.[20] It is perhaps a little fable to soothe the anxieties of changing artistic status. Pegasus, says a late sixteenth-century interpreter, was born from the Medusa's blood and is therefore the fame

19. Rudolf and Margot Wittkower consider Giovanni Battista della Palla in the 1520s to be "the first international art dealer," thus marking another separation of the trade in painting and sculpture from that of their more locally oriented fellow crafts.
20. Although glass mirrors had existed since the Middle Ages, they began to appear in quantity, mainly from Venice, in the sixteenth century. Plate glass, which allowed a full view along with surroundings came somewhat later. Throughout the painting of the fifteenth to seventeenth centuries, there is an increasing emphasis on the eye—what it sees and how it might be tricked. Perspective becomes the hallmark of the new modernity, in contrast to the evenly lit and holy balance of most earlier religious painting. Mythic figures associated with mirrors, like Perseus, or eyes, like Argus, the thousand-eyed guardian of the gods, are frequent subjects. The myriad eyes and tongues of fame and the Renaissance love poet's preoccupation with his loved one's eyes—so praised when looking at him and so heartbreaking when turned away—are part of the general preoccupation with seeing and being seen.

that comes when virtue destroys terror. In the old artisan world, any aspiration had been subsumed in the contract and details of the job to be done. With the new artistic world of playing to an audience, there is more to be gained and more danger as well. By our own time all this rich elaboration of myth has been reduced to the great actor revealing to an interviewer that he invariably gets stage fright. But in sixteenth-century terms the surge of artists to center stage might be most succinctly expressed by observing that one of the most notable works sculpted by Benvenuto Cellini, author of one of the first extended autobiographies written by an artist, is a triumphant *Perseus with the Head of Medusa,* the struggles of whose creation and reception take up a large part of Cellini's narrative.[21]

Using classical myths in the service of new definition of artistic status accords well with the Petrarchan effort to connect one's aspiration with the models of the classical past. But with the new aspirations to ride to heaven on Pegasus came new hesitations and denials as well. In innumerable emblem books of the fifteenth, sixteenth, and seventeenth centuries, artists, engravers, and printers included a contrast between good fame (or pure fame) and bad fame as part of their explications of visual images. Sometimes the engravings were based directly on Petrarch's *Triumphs,* especially "The Triumph of Fame." Increasingly, the image of the goddess Fame herself separates from the Virgilian bird-monster or even the Chaucerian arbitrary monarch. Painters depict her in soft and languorous tones, holding a horn borrowed from Triton or standing atop the orb of the world. Rumors, in contrast, are carried by Mercury (pockmarked with *Fama*-style eyes and ears) and aided by Pegasus, who soars through the sky with or without Perseus. For some, fame precedes war and is primarily the herald of military men. For others, fame trumpets the worth of a good ruler or a great wise man and writer. Whatever the form, visual or verbal, fame has become a prime subject of interpretation, an emblem of the new interest in the audience of the world and in those who are its prime purveyors of information and opinion.

The imagistic preoccupation with fame from the fifteenth to the seventeenth centuries therefore indicates the way artists identified their cultural importance with that of the public men they celebrated at the same time that they questioned their place in a society in which fame and celebrity, fueled by the spread of printing, were becoming increasingly commonplace. Petrarch, still living in a manuscript culture, revives Virgil's contrast in the *Aeneid* between the rumor of crowds and cities, on the one hand, and the good fame bestowed by wise men, historians, and poets, on the other: He praises Laura for pulling him out of the "common way" and turning him away from the "common herd" who wouldn't be able to appreciate his works. But for artists and writers in the new world of print, the contrast between good and bad fame was less decisive. Along with the proud asser-

21. Cellini died in 1571. The *Autobiography* circulated in many manuscript copies, but was not published until 1730. The *Commentaries* of Lorenzo Ghiberti (d. 1455) are usually considered the first autobiographical writing by an artist.

tion also came the humble denial, just as the rituals of political power often included an act of humbling to minimize the moral and spiritual insufficiency of triumphing so totally in the eyes of others. Like the Turkish sultans who entered Santa Sophia wearing a hat in the shape of Mohammed's foot, even artists of monarchical ambition exploited motifs of assertive humility, especially where religious subject matter was concerned. In another popular sixteenth-century motif, the descent from the cross is the complement of Pegasan assertion. Usually there are three main figures—Jesus, of course, and, carrying him, Joseph of Arimathea and Nicodemus. Since Joseph is well-to-do, he carries the shoulders of Jesus, while the beggar Nicodemus carries the feet. What is intriguing here is the frequency with which the face of Joseph is made to resemble that of the patron and the face of Nicodemus that of the painter. In this religious context, the painter thus is not quite the assertive aspirant to renown he may be elsewhere. But in a striking example, Michelangelo, who was very much concerned with social status, has it both ways by sculpting himself as Nicodemus, but in the position usually reserved for Joseph. The combination of assertion and humbleness is fascinating, similar in its way to the hedging of those public men who included in their publicity an image of themselves as pensive lovers, validating their worldly power by their other-worldly and often explicitly noncarnal commitment to love. Such love replaced the monkish habit or the pious look, an indication of the knowledge of a realm beyond the flesh, but one that, like the royal dynasty, was a rival to the spiritual realm of the Church.[22]

Mantegna and Dürer

Depending on a country's political and religious traditions, the imagery of artistic renown took on different aspects. The frequent use of classical Roman models—especially outside Rome—meant for patrons an independence from Catholic Roman definitions of appropriate power and for artists an independence from traditional definitions of artistic status. The farther away one was from the Rome of the present, the easier it was to call upon an older Rome (and, as did Protestantism, an older Christianity)

22. This pietà was intended by Michelangelo for his own tomb but abandoned because of defects in the stone. Michelangelo also did three known drawings on the theme of the fall of Phaëton and, perhaps most centrally in this series of ambivalent images of artistic aspiration, depicts himself in the Sistine Chapel *Last Judgment* next to Jesus and Mary in the form of the flayed skin of St. Bartholomew, thus invoking as well the flayed Marsyas, punished for his competition with Apollo. For the connection of classical and Christian motifs, see Wind, *Pagan Mysteries*. Liebert in *Michelangelo*, although aware of the general history of the Marsyas motif and its importance to Titian and Raphael as well, nevertheless makes Michelangelo's psychology the primary generator of meaning: "Bartholomew's fate of being flayed alive served as a vehicle for expressing in a sacred work the personal significance the theme of flaying held for the artist" (352).

for imagistic and ideological support. Although many of the basic motifs of classical portraiture were first revived in Florence, the most fertile field for the parallel growth of monarchical and artistic status was therefore in northern Europe, the Netherlands, and England. Although the boast that artists had a special perception of the world was first sounded in Italy, it took the artists of the North to sharpen the polemical edge. Two overlapping styles of artistic self-definition might be distinguished here, each construing the revival of the classical world somewhat differently. In terms of their relation to ancient Rome, we might call one the artist as Roman general-politician and the other the artist as Roman writer-philosopher. Cicero therefore could easily be a hero of both, particularly the Cicero of the *Letters,* rediscovered by Petrarch. But while artists in the general-politician style are pugnaciously optimistic about their status in the world, those in the writer-philosopher mode are more withdrawn and contemplative. For the first, who tend to live and work in southern, Catholic Europe, there is a close relation between themselves and the heroes they depict, and their personal goals often include worldly status. For the second, who tend to live and work in northern and (in the course of the sixteenth century) Protestant Europe, there is a distance between themselves and those they depict and a clear if implicit effort to aspire to status not by the grant of preexisting power so much as by creating a new, artistic power of their own.

The political contrasts are comparable. The Medici, for example, seemed satisfied with using their commercial and financial power to fill the time-honored political and religious bureaucracy with their own people, even their own popes. But the princes and kings of the North, fired by the new political spirit of Protestantism, sought to replace the lines of popes with a new history based on national dynasties. Thus the striking self-consciousness of the Florentine artists yet remains within a social hierarchy where revival of the Roman past is a revival of native traditions. But in the north artistic self-consciousness has a much more separatist tinge, recasting the humble artisan as the divinely inspired artist, who through study and grace partook of what the Protestant theologians might call "election." As both grace and study were needed to confirm religious election, so both divine inspiration and the ability to generate aesthetic theories constituted the twin justification for the artist's new status. Art might gather validity by demonstrating its relation to mathematics and geometry, as Alberti proposed early in the fifteenth century. But it based its special authority among human activities on the sensibility of the artist.[23]

Since broad distinctions need actual individuals to give them life, the first type might be represented by Mantegna (1431–1506) and the second by Dürer (1471–1528). In the work and careers of both men, we can glimpse the new artist of the Renaissance, supporting and serving his

23. The word Vasari uses most frequently to describe the special quality of great paintings is *grazia* (grace), an interesting example of the secularizing of religious terms in art criticism.

patrons but also striking back at them not by Wheels of Fortune or Dances of Death or Mirrors for Magistrates—in which the great are chastised—but by their own self-assertion. Mantegna was born the son of a carpenter. In his early teens he was adopted by a Paduan painter and registered in the painters guild, and by the age of thirty was the court painter for the rulers of Mantua, an important center for the revival of classical culture. But long before he had an official connection with Mantua, Mantegna was asserting that he embodied its cultural heritage. His father was named Biagio. When Mantegna was adopted, his own name was changed to Squarcione, the name of his painter stepfather. At the age of seventeen, as if to commemorate his release from his apprenticeship, he signed an altarpiece with the name, Andrea Matinea Pat., that is, Andrea, the Mantuan born in Padua, although he was still referred to as Andrea Squarcione as late as 1467. Mantegna, a name that appears somewhat later in his works, is the Italian equivalent of the more Latinized form of Mantinea. By these indications alone, we are pointed toward the context of classical Rome in which Mantegna created his career and himself. He would be the inheritor of Virgil, the other great Mantuan. Fascinated by classical ruins, his duties as court painter to the Gonzagas included being a librarian and supervisor of archeological collections as well. In his early thirties, according to letters, he went on a trip with friends to search for classical remains. Along the way, they referred to each other by Roman titles—Mantegna was the "consul"— and they sang the praises of Christianity, using pagan metaphors and the invocation of pagan gods. Like Dante, Mantegna considered himself a mediator between what was best in the classical and Christian traditions. In general his work deals with Christian subject matter amid the classical grandeur of Roman "masterpiece" architecture. One of his early assignments in Mantua was a room decorated with figures of Caesar and seven other Roman emperors. Not yet forty, he began to let people know that he would like to be a Count, an ambition that had been achieved by his mid-fifties, perhaps about the time when he was working on one of his most ambitious projects, a series of paintings called *The Triumph of Caesar,* which combined a multitude of classical sources and his own invention to depict Caesar's entry into Rome after the conquest of Gaul.[24]

The revival of classical antiquity was therefore for Mantegna closely related to both his Christian political beliefs and his sense of his own status as an artist. Turning his back on the guild world to which he owed his early training, he chose instead to be a student of antiquity, a creator whose signature on his work was not merely a monogram indication of its provenance but a part of the antique world he drew upon for inspiration— as if it had been chiseled there for more than a thousand years. His fascination with the problems of perspective and his inclination toward the sculptural accord with his view of himself as a kind of Roman public man, while

24. For a sardonic account of the widespread masculine urge to imitate classical models in work and personality from the Renaissance to the nineteenth century, see Adams, *The Roman Stamp.*

in his private life he was constantly engaged in law suits and public bickering with his neighbors, who didn't quite appreciate his frequently highhanded ways. In the *Autobiography* of Cellini we read the self-justifying stories of a similar temperament, born some seventy years later, constantly ready to fight those who have injured him in even the slightest way, constantly competing with other men, and particularly with other artists, for the rewards of greatness. For Mantegna and Cellini, as well as for many other artists of the period, art was a political as well as a personal statement, in which you took up a sword in the name of whoever had the good taste to recognize your genius. Partisan and often powerful, art was a force that had an immediate public dimension. In about the middle of Mantegna's career, for example, a conspiracy supported by the pope failed to assassinate Lorenzo de' Medici, and the Pope excommunicated the city of Florence instead. When negotiations began, the pope insisted that the final settlement should include the total erasure from the wall of the City Hall of the fresco Botticelli had done of the hanging of the conspirators.

In a work like *The Triumph of Caesar* or through evidence like the placement and evolution of his signature, we can understand Mantegna's effort to create an artistic identity that partook of the sanction of the Roman public man. So he appears in the austere and unflattering patrician bust done for his tomb. But, like many of his fellow painters at the time, Mantegna never depicted himself as an artist or included his studio in a painting. That kind of visual self-presentation was much more typical of the artists of the North, from Dürer down to Rembrandt and Vermeer, when the two styles of artistic self-assertion, never wholly separate, were already beginning to mix in figures like Rubens and Velázquez. At the age of thirteen Dürer was already beginning a series of self-portraits that would be a continuing interest throughout his life. Like the Italian artists, he adopted the practice of signing his works in a distinctive way, often calling special attention to the "making" by hanging it like a tag among trees or engraving it on a stone within the engraving. In his later years he further elaborated the project of his artistic individuality by writing a treatise on the theory of painting and graphic representation. These combined impulses—toward an emphasis on the artist's personal style, toward a fascination with method, and toward an interest in making theoretic statements about "art"—summarize the prime ways in which fifteenth- and sixteenth-century art sought to demonstrate its special nature and justify the special regard in which artists should be held. In a sense Dürer wanted to be his own Alberti and Vasari, his own theorist and biographer. With Rembrandt, who lives more than a hundred years later, he also shares a preoccupation with the processes of printing and engraving—and thereby a sense of an audience beyond the court or papal patron—that provides the context for their similar experiments with self-portraiture and their meditations on the nature of the artist.[25]

25. Dürer's self-portraits include one of himself naked in his early thirties and another in a letter to a doctor in which he is pointing at the place that hurts and

As the unprecedented possibility for personal fame inspired the visual artist ever onward, his calling began to appear much more problematic than it was when he was a hired artisan. So Erwin Panofsky writes of the dilemma of Agnes Frey, Dürer's wife:

> Agnes Frey thought that the man she had married was a painter in the late medieval sense, an honest craftsman who produced pictures as a tailor made coats and suits; but to her misfortune her husband discovered that art was a divine gift and an intellectual achievement requiring humanistic learning, a knowledge of mathematics, and the general attainments of a "liberal culture" (9).

Visual art as a vocation imposed specific limits, but as a calling its search for glory might end in despair. In 1513 and 1514, when Dürer was in his early forties, he created three masterful engravings that particularly illuminate his own uncertainties over the urge for artistic fame that animates so many in the Renaissance—*Knight, Death, and Devil; St. Jerome in His Study;* and *Melencolia I.* In the first a knight rides through a craggy landscape, his dog running beside him, while a rotted and crowned Satan and a boar-faced, harrow-carrying Death stand ineffectually beside the road. In the second St. Jerome sits at work, his dog and his lion resting on the floor in front of him. In the third a winged woman sits next to an unfinished monument or building. Beside her a winged boy sits perched on a column capital and a sheep sleeps at her feet. All three are documents of Dürer's quest for precedents that would help him understand exactly what it was that distinguished an artist from other men, and all three works require interpretation, demanding from the viewer something more than mere seeing. In each we see a central figure engaged in a vocation, a way of life. The difference lies in the assurance and direction of that way. The knight moves through a rough world, hardly bothered by the threats along his way. In fact Dürer depicts both the Devil and Death as somewhat comical figures, as if the engraving were done by the knight, for whom they are only empty costumes meant to scare children. St. Jerome, on the other hand, is bent over his desk, writing. Around him his world is ordered, comfortable, and complete, the normally assertive (and kingly) lion as placid as a lapdog. Like the knight, Jerome has a clear sense of where his work is going and he commits himself to it wholeheartedly. Melencolia, however, is upset. Around her are implements of measure, tools, and building blocks. But whether she is in the middle of a project or just beginning, either she doesn't know what to do with them or what she can do is insufficient for her aspiration. In our terms she is blocked. All the practical means are at hand, but without the shaping vision, they are useless.

---

asking for a diagnosis. The interest fostered by portraiture in perceiving one's body as an object is also illustrated by the story of the Englishman who explained that he wanted to have his picture painted again in his old age because, while his mirror showed him what he looked like in the moment, the difference between the pictures would show him how much he had changed (Strong, *Icon*). Rembrandt's self-portraits are also remarkable for the number of uncompromising views of his aging.

Just as the knight and St. Jerome can be understood as models for the artist in a mood of assurance, Melencolia is an emblem of his uncertainty, about both his artistic calling and what that calling implies in actual work. The knight and St. Jerome are self-contained and self-willed, perhaps because they have missions outside themselves, whether chivalric or religious. Melencolia, however, lacks that inner certainty of mission. Independent of any master, she does not know how to become a master herself. On a painting of Virtue throwing out Vice, Mantegna inscribed a motto that roughly translated reads: "If you get rid of leisure, you break Cupid's bow." In other words, if you get to work, the disruptions of passion won't be able to bother you. But Melencolia's problems can't be solved by such hearty exhortations. Although she has the wings of Pegasus or *Fama,* she remains earthbound, not knowing where or why to fly. The Christian knight and the literary saint have clear and compelling missions. But what is the mission of the artist? Is he all assertion and no subject matter?

Unlike the other two engravings, one set on the road and the other in a room, *Melencolia I* is cluttered with objects and depicts an essentially unrealistic space. Unlike the *Knight* or *St. Jerome, Melencolia I* is a work that exists totally in the mind. There may be questions of interpretation about the *Knight* and *St. Jerome,* but hardly of the order that exists in *Melencolia I.* At the point where Dürer most directly dramatizes his fears about his artistic vocation, he also requires the viewer to match his own intelligence to the demands of the engraving. Its clear paradox is that, while artists especially may suffer the tortures of despair about their skills and their understanding, yet their own depiction of that struggle can become subject matter itself. Strikingly enough, after his conversion to Lutheranism in 1521, Dürer turned to religious subjects almost entirely. The wakening freedom of artistic individuality had brought with it the problem of what to depict and how to do it. Conversion offered not only spiritual solace but also subject matter, and *Melencolia I* shows how closely the two were connected for Dürer. There is no *Melencolia II.*[26]

Dürer's distinctive signature, his self-portraits, and his treatises on anatomy and perspective as well as the evidence of his subject matter indicate the degree to which both his talent and his temperament inclined him to see himself from the outside. He crystallizes dilemmas that will be written large throughout the sixteenth century, particularly those of artists caught between capitalizing on and being victimized by their own new status. The *Knight* and *St. Jerome* face inward. The engraving cannot depict the content of their assurance, only that they are assured. But *Melencolia* has a visible and a disturbed soul, and therefore one much more suited for depiction. In contrast to the portraits of temporal power—robed, on horseback,

26. Even geniuses, or perhaps geniuses most of all, need subject matter. Compare John Berger's observation that Picasso's outpouring of new imagery and work in the late 1930s is due at least in part to his decision to join the Communist party (*Success and Failure of Picasso,* 174–79).

or otherwise superior to the viewer—the portraits of humanist thinkers and artists in the sixteenth century (as well as some of their more thoughtful patrons) attempt a similar look into the contents of the mind and soul. Dürer may have been the first artist to turn melancholy into a special attribute of artists. But by the end of the sixteenth century every young man who wants to be thought sensitive will be wearing the melancholic look and dressing in whatever the melancholic style demands. Even the rambunctious Cellini confides that his "natural tendency was melancholy." [27] Thus, while many visual artists were furnishing models for monarchical authority, they were also developing images by which inner life might be known more directly. Unlike Mantegna, Dürer faces the difficulties of artistic aspiration without the safety net of the classical paradox of the humble grandeur of good fame. But, like Chaucer's, his example was nevertheless a source of solace and inspiration to his fellow artists. Barely twenty years after his death, the guild of St. Luke, the artist guild of Antwerp, possessed a ceremonial goblet decorated with portraits of Apelles, Zeuxis, Raphael, and Dürer.

Humanists, the Reformation, and the Herald of Print

A touch of self-esteem prods the beginner to great endeavors.
—ERASMUS, *Antibarbari*

In different but interlocking ways, the revival of classical culture we associate with the Renaissance and the revival of a primitive and more personal Christianity professed by the Reformation both mark a flow of opportunity to the individual after the more socially restricted world of the Middle Ages. Reforming the present by infusing it with the spirit of the past, they imply that such a spirit is available for all who can find it in themselves. For the last few pages I have been considering the Renaissance conception of the artist and his fame, particularly in terms of the partnership with public power. But works like Dürer's three engravings exemplify a different concept of what art and artists can do. Instead of allying itself with an imagery of royal power, this art, like the humanist learning to which it is often allied, seeks to engage an audience and change its mind, its way of perceiving. Where the artistic images of temporal power invoke the classical gods and heroes to portray the great men of the present, this art seeks to foster an inner life of thought. A Protestant ruler like Elizabeth I might be the beneficiary of both impulses. Even in the midst of the chivalric and

27. In *Born Under Saturn*, the Wittkowers discuss the cultural shift by which artists, previously defined as born under Mercury (the patron of art understood as artisanship and commerce), were considered by themselves and their audiences to be born under Saturn, the sign of extreme states of personal sensibility.

monarchical display of Henry VIII's court, there had been room for such austere and learned figures as Erasmus, Thomas More, and Elizabeth's teacher, Roger Ascham, whose allegiances stretched beyond nation and institutional religion to a new international intellectual community, for a time within the Church although not necessarily of it.

But the potential conflict between the nationalist monarchs and the international humanists and artists lay clearly beneath the surface of their partnership. It is aptly symbolized by the execution of Thomas More by Henry VIII or, in a milder way, by the moment when an exasperated Francis I tells Cellini that the only reason his works were great was that a monarch had given him the opportunity to do them. Like royal iconographers and historians across Europe, such writers and artists may have once strenuously supported their royal patrons. But their support derived from a Petrarchan project of half discovering and half creating a family of wisdom and sensibility beyond wealth and royal genealogy. The potential paradox becomes more acute with the spread of printing in the sixteenth cenutry along with the appearance of a whole new generation of painters and visual artists, publishers, and engravers whose aspirations are transformed by the new medium. Writers are the first to capitalize on the expanded audience print supplies. But visual artists do not lag behind for long.

Recovering the past is always linked to celebrating an aspect of the present. The renewed fame of the classical author enlarges the reputation of his editor/translator/critic, the testament of language outlasting the frailty of the individual body. Of course, by our own time writers and artists have been so successful at publicizing their superior claims to historical importance that we remember their names better than those of all but a few of the most notable Renaissance rulers. But until the invention of printing, such propaganda (a postprint word) was hardly possible. Petrarch sought by scholarship to rescue language from corruption and writers from being forgotten. How much easier would the task be when aided with the new technology of movable-type printing. How much more certain would be the way out of personal death and into posterity. No longer would the great books of the classical past or the Christian religion be confined to the use only of those wealthy enough to have them copied. Like the change from the parchment roll to the codex that accompanied the intellectual expansion of early Christianity or the introduction of cheaper scribal production methods that formed a part of the so-called twelfth-century Renaissance, the printing press allowed an enormous expansion of audience and a more direct relation between writer and reader. Whether the language was Latin or English or French or German, printing had helped the humanist philologists to fulfill the dream of comparing manuscripts and thereby publishing in many copies a final and attested version of whatever ancient book, Cicero or Homer or the Bible, they wished. In previous centuries the prime theological issues had been as various as the divinity of Jesus, transubstantiation, and the proper relation of Church and

State. In the sixteenth century the issue was usually the question of the true text.

The first best-selling printed book was Thomas à Kempis's *Imitatio Christi* (*The Imitation of Christ*) (1473), which by the end of the century had already gone through ninety-nine editions and kept its momentum through the sixteenth century as well. Following in the path first laid down by St. Francis, à Kempis had conceived of his work not as a piece of argumentative theology but as a guide to Christ's life as a pattern for personal piety and behavior. But what may have originally been a handbook for members of his monastic order became through the dissemination of printing a guide for readers all over Europe. Like the vernacular Bibles that were appearing in numbers even before Luther's more notorious translation, or the engravings of rulers available in quantity to those who couldn't afford paintings, the popularity of a spiritual guide like the *Imitation* illuminates the remarkable way in which printing fed on the paradox of reproducing the unique and bringing matters previously rarefied and elite into the possession of many. Not long after the Medici Pope Leo X instituted a censorship of biblical translations, for example, Henry VIII's Reformed England expanded all vernacular publication of both religious and secular works, including the Bible.

The emphasis on the personal mediation of religious truth that permeated much of Protestantism was thus helped on its way by a new means of communication that was as important to writers and their patrons as it was to the theologians. When Luther posted and quickly published his ninety-five theses in 1517, a book and pamphlet battle that spread over Europe had already begun. Every class of readers, whether lay, spiritual, or noble, was becoming more attuned to the new doctrinal self-consciousness, the bringing of previously arcane matters into the streets of everyday discourse. Like political power, religious belief had to stage its importance, instead of merely asserting it. Standing back, self-aware, the reformers, aided by the printing press, could both criticize the traditional formats of assertion as well as invent new ones. We have little accurate information about who Thomas à Kempis was, and scholarship in its careful way usually ascribes the authorship of the *Imitation* to one or more anonymous members of the Brethren of the Common Life, Thomas's order, which stressed devotion to Christ and distrusted the excessive use of the intellect. But early in the sixteenth century another Dutch author, a member of the same order and schooled in the same town as Thomas, yet much less ambiguous about both the operations of intellect and having his name on the title page, began to pour forth an enormous flow of works that popularized the new humanist way of looking at religious belief and moral action. In the process he became second only to Thomas in book sales. This visionary who perceived the intimate connection between the spiritual life and the new technology of printing was Erasmus, the first author deliberately to seek out a suitable publisher and to try to mold the publishing policy of a firm as well as to make agreements that stipulated authors' fees—an innovation which was not taken up again by either publishers or authors for about two hundred years.[28]

For much of sixteenth-century Europe, Erasmus is a prime interpreter of the biblical and classical texts ever more voluminously appearing in print. As Dürer wrote in a diary in 1521, after hearing rumors of an assassination of Luther:

> O God, if Luther is dead, who shall henceforth so clearly expound to us the Holy Gospels? O God, what might he still have written for us in ten or twenty years? O all ye pious Christians, help me to weep over this God-illumined man and beg Him to send us another enlightened one. O Erasme Roderodame [of Rotterdam], where wilt thou take thy stand? Look, of what avail is the unjust tyranny of worldly might and the power of darkness? Hark, thou Knight of Christ, ride forth at the side of Christ our Lord, protect the truth, obtain the crown of Martyrs! (Panofsky, 151, 198–99)

Dürer might think that Erasmus needs some prodding to be as important an interpreter as Luther. But he wants someone to assume that role, just as he himself had taken it up as painter and engraver. And he insisted that the interpreter be known by name. Whether they were writers or artists, Catholics or Protestants, the medium of the book made these new interpreters aware of their own histories as well, not as a disjunctive collection of commissions and contracts, but as a moral and aesthetic career. In 1509–1511 Dürer had published two books, generally referred to as *The Large Passion* and *The Small Passion,* which depicted the life of Christ through engravings accompanied by the poems of Benedict of Chelidon. On the title page Dürer's authorship is clearly noted in elaborate gothic lettering: *Passio Christi ab Albrecht Dürer* (The Passion of Christ by Albrecht Dürer).[29]

By its appeal to the private person sitting alone rather than the worshiper being preached at in a crowd or the spectator in awe of public grandeur, the printed book invoked the relation of the individual to God's truth that had been implied by the saintly and philosophic image of Jesus, as opposed to the imperial. Even though Erasmus, like his friend More, was inclined to support the Church rather than those monarchs who, for religious or political reasons, were beginning to embrace varieties of Protestantism, yet they—together with Luther, Melanchthon, Calvin, and many

28. Besides the *Imitation* and the works of Erasmus, the only other sixteenth-century book worthy of being called a best-seller is Ariosto's chivalric epic *Orlando Furioso,* final version, 1532 (Steinberg, 141–42).

29. In addition to his name on the title page, Dürer's humble assertion of himself as a religious artist is reflected as well in the several versions he does of a particularly "artistic" event in the life of Christ: St. Veronica's discovery that the cloth she has used to wipe Christ's brow has absorbed his features. In later editions the cloth itself appears more prominently, like an artist's canvas, separated from the event in Christ's life from which it sprung, displayed now by the angels.

more—all used the fairly new medium of the printed page to supply what audiences discovered they were hungry for: the mediation of an intercessor who would explain and describe what had been too long considered beyond explanation and description. The humanist vocation was essentially that of teacher, and the international celebrity of Erasmus was an inspiration to all who wanted to link their learning and intellectual authority to political power. Acquiring a humanist as counselor and cultural ornament was a goal of rulers all over Europe. Augustine, who thought the Christian a wanderer in the world, could never have foreseen the amount of trekking from country to country and court to court the sixteenth-century humanists thrived upon in a world where they could be known long before they were seen. In contrast to the chivalric knight whose virtues aristocratic publicists were now celebrating as part of an almost lost golden age, the humanists were spiritual knights, sallying forth in the name of learning. Erasmus even wrote a book about the new spiritual mission, the *Manual of the Christian Knight* (1503), and Dürer's knight intent on his mission, disdainful of Satan and Death, may owe much to his inspiration.

Erasmus and More thus stand between a Petrarchan contemplative withdrawal from civil life and a new age of secular administrators infused with classical political precepts. All over Europe, but particularly in England with its long-centralized monarchy, the knightly and chivalric class was losing its importance in government. Taking their place was a new class of political and intellectual humanists, often barely emerged from the monastery or otherwise low social backgrounds, who turned their classical and Christian learning to the uses of a new science of statecraft. In *Utopia*, the immensely popular book about an ideal commonwealth (Latin, 1516; English, 1551) that gave its name to a whole new genre of political literature, Thomas More not so coincidentally also attacked the whole idea of chivalric military fame. In a mode that had survived through the Middle Ages, techniques of good government were also still being cast in the form of advice from Aristotle to Alexander. So Guillaume Budé, for example, instructed Francis I. But the possible ways of being a public man, or of just being a person in front of others, was becoming as various and as complicated as the new modes of visual depiction. The king was at the top, but everything else seemed in doubt. Such medieval questions as the nature of true nobility, which Dante had considered in the *Convivio* (and decided it lay in personal virtue), took on a greater urgency as clashes between the Church and reformers gave birth to new political alignments and writers began to speculate about the resulting changes in the social order. More's *Utopia* and Erasmus's *The Education of a Christian Prince* (1515, written for Charles V, the Holy Roman Emperor) sound concerns that are echoed in Castiglione's *The Courtier* (1528; English translation, 1561), and Machiavelli's *The Prince* (written 1513; published 1532; first English translation, except for manuscripts, 1640). By the end of the century they have become the prime subject matter of Shakespeare's history plays.

Erasmus, like many other writers of the period, had a self-consciousness intricately related to the forms of human depiction then being pioneered. But in essence he was still a word man, somewhat suspicious of the place of images in belief and particularly in worship. He condemned the more macabre versions of the tortured Christ coming into vogue, denounced relics, and thought that the unadorned cross was the only truly effective and justifiable Christian symbol, because all the others roused the passions without engaging either belief or understanding. For all his classical learning, he sought to bring that learning solely to bear on the Church, which for him was the central cultural fact, capacious enough to absorb all differences. Unlike St. Jerome, a thousand years before, who worried that he was more Ciceronian than Christian, Erasmus believed that Ciceronian learning and vocabulary could easily be subsumed into Christianity. In effect reenacting as well as superseding his forerunner Jerome, he spent a vast portion of his intellectual energy on a massive new Latin edition of the Greek New Testament, which attacked Jerome's traditional translation by pointing to innumerable problems in the transmission and interpretation of the original. In the process of working on his edition, Erasmus had discovered the notes Lorenzo Valla had made for a similar work, and the connection through Valla back to Petrarch underlines Erasmus's inheritance of Petrarch's view of words as the prime way into history. Without attachment to any particular country—and often strongly opposed to nationalism—Erasmus was attempting what has been called the last effort to make a medieval theological vocabulary relevant to a world in which the political and the theological were becoming separate, even opposed, realms of experience. His Christianity was more personal than institutional, and his Christ not the king but the teacher, a figure akin to the man he called "Saint Socrates" and to Cicero.

Erasmus's emphasis on Christianity as a way of life complemented his distaste for the great prince in the state, unless, of course, that prince could take good instruction from the learned. To the end of his life he tried to maintain his distance from both State and Church, continuing to write especially against the concept of purgatory and the use of relics and indulgences, because they substituted the merits of the saints for one's own. But even though his writings invariably argued for a universal Christian culture, they were easily adapted by national rulers who wanted to buttress their own authority and belief against the pressures of the Church. More's execution was similarly open to ambiguous interpretation: What from the Catholic point of view was celebrated as a martyrdom in the name of the Church, from a later Anglican and Protestant view was a radical assertion of personal conscience against an absolute monarch. In their different ways, both Erasmus and More, like many others who had entered the quest of letters, found that their pilgrimages demanded either an accommodation or a competition with temporal power. The Christian knight, wandering the world in search of truth and in defense of virtue, finally had become a figure opposed to the papacy. More than twenty years after his death, all the works of Erasmus the author are condemned on the first appearance of the Catholic "Index of Forbidden Books." [30]

With an enthusiasm that had inspired so many others, Erasmus had greeted printing as a miraculous new vehicle for learning, the seven-league boots needed for God's work to stride across Europe. From the beginning of his career, he is attuned to the importance of the printed book in the dissemination of ideas and reputation; at first he believes that it is a purely benevolent way to supersede the work of Jerome and Petrarch by a grand new invention they would have used if they could. Even when Erasmus published his *New Testament* (1516) and Luther's ninety-five theses appeared (1517), neither expected his work to have the impact it did, for they still lived within a medieval tradition of scholarly argument and discussion. (Luther's own controversies with the Church began over whether Hebrew should be taught to priests.) Yet printing, although celebrated as the instrument of a rebirth of piety and learning, was also a form that insensibly molded the aims of its users. As Elizabeth Eisenstein points out in reference to theological controversy, "with typographical fixity [and the wide dissemination of works] . . . positions once taken were difficult to reverse" (326)—or, one might add, to rein in. Scholarly editions, dictionaries, and compendia of all sorts of knowledge were becoming widely available for the first time in history. But the pressures of the new nationalisms and the awakened power of the new medium of communication swept their authors inexorably toward the future.

The various editions of Erasmus's *Adagia,* a collection of commentaries on proverbial wisdom, illustrate the evolution of his attitude toward printing from wondrous welcome to wary ambivalence. In 1508, in the midst, appropriately, of his remarks on *festina lente* (make haste slowly), he pauses to lavish praise on the Roman printer Aldus Manutius, whose books are meant for "those who are weary of that old, crass, barbarous doctrine and aspire to true and antique learning" and whose library, unlike that of Ptolemy at Alexandria, because of printing "has no other limits than the world itself" (M. Phillips, 179, 181). As soon as manuscripts are collected and collated, the new art of printing will publish to the world the finest editions ever done. "Publish" for Erasmus is a literal bringing to the light of what had remained hidden and secret in the possessive clutches of the elite. But by the 1525 edition of *Adagia,* the situation has already changed. No longer are printers characterized only by the learned care of Manutius or Froben (the publisher of Erasmus's *New Testament*), true

30. The concept of a forbidden book has little meaning without the broad availability of books in general that printing enabled. Although lists of forbidden books had been drawn up from time to time by different popes, the first to bear the now familiar name "Index" was published in 1559, revised in 1564, and updated irregularly afterward. Its origins thus commemorate the enormous usefulness of printing for theological polemics that forced the papacy beyond the kind of censorship Leo X tried to exercise and into outright prohibition. It might also be noted here that the first prominent use of the term "propaganda" appears in the name of the office established in 1622 to direct Catholic mission activities, the *Congregatio de propaganda fide* (Congregation for the Propagation of the Faith).

partners in the humanist quest. Now, there are swarms of them everywhere, sowing confusion in their wake, driven only by greed. After welcoming the new art as a companion in the search of truth, Erasmus finds himself caught between the elitist secrecy he mocks and the commercial debasement he deplores. His assumption that images impose on men, while words are the way to freedom, has come face to face with the realization that words too can obscure the truth, especially when everyone with something to say has access to a printing press.[31]

The Rise of the Graven Image

We are so used to seeing the faces of the past peering at us from museum walls or the pages of art history that we forget the usually narrow circle of their viewers in the ages before art became an object of public attention and scholarship put otherwise private objects on public display. This democratization of the eye often has ironic historical effect, especially when we view with our museumgoer's detachment the nude mistresses of those who wished to symbolize personal possession by visual possession. Even the portraits of Elizabeth based on the approved patterns were available only to the richest and most loyal of her subjects. Otherwise, portraiture was a private entry on the record of time, with a small circle of appreciation, a reminder to family and friends and perhaps even to an older self that one had lived and wanted to be remembered as looking a certain way.

In a world more attuned than before to the varieties of public display, painting offered not only the temporally powerful an important way both to see oneself from the outside and to define how one ought to be seen. But writers and others who sought the fame of virtue and learning at first took slowly to the vogue for portraiture, and paintings of them often featured books, letters, or some collection of intriguing objects, as if to display with bare adequacy the more complex furniture of the mind. (Strict Protestants might extend their iconoclasm to a refusal to admit even the images of their favorite religious reformers.) Erasmus himself doodled small self-caricatures, visual as well as verbal, on the margins of his books. But for all his remarkable awareness of the place of personal publicity in the dis-

---

31. Eisenstein remarks on Erasmus's "blindness about his own historical role" (341), but there is also something self-consciously protective in his pose. He could not help but be aware that the wide dissemination of uniform texts allowed by printing was an important tool of Reformation propaganda. During the reign of Edward VI, for example, Erasmus's *Paraphrases of the New Testament,* translated by Nicholas Udall and others under the sponsorship of Henry VIII's last queen, Catherine Parr, "were to be set up in all of the churches" as compulsory reading at a time when Sunday attendance was compulsory as well (Bainton, 141). A similar confusion about audience is characteristic of the contemporary "avant-garde" artist, who still believes he is on the cutting edge of culture, while he gives interviews to mass-market magazines.

semination of thought, Erasmus generally considered the portrait to be primarily a talismanic link between friends rather than something to pique the interest of a public audience. Shortly after the publication of his edition of the New Testament, he sent to Thomas More a diptych portrait of himself and Petrus Aegidius, who figures prominently in More's *Utopia*. Thus, no matter how separated the members of Erasmus's international friendship would be, they might have images of each other around them for inspiration.[32] Somewhat later Erasmus sends Hans Holbein to England to stay with the More family and paint their portraits with those of Erasmus's other friends in England. As he had written to a friend a few years earlier who had asked for a portrait of More, it would require an artist talented enough to portray Alexander the Great or Achilles. In a later visit Holbein was employed by Thomas Cromwell, who had replaced More as Henry VIII's chief minister and supervised the confiscation of church property. It was through Cromwell that Holbein was introduced to Henry VIII.

That Hans Holbein could so well serve both Thomas More and Henry VIII indicates the potentially uneasy balance in the coalition of the painter and the king for worldly sway, and the painter and the humanist for sovereignty of the inner life. In a sense the new portrait painters were serving two masters, the man of public power and the man of private learning and understanding, the one requiring a portraiture that emphasized grandeur, the other a portraiture that indicated the inner life.

The appeal of Holbein to More and Erasmus, as to us, comes from his ability to suggest a character beyond the visible and thereby to become part of the general humanist publicity for inner worth and personal virtue, the positive side of Dürer's more distracted Melencolia. Holbein's Henry VIII looks out and down at us. But in Holbein's painting of More and his family, each member, while physically in a very precise relation to all the others in the painting, yet gazes somewhere off into the space of the painting itself, their gazes crossing without quite meeting, a family of individuals without the need to impose visually on others, each palpably thinking. In the center background is a clock, ticking an earthly time to which such spirits are clearly not bound. Similarly, in many other sixteenth-century portraits, the skull is close at hand, as if in the Roman style to undercut the ostentatious visibility by a professed awareness of the nearness of the grave and dissolution, just as Holbein balances his portraits of temporal power with his *Dance of Death*. In a way that the public patron can never quite manage, the writer or painter thus gathers moral strength from the confession of his weakness and thereby turns it into an emblem of another kind of greatness, not worldly greatness of course, but a greatness of the spirit, a breadth of vision.

32. The painter of these portraits, Quentin Matsys, was the first Dutch painter to imitate Italian medallion making in the classical manner. Twenty-five years before he did the portraits of Erasmus and Aegidius, he had done one of himself (Voet, 346). The vogue for self-portraits of painters, paintings of painters and their families, and paintings of events in which painters participate is especially characteristic of the Low Countries in this period.

The contrast between the portraits of More and his family and those of Henry VIII and his has virtually dissolved by 1593, when Thomas More II (More's grandson) commissions Rowland Lockey to create a painting incorporating the Holbein original (minus three family members) with portraits of his own family in a pictorial genealogy. In the second More family portrait, the monarchical style has triumphed, but now as an emblem of spirit rather than of worldly power. Each of Thomas More's family still preserves his or her original internal gaze, while his grandson's family looks out directly at the viewer, with a stronger visual relation to the one who looks at them than they have to each other. Thus in the course of the sixteenth century, the humanist effort to capture a natural image of thought crosses with royal portraiture to create an image meant to convey the iconographic meaning of an individual, not subordinating the viewer (as the king had done) but personalizing the viewer by locking his eyes with those in the painting. The full face is not the full face of Henry VIII, swollen with power, but a more pleading, beguiling face looking toward an outside world, an audience, that must be engaged, beseeched, and even placated. In the older world the patron had authenticated the painter. Now, the painter and his painting authenticate the patron, remove him from the toils of the moment, and place him into history, while the viewer stands witness to their own witnessing of their heritage. Like the eyes in the Chandos portrait of Shakespeare some years later, the eyes of the family of Thomas More II look into those who look at them, affirming a bond of human nature.[33]

But paintings in private homes or even those in public places were hardly responsible for the sixteenth-century rush toward self-display and ancestral brandishing. It required as well the growing popularity of copper engraving—with which a group of printers and engravers, almost entirely based in the Low Countries, broadcast images of monarchs, adventurers, intellectuals, theologians, and artists themselves to a European world that seemed eager to collect their images—a roster of new saints to rival the whole Catholic calendar, possibilities and inspirations for men on earth. Erasmus had considered More's family a Platonic Academy. But in the new age of visual media and propaganda, the knowledge of that stature would never be confined only to intimate friends or a narrowly selected audience. The outpouring of pamphlets and books that accompanied the Reformation emphasized standing up and signing one's name and honoring those of one's party or persuasion who had done so. A rich patron might commission portraits of Luther and Melanchthon from a distinguished artist like Lucas Cranach. But by mid-century pattern-portraits of Luther and Elizabeth and perhaps others were circulating, with holes along the

33. As uncompromising Catholics during a particularly anti-Catholic part of Elizabeth's reign, Thomas More II and his family have good reason to affirm their personal history as a testament of their faith. In fact their portrait—along with a preliminary drawing by Holbein and a copy made by Lockey—is the main evidence we have for the look of the original, which has been lost.

lines of the drawing so that they could be duplicated by the most inept artist.

Portrait painting, like the religious painting it replaced, sought for an intersection of the individual with the eternal. But printing and engraving brought the news. The first subjects of the new techniques of visual representation had been less emblematic (like royal portraits) than analytic—looking into the human body through anatomy and looking beyond the traditional bounds of nation through the documents of exploration.[34] New maps of the body and new maps of the world poured from the presses and through them all runs an intoxicating sense of new beginnings. The hero was not the one who was born well or who best replicated the great actions of the past. He was the one who was first. Mapmakers and printers were redrawing the relations of the countries of the world, putting western Europe definitely at the center, looking at their own cities from above like birds or like God, and celebrating the great naval heroes, not only those who fought battles, but also those who made the great discoveries.

Soon enough the mapmakers and engravers were depicted as heroes themselves, Hendrik Hondius and Gerardus Mercator companions in daring with Sir Francis Drake and Thomas Cavendish. In 1560 Mercator and Abraham Ortelius, two pioneering mapmakers, visited a Neolithic burial chamber in France, where they wrote their names along with those of other, mainly Flemish and Netherlandish, visitors. A short time later a new engraving was for sale in Antwerp, showing the dolmen, with all the famous names written on it. The impulse has precedents back at least to classic Rome and descendants down to the graffiti-streaked present. But Mercator and Ortelius, like Dürer devising his monogram, were placing themselves in a longer vista, two very respectable merchant-savants inscribing their names on a massive monument that itself transcended time and death to speak to the future. Antwerp especially had been a center of publicity for exploration and seafaring since the end of the fifteenth century when its printers were among the early publishers of Columbus's letter to Gabriel Sanchez (King Ferdinand's treasurer) about his voyages, and later the letters of Amerigo Vespucci to Lorenzo de Piero Francesco de' Medici (the Magnificent's cousin) about similar discoveries in the Western Hemisphere. Perhaps it indicates something about our own relation to this newly heroic world of Renaissance printing, mapmaking, and geographical discovery that we live in a country named not for its indigenous people or its physical features or even its European discoverer, but for a best-selling author and navigator noted primarily for his fashioning of a new method to compute exact longitude.[35]

34. The first elaborate use of engraving, which helped repopularize it as a method, was Plantin's edition of Vesalius's pioneering work of human anatomy (1563).

35. Columbus's letter *De Insulis nuper inventis* (On the recently discovered islands) had first appeared in 1493 and Vespucci's *Mundus novus* in 1502–1504. The general practice of using "America" for all the newly discovered lands dates from the *Cosmographiae introductio* (1507). There, the geographer Martin Waldseemüller argued

With the expansion of the book trade in the sixteenth century, and especially with the increasing use of copper engraving (previously considered too expensive) after the middle of the century to supply portraits more detailed than the old woodblocks, printed portraiture becomes a widespread way to merchandise faces other than royal. Of course, royalty and the supporters of royalty were quick to adopt the new methods as well, and triumphal entries flourished on frontispieces along with noble faces and figures adorned with all the trappings of their social power. The late 1590s in England especially saw an outpouring of pictorial propaganda about kingship and continuity sponsored by the Elizabethan atmosphere if not in most cases by Elizabeth herself. Without children of her own, she ensured that England after her death would search for or spawn children of her royal image. No longer could the idealized kingly images of the medieval period, or even the more elaborate versions of More's brother-in-law Rastell sufficiently determine loyalty. The king business was clearly being reconceived as a matter of creating a self-conscious and personalized iconography. More and more detail, "realistic" as well as symbolic, was being demanded by newly sophisticated print and book buyers. In 1584 the Franciscan monk André Thevet advertised that his book contained *"les vrais pourtraits"* of illustrious Greeks and Romans, as taken from paintings, books, and medals. In 1597 "T. T." published a book heralding itself "The True Portraiture of the Countenances and Attires of the Kings of England, from William Conqueror unto our Soveraigne Lady Queene Elizabeth now raigning" that established the faces of English kings for a hundred years and more. With the proliferation of engravings, the emblematic power of Renaissance portraiture began its long march to the walls of post offices, where the official images of rulers preside over the equally official images of sheafs of wanted criminals. The growing industry of copper engraving had taken the step from the formal portrait to the book. From the halls of those who could afford painted versions of the royal image descended engraved portraits that could be purchased by hero-worshipers and political supporters of more modest means and often different loyalties.

As we have seen, portrait painting had a close relation to temporal power. Even more in the past than in the present, having the money and power to be painted made you worth looking at. We wonder now that

---

that Vespucci's descriptions, which were included in the *Cosmographiae* and took up more space than Waldseemüller's arguments and computations, implied that a whole new continent had been discovered. Jantz (*Images of America*) constructs an ingenious etymological argument why the name should have been based on Vespucci's first name rather than last and why it should have been in the feminine form rather than the masculine. Whatever its origin, after a brief period the usage becomes widespread. Quinn, for example, points out that Vespucci, "a better publicist than Columbus . . . who brought the New World to life" (II, 640), thought the new world was a whole new mainland, albeit connected to Asia, while Columbus in most of his writings considered the land to be only islands off the Asian coast. Vespucci's accounts appeared on almost three times as many editions and issues as those of Columbus. See also Hirsch, "Printed Reports on the Early Discoveries and Their Reception."

some of those people looked so ugly or allowed themselves to be portrayed with such transparently devious expressions. But it was only when painters began to write treatises on painting that concepts like beauty and proportion emerged as ways of imposing the vision of the artist on the patron's urge to be seen. With engraving, the balance of power had definitely shifted from the subject to the artist, the engraver, and the publisher. Engraved royal portraiture and the tightening of standards for an authentic image became a less significant aspect of sixteenth-century printing than the appearance of a whole new galaxy of heroes, who, like the self-made artists and engravers who celebrated them, had accomplished their fame on their own, without or despite the burden of heredity. With burin in hand, the engraver would choose which faces to celebrate and which to degrade. The humanist genealogy of heroes could constitute a more secular and (for the new age) a more psychically powerful lineage than the distant icons of the medieval past. Like Augustine, amazed that St. Antony had lived virtually in his own time, men and women could read Foxe's *The Actes and Monuments of These Latter and Perilous Dayes* (Latin: 1554, 1559; English, 1563) and be inspired. The *Book of Martyrs,* as it was called, was one of the earliest examples of a combined religious and national polemic to employ portraits and illustrations, and it had a lavish progeny.

No longer did rulers and the temporally powerful have a monopoly over the commerce of remembering and being remembered. With their comparative lack of a royal focus, printers, painters, and engravers initiated a whole new market in faces and reputations from such mercantile and outward-looking cities as Antwerp and Frankfurt, home of a biannual book fair. In Antwerp, for example, the printing house of Christophe Plantin was an economically successful business that necessarily evolved a very different attitude toward who was a great man and why. With the need for buyers rather than for patrons, and a position in a commercial community, the printer sought to satisfy a new audience and along the way helped to create new tastes in heroism and fame. Of course, there were still many books and pictures to elaborate the cult of royalty that printing had done so much to help establish. Royal genealogies remained popular, and the ascension of James I especially witnessed an outpouring of charts depicting through the appropriate royal heads the descent of the Stuarts, down to the most elaborate of such books, Henry Holland's *Baziliωlogia* of 1618. A century or more of evolving royal portraiture had brought the kingly image firmly into the minds and possession of their subjects, even to the point of a certain luxurious trivializing: The Victoria and Albert Museum displays a fourteen-piece set of knives (dated 1607) with ivory handles carved with the heads of fourteen English monarchs that clearly marks the passage from history to souvenir. Well into the seventeenth century and beyond, propagandists for the nobility like Sylvanus Morgan in his *Sphere of Gentry* (1661) intricately limned the orders and emblems of social hierarchy.

But, more often than not, the new heroes were not monarchs, even Protestant ones. In the beginning of the fifteenth century the international community of humanist arts and letters could buttress monarchical claims to secular power with its own claim to reviving a classical past. But once those claims were stated, England became a battleground of rival heroic families and genealogies. Marcus Gheeraerts the Elder's engraving *The Procession of the Knights of the Garter* (1576) is an early example of such an anatomizing of the highest chivalric order in England that is analogous in its way to the anatomies of human bodies and the maps of the world that others were publishing. But mapping also implies the ability to stand apart, and the engraver could as easily compete with as support the royal perspective. In contrast with the official procession of the Knights of the Garter in all their regalia, we might look at Theodor de Bry and Thomas Lant's *The Funeral Procession of Sir Philip Sidney* (1588), a series of some thirty engravings that in at least one person's home was mounted over the fireplace on rotating pins—an early "movie" commemorating a somewhat different kind of heroism. Behind Sidney's cortege march a whole panorama of English society, including artisans as well as aristocrats—an almost classically ordered ritual procession of the new political order of society in honor not of a monarch but of an aristocrat not much in favor at court, a writer, literary theorist, and patron of the arts, who died defending the Protestant cause in the Netherlands.[36] Similarly, in about 1602 William Elstrack publishes a conventional genealogical celebration of the monarchy entitled *Henry VIII and His Successors,* but at the same time he also publishes *The Progenei of Geffrey Chaucer.* New traditions of art, learning, and adventure were being formed by innumerable illustrated handbooks along the lines of J. J. Boissard and Theodor de Bry's four-volume *Icones virorum illustrium et praestantium* (Frankfurt, 1597–1599), which displayed a whole new constellation of humanist saints—a hagiography of great men stretching back to Petrarch and Dante, including Luther and Calvin, and increased by forty or fifty portraits and short biographies in each volume, where, with a slight blurring of the eyes the title might read not only "Images of illustrious and outstanding men" but also "Images of men, illustrious and Protestant." In 1620, two years after Holland's *Baziliωlogia,* his *Herωologia* appears—with a full cast of English heroes, to complement the previous book of kings, which, in at least one volume, included Pocahontas.[37]

Even as the great sought to control their images before the world, and the availability of more efficient methods of visual representation encouraged the proposal of alternate ranks of heroes, so the way was also

36. For Sidney's own efforts and those of his friends to create his image, see Hager, "The Exemplary Mirage." The engravings of Sidney's funeral are included in Hind, *Engraving in England.*

37. Each portrait in Boissard has a Latin poem attached praising the subject. The one of Boissard himself compares his project to that of Apelles painting Alexander. Holland's work is modeled to a great extent on Verheiden's *Praestantium aliquot theologorum qui Romanum antichristum praecipue oppugnarent* (Hague, 1602), whose title—"Some of the outstanding theologians who have especially combated the Roman Antichrist"—makes the polemic edge even more explicit.

opened for those who wished primarily to promote themselves. In a bizarre impulse conditioned by the fascination with secular portraiture, John Lord Lumley turned his home into a monument dedicated to what were supposed to be his illustrious ancestors, complete with statues, paintings, and newly constructed tombs, as well as a repository of portraits of both family members and other notable Englishmen. Lumley, who had lost all three of his children in infancy, clearly found in his obsession with portraiture a restorative against the triumph of time and death. Unlike our conception of a collector, Lumley collected to mark not the eternity of art but the way painting made the human presence last through time and persist in memory by its preservation of a face, an image.

Elizabeth may have shown the way to those of her countrymen who could understand the place of promotion and performance in an effective monarchical nationalism. But by the last years of her reign her own efforts were superseded by the self-consciousness she had helped to bring into being. While on an embassy to Henry IV of France in the early 1590s, Sir Henry Unton had brought along a miniature of Elizabeth to show to the king. Henry immediately kissed it several times, although Unton refused to give it up. The image of the queen, her ambassador flatteringly reported, "had more effect than all his wasted eloquence" (Strong, *Elizabeth,* 28).[38] In 1596, after Unton himself had died, his widow commissioned a very different kind of portrait than the Elizabeth icon-pattern: a painting of her husband seated among the scenes of his own life, triumphs, and even his own funeral procession, a human being expressed not in the frozen moment of conventional portraiture but through a kind of story. A supporter of both Leicester and Essex, two of the prime favorites of Elizabeth I, Unton had been at Zutphen when Sidney died, was himself knighted a few days later, and after his death was, like Sidney, the subject of a book of elegies published at Oxford. As de Bry and Lant's engravings of Sidney's funeral procession place private mourning in a social context, the strange and complex portrait of Unton tries to crystalize the nature of an indivdual through the prism of his social roles. Coming at the end of a sixteenth-century tradition of royal and noble portraiture, its effort to supplement the image of Unton with scenes from his life reflects the growing interest in the anecdotal and the narrative—an individual's *story* as much as his unchanging image.

Guided by intuition and pressed by necessity, Elizabeth had sensed the need to become a ruler of new symbolic intensity to head a nation so recently separated from the imagistic monopoly of the international Church. But although the fame she so crucially helps develop was in her view exclusively monarchical, the availability of its new language easily engendered aspiration in others, both political and artistic. Toward the end of her reign there were already many who did not agree that there was room for only one star, one prime object for all eyes, of whose glory all

38. According to Sidney Lee's entry for Unton in the *Dictionary of National Biography,* Elizabeth had earlier accused Unton himself of "seeking a vain popularity."

other fame is merely a reflection. In great part, for example, the engravings of Sir Philip Sidney's funeral procession mark how his career and death could become the focus for a kind of fame backlash in Elizabethan England, aimed specifically at the publicity that Elizabeth and her advisors were fashioning so well for the monarchy. Sidney both partook of that fame and denied its sole validity. Thus the death of a man who was not much in favor at Elizabeth's court, nor one of the prominent nobles who might oppose her, caused widespread reaction in England and across Europe. The United Provinces (Netherlands) offered to give him a state funeral of their own. He was the "Scipio, Cicero, and Petrarch of our time" wrote Raleigh in an epitaph, whose virtue was "the best monument" (135–37), and his funeral was elaborately staged, numerously attended, and widely publicized. It was a different kind of fame from Elizabeth's, although seductive enough to rulers that even King James, as a young man, could write a eulogistic Latin poem in Sidney's honor. But the event of Sidney's funeral and the celebration throughout Europe of Sidney as a belated chivalric knight fallen on evil times, an ideal synthesis of literary man and military spirit, highlighted the uneasiness with kingship itself as an absolute value. He was an emissary, the Sidney myth went, from an older England, the embodiment of that double tradition of honor and humility that underlay the idea of the Christian knight.

For Sidney and his audience, such true greatness was also exemplified in the choice of love over fame that underlies so many of the sonnets in the sequence called *Astrophil and Stella*. If we recall the medieval troubadours singing of their mistresses, the knights paying court to ladies, and even Petrarch, who said that love of Laura impelled him to seek a forever-enduring fame, the opposition between fame and love in Sidney's poem might seem puzzling. But Sidney's praise of love reflects a similar revulsion from the fame of noble and royal ostentation—the "brazen fame" of courts and worldly hierarchy—that is an essential part of the English tradition from Chaucer on. Don't try to find elaborate meanings in my poems, says Sidney. I am interested in neither the fame of military ostentation nor in the fame of scholarly obscurity:

> I list not dig so deep for brazen fame.
> When I say Stella I do mean the same
> Princess of beauty for whose only sake
> The reins of Love I love, though never slake,
> And joy therein, though nations count it shame (xxviii, 4–8).

The woman he celebrates is Stella, a real woman, not an allegorical creature. Although he calls her Stella, star, and himself Astrophil, star lover, this is not the stellification of worldly fame, by which the gods turn their favorites into constellations, but a love celebrated in a personal poetry that the public world rejects. The sentiment is a strong one, and it is reflected in the words of chivalric heroes throughout the seventeenth century who, as in Dryden's version of Shakespeare's *Antony and Cleopatra,* make the choice of love over military and political fame: "All for Love, or, the World Well Lost." The values of this tradition stress privacy, even anonymity. Its heroes evade worldly recognition, for they know or they discover that to court it in the manner of the Renaissance princes would undermine the values they cherish. Like Chaucer, and in a manner typically English, they are torn about fame: It is a problem, at its best to be sought for, at its worst to be avoided. But who can tell the difference between best and worst?

By dying at thirty-two Sidney preserves the ambiguity and the ideal at once. The cautionary hero of an antipolitics, he becomes a secular martyr in the cause of personal feelings, conscience, and noblesse oblige against a world so taken up with itself and its own empty self-display that it has left those more private and spiritual virtues behind. As James I says in his youthful poem, Sidney united military and artistic virtues. But his literary works were not published until after his death. Like many writers of the sixteenth and seventeenth centuries, he preserved an aristocratic amateurism by circulating them only in manuscript. To have them printed would be to become a hardworking professional rather than someone through whom culture flowed as naturally as blood.[39]

But just as Sidney's style of virtuous withdrawal was admired by kings like the youthful James I, so Elizabethan self-display could be imitated by aspirants of all sorts. By the late 1590s the English inclination to self-presentation can be illustrated by the particularly elaborate case of a young medical student named Richard Haydock. On the title page of his translation of an Italian treatise on painting, he modestly says that it was "Englished by R. H.," yet also includes a full-sized folio picture of himself for the frontispiece. The elements are suggestive—a translation of a work about the theory of visual representation published by someone reticent about his name, yet very eager to show his face. But perhaps Haydock is only an extreme version of the ambivalence about artistic self-presentation in a decade that witnessed university-trained writers like Thomas Nashe working his own name into the titles of some of his works while the first individual publications of Shakespeare's plays were usually identified with only a note about when and by whom they were performed. For Haydock, as for others involved in the visual arts, the growing self-consciousness about the medium itself was connected to a personal self-consciousness about the figure the artist (or the translator of a work about art) made before the world. A few years later, Haydock pretended to be able to preach in his sleep. After taking in several members of James I's court, he was fortuitously exposed by James himself, to whom he made a full confession: "He apprehended himself as a buried man in the University, being of low condition, and if something eminent and remarkable

39. George Puttenham, in *The Arte of English Poesie* (1589), establishes a literary genealogy that stretches from Chaucer down to Sidney. In another sort of genealogical connection, the Earl of Essex in 1590 marries Frances Walsingham, Sidney's widow.

did not spring from him, to give life to his reputation, he should never appear anybody, which made him attempt this novelty to be taken notice of" (quoted by Hind, I, 33). Haydock should perhaps be proverbial as the archetypal humanist college man, with high expectations of himself nurtured from his studies of the greats of past and present, whose desire for personal justification through fame is so overwhelming that fraud and self-promotion are as necessary to his identity as scholarship and learning. Haydock's desire to be seen and to make a figure in the world somehow meets its complement in James I's nervous loathing of being looked at, reflecting the part-cooperative and potentially competitive interplay between the monarchs who used the new methods of self-representation and the artists and aspirers to fame who came into their service. James, although a king by birth, seemed to recognize in Haydock a kindred anxiety of dissimulation. After exposing Haydock's pretense and questioning him about his motives, he pardoned the amateur poseur and gave him ecclesiastical preferment.

For a moment at least, in the relation between Haydock and James, the king remains the prime dispenser of honor and status. But for how long? The publicizing activities of sixteenth-century art and engraving had established the context for a status and a fame independent of royal values, tradition, and control. What would happen when the interests of the king and those of the state diverged? Fulke Greville's poem, *An Inquisition Upon Fame and Honour* (1633?), prophesies the coming conflict over kinds of fame and kinds of public men with the pinpoint accuracy of someone who was the lifelong friend (and biographer) of Sir Philip Sidney and one of the chief publicists of his heroic image. In Greville's poem, the argument that fame has meaning only in the context of the state is juxtaposed uneasily and often abruptly with the progress of the soul to its heavenly rest. Greville does not seem to know or to accept the Petrarchan belief that heavenly fame is the realization of good fame on earth. He is Puritan and perhaps Augustinian enough to consider them opposed. "Fame" to him means only recognition on earth. Like "gain" and "pleasure," it is one of the three material ways men fight off the terror of death. Kings should therefore promote the possibilities for fame, for "never any state / Could rise or stand, without this thirst of glory, / Of noble werkes, as well the mould as story" (st. 6). It is the prime lure alike for rulers, warriors, intellectuals, and even "silly artisans" because it "doth enlarge States, by enlarging hearts" (st. 8).

But quickly the argument moves in another direction, seeking out the inadequacies of its own perspective. Fame on earth, continues Greville, sets man up as "his selfe-constellation," turning him away from God toward false learning, false action, and a false sense of self—"Selfenesse even apt to teare it selfe asunder" (st. 14)—which smothers true virtue under the trivialities of show. Yet, says Greville in another twist of the argument, the spiritual live on earth as much as do the aspiring, and those who condemn earthly fame put nothing in its place but their own self-promotion: "As while the pride of action wee suppresse, / Man growes no better, and yet States grow lesse" (st. 20). The word people attack the action people, but neither praises God, for they both consider man to be the measure of all things: "With things as vaine, they vanities beat downe. . . . Glory's dispraise being thus with glory tainted" (st. 23–24).

The selfishness that Greville identifies with the "thirst of glory" comes from the Roman, "the montebanks of fame." But, since Sidney's post-humous fame rests on his synthesis of the warrior who fights for England's material defense and the artist who defends (and defines) its soul, Greville is too much his admirer to accept totally the opposition between Roman state fame and Christian spiritual anonymity. The possibility is still open for a new definition of selflessness that would be assertive without being fraudulent, committed to the support of the state without being corrupted by worldly goals. If we lose the urge for fame, then all of human life is dark, for fame belongs to "human commerce" and there it should remain, "an outward mirrour of the inward mind" (st. 28). Just don't think it brings any inner peace. Fame and philosophy are both deluded because they measure everything by man. Such pride caused the fall of Adam, whose true fault was to try to be as famous as God: "Since to be like his Maker he affected, / And being lesse still thought himselfe neglected" (st. 34). Adam's mistake, like ours, is to believe that fame makes you more than human. But all it means is that you're more visible and there-fore have more enemies: "For who be throughly knowne, are ever losers" (st. 41), the possession of those who praise them. No matter how neces-sary or constant fame is in human affairs, it is an empty desire, "difficult to keepe, and desperate to lose" (st. 52), impossible to control, changing all the time, and never satisfied. Men seek it from "pride of heart and singularity," because they overvalue their own qualities, because they value political position more than personal worth, and because they love ap-plause. But if men have good consciences, they need no other trumpet, and they have more true fame than those who seem to reap its rewards (st. 47). Even when they become famous, they can't hold onto it without constant labor, and even then it can easily be lost, just as the World and Fame, "twinnes of one wombe," always lose to God:

> Lastly, this fame hard gotten, worse to keepe,
> Is never lost but with despaire and shame;
> Which makes man-nature, once fallen from this steepe,
> Disdaine that being should out-last their name:
> Some in self-pitty, some in exile languish,
> Others revell, some kill themselves in anguish (st. 71).

After his circuitous worrying of this issue that so gnaws at him, Gre-ville finishes by again praising the inner life and virtue that is responsible for anything valuable that we do and any true fame we receive. To love God is to get glory by his name, to worship fame is an idolatry of Time and Fortune: "man-pleasing, God's displeasing is" (st. 85). For all his struggles to resolve the conflict between the fame of the world and the fame of the spirit, Greville has wound up with an uneasy compromise between the values of Church and State, piety and public action. As the series of engravings illustrating Sidney's funeral indicate, along with Greville's own writing of Sidney's biography, the ancient distinction between material and immaterial fame was becoming difficult to maintain in a world of new pictures, theaters, and ceremonies. Greville himself says that if any "artificer of extraordinary fame" made himself "known to this famous spirit," they found Sidney a "true friend without hire" (*Life,* 34). Even such an heroic spirit might welcome the chance for being properly portrayed.

V

THE
DEMOCRATIZATION
OF FAME

From Monarchs to Individualists

The Public Eye

At most, the greatest persons, are but great wens, and excrescences; men of wit and delightful conversation, but as moales for ornament, except they be so incorporated into the body of the world that they contribute something to the sustenation of the whole.
                    —JOHN DONNE, Letter to Sir Henry Goodyer (1608)[1]

The word Person is latine . . . [and] signifies the *disguise,* or *outward appearance* of a man, counterfeited on the Stage. . . . So that a *Person,* is the same that an *Actor* is, both on the Stage and in common Conversation.   —HOBBES, *Leviathan*

Even though he took center stage in the controversies of the Reformation, Erasmus had generally only polemical disgust for the explicitly theatrical, whether in the State or the Church. Erasmus's sensitivity to the world of visual media was therefore confined primarily to the portraits that constantly reminded himself and his friends of their spiritual presences. But in the course of the sixteenth century, visual and theatrical art especially became the new-found support of religious and political polemic. With the Renaissance exaltation of the importance of painting and sculpture as well as the print-spawned ability of artists and writers to reach wider and wider audiences, art began to move away from an intercessory role between earth and heaven, or between temporal power and spiritual authority, to achieve a status of its own. The reformers may have at first been more sensitive to the uses of printing than was the papacy, but with the Counter-Reformation of midcentury the Church was fighting back on all fronts, the newly formed Jesuit order in particular producing an enormous pamphlet and scholarly literature, while promoting art that would glorify the Church and the

---

1. *Letters,* I, 191 (September 1608). Donne goes on to condemn himself from having been diverted from his studies of law "by the worst voluptuousness, which is a hydroptic, immoderate desire of human learning and languages—beautiful ornaments to great fortunes; but mine needed an occupation."

Catholic Reformers.[2] All through Europe, but particularly in France, England, and Spain, the struggles left an abiding conviction that all renown had to be properly staged, to create what Stephen Orgel has termed with double-edged precision "the illusion of power." The poetic and pictorial *Triumphs* of Petrarch, Mantegna, Titian, and many others began being imitated in real life. When sovereigns ritually entered a major city or when coronations occurred, artists, architects, and builders were at work for months in advance constructing elaborate triumphal arches, gateways, and adjoining mansions, bedecked with allegorical devices of fame and glory celebrating national unity and prosperity, festooned with precious metals, covered with flowers, and accompanied by a cheering populace gathered for the occasion. Statues of heroes welcomed the hero-ruler, not quite as comically as Venus de Milo gives Hitler the Nazi salute in Chaplin's *The Great Dictator,* but with the same voracious assimilation of past history and art to present purposes.

From Henry VII's problems with imposters who threatened his rule, we have come in the course of barely a century to a time when the monarch, like it or not, must be preoccupied with the place of theater in legitimizing and presenting himself and his reign to a national and even an international public. When James I succeeds Elizabeth to the throne, the English antagonism to the Scottish line inspires an immense increase in the propaganda of kingship, both political and artistic. While king of Scotland, James had written *Basilikon Doron,* a manual of kingship for his son Henry, stressing the divine right of kings, and he finally somewhat grudgingly submitted to the coronation display. But whatever his own reluctance, all around him new signs of visible heroism within the state were being experimented with and old ones were being codified. The funeral of Sir Philip Sidney and the subsequent growth of his myth, like the later masques and ceremonies put on for and acted in by the royal court, were both responses to the need to redefine the public man.[3] Through every attempt either to secure traditional public authority or to justify innovations runs a central concern with the importance of the theater of state to individual glory, honor, and fame. In public triumphal displays as well as in ceremonies directed at the audience of the court, the politics of monarchy gathered strength from the new sophistication of theatrical methods. The contrast between the king's two bodies, physical and eternal, which so preoccupied late medieval jurists, would be healed by an artistically organized ceremony witnessed by an appreciative audience. The superindividual nature that was the source of the ruler's authority would be staged, not just

2. The papal monopoly on saintly cults had been asserted first in the thirteenth century after generations of conflict. It was reaffirmed in the early seventeenth century as part of the Counter-Reformation effort to win back the iconographic power that had been seized by the Protestants.

3. For a time in the beginning of the seventeenth century, it looked as if James I's son Henry would satisfy the longing for a Sidney-like humanist knight to define the core of national heroism. But Henry died in 1612, and later efforts to define the English king as a god-hero on earth had much less success than they did in France under Louis XIV.

at coronation and death, but at important occasions all through the reign. Aided by the new technologies of picture making and printing, the new status of artists and writers, and the newly revived fascination with the possibilities of theater, the Renaissance monarchs bring an older form of imperial ceremony back into vogue. But, instead of being confined to the audience in front of them, the new rituals could be published in books available for the loyal citizen to purchase. In *The New Arabia Felix* (1604), for example, Thomas Dekker published engravings of the triumphal arch he designed for the coronation of James I. As the king passed under the arch, Fame blew her trumpet and the Five Senses woke from their rest to defeat Detraction and Oblivion, who try to destroy the new flowing Fount of Virtue.

The *theatrum mundi* (theater of the world), with its tones of medieval gloom, remained a popular image for writers who wanted to cast a jaundiced eye on earthly things and align their gaze with the audience of heaven. But in the unparalleled richness of English Renaissance theater the new audience clamored to pay admission. Theater mirrored the social world. Through it audiences could see up close behavior visible only at a distance in normal life. Even when its sympathies were divided, this theater continues to explore the ideology of the exterior, what it means to be a public person, a person before others, through a form that itself deals in surfaces. After the visually confined hierarchies of the Middle Ages, when willful ostentation was limited to very few and only the wellborn could be remembered through monuments or tombs, the way was now open for others to present themselves profusely to the world. In the private and many of the public theaters, aristocratic patrons could sit on the stage, as if to identify themselves with the actors as equally appropriate objects of the audience's attention. More and more people were getting into the act. Merchants, tradesmen, and lawyers put on festivities as elaborately theatrical as those of royalty. Depending on who was paying the bill, the play or masque, procession or festive parade, conveyed their image of what society should imitate and what avoid.

Against the attacks of those who condemned both theater and acting as devilish distortions of truth, writers like Thomas Heywood argued (in *An Apology for Actors,* 1612) the superiority of the stage to both painting and the written word as a way of preserving the fame of the great men of the past. For this reason, says Heywood, Romulus built a theater as one of his first acts in founding Rome. Theaters have always been part of great cities and an essential part of their success and prosperity. The shape and size of the theater reflects the wealth and power of the commonwealth. In Julius Caesar's theater, which Heywood considers the greatest model for all subsequent theaters, the whole universe is mirrored: "in that little compass were comprehended the perfect model of the firmament, the whole frame of the heavens, with all grounds of astronomicall conjecture" (35), while the seating arrangement was a perfect mirror of the hierarchy of society.

Heywood's theater is thus an entire world, and to reject its importance and influence is to reject all that is valuable on earth. The word "famous" runs all through *An Apology for Actors* and it's always positive, for the disdainers of fame (Heywood particularly dislikes Marcus Aurelius) are disdainers of theater as well. Heywood's theater thus does not promulgate fiction but myth, specifically a myth of political and social harmony. To attack theater, argues Heywood in his reformulation of the Roman link between the stage and public action, is to attack England itself. While arguing for the dignity and status of his own profession, he is also making explicit the way monarchs in England, France, and in other parts of Europe were wholeheartedly accepting the connection between the structure of the playhouse and the structure of the nation, between the plot of a play and the plot of history, between what they did on the throne and what actors did on stage.

*   *   *

Although Elizabeth's successes indicate the importance of theater to the fortunes of Renaissance monarchy, James's self-protective reticence about public display was understandable also. In the past the arts had generally interceded to support public power, whether lay or clerical. Neither poets nor painters had yet quite separated themselves from their traditional celebration of the patron. But in theater the demands of the medium itself could nurture a growing uncertainty about the nature of public power and authority. Retrospective fame tends to pick out someone from the past to be rescued from death and oblivion. But fame in one's lifetime, when it does not look toward a justifying future (for example, in the case of the avant-garde) often serves to exempt a special individual from the erosion and flux of normal life, preserving him not necessarily from death so much as from change. In the newly elaborated publicity of monarchy, the ritual and ceremony of rule creates a context of permanent and unchanging form. But even as it contributes to the persuasiveness of monarchical power, theater undermines it by calling attention to its existence *as theater* and to kingship *as a role*. English rulers and aristocrats, for example, were often great patrons of the theater. But it is extraordinary how many of the greatest and most long-lived Elizabethan and Jacobean plays crucially engage the issue of personal ostentation—what the age called "magnificence"—only finally to condemn it in favor of some more inward, less visible, and less theatrical virtues.

Heywood's analogy between the structure of the state and the architecture of theater asserted to all those who considered the public world to be in disarray that there was a clearly visible, articulated, and stable public order that the theater was both encouraging and supporting through its set designers, architects, playwrights, and actors. But an underlying formal subversiveness turns Heywood's socially mirroring theater into a potential critic of the royal display to which it is nominally an obedient servant, and begins to foreshadow an alternate definition of civic fame.

For those brought up in the revival of classical imagery and values, a fame outside the traditions of the state, however defined, might be inconceivable, and for those with hereditary claims, the state and its history might be bulwark or backdrop. But to others it might be a necessary evil and even an antagonist to their aspiration.

For moralists like Greville, the state was cut off from the realm of the spirit and only the urge for fame could in its haphazard and unpredictable way supply a nexus for the transformation of private virtue into public service. He gives no examples of such behavior from his own time, or even from the recent past. Perhaps he thinks that only Sidney could have managed such a transformation of selfishness into selflessness. There were many who, following the Elizabethan model, were willing and eager to put theater at the service of the monarchical view of the state. But the theater of which I speak, especially the theater of Shakespeare, questions the ease with which the state's traditions and values are both defined and embodied. In the course of the English seventeenth century, that privilege of definition and embodiment, previously the sole right of the governing classes, undergoes a tremendous change, from the absolute and divine power of the king to the economic and legislative power of Parliament, from the sanction of biblical monarchy to the sanction of political theory. Heywood, as suited his monarchical view of theater, considered the perfect state to be ordered, harmonious, and hierarchical. But in the English civil wars of the 1640s, both monarchy and the hierarchy it supported had become open to political question. When many could believe that the king was an enemy acting against the best interests of the people, then the nature of the state had changed, and with it the way fame could be achieved.

In the history of fame, the seventeenth century thus marks the increasing importance of theater not only for the self-presentation of public men, but also for the way in which all individuals contemplate the nature of their rulers and themselves as social beings. Without Elizabethan and Jacobean theater, the theories of personality pioneered by writers like Hobbes and Locke are impossible to understand. They arose not from abstruse philosophical study but from an awareness nurtured by the art and culture of their own times. Stephen Orgel has shown how through gradual stages the English theater was transformed from a hall in which the king not only had the best view, but was also part of the show, to the public theaters of Shakespeare, in which the stage is visible from all parts of the house. Similarly, when this theater deals with rulers as its subject matter, it takes earlier works intended to counsel or admonish the great and dramatizes them, putting the great on stage and making them the object of an audience's gaze. The importance of the implicit political revolution is hard to exaggerate. Kingship and rule are turned into a show in which one might play a good part or a bad one, but always a part, while the audience, usually the subordinates of the great, for a time become their judges. Such earlier monarchs as Henry VIII, Charles V, and Francis I had commissioned elaborate ceremonies and festivities in which they were the star performers as well as the audience for what everyone else did. But in both the layout and the conception of the English Renaissance theater, the importance of the audience and what it wanted to see was increasing all the time.

*　　*　　*

The plays of William Shakespeare (1564–1616) and Ben Jonson (1573?–1637), the two greatest playwrights of the Elizabethan and Jacobean period, indicate the major political impact theater has in its impact on the relationship of monarchy to its audience. In Shakespeare's English history plays, his Roman plays, and his tragedies of office (such as *Macbeth, Othello,* and *King Lear*), the question of having and (even more important) retaining public status is crucial. Sometimes the play's own standards of value—Who is the main character? What is the plot?—accords with the world outside the theater—who is famous and important? What happened in history? Sometimes the relation is more ironic and aslant. But invariably Shakespeare separates himself and his audience from the action by invoking the context of theater and the importance of acting in the "real life" of his powerful characters. Buttressed by history, but history turned to dramatic purposes, the plays present our rulers to us and thereby furnish a kind of permanent Saturnalia in which hierarchy is questioned so that those without political power are taught the skills of irony and moral judgment—the sources of another kind of authority. When Shakespeare in *Macbeth* compares the world to a stage, he stands between the old and new. Macbeth, who speaks the lines, finally realizes his powerlessness in a plot created by others: The play is his life and the playwright is God. But the audience watching *Macbeth* shares in that Godlike detachment from the ills of this ambitious and assertive public man and will judge him in their turn.

What would Henry VIII have thought of Shakespeare's theater, where the private moments of kings are exposed to a scrutiny as intense as that invited by their public ceremonies? With Shakespeare, acting has become a dominant metaphor for all social behavior, especially that of the great. He takes the theological and political concept of the king's two bodies, with its separation of the eternal spiritual body and the time-bound physical body, and turns it into a social and psychological concept. In *Richard II,* for example, Shakespeare dramatizes how, in the monarchical state, the problem of fame is the problem of inadequate kings. Like Falstaff's "honor," "king" too can be a "mere scutcheon," a social name that may accord with individual reality but just as often fails to measure up. This is the core of Shakespeare's fascination with what theater can show of the distinction between name and person, and he pursues it as much in the gap between "Shylock" and "Jew" or "Othello" and "Moor" as between "Richard II" and "King." Shylock and Othello are the victims of social generalizations and so can rise in our estimation only when their individuality is explored. But Richard, like so many other Shakespearian kings, has benefited too much from the same process and so can easily fail. Kingship in Shakespeare's theater is always a role. Some play their parts well, others badly, depending on their personal nature and their grasp of how a king ought to act. In Shakespeare's plays, the "timeless" rituals of kingship have been taken out of the cathedral and put into a theater. As in the portrait of Sir Henry Unton, surrounding the otherwise iconographic image is the narrative of individual human events. The implication is clearly that kingship is not a unique and unquestionable source of power and authority. It is instead a prime style of social self-consciousness that uses historical, political, and spiritual sanctions—as its sense of performance dictates. Therefore, it can be criticized, as is acting, in terms of the effectiveness of the portrayal—a category that includes whatever actions and policies are promulgated. As Shakespeare's prologues and epilogues emphasize his interest in the difference between fit and unfit audiences, so his characters constantly invite those in the audience who can appreciate the delicate nature of illusion to judge the difference between proper and improper performances, appropriate and inappropriate self-awareness. Monarchical display after Shakespeare can no longer merely invoke the heroic analogies of the past amid the rich display of the present. Now, the audience must be convinced as well as dazzled. Elizabeth herself, seeking to censor *Richard II,* said "I am Richard II, know ye not that?" With that insight or that willingness to be affected by Shakespeare's conception of kingship, Elizabeth has in effect concluded that Shakespeare has won.[3]

That a large portion of the English, who had revered Elizabeth as the emblem of their nation, would in less than fifty years war against and execute the son of her successor argues a change in the perception of kingship that is greatly influenced by the portrayal of royalty in theater, not even as satiric butts but as actors, like the rest of us. John Ford's play *Perkin Warbeck* (1634), based on the story of the pretenders to Henry VII's throne, takes the perception a step further. In the play Lambert Simnel, who also claims that he is one of the little princes supposedly murdered by Richard III, is easily bought off by a job in the palace kitchen. But Perkin Warbeck continues to fight, convincing others by the power of his belief in himself. The historical Henry VII had consolidated his military defeat of the rebels with extensive propaganda supporting his dynastic claims, as well as an expanded royal administration and new economic policies. But in Ford's play the fictional Henry VII clearly loses the contest to the inner force of the undaunted Perkin. Authenticated by

3. According to J. E. Neale, Elizabeth makes the remark in conversation with the antiquary William Lambarde, after the defeat of Essex's rebellion (381). Since several of Essex's associates, to drum up popular support, had bribed Shakespeare's company to put on the play ("bribe" because the company considered it too old-fashioned), and Elizabeth goes on to associate the king with the play, no doubt the connection was a familiar one. In 1597 the play had already been ordered printed without the scene in which Richard is deposed.

his sincerity rather than by his genealogy, Perkin turns the theater into an arena of combat for the national psyche to replace Heywood's mirror of national order.

As Elizabeth's remark about *Richard II* indicates, her own extraordinary ability to fuse political and cultural centrality begins to falter in the last years of her reign. *Perkin Warbeck* appears in the midst of a period of eleven years in which Charles I has dismissed Parliament to rule alone. Thus, in its immediate political context the play casts severe doubt on those who believe that the king rules by divine right. But its message hardly penetrated the court, where the plays and masques Charles watched all reinforced the ideal view his style of kingship had of itself. Like Heywood's, this was a theater of perfected form, where the spiritual ascendance of the monarch was imaged in the material profusion of the presentation. As such, it stood in implicit contrast with the other theater, which exposed the connection between costume and social power, as well as the potential fluidity of social identity for those who learned to look behind the scenes.

To a great extent it was Ben Jonson who was chiefly responsible for developing the techniques and themes in which the monarchical ideology of these court masques was expressed. As much a man of the theater as Shakespeare and as keenly aware of the nature of theatrical illusion, Jonson nevertheless exemplifies a contrasting urge to found his public fame in royal patronage. Coming to prominence a few years after Shakespeare, his plays first began appearing in the late 1590s. By 1605 he was already writing masques for exclusive performance at the court of James I and continued to do so until 1630, when he fell out of favor with Charles I. Far from using the theater to demystify temporal power, Jonson accepts the stoic preoccupation with "playing one's part" in a cosmic order and positions himself as both the chastiser and celebrator of the theater of the world. "In my *Theater,*" he writes, *"CATO,* if he lived, might enter without scandall" (*Complete Poetry,* 4). While Shakespeare takes his distance from all social roles, Jonson implies an ideal seamlessness of man and role. His theater is finally political, while Shakespeare's is psychological, just as he considers disguise to be an evil sham, while Shakespeare's characters often take on disguises to become more free and express some part of their nature otherwise socially restricted. Steeped in classical literature, Jonson's conception of himself as a playwright harkens back to Virgil, Horace, and Ovid (or to Erasmus and More) in his belief that he can teach the great by birth to be great by virtue as well. Like many writers in both England and France in the seventeenth century, he considers himself to be a civic figure, a poet-priest. His theater thus can in one mood satirically expose social irregularity and in another establish an ideal place where monarchical symbols as well as monarchs mean exactly what they say. Like many a purist, Jonson seems to recognize no middle ground between venom and unction. In his sensibility the promotion of an aristocratic mythology in his poems and plays coexists with an urge to demolish revered figures with a gossipy personal anecdote. When in 1618, for example, one of his hosts on a trip to Scotland praises Sir Philip Sidney and Queen Elizabeth, Jonson gives a vivid description of Sidney's pimpled face and confides that Queen Elizabeth had tried many lovers but couldn't finish the act because her "aperture" was too small.

For the monarch who was not or could not be perfect already, the writer as exemplary teacher would furnish the pattern, and so Jonson in his court masques stresses a true fame that may be ostentatious and theatrical but is nevertheless founded upon inner virtue. In one of his earliest, *The Masque of Queens* (1609), Jonson states in the preface that he wanted "the nobility" of his work to "be answerable to the dignity" of the Queen and the other noblewomen playing parts, "for which reason I chose the argument to be a celebration of honorable and true fame bred out of virtue" (*Complete Masques,* 80). The masque begins with an antimasque of hags and witches representing "Ignorance, Suspicion, Credulity, etc., the opposites to good Fame." After they go through elaborate curses and diabolical plots in the manner of *Macbeth* (James I was an expert on witchcraft and author of a book called *Demonologie*), their horrid setting magically transforms itself into a House of Fame, topped with the Queen and her eleven noble ladies-in-waiting. From the House comes Perseus, "expressing heroic and masculine virtue," who tells how he slew the Gorgon, not "for an empty name," but to show how Virtue begat Fame when Terror was slain. Fame is therefore his daughter (not Chaucer's arbitrary monarch), and her house is built with columns that celebrate the greatest "men-making poets." Then Perseus sings the praises of famous women as well, from the great warrior women of the past down to James's wife Anne, concluding with the praise of James himself, "you, that cherish every great example" (95). Whereupon *Fama bona* (good fame) appears, her feet on earth and her head in the clouds, carrying a trumpet and an olive branch, and praising Virtue, "my father and my honor." [4]

Inigo Jones's design for this masque follows Chaucer's description of the reception hall of Fame. But, in the same way that Jonson has taken the Virgilian and Chaucerian descriptions and stressed only their positive aspects (for example, the echo in Fame's house implies its infinity rather than its emptiness), Jones makes the columns of the poets uphold not the fame of nations but of individual heroes—Achilles, Aeneas, Caesar, and so on—"For who doth Fame neglect doth Virtue scorn" (97). Empty fame dies; good fame lasts forever. The Chaucerian ambiguity of the appearance of an unnamed "man of great authority" at the end of a poem that seems to undermine all authority is contrasted in Jonson's masque by a direct address to the king and queen and to the court that both watches as well as performs. Publicity to Jonson has a tangible connection with true worth, and in his last masque, written for Charles I more than twenty years later, he again introduces Fame, who praises heroic action but warns that if Fame is neglected, Virtue often dies. Jonson's attitude toward public fame,

4. For the "look" of these masques as designed by Inigo Jones and the sources of their imagery, see Orgel and Strong, *Inigo Jones.*

unlike Shakespeare's questioning or Greville's disdainful resignation, is thus optimistic or at least hopeful. Indeed we owe to Jonson the beginnings of literature in England as a profession. In 1616, seven years before Shakespeare's death and the publication of the First Folio, Jonson published his *Works,* to the ridicule of many who thought that plays were too ephemeral and popular to be called "works," but to the satisfaction of anyone who thought that the profession of literature deserved as much respect as that of priest or lawyer or king. In the same year he began receiving a yearly pension as the informal poet laureate.

From our point of view both Shakespeare and Jonson are engaged in the race for artistic glory: reenacting the past as playwrights while presenting themselves to the public as authors. But Shakespeare is hardly the best example of the new power of the spoken and printed word in the sixteenth century, since he was a playwright whose name did not grace the title pages of his individually published plays until well on in his career. The company of actors and the place of performance were the information the public wanted, and it was not until the late 1590s, after almost a decade of work, that Shakespeare's name was considered to be selling point enough to begin appearing as well. Shakespeare's reticence on his early title pages may have something to do with the fact that he was one of the owners of his acting company. But Jonson's authorial assertiveness is definitely linked with his position as perhaps the first writer in England to make a free-lance living through individual contracts. As the independent representative of a classical tradition of authors, he was for hire by those he considered to be worthy of his talents. The potential conflict we might glimpse between his own beliefs and the beliefs of his patron seemed to bother him as little as it did such court painters as Titian or Velázquez. So too, the status of the patron was a model for his own constant self-reference and self-promotion. When he publishes his masques as part of the 1616 *Works,* Jonson bestows appropriate credit on Inigo Jones as well as on the dancers, musicians, and performers who had brought them to the royal stage. But he still emphasizes that it is primarily his words that have created this world, and he loads the text of the masques with stage directions and asides that stress the need for a subtle interpretation of the relation to their classical originals.

Although Jonson was himself nurtured on the example of Sir Philip Sidney, his use of theater aligns him with views of fame that Greville spends a good deal of time attacking on Sidney's behalf. Drawing on similar classical and Renaissance sources, Jonson believes that the urge to fame and the cautions of an ethical self-awareness are not incompatible. He will be able to pull it off. As he says in his poem, "To Sir Thomas Roe,"

> Be alwayes to thy gather'd selfe the same,
> And studie conscience, more then thou would'st fame.
> Though both be good, the latter yet is worst,
> And ever is ill got without the first (9–12).

The sentiment of self-containment, as Jonson fully knows, goes back to Horace with its implication that the poet can teach the patron how best to merge conscience with fame. The fames of great men and poets are mutually supportive, and the best praise comes from a muse "that serves nor fame, nor titles; but doth chuse / Where vertue makes them both . . ." ("To Sir Henry Nevil," 2–3).

Blinded by his chosen progenitors, Jonson was unable to understand the extent to which the new age dictated that his artistic interests would ultimately diverge from those of the monarchy. In the argument that gave rise to his dismissal from the court, Charles I was asked to decide whether Jonson's words should be changed to suit Jones's sets and costumes, or vice versa. As we might expect in hindsight, Charles sided with the visual artist over the verbal. Jonson wrote satiric poems against Jones, but other writers were hired to help him create the masques. In the beginnings of Elizabethan theater, the monarch had been the ideal audience, defining the occasion by his gaze. By the end of the reign of Charles I, the royal theater had become a mirror that reflected monarchical ideals back to the king's uncritical eye, with hardly even the shred of Jonsonian moral uplift. In one masque of the early 1630s, Charles I and his Queen Henrietta Maria are praised for "that Heroicke vertue / For which Antiquity hath left no name, / But patternes onely, such as Hercules, / Achilles, Theseus" and told that "their faire Fame, like incense hurl'd / On Altars, hath perfum'd the world" (Carew, *Coelum Britannicum,* 170, 184).[5]

Until he loses royal favor, Jonson plays a central role in the Jacobean and Stuart courts' effort to convince itself (and some potentially fractious nobles) of its own supreme place in the history of fame. For the free-lance playwright and poet, whatever his low opinion of courts, court patronage was the highest possible goal, because it validated his own estimation of his status as a writer. Along with his classical and Renaissance forebears, he believed in that connection between the highest art and the grandest political power, and he sought that monarchical self-sufficiency and singularity for himself. Self-promotion as an artist therefore accorded with both the needs of his career and his philosophical belief that the urge to fame is an integral part of the combination of action and virtue that produces both artists and kings. Theatrical presentation for Jonson enhances personal nature and properly dramatizes true virtue, while Shakespeare uses theater as a way of evading public display for himself, even while he meditates on the assertive characters who are so often at the center of his actions. His sympathies caught between Falstaff and Hal, Shakespeare considers public behavior not as it is motivated by the desire for fame but as it is indebted to theater. Hotspur's blustering chivalry and Falstaff's overwhelming personal style must be both superseded by Hal's cooler manipu-

---

5. The prime statement of Jonson's argument with Jones is "An Expostulation with Inigo Jones." See the notes in *Complete Poetry,* 391–95, and the discussion by Gordon in "Poet and Architect."

lation of many of the same poses. Shakespeare doesn't say he likes it; he exhibits it for our understanding.

Portrait of a Painting

> Let fame, that all hunt after in their lives,
> Live regist'red upon our brazen tombs
> And then grace us in the disgrace of death;
> When, spite of cormorant devouring Time,
> Th' endeavor of this present breath may buy
> That honor which shall bate his scythe's keen edge
> And make us heirs of all eternity.

So speaks the king at the beginning of Shakespeare's *Love's Labor's Lost* (about 1596) and the sentiment is Roman: The tomb best conveys the majestic parade of the virtues of the departed—the chiseled lists of honors and victories, the painting of faces on shrouds—to intimidate the present and amaze the future. But even as kingship in England (and in France with more success) was wrapping itself tightly in the panoply of classical celebrity, artists and playwrights were exploring the more self-interested implication that, since their work created fame, they should have something approaching equal status. Such assertions might take either a Jonsonian line of direct emulation of the ruler or a Shakespearian emphasis on a vision in contrast with public power. So far as painters are concerned, the most interesting examples occur not so much among the English, where the development of painting tends to lag behind that of theater and poetry, but in Europe, where the Renaissance conception of the great man as painter continues with tenacious strength. Among the royal propagandists, Titian (1490–1576), for example, had been instrumental in creating the figure of Charles V; Van Dyck (1599–1641) established the style of Charles I; Rubens (1577–1640) worked as both artist and royal diplomat; and the Spanish royal family of the Hapsburgs appears to us (and to itself) through the eyes and brush of Velázquez (1599–1660). Velázquez's great painting of 1656, *Las Meninas* (*The Maids*), shows the painter in front of his easel, while around him stands the princess with her attendants and several of the court dwarfs. Like the masque designed for the king and queen, the point of view of the painting is that of the sitter, that is, the king and queen who seem to be watching the painter paint them, their real or painted faces reflected in a mirror in the background of the painting. Several elements in this much discussed painting deserve comment for their explicit indications of Velázquez's understanding of his relation to the monarchs he portrayed. Like many artists of the period, Velázquez was depicting something like actual studio conditions in his painting, getting behind the iconic nature of the image to reveal the processes by which it was created and thereby presenting himself more forcefully as the creator. Yet at the same time, he resolutely does not presume too much. In his relation to Philip IV, like Titian to Charles V, or Holbein to Henry VIII, Velázquez may have the Apelles/Alexander analogy in mind. But any possibility of direct competition is specifically denied: On the back wall of the room are two paintings, based on Ovid's *Metamorphoses,* that display the dire results of more artists competing with the gods—the punishment of Marsyas by Apollo and of Arachne by Minerva. Thus, even the indirectness of *Las Meninas,* a painting about court status as well as artistic representation in general, does not undermine the majesty of the sitters but enhances it by Velázquez's obeisance to their overwhelming stature, akin to that of the gods. By invoking the Marsyas analogy made by Raphael, Titian, Michelangelo, and others, Velázquez combines motifs of artistic assertion with motifs that stress the limits of what an artist can be.

But once the artist makes a point of saying he can never be a king, other forms of status are still open, beyond those of a skilled craftsman, and Velázquez is sensitive to that aspiration as well. In England both Rubens and Van Dyck are knighted (by Charles I), and Velázquez for most of his career sought court positions that had nothing to do with painting in order to characterize himself not as an artisan who worked for money, but as a loyal supporter of the king who happened to be a great painter as well.[6] For some time before he painted *Las Meninas,* for example, Velázquez had been petitioning the king to be admitted to the aristocratic military Order of Santiago. Among other qualifications, it was essential that the candidate practiced no craft or profession or business that required payment for services. Eight months before his death, he was inducted into the order, but in *Las Meninas,* painted four years earlier, the cross of the order is already on his chest. No doubt it was painted in later, whether by an associate, by Velázquez himself, or (as one story goes) by the king is unknown. But it completes the delicate balance of artistic and royal status that is one of the main subjects of the painting. The Ovidian stories of Marsyas and Arachne can be read as either cautions to the aspiring artist or attacks on the tyrannic god-patron, who (like Francis I chastising Cellini) takes credit for what the artist has accomplished himself. By having the sign of nobility bestowed upon him by the king painted in later, Velázquez indicates that his message has been received.

When painters desire aristocratic status, they seek a confirmation in worldly terms of the special sensibility that they believe is their portion

6. The Duke of Buckingham, James I's favorite and a great patron of the arts, frequently used painters, including Rubens, as diplomatic agents. On a trip to England (1629–1630), during which he is knighted and receives an honorary M.A. from Cambridge, Rubens also paints a *Landscape with St. George,* in which the patron saint of England wears the face of Charles I. Madlyn Miller Kahr suggests that Rubens's visit to Madrid at the same time inspired Velázquez to gain similar status for himself. Foucault memorably interprets *Las Meninas* in *The Order of Things.* See also Alpers, "Interpretation without Representation," for a critique and extension of Foucault, and Snyder for an intricate discussion of the painting's technical use of perspective.

both as individuals and as members of this newly assertive profession. This complex balance of aspiration and humility ('not a king but like one') is based on an assertion of sublime craft that denies it can be bought and paid for in any earthly terms—except by the bestowal of the status of "gentleman."[7] "We" look at and try to interpret *Las Meninas*. But in a sense we are not supposed to see it; only the king and queen are. They are the occasion of the painting, they "authorize" its scene by their perspective, and almost all the figures, including that of the artist, directly respond to their presence. The painting, like Jonson's masques, exists only for the eyes of the monarch. Like most other paintings of the period, it has no title until the nineteenth century, when it needs a name because it is being seen by those for whom it was not painted.

In contrast, when the artist, like Shakespeare, writes for a popular audience, or, like Rembrandt (1606–1669), receives commissions from many sources, or, like Vermeer (1632–1675), seems to paint primarily what he wants to paint, the traditional motifs of fame and social status are perceived with a cooler eye. Without a monarch as the prime see-er atop a hierarchy of fame and character, the way is open for much different definitions of what value is. Essentially, I would say, such artists attack the tradition of patronage by denying the patron has any more status than his position as employee affords him. Velázquez's sensitivity to his monarchical audience emphasizes the nobility of his own art even while he places himself along with courtiers and dwarfs in an obsequious but potentially defiant marginality. Like the king, he is separate from the scene he depicts and, again like the king, his gaze creates, orders, and makes permanent what he sees. The glimpse into the process of artistic creation allowed by *Las Meninas* unsettles the viewer's relation to the space of the artist, the models, and the viewer himself in the service of a claim to artistic transcendence of material reality. But, as paintings of Vermeer and Rembrandt imply, looking behind the scenes of painting, like acknowledging the setting of theater, can also call into question the divine and noble nature of art even while it asserts that it is the artist that makes art happen. Shakespeare's fascination with theatricality and social role is mirrored in Rembrandt's preoccupation with technique—the quality and texture of paint—and costume. Shakespeare's ability to submerge himself in his characters could be likened to Rembrandt's numerous self-portraits, always done in

7. The concept of the "gentleman," like the concept of honor, preoccupies seventeenth-century writers trying to strike a balance between "true," that is, innate worth, and what Lawrence Stone has called the "cult of reputation," that is, external show, that sweeps through at least the English aristocracy in the first half of the century. Stone cites "expenditure as the acid test of rank," in both charity and philanthropy as well as personal display (*Crisis of the Aristocracy*, 26). Books like Sir John Doderidge's *Honors Pedigree* (1652) and Sylvanus Morgan's *Sphere of Gentry* (1661) defined nuances in rank and escutcheon for new crowds of aspirants. As Doderidge writes, "[W]hosoever studieth in the universities, who professeth the liberall sciences and to be short who can live idly and without manuall labour and will beare the port charge and countenance of a gentleman, he shall be called master" (quoted by Stone, 49).

some strange guise, usually exotic or beggarly, that yet paradoxically allows us to see further into his changing view of himself than would any more straightforward depictions of "the Artist." When Jan Steen (1626–1679), for example, paints himself as a drunken lute player, it is hardly the ritual humility of Michelangelo sculpting himself as Nicodemus at the Crucifixion, but a more boisterously autobiographical image.

In place of the grand assertions of Velázquez or Jonson, with their paeans to self-sufficiency, such self-portrayals celebrate the artist as a protean figure who gains his power from his ability to transform, to see beneath the surface instead of enhancing its sway. *Las Meninas* reveals the occasion of painting only to enhance the artist's magical status, just as Jonson's interminable notes and prefaces to his masques root occasion and method in history and moral perception. No wonder Jonson was so angry at Inigo Jones's increasing importance in the production of royal masques. He had acquiesced in the need for such trappings to support his words and praised them highly; now, they were superseding the art that all along he had inwardly considered their superior. Shakespeare and Rembrandt, on the other hand, move more easily between art as exaltation and art as the manipulation of properties. For such an artist in a satiric mood, there were a few hundred years of pompous assertion to deflate. Velázquez's easel, for example, stands heavily in the corner of *Las Meninas,* fully the size of the painting itself, a heroic framework for his vision. In contrast we might first place Rembrandt's *The Artist in His Studio,* in which a somewhat apprehensive painter contemplates a huge easel in a virtually bare studio. No patrons or models or passersby surround him. The door to the outside world is locked, and he is alone with the basic problem of any art: what to do next, how to begin. The final work in this seventeenth-century triptych of painters on painting would then be Vermeer's *The Art of Painting,* called the Czernin Vermeer. As so often in Vermeer's paintings, there is a drawn curtain at the side, a pseudotheatrical frame that calls attention instead to the depiction of a moment that in actuality is beyond theater. Here we stand behind a painter before whom sits a young model resting between sittings. By the model's side is a long trumpet, the Roman *tuba* revived by painters like Mantegna for their triumphs of worldly glory. The painting in production is an allegory of Fame or perhaps of History, but we do not see its final (and perhaps too familiar) form, only its sketchy beginnings—in a rest period before the heightening and artifice have begun to do their work.

Because of their direct connection with the panoply of visible status, the painter and sculptor are more likely than the writer or playwright to aspire to an actual position of wealth and power. But, whatever the formal nature of their art, such an ambition continues to be true of those artists who design their careers on a style of fame that generally imitated that of their patrons. Such was the inheritance of the Renaissance replacement of the Church by the politician and ruler as prime customer for art. But, as the contrast between Shakespeare and Jonson, Rembrandt and Velázquez, indicates, many seventeenth-century artists were also moving away from being intercessors for worldly power and into a self-awareness *as artists* that would exclude such a role and even finally stigmatize it as the worst kind of servitude. Instead of defining its goals and status in terms of pre-existing wordly hierarchies, this art gradually began to develop a fame of its own, uninterested in nobility or riches except on its own terms. Even as he courted royal favor, for example, Jonson was the central figure in the development of "the tribe of Ben," a group of friends and younger writers, among whom those who wrote for each other began to establish an alternate genealogy and an alternate definition of national values.

This new attitude owed a good deal to the Reformation attack on the saint as intercessor between God and man together with its stress on the individual's direct relation to Christ—theological views that simultaneously threatened to diminish the importance both of the earthly ruler as an intermediary with the kingdom of heaven and of the earthly artist as a conduit of divine glory. In paintings influenced by Reformation ideas, the Christ in majesty of the past is replaced by a more reticent figure, not the center of dramatic attention, like Michelangelo's Christ as Judge in the Sistine Chapel, but often virtually submerged in the crowd among whom he appears, preaching. Such a Christ stands not at the apex of visual hierarchy, but in a more "democratic" position, without monarchical analogies to his power. Instead of the work of art as a grand statement of human aspiration on the Renaissance model, it is a more humble gift, as befits its subject matter. Rembrandt's attraction for the story of Joseph, the nomadic Jew successful in the city of the Gentiles for his gifts of interpretation, gives some taste of his own dignified separation from the type of artistic status and insight asserted by a Velázquez or a Jonson. Shakespeare's evasion of personal display is similarly reminiscent of that of Jesus, willing to display his power only if he can avoid being forced by crowds to turn it into mere magic. In seventeenth-century terms the distinction parallels that between the frequent Catholic belief that art primarily connects earthly with divine status and the Protestant belief, growing out of iconoclasm, that seeks to strip from both religion and politics the mystifying panoply of hierarchy and power. The result is not a denial of the artistic status that was first heralded in fourteenth-century Italy. But it does seek to refound that status not on the sanction of classical antiquity or on the artist's mastery of historical themes and motifs so much as on a recognition of art as a special kind of human activity that owes its importance not to analogies with other kinds of status but to its own processes and modes of understanding. Analogies with Alexander and Apelles are no longer relevant to such a goal. In their depictions of majesty, Jonson and Velázquez seize on the idealized moment. But Shakespeare and Vermeer focus instead on the many moments between, which give continuity and history to the isolated public images by revealing the context from which they arise and thereby undermining their claim to exclusive truth.

The Royal Actor

Our scenes afford thee store of men to shape your lives by.
—HEYWOOD, *An Apology for Actors*

But I have that within which passeth show.
—SHAKESPEARE, *Hamlet*

We may later wonder at the degree of awareness of his own media manipulations that induced Adolf Hitler to put Vermeer's *The Art of Painting* at the top of his list for confiscation when he began amassing European art for a projected museum in his hometown of Linz, and one may be intrigued as well by the possible crisis in his sense of artistic status that may have induced Picasso in 1957 to paint forty-five different studies of all or parts of *Las Meninas* in nine months. But back in the seventeenth century, the formerly cozy relation between temporal power and the artistic promoters of visual status was becoming increasingly uneasy. Charles I had long been accused of spending more money on his art collection, especially his purchase of Mantegna's *Triumph of Caesar* and other paintings from the Sforza collection, than on the welfare of his country. A few years before Velázquez painted *Las Meninas* and made his bid for noble status, Charles, his collection confiscated, had been tried and executed by the parliamentary armies under Oliver Cromwell for treason to England.

Theater in particular proved to be a double-edged sword in the establishment of monarchical status. At the heart of its ambivalence was the figure of the actor. With the increasing importance of the actor as a cultural figure in the sixteenth and seventeenth centuries, the duality of earthly body and heavenly soul has been complicated by the distinction between self alone and self before others, between individual nature and that nature displayed through art. The perception that the king may not be playing his role as well as others would also get its edge from the increased sensitivity to acting. Ideally, the monarch is the good actor, whose appearance in the world matches the virtue of his or her inner nature. But once acting has become a familiar experience and audiences become increasingly sophisticated about its styles and varieties, then the relation between monarch and actor might just as easily work to the king's discredit as to his benefit. When, for example, James I entered London as part of his coronation festivities, he was welcomed by the actor Edward Alleyn, who played the Genius of the City. What an instructive contrast that must have been to those ready for the lesson! The dumpy, somewhat unattractive real king greeted by the six-foot-six, extraordinarily handsome actor—who had already made a striking career playing the world-shattering heroes of Christopher Marlowe in plays like *Tamburlaine* and *Faustus,* was part-owner of two London theaters, and later founded an Oxford college. Borrowing the technique and power of the performer could be dangerous for the ruler who could not measure up either to the actor's physical presence or to his command of his part.

Writers from antiquity on had condemned the influence of actors on public men for their focus on appearance and their inadequate ability to convey the great man's fame (inadequate, that is, compared to writers). Horace tells Augustus that the poorest stage shows are celebrated more than good writers; Plutarch points to the number of actors who were companions of the fame-obsessed Romans; Boethius turns away from the theatrical Muses and toward Lady Philosophy; Chaucer characterizes the hangers-on at the door to the House of Fame as a motley collection of traveling musicians, balladeers, and actors. The attack heats up in the Elizabethan period when the actor's depiction of kingship is perceived as a blasphemous diminution of kingship's divine sanction. Already in the 1590s the satirist Joseph Hall seems to aim one of his poems specifically at Alleyn's performance in Marlowe's plays, not only because of his presumption in acting "some upreared, high-aspiring swain," but also because of the effect the plays and players have on an impressionable audience. Plays about royalty, says Hall, debase what they portray, inciting their audience to aspirations it should never be allowed to entertain. Hall's theater is thus hardly the mirror of social harmony celebrated by Heywood, but a vile chaos that defines God's order by mingling all of society into one undifferentiated pit:

> A goodly *hoch-poch*, when vile *Russettings* [country people],
> Are match't with monarchs, & with mighty kings.
> A goodly grace to sober *Tragike Muse*,
> When each base clown [peasant], his clumbsie fist doth bruise,
> And show his teeth in double rotten-row,
> For laughter at his self-resembled show. . . .
> Shame that the Muses should be bought and sold,
> For every peasants Brasse [money], on each scaffold [stage].
>
> (*Virgidemiarum*, III, 39–44, 57–58)

Monarchical theater had turned the iconographic portraiture of the sixteenth century into a series of ritual tableaus elaborating all the ceremonies that enhance a king. But acting, a crucial element in those ceremonies, also had its roots in Renaissance self-creation, where artists and writers renounced their nominal parentage to take on new names and status, vaulting themselves out of the restricted past and into the open future. Heightened costume could strengthen eternal ritual, but it also implied the ease of change.

The ambiguous implications of being on stage thus inflected the theater of rule in four ways. First, preeminently through Shakespeare, it emphasized the distinction between king and man and suggested that kingship might be a burden rather than an exaltation: Hal's realization that "uneasy rests the head that wears a crown." Second, through the awareness of acting as a craft and embryonic profession, it made the self-conscious playing of the role a prerequisite to effective kingship. Third, it added to the political and religious question of kingship the factor of psychological fitness, so that, in a play like *Perkin Warbeck,* for example, the main character is seen as a genuine imposter whose sincerity is superior to that of the precariously legitimate King Henry VII.

The fourth element in the influence of the theater on fame in the seventeenth century, as Joseph Hall clearly sees, rested in the audience. The audience of theater, especially as sophisticated an audience as seventeenth-century theater implies, views the play simultaneously as self-contained action within the frame of theater as well as an intervention with the outside world. It alludes both to historical events as well as to its own existence as a performance created by certain playwrights, managers, set designers, and performers. In the small urban worlds of Paris and London, such awareness was intensified, as it is in New York and London and Paris today, by the somewhat artificial means of gossip columns and public relations men who keep the backstage constantly in the minds of the audience. One result of this double apprehension of theater is the way we sympathize with the performer *as a performer,* playing his role as both character and star. In the theater developed in England and Europe in the sixteenth and seventeenth centuries, the audience is not a passive observer but an accomplice. We are instinctively, for example, on the side of the disguised person because the disguise is our special knowledge, our power over everyone else in the play, our wink along with the playwright and the disguised character. Two kinds of characters that intrigued this drama stand out for the mingled roles of accomplice and judge we play in their presence: the Machiavel, whose premeditated revenges compensate us for the feeling of passivity in the face of history, linking us imaginatively with the plotting playwright; and the hypocrite, whose pious self-promotion turns the tables on the arbitrary standards of society, linking us imaginatively with the impersonating actor. Both characters mingle in that more ancient antihero, Satan, who enjoys a stirring theological and literary revival in the seventeenth century as the adversary of God—his aspiration warning us not so much against aspiration itself, as against its mistakes and excesses.

England in the Renaissance had emerged as one of the most powerful monarchical states in Europe, as well as the home of a flourishing national theater (often under royal or aristocratic patronage) and the source of an unending stream of theoretical writings on acting and the stage, in both support and denunciation. Royalists and writers from within theater were, of course, generally positive. So long as the monarch maintained his place as the central symbolic figure for his kingdom, his combined personal and emblematic nature was the prime focus for his subjects. Under both James I and Charles I the propaganda of divine right had been accompanied with an enormous expansion of the number of holders of aristocratic titles. James had even invented a new one, the baronet. Hierarchy and divine right would support each other. Under Richelieu's guidance it was already working in France, and the Stuarts would try it in England. Swelling the ranks of privilege, presiding over more and more conspicuous displays of aristocratic wealth and magnanimity, could in the royal view only increase the stature of the monarchy and tie the newly titled more firmly to its political destiny. With so many newly created aristocrats invited to swell the public stage, writers pressed forward to detail the intricate insignia of heraldry for audiences made up more of aspiring businessmen and merchants than of actual aristocrats. Aristocracy was a show to be observed.[8] Suetonius was translated and published to great success, and early gossip columns about court behavior flourished. Royal propagandists in early seventeenth-century England were hardly so organized as they were to become in France. But they furnished influential models. Sir Francis Bacon, for example, in his essay "Of Honour and Reputation," followed Machiavelli in placing at the top of his five-level pyramid of fame the founders of states—like Romulus, Cyrus, Julius Caesar, Ottoman, and Ismael. Then came legislators, those who deliver their countries from civil war or servitude, those who honorably enlarge their territory or nobly defend against invaders, and finally, the *patres patriae,* who rule justly. Thus true fame was still being organized in the context of the state, and when Charles I's court artist, Sir Anthony Van Dyck, began work on an *Iconographie* that would include portraits of the great, he divided it into three series: princes and military commanders, statesmen and thinkers, and, the largest category, artists and amateurs of art, including Van Dyck himself.

Yet the patrons of this art breathed in an atmosphere of unreflective self-congratulation that gradually corrupted the whole project. The artistic enabler of fame was doing his supportive but subversive part to press forward the development of a nationalism seemingly based on royal genealogy but more solidly founded on a growing sense of national culture and style that could ultimately be separated from the royal line. Already in the time from Henry VIII to Elizabeth, England was in the process of evolving from a kingdom to a nation, in which there could be many different, and perhaps competitive, ways of defining "England." Elizabeth had helped the process along by her identification of herself with England; James contributed his share with his own writings and propaganda of divine rule; Charles would fail miserably to further their legacy. All along, the clearly voiced fear, from antitheatrical writers of both the High Church right and the Puritan left, is that theater will expose to otherwise loyal audiences the dangerous possibility that social hierarchy, from top to bottom, was merely a construction of roles to be played. Comic plays or allegorical stories of religion and virtue were all very well. But acting took kings and turned them into

8. The role of appearance was so important in all aspects of public that, it is said, William Laud, later Archbishop of Canterbury, sought to dissuade James Shirley, embryonic playwright and staunch defender of the stage, from taking holy orders because Shirley had a disfiguring mole on his cheek.

possibilities that anyone could aspire to imitate. When the king begins to compete visually with other men, how long will it be until he must compete politically? To a great extent, the English civil wars, in which the adherents of the king battle the adherents of Parliament, can be considered a falling out between the prime public man and his newly discontented audience, a result perhaps of his belief that their adulation and support requires no special courtship or expert role playing of his own.

In contrast to the passive self-assurance of the English monarchy's patronage, the French monarchy, especially in the person of Louis XIV, more effectively organized its artists and writers to stage his authority. As the eighteenth-century English statesman Viscount Bolingbroke later remarked about Louis, "If he was not the greatest king, he was the best actor of majesty at least that ever filled a throne" (I, 262). Coming to the throne at the age of five (1643), but not ruling until 1661, Louis XIV revolutionized French government by introducing a strongly centralized rule and by making the nobility financially dependent on royal favor. Absorbing and promoting the lessons of heroic greatness outlined through the plays of Corneille (1606–1684) and Racine (1639–1699), Louis established lessons and rituals of his own to further envelop the French nobility into a theater of courtiership for which he was both playwright and star, extending his absolute sway into the next century. All the moves Elizabeth made instinctively toward a combined cult of herself and her country, Louis and Colbert, his minister of finance, turned into a premeditated program. Any potentially overmighty subject was quickly enmeshed in a tremendously expensive personal preoccupation with the minute distinctions of status required by court protocol, down even to the hours spent watching Louis eat. In the arts Louis and Colbert initiated a bureaucratized patronage directly supported by the state. Louis XIV wanted to show that history ended in himself and his reign, and his lieutenants in infinite elaborate ways devised buildings, contrived ceremonies, set up academies, and commissioned works that would celebrate Louis as the unparalleled Sun King, the source of all individual glory. As Louis said to the assembly of writers who were commissioned to be his historians, "I entrust you with the most precious thing in the world to me, my glory." He would be both the center and dispenser of fame, the fountainhead of a monarchical fame industry, and perhaps the last such hereditary ruler to make his central cultural importance stick. The mercantile middle class became his employees, and the whole country, but especially the aristocracy, was his audience. They may have wanted honor and power. He made them be satisfied with honors and status.[9]

---

9. Louis XIV was especially fond of being portrayed as Alexander. Racine dedicated his play *Alexandre le grand* (1665) to him, adapting Arrian's claim to assure Louis that, unlike Alexander, he would have no reason to worry that he would be insufficiently celebrated. Among the many versions of Louis as Alexander is a sculpture by Bernini. William III in England (reigned, 1689–1702) was also fond of Alexander. But his version is Alexander the dynamic individual rather than Louis's patron saint of cultural and military expansionism.

If Louis XIV may have elaborated the cues he picked up from Elizabeth, he also had an excellent cautionary example before him in the beheaded person of his uncle, Charles I of England. As we move into the centuries of democratic fame, I will not have much more opportunity to contemplate the fame of kings. Louis XIV and Charles I well define two prime routes in this last century when monarchy set the standards instead of (at best) tagging after philosophers, performers, and politicians or relapsing into purely superficial social sway. Louis believed kingship was a profession, to be worked at full time. His court rituals, in which every detail of dress and social behavior was dictated by forms laid down by and perfected in the actions of the king, were only one of his several responses to the general theatricalization of monarchy and nationhood that marks the period. As Garrett Mattingly has remarked about the incessant military and political conflicts of the Renaissance, "war dramatized the state" (49), and Louis XIV was a ruler who wished to take center stage in every possible way. In addition to rebuilding France into a centralized political and cultural unit with absolute kingship at the core of its being, he sought to expand France's power in Europe as well through a series of military and political maneuvers that lasted well into the eighteenth century, although with much diminished success for his dynastic and national ambitions.

Louis XIV's aggrandizement of all national glory into the figure of the monarch takes essentially Roman imperial concepts and stages them on a scale unparalleled since the classical period. But the danger of monarchical theater, as illustrated in the career of Charles I, was the possibility of losing the entire realistic social context of achievement, except for the self-justifying audience of the court. Charles disastrously indulged the aesthetics of kingship with little sense of the tangible political power that art and theater might represent and even facilitate. Instead of understanding the many political compromises through which the Bourbon dynasty and his father-in-law, Henri IV, had succeeded in France, he commissioned Inigo Jones to build him a palace that would surpass the Louvre. In England from Elizabeth to James to Charles, the show of monarchy gradually overwhelms the content until it smothers its occupants.

If the building of the Palace of Versailles and the moving of the French court there in 1682 is the ultimate statement of Louis XIV's image of theatrical monarchy, the emblem of Charles I's much more uncertain playing of his role is the book published after his execution, supposedly written by himself, and a sacred work to English royalists ever since—*Eikon Basilike* [The Royal Image], *The Pourtraicture of His Sacred Majestie in His Solitudes and Sufferings,* already circulating in manuscript when Charles was executed.[10] As Charles may have read in Bacon's *Essays,* "if a man can be partaker of God's theater, he shall likewise be partaker of God's rest" ("Of Great Place," 30). In *Eikon Basilike,* by appealing be-

10. It is generally believed among scholars, although not definitively proven, that *Eikon Basilike* was written by John Gauden, made bishop of Exeter after the restoration of the monarchy in 1660 by Charles II, Charles I's son.

yond the usual trappings of monarchical theater to a realm of private spirituality, Charles and his supporters sought in part to justify his political and military losses by identifying kingship and this particular king not as the soldier of God and *Defensor Pacis* so much as the Christlike Suffering Servant of his people.

Bacon, like William Camden in *Britannia* (1586)—the first great conspectus of British history as a function of British geography—or like the more jaundiced Fulke Greville, still believed that personal honor was also an important civic concept, especially when it was ratified by the honor of the greatest individual in the state, the monarch. But in *Eikon Basilike* all this effort to tap the willingness of the aristocracy and the rising members of the gentry to acquiesce in the propriety of the king's conferral of individual honor in the state is shunted aside. Through Van Dyck, Charles I had presided over an unparalleled expansion of portraiture in England, comparable only to the impact Holbein had made a century before. But *Eikon Basilike* returns instead to a more private and spiritual kind of image, visually influenced, as Roy Strong argues, by some of Van Dyck's details, but still trying to gather its power not from the imagery of rule but from that of suffering, not from civic but from Christian virtue. Machiavelli had argued that Christian virtue was opposed to civic virtue, which was based both on modeling oneself on the great men of the past and, for the prince, on the constant willingness to go to war. But the *Eikon Basilike* conception of Charles I as "king and priest and prophet" recasts him in the mold not of Caesar but of David, the priestly ruler of a spiritually founded state:

> I know no resolutions more worthy a Christian king than to prefer his conscience before his kingdoms. . . . And, indeed, I desire always more to remember I am a Christian than a king, for what the majesty of one might justly abhor, the charity of the other is willing to bear; what the height of a king tempteth to revenge, the humility of a Christian teacheth to forgive (28, 34–35).[11]

The pose is familiar to us from its medieval precedents. But it rings strangely here in the midst of the seventeenth century, although it is easy to see its utility for a king defeated politically and militarily by his own subjects, as well as its echoes of the death and legend of Sidney, the last Christian Knight. Parliamentary leaders like Thomas Fairfax and Oliver Cromwell were celebrated in equestrian portraits whose style was taken directly from those first devised by painters like Rubens and Velázquez to praise kings and emperors. Why not then turn aside from the traditions of classical monarchical virtue and stress instead the king as spiritual leader, who takes arms against his own people only because he does not

11. "State" is frequently used by later seventeenth-century royalist writers as a word for nonmonarchical governments without religious ties. *The Oxford English Dictionary* quotes John Dryden: "Monarchies may own religion's name / But states are Atheists in their very frame." The modern distinction between Church and State is also of seventeenth-century origin.

wish to be "infamous . . . to all posterity" as the first Christian king of England to consent to the oppression of the national church. Yet the age was demanding more self-awareness in its kings than Charles could muster. In his 1650 poem, "An Horatian Ode," Andrew Marvell celebrates Oliver Cromwell's brutally successful campaign in Ireland and contrasts Cromwell who "does both act and know" (76) with Charles I on his scaffold, the Royal Actor, playing his part to the end, trapped by the audience he has created. By being the Royal Playwright, Louis XIV will manage to dazzle the French audience and preserve France's absolute monarchy for more than another century. *Eikon Basilike* may attempt to fashion a kind of self-effacing theater for Charles's monarchical self-justifications, but theater it still is, needing as much publicity as more wordly aspirations. So it is perceived by writers like Marvell or, even more explicitly, John Milton, who is asked by the parliamentary government to take on the unwelcome task of answering the work of the "royal martyr," after whose execution his admirers dipped their handkerchiefs in his blood. Milton condemns the "civil kind of idolatry" that people are prone to before kings and counters the more substantive charges against Parliament and its leaders leveled in *Eikon Basilike*. But running under his argument is a concurrent pattern of comments on the theater of kingship—the "licentious remissness" of the theater Charles watched even on Sundays and the ineptness of his own efforts to play the kingly role: "[T]he general voice of the people almost hissing him and his ill-acted regality off the stage" (789).

Once the court loses its central place in the nation's eye, its rewards are no longer the only definition of public recognition. The victor in the battle between king and Parliament is Oliver Cromwell, not a descendant of kings but a "private man," who has led the parliamentary forces against Charles I, reestablishes English military power in Europe, and becomes the first Englishman to rule over all of the British Isles. In an emblematic act, when Cromwell becomes Lord Protector after the execution of Charles I, he asks that his portrait be done, "warts and all." The moment is apt. "Warts and all" not only announces a face that would be unprettified by aristocratic fictions of appearance. It also makes that look a worthy subject of painting. After Cromwell dies and his son resigns, Charles II will be restored. But the possibility that rule was not only hereditary, but also had something to do with abilities that might be found outside the royal family, and even outside the aristocratic classes, was firmly fixed in the national experience. This is Shakespeare's legacy: Behind the panoply of the king is the man, and behind both is the actor. If the man is inadequate, if the actor cannot draw on his reservoirs of psychic energy, the king will remain a posturing shell. Thus acting turns political authority into a problem, one of whose solutions is Cromwell— "warts and all," the style of unadorned self-presentation—although for his troubles Cromwell will be continually attacked by the royalists for being

1

The Codification of the New Heroes. (1) Title page from Henry Holland's *Herωologia* (1620), one of an outpouring of books celebrating contemporary fame. The Latin reads: "the most famous and wisest among the English, who flourished from the time of Christ to the present year." The Latin title, with its Greek omega (ω), connects the book to the heroes of the classical past. *Henry E. Huntington Library*

2

(2) Pocahontas, from Holland's previous work, *Baziliωlogia* (1618), which dealt primarily with rulers. According to H. C. Levis, different versions of the work included Mahomet the Great; Mary, Queen of Scots; and other figures. Pocahontas died in 1617, shortly after her marriage to Thomas Rolfe and her voyage from America to England. *National Portrait Gallery, Smithsonian Institution, Washington, D.C.*

ORLANDO

FVRIOSO

IN ENGLISH

HEROICAL VERSE, BY

IOHN HARINGTŌ

Principibus placuiſſe viris non vltima laus eſt.

Horace

The Author as Aristocrat. In the 1590s, at the same time that professional writers like Shakespeare were only beginning to put their names on their books, the growing status of authorship lured aristocratic amateurs, for whom it constituted a new style of honor. (1) Title page of John Harington's translation of *Orlando Furioso*, one of the best-sellers of the sixteenth century. Although this translation appeared less than sixty years after Ariosto's death, the author is depicted (above the title) as an antique Roman, complete with laurel wreath, while the translator's much larger picture is that of an Elizabethan gentleman, complete with up-to-date timepiece. *Henry E. Huntington Library* (2) *The Progenei of Geffrey Chaucer*. Although he is dressed in a simple medieval costume, Chaucer is surrounded by the heraldic shields of his descendants. *Henry E. Huntington Library* (3) Richard Haydock, "student in Physik," made his bid for fame by translating Lomazzo's treatise on painting. He also designed the title page, which features a large portrait of himself that belies the modest "R.H." with which he signed the work. *Henry E. Huntington Library*

Monarchy: Spiritual and Political. (1) William Marshall's engraving for *Eikon Basil[...]* (1649), supposedly written by Charles I, shows the king at prayer before his execution, [...] spired by the glory that comes from heaven and discarding his earthly crown for the th[...] wreath of grace. *Henry E. Huntington Library* (2) Title page of Thomas Hobb[...] *Leviathan* (1651), his disquisition on the nature of monarchical power, featuring a giga[...] king, looming over the countryside, scepter in one hand and sword in the other, his b[...] made up of the bodies of his subjects. *Henry E. Huntington Library*

Non est potestas Super Terram quæ Comparetur ei. Iob. 41. 24.

LEVIATHAN
Or
THE MATTER, FORME
and POWER of A COMMON-
WEALTH ECCLESIASTICALL
and CIVIL

By THOMAS HOBBES
of MALMESBVRY.

London
Printed for Andrew Crooke
1651.

1

Writers versus Patrons. God is on whose side? (1) *Fama Fraternitatis* (1618): The Invisible College of the Rose Cross Fraternity. An elaborate and perhaps impenetrable visual allegory featuring warriors waving swords and quill pens in an effort to protect a mobile and self-contained castle. A kingdom unto itself, the castle trumpets its own coming while God's hand supports it from above. *From Theophilus Schweighardt, Speculum Sophicum Rhodo-Stauroticum (1618). By permission of the British Library*

2

(2) The Fame of the Royal Society (1667). Fame crowns
Charles II, Charles I's son, patron of the Royal Society.
The orderly world of books and instruments of measure-
ment surrounding him imply the need for a monarchical
patron to keep order in the world of the intellect as well.
Compare the same symbols in disarray in *Melencolia I.*
From Thomas Sprat, History of the Royal Society (1667).
By permission of the British Library

Published according to act of Parliament.
Sept. 15. 17

1

AN
ESSAY
ON
MAN.
BY
ALEXANDER POPE, Esq;
Enlarged and Improved by the AUTHOR.
Together with his MS. Additions and Variations
as in the Laſt Edition of his Works.
With the NOTES of
WILLIAM, Lord Biſhop of GLOUCESTER.

LONDON:
Printed for W. STRAHAN; and T. CADELL, in
the Strand. MDCCLXXIV.
[Pr. 1 s. 6 d.]

2

Studious he sate, with all his books around,
Sinking from thought to thought, a vast profound:

Plung'd for his sense, but found no bottom there;
Then writ, and flound'd on, in mere despair.

DUNCIAD. Book I. line 111.

3

4

Varieties of Artistic Self-Consciousness: Eighteenth-Century Versions. (1) The frontispiece, drawn by Alexander Pope, of his *Essay on Man* (1731–33) features a wise man
(perhaps a writer) blowing bubbles amidst the broken columns and headless statues of
the classical past. *Henry E. Huntington Library* (2) In Hogarth's *A Grub Street Poet*, the
struggling author toils in his garret while the landlady comes to demand the rent. In this
version he is working on "Poverty, A Poem"; in another it is "Riches, A Poem." Below
the engraving Hogarth quotes from Pope's *Dunciad*. *Henry E. Huntington Library* (3)
The young Sir Joshua Reynolds looks out at the viewer, brush and palette in hand.
National Portrait Gallery, London (4) The older Sir Joshua Reynolds, now laden with
honors, has secured a place for himself in the history of art with a self-portrait reminiscent of Rembrandt's *Aristotle Contemplating the Bust of Homer*. Here the bust is of
Michelangelo. *Royal Academy, London; Bridgeman/Art Resource*

1

2

Images of America. In Europe a
personified figure of Fame virtually
vanished by the nineteenth century.
But in the newest nation both heroism
and symbolism had to be invented
from the ground up. (1) The earliest
depictions of America were as the
Indian Princess, perhaps a residue of
the fame of Pocahontas. The *Triumph
of America*, drawn by Madame
Plantou and engraved by Chataigner
to commemorate the Peace of Ghent
(1814), continues to use the Indian
Princess, here shown in a Roman
triumphal procession, with Fame, at
left, flying aloft and blowing her
trumpet. *Courtesy, Winterthur
Museum* (2) Washington in white and
orange robes is carried to heaven by
an angel (Fame?) and Time, while
Liberty and an Indian weep in this
painting on glass based on John J.
Barralet's 1802 engraving. *Courtesy,
Winterthur Museum*

3

(3) This detail of the soup tureen from Washington's dinner service, a gift of the Society of Cincinnati, features Fame holding the insignia of the society. *Courtesy, Winterthur Museum*

5

4

(4) Although Washington and Franklin were the two most famous Americans, sometimes it was hard for Europeans to tell them apart. This English souvenir statue, made of pearlware, dates from the mid-nineteenth century. *Courtesy, Winterthur Museum* (5) In this etching by Marguerite Gérard after a drawing by Fragonard entitled "To the Genius of Franklin," the classical severity of Barralet's apotheosis of Washington finds its Romantic counterpart. *Courtesy, Winterthur Museum*

1

Napoleonic imagery, like that of the American Revolution, explicitly revived Roman motifs to reinforce his authority. But Napoleon also invoked less usual sanctions. (1) In Girodet-Trioson's *Ossian Receiving Napoleonic Officers into Valhalla* (1802), commissioned by Napoleon, Ossian's epics of primitive greatness serve the same inspirational function for Napoleon as Homer did for Alexander. *Malmaison. Chateau; Giraudon/Art Resource* (2) Napoleon is depicted as a Roman emperor on the medal commemorating the passages of the Rhine, with the reverse showing the imperial eagle before the throne. *Numismatic Fine Arts, Beverly Hills*

2

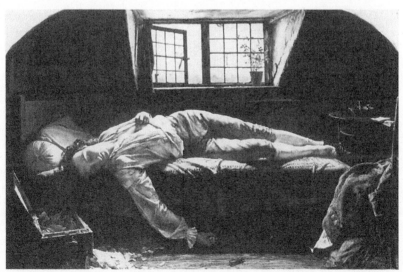

Two Nineteenth-Century Views of Artistic Death. (1) Painted by Ingres for a royalist patron after the restoration of the French monarchy, *The Death of Leonardo da Vinci* (1818) shows Francis I embracing the dying Leonardo while a member of the court looks disapprovingly from the foot of the deathbed. *Petit Palais, Paris; Kavaler/Art Resource* (2) The product of a later conception of the writer (and artist) as alienated from society, Henry Wallis's *Death of Chatterton* (1856) depicts the suicide of the young aspirant who failed to achieve the fame he felt he deserved. Wallis painted the work in the same garret where Chatterton had actually died. The model was the young novelist George Meredith. Two years later Wallis ran off with his wife. *Tate Gallery, London*

1

2

Like Franklin, Abraham Li**n**
did not look like a classicall**y**
approved "great man," and **p**
tography was instrumental i**n**
bringing his new physiogno**my**
the public. (1) This is the *ca**rte**
visite* made by Mathew Brad**y**
February 27, 1860, when Li**n**
was in New York to give a s**p**
at the Cooper Union. Linco**ln**
considered it a crucial facto**r**
his election. *George Eastma**n**
House, Rochester, New York*
drawing of Lincoln from a **now**
vanished portrait, intriguing
the way it assimilates the fea**tures**
of Lincoln, with tousled hai**r**
cleft chin, to those of Lord **B**
(with a suggestion of the lio**n**
mane of Alexander?). Maki**ng**
great men look like Byron w**as**
common in the early ninetee**nth**
century. There are several su**ch**
images of Daniel Webster, fo**r**
example. Stefan Lorant date**s** **a**
similar image of Lincoln to **1858**
*Henry E. Huntington Librar**y***

Barnum. (1) An example of just one of the many types of self-advertising stationery used by P. T. Barnum. This is a letter written in 1878 to Mark Twain, asking for some public praise for Barnum's show from "Mark." Barnum had asked several times previously and Twain never agreed to do it. In another letter to Twain he says, "You know I had rather be laughed *at* than not noticed at all. . . ." *The Mark Twain Project, Bancroft Library*

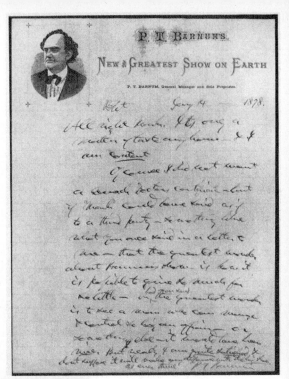

1

(2) A Brady portrait of Barnum with the ballerina Ernestine de Faiber that neatly expresses the way in which Barnum both presented his attractions and was onstage himself. *National Portrait Gallery, Smithsonian Institution, Washington, D.C.*

2

Teddy Roosevelt was the first president since Lincoln to become a central figure in the eyes of the American public. In an early example of his sense of self-presentation (1886), he is here photographed after successfully tracking some men who had stolen a boat from his North Dakota farm. At least that was the story up until a few years ago, when it was discovered that the photograph had been restaged with some of Roosevelt's own men "playing" the thieves. Perhaps that makes the point even more clearly. *Theodore Roosevelt Collection, Harvard College Library*

The Performer and His Roles. (1) Sheet music cover for the Virginia Serenaders (1863) showing the performers in their minstrel show costumes and "as themselves." *Harvard Theater Collection* (2) Julian Eltinge, a famous female impersonator of the early twentieth century, appeared in the *Julian Eltinge Magazine* as both bride and groom. The magazine featured such photomontages of Eltinge's many female roles, hints on cosmetics and exercise, and a certain number of shots of Eltinge (whose real name was Bill Dalton) smoking cigars or boxing with James J. Corbett, just in case you wondered. *Billy Rose Theatre Collection, The New York Public Library at Lincoln Center, Astor, Lenox and Tilden Foundations*

SONGS OF THE VIRGINIA SERENADERS.

PIANO FORTE,
J.W. TURNER.

The basic problem of fame has often involved an effort to avoid the charge of mere personal ambition. In being depicted by Jonathan Richardson with the features of Milton, Alexander Pope placed himself securely in literary history. *Cornell University Library*

"WE"

In a more modern assertion, Charles A. Lindbergh qualified his own aspiration by insisting that "we"—the man and the machine—did it together. *AP/ Wide World Photo*

In 1958 Richard Avedon photographed Marilyn Monroe in the guises of the great and glamorous stars of the past. Here she is as Jean Harlow. The analogy with Pope's impersonations is obvious. But in light of the movie-star immediacy exemplified by Monroe, the appeal to the sanction of past fame only emphasizes its irrelevance. This is more play-acting than homage, and the impersonation is perhaps too complete. *Photography by Richard Avedon, copyright © 1958 by Richard Avedon, Inc. All rights reserved.*

the quintessence of a sevententh-century bad actor, both hypocrite and Machiavel.[12]

So long as there remains a belief that the king is the one person in whom character and role are indistinguishable, monarchs remain attracted to actors. But the theatrical support of royal power present in the Stuart masques or the layout of Versailles is less humanly compelling than in the frequent loans Charles II makes of his coronation robes to his favorite theater company and his frequent selection of actresses to be his mistresses. After Charles II kingship in England loosens or even severs its ties with the stage. Theater becomes associated with the aristocratic classes, and when aristocracy was attacked for its immorality in the later seventeenth century, theater is the focus of the attack, for the rarefied, artificial, and repressive view of the world that its forms supposedly embodied. By the eighteenth century, as the arts begin to be employed by an increasingly wealthy part of the population to express its own desire for a place in the public eye, the sanction of theater has degenerated into the spectacle of a certain Welshman named Apreece, who paid the actor-playwright Samuel Foote to put him into a play (and supplied his own costume) so that he would be a success at court. Like so many aspiring fops in Restoration comedy, all he got out of his desire to make a figure in the world was ridicule. Yet one can look with similar melancholy on the possibility that, for all his artistic patronage, many people now remember Charles I primarily because he had a "Van Dyck" beard. Monarchs had begun to discover that tapping the power of theater and visual imagery to enhance one's own never quite works out as planned. Some wound up like Louis XIV, forced by his own success to mount grander and more foolhardy plans; others, like Charles I in the visionary painting by the Dutch artist Weesop, succeeded only in becoming their own executioners.[13]

12. "Warts and all" is the usual short rendition of Cromwell's supposed instructions to Sir Peter Lely: "I desire you would use all your skill to paint my picture truly like me and Flatter me not at all. But remark all these roughness, pimples, and warts and everything as you see me. Otherwise I will never pay a farthing for it" (quoted by Fraser in *Cromwell*, 472, from the 1721 account of George Vertue in *Anecdotes of Painting*). Fraser also argues that it was Samuel Cooper the miniaturist rather than Lely who did the original version.

13. In our own century, as café society metamorphosed into the jet set, we have been treated, particularly since the 1920s, to the sight of minor European royalty pressing into a spotlight held more firmly by actors and society painters, an urge the bourgeois monarchs of the nineteenth century did not seem to have. Political leaders from Napoleon to John F. Kennedy and beyond have sought the advice and company of performers. In a more malevolent vein, twentieth-century dictators like Hitler and Mussolini have acted in power like warped versions of performers, constantly staging their power. In this competition they are reminiscent of monarchs like Louis XIV as well as of frustrated performers like Nero, whose tendencies to violence and supreme artistic stature are intricately intertwined.

Aristocrats Without Ancestors

Simply the thing I am / Shall make me live.
—PAROLLES in *All's Well That Ends Well*

. . . as in other things, so in men, not the seller, but the buyer determines the Price. For let a man (as most men do), rate themselves at the highest Value they can; yet their true Value is no more than it is esteemed by others.   —HOBBES, *Leviathan*

The tendency to periodize human history, although it often produces grotesque efforts to decide whether some human production is "truly" medieval or "truly" Renaissance, nevertheless does correspond to the perception that the general atmosphere has changed enough for us to conclude that the times themselves must be different as well. In the history of fame especially, the appearance of a multitude of striking individuals allows us to mark not the "idea" of the Renaissance, for example, so much as a period—like the Mediterranean world in the two hundred years around the birth of Christ or the twelfth and thirteenth centuries in Europe—when the parameters of human nature and human action are being redefined. Until societies move toward a system of political representation, fame is important primarily for those classes and families who control all power and authority, and for those who are their celebrators. But when that power can be sought and effectively wielded by new groups and individuals, fame becomes a political issue, a goal for many who had otherwise never considered it a potential of their characters. Jakob Burckhardt, the great nineteenth-century historian, considered the promotion of personal fame to be one of the essential activities of the Renaissance, although mainly, as we have seen, a concern of rulers and artists. Yet other groups were beginning to press forward as well. Rising English businessmen in the early seventeenth century, for example, had eagerly adopted the chivalric imagery and allegorical processions that had been reintroduced into London public life by Henry VII and Henry VIII. Where else to find the imagery of status but among the court and the aristocracy? But gradually the aristocratic disdain for profession and craft (which in Spain had produced the spectacle of Velázquez denying that he was paid for his paintings) was giving way to a host of propagandists who spoke up on behalf of the special qualities required to be professional—in the law, in medicine, in science, in literature, and in art. Kings like James I and Louis XIV argued both the divine sanction for kingship as well as the particular anointing of their own genealogical line. The need to make such arguments explicit indicates the actually growing resistance to the monarch's claim to represent and embody the nation, and the growing importance of the elected representatives of the people, or at least of those people who were entitled to vote.

Even Henry VIII, with his absolute power, was pressed to share authority with aristocrats and rising civil servants. By the time of Charles I's period of "personal rule," there was a large body of opinion that disputed not only the king's right to run the country exclusively but also the historical and spiritual sanctions for the royal claim. In the fifteenth century Henry VII had emerged victorious from a civil war that was fought between different branches of the aristocracy. In the seventeenth century the civil war was fought between the partisans of monarchy and those of parliament.[14]

The efforts of late Renaissance monarchs like Charles I and Louis XIV to situate themselves at the intersection of a spiritual and a secular nationhood celebrated by the greatest artists and writers was in part the result of the doctrinal schism within Christianity. When the Reformers protested the authority of the Scripture, that is, of written tradition, against the authority of the popes, that is, a centralized political tradition, they hardly foresaw the proliferation of new institutions their anti-institutional views would spawn, nor the way that rulers who protected them absorbed their sanction into a new politics. New Romes, Jerusalems, and Troys sprouted everywhere. Identity was once again vested in the city and state to award, although their exclusive control over fame was more difficult to maintain, since Reformation Protestantism had opened the possibility that "visible saints" might walk the earth now in shapes unrecognizable to the connoisseurs of social status. Luther had translated the New Testament into German and made everyman his own interpreter. Similarly, he reduced the sacraments from seven to two (baptism and the Eucharist), making marriage, for example, a civil ceremony. Monasticism and clerical celibacy, he said, should be abolished, because everyone in some way was a priest. There was no special "call" to the priesthood. Everything that one did in life was a calling. Whatever the different emphases of other theologians, the inclination of what became known as Protestantism was clearly away from the separation of priesthood and laity and toward a reinfusion of spiritual values into everyday life, whether it took the form of Calvin's religious state in Geneva or John Bunyan's conviction that just beneath

14. The growing explicitness of monarchical political self-justification in theories of divine right and cultural self-justification in theories of heroic and epic literature that characterize the seventeenth century in Europe are paralleled on the visual plane not only by the court masques of the Stuarts, but also by the dwarfs, fools, and other court grotesques of the Spanish Hapsburgs. Shakespeare, with his unmatched theatrical irony, invariably casts the fools as elliptical wisemen, an inner reproach to monarchs who otherwise seem even grander by comparison. More than a tinge of this attitude shadows *Las Meninas,* although it is hard to think of Velázquez explicitly linking the monarch, the infanta, the grotesques, and himself as similar partakers in a grand social marginality on the order of 'If I were not Alexander, I would like to be Diogenes.' During the Restoration, Thomas Killigrew played the double roles of occasional fool to Charles II and full-time head of the King's Servants, one of the two officially licensed theaters. (The other was sponsored by the King's brother, the Duke of York.) On the simpler level, like the relation of television talk-show host to visiting comedian, the king's condescension to and protection of the fool is the humanizing touch that underlines the actual power.

the surface of the English countryside lay all the ultimate conflicts between God and Satan for the human soul. The Elect had to be identified in life in order to be prepared properly for heaven.

The medieval sense of a human transcendence required placing oneself into divine situations. For those who turned away from the "normal" social world, the desire for fame was expressed in a desire to be symbolic, to escape an individuality that was defined wholly in social and emotional terms. Fame in the eye of God required turning away from the body, the tangible, visible self, as well as from the gaze of other people that constitutes society. But the kinds of individuality that were being formulated in the seventeenth century, although often religiously based, stand in strong contrast to such a purely spiritual conception of human nature. All the general factors historians have discerned in the period—the erosion of monarchical power and the rise of Parliament in England, the growth of an individualism fostered by Protestant theology, the expansion of economic markets across Europe and around the world, the emergence of London as the largest city in the world (with the possible exception of Tokyo), a rise in the literacy rate that encouraged the growth of new modes of communication (including newspapers, mail service, circulating libraries, and cheap editions)—encourage a myriad of new ways for individuals to engage in activities and achieve status that had previously either been barred to them or not even existed. Depending on their angle of explanation, a historian might decide that one underlying social, economic, or political factor or trend is basic to such a transformation. But in a history of fame, we must point out the central enabling necessity of a change of self-conception that must accompany and often precedes the more obvious shifts in social, economic, and political organizations. In the kind of massive shift marked by the seventeenth century, the forces of psychic change clearly interweave with and often influence the forces of political change. The overthrow of kings requires not just an explicit political theory or a set of grievances but also a deep-seated conviction that kings *can* be overthrown; that their authority and power, their "true" fame, is not sufficient either to protect them or make them innately superior to anyone else. Thus matters of political theory as well the development of theater have their place in understanding how the seventeenth century in England particularly gave birth to the modern conception of a marketplace of fame in which all might sell their wares. Before verbal and visual media began to inundate the world with the names and faces of the famous, it was necessary that there be a new sense of what it meant to be an individual.

Eikon Basilike condemns those rebelling against royal authority for their ambition rather than for their disloyalty. Kingship, properly understood, it argues, is a transcendental individuality that subdues the otherwise incessant competition for preeminence and singularity, "the proud ostentation of men's abilities for invention and the vain affectation of variety for expressions in public prayer" (96). But Charles's effort at spiritual and political self-justification has little sensitivity to the growing conflict between the needs of the individual and the needs of the state that would become the crux of so much later political and social argument. He could not see that the royal oak was no longer the only tree in the forest striving for the heavens. By the eighteenth century, the rest of Europe would wake up to what England, with its more active and more popular theater, did much earlier: Kings are as various as people and must justify themselves by their actions rather than by their genealogy.

The word "individual" itself begins to appear with more frequency in English after the middle of the seventeenth century, often in not always positive contrast to "namelesse." With its implication of a core of personal distinctiveness yet visible to the world, it would have been a strange concept to use (except negatively) in the Middle Ages, since it seems sharply at odds with the Christian belief that the purest form of each person is the soul, which seamlessly links one with all other human beings before God. In some sense modern individuality, with its characteristic valuing and vaunting of completeness and self-sufficiency, is more akin to the preordained social self protected by the Roman *genius,* the personal star that Horace says every man has in the heavens. But in the seventeenth century that genius begins to be separated from ostentatiously famous (and Roman-style) careers and discussed instead as a general concept, to which a Christian sort of spiritual self-definition might be relevant as well.[15]

By seeking to reroot monarchical authority in Christian virtue, *Eikon Basilike* inadvertently implies that justification might also work in the opposite direction. In effect such an implication was at the root of the new politics, and two aspects can be distinguished: one linked to the way Renaissance artists were reshaping the forms of human self-presentation and the other to the Reformation redefinition of the role of spirituality in secular life. In the first—identity as an external continuity in history and law—I am perceived by others; in the second—identity as a continuity within—I perceive myself. In England particularly, out of this ferment over the place of individual self-awareness and "conscience" in determining one's allegiance to the state and to its religion, arose the beginnings of modern political philosophy in the writings of Thomas Hobbes and John Locke. Despite their explicit political inclinations, Hobbes to the monarchy and Locke to the Parliament, they both rested the source of authority in the people, the nation. On the cover of Hobbes's *Leviathan* (1651), published two years after the execution of Charles I, an enormous crowned body looms over the landscape, his form made up of individual heads. No longer merely part of a passive audience for the displays of monarchy, the seventeenth-century Englishman was seeking a more active role in rule. The place of kingship in the nation had become more a political question

---

15. For a concise consideration of the history of the concept, see Lukes's, *Individualism.* Raymond Williams in *Keywords* makes some acute comments on the history of usage, especially the distinction between *individualism* and *individuality* (133–36).

than a theological one, and so there was a need as well to develop a political philosophy, an explicit theory of mutual relations between king and subjects, rather than the arguments either from the Bible or the ancients or mere force of arms that had been common before. Society and the national had become concepts about which it was possible to generalize and theorize. The Englishman did not just accept the order he found himself in; he was beginning to argue about it.

Hobbes's argument, while emphasizing the importance of law as the basic structure of society, concentrates particularly on the self-awareness by which the individual represses unsocial desires for the good of others, much as the king rises above his private nature to act for the good of the state. Locke, in his later view of the contract by which monarch and subjects organize society, is more concerned with identity as a legal concept: Is the person standing before us today the same person who committed that crime before witnesses yesterday? Is there a continuity in self that goes beyond mere temporal sequence? But both similarly insist on the individual as the carrier of a personal continuity that might be called identity. Hobbes emphasizes the continuity of an active mind, while Locke explores the implications of continuous physical presence. But for both the individual is firmly on earth, within a society.

These two forms of individual identity still define our ongoing cultural argument between the demands of society and the demands of personal nature, the urge to be the same and the urge to be different. In both, the transcendental status that divine-right monarchs sought for themselves is turned against the idea of monarchy, subverting the belief that there was only one most famous person in the state by making that autonomy open to anyone bold enough to claim it. Louis XIV's establishment of royal patronage as the goal of all writers and artists holds off for a time in France the search for other roads to fame. But in England the execution of Charles I along with the political and military successes of Cromwell, the "private" man who had ruled without the sky falling in, left the growing impression that human aspiration need not depend on the monarch's approval to define its goals or its achievement. A year after Cromwell has been made Lord Protector, Andrew Marvell, taking on the voice of a foreign prince amazed at England's prosperity and strength, sings his unprecedented virtues:

> Where did he learn those Arts that cost us dear?
> Where below Earth, or where above the Sphere?
> He seems a King by long succession born,
> And yet the same to be a King does scorn.
> Abroad a King he seems, and something more,
> At home a Subject on the equal Floor.
>
> ("First Anniversary," 385–92).

The example was appealing, even to monarchs. By the end of the century Daniel Defoe will celebrate the Dutch-born William III not as a king so much as a person:

He needs no character but his own fame,
Nor any flattering titles, but his name. . . .
For fame of families is all a cheat,
'Tis personal virtue only makes us great.
—("The True-Born Englishman," 929–30, 1215–16).

Even for a king, Defoe implies, the awakening to the possibility of personal fame allows a freer access to the daily theater of politics and society. In just over two hundred years, we will have moved from Henry VIII and Elizabeth, identifying their personal interest with the interests of England, down to Edmund Burke, in the late eighteenth century, who tells the electors of Bristol that they voted for him personally, not for his willingness to reflect all their specific views.

These more gradual changes in the political sphere were reflected and stimulated by changing scientific attitudes toward knowledge in general and how it was acquired. Descartes, Galileo, Hobbes, Locke, Newton, Spinoza, Kepler, Leibnitz—throughout the seventeenth century appear a group of men who establish a tradition of the wise man, within the state, often interested in theological subjects, but whose main work is a systematic attempt to bring knowledge into an order that relies not on conceptions of divinity but on experiment and reason. Turning against the knowledge determined by precedent or religious doctrine, they searched for truth directly in front of them in the world, perceiving and testing it through the powers of human thought. In the late 1630s Descartes had written with resonant effect, "I think, therefore I am." The first principle of philosophy and understanding, he argued, was an affirmation of personal nature based on the self-conscious perception that one was essentially a being that thinks. As Locke was to write later, "Consciousness always accompanies thinking . . . in this alone consists *personal Identity, i.e.,* the sameness of a rational Being" (9). Aquinas and other medieval theologians had assumed that the end of philosophy was to know God through things. But Descartes among others decisively and influentially separated the order of things from the order of God. Since human consciousness—thinking—is the core of individual identity and since it is impossible to know God, we should instead discover and refine a host of new ways to know. In the traditional social order the world was a stage. But the new knowing would bring new freedom because it allowed the knower "to be a spectator rather than actor in all the comedies which were being played there" (50).

Without minimizing the distinctions among the group of great scientists who began appearing on the European scene toward the end of the sixteenth century and throughout the seventeenth century—the different ways they break away from, yet still remain attached to previous assumptions about, say, physiology and astronomy—their similarities are apparent. Descartes in some ways looms the largest because he is the most explicit about the man-centered interpretation that the new knowing requires. Like so many of the new wise men, Descartes chose in particular two objects of contemplation, the human body and the universe, and in both he sought to find coherences that he will have been the first to discern. "My design," he says in the *Discourse on Method,* "has never gone beyond trying to reform my own thoughts and to build on a foundation which is wholly my own" (38). Unlike Don Quixote, Descartes believes that preexisting books are only of limited use in this project. If they are relied on too heavily, they, like too much traveling, alienate the reader from the reality of his own country, which lies in front of him. Thus, seeking "no other science than that which I could find within myself or else in the great book of the world" (33), Descartes begins his plan of understanding.

Descartes's tone is simultaneously modest in its limitation of enquiry to what he can perceive and reason by himself and assertive in its clear assumption that he is the first man to begin at the beginning of true knowledge, sweeping aside, or at least putting in reserve, whatever has been thought and written about these subjects in the past. The *Discourse on Method* therefore includes few acknowledgments of the trailbreaking being done by other scientists in Descartes's own time or before. The main exception is William Harvey, whose treatise on the circulation of the blood Descartes cites approvingly, only to say that Harvey has remained too content to examine the phenomena of the body without exploring why it is the body works that way. For Descartes, the body is a machine and therefore understandable as a system of mechanical relationships. His exposition of its mechanical coherence may not be as moving as Johannes Kepler's description of the harmonies in the universe unperceived by most previous astronomers. But both discover an almost aesthetic unity of design in what they contemplate. Augustine's God was the audience that was the sufficient observer for all the actions of man. But the celebration of exploration and anatomizing so frequently illustrated by sixteenth-century engravers popularized the taste for explorations of mind as well as of space and matter. The God of Descartes or Kepler, to the extent that he plays a role at all in their human-centered perception, is a kind of consummate artist who creates intricate harmonies that men can discover on their own, becoming his appreciative audience and finding audiences themselves for their exposition of such true knowledge.

Thus throughout the seventeenth century, the political structure of countries was often changing less quickly than the psychic scope for the enlargement of personal will and identity. With wise men offering models of universal comprehension, actors of social self-awareness and manipulation, artists of aesthetic insight into the fame of the future, it is easy to understand how the old assumption of kingship as the only measure of true fame was in jeopardy. As avant-garde science was attempting to explain the harmonies of change, and that growing branch of Anglican Protestantism we call puritanism was arguing the greater claim of individual conscience over the coercion of social duty, the idea of fame and achievement was changing as well. On the one hand stood the lavish volumes of the genealogists and heralds, while on the other stood the increasing number of spiritual autobiographies, which all told the story of a discovery of a spirituality that exists in full interplay with the world, a kind of monastery within, which allowed a transcendence on earth beyond the material status of monarchs and aristocrats.

In a world that scientists and philosophers were beginning to see in dynamic motion rather than eternally and perfectly still, the individual was moving as well. Books on etiquette and courtesy (middle-class versions of earlier arguments over true nobility and the nature of the courtier) taught new men of wealth and talent how to behave in the higher social reaches they had attained or hoped to. A taste for character sketches was complemented by a tremendous expansion of biography, especially the lives of the great men of the new age, which would authenticate the country and its history. Villani's late fourteenth-century Latin compendium of the most famous citizens of Florence set the standards of local pride in a world before printing. But now such annotated lists of greatness could be even more broadly circulated. Thomas Fuller's *The Worthies of England* (1662), for example, the first full-scale compendium of English biography, followed the outline of Camden's *Britannia* by writing the lives of the great men county by county—just as saints had become the geniuses of place for little towns around the Mediterranean a thousand years before. Charles Perrault, the author of "Cinderella" and "Sleeping Beauty" and a great promoter of the superiority of modern to ancient literature, produced at the end of the century a two-volume *Hommes illustres qui ont paru en France pendant ce siècle* (1697, 1700); and Pierre Bayle's *Dictionnaire historique et critique* (1697), the first great blast of the intellectual movement that would be called the Enlightenment, was cast as a commentary on a series of exemplary biographies. Fame was infectious. Like the printers and engravers who shared in fame by promoting it, the genealogists, delineators of honors, biographers, and embryonic encyclopedists of the new fame sometimes obviously (by large pictures of themselves on the title page) and sometimes less overtly (by modestly saying they didn't work for personal fame) assert their eminence. Fuller provides a nicely rounded model of the "ends" of biography when he explains that he writes first for the glory of God, second to preserve the memory of the dead, third as examples to the living, fourth to entertain the reader, and finally "(which I am not ashamed publicly to profess) to procure some honest profit to myself" (1).

So many new mirrors and models could not help but have an evolutionary effect on social and political life. In less than a hundred years the political organization of England changed from an assertive divine-right monarchy to a commonwealth in which the legislative power of Parliament was virtually unchallenged. Fuller himself, writing shortly after the restoration of Charles II, laments the loss of so many records during the civil wars and apologizes for using the word "Parliament" as if it excluded the king. But his own book, with its detailing of the tangible virtues of England as well as the personal characters of its most worthy inhabitants, marks the shift of authority. Both the summoning of Charles II and the replacement in 1688 of James II by William III happened because the majority of the politically aware and powerful wished it to happen. Even though in both cases they could not really conceive of an England without the traditional sanction of monarchy, the king was in effect removed from his position as the sole determinant of honor and public value. Medieval imagery had made fame the often arbitrary gift of fortune. But with the new political and legal awareness of the late Renaissance, what had been seen as a gamble on the Wheel of Fortune became something to learn about and manipulate. The prime model for all aspiring behavior, all real fame, was still the aristocrat. The lavish consumption that marked aristocratic style, the fervent amateurism of aristocratic intelligence, and the power that aristocratic lineage entitled one to were the standards by which all other style, learning, and authority were judged.

In seventeenth-century theater the aristocrats had often sat on the stage, intermediaries between the audience and the world of the play. But the actors and playwrights and set designers and artists were themselves becoming the intermediaries in a society increasingly determined by a market economy in which gain and glory were becoming indistinguishable. The previously unquestioned value of being an aristocrat had to face a world of judging observers in which, in Hobbes's phrase, "true Value is no more than it is esteemed by others." Aristocracy, so used to considering its style a by-product of its status, now had to convince of status by its style. Those who longed for status at the top of the social pyramid ransacked past ages, particularly the chivalric and knightly, for even more elaborate devices. Books delineating the infinite degrees and accompanying visual standards of rank flourished. New coats of arms were designed and new portraits of the king commissioned to affirm loyalty. Because the aristocracy was no longer doing its old duty of heroic example and chivalric defense, many of those who deplored but tried to come to terms with the new political realities, including Hobbes, set to work devising a literary etiquette for the "true hero," whose example might restore the values and perhaps even the politics of the past.[16] Public poets like John Dryden considered a large part of their task to make aristocratic values explicit, so that they might be retaught to the class that had somehow forgotten them along with their special relation to the nation. But even among these monarchically inclined writers and playwrights, the aristocratic sanction was turning increasingly into a personal rather than a class distinction. Unlike the

16. In a manner similar to that of the American western film in the 1950s, the "heroic play" is an important feature of late seventeenth-century English drama both as an effort to define ideal heroism and as a mirror to contemporary political conflicts, especially those between the monarchy and the Parliament. For Hobbes's views, see "The Answer of Mr. Hobbes to Sir Will. D'Avenant's Preface Before Gondibert."

same effort two hundred years before, there was little promotion of a cult of knighthood at court. They were all too busy at the theater.

In the seventeenth-century decline of the English aristocracy as the emblematic national class, we watch as well the rise of an aristocratic sense of self that refuses to be judged by any standards the world values, together with an aristocratic perspective that views the operation of society from a vantage point on the highest hill. In these terms aristocracy is less a social and political category than a psychological or stylistic one, designating not money or power or lineage so much as character, sensibility, and "individuality." In more hierarchical societies Velázquez could consider his admission to a noble order as the crown of his career as a painter and Racine could give up writing plays as soon as he secured a court appointment as Louis XIV's royal historiographer. But in the England of Cromwell and Charles II, and of Milton, Dryden, Defoe, and Pope, the contestants were not just a hereditary aristocracy with a few "new men" whose destinies were linked to their patrons, but an increasing crowd of men and women of talent and ambition who, through the intellectual and spiritual self-sanctioning the age was beginning to allow, were making emphatic social and political claims. In France the political usefulness of public monuments to stir men of ambition to emulation remained vital because of Louis XIV's sponsorship of the state's "glory" as embodied in himself. But in England, a society increasingly held together by cash, competition, and contract instead of the old blood ties, the desire for such recognition has become much more generalized. The process had ironically begun when the efforts of James I and Charles I to solidify social and political hierarchy had backfired. Their inept promotion of honors and status may have, as Lawrence Stone says, created "hardening lines of social cleavage" (19), but they also undermined the moral justification for aristocratic privilege. With this corruption or at least watering down of the entitled aristocracy, an alternate cultural aristocracy, neither economically oppressive nor politically hostile to rising talent, found it easier to emerge. "Aristocrat" in this expanding sense abutted and coincided with the inward assurance and "conscience" of the many Protestant groups that arose in the course of the civil wars. Whatever their differences, their effect on English psychic life tended in the same direction—away from hierarchy and toward individuality, away from tradition and toward sensibility. Among actual aristocrats, on the other hand, the urge to justify one's singularity might express itself in antisocial actions that spurned the standards of society entirely. On the crudest level, numbers of the defeated royalist captains of Charles I took to the forests and backroads of England to become dashing highwaymen and even in the Restoration never tried to regain their old social status. In more rarefied realms, the figure of the rake, the rebel against God and man first depicted in sixteenth-century Spanish drama as Don Juan, reappeared in both England and France as the forerunner of a libertine philosophy of freedom that stressed the unnaturalness of social codes. When that style of individualism was united to a literary perspective, we find the Earl of Rochester, in his own time considered by both the outraged and the fascinated as a kind of Satan, and we shall later discover his late-blooming inheritor, Lord Byron.[17]

By the end of the century, aristocracy was becoming such an abstract aspect of identity that every man might be one, at least in his heart. Unlike Perkin Warbeck, he had no need to go to war to prove his sincerity, since the urge toward an aristocracy of the spirit often also entailed a desire to retreat to some special nonsocial place and there leave the growing competition behind. Throughout the seventeenth century moralists cite the figure of Herostratus (as had Chaucer) as an example of the wickedness that was done for fame. But they do not contrast Herostratus's burning of the Temple of Diana with the more legitimate military and political conquests of Alexander. They lament instead the architects of the temple, whose names, they say, are lost, although the destructive name and bad fame of Herostratus lives on. In another period, such contrast between honorable and false glory would support a Christian aversion from the urge of fame. But in the writings of seventeenth-century literary men, it invokes instead the possibility of a fame other than that of military or political power. From this angle Herostratus is not Alexander's opposite but his parody, for both are destroyers, while the fame of the architect is that of the builder and the civilizer: "To be namelesse in worthy deed exceeds an infamous history" (282), Thomas Browne could still write in 1658.[18] But the time for such a high-minded ideal was growing short. No longer could a moral or spiritual position be made simply equivalent to a praiseworthy lack of self-consciousness. In the new world of publicity, even the reclusive needed a public format if they wanted to have an effect. The scope for will to effect personal and social change was opening every day. (If the king can be executed, what can't be done?) The new problem would be vested in the individual: If you don't succeed, it may just be your own fault. Now that there was intricate advice on how to be a good courtier, or a diplomat, or a ruler, it was getting more and more difficult to excuse

17. Rochester's brief life (1647–1680) is a fascinating epitome of the situation of the English aristocrat at a time when the aristocracy is losing its symbolic centrality for the nation. On his life, see Greene, *Lord Rochester's Monkey*, and on his work, *Complete Poems*, ed. Vieth. Toward the end of the seventeenth century in England, engravings of criminals (including one famous for picking Oliver Cromwell's pocket) and oddities (like the man who could eat stones) begin appearing along with biographies detailing their crimes and eccentricities. But it is not really until the publications of William Caulfield in the late eighteenth century—such as *Portraits of Remarkable Persons* (1794) and *Blackguardiana* (1795)—that such figures get a biographical dictionary of their own.

18. Browne's essay *Hydriotaphia, or Urne Buriall* (1658) was inspired by the discovery of Roman funerary urns in Norfolk and is a wonderful meditation on death and aspiration as they are understood in the classical and Christian world: "To subsist in lasting Monuments, to live in their productions, to exist in their names, and praedicaments of *Chymera's*, was large satisfaction unto old expectations, and made one part of their *Elyziums*. But all this is nothing in the Metaphysics of true belief" (285).

oneself for failure by invoking God or Fate or Fortune. Individualism, with its new opportunities, brought new anxieties as well. Man could now more freely explore the world and understand the universe. But both seemed much bigger places than they ever had before.

The Sincerity of Solitude

> Ambition is far from being a Vice in Poets, that 'tis almost impossible for them to succeed without it. Imagination must be raised, by a desire of Fame, to a desire of Pleasing. And they whom in all Ages Poets have endeavour'd most to please, have been the Beautiful and the Great.
> —DRYDEN, Preface to *The State of Innocence*

> Famous he was in Heaven, on Earth less known;
> Where glory is false glory, attributed
> To things not glorious, men not worthy of fame.
> —MILTON, *Paradise Regained* [19]

Along with the sense of personal opportunity that was fed by the social and political changes brewing in seventeenth-century England came a new sense of uncertainty as well. I have been stressing the influence of models of spiritual and political self-sufficiency that were affecting England. But the transition from monarchs to individualists, from writers supported by patrons to writers supported by audiences, was hardly very abrupt. Especially after the Restoration of Charles II, there were still many who identified the cultural elite with the political elite. The older model of the artist's patronage by the great thus survived and even flourished. Although there were now more writers who, like Dryden, were at some pains to keep reminding the aristocracy of its ideals and true business, aristocratic support still linked the names of artist and patron together for an admiring posterity as mutual celebrants of national glory. The patron guaranteed the social virtues of art by being the ideal audience, authenticating artistic value by his recognition that it and its maker were somehow beyond class.

But the increasingly popular French word for fame, *renommée,* literally "renamed," indicates the potential separation of the writer from his royal, aristocratic, or merely wealthy patrons to achieve a status of his own. One aspect of this new status was mocked as early as 1663 by Samuel Butler, when he says that every book now published features "the praises of the

---

19. *The State of Innocence* is Dryden's versified and dramatized version of Milton's *Paradise Lost.* The Preface is dedicated to Mary of Modena, the wife of the Duke of York, Charles II's brother and the future James II. At this point in *Paradise Regained,* Satan is chiding Jesus because so many others had achieved so much at his age (Alexander, Scipio, Pompey, Caesar). In answer, Jesus speaks of Job. For some shrewd and far-reaching comments on Milton's conflict over fame, see Grossman, "Milton's sonnet 'On the Late Massacre in Piemont'."

Author, penn'd / By himself, or wit-ensuring friend, / The Itch of Picture in the Front, / With Bays, and wicked Rhyme upon't" (*Hudibras,* I, 647–50). In such a satiric jab at the visual self-promotion of authors we can begin to glimpse the evolution of the artist and writer from the socially oriented, patron-pleasing creature of most of human history to the artist and writer of the present, who seeks acceptance only on his own terms and who characterizes himself as an outsider. Of course, this separation from society is a myth, and one easy to undermine by pointing at the care artists and writers take with their own careers. But it is a myth stronger than any of the facts of the situation, and one that has conditioned the way both artists and their audiences view what it is that art does.

The patron may still have been accorded a measure of social obeisance, but the nature of patronage had changed. Charles Churchill in 1763 satirizes the corruption of Grub Street writers and, looking back in nostalgia, wonders,

> [I]s this the land
> Where Merit and Reward went hand in hand
> Where heroes, parent-like, the Poet view'd,
> By whom they saw their glorious deeds renew'd;
> Where Poets, true to honour, tun'd their lays,
> And by their patrons sanctify'd their praise? ("The Author," 50–56).

Even by the mid-seventeenth century writers who allied themselves with patrons and praised aristocratic virtues had already become more censorious. As the system of politics became more representative, the patron became a source of public appointments rather than of exclusive support. Locke, for example, lived for most of his life in the service of the Earl of Shaftesbury or in sinecures owing to Shaftesbury's influence until the appearance of the second edition of the *Essay Concerning Human Understanding* in 1694 (with his name on the title page) made his name known to a larger audience. Pope, with the publication by subscription of his translations of the *Iliad* and the *Odyssey* (when he was in his mid-thirties) became the first English writer to make an independent income from his writing. And Samuel Johnson in the midcentury refused Lord Chesterfield's offer to have the *Dictionary* dedicated to him with a ringing denunciation of the whole system of patronage and the encumbrance it was on the writer—which Boswell reprinted in full in the *Life of Johnson* as one of his proudest moments. No longer would the patron assume his Renaissance role as the only audience whose opinion counted, the ideal to be celebrated, whose money and power released artists and intellectuals alike from a need to depend on the Church. The new audiences were less defined, but they offered the promise of an even greater independence: the "fit audience" who would understand the artist's true meaning; "the public" whose new literacy and increased income would guarantee widespread support; posterity, an audience untainted by the present; and, finally, a noninstitutional God, whose disestablished gaze might infuse all of the other three. Each in its different way took the artist away from the social support of either institutional religion or the patron and turned him into a solitary forerunner of human sensibility, whose isolation sought out his audience not as a theatrical social entity, but as a collection of individuals like himself. Artists and composers require the support of patronage much longer. But Johnson's letter to Chesterfield, like Churchill's nostalgia, marks the end of an entente between writers and patrons in England that had been unraveling for over a century. Ben Jonson, in the first decade of the seventeenth century, writes a poem celebrating the true aristocratic virtues embodied in the character and family of the Sidneys. In the poem, Jonson sits at the Sidney table among other retainers and servants, toasting their virtue and the magnanimity of their hospitality. In the last decade of the century, John Dryden writes a similar poem, celebrating similar virtues as the backbone of England. This time, however, the person honored is not an aristocrat, but a country justice of the peace, Dryden's cousin, who, appropriately enough, is also named John Dryden.

In the last few pages, I realize that I have frequently used "artist" as a general term, because by our own time the special fame and status of artists of all sorts has become familiar. But in the seventeenth-century erosion of the upper-class claim to central cultural importance, it is writers who primarily establish a status that is superior to the temporal power that nominally employs them. The tradition they drew upon might be called Protestant in origin, although its influence was already much more general. The Reformation had emphasized the spiritual authority of the unadorned word in opposition to the power of centralized and historically validated institutions like the Church and its priesthood. As Descartes extended the argument, it was the ability to innovate in language that separated human beings from animals. To this formulation, Hobbes added an emphasis on language as the binder of all social behavior, and Locke emphasized language as part of the contract that members of a society willfully enter with each other. As Charles I (or his author) in *Eikon Basilike* attempted to justify monarchical authority by appealing to the sanction of a God whose medium is language, so the wise man or poet whose picture appears prominently on the frontispiece felt impelled to search for a transcendent (although not necessarily religious) truth that would compensate for the personal assertion of his quest. Thus writers of all sorts throughout the seventeenth and eighteenth centuries can with virtually one voice assert their overwhelming desire for literary fame at the same time that they trumpet their personal insignificance before the innate, natural, or spiritual truth they have discovered.

It is characteristic of the world that comes into being after the Renaissance that, as each new expansion of literacy occurs, as each new change in the political or social order happens or is thought to have happened, writers especially become uncertain about whom it is they are addressing and how they should speak to be best heard. The search for, in Milton's phrase, the "fit audience . . . though few" (*Paradise Lost,* VII, 31) is a recurrent preoccupation of the period. The twin dangers are the theatrical desire to please the crowd, on one side, and the retreat to a self-regarding narcissism, on the other. For writers who had to make a living, the need to find oneself in the mirror of an audience, while trying not to be a posturer or performer, was a difficult task without some greater sanction for what they were doing. The Earl of Rochester, who had been Dryden's patron, mocked the playwright and poet laureate for his attempts to please the crowd. Why do you need their praise? he asked. All that is necessary is the approval of a few judicious and trustworthy friends ("An Allusion to Horace," 120–26). Rochester himself takes the way of the solitary aristocrat—like Sir Walter Raleigh before and Lord Byron later—who uses his writings to gather support from an audience beyond the visual immediacy of his courtly self-dramatizing. His poems are published only after his death. Before then, they were circulated in manuscript—an emblem of his disdain for a larger and therefore less discriminating audience.

But for the swelling ranks of professional writers, the question of their appeal to an audience was not as easy to evade, and it was becoming increasingly clear that postures of self-sufficiency were most effective when they were embodied in books. The "solitudes and sufferings" of Charles I in *Eikon Basilike* were still the privilege of the king; otherwise, "the private man by his solitary abilities" had less to offer than "the joint abilities and concurrent gifts of many learned and godly men" (97). But such an officially limited spirituality is countered in the works of Milton, Pascal, and others by an unofficial and personal spirituality sanctioned by a direct relation to God—essentially unmediated by earthly institutions. Solitude, whether that of the aristocrat or the saint or the inspired poet, is a support for singularity, and in the one-to-one relation of reader and book, the message of singularity is carried by the situation itself. Bound by the book, readers constitute a secret fraternity, a "fit audience" already formed.

An intriguing image of the situation appears early in the seventeenth century when, between 1614 and 1617, the manifesto of the Rosicrucian Brotherhood appeared in nine editions and four languages. It was entitled *Fama Fraternitatis (The Fame of the Brotherhood)* and told of a secret organization of wise men that was now opening its doors to all who shared its beliefs. Almost immediately, books and pamphlets appeared either denouncing the Rosicrucians or praising them for their stand against greed and the self-seeking of philosophers who think that the point of knowledge is the ability to make gold from base metal. To this day no one knows the real author of the manifesto, why precisely it was written, or whether it might not have been an elaborate hoax. But if we are in quest not of precision but of images and events that can let us penetrate to an age's attitudes toward fame, the *Fama Fraternitatis* manifesto and the reaction of its readers has all the necessary ingredients. As printing was opening the eyes of Europe to worlds and people previously unheard of or unseen, so the Rosicrucian manifesto is the evidence of a community of book readers who all want to be in on the tremendous secret of how book reading itself links together all the wise men of the world in a "fame" beyond all boundaries of class or nation. Through the part-material, part-intangible medium of the book, then, the self-enhancing solitude that was the monarch and the aristocrat's social legacy could be transformed into a spiritual and individualistic mode available to anyone who wrote. If assertion was imaged in visible ostentation, then the book and its words displayed a trope of humbleness, especially when their content was explicitly religious and the writer, like the publican in Jesus' parable, might hope for his just reward: "[F]or every one that exalted himself shall be abased; and he that humbleth himself shall be exalted" (Luke, 18:14).

Perhaps the most famous line about fame in English literature we owe to John Milton, in whose career and work the seventeenth-century conflict over the charge of fame seeking is illustrated at its most elaborate. In *Lycidas* (1638), an elegy for a dead young poet, Milton asks why anyone should write poetry:

> *Fame* is the spur that the clear spirit doth raise
> (That last infirmity of Noble mind)
> To scorn delights, and live laborious days (70–72).

"Last" here means final or only infirmity, echoing Augustine's conclusion that the love of praise is the most difficult of all imperfections to expunge from oneself. But Milton's mode here is less Augustinian than Petrarchan. It is worthy to strive for literary fame on earth, although the shadow of death is always present:

> But the fair Guerdon when we hope to find,
> And think to burst out into sudden blaze,
> Comes the blind *Fury* with th' abhorred shears,
> And slits the thin-spun life (73–76).

Even the chivalric reward of the "Guerdon," like the favor a lady gives a knight for winning a tournament, is abruptly snatched away by the unforeseeable fatality of death. But, although the prize may have vanished, fame itself does not necessarily die with the death of the aspirant:

> Fame is no plant that grows on mortal soil . . .
> But lives and spreads aloft by those pure eyes
> And perfect witness of all-judging *Jove* (79, 82–83).

True fame, in the Petrarchan way, comes in Heaven, but it also is reflected by enhanced fame on earth, just as Milton's own poem participates in a tradition of elegies that celebrate the special status of poetry and the special fellowship of poets. Jove is the audience that validates poetic aspiration and, because it is Jove rather than God, it is a validation that can occur on earth as well as in Heaven, after one is dead. A few years later, Milton writes of his own self-consciousness of a writer's destiny:

> [A]n inward prompting which now grew daily upon me, that by labor
> and intent study (which I take to be my portion in this life) joined

with the strong propensity of nature, I must perhaps leave something
so written to aftertimes, as they should not willingly let it die (668).

These words appear in one of his early pamphlets against the episcopal
government of the Anglican Church—*The Reason of Church Government*
(1642), published when he is about thirty-three—to explain why he has
turned from his dreams of writing "to the adorning of my native tongue."
Because of the times, he must leave the "calm and pleasing solitariness" of
poetry and serve God by creating powerful arguments in prose against
those he believes to be destroying his country and its church. Whereas
poets are licensed to speak of themselves in their works, the business of
prose is more public and therefore cannot justify the same sort of personal
assertion. Civic and religious duty require a firm subordination of self to
the truth one seeks to demonstrate. Thus through the pamphlets Milton
writes in the twenty or so years he participates in the English Revolution as
publicist, apologist, and, in Cromwell's government, as Secretary of Foreign
Tongues, runs a counterstrain of what he might have done if he had not
chosen the world of politics and "the cool element of prose" rather than
that of poetry. While the poet strives for eternal fame, he will restrict himself to his own country and his "mother dialect":

> That what the greatest and choicest wits of Athens, Rome, or modern
> Italy, and those Hebrews of old did for their country, I, in my propor-
> tion, with this over and above of being a Christian, might do for mine;
> not caring to be once named abroad, though perhaps I could attain to
> that, but content with these British islands as my world (668).

His goals are less personal than national. As he writes in the preface to
Eikonoklastes:

> Neither was it fond ambition or the vanity to get a name, present or
> with posterity, by writing against a king. I never was so thirsty after
> fame nor so destitute of other hopes and means, better and more cer-
> tain to attain it (781).

It is an attitude, as we have seen, that reaches back to Chaucer's *Retraction* in its effort to ensure that all literary words are the reflection of the
Word. But the praise of solitude, and the desire for no audience other than
the audience of God, has a problematic ring in a world of print and propaganda, making Christian humbleness chime oddly with classical ambition.

Because he devotes himself so thoroughly to God's truth in both prose
and poetry at the same time that he is steeped in classical language and
literature, Milton's work and career concisely express the intertwined
classical (and aristocratic) ideals of the public man and the Christian (and
saintly) ideals of the private man in the early seedtime of modern individualism. Almost thirty years after *Lycidas*, Milton is spared the retribution
of Charles II's government for his part in the execution of Charles I, and
he returns from pamphleteering to poetry with two great works, *Paradise
Lost* and *Paradise Regained,* that explore the question of fame first through

the misguided ambition of Satan, then through the ideal ambition of Jesus. Neither poem is dedicated to any specific patron. They are, he says, inspired by a divine muse, who justifies his authority to praise in "unpremeditated verse" an authority beyond the world. It is a new role for the writer. No longer performing before a great man or an immediate audience, instead he is private, "in darkness, and with dangers compast round, / And solitude; yet not alone" (*Paradise Lost,* VII, 27–28).

As a young man Milton had aspired to write an epic poem and wondered "what king or knight before the conquest might be chosen in whom to lay the pattern of a Christian hero" (*Reason of Church Government,* 668), deciding at different times to center the work on Alfred, the scholar-king, or Arthur, the model of Christian chivalry. But in *Paradise Lost* and *Paradise Regained,* he turns away from royalist efforts to identify Christian heroism with the warrior aristocracy. Instead he characterizes Satan as an epic showoff—the distilled essence of Achilles, Odysseus, Aeneas, the Arthurian knights, and the national heroes of the Renaissance. Rebel against God, competitor with Christ for God's favor, enemy and betrayer of man to enhance his own theatrical self-assertion—Satan's major flaw in *Paradise Lost* is that he measures everything by its outward nature rather than its inward essence. Satan always vaunts, always plays to an audience. Deluded totally by the snares of ostentation, he is an emblem of "all who in vain things / Built thir fond hopes of Glory or lasting fame, / Or happiness in this or th'other life; / All who have thir reward on Earth . . . / Naught seeking but the praise of men . . . empty as thir deeds" (III, 448–454). The real heroism, the true glory, belongs to private, domestic individuals like Adam and Eve, whose actions are virtually the opposite of aristocratic and epic display. When Milton comes to the scene of the Fall itself, he says it is a "tragic" story he must tell, but one "Not less but more Heroic" than those told in the *Iliad,* the *Odyssey* and the *Aeneid* (IX, 6, 14). Uninterested in writing about wars, "hitherto the only Argument / Heroic deem'd," he recounts instead "the better fortitude / Of Patience and Heroic Martyrdom," and turns his back on all chivalric display as "Not that which justly gives Heroic name / To Person or to Poem" (28–29, 31–32, 40–41). The implicit humanist attack against aristocratic and knightly fame here has clearly come out into the open; the Augustinian division between the two cities has become a direct conflict. The hero no longer adds Christian virtue to his other accomplishments in the world; instead the Christian sense of self is the core of whatever he hopes to achieve, and the martyrdom that had defined the outer limit of the Christian attack on classical fame becomes nationalized, politicized, and domesticated.

By insisting that the actions of Adam and Eve are heroic, Milton sets their private and domestic virtue in the lists against the ostentation of Satan, which unites the epic hero of the past with the self-centered entrepreneur of the present. But, unlike so many of his philosophic ancestors, Milton also insists on the aggressiveness *in the world* of the private heroism he celebrates. Cromwell's career had shown that the efficient wielding of political power had nothing to do with the fortunes of birth or riches. The assurance of spiritual sanction that animated those who warred against the monarchy forced conscience and personal virtue into the streets, where it became a spiritual individualism that might create a new commonwealth. From their different positions, both Hobbes and Milton saw that the new age was one of individuals. But while Hobbes considered the essence of individuality to be competitive and self-preserving, Milton tried to show that it might also be communal and self-sacrificing.

When an artistic and spiritual fame that is separate from social demands yet demands social status, the question of narcissism becomes central. When Eve in *Paradise Lost* looks into a pool and wonders what beautiful being it is she sees there, she is expressing a sentiment that is pure only in Eden, and her desire to be appreciated by Adam for her integrity and self-sufficiency obviously reflects Milton's own aims as a writer. Yet this same desire to be appreciated is of course also the aspect of character most vulnerable to the attack of Satan, himself racked with a sense of injured merit, unappreciated by God, less preferred than Christ. Guised as the serpent, he therefore not only praises Eve's beauty, but also slyly points to the smallness of the audience in Eden who can appreciate it. She would be universally admired, he says, but here only the rude beasts and one man have the chance:

> Who sees thee? (and what is one?) who shouldst be seen
> A Goddess among Gods, ador'd and serv'd
> By Angels numberless, thy daily Train (IX, 546–48).

Caught by Satan's appeal to her desire to have her beauty more well-known, Eve falls as a lesson to all those, including Milton himself, who would seek more admirers than the "fit audience . . . though few." The sin of Satan is not pride so much as an unquenchable desire for more and more appreciators, and a ravaging envy of anyone whom he thinks is celebrated in his stead.

By his commitment to an active spiritual virtue Milton has made the Christian paradox of public humbleness or the fame of private life even more acute than it was through the Middle Ages. In *Paradise Regained,* the paradox occupies center stage. In this retelling of the temptations in the wilderness, Jesus is a private and solitary man—"obscure / Unmarkt, unknown"—who has accomplished "deeds / Above Heroic, though in secret done, / And unrecorded left through many an Age" (I, 24–25, 14–16). Playing on the urge of Jesus to do "public good," Satan first presents himself as an admirer who, although evil, has something to learn from his example. Then, twitting Jesus for aspiring to greatness even though he is lowborn, Satan offers wealth. But Jesus refuses the offer along with the power and praise it implies. Even being a king, he says, is filled with boredom and lies, far better to enhance "the inner man, the nobler part" (II, 477) and reign within yourself. Satan rebounds with an argument like that he used on Eve. By your age Alexander, Scipio, and Pompey had done great deeds known to all:

> . . . wherefore deprive
> All Earth her wonder at thy acts, thyself
> The fame and glory, glory the reward
> That sole excites to high attempts the flame
> Of most erected spirits . . . (III, 23–27).

But Jesus continues his refusal to accept any fame that is dependent on an audience, even when that fame happens to be called glory:

> For what is glory but the blaze of fame,
> The people's praise, if always praise unmixt?
> And what the people but a herd confus'd,
> A miscellaneous rabble, who extol
> Things vulgar, and well weigh'd, scarce worth the praise? (III, 47–51).

Not soldiers and conquerors, but the just man, who seeks to be "singularly good," is truly worthy: "Famous he was in Heaven, on Earth less known; / Where glory is false glory, attributed / To things not glorious, men not worthy of fame" (III, 68–70). Job and Socrates, who suffered alone for truth, are the true heroes, while all who say they strive for fame really seek only words of praise, unrelated to their virtue or their deeds.[20]

Satan then offers worldly power and wealth to Jesus in return for his worship. But again Jesus refuses: His kingdom, he says, is not a monarchy in which one man rules and he need not hurry its coming. Now, Satan finally believes he has understood the true desires of his adversary. He takes away the glorious panorama of Rome and the kingdoms of political power and shows instead Athens, the city of intellect:

> Be famous then
> By wisdom; as thy Empire extend,
> So let extend thy mind o'er all the world (IV, 221–23).

Then, in a passage that has upset generations of critics, Jesus seems to reject all of classical philosophy, preferring the Bible to Greek literature and Roman political thought. Exasperated, Satan asks him why he is in the world at all and takes him back to the wilderness where he found him, giving him a few bad dreams as a parting malediction. The next morning finding Christ again unruffled, Satan briefly tries the third temptation—will God save him from death?—and again Christ refuses to be tempted. Satan

---

20. In answer, Satan slyly protests that God himself seeks glory through the praise of men. No, responds Jesus, God acts only to impart his goodness to all. The glory we give him is merely our thanks: "The slightest, easiest, readiest recompense / From them who could return him nothing else" (III, 128–29). The distinction is analogous to one that might be made between a sterile narcissism that seeks only applause and a fruitful narcissism in which self-awareness leads one to better serve others. In eighteenth-century terms, the latter is the self-love that can generate social virtue (in Pope's *Essay on Man*) or the self-interest that can benefit others (in Adam Smith's *The Wealth of Nations*).

has lost, paradise has been regained, and angels come to refresh Christ, cheering him on until "hee unobserv'd / Home to his Mother's house private return'd" (IV, 638–639).

Paradise Regained gives a concise statement of the late seventeenth-century connection of the idea of fame to a new and persuasive definition of the individual, not as a member of a particular class but as a communicant with God. In the chivalric definition of fame, private pleasures and private qualities were a deviation from heroic ostentation and visible status. But by the late seventeenth century in England, privacy had become the emblem of a fame that asserted its superiority in Christian commitment as well as in patriotism. Milton makes the Gospel Jesus, who evades fame, into the new model for human nature in general and for the writer in particular, in whose books the theatrical orations of the classical past can be morally overturned. The sincere solitude of Jesus, like that of the writer, is a stillpoint to which others are drawn, a prelude in its way to that of the self-sufficient adventurer of the eighteenth century—Robinson Crusoe on his island or George Washington with his eyes fixed on some nameless destiny. Clearly, the pose of solitude will become a useful weapon in the age of democratic revolutions, for it is the image of a self-ratification that cares little for the burdensome past or the noisy present.[21] In *Samson Agonistes,* Milton's last work, the celebrity Dalila (Delilah) claims for herself ("I shall be nam'd among the famousest / Of Women") is mockingly contrasted with the "eternal fame" that Samson's annihilation of the Philistines has brought to himself and Israel. A turning toward the self is no longer a diversion from either the public fame of the upper classes or the spiritual fame of the saint and the martyr.

In *Paradise Lost* Milton had mocked the philosophers who hope to become gods through suicide. But in *Samson Agonistes,* Samson's suicide is a personal act that yet has both a spiritual and a social dimension. The chorus in the play compares him to the phoenix, "that self-begott'n bird. . . That no second knows nor third" (1699–1701). Throughout the Middle Ages and into the Renaissance, the phoenix had been the emblem of kings, the sign both of dynastic succession as well as of the legal and theological doctrine that the individual king may die but kingship goes on

21. The use of Jesus as a talismanic figure whose invocation can exonerate one from the crassness of seeking fame and success on earth is constant into the twentieth century. For a characteristically complex turn on this invocation, see the note Cotton Mather wrote in his diary when, for the second time, his candidacy for the presidency of Harvard had been rejected by the corporation: "I rejoice, I rejoice, I feel a secret Joy in it that I am thus conformed unto Him who was despised and rejected of men" (Silverman, *Mather,* 391). Not long before, Mather had solicited membership in the Royal Society by simultaneously inundating its officials with curious "scientific" observations while proclaiming his "unworthiness" (254). Compare the response of his father, who had left the Harvard presidency some years before after preaching a final sermon to the students to expect not honor from their service to Christ, but "rather to be *Despised and Rejected of Men;* rather to have all manner of *Indignities* heaped upon you" (178). For an intricate and suggestive exposition of the forces of abnegation and assertion in Mather's ideas of individual nature, see also Bercovitch, *Puritan Origins of the American Self.*

eternally. But in the period after the English civil wars such an emblem suits much better with the double life of the individual, who mediates between the demands of the social and the spiritual order. Milton's version is grand, heroic, and largely unconnected with any immediate context. As he writes of the phoenix, "though her body die, her fame survives, / A secular bird [through] ages of lives" (1706–1707). But his definition of appropriate fame is reflected as well in a lighter but no less compelling story written by someone who identified himself much more closely with a hierarchical social order—"Cinderella" by Charles Perrault, who has previously appeared in these pages as the great publicist of the glory of the age of Louis XIV. In Perrault's story, of course, Cinderella's sisters rely on her advice and good taste to help them make a mark in the fashionable world, while her own beauty remains unknown. Then, by the intervention of her fairy godmother (muse and genius combined?), she can go to the great ball and appear as an unknown beauty. She loses the slipper, the prince searches the kingdom for the foot that fits, and then raises her to the status she deserves.[22]

Pope, Swift, and Franklin: *The Stage of the Book*

Much better it is, certainly, at some times, to endeavour to grow wise at home in private; then by the hasty divulgation of such things, to the knowledge whereof you have attained with vast labour, to stir up tempests that may deprive you of your Leasure and Quiet for the future.   —WILLIAM HARVEY, Epistle Dedicatory to *Anatomical Exercitations* (1653)

Why did I write? What sin to me unknown
Dipt me in Ink, my Parents', or my own?
As yet a Child, nor yet a Fool to Fame,
I lisp'd in Numbers, for the Numbers came. . . .
I sought no homage from the Race that write;
I kept, like *Asian* Monarchs, from their sight.
        —ALEXANDER POPE, "Epistle to Dr. Arbuthnot" (1735)

By the end of the seventeenth century the book was defining itself as a prime new place of fame, not (like the stage) tied to the world of political and military action, but somehow hovering above it, judging it, and finding it deficient. In their different ways, both Perrault's fable of social mobility and Milton's dramatization of the contest between Satan and Jesus under-

22. The original versions of Perrault's stories are often very unlike the nursery stories we know in English. On Perrault's career in cultural politics, see Ranum, *Artisans of Glory,* and Soriano, *Le Dossier Charles Perrault.*

line the mingled anticipation and apprehension of the writer at the end of the seventeenth century. In the future lay a world that would be open to the exercise of individual will in ways virtually unparalleled in European history. No wonder that William Blake at the end of the eighteenth century thought that Milton was "of the Devil's party without knowing it" ("The Marriage of Heaven and Hell," 124). By then, after the American and French revolutions, Satan could be recast as the rebel against God's arbitrary power who had been given a bad press in the centuries of monarchical and paternal control. But Milton's awareness of his complicity in Satan's assertion is hardly as unknowing as Blake believes, for he is well aware that it comes uncomfortably close to the pride of the writer, alone with himself, imagining worlds. Only by paying tribute to the inspiration of God's heavenly muse can the blind and solitary poet, like the Jesus he celebrates ("Private, unactive, calm, contemplative, / Little suspicious to any King"), qualify what in another mood is an exuberant poetic celebration of "my advent'rous song, / That with no middle flight . . . pursues / Things unattempted yet in Prose or Rhyme" (*Paradise Regained,* II, 81–82; *Paradise Lost,* I, 13–16).

By calling on the muse, the writer becomes at least rhetorically a transmitter of poetic language, a conduit for divine guidance (since no one invokes the muse to talk to himself). Whether the muse is pagan or Christian, her appearance displaces attention away from the writer and toward the message. In this sense the Renaissance reemphasis on the invocation of the muse, with all its classical allusions, marks another effort to go beyond the craftsman's emphasis on the work rather than the maker to dramatize instead the artist's special connection with a truth unavailable to his audience. Alexander Pope (1688–1744) is perhaps the last major English poet to invoke the muse as a source of inspiration by whose force the poet can go beyond his mortal self to write for the moment with the power and insight of an immortal being. Later in the eighteenth century, the muse will be forgotten, except as a mere flourish. By then the poem no longer needs an extraterrestrial sanction, for it is important primarily as a production of the writer, an element in his career. Even when it is presented as inspired, as many Romantic poems are, the inspiration comes from within.

The vital change from the classical to the modern view of artistic fame is thus the loss of the patron as the touchstone of artistic identity and his replacement by the critic, and the loss of the muse as the source of inspiration and her replacement by the artist's own sensibility. In England at least Dryden lays the groundwork for this change by establishing the professional writer as someone with a special insight into the institutions and traditions of his country. Dryden still works under a patronage system, even though he often treats that system ironically. But with the eighteenth century, and especially with a figure like Pope, admired all over Europe as well as in England, the writer becomes a member of what might be called a language class or, as Locke called it, a "republic of letters" that understands writing as a tool of class power for itself rather than for others. The class to which patrons belonged was no longer perceived by writers, artists, or the audience in general as having any special claim to identity with the essence of national culture. Individuals might still be courted for their ability to pay and be praised as part of the bargain, but as social inspirations their power was quickly lapsing. Patrons were on the way to becoming employers, if they existed at all. Until the eighteenth century, the poet's assertion had been, 'I create works that last through time,' and the patron's response had been 'Make me your subject, or at least an important bystander.' But with the eighteenth century the artist himself becomes the recipient of that lasting fame, and the search for it becomes one of his prime subjects and vexations.

With the transformation of the European and particularly the English economy that characterizes the eighteenth century, the old assertion of working for fame rather than pay—which separated artists from mere artisans and connected them to the aristocracy—also assumes a new significance. Since aristocrats as well as merchants and tradesmen were taking part in the creation of the new economy of money and extended credit that would foster the expansion of European imperialism, the artist's desire for fame rather than money could have either an archaic or a revolutionary air. To the extent that writers were opposed to the prevailing social forms, or ignored them, they might claim or seem to be Christlike in their martyrdom to the crowd of moneylenders and money changers. In the seventeenth century the poet laureateship in England could boast names of lasting importance like Jonson or Dryden. But by the eighteenth century, the laureateship, the public post of poetry, became clearly a niche for timeservers and government favorites. The true poet's public could therefore never be official, but one that, like the family of art itself, had members in every corner of the kingdom, similarly garbed in their solitary virtue.

Perhaps artists of all sorts always felt that way, especially since the Renaissance. But, as Milton had expressed the fear, the model of Jesus for writers might be difficult to distinguish from that of Satan, and the urge to spiritual and intellectual achievement could turn into a Satanic obliviousness to everything but applause. More than ever before, the stock in trade of eighteenth-century writers was beginning to be their private nature, their personal view of the world. Milton's attack against classical learning, as well as his frequent implications that science teaches nothing but metaphors through which we can dimly know the truth about the universe, leads him to a kind of aesthetic implosion, by which he uses inspired words to undermine their secular authority. Yet, the paradox continued, it was also only through the inspired operations of mind as embodied in the book that true achievement could be measured. It is a theme that will have many imitators during the eighteenth century, particularly among those writers most anxious about the ill effects of fame and reputation on the reception of their message. At virtually the same time Pope is arranging for his private letters to be published by an enemy (so that he can bring out an "authorized" edition), he mocks fame as "a second life in another's breath" and says that the appreciation of friends and "one self-approving hour" is worth all the cheers of the ignorant mob. The sentiments are from the philosophical *Essay on Man,* which, by the way, Pope published anonymously, even while he was putting his own name onto other, more satiric, poems. Like Defoe's Robinson Crusoe, whose "editor" wonders if the story of a "private man" would ever interest the public, or Moll Flanders, who is "famous" on the title page of her book, yet frequently tells us that's not her real name, Pope's manipulations seem an effort to divide himself into famous and anonymous parts, the outward assertion justified by the inward solitude—held together by the simultaneous public and private gesture of writing one's story in a book. In a world where books were an increasing part of visual self-importance and authors, urged by "the itch of picture," put themselves irresistibly forward, Pope, whose picture was painted perhaps more different ways than that of any other English writer, sought refuge in the book as a stage for the self, on which modesty and assertion could harmonize comfortably together. When Pope revises Chaucer's *House of Fame* as *The Temple of Fame,* he emphasizes not the books that promote nations and great individuals but the books that promote their authors, and he concludes by delineating the kind of moral fame he will himself accept. In such an assertion, the mediation of the patron and even the muse has been effectively stripped away.

Many of the early propagandists of this view of art—Pope, Addison, and even Swift—thought that their standards were those of the upper classes of the previous generation. But because they believed these standards could be learned in the relation between writer and reader, the implication of their work was egalitarian. Since the artist was in touch with ultimate social and spiritual values, both he and his audience could consider themselves members of a new class, specialists in the eternal. When patron, muse, and writer center in the same person, the audience is often called on to appreciate works about the process by which writing is created. The maniacal extremes of such self-regard are satirized by Swift (in almost always anonymous works) as the essence of the modern search for literary fame, which has been created by both an ignorant audience, whose bare literacy has no base in taste or religion, and the empty author, whose goal is only personal notoriety. All writing, he implies, including his own, is a doomed effort to bolster self-esteem in the face of onrushing time and death. Such an attack had already been made by writers who discovered that the chivalric and aristocratic fame they both praised and coveted was too easily sought by those without the requisite credentials. Dryden, for example, in a poem addressed to the court painter, Sir Godfrey Kneller, acknowledged the importance of painting the right people, but deplored the need to paint the wrong as well, and reminded Kneller that the older, more invisible, and therefore truer art of writing might correct the painter's lack of discrimination in subject matter:

Good Heav'n! that Sots and Knaves shou'd be so vain,
To wish their vile Resemblance may remain!
And stand recorded, at their own request,
To future Days, a Libel or a Jest (160–63).

Although Swift, who hated Dryden, would be disgusted with the association, he and Dryden stand together in their disdain for the way individuals without either talent or values yet use the book and the picture to place themselves on the public stage. By selling wisdom through the book and the engraved portrait, publishing leaves one defenseless before those with whom one has no cultural sympathy at all. Swift is still in a world in which the writer offers his services to individuals and causes, and his refusal to put his own name to most of his works reflects at best the Christian sense that the truth of the work is more important than the identity of the author. To be singular, to seek literary and philosophical fame, is in some basic way to be private. Swift appreciated that privacy, and it forms part of his real ambivalence about the act of writing and publishing. In "Verses on the Death of Dr. Swift" he wonders what the use of a life devoted to writing has been. Even your friends quickly forget you, he says, and your books are used for wrapping fish or worse. He values his political works the most, because they seemed to have accomplished something tangible, changing a few laws and some opinions. (*Gulliver's Travels* isn't even mentioned.) Even so, he concludes, none of his works will be remembered for long. Only this poem will preserve their memory, and he must write it himself because no one else can be trusted to carry the message to posterity.

At his most bitter and ironic, Swift has written a poem to inform the future about all his writings that have vanished. By midcentury, in a very different poem, the famous "Elegy Written in a Country Churchyard," Thomas Gray has taken the same paradox a step further. "The paths of glory lead but to the grave" (36), says the poet, contemplating the tombs of the unaspiring unknowns buried in the churchyard rather than under the monuments and plaques within the church. The onrushing specter of death, as so often in English eighteenth-century poetry, undermines all ambition, even that of poetry itself. As the poem continues, the walker in the graveyard gives way to another speaker, who paradoxically celebrates the "youth to Fortune and to Fame unknown." Behind the shifting masks, Gray's evasion is total and perplexing, understandable only through his urge to be an author without risking either the glare of reputation or the scrabbling for success that has thrown authorship into disrepute. In eighteenth-century England, to be an author in the old way, a respected man of distinction, often requires pretending not only that one does not get any money from it, but even that no one has written the poem at all. Neither the intercession of the muse with the gods or God nor that of the patron with social power will truly survive the age of democratic revolutions. Even in those countries untouched directly by revolutionary politics, painters and poets were attracted to the image of themselves not so much as masters of language, sound, or visual design, but as the antennae of the human race, "the unacknowledged legislators of the world" Shelley will write in *A Defense of Poetry,* geniuses not of substance but of sensibility.

*   *   *

When we see how cruel statesmen and warriors can be to the human race, and how absurd distinguished men can be to their acquaintance, it will be instructive to observe the instances multiply of pacific, acquiescing manners; and to find how compatible it is to be great and domestic, enviable and yet good-humored.
      —BENJAMIN VAUGHAN, Letter to Benjamin Franklin[23]

In England writers were beginning to reject their traditional association with royalty and social power. But the models of an aristocratic fame were still infectious, and the only alternatives seemed to be a masquerading manipulation or a high-minded rejection. Whereas in the seventeenth century a common poetic rhyme is "fame/name," in the eighteenth century it is more often "fame/shame," and Pope writes wistfully of Shakespeare as a writer who could work "without any views of Reputation, and of what Poets are pleas'd to call Immortality: Some or all of which have encourag'd the vanity, or animated the ambition, of other writers" ("Preface to Shakespeare," 463). But in America, still the colonies, the competitive pressure of a large number of people in a small space was not yet present: Opportunity was the air they breathed, and their model was not the cautionary classicism of Milton so much as the expansive self-making celebrated by Defoe, whose greatest praise for William III rejected all previous traditions of royal celebration.

The living emblem of the self-created and self-described for the eighteenth century was Benjamin Franklin, whose career marks a stillpoint of harmony in the otherwise baroque wrestling with the question of earthly fame that characterizes that of so many other public figures of the period. That Franklin seems calm before impulses that shatter others owes much to the European belief that America was the open place, the unconditioned land of one's dreams, where the individual might stand on his own, unburdened with the outworn baggage of the past. In America, it seemed, one might create a name entirely from one's own efforts. Defoe's Moll Flanders, for example, is a woman with tremendous energy and talent but no arena save crime in which to display it. Forever evading the law through disguises and pseudonyms in England, she tells us that only when she arrives in America can she take her "real name in Virginia." Both Moll and Robinson Crusoe plainly tell us that their English names are what people have called them rather than who they really are. Defoe thus invokes the social rebaptising the America space allows, and the born-again virginity

---

23. Franklin's *Autobiography* (69). Vaughan had edited Franklin's nonscientific papers and essays in 1779, and Franklin includes his letter in the manuscript of the *Autobiography.* Although seemingly complete before Franklin's death in 1790, the *Autobiography* was first published (in an incomplete version) in 1818.

of using one's real name echoes throughout his novels: England is the place of confinement; France and Europe the place of costume and elaborate social disguise; America the place where the true self and the real name can be made plain.

When Franklin is four years old, the uncle for whom he was named writes an acrostic poem of moral instruction that admonished him (under the letter "M") that "Man's danger lies in Satan, sin, and self." But something in Franklin's own nature and in that of the country in which he was born allows him to translate this seemingly self-denying precept into a cue for social action. In his twenties, already a skilled printer and flourishing member of the Philadelphia community, he lays out for himself a program to become perfect through the careful exercise of twelve virtues. "Self-education" and "self-examination" are two of the most frequent compounds in Franklin's *Autobiography*. They are, he says, the cornerstones of his own worldly success. Like Defoe's heroes, he has the talent of seeing himself as a living object to be shaped by his mind and will. Like Marvell's Cromwell, he urges his "active star" instead of, like Cinderella, waiting to be recognized. The project to become perfect is just a youthfully exuberant example of his general tendency to consider his character as something not fatally inherited, but something to be formed for use within a world of other people. At the same time that novelists like Defoe, Richardson, and Fielding were introducing a new sensitivity to the nuances of inner nature and personal relations, Franklin was training himself in a self-monitoring awareness of the impact he was making on others and how that might be bettered both for their benefit and for his own.

Just about the time that he is drawing up his plan for moral perfection, Franklin is told that many consider him to be insolent and ambitious, and so he promptly makes Humility the thirteenth virtue on his list and enjoins himself to imitate Jesus and Socrates. Like Milton or Cotton Mather, Franklin's ambition draws him toward the compensating virtue of humility. But whereas Milton displaces his conflict into, say, the spectacle of Samson assertively sacrificing himself for the Israelites, and Mather recommends himself by his unworthiness, Franklin is willing to recognize the urge to wordly distinction for one's virtue as a necessary though paradoxical component of social character.

> I cannot boast of much success in acquiring the *reality* of this virtue, but I had a good deal with regard to the *appearance* of it. . . . For even if I could conceive that I had completely overcome it, I should probably be proud of my humility (87, 88).

So sensitive to the way others are bothered by any assertion of singular importance, Franklin says that he constantly strives to minimize his own role in promoting any public project. In a sense he takes Descartes's postulation of the untouched and unaffected observer and applies it not only to his experiments with the physical world, but also to the investigation of himself.

Franklin's regard for appearances, so often attacked by literacy critics for its manipulativeness, is yet intimately related to his commitment to social and personal progress. Much to the disgust of moralizing commentators who want to believe that self-concern and great achievement are incompatible, he demonstrates that exemplary humility can be a virtue in appearance as well as in reality. His self-monitoring is therefore closely related to what I might call his civic narcissism, his desire to connect what is best for himself with what is best for those around him. His career is central to the development of the public organization of the city as an administrative unit that draws upon the civic spirit of the inhabitants; and he is constantly raising funds for hospitals, universities, intellectual groups, street lamps, street sweepings, and all the amenities of city life that we now take for granted. His incessant plans and projects (a characteristic he shares with Defoe) search for general principles by which useful actions might be accomplished. In an age of awakening cultural relativism, he is acutely alert to the useful customs of otherwise separate groups and filled with the desire to diffuse them generally.

As the career of Cicero may first exemplify, the awareness of being seen by others always accompanies the new man in the new place, and Franklin's America was a land of new men and women in the newest place in the world. The sense of starting afresh, without the overhang of the European past, was there to be built upon, and, shortly after the Revolution, Benjamin Vaughan writes to Franklin to encourage him to continue the *Autobiography* that Vaughan has read in its earliest version. Franklin, says Vaughan, should write it because it will advertise America to a Europe eager for information about "the manners and situation of a rising people." Part of the lesson of Franklin's own career, says Vaughan, is the way he is responsible for his own success and is not ashamed of the origins from which he has risen: "You prove how little necessary all origin is to happiness, virtue, or greatness" (69). Since America, unlike Europe, has no distinguished past, only the past of nature, the status of its inhabitants and of the country itself must come from their inner lives, which are revealed in social and civic activity in a premeditated exercise of mind improving nature that Vaughan, following Franklin, calls "the art of virtue." Such an art is superior to the race for glory in the old world because it regulates itself instead of being determined by the false standards of the past. Vaughan, like Franklin himself, thus mingles Miltonic injunctions to privacy and patience with a more eighteenth-century commitment to personal growth and social progress. The nation, like the society, is not a time-honored structure into which individuals fit; it is the sum of all individuals: "When [the English] think well of individuals in your native country, they will go nearer to thinking well of your country" (71). Fame in such a society is not the tarnished possession of an aristocratic class, now available to less favored aspirants, but a possibility of the ambitious spirit who desires to put his talents at the service of his fellow citizens.

The spiritual fame released from privacy and isolation that is represented by the career of Franklin becomes a central model for fame in America. But it should again be noted how important to this concept of a personal fame "ashamed of no origin" is the special situation of the writer. Throughout his *Autobiography,* Franklin refers to his life as a book, sometimes marred with "errata." The analogy is a familiar one in late seventeenth-century funeral inscriptions, but one that Franklin carries perhaps to its most elaborate statement, especially in the epitaph he composed for himself (he said) at the age of twenty-two:

> The Body of BENJAMIN FRANKLIN,
> Printer.
> Like the Covering of an old Book,
> Its Contents torn out,
> And stript of its Lettering and Guilding,
> Lies here, Food for Worms;
> But the Work shall not be lost,
> It will (as he believed) appear once more,
> In a new and more beautiful Edition,
> Corrected and Amended
> By the Author.[24]

In this brief bit of wordplay, Franklin echoes Horace's assertion that poems last longer than empires, as well as Erasmus's celebration of the new world made possible by the printing press. Without a worry over an assertion of authorship that in England had often taken refuge in either a refusal to publish or a refusal to name oneself as the author, Franklin blithely fuses the body authored by God with the book authored and made by himself. The body may be God's authorship, but the life is Franklin's, in which, as he says in the *Autobiography,* he can retrospectively indicate where corrections should be made. As the epitaph emphasizes, the book is a better body, a compensation for illness and mortality, a hedge against death that preserves the writer's individuality, just as religion will preserve his soul.[25] The metaphor and the literary seizing of personal initiative it implies gathers strength from Franklin's own profession of printing, with its keen sense of the self-objectifying interplay between the author's mind and the

24. This is the first printed version in *Ames Almanack* for 1771. See Butterfield, "Franklin's Epitaph."

25. The objectification of the body is a frequent theme of eighteenth-century literature. As Dr. John Arbuthnot writes in "Know Yourself" (1734),

> This frame, compacted with transcendent skill,
> Of moving joints obedient to my will;
> Nursed from the fruitful glebe, like yonder tree,
> Waxes and wastes; I call it mine, not me (436).

Philosophes like La Mettrie in *L'Homme-machine* (1748) were building on Descartes and Locke to lay the groundwork for an experimental biology and medicine by considering the body as a machine made of causally related parts. Bodies were often compared to watches, and God was becoming to be known as a watchmaker also, who made both man and the world as wondrous pieces of intricate machinery. The suitability of such a view to the new possibilities for self-promotion and self-monitoring seems clear.

words on the page. When Franklin gives an early account of his principles and morals and then concludes, "I had, therefore, a tolerable character to begin the world with" (57), it is difficult not to hear "character" in its printing sense—the letters and numbers and figures that make up a book. Such a "character" mediates between the inward-turning self and the public world of readers. Unlike the selfish self, "character" is self-aware without being self-conscious. "Extremely ambitious" to become "a tolerable English writer," Franklin thought that most of his advancement in the world came from his prose writing (13). He created himself as writer by studying models like the *Spectator*. But he also purged from himself some of the hack's naked assertion by writing under pseudonyms. It is Poor Richard, not Ben Franklin, who publicly confesses his desire to become famous by complaining of the lack of public esteem for him. This early channeling of a tremendous literary ambition into pseudonym and parody is reminiscent of Swift, but without Swift's despair over the ability of words to accomplish anything. Swift was still writing for the enlightened few who would truly understand, while Franklin was writing for all who would listen. Unlike the English writer who disgustedly saw the existence of a new and wider audience as an irredeemable watering down of literary quality and the writer's own status, Franklin considered the newly expanding commerce of the book to be the bridge between personal success and social good. In an *Essay on Man* Pope argues the development from self-love to social love as a necessary process. But for Franklin they interconnect in almost effortless reciprocity.

Central to the mutation in the history of fame marked by Franklin's career is the increasing tendency for the most articulate and assertive to consider their minds, their careers, and their characters to be in their own power to shape and change, to be, in short, their own possession rather than that of God or the king. As C. B. Macpherson points out, the tradition of political philosophy culminating in Locke argues that you are your own property and therefore only you can sell yourself. Such political theories of self-possession, which also seek to define the "natural rights" of all human beings as a basis for reforming that state, dramatize as well the lack of any necessary obligation the individual owes authority if it is not legitimate. There is no innate truth to the state or religion as worldly authorities, only as they have legally evolved. Divine right was giving way to politics. Instead of being a mere cog in the machine of time, the individual could potentially vault himself into its seat. So long as one possessed oneself, one could do with that self what one desired.

But of course what you did with your self was limited by what you were, and the example of Franklin's self-monitored career assumes even larger significance in America—a country soon to be freed from the domination of Europe, with all its past and traditions, and hungry for new models of behavior. To sell oneself is better than being sold by others, even though ahead might lie an alienation from one's work. So too, to consider one's public image as something to be fashioned and sold may heighten the feeling of personal will, even though psychic alienation and the commodity self may loom in the future.

Warlocks of Individualism

BOSWELL. "Is it possible to live amongst other men and retain one's singularity?" ROUSSEAU. "Yes, I have done it." BOSWELL. "But to remain on good terms with them?" ROUSSEAU. "Oh, if you want to be a wolf, you must howl."

—*Boswell's Journal*, 3 December 1764

The eighteenth century marks the beginning of an international European fame culture in which an enormous variety of new social, economic, and political groups use the expanded powers of media to press themselves and their individual members into the vacuum of cultural authority, challenging the monarchies and aristocracies that had previously been the sole custodians of such singularity. The concepts of both honor and fame are by the eighteenth century firmly along the way to losing the exclusively public definition from which they had been inseparable through the ages. Once the validation of a class distinction, they, like identity itself, have become personal possessions, not only distinguishable from class, but perhaps even opposed to it. Earlier social myths that featured aristocrats who disguised themselves as primitives or members of the lower classes were replaced by the Cinderella-like myths of the Industrial Revolution, which featured instead a seemingly lower-class person who turns out to be an aristocrat in disguise. The attack on external authority had resulted in a confusion over what a valid authority was, and the most intriguing (perhaps because most imitable) patterns of assertion were those whose energies seemed to come from within. "God," said Franklin's Poor Richard, "helps them who help themselves."

Into that gap of authority stepped those warlocks of individualism, the sages and wise men of the eighteenth century—men such as Voltaire, Denis Diderot, David Hume, Samuel Johnson, Benjamin Franklin, Thomas Jefferson, and the most singular of the singular, Jean Jacques Rousseau. In Rousseau's strange career, we can watch Franklin's amalgam of soul and civility mixed in very different proportions. I place Franklin and Rousseau next to each other in the face of so much analysis (the most acerbic and familiar, that of D. H. Lawrence) that they are entirely opposite: Franklin the premeditated manipulator, Rousseau the apostle of equality and nature. Yet in the history of fame both firmly mark the eighteenth century as an age preoccupied with the question of self-definition in public. Both Franklin and Rousseau practice an assertiveness, a willingness to take the stage, that is justified not by blood or money but by a paradoxical uniqueness: Praise me because I am unique, but praise me as well because my uniqueness is only a more intense and more public version of your own. In the taxonomy of fame, this nexus of the unique and the general, the individual and the community, bears some strong resemblances to the special status of the saint and the participation of the individual soul in the community of believers. But with the eighteenth century that spiritual distinction and the spiritual fame it often entailed had become part of a new social, political, and economic justification for individual will and action—in the world. Rousseau's *Confessions,* for example, is as much about the evolution of his feelings and beliefs as is St. Augustine's. But they are not feelings whose true audience is God, only to be overheard by men. Instead Rousseau is constantly expressing his feelings to have them and thereby himself validated by the crowd of discriminating readers whom he would like to win over.

Rousseau strikes a wholly modern note in the history of fame by his preoccupation with the expectation of being recognized for what he "really" is. He seeks a fame for naturalness, a fame for inner qualities, for what one is without the overlay of social forms. It is a fame of feeling, a "natural fame" that is held personally, without forebears or tradition, and rejects any honor or virtue that must be validated by social position and social visibility. In Rousseau's career, as in those of Voltaire, Johnson, Laurence Sterne, Franklin, and many others, we can observe what happens when fame ceases to be exclusively associated with any social class or vocation and becomes instead an attribute of the self, a justification of the individual in opposition to traditional standards of identity, a spiritual essence that is on view for the world. Voltaire expresses it by choosing to live like an aristocrat of old, constantly in a crowd, casting his entourage in plays of his own devising, onstage and off. Johnson balances his physical eccentricity and brutish power with a ferocious fealty to orthodox Christianity. Sterne, like Don Quixote sallying forth in search of both adventures and an author to sing them, blithely capers through a celebrity for being the author of *Tristram Shandy,* as well as the mind and personality that is its subject.

But Rousseau's own temperament, coupled with his commitment to the concepts of political and social freedom, carves such exemplary self-display in high relief. Rousseau's definition of the state, like that of Jefferson later, justifies it by the order neither of religious revelation nor of dynastic continuity but of nature. In *The Social Contract* (1762) he poses the basic modern political question of the relation between social duty and personal freedom. In answering such questions, the past has no privilege for Rousseau. The unchanging human spirit, once scraped clean of all illegitimate growths and disguises, must be consulted instead. With neither embarrassment nor excuse, Rousseau traces his beliefs about the tyranny of society to his personal grievances, not reducing them to the individual as would a psychohistorian but assuming that personal experience is the necessary beginning of all social order, the vital root that institutions have historically repressed and warped. Although he claims to have lived "a life unparalleled among humankind," that life is also a key to general human truths (389).

Like his vision of man caught in the confines of society, Rousseau himself only gradually emerges from a dependence on the opinion of the world as the guarantee of his success. Neither his experiences of politics in Venice (as a footman) nor of art in Paris (as a musician and copyist) particularly satisfies his desires, for he constantly tests the world to see if he is being treated according to his merit. In the array of eighteenth-century sages and wise men whose writing and personal nature so fascinated their contemporaries, Rousseau also deserves a special place because of the extreme contrast between his urge to be recognized and his urge to retreat. "The horror of being found out" (88) complements the desire to be known. In form the impulse resembles that of Satan in *Paradise Lost,* with his sense of injured merit, or Eve, who wants others to recognize the independence of her will and judgment. But, as he does with his fame, Rousseau takes such desires for personal justification and redefines them as the disappointed dreams of a good proportion of humankind. In a world becoming more and more free of traditional restrictions on ambition, all sought to be treated according to their self-esteem—only to discover they are being treated in accordance with their self-hatred.

Franklin's relative lack of explicit irony in his writings and his unruffled embrace of role playing, costumes, and impersonation may ultimately be due to the fact that, as an American, he could be the unaccommodated, unconditioned man without constantly having to prove it. But Rousseau's paranoia is inseparable from his self-esteem and a portent of one important strand of the future fabric of fame. The process begins in earnest when at the age of thirty-eight he wins the prize of the Dijon Academy for the best essay on whether the advance of civilization has improved the nature of man. Rousseau's answer, of course, is no, and his subsequent celebrity changes his life entirely:

> So long as I had lived unknown to the public, I was loved by all who knew me, and had not a single enemy. But as soon as I had a name, I ceased to have friends (338).

Voltaire, he says in the *Confessions,* is "weighed down by fame and prosperity," and to a certain extent he sees Voltaire as his antitype, an extreme statement of the man of letters who is not torn between society and solitude but wallows in the constant embrace of his audience and entourage. Nevertheless Rousseau's involvement in his own celebrity is hardly more free than Voltaire's. Both realize that the fame they sought as ennoblement and self-justification has become, in this new world of celebrity seekers and publicity, a trap for action and thought. Voltaire, like Samuel Johnson, deals with the problem by setting up his own intellectual court, becoming both playwright and center of attention. In contrast, as Rousseau becomes increasingly fashionable, he also becomes more antisocial, condemning, as did Augustine, all the falseness of social identity through the figure of the actor. If you need to be seen this way, he writes, you are empty inside, the hollow product of an urban life that values show over true virtue. In his *Letter to M. D'Alembert on the Theater* (1758), Rousseau ferociously rejects the suggestion that Geneva needs a public theater. Such an institution, he argues, would only undermine or destroy all possibilities for a worthwhile society. Standing the old association of actors with public men on its moral head, Rousseau turns it into a condemnation of the obsessive fealty to past power that is imaged in the actor's imitations and role playings. Actors, he concludes, are hirelings who imitate for money, the models of everything a good citizen is not.

Rousseau's vehemence against the actor and against theater is clearly in the service of his desire to throw off inherited social roles so that man can be free and build anew. Like Diderot in his *Paradox of the Actor,* a product of the early 1770s, Rousseau contrasts the actor with the man of sensibility. But whereas Diderot considers acting to be a possible model of self-awareness that can help the individual to move effectively through society, Rousseau believes that the social, acting self must be purged almost entirely, like an infection that once contracted can never truly be cured.

Yet the very ferocity of his attack indicates the pressures of his own division—to be private and yet to publicize his ideas—as well as the increasing avidness with which he was being courted and observed in a Europe where the dissemination of the images of great men and the spread of their often liberal and democratic ideas were closely linked. After Rousseau has fled to England under the protection of Hume, he and Hume go to a play starring David Garrick, where, says Hume, "the king and queen looked more at him than at the players." But, says Hume, despite the public interest in the social philosopher whose works had been banned and burned in France and Geneva, Rousseau maintained his strange separateness:

> What has chiefly begot a doubt of his sincerity, are his great singularities, which some people take for affectation, and an art to gain celebrity: but his greatest singularity is the love of solitude, which, in a man so well calculated for the entertainment of company, and seemingly so sociable, appears very extraordinary (Grieg, II, 15).

Unlike the philosopher whom Diderot's *Encyclopédie* defined as one who loves society, Rousseau constantly fears that society and its web will swallow him up. In society one can never be more than a mere actor, when the true goal should be to become an author, a creator, and generator rather than a servant and agent. As Rousseau becomes more and more famous, he also becomes increasingly paranoid about what he perceives as threats to his independence. Other wise men, sages, philosophes, and writers of the eighteenth century, whether persecuted or not in their native lands, would often band together in clubs, personal courts, or intellectual families as protection against the newly invisible and powerful audience. But Rousseau invariably goes it alone and, when he is invited in by friends, soon turns against them in what can only be understood as a flailing revenge for their presumption to believe that he might be dependent on their protection in any way. After Hume has brought him to England as a victim of intellectual and political persecution and attempts to get a pension for him from the king, Rousseau amazes his host and virtually all of his other friends and supporters in England and Europe by denouncing what he believes to be a plot against him hatched by Hume, Horace Walpole, d'Alembert, and baron d'Holbach. In essence he was rejecting the international culture of which they all considered themselves to be part. Unlike Hume or Voltaire or Franklin, who disliked solitude, Rousseau was the public solitary for whom acceptance by others was always a prelude to co-optation and dependence. For all his interest in social theory, he was not himself sociable or, in Dr. Johnson's word, "clubbable." His philosophical explorations of the institutional restrictions on human freedom reciprocally strengthened his personal sensitivities. Gifts of money and position, which his supporters considered to be the traditional reward for authorial eminence, conveyed instead to him the awful weight of psychic obligation and servitude. With an almost fatal necessity, the Hume whom he addresses as *"mon très cher Patron"* in his early letters turns into the rich patron whose yoke he must publicly throw off to proclaim his freedom once again.

In his continuing effort to retain his singularity and his freedom at the same time that he produces works whose primary goal is to convert their readers to a new vision of man and society, Rousseau is a striking early example of a more common modern phenomenon: the person who desires to be spiritually public and physically private, the shy star. In part, these seemingly contradictory urges are materially connected with his chronic urinary problems: the embarrassing need to catheterize himself frequently and to leave social gatherings abruptly to relieve himself. But the physical symptoms, the psychic urge, and the intellectual understanding mesh with almost seamless precision. Faced with what he considers to be the distortion both his enemies and friends have made of his name and personal significance, Rousseau sets out in the *Confessions* to tell his own story, to exonerate himself by telling the absolute truth rather than apologizing:

> [S]ince my name is fated to live, I must endeavour to transmit with it the memory of that unfortunate man who bore it, as he actually was and not as his unjust enemies unremittingly endeavour to paint him (373).[26]

His writings will carry the truth about him forward, out of the malice of the present and into the deserving future. They are the history of "my inner

26. Rousseau's urge to self-exoneration and his paranoia about being controlled through being written about was infectious. Since he had begun writing his *Confessions* while in England, Hume and some of his supporters were fearful of their effect when published, although others warned him against getting into a pamphlet war with Rousseau. To present his own side of the controversy, Hume in 1766 therefore published in Paris (although the title says "Londres") the *Exposé succinct de la contestation qui s'est élevée entre M. Hume et M. Rousseau, avec les pièces justificatives.*

self" (262) and the movements of his soul, not toward union with God, in the manner of Augustine, but toward the ideal of total self-expression, which in Rousseau's view can never be untruthful and, when seen, must be loved. While Franklin's *Autobiography* teaches "character," the acquiring of a public self, Rousseau's *Confessions* defines character as the exposure in writing of the self within, as it might exist before civilization did its evil work. Disgusted with theater, virtually unable to speak in front of any public audience, Rousseau tells us he wants to be free of public opinion, but only to seek another public, in posterity, reachable only through the book:

> Even today, when I can see the most baleful and terrifying plot that has ever been hatched against a man's memory advancing unchecked towards its execution, I shall die a great deal more peacefully, in the certainty that I am leaving behind in my writings a witness in my favour that will sooner or later triumph over the machinations of men (525).

In his desire to be recognized for what he is himself, Rousseau is the true child of a new world of books and pictures, increased literacy and widely expanded audiences, which burgeon and thrive because they are unhampered by national boundaries and class tastes. Instead of being part of the traditional historical dialogue between the wise of the world, carried on within the confines of books, the writings of Voltaire, Rousseau, Franklin, and so many others are "news" that strike the eighteenth-century reading public directly, with the freshness of a wind blowing away the dust of centuries. Whatever their own commitment or hostility to traditional values, they must come to some accommodation with the new audience that has given them their power. Of all, Rousseau is the most seemingly unaccommodated. Yet in different ways both he and Franklin yet share this quite new sense of a public career for themselves. They looked forward to it, they expected it, and they believed it was a necessary concomitant of their abilities. Until Franklin and Rousseau, autobiography concentrates almost exclusively on the world of internal spiritual change, with scant attention to the social and the visual. But Franklin considers it of prime importance in his autobiography to tell what he looked like when he came into Philadelphia for the first time—disheveled from his long journey from Boston and carrying three loaves of bread, one under each arm and one that he was eating—to illustrate both the disparity between his appearance then and what he became later, as well as his present continuity with that strange apparition. Similarly, Rousseau, despite his professed desire for solitude and retreat, pours himself out in his writings and in person with the modern performer's unique combination of absolute sincerity and absolute premeditation. Diderot distinguishes the actor from the man of sensibility, but Rousseau is the actor as man of sensibility, creating a social space for behavior and attitudes that had previously characterized society as a maze of unavoidable hypocrisies. His political views emphasize the primitive freedom of human beings, but in his own autobiography, and in his life, he shows how dependent that freedom is on the observation of others. It is not a monkish retreat but a retreat in public and an affirmation of the need for personal freedom even in the midst of a world of social obligations.

Before the eighteenth century there were many attitudes toward the desire for fame, but with its arrival those attitudes had to include the new question of what it *meant* to be famous. The rarefied dissemination of words and images among members of similar social, political, or religious groups had expanded enormously to include potentially an entire civilized world. Beyond any previous period, the eighteenth century marks a diffusion of the image of the famous into places, social as well as geographical, it had never gone before. Toward the end of the seventeenth century John Locke had asked Sir Godfrey Kneller to put Locke's name on the back of a portrait, because after a few generations the names of "private men" are lost and the faces on the paintings unidentifiable (Tiffin, 138). He may have been the last important English writer to be able to make such a plea unself-consciously. Just over half a century later writers and artists were representing their countries to the world much more decisively than any traditional king ever could, while monarchy itself tried to take on some of the philosopher's cachet in the persons of the "enlightened" Frederick and Catherine, celebrated by their admirers as the Greats. When Franklin was a young man visiting London, he hoped to catch a glimpse of Sir Isaac Newton but was unsuccessful. By the time he was as old as Newton had been then, his own face was displayed all over Europe in the shape of engravings, busts, statues, paintings, and even little statuettes and painted fans that looked like souvenir keepsakes.

One intriguing difference between the selves Franklin and Rousseau projected to the world lies in their differing attitudes toward the future. As individual nature became filled with possibility, so history could be seen in motion. Rousseau, on the evidence of his *Confessions,* is constantly dreaming of what he doesn't have but ought to, while Franklin presents himself as methodically accumulating the elements that will make up his future life, sometimes, as he says, committing "errata" but usually building clearly toward the future. In other words, progress, that great eighteenth-century watchword, for Franklin seems to involve a constant movement forward from what has already been done, while for Rousseau it is an equally constant awareness of a lack that must be remedied, an emptiness that must be filled. In part the difference is that between America, where the possibilities were open and the new materials abundant, and Europe, where the possibilities all seemed well-defined and closed, and the only options either to demolish or to strip down to basics.[27]

Once it appears possible that life on earth can be improved, then justification by heaven is no longer so clearly inferior to the recognition possible

27. The Romantic poets will similarly be more stimulated by the French Revolution than by the American because its overthrowing of oppression comes closer to home than the American plunge into the open landscape.

on earth, now and in the future. In the Christian humanist view of fame elaborated by Petrarch, earthly fame is both a noble goal and an empty desire because it is the shadow of the true fame of heavenly glory. Heaven makes earthly fame perfect. Samuel Johnson, in "The Vanity of Human Wishes" (1749) had indicted the "fever of renown" that led men to aspire to political power and military victory at the expense of the lives of others. He concluded that all aspiration (including scholarly ambition) was thereby suspect and only "hope of heaven" possible. But for Rousseau, as for Franklin, hope was the psychological and spiritual equivalent of progress, a belief that present energy heralded future success for the individual as well as for the society, even after that individual's death. The most popular English poem of the fifty-year period between the death of Pope and the first publications of Wordsworth was Edward Young's *Night Thoughts on Life, Death, and Immortality*. Some years before, Young had written another long poem entitled *Love of Fame: The Universal Passion* (1725–1728). But now that everywhere in the new world of intellectual and material progress time was rushing on with more precision than ever before, his subject had become the musings of a solitary wanderer among graveyards. When we note the many works like *Night Thoughts* in the midcentury English "graveyard" school of poetry, consider the enormous pressure of onrushing death in novels like *Tristram Shandy* as well as the new genre of gothic horror, and observe the number of literary men and women afflicted alike by both the Renaissance disease of melancholy and the more up-to-date eighteenth-century upset known as hypochondria, it is tempting to characterize the latter part of the eighteenth century as a world in which the waning of belief in an afterlife has bred a twin obsession with posterity and death.

Theologically, the eighteenth century is preoccupied with the question of hope, which often translates into the linked questions of immortality—Does each individual have an immortal soul?—and the problem of evil—Would a just God create an unjust world? It is difficult not to align this new doctrinal preoccupation with the new definitions of individuality arising in political and economic theory as well as in daily life. Faced with a materialist and mechanistic empirical science that seemed to deny spirituality altogether, many theologians no longer considered the immateriality of the soul a prerequisite to its immortality. Instead they took the Petrarchan triumph of eternity one step further and argued that it is precisely the widespread aspiration to fame on earth, the vanity of human wishes, that proves the existence of an immortal soul and an afterlife, because a good God would not create a universe in which man was forever incomplete. Thus both the new vision of earthly history—that progress would bring perfection—as well as popular Christian theology instilled in the individual a feeling of being unfinished, forever in motion toward an integral self that existed either in the future or after death. In a culture where talk of the afterlife was becoming less and less important to theology, let alone the ordinary believer, the hope of fame on earth was part of the expectation that one might be fulfilled, that is, recognized in one's lifetime. Hope of heaven, hope of immediate fame, and hope of fame in posterity were becoming difficult to distinguish.

Between 1765 and 1767, when Rousseau and Hume are discovering their differences over the care and feeling of contemporary celebrity, the writer and encyclopedist Diderot and the sculptor Falconet carry on an extensive correspondence arguing whether it is better to have fame in one's lifetime or in posterity. Through all the exchange, through all the discussions of classical precedents and other issues, the question is fame in the present or fame in posterity, never whether fame is worth having at all. In posterity, argues Diderot, fame will redeem the individual and his work from the envy of the present, much as the Christian afterlife redeems the reputation of the virtuous from the persecuting world of the wicked. Posterity guarantees a freedom where printing preserves the truth forever. Falconet, the visual artist, argues in response that he doesn't need to be heated by the fire of posterity in order to be inspired. Before him are his materials and the nature that inspires his forms. To look to posterity for his true audience is to look for status in a world where he does not exist and can never therefore be really appreciated except as a disembodied phantom.

Appropriately enough, a few years later, Falconet publishes the correspondence. Yet it is Diderot's more literary view that becomes the persuasive model for much of future aspiration. When God is no longer the universally accepted ground of both history and eternity, then what Constantine had considered to be the essence of the Christian message—the victory over death—is hard-pressed to maintain its exclusivity. If the soul might not be immortal, if man, like the rest of the physical world, was only matter in motion, then the urge to fame and recognition would especially press those who wrote to lay claim to the attention of memory and time. Lay and clergy, priests and philosophers, rushed to London, Paris, and Geneva with their sermons and pamphlets under their arms, ready for publication. The Petrarchan victory of fame over death had returned as a prime theme of literary culture, with the difference that the reward would not be in heaven but in posterity and perhaps even sooner. The individual might be carried away by death, but his character could be projected into the future by his work. No matter what their religious or irreligious orientation, eighteenth-century writers faced the identity-destroying power of death by looking beyond their own lives for their justification. Within one's own time, the frailty of the body and the meanness of contemporaries deprived the author of his due. But fame might be the promise of a spiritual health—on earth, in posterity, or both—that would allow him to leave his diseased body behind without regret. No wonder the eighteenth century was the first great age of biography and autobiography. And in its worries over the judgment of posterity we can glimpse the seeds of the avant-garde art soon to be celebrated by Romanticism. For the idea of an avant-garde is yet a further refinement of the idea of posterity: Justification can occur only in the future, when new audiences will come into existence. To celebrate any living artist as avant-garde is a contradiction in terms. To be avant-garde is to belong to the future; the judgment of the present is irrelevant.

The Advent of the Fan

[I met] officers or other people who had no taste for literature, most of whom had not even read my works, but who nevertheless, from what they told me, had travelled a hundred, a hundred and fifty, two hundred, or three hundred miles in order to see and admire the illustrious man, the celebrated man, the most celebrated man, etc. . . . So I waited for them to start the conversation, since it was up to them to know and to inform me why they had come to see me. Naturally this did not lead to discussions which interested me very much, though they may have interested them. —Rousseau, *Confessions*

It is certain that I am not a great man, but I have an enthusiastic love of great men, and I derive a kind of glory from it. —Boswell, 1764

The avant-garde and the justification by posterity lay in the future. But in his own time, while the great man of the eighteenth century ignored the usual categories of social status, he also cloaked himself in a personal uniqueness that drew a whole new audience of admirers, who sought not to share his knowledge so much as his special reality. The greater immediacy of eighteenth-century publicity—the rapid diffusion of books and pamphlets, portraits and caricatures—plays a material role in introducing the famous to the fan, perhaps a more appropriate word here than audience, if only to distinguish a new quality of psychic connection between those who watch and those who, willingly or not, perform on the public stage.

We now live well along in an age when curiosity about the celebrated is considered reason enough to press into their privacy, and the pathologies of the fan's identification with his idol has led to murders and attempted murders by fans who believe their identities have been destroyed by their love and therefore must be revenged. But the eighteenth century is only the dawn of such an era. Fame and the famous are just beginning to be discovered as a species of sympathetic magic by which the nonfamous can negotiate with the world. And it is expatriates like Voltaire and Rousseau who first become way stations for the ambitious to visit, like natural wonders or historical monuments. With the specter of change threatening all traditional forms of social distinction, the fame of the eighteenth-century wise man protests against human transience while affirming the power of individual nature to make a difference. In a world that had newly discovered its incompletenesses and imperfections, the famous gave the illusion of being holy because they were integrally themselves—and they had the reputations to prove it.

Few if any understood why they were being so suddenly sought out. They ascribed the interest to their literary celebrity or to the desire to imitate their success or to understand their ideas more fully. Yet underneath it all, they may have suspected it had more to do with their perceived personalities than with any tangible achievement or idea. Rousseau does seem genuinely puzzled by visitors on whom the independence and freedom he personally symbolizes has more impact than any of his political ideas. His own ambitions he believes to be more traditional. In the *Confessions* he traces them to his youth in Switzerland, his admiration for his father, and his reading of Plutarch—all of which inspired him with a desire for "heroism and virtue." But despite their classical resonance, such concepts for Rousseau have little to do with political or military renown. He extracts from Plutarch an ideal of individual heroism virtually opposed to its usual public embodiment. Unlike Napoleon, who begins his study of Plutarch not much later, Rousseau aspires to be appreciated like those heroes, but without actually imitating any of their actions.

No wonder perhaps that fame, instead of making Rousseau the heir of Plutarch's heroes, had turned him into a name, a face, and an aura—an object not of attention but of curiosity, consorting not with kindred spirits but with fans. Unused to the new phenomenon of an audience that seeks to shape public figures by its own desires, Rousseau begins to believe that some of those who visit have been sent as spies by governments his political and religious works have offended. Looking back, we can be fairly sure this is not true. But before pigeonholing it as another example of his general paranoia, we might savor the ambiguous truth his reaction contains. Rousseau wonders why people who have never read his books want to see and talk with him. But he already believes he has been outlawed because of his character as much as his works, and his *Confessions* will exonerate him by telling all. Why not then be admired for his exemplary fame rather than for what he has done? Few of those who flocked to visit him in Switzerland, after he had fled from France, were there to learn how to be writers or political thinkers, just as few of those who pestered Alexander Pope some years before ("What Walls can guard me, or what Shades can hide? / They pierce my Thickets, thro' my Grot they glide") were interested in learning how to become poets. But they were interested in learning how to become their true selves, whatever that might be, and soaking in the famous man's aura of completeness was the first step in dealing with their own sense of personal and social fragmentation.

Thus the most unprecedented element in the crucial changes the eighteenth century makes in the concept of fame is the appearance of an audience that, instead of passively responding to its idols, takes an active role in defining them, an audience that is willing to be manipulated but eager to convey how that ought to be done more expertly. In no one are these contrary impulses of hero worship and self-importance displayed as in the life of James Boswell. Boswell, like so many later fans, continually crosses the line between admiring and wanting to be like his idols. But he is perhaps unique in his time for the number of such idols he had and his own talent for drawing them out and recreating them for the future. In 1763, at the age of twenty-four, Boswell, oldest son of a Scottish judge, presented himself in Switzerland to Rousseau. Just before he had left England on his tour, he had met Samuel Johnson, later to become the subject of Boswell's famous biography. Shortly after meeting Rousseau, he met Voltaire and later, through Rousseau's introduction, the Corsican leader Pasquale Paoli, another great reader of Plutarch, who would become the central figure in Boswell's celebration of the Corsican battle for independence from France.

Like so many of his heroes, Boswell considered self-consciousness and writing to be inseparable. Even before his meetings with the great, he had embarked on an extraordinarily elaborate series of personal memoranda and private journals that he was to continue for the rest of his life. Like Franklin, he had early in life set forth an "Inviolable Plan" for his own conduct, addressing himself like a lax student:

> This is a great era in your life, for from this time you fairly set out
> upon solid principles to be a man. . . . You have been long without
> a fixed plan and have felt the misery of being unsettled (Pottle, 127).

Such resolutions often went guiltily unheeded by Boswell, but he remained committed to the greater meaning of individual nature as it is displayed in writing, the larger being that literature allows one to have before the world. The incessant journals he wrote about himself, the endlessly expanding pages of autobiography, are complemented by the worship of great men that produced his *Life of Johnson,* in which, Boswell boasted, Johnson would be seen "more completely than any man who has ever yet lived" (22). All his writings embody the eighteenth-century urge to make the most fleeting fame—the fame of voices spoken into ears, the fame of *talk,* so long considered impermanent—into something permanent and even artistic. Like the young Franklin posing as Silence Dogood the Boston gossip, Boswell looks forward to the characteristically modern desire to record almost everything. To print gossip, as well as to make oneself the subject of gossip, is to pinion the far-flying *Fama* of Virgil in order to ride her oneself. The urge to publish details of the private lives of individuals we hardly owe entirely to the eighteenth-century frenzy for fame. But in its figures and their fans we can see the seeds that blossom today, when the fashioning of public personality has become a major artform.

The eighteenth-century preoccupation with personal immortality is expressed chiefly in the desire to fix one's name and image for eternity. Voltaire manipulated the theater of his reputation all through his career. Franklin similarly was well aware of the possible ways to fine-tune one's impact on others. Rousseau and Johnson, in contrast, asserted an imperviousness to the opinions of the world even while they unself-consciously created public characters that drew to them others fascinated with how such eccentricity and independence could survive. But for Boswell, more star-struck than star, literary fame offered the most tempting possibility because it allowed the projection of a personal image that was imposing and yet evasive—a distillation of the grand public personalities of such as Johnson or Voltaire or Rousseau that could magically protect the tender aspirant as he made his own raid on literary celebrity. For Boswell, writing is thus simultaneously a disguise and a revelation, a staging of individual nature that seeks to monitor its growth at the same time that it enhances its stature:

> [Literature] is making another self which can be present in many places and is not subject to the inconsistencies of passion, which the man himself is (Pottle, 94).

By engaging with the great and writing about them, Boswell, like a poet in touch with the muse, nominated himself as the spokesman for earthly immortality. As a quintessential representative of the new audience, he would choose the appropriate objects of attention, and, in the name of an author's fealty to the great, he in some sense also replaces them, turning, say, Samuel Johnson into 'Boswell's Life of Johnson' or Paoli's struggle into 'Boswell's Account of Corsica.'

Boswell was a person in whom the fame ferment of his time was constantly bubbling. He may not invent, but he certainly popularizes the grand tour of Europe, not as a way of seeing the great works of the past, but of meeting and talking with the great men of the present, whose natures stand above nationality or culture. Instinctively allied with a patriarchal, almost feudal, politics, loath to give women any status beyond housewife and mother, and committed to Christian religious orthodoxy, he yet feels drawn to men and women who exemplify an independence from conventional standards, as if in their dynamic separateness he might discover the key to a heroism of his own. His desires to learn more about them are inextricably intertwined with his need for them to tell him more about himself, through explicit advice as well as through the implicit and continual restaging of aspects of his own personality in their heightened costumes. In one mood he could write that nothing about himself should be secret, and in another pour forth innumerable pamphlets, either written anonymously or under false names. Before he presents himself to Rousseau, he writes a brief sketch of his life beseeching the master of feeling to sort out his emotions for him. With Voltaire a few weeks later he argues theological and political questions with wit and force. With Johnson, he is the eager, inquisitive companion. Like his journals, his attitude toward those he admired was the product of his premeditations. Sincerity could hardly be an issue when Boswell's basic questions were 'How have you come to be the way you are?' and 'How might I become that way too?' Boswell's biographer, Frederick Pottle, says that Boswell could tune himself to other people in the way that others enter into the natures of fictional characters. But perhaps Boswell also perceived how fictional other people, especially the famous, were becoming, how readable and imitable they could be.[28]

Although he was attracted to Voltaire and attempted unsuccessfully to be presented to Frederick the Great, it was Rousseau and Johnson who determined the parameters of Boswell's personal search for recognition. Despite his own monarchical and conservative politics, he was irresistibly drawn to those who by belief or by nature, or both, were on the fringes, who in some sense flirted with the no-man's-land beyond the rigid social forms in which Boswell was brought up. Sexuality was for him, as it was for his contemporary Casanova, just a more socially sanctioned form of the same flirtation. Through his promiscuity he plunged into a world of immediacy and directness that tested a personal nature undetermined (he thought) by traditional status. Once he had survived the contest, he felt more real, just as he felt when applauded by others for his literary accomplishments. A great mimic when he was young, Boswell tried on the lives of others to find himself. The value of acting was one of the few articles of faith he continued to defend in the face of Johnson's sarcasm, and two of his earliest works dealt with theater: one supposedly written "by a Society of Gentlemen"; the other "by a Genius." A few years later Boswell commented in his journals that he had the desire to write but no subject. In the same way, he wanted to be recognized but wasn't sure either why or how.

Intriguingly enough, neither Johnson nor Rousseau seemed to understand the link between Boswell's self-observing, "theatrical" sexuality and his desire for fame. But Hume did. In Boswell's greatest foray into celebrity sex, the twenty-four-year-old adventurer offered to accompany Rousseau's forty-five-year-old mistress Thérèse Le Vasseur to England, where Hume had taken Rousseau after his flight from Switzerland. Eleven pages

28. In 1769, only a few years after Boswell sets out on his tour, the most elaborate biographical history of England ever to appear is published. It is worth quoting the grandly assertive title of these six large volumes in full: "A Biographical History of England, from Egbert the Great to the Revolution: consisting of CHARACTERS disposed in different CLASSES, and adapted to a METHODICAL CATALOGUE of Engraved BRITISH HEADS. INTENDED as An Essay towards reducing our BIOGRAPHY to SYSTEM, and a HELP to the Knowledge of PORTRAITS. INTERSPERSED WITH variety of ANECDOTES, and MEMOIRS of a great number of PERSONS, not to be found in any other Biographical Work. With a PREFACE, shewing the Utility of a Collection of ENGRAVED PORTRAITS to supply the Defect, and answer the various Purposes of MEDALS." The author, an Oxfordshire vicar named James Granger, divided the great into twelve classes. Beginning with the royal family, in a class by itself, the first eight classes were aristocrats, statesmen, and divines; the ninth was made up of "physicians, poets, and other ingenious Persons who have distinguished themselves by their Writings"; the tenth of "Painters, Artificers, and Mechanics" and others of "inferior Professions"; the eleventh was reserved entirely for women "according to their rank"; and the twelfth a grab-bag for everyone else who had ever been heard of because of peculiar circumstances, "such as live to a great Age, deformed Persons, Convicts, &c." Granger himself says in his dedication to Horace Walpole that he writes "neither for fame nor bread," only to amuse himself: "I have attempted to act the part of an humble author; but have no kind of anxiety for fame." Any commentary on the relation between his fame taxonomy and his own disavowals is unnecessary.

from Boswell's journal are missing that describe the journey, but according to one who saw them before they were burned by Boswell's descendants, they recount the affair between Boswell and Thérèse, her condemnation of his lovemaking as inferior to Rousseau's, and his constant pressing of her for more anecdotes about the master. It would be wonderful to have the details, but we do have Hume's comment to a friend even before the journey began:

> . . . I learn that Mademoiselle sets out post, in company with a friend of mine; a young gentleman, very good-humoured, very agreeable, and very mad. . . . He has such a rage for literature, that I dread some event fatal to our friend's honour. You remember the story of Terentia, who was first married to Cicero, then to Sallust, and at last, in her old age, married a young nobleman, who imagined that she must possess some secret, which would convey to him eloquence and genius (Grieg, II, 11).

Boswell's biographers, including Pottle, have wagged a stern finger at what they consider his "betrayal" of Rousseau. But Hume's insight is deeper. Boswell sought from Rousseau an intangible self-contained virtue, which might be expressed in terms of wisdom, literature, or some other values, but was ultimately unrelated to them. Through sex with Thérèse, that intangible aura of fame might rub off on him. Long before Freud in his summary way remarked that the basic human (i.e., male) desires were "honor, power, and the love of women," Rousseau himself associated the urge to be famous with the need to be properly recognized and therefore loved and desired by women. For Boswell, raised in a culture of extreme patriarchal chauvinism, the new antimonarchical fame was also authenticated and conveyed by the sacramental participation of women. In the standards of the time, direct power ran a distant third in Freud's triad—if it finished at all—because it made the desire for fame impure, while fame and the love of women were often interchangeable.

With the appearance of Boswell's book on Paoli and the struggle for Corsican independence, Boswell at twenty-seven seemed to get the public attention and esteem his inner sense of merit demanded. The book's success, he thought, would allow him to be "uniform":

> I am always fixing some period for my perfection as far as possible. Let it be when my *Account of Corsica* is published. I shall then have a character which I must support (Pottle, 344).

Although he still wrote anonymously and still often dressed in disguise, he became a recognized public figure, highly praised, highly esteemed, and highly sought after. Yet the satisfaction he was looking for never quite materialized. For once, the world's opinion of him had seemed to correspond with his own, but the gap quickly widened again. With the publication of *An Account of Corsica,* the feeling that he was not praised enough turned into the belief that he was being praised falsely:

I was quite as I wished to be, only I am positive I had not so high an opinion of myself as other people had. I look back with wonder on the mysterious and respectful notions I used to have of authors (354).

It would be a mistake to dismiss Boswell's reactions as if they were the expressions of his personal inability to be satisfied with the praise for what he had accomplished. Much more interesting is the way his personal and explicit response to fame two hundred years ago so well lays out a syndrome of aspiration, achievement, and disgust with achievement that has become so familiar. Boswell's elaborate self-examination makes him a prime modern case of those who believe that fame and recognition will satisfy their desires to be complete, "uniform," and filled with character, only to discover that nothing is really sufficient to satisfy the hunger within. By the eighteenth century, signs of progress were everywhere. The introduction of new industrial techniques, the opening of new markets, the creation of new crafts and professions, had turned the unappeasable hunger and incompleteness described by Ovid and Augustine into a social and historical virtue, to which Boswell's sense of despair at the moment of greatest achievement is one of the crucial psychological responses. The movement of artists away from medieval craft status, writers away from courtiership, and both away from patronage had by the later eighteenth century reached a point of socially functional social alienation. In an updated version of Cesare Borgia's Renaissance motto, *aut Caesar aut nihil* (either Caesar or nothing), the gap between success and failure widened to swallow even the loftiest ambitions. Since there was no longer a clearly graduated hierarchy of offices or achievements, nothing in between could truly satisfy. "Real" success was beginning to be defined as the entry into a realm of fame and self-possession that was virtually impossible to achieve—an escape from death through immortality on earth. Yet figures like Rousseau or Franklin, Napoleon or Byron, still promised that you might be next in the pantheon. Thus arises that "fever" or "thirst" for recognition that preoccupies so many real and fictional characters throughout the eighteenth century down to one whose desire has given this book its title, the hero of Matthew Lewis's *The Monk,* Ambrosio, called "The Man of Holiness" for his pure life and his mesmeric ability to preach to huge audiences. At first Ambrosio is considered an unworldly saint by all who know him. But his ever-growing "frenzy of renown" leads him finally to a pact with the Devil for even greater powers over others and particularly the power over death. From the sensational debaucheries of *The Monk* and the novels of the Marquis de Sade to the more complex aspirations of Goethe's *Faust,* such stories of limitless ambition typify the later eighteenth-century preoccupation with the possibility that a fame linked with power could surmount death and compensate for the lost hope of heaven.[29]

29. To emphasize that Ambrose's "frenzy" is an aspiration to spiritual grandeur, Lewis includes a colossal statue of St. Francis as one of the looming sights of his cloistered life. The late eighteenth-century link between the hunger for fame and the hunger for sex may also be inherent in the frequent discovery that characters like

When Hume was dying, Boswell rushed to his deathbed to see if the philosopher's unbelief had dissolved in the face of physical annihilation and was chagrined to discover him composed and calm. Without religion, Boswell seemed to believe, there was no assurance that one would last in any way, no permanence, only flux and chaos. To appeal equally to an immediate audience, to posterity, and to the Christian afterlife ensured that some residue of the self, whether as name or soul, would last beyond death. Rousseau had tried to disentangle the writer from his place in an actual society with all its repressions and make him instead a member of a society of the future, which he would help to bring into existence. But the genial identification of body and book in Franklin's epitaph could also take on the darker Swiftian tones of body and book perishing together, and so Boswell courted fame in the present as well, attempting to be both author and actor. Thus he continually put himself in the public eye, even while he seemed to subordinate his own assertions to those heroes he admired, particularly and finally Johnson, the rock of eccentricity. Fame to Boswell was like the flame to the moth: It signified both transcendence and annihilation. Throughout his life, he was attracted not only to the famous, but also to public executions, searching for the tightrope between death and life, cavorting over the abyss. Like the ancient Romans whose greatest personal assertion came in the monuments raised to their death, those condemned to die publicly made the moment of fame and the moment of death one. As he did with Hume, Boswell would try to question them before their executions, only to emerge frequently puzzled and irritated by their seeming calm or diffidence. Perhaps through his costumes and impersonations, like Laurence Sterne running from death in the guise of Tristram Shandy and Parson Yorick, Boswell dimly thought that he might not be recognized by Death because he was so openly available for the attention of Life.

In the centuries of chivalry and aristocratic power, the urge to fame had been the capstone of human greatness. If you were not of that class, singularity could be supported only in the service of God or some similar spiritual ideal. But with the decline of aristocracy's virtual monopoly on fame and honor, artistic fame particularly drew its sustenance from an ideal of solitude, separation, and difference, in which life itself was an expatriation from final justification. Instead of being defined solely in terms of a supreme social grandeur, as the chivalric and classical fame would have been, modern fame took on a stance of isolated virtue to praise a human nature unbeholding to anything the aristocratic world had explicitly valued in terms of tradition and class alignments. Sometimes it furnished actual achievements. But as often as not it celebrated an aspect of personality, a sense of uniqueness, which, thanks to Max Weber, we have come to call "charisma" (and Napoleon would call "prestige")—the new property both of politicians who professed to be beyond politics and artists be-

---

Ambrose make of "disgust after achievement"—the emptiness that follows their most elaborate seductions.

yond the pressures of a social conformity. For their audiences, such figures kept the promise of the individual alive.

But in a world of increasing publicity, even social alienation had to be staged. Rousseau's attraction to islands and isolated retreats, his constant search for security, and his constant flight from paranoia brought Robinson Crusoe into daily life: a search for exotic circumstances that would match the sense of uniqueness within. In just this way the monarchical and authoritarian Boswell was drawn toward the struggles of Corsica to assert its political freedom from the weight of the older countries of Europe. There the ancient virtues would be self-consciously revived, by a Paoli who read Plutarch. There one might find the brilliant combination of a primitive spirit of independence that was also self-aware. This self-conscious naivete sincerely manipulated for political effect could be embodied by Boswell's appearance at Garrick's celebration of Shakespeare's bicentennial dressed as a Corsican chief, or by Benjamin Franklin's presentation in the courts of Europe dressed in nicely tailored goatskins—Robinson Crusoe walking among us. Such primitivism is a satiric demonstration that a culture's claims to civilization may be hollow. Performed by those who are nominal outsiders, its political polemic is inseparable from its personal statement of individual alienation.[30]

Through books and images, social and political powerlessness become a larger self, intent on changing the world psychically as well as materially. Boswell, like so many other writers and later politicians in the eighteenth century, had sensed the analogy between the new money system of paper credit, which allowed capitalist speculation to fuel an expanding economy, and the newly expanding system of journals and publicity, which fostered the expanding leverage of reputation. As the discovery of gold and new wealth in the Americas had helped buoy the imagery of aspiration throughout Renaissance Europe, so the invention of credit extended the shadows of individuals in both finance and fame. Fame in a commodity world where everyone is democratically free to sell himself might be defined as an effort to erase the disparity between the value you put on yourself and the value put upon you by the world. The search for fame is the search for the unity between the two, and the despair comes with Boswell's recognition that the disparity between those standards of value was absolute. As Pope had pointed out, the world's approval could never match an individual's self-approval or make up for its absence.

For public figure and audience alike in the eighteenth century, all the progress, enlightenment, and revolutionary social change furnished both a shining vision and a gloomy specter: Would you be able to measure up? After searching for the secret of integrity in the great men of his time, Bos-

---

30. The American artist Benjamin West, who would later become the head of the British Royal Academy, was on his first trip to Italy, in 1760, when he was shown the Apollo Belvedere. To the primitivist delight of the Italian noblemen showing him around, he immediately compared the statue to the figure of "a Mohawk warrior"—a true "natural man's" reaction to the great works of the classical past (Brooks, 1–2).

well came finally to Johnson, in whose obdurate and undisguised peculiarities, his slovenly dress and peculiar gyrations, he could clearly see the victory over physical frailty and even death that might be achieved by an act of mind and will whose most perfect form was writing. Out of the depths of his own strangeness, Johnson had fashioned an authoritative personal voice that was all the more appreciated because it was so obviously the fruits of a tremendous struggle. In that repression and shaping of the self was a message for the more fragile sensibilities of the new age, caught between opportunity and anxiety. Johnson was not the heroic-aristocratic writer, easily coming into his birthright, but the uncommon man, whose achievement was built on adversity. By becoming his biographer, Boswell might allay his own uncertainty before the gaze of the world, immortalizing Johnson's authority through his own authorship. As he wrote in 1793, barely two years before his death, in the preface to the second edition,

> There are some men, I believe, who have, or think they have, a very small share of vanity. Such may speak of their literary fame in a decorous style of diffidence. But I confess, that I am so formed by nature and by habit, that to restrain the effusion of delight, on having attained such fame, to me would be truly painful. Why then should I repress it? . . . I have *Johnsonized* the land; and I trust they will not only *talk*, but *think*, Johnson (8).

The Posture of Reticence
and the Sanction of Neglect

Reality is always the foe of famous names.
—PETRARCH to Giovanni Colonna (March 1337)

Rarely can anyone given to acquisition of wealth acquire renown.
—ALBERTI, *On Painting*

By the end of the eighteenth century, the sincere solitude of the seventeenth-century writer, the turning away from crowds and city life reminiscent of the saint in the desert, could no longer be maintained in the face of an embryonic mass society in which the fascination with public figures fed the commitment to representational politics. "My shame in crowds, my solitary pride" (412), Oliver Goldsmith calls Poetry at the end of *The Deserted Village* (1770), a poem lamenting the decay of village life owing to the flourishing of cities. The "honest fame" that writing could once bring is an ideal as fleeting for Goldsmith as the lost villages. Hume remarks at one point that the Scottish soldier George Keith is "the only Man who has yet been able to make [Rousseau] accept money" (Greig, II, 29), and if anything tangible is at the root of Rousseau's outrage at Hume's efforts to help him, it is the royal pension, which Rousseau views, like all financial reward that doesn't come from his own efforts, as a way of buying him off. With such a view of writing, the gifts of patrons might be either accepted or rejected, but it would always be with scorn. For a time during the decline of patronage and the expansion of commercial publishing—as Johnson's remark that "no man but a blockhead ever wrote, except for money" implies—writers could maintain the distinction between money as the support for manly self-sufficiency and money as the debilitating largesse of a patron. Thus Goldsmith and Johnson would reverse the snobbery about "Grub Street" by praising what was written for money (i.e., to please a public) and attacking what was written for fame (i.e., to please a patron).[1]

As we shall see, this essentially antiaristocratic attitude vanishes quickly when the ignorant public for commercial literature replaces patronage as

1. Goldsmith once remarked ironically to the playwright Richard Cumberland: "You and I . . . have very different motives for resorting to the stage. I write for money, and care little about fame" (Dircks, 17). Cumberland took it as a compliment.

the enemy.[2] But, like Johnson, Goldsmith wrote in order to live. Both considered their writing to be work, a career, and Johnson's last great work, *Lives of the Poets* (1779–1781), is a polemic about the many ways a life might be devoted to literature. The word "career" itself begins to take on its modern meaning in the early nineteenth century. From its early meaning as a race course, it evolved to mean a life marked by important deeds and finally to designate an individual's public life of vocational and professional work. Rather than a group of paintings or a collection of books, an artist's life was beginning, with the rise of art and literary criticism, to be considered as a developing organic unity, akin to personal character. But even as the language of social success was being codified and agreed upon, the countervailing urge to solitude and alienation remained strong. "Career" enters common usage in 1803 (according to *The Oxford English Dictionary*), just about the time that Wordsworth was writing his 'Immortality Ode' ("Ode: Intimations of Immortality from Recollections of Early Childhood"), with its crucial contrast between the achievements approved by the world and that greater aspiration, present in youth and urged by love of nature, that adulthood has almost obliterated.

Amid the welter of new avenues to renown and the anxiety about choosing the right one, the distinction between classically rooted civic fame and religiously rooted spiritual fame was difficult to maintain. The decisive change was the movement away from a sole reliance on monarchical metaphors to define status—even in countries that still had kings. In terms of fame, monarchy may be described as a social system in which there is always one person who plays a social role that identifies him or her totally with the system's organization of public life. In the feudal oligarchies there were many centers of honor. With the rise of centralized kingship and monarchy, the court and king became the center that organized the ceremonies and rituals of public life and conferred honor on those who helped foster it. The king was at the top of the earthly hierarchy and, as God's representative on earth, he was also the bridge between earth and heaven. The belief that the monarch has a private life in any significant way separable from his public life comes from a modern view of character imposed on the past. Charles II's mistresses were as much a political gesture as Prince Hal's forays to the Boar's Head Tavern with Falstaff. Within the monarchical context, the question is not 'What constitutes private life?' but 'How should private life be expressed publicly?' The realm of the spirit is always a potential of Christian monarchy—and Charles I of England calls upon it frequently in *Eikon Basilike*. But in no way can the spiritual or the religious aspect of

---

2. In his lectures on *English Humorists of the Eighteenth Century* (1851), for example, Thackeray scornfully remarked that Sterne wept for fame and money. But, at the time, Boswell had begun a "Poetical Epistle" to Sterne in celebration of the merits of *Tristram Shandy* with somewhat different sentiments:

> Great erudition, polish'd taste,
> Pure language tho' you write in haste,
> Sweet sentiments on Human life—
> This I am sure, 'tis not for gain—(Howes, 84)

the monarch be identified with what *we* mean when we refer to private life. Private life in our sense is a concept that slowly emerges in the course of the eighteenth century. It refers neither to public behavior (before man) nor to religious behavior (before God), but to something in between: the individual before his family, friends, his posterity, and himself.

With the influence of a Protestant emphasis on the possibility of an individual relation to God without earthly intermediaries, the central importance of the king—particularly in the Protestant monarchies—began to be displaced by other sources of validation. Before the late eighteenth century there were always some who courted the immediate publicity of the eye and others who sought justification in less visible realms. But the historical shape of those differing attitudes then seemed clearer. As we move closer to our own time, however, into a period inaugurated by the overthrow of the monarchical concept of political power in America and France and marked by the rapid expansion of visual and verbal communication, the fame of ostentation and the fame of evasion begin to intertwine. In *Lives of the Poets,* Johnson can compare the literary virtues of Dryden and Pope with hardly a word about the way they presented themselves to their immediate audiences. By the 1820s, with William Hazlitt's comparison of Sir Walter Scott and Lord Byron in *The Spirit of the Age,* that issue is intimately connected to Hazlitt's discussion of their works. In barely forty years, fame has become inseparable from audience attention to one's personal nature.[3]

Founded in Fame

And they said, Go to, let us build us a city, and a tower, whose top *may reach* unto heaven; and let us make a name, lest we be scattered abroad upon the face of the whole earth.   —GENESIS 11:4

It *was* the brave Columbus,
A sailing o'er the tide,
Who notified the nations
Of where I would reside!
—EMILY DICKINSON

In great part the history of public fame since the eighteenth century is a history of successive efforts to reach beyond conventions of recognition and create a perceived self that is unprecedented without being unrecog-

3. By the twentieth century such seeming contradictions will become all too familiar, even though biographers, ignorant of the history of fame, still wonder why it is that their subjects both demand and try to evade public attention, struggle to become public figures, and then go into seclusion. What Byron, Napoleon, Emily Dickinson, or a hundred others felt in their marrow now blithely becomes part of a song called "Fame," in which going to heaven and having your name remembered amount to the same thing.

nizable. When politicians and generals parade their unconcern with customary honor, when poets and artists take the public stage to proclaim their lack of fealty to any established order, paradox has become the very atmosphere of fame. Previously nurtured as a class attribute, fame in its spiritual and artistic dimension had transcended class to offer the individual a status unrelated to his background. Johnson would have scorned it, but Boswell's celebration of his solitary rectitude stands behind the self-celebration of a figure like Byron, who sallies forth to free each individual reader from the trammels of social order. Coming in the midst of this ferment over who deserved fame and why, the American and French revolutions mark an epoch in the history of fame because they enfranchise the largest audience for the actions of the famous that had ever existed. In the process they offer the first demonstrations that there may be practical political dimension to the new individualism after all, if alienation from society could be redefined as alienation from society's traditions. As we shall see, no aspiration, even the aspiration to be neglected (and thereby show one's greater virtue) can escape the widespread self-consciousness about fame this audience helps create. The growing eighteenth-century fascination with the question of individual political and economic freedom, culminating in the American and French revolutions, creates a potent free market of fame, in which the use of media—writing, painting, and engraving—becomes a lever to power.

In America especially the legacy of the ages might be overturned entirely. At the end of the seventeenth century, Locke and his patron Shaftesbury had discussed the possibility of building a whole new society in the American wilderness, shaped by the free consent of independent individuals. The French revolutionaries institute a new calendar as part of their disruption of aristocratic time, beginning with the Year One, renaming the months, and reburying Rousseau, Voltaire, and other heroes in the Pantheon of Paris. But America seemed to have no need to rebegin because it was already new, a land that fed and was fed by the eighteenth-century fascination with origins and originality, islands and primitive peoples, where the roots of true individuality might be found. The orphans whose stories furnish so many plots to eighteenth-century fiction came to life in the new American individual, who rose out of the dunghill and went on to greatness, self-generated and therefore regenerated as well. In Europe, with its overhanging past, such open assertions appear most often in the guise of the outsider. But as the newest nation, taking as its audience all of Europe, America had been founded in fame. Its dynamic present superseded the past of all those who made it up, and its national self-consciousness was the support or crutch for the individual aspiration of each of its inhabitants.[4]

4. The power of this belief serves to justify later absorptions either by conquest or assimilation of any peoples the colonists found already in America, such as the native Americans and the Spanish, whose histories were older than the history of the nation itself.

In its demonstration of the ease with which an image of the nation could gather the allegiance previously given primarily to the ruler, America foretells the basic pattern of national fame in nineteenth-century Europe, where empire building proceeded as much by cultural and economic conquest as by military. The urge to cultural conquest may have had Alexandrian precedents, but a good portion of its imagery was originally Roman. Throughout late eighteenth-century art and literature recurs the image of the grand ruins of the past. In both revolutionary America and France, Roman architecture and imagery were elaborately revived to denote a restoration of classical Republican virtue that had been corrupted by the monarchical and aristocratic political system. In America, Corinthian capitals used as ballast in English or European sailing ships turn up as garden centerpieces in southern plantations or northern estates. *Fama* the raging monster of scandal and falsehood was decisively replaced by the benevolent herald, the newspaper gossip, and the eulogistic mourner. Death in post-Revolutionary America, as it had in classical Rome, especially summoned up images of heroic fame, and in innumerable homemade as well as printed mourning pictures, the solitary maiden grieving by the urn of the departed coincided with the tears of Columbia, Liberty, or even *Fama* herself mourning lost greatness.[5] In Europe, as Napoleon's career will illustrate, the Roman precedent ultimately justified the empire, but in America there was a more concerted effort to maintain the liberty of the Republic. Philip Freneau's verse depiction of George Washington may be influenced by Defoe's account of the personal virtues of William III, but popular prints after Washington's death showed him ascending to heaven wearing a Roman toga.

Down into the nineteenth century and beyond the tendency to link American leaders visually with Roman insignia is strong, until the rise of Fascist Italy gives such details as the Roman fasces on Lincoln's statue in the Lincoln Memorial, and his togalike cloak, an uncomfortable resonance. The model was less any particular Roman great man (although Cato and Cincinnatus are often mentioned) than the general image of personal ambition at the service of the state. The danger of the Republican analogy was that it carried with it a tinge of that competition among such as Pompey, Catiline, Caesar, and Cicero to determine who had the proper vision of Rome. But the gift of the American Revolution to its champions was that for a time at least it seemed that all energies were in accord, and the fame they aimed to create was not the fame of any individual so much as the fame of America, the newest and greatest of nations, where new kinds of men and therefore new kinds of fame would be made possible. So Douglass Adair, in his trailblazing essay, "Fame and the Founding Fathers" describes in detail how pervasive the desire for fame was among the Founding Fathers: It "transmuted the leaden desire for self-aggrandizement and

---

5. The credit for the artistic conflation of the grieving woman—America or Liberty—and *Fama* into one figure has been given to the Swiss-born English painter Angelica Kauffman (1741–1807). See Schorsch, *Mourning Becomes America*.

personal reward into a golden concern for public service and the promotion of the commonwealth" (24). In Revolutionary America, unlike Fulke Greville's more ambiguous celebration of the classic urge to fame more than 150 years before, the argument justified the founding of a new state, instead of the preservation of an old.

Questions of political liberty, representative democracy, popular war, the power of "the people," and the access to media are only a few of the political themes of the half-century or so from the American Revolution to the death of Napoleon. But accompanying and shaping them is the self-conscious effort to define the essence of America as a nation through visual and verbal art. Cultural historians such as Kenneth Silverman, Neil Harris, and E. McClung Fleming have documented the extent to which artists and writers in the late eighteenth and early nineteenth centuries were passionately involved in a search for the appropriate image of America. The countries of Europe in the eighteenth century had moved away from the monarch as the symbolic figure to an abstraction of the nation: Elizabeth gave way to John Bull, Louis XIV to Marianne. America as the New World had been symbolically depicted as the Indian Princess. Later, mythological figures like Minerva and Hercules (proposed by Franklin and John Adams) were used, neoclassical goddesses with helmets and plumes, as well as less individual figures like Columbia and Liberty, until iconography settled down with the toga-draped Liberty for ceremonial occasions and the indigenous Brother Jonathan and Uncle Sam for the more raucous popular events.

Portraiture especially presents individuals, king or commoner, not as part of a system so much as autonomous and free, while defining the viewer as a member of an audience for whomever is depicted. After the Revolution, Americans were eager to see pictures and hear poems that celebrated their great men and heroic actions. Without a glorious past, they had nevertheless a glorious present and in celebrating Washington or Franklin or Jefferson, they were celebrating themselves as well. While in Europe the overthrow of a monarch might inspire others to assume that role, in America there was never any single niche to be filled. The most familiar motto on the Great Seal—*e pluribus unum*—equally implied the one nation created from many individuals and the one individual who might arise from the audience to represent the nation. Finally, no one represented America but the American. In the person of Franklin particularly, the American was the new person, not just in the Roman sense of someone entering public office who came from a nonruling family, but as both historically unprecedented and humanly basic. What individual or figure represented and summarized America was therefore a question constantly at issue, and the history of the United States can be easily written in terms of the shifting definition of what an American is or might be.

In the context of self-saluting, the flag was another intriguing revamping of Roman precedent. It was the first national flag to dispense with crosses or the armorial bearings of its rulers to create a new design, each state a star, each state with its own Roman Genius, starring itself and making itself immortal.[6] In such an exuberant context, Fame herself, in England and Europe a virtually archaic classical motif, regained a final dying bloom before the nineteenth century essentially dropped such overt classical motifs. In 1788 the *Columbian Magazine* featured an engraving of Columbia, "the Genius of the United States," in front of a temple representing the (recently ratified) Constitution. Clio, the Muse of history, kneels at her feet. The next year the *Columbian*'s frontispiece showed Columbia seated, with books, a globe, and a shield depicting the American eagle and the constellation of stars representing the new states. Behind her a figure with a lyre points to another temple, this time clearly the Temple of Fame, while he lays out her destiny:

> America! with Peace and Freedom blest,
> Pant for true Fame, and scorn inglorious rest:
> Science invited; urg'd by the Voice divine,
> Exert thy self, 'till every Art be thine (Fleming, 61).

Public fame from the time of the American and French revolutions is thus shaped by a world where the image and idea of fame can be reproduced and disseminated in unprecedented quantities—enough to make the introduction of the engraved portrait and the printed text in the fifteenth and sixteenth centuries seem like only a dabbling in the waters of renown. Even before the revolutions pressed a new political action on larger numbers of people, the culture of the eighteenth century in Europe was showing a greater and greater fascination with the question of being seen and the act of seeing, not only in terms of a scientific and experimental empiricism, for which the Enlightenment is usually celebrated, but also in terms of seeing *other people* and being seen by them. In the course of the century in England, acting styles shift from the bombastic and oratorical styles of the early part of the century to the more "natural" style of David Garrick by midcentury, where the prime performer, although still recognized as a virtuoso artist, yet seeks to impersonate a character and a sensibility instead of rhetorically declaiming its nature. Diderot's *Paradox of the Actor* takes its lead and inspiration from Garrick himself to theorize elaborately on the actor as a public performer, who coolly renders the most extreme passions,

6. Washington's first flag in 1776 still includes the British crosses of St. Andrew and St. George. By 1777 the new flag has replaced their imagery with its own. For the Great Seal of the United States, it took three submissions over three years before a revamped version of the third submission was adopted in 1782, with two mottoes from Virgil, one from the *Aeneid* (*annuit coeptis*) and the other (*novus ordo seclorum*) from the fourth or "messianic" eclogue originally meant to herald the coming to power of Augustus and later interpreted as a prediction of the appearance of Jesus. Thus, after more than two centuries of monarchical propaganda invoking Virgil's image of the restored Golden Age, the language is reapplied not to an individual but to a nation. *E pluribus unum*, in contrast, ultimately derives from Horace's *de pluribus una*, a phrase from the poem (*Epistles*, II, ii) in which he describes the nature of personal *genius*. In the eighteenth century *e pluribus unum* is the motto of *The Gentleman's Magazine*, one of the early publications to address an audience interested in sampling the varieties of knowledge (Silverman, 658n).

submerged in his role, but detached enough to make it convincing and committed. The analysis is a virtual prophecy of the public stances that will soon be taken by figures like Washington, Napoleon, and Byron: As the audience develops a greater and greater taste for sincerity, passion, and involvement, it also appreciates best the actor who expresses those traits with coolness, detachment, and self-awareness. Thus Diderot's actor appeals simultaneously to the audience that wants to believe his impersonation of the passionate character and to the audience that will appreciate the skill and genius of that impersonation.

Although the American and French revolutions decisively open the question of how to define the face of liberty and freedom in a world whose public imagery had been derived almost exclusively from its ruling houses, their efforts arose out of a general European movement in the later eighteenth century to discover what the distinctive individual was like, apart from his background or origins. From the midcentury onward more and more novels, for example, devoted themselves to the question of education: What and how should men or women be taught so they might best realize not their national or class heritage but their human nature? Rousseau himself made an influential contribution in his novel *Émile* (1762), but he was only one of a number of writers across Europe fascinated with education as a way of creating a different kind of person, as free as possible from the prejudices of the past.

The leader, the most admired man, in such a cultural atmosphere is the enabling figure who sponsors the greatest amount of self-expression and self-enhancement. Few think of a "career" when social identity is fairly fixed by the circumstances of birth. At most the soul can develop, since the body is doomed to labor within predetermined confines. But eighteenth-century culture introduced the individual to an awareness that his life could be contemplated, shaped, and sold. Until the eighteenth century, "ego" was a word that tended to appear in English as "egoity," an English version of the medieval theological term used primarily to describe the self-obsession of Satan. But in the course of the eighteenth century, *egoism* (the philosophy that only the mind exists) and *egotism* ("the excessive use of the first person singular" said Joseph Addison) became more and more prominent, until the use of *ego* to designate self-consciousness became popular enough to begin to appear frequently in popular literary magazines. Addison himself had picked up *egotist* from the writings of the grammarians and logicians of Port-Royal, whose interest in making language express what was invariably true no doubt spawned their disdain for such subjective distortions. But he was writing at the beginning of an age more interested in the varieties of individual nature as well as in the impact individual perspective makes on both observation and language. Up-to-date moralists like John Mason, author of *Self-Knowledge: A Treatise Shewing the Nature and Benefit of That Important Science, and the Way to Attain It* (which had gone through twelve editions by 1791), might argue that knowing the self fully led to greater self*less*ness and Christian humility. But there was an equally strong line of argument marked by such works as Pope's *Essay on Man* (1733) and Adam Smith's *Wealth of Nations* (1776) that stressed the social usefulness, especially on the economic plane, of allowing everyone to exercise his will freely. As the paradigmatic open place, America was, of course, the situation where such freedom could best be exercised, and J. Hector St. John Crèvecoeur, in his celebrated "What is an American?" essay in *Letters from an American Farmer* (1782), calls self-interest "the basis of nature" and frequently uses "selfish" as a positive description of behavior.[7]

In America and France especially, the lack or the overthrow of monarchy thus engenders a gap of public gaze that will be filled in different ways by figures such as Washington, Napoleon, and Byron. The audience no longer merely seems to watch and passively take in the self-constructions of its society's great men. Its gaze now creates and shapes those who move before it, forcing greatness to occupy a certain space in its eye. It is an audience, perhaps the first such in modern history, sophisticated enough to be titillated by a refusal of its most obvious applause. It is no longer willing to accept public figures who merely fill their roles, but is intent instead on those who play them with a passion generated by self-consciousness. Unlike Renaissance monarchs such as Elizabeth or Louis XIV, who validated their stature by hiring and inspiring writers and artists to associate them with the greats of the classical and their own national pasts, late eighteenth-century political figures like Napoleon and Washington emphasized their willingness to support what was new and changing in their worlds, the social imperative of self-fulfillment summarized by the Declaration of Independence—"life, liberty, and the pursuit of happiness"—and the Declaration of the Rights of Man—"life, liberty, and property." The new public man proclaims that he does not take on his role because of his heredity but because he *must*. Marcus Aurelius considered rule to be an obligation undertaken for the good of the state, but he still longed to retire. Similarly, the fame of such figures as Napoleon or Washington contained at its most compelling more than a hint of possible refusal: If it were not for the needs of the audience, the task would never have been taken up. Simultaneously, the audience is flattered and yet held at a distance. Unlike the monarchs who take it as their due to be celebrated in public, the new public man expresses the painful but necessary self-consciousness of appearing before others at all. *Eikon Basilike* may have defined kingship as a

---

7. The difference between Addison's and Emerson's attitude toward Montaigne is indicative of the change in the implication of "ego" and its cognates. For Addison, Montaigne is "the most eminent egotist that ever appeared in the world," who constantly talks about himself and brings every discussion back to himself: "Had he kept his own counsel, he might have passed for a much better man, though perhaps he would not have been so diverting an author" (*Spectator*, 2 July 1714, No. 562). Carlyle similarly contrasts what he considers to be the showoff Boswell and the "silent" Samuel Johnson, who stayed at home (264). But for Emerson, "Montaigne is the frankest and honestest of all writers" (698): "The sincerity and marrow of the man reaches to his sentences" (700), and the book is realized—in Montaigne's own terms—by being as close to the self of the author as possible.

calling as well as a hereditary right. But the president served because he was elected, the first consul and emperor because of his star. And so Napoleon associated himself with Joan of Arc, the saint God had forced into armor for France, and Washington invoked Cincinnatus, the farmer urged into civic duty by the times and his fellow citizens.

The French and American revolutions had begun an age of citizen-armies who defend a nation rather than the privileges of a particular group. Accordingly, the nation itself became a part-psychological, part-spiritual concept, whose nature is constantly being defined and appealed to by those who would lead; and political leaders take on the performing necessity of frequently subordinating policy to the courting of audience assent. If the leader is a larger version of the individual citizen as well as a concentration of the meaning of the nation, then advertisement, the proliferation of his imagery, is required to make those equations a daily reality. George Washington may have hated to sit for his portrait and Napoleon may have enjoyed it, but the need for such portraiture was common to the evolving political and cultural life of both countries—the need to lure allegiance through the eye as much as through the mind. Contrasted with the secrecy of the power of the past, the increasingly visual form taken by the power and assertion of the postrevolutionary period was presented as a new sincerity, a willingness to face the public in order to be recognized and to be identified with. The early portrait of Washington by Charles Willson Peale in 1779, showing him solid and triumphant after the Battle of Princeton, and the later Washington of John Trumbull (1792) after the Battle of Charleston, appearing shadowy and powerful, illustrate the contrast. Peale's Washington is still the traditional military hero; Trumbull's has become the symbolic leader. Peale's Washington looks directly at us; Trumbull's, in a pose akin to David's of Napoleon (who admired Washington and frequently imitated his iconography), looks away. In these gazes outside the frame, into eternity or posterity or destiny, we find the eighteenth-century expansion of the self-contained spirituality of the family portrait into a political program. The portrait of a great man looking at the viewer denotes a self-satisfaction with social status. But his looking away conveys an assurance of personal destiny that makes a direct appeal to the viewer unnecessary and irrelevant. It is this pose of independence and self-sufficiency that typifies the most famous figures of the age, whether they are in the sphere of politics or art. In paintings the viewer is either ignored or treated as a kind of intrusion on the vital inwardness of the depicted celebrity. Thus one viewer, the ignorant and sycophantic interloper, is dismissed to flatter another—the self-absorbed activist, who appreciates the great man in part as an image of himself.

Such paradoxes of the image of popular sovereignty spring from the basic eighteenth-century argument over the relative claims of social and individual rights. To the extent that we believe that virtue comes from the willingness to submit to social rules and social order, we can accept a designedly theatrical or dramatic self-presentation in our leaders and in ourselves. To the extent that we believe that virtue comes from the individual and that society can be an illegitimate imposition on personal freedom, we will consider virtually any social staging of ourselves as corrupt at the core. The first view might be identified with those who argue our obligation to support the society that exists, and the second with those who argue our obligation to create the society that ought to be. But the distinction is also one between inextricably connected ways of defining human nature. Unlike the monarchies, where social hierarchy tried to ensure that everyone might have a preexisting social role, the new political societies were predicated on the assumption that personal ability and personal will are stronger than inheritance. When social roles are thus so mobile and shifting, individual nature, "character," becomes the stable concept that public behavior aims to stage. Thus in the imagery of the public men of the democratic revolutions, the belief in God's providential eye on the world turns into the personal trait of the great man's "destiny"—the dynamic individual's inevitable progress toward the achievements and rewards that both history and eternity had decreed to be necessary.

For the great man or the great country on the stage of this newly alive history, the goal was usually unspecified, for that would be to limit its scope. "Destiny" meant instead the compelling future, where growth and achievement would endlessly unfold for the ages to come, and to which one must be committed because one could not do otherwise. In a certain light this destiny might resemble the old literary idea of posterity. But in fact it was quite different. No longer was posterity defined as a Horatian future where poems will be honored for outlasting all the seemingly more tangible triumphs of the great general-politicians. The new destiny/posterity superseded the Renaissance opposition between arms and letters by gathering the sanction of otherworldly detachment into the hero of the present. Like the saint, looking to heaven, or the writer, looking to a more "fit audience," the new hero believed that action in the present carried with it the awareness of a gaze from the future. The detachment of the writer contemplating posterity complements the detachment of the public man with an eye ostentatiously on that day when he will be judged whole and entire, uncompromised by the enmities and imperceptions of the present. Byron in 1812 only half-jokingly refers to the contemplation of his correspondence with Lady Melbourne by readers in the twentieth century (Marchand, *Letters,* II, 240). And Napoleon in exile on St. Helena will plan for the creation of his most lasting work, the Napoleonic legend.

The Lineage of the Unprecedented

Formerly *Poets* made *Players,* but nowadays 'tis generally the *Player* that makes the *Poet.*

—ABEL BOYER, *The English Theophrastus* (1702)

Military politicians like Washington and Napoleon as well as figures of art and fashion like Lord Byron and Beau Brummell crystalize the search for a new variety of great man in the age of revolution. Not even Rousseau had been as acute a psychosocial barometer for his society or his age. The distant monarchs had been replaced by men in whom their audiences saw a simultaneous reflection and enhancement of themselves. By exposing the uncertain line between public and private nature, their self-stagings implied that buried in each spectator was a greatness that could be exposed for public display and fascination. Disrupting the regular history of royal dynasties, Napoleon, for example, embodies a desire for national rather than class glory, and with his proclamation of "careers open to talents" he tapped the urge of many to claim their own place in the new dispensation. Emerging from the bosom of the aristocracy, Byron is similarly celebrated not for his position or his poetic ability so much as for the literary display of 'himself'—a swirling whirlpool of almost sexual allure in which his audience might glimpse an image not of their public selves so much as those desires and aspirations that had seemed socially unfit or irrelevant, now writ large and grand. In the letters that poured in to him from every part of England spoke the voices of private loneliness and singularity in response to their public model and the catalyst of their own self-regard. To have a public personality and thus appear larger in the eyes of others was no longer the sole prerogative of inheritance and birth or even of talent. As Napoleon makes honor and glory the possible goal of every Frenchman, rather than the possession of a particular class or occupation, so Byron marks the point at which the desire for fame, the aristocracy of the spirit, might be vicariously enjoyed by every reader.

If we try to generalize the appeal of such figures, one trait that stands out is the seeming elusiveness of character on which so many of their contemporaries remarked. However public they are, all convey an atmosphere of solitude and self-sufficiency to which their admirers and supporters are drawn without quite knowing why. In both Napoleon and Byron, for example, the talk of their "destiny"—which Napoleon identified with that of France and Byron with some darker fate—expressed a fusion of earthly aspiration with spiritual withdrawal that was to be appreciated by the audience of God. Butler had mocked the "itch of picture" among writers and Pope in 1730 indicated how the wealthy and titled had joined the competition: "My Lord advance with majestic mien, / Smit with the mighty pleasure, to be seen" ("Epistle to Burlington," 127–128).

But, in response to this new age of communications and mass audiences, it was becoming paradoxically appropriate that the greatest authority might be gained and even justified by a display of spiritual or emotional intensity that implied it did not need an audience. In tandem with a wider vocabulary of public exposure come words like Napoleon's "prestige," the personal force by which an individual holds together a nation, and what might be called Byron's "glamor," Sir Walter Scott's word for the magic and mystery of the visible.[8]

Even as more visual representations than ever were becoming available, the greatest seemed both to exploit and to elude that specificity. The latter half of the eighteenth century, for example, had witnessed a European craze for physiognomy. The seminal work was a treatise by Johann Kaspar Lavater (1775–1778; English, 1789–1798) in which he—like James Granger organizing English biography or Linnaeus classifying plants, animals, minerals, and diseases—tried to create a "science" of the face and its expressions by which character might be read directly. The subject had been around since antiquity. But the enormous popularity of Lavater's book illustrates how intense the fascination had become, particularly with the face of greatness. The more detailed Lavater was (he used engravings primarily of writers, artists, and philosophers), the easier it would be for his audience to tell the heroic "truth" of an individual face from the ostentatious costumes to which they had been accustomed. By the early nineteenth century, virtually all those who wrote about the significant people of the period fancied themselves expert physiognomists and we are treated to innumerable shapes of ears, turns of lips, and tones of complexion that are presented in an effort to convey to the reader the uniqueness of the person being described. Usually, the writer or diarist then concludes with a balanced flourish that lets us know this great figure has been properly and totally plumbed. But, in the descriptions of Byron and Napoleon, despite the care taken to note the twist of Byron's mouth or the color of Napoleon's eyes, there is little such finality. We are told that both had pallid (or ivory) complexions and that both bit their nails.[9] But Byron's character is finally a mystery and Napoleon's is without any common shape—to his enemies entirely opportunistic, to his admirers, magisterially transcendent. Like a "destiny," prestige and glamor were powerful gifts, emanating from oneself yet raising strong emotions in others, that at best one could coolly stand back from rather than totally control. Diderot's

8. Scott's use of "glamor" is a self-conscious revival. Until the late fifteenth century, "gramarye" could mean either the ability to read and write or the ability to cast spells, since to the Middle Ages these talents were usually equivalent. Then—with the expanded literacy opened by the invention of movable-type printing?—the two words took their separate ways: "gramarye" = magic turning into "glamor"; and "gramarye" = the knowledge of words turning into "grammar."

9. Quennell in *Byron: The Years of Fame* suggests that Byron's pale face came from a lifelong habit of using purgatives. But the intersection of an image of purified humanity with one of the melancholic mime seems more intriguing for our purposes.

actor had stepped off the stage and into the court, the drawing room, and, as Jane Austen makes clear, the afternoon tea party.

An important element in the sway that Napoleon and Byron had over those around them was their sincere willingness to stage themselves theatrically and premeditatively. Napoleon frequently flew into calculated rages, while Byron, for reasons that sympathetic writers have ascribed to his club foot and unsympathetic ones to his penchant for self-display, would frequently stand alone and seemingly disconsolate in the foyers and anterooms of large gatherings. Both were characterized by a shyness and reserve on social occasions, which vanished for Napoleon when he was in his public role as military and political decision maker and for Byron when he sat down to write. Napoleon, it is said, took lessons from the actor Talma in how to make small talk, while Byron took great pains with his appearance, along the lines of the melancholic foppery made fashionable by Beau Brummell. (Byron once said that the three greatest men of the nineteenth century were Beau Brummell, himself, and Napoleon—in that order.)[10] Thus the theater of their public self-presentation was itself a sincere effort to stage with desperation or exuberance their overwhelming self-consciousness, at a time when the stage for so many forms of unreflective ostentation had immeasurably widened. As the combination of social uneasiness and personal magnetism characteristic of both Napoleon and Byron (like that of Rousseau) indicates, the painfully shy person along with the star are the twin children of modern fame. The Christian expectation of the security of eternity, which requires a subordination of personal desires and eccentricities, has in effect been laid aside for the social expectation of security on earth, which requires self-assertion. Yet society's standards for success, particularly the economic, still carry the old stigma of moral and spiritual insufficiency. Thus an important element in the nature of the best fame was its aloneness, its separation from the crowd, even though the famous, more clearly than ever, had emerged from the crowd to assert their personal distinctiveness and thereby demonstrate its potentiality in every member of their audience.[11]

10. "He used to say there were three great men ruined in one year [1814], Brummell, himself, and Napoleon!" (Medwin, 72). In other moods Byron believed that Sir Walter Scott was "undoubtedly the first man of his time" (Quennell, 221). The urge to draw up lists of the great, often including oneself, is a hallmark of the period. Compare Byron's barely ironic remark after reading an article published in Java that compared his poetry to Tom Moore's: "But, there is *fame* for you at six and twenty! Alexander had conquered India at the same age; but I doubt if he was disputed about, or his conquests compared with those of Indian Bacchus, at Java" (*Selected Letters*, 247).

11. Until now one important theme of this book has been a particularly male sort of self-importance, designed to be viewed primarily by other men. Sometimes it appears unadorned and others parodied, sometimes undermining itself and sometimes assertive. In the new world of revolution and publicity, where the cult of primitivism and the natural helps support attacks on inherited authority and traditional conceptions of masculinity, the male urge to fame begins to seek audiences of women as often as those of men. Both Byron and Napoleon had a low opinion of the capacity of women to do anything beyond the domestic and often a contempt for those who

Robert Burns in 1786 had voiced the new anxiety of the day in the comforting tones of Scottish dialect when he wrote "O wad some Power the giftie gie us / To see oursels as ithers see us!" Burns was writing in the voice of a speaker observing a louse crawling unnoticed on the bonnet of a woman in church. But the desire to stand aside from oneself to regulate one's image before the world was hardly confined to those who wanted to compose an unblemished picture of fashionable piety. Not long after, Beau Brummell became famous for the care he took with his appearance, to the extent of tying his tie some forty or fifty times until the look he wanted was right—and discarding every tie that was inadequately tied because its rumples would betray its lack of spontaneous perfection.[12] But in this fervent dawn of ostentatious self-absorption, where a reputation might be had for owning an extraordinary number of shoes or snuffboxes, Brummell represented not a fastidious vexing of detail so much as the pressure of self-consciousness applied to the appearance of the public self. Contrary to how Brummell's dandyism was later imitated, his own style was a study in reticence. He sought to be noticed not for his lavish dress but for the intricate self-consciousness of his restraint. His clothes and his behavior, unlike those of the gaudy and feathered fop of the seventeenth century, are characterized by austerity. Like Byron going to parties and standing on the fringes and in the corners, Brummell's version of the dandy conveys a sense of separation and melancholy, as if he were in mourning for society itself with all its misdirected splendor. Instead of clothes as an externalized, disguising costume, the dress of the dandy implies that some purified self is being expressed, some controlled self-will. Just as Byron tests his isolation against crowds, the dandy's disdain for the imperfect behavior of others must be repeatedly staged within a social world. Whether their actual origins were low or high, both combine the social sanction of the aristocrat with the spiritual authority of the desert saint to fashion themselves as phenomena out of nowhere.

For the aristocrats of his day and their growing crowd of imitators, Brummell especially was the embodiment of a crucially separate point of view from which perfect value can be discerned, and the vogue and scope of his influence implies a world hungry for such models and assessments. Although his position as social arbiter would seem to make him more sensitive to the nuances of social standing, Brummell yet emphasized his own self-creation and even minimized what position his father did have:

---

did more. But Napoleon's audience was almost entirely men and Byron's preponderantly women. The crucial issue is the distinction between the literary audience in which women dominate and the political audience in which they have little power until the age of their enfranchisement begins in the late nineteenth and early twentieth centuries. Yet the influence of a newly widespread audience of women for fame is apparent long before they get the vote, as souvenir sewing boxes distributed during the 1824 American presidential campaign may attest.

12. As the admiring author of a two-volume biography of Brummell noted a few years after Brummell's death in poverty, "his tie became a model that was imitated, but never equalled" (Jesse, I, 55).

Who ever heard of George B.'s father and who would ever have heard
of George B. himself, if he had been anything but what he is?[13]

By telling the oafish Prince Regent (later George IV) what to wear in
order to look like a ruler, he illustrates the pitiful inadequacy of both the
monarchical version of the hero and the courtier version of the audience
that for so long had been the only model of fame. Brummell, like Byron
and Napoleon, represented a new kind of self-projected power, compounded of concentration, austerity, and self-sufficiency. Although he
seemed thoroughly inside the social world, he yet gained his sway by his
self-conscious ability to stand aside, premeditating what for others was
barely semiconscious. Like the great poet or the man of the people, the
supreme arbiter of fashion invoked only his own unprecedented personal
nature as the source and sanction of his insight and power.

Much like Byron, the aristocrat who signals the effective end of aristocracy because he also wants to be famous, the dandy as formulated by
Brummell is the exquisite flower of a decayed aristocratic world whose
beauty seems to justify its existence but actually predicts its quick demise,
because such style is necessarily premeditated. Thus in the nineteenth century the dandy shares some characteristics with both the conservative politician and the political revolutionary. Their temperaments are innately
critical of society because they take its forms so seriously, sometimes to
perfect and sometimes to overturn. The career of Beau Brummell, who
achieved his special social status through an exemplary detachment from
himself, a self-honing if not quite a self-making, looks forward barely a
decade to that of Benjamin Disraeli, the young dandy novelist (and later
prime minister) who is celebrated for the picture of high society in his
novel *Vivian Grey* until it is discovered that he is an outsider and a Jew
who in some basic sense made it all up. It might have been well for his
snobbish critics to remember that the American Revolution began with
the colonists adopting as their own the British mockery of "Yankee Doodle
Dandy" and ended with them singing "The World Turned Upside Down."

In our own time, of course, the acute awareness of how we appear to
others is so obviously indebted to the innumerable forms of modern visual
representation that we may miss the revolution in self-awareness marked
by the career of Brummell, with its intriguing analogues in those of Byron,
Napoleon, and others. It crystalizes as well a growing fascination with the
visible nature of public people that helps engender the growth of caricature, vaudeville, and variety theater; seizes ravenously on the new invention of photography; and later battens on movies, radio, and television. A
few years ago Rich Little—an impressionist and therefore a member of a
theatrical group whose careers are based entirely on an audience aware of
how certain public people sound, look, and behave—told an anecdote about
meeting John Wayne, whom he had been imitating for years. Worried that

13. Quoted by Ellen Moers, *The Dandy*, 18, from Lady Hester Stanhope, *Memoirs
in Conversation with Her Physician C. L. Meryon* (1845), I, 281. Brummell habitu-
ally talked about himself in the third person.

Wayne had been offended, Little was cautious until Wayne welcomed him heartily and thanked him for keeping Wayne's own career afloat by reminding the audience of his image. Then he asked Little for a favor. He was doing a show that night and hadn't had time to read the script. Could Little read it with Wayne's voice and Wayne's gestures so that Wayne could see if it was right for him? Like dukes coming to Brummell to have him pass judgment on their clothes to see if they measure up to what a duke should wear, Wayne wants Little to see if the script is fitting. The difference, of course, is that Brummell has made himself into the standard to which these aristocrats and gentlemen must adhere, while Wayne is using the imitative caricaturist Little to fine-tune his own sense of the image he wants to project. Like all modern performers, he has his own Brummell inside.

In the cult of Byron we see the early nineteenth-century fascination with a kind of visual glamor that takes its material from surfaces only to hint at what lies behind and beyond them. Because of his delicate sense of fashion, Brummell's admirers ascribed to him a secure inner seat from which such judgments were made, while Byron's own fame in society was increased enormously by the besetting sense of what was unsaid and invisible about his nature. Garbed in the characteristic black of the early nineteenth-century dandy, Byron's somberness could imply an awful destiny and a mysterious past behind the public self. The lure of even his best works for his contemporaries depended to an enormous extent on reading him through the poems, the dashing and melancholic naif wandering through the world. Achilles, the hero sulking in his tent because his honor has been usurped by Agamemnon, the mere commander, turns into the Byronic hero, publicly ravaged by a secret he cannot tell. Capitalizing on the paradoxes of fame and its new separation from any political or civic life, gifted by birth with all the social privileges that stability and acquiescence could bring, he yet chose to reject political and social aristocracy to become a writer, an aristocrat of the spirit, committed to the ideals of liberty and freedom. The image was appealing, even infectious. Byron died of it in Greece, offering his now totally tangible fame as a weapon in the fight for independence. From Boswell masquerading as a Corsican rebel at a fashionable ball to Byron dying of fever at Missolonghi, the costume of self-sufficiency has merged with the flesh beneath. Ernest Hemingway sparely and succinctly summed up the ideal of the questing writer as it is carried into our own times. It's lonely, he writes to his publisher Charles Scribner, "when you have the point" (Letters, 800).

Ever since Byron's four years of greatest fame[14] ended with his formal separation from his wife of barely more than a year, gossips and biographers alike have labored to deduce something specific about the "sin" that forced the breakup of his marriage and the exile that ended only with his

14. The "years of fame" are 1812 to 1816, although Byron himself counted his period of greatest fame as six weeks. He left England on 25 April 1816, less than a month before Brummell fled to escape his creditors (12 May).

death in Greece eight years later. For those who like such specifics, it is usually accepted now that Byron had an affair with his half sister Augusta Leigh in 1813 and may have been the father of her daughter Medora, born the next year. Then uncertainty enters, for only speculation ties Byron's guilt for the "sin" to his increasing rages during the first year of his marriage, resulting in a separation that became permanent. Yet, long before these events took place, a hero with a brooding awareness of some enormous sin or unfulfilled destiny is a characteristic of Byron's poetry and his public appearance. The most interesting question for Byron's contribution to the history of fame is therefore not what he and his half sister may have done, but how whatever happened fit in with the already well-established implication that some unutterable dark secret was the diabolical or angelic source of his poetic insight.

In other efforts to ground Byron's "secret" in biographical fact, writers have concluded that Byron stood to one side at parties and rarely circulated because of his embarrassment about his clubfoot. Yet the clubfoot and the "sin" were both part of Byron's sense of himself in public, two wounds, one inherited and the other voluntarily inflicted, that appropriately shadowed the image to which so many of his readers and admirers responded. They bodied forth the dark uncertainty of his inner life, while furnishing personal dissatisfactions that helped Byron justify his preoccupation with his singularity. Like so many in the present, Byron was a fan before he was a star. So preoccupied was he by some posterity lobe in his brain that he was perpetually revising the fame hit parade of his times. All sorts of fame intrigued him. He collected hair from friends and notables and had his own collected. On his travels he carried a screen, as Peter Quennell notes, "pasted with scraps of boxers and actresses" (166). At the point when his marriage was clearly coming to an end, he considered himself "the greatest man existing" and would not allow even Napoleon equal time. Clearly the most encompassing definition of the Byronic "sin" is that it is self-consciousness itself, the sense of unappreciated merit, the overwhelming desire to appeal to the public—necessary and worthy because retirement is both antisocial and hypocritical, disgusting because of the new public world into which such appeal has to be made.

Many writers have remarked on Byron's penchant for displaying what are usually private matters in the newspapers of Europe, while they point to the fact that he was outraged when his life became the subject of popular rumor. But the paradox is only superficial. Byron and Napoleon were men whose temperaments allowed them without premeditation to promote their undoubted talents by an atmosphere of anecdote and innuendo that made them larger than human. So far, they resemble Alexander, Jesus, and all those in the history of fame whose names have lasted to the present. But Napoleon and Byron also lived in a world in which the audience was beginning to expect some participation in creating the greatness of their idols as a mirror of their own. Once the message of fame was sent out by their very visible careers, it could return in an incredibly expanded form.

Some might evade its pressure, few could measure up to it, and most would fail. In America, at least in the generation of the Founding Fathers, the great man managed to escape the demands of his audience with relatively few scars. But Byron and Napoleon are prime examples of public figures undone by their own vogue and success. The paradoxical salvation promised by modern fame of a transcendence through publicity was well under way. Byron had said after the publication of *Childe Harold* that he awoke to find himself famous. He was not yet aware that the new machine of literary celebrity had fallen upon him as its first hero-victim. In his effort to understand his image, Byron kept virtually all the letters sent to "him" by his fans, as if in the accumulation he might discover the charm by which to keep it under control.

* * *

> The French and American Revolutions differed from each other in many things, but they were alike in one particular—the former gave all its *power* to a single man, the latter all its *fame*.
> —BENJAMIN RUSH to John Adams, 14 August 1805

As general and politician, Napoleon was much more interested than Byron in adapting his public self to the ends of direct power over others. Born in the year after Boswell publishes the *Account of Corsica,* nurtured in his youth on Rousseau's projected constitution for Corsica and Plutarch's patterns of classical political and military greatness, Napoleon is also the beneficiary of a revolution that wrested military authority from the exclusive hands of the rich and titled. For better or worse, he was the man of the present, and whatever attempts he made later to establish his own family as a kind of royal dynasty, his greatest strength and the strongest link to his admirers was his commitment to both the overthrow of past sanctions and the ennobling of individual effort. In contrast to the hereditary monarch's dependence on lineage, the Napoleonic general and the Napoleonic ruler made every decision a test of personal worthiness.

In a frequently used metaphor, Napoleon considered himself an arch between the old order and the new. His commitment to the moment of triumph and the glory of France thus required some historical dimension as well. Like the iconographers of the American Revolution, Napoleon sponsored and expanded the analogy with Republican Rome already begun after the fall of Louis XVI and Marie Antoinette. As he proclaimed to his army in Italy while he was still only a highly successful general:

> . . . [W]e are friends to all peoples, and particularly to the descendants of Brutus, of Scipio and the great men whom we have taken for models. To rebuild the Capitol and place in honour there the statues of the famous heroes, to awaken the Roman people benumbed by centuries of slavery, such will be the fruit of your victories (Hutt, 17).

Thus he begins his characteristic project of making the appeal to glory, formerly the clarion of courtiers and other royal flatterers, into a tool of national unity, a patriotic appeal to bind men together, rather than the narrow appeal to the interests of a particular dynasty. In the new atmosphere of democratic revolution, Napoleon represented himself as the archetypal Frenchman who would restore the national glory that the nominal conservers—the aristocracy and the royal family—had so derelictly allowed to decay. In the manner of most civil wars, the French Revolution had been essentially fought over which Frenchmen would be allowed to call themselves and their actions "France." By his own self-conception, which accorded so well with the desires of his audience, Napoleon defined his singularity as an ability to be the container for the aspirations of all. The steps in his career bear striking and publicly stressed analogies to the rise of the young Augustus. Courting factions otherwise totally at odds, forcing enemies to work together on state projects, he placed himself beyond faction and class. But unlike Augustus's appeal to the sanction of Julius Caesar, Napoleon invoked first "France," the national entity that was larger than any particular class or faction, and then the sanction of his own extraordinary success, his "destiny," his "star." As in America, the state itself, as a heightened image of its inhabitants and its history, would supersede any other justifications for power.

Like Augustus, Napoleon first appears as the child of the Revolution, then quickly becomes, in turn, the victorious general, the patriotic consul, and finally the supreme emperor. Along the way he developed the ability to highlight everything he did with both laudatory dispatches (whatever the truth of the situation) and paintings that celebrated his victories and solidified his image as the man of destiny France needed; the Roman past was to be realized and made perfect in the actions of the present. Art could be news, even though sometimes the revolutionary tide of events would move so quickly that paintings might sit half-finished in the studio, their previously patriotic subjects already made obsolete by the politics of a month later. Into such a whirlwind, where the honoring images of the past were constantly being reexamined for their applicability to the present, stepped Napoleon, the Corsican outsider, to whom French culture was something to be understood as a whole, then reorganized and reshaped. Nothing marks his visible career more than his self-conscious self-creation of himself as a figure of national and historical unity. Unlike the Americans, who asserted that they were beginning anew, and so were often ill at ease with the trappings of earlier power and authority, Napoleon, like Augustus, clearly put on his power with his authority. He was at once the man of destiny—melancholic, brooding, striving alone—and the man of classic order, ensuring the survival of all those institutions, the nation itself, at whose center he stood. Galvanizing those who saw him and those who knew only his reputation, Napoleon displayed a remarkable ability to claim constant significance for all his actions. Those with him, his injunctions and commands continually implied, were on the forward wave of time and history. The Revolution had begun the calendar again; he would give France a constant series of new beginnings, new victories, new expansions, in which there were no private moments, only moments in history. Everyone in France walked on the stage of history, the object of all eyes in Europe and therefore in the world. He would be the inspiration for a revolution in political and personal self-display, inspiring a whole nation to greatness. On his establishment as first consul and the appearance of coins featuring Napoleon in profile crowned with laurel wreaths, the analogy with Roman images of authority is complete, and the subsequent administrative centralization of France and reform of the legal system makes the Augustan analogy even more tangible.[15]

With Napoleon, the great man becomes not only the realization of the past but its salvation and justification as well. Already as a young Revolutionary general, he had marched over the St. Bernard Pass into Italy, explicitly following in the footsteps of Hannibal and Charlemagne, then surpassing them by conquering Rome. From these campaigns he sent back to Paris huge quantities of artistic treasures from the classical and Renaissance worlds—paintings, sculpture, manuscripts—exacted as tribute in peace settlements and designed for a new museum of art in the old royal palace of the Louvre. With the Consulate (1799–1804) the paraphernalia of Roman Republican titles and imagery liberally adorned a government over which Napoleon was nevertheless soon in sole charge, even while the images of Brutus and Washington, Alexander and Caesar, were honored in statues and paintings all over the royal precincts. It was like a material version of the *translatio studii,* by which Renaissance writers had celebrated the gradual movement of culture from Greece to Rome to France and England. The French Revolution had given the spark and Napoleon encouraged the assumption that French Republican virtue 'deserved' the tribute of the great art of the past because it was the prime inheritor of past greatness. As he wrote in 1796, "All men of genius, all those who have attained distinction in the republic of letters, are French no matter in what country they may have been born."[16] Like Alexander's diffusion of Greek art and customs across Asia or Hitler's enormous art confiscations during World War Two, it was a convenient assumption of cultural centrality in order to buttress imperial military ambition. Already in 1794, French campaigns in the Rhineland had brought back to Paris the pillars from Charlemagne's chapel at Aix-la-Chapelle (that he himself had gathered from Trier, Ravenna, and Rome) along with the Roman sarcophagus that had been traditionally identified as Charlemagne's tomb. In David's 1801 painting of Napoleon on horseback crossing the Alps to

---

15. The 1790s were a particularly bad economic time for artists, who retained a high social prestige but were only beginning to understand the new sources of income available from the revolutionary state and its partisans, as opposed to their previous patrons. Many artistic supporters of Robespierre had been among the guillotined. Napoleon's reorganization of art for national propaganda turned their talents to less dangerous use.

16. Quinn, "Art Confiscations," quoting from Albert Sorel's *L'Europe et la révolution française* (Paris, 1892), IV, 154. Quinn's article is an invaluable resource from which I have extracted some of the information in this paragraph.

begin the Italian campaign, engraved in the rocks under his horse, like the graffiti of past greatness, are the names Hannibal and Carolus Magnus.

In 1804, as if to complete the supersession of the past, Napoleon is crowned emperor, not at Rome but in Notre Dame de Paris, and not by the pope but by himself, thus resolving the ambiguity of Charlemagne's relation to the Church within his own person, barely a thousand years later.[17] Charlemagne, who probably spoke something more like German than like French and whose court resided in what was then and later considered Germany, nevertheless became a sanctioning figure for his French Empire. But the analogies between Napoleon and Augustus or between Napoleon and Charlemagne also carried with them something beyond the validation sought by previous great generals, founders of dynasties, or lawgivers. It was a more mystical sanction, akin to Augustan *auctoritas,* that accorded curiously with Napoleon's own position outside official French society as a Corsican and outside official European monarchs as a nonhereditary ruler. He ruled, such nuances emphasized, not so much by power and certainly not by genealogy as by his personal force and the mysterious authority it afforded him. He pressed the analogy with Charlemagne, and it would be pressed even further by his nephew Napoleon III, who sat on a throne with a place for the forearm of Charlemagne worked into its structure. But he also enthusiastically promoted the cult of Joan of Arc, the French soldier-saint whose efforts to unify her country against England could easily be seen as evidence of God's willingness to invest a previously unknown individual with the future of France. Girodet's 1802 painting, commissioned by Napoleon, which depicts the (fictional) Welsh bard Ossian welcoming Napoleon's officers into heaven, similarly captures the prophetic and visionary sanction that Napoleon also wanted. He was consul, soon to be emperor, but he also considered himself to be a seer.

It is unclear where Napoleon got the idea of making his Italian campaign a raid on the history of Italian art as well as a political and military defeat for Italy and the Papal States. It certainly is completely in accord with his later goal of both centralizing European culture in France (rather than Rome or Vienna) and centralizing French culture and history in himself. Voltaire had argued that the cultural grandeur ruled over by Louis XIV was in a direct line from Alexander, Augustus, and Leo X (the sixteenth-century Medici pope). Napoleon's Italian victories absorbed that literary sense of historical continuity and made it tangible through his accumulation of Italian artistic treasure. At twenty-nine, after sweeping through Italy, he went to Egypt, taking not only an army but also a whole scientific commission to measure, detail, and annotate the remnants of that ancient civilization so that, like Alexander and Caesar before him, he might assert his preeminence as the vanguard not merely of great military victories but of a newly powerful culture as well.

17. To placate the pope, Napoleon allowed the coronation to pass without mention in the *Moniteur,* the official account of daily government occurrences. Later, however, he commissioned a gigantic painting of the scene for posterity.

The late eighteenth- and early nineteenth-century recovery of the ancient past—in Greece, Rome, and Egypt especially—seems an integral part of the political and economic expansionism of most of the imperial powers, a historical and cultural justification of their own position as inheritors. Not just scholars but political and military leaders as well looked for fame and glory in these terms. In the eighteenth century the British had added to economic and political conquest the relatively new component of cultural conquest. The British Museum, founded in 1753, turned into a government institution what had previously been the province of rich amateurs—the collecting and amassing of the artifacts of other civilizations, past and present—thus making the English the inheritors of history because they defined its meaning and importance in the endless cases of their museums. Similarly, the message of power that the pharaohs had sent to the beyond would be codified and organized by the French savants and cultural commissars Napoleon had brought with his army. Taken from their tombs, the artifacts and mummified bodies that were to make a claim on eternity would be displayed instead to the museumgoers of France, England, Germany, and America—each nicely annotated with a curator's explanation and an accession number.[18]

Just as Egypt pressed Alexander, Julius Caesar, and Marc Antony to greater competition with the gods, so Napoleon received an extra charge of psychic energy there. He grandly called the battle he won at Embaba "the Battle of the Pyramids," even though they were ten miles away, and he remained in Egypt supporting what historians have called a "make-believe" government for almost a year.[19] Unlike his predecessors, Napoleon heard no oracle whisper that he was the son of a god. In any case that mode of fame was outdated. He aspired instead to be the embodiment of the ambitions of an entire country or even of the whole European continent. In his role as a promoter of national culture, he climaxed a century of "enlightened monarchs" (like Frederick of Prussia and Catherine of Russia) who looked to France as the center of European civilization and sought to import it for their own uses. Similarly, he inherited Louis XIV's project of unifying the nation. *"Une foi, une loi, un roi"* ("one faith, one law, one king"), said Louis in 1685 and revoked the edict that tolerated Protestants in France, driving them to England, America, and over Europe. Napoleon's commitment to religious purity was more political than spiritual, and his cultural embrace wider still. So long as liberty and equality and fraternity were the rallying cries of the new freedom for France and Frenchman, and

18. The art confiscations that mark the Napoleonic combination of political and cultural imperialism are repeated a century or so later by Hitler, whose agents combed Europe for treasures that would be the collection for the world's greatest museum, to be built in his hometown.

19. With a similar reach for resonance, Admiral Nelson called his victory at the bay of Aboukir, "the Battle of the Nile." Byron in Greece, Gordon at Khartoum, Lawrence of Arabia—throughout the nineteenth and into the twentieth century, the English especially were lured by the fame that comes from traveling in exotic places, Alexanders perhaps, with a touch of Robinson Crusoe.

the forces of the old legitimacy were successfully defeated, Napoleon's rule seems hard to fault substantially. "And to all states not free / Shall *Clymacterick* be," wrote Marvell in the "Horatian Ode" (103–104), equating Cromwell's restless individual energy with the coming of political freedom. In his retirement, Napoleon, speaking like a Rousseau in arms, later proclaimed that all his actions were aimed to lift the yoke of oppression from every aspect of the human spirit. But his reign had quickly begun to reveal the less attractive imperialist dimension of that boundless assertion. Soon enough, he decided that the survival of his rule depended on a state constantly at war, reputedly proving itself against the arms of others. The sweeping career that had been so liberating to the potential of others narrowed for Napoleon himself to a demand for absolute centrality. The sense of drama with which he infused every decision was complemented by an inability or an unwillingness to delegate decisions to anyone independent of his own views. Increasingly, as he translated his military victories and his personal fame into political power, Napoleon made himself the indispensable avenue for every action of any significance within France. "Men need distinctions," said Napoleon, and so he restored under the empire many of the old ranks and privileges that had existed before the Revolution and founded the Légion d'honneur to tangibly embody his creation and bestowal of the nation's new emblems of honor and glory.

Unlike many of his modern imitators, however, Napoleon left a better legacy than the pattern of his career. Reading accounts of his brief return to power after the exile on Elba, it is hard not to see that march on Paris as the triumph of an image he had created of being the only necessary man, the repository and inheritor of the ages, and therefore the only hope for the future. No wonder that he remained fixed in the imagination of Europe long after Waterloo had become a matter only for the historians of military strategy. He was a guide rather than a model, and guides are valuable for the directions they show rather than for the behavior they illustrate. As an emblem of the right of the people to determine the politics of their own country, he was an inspiration to the enemies of privilege everywhere. But so far as he believed that he himself was the only true expression of that right, he was a despot and a tyrant, even, if, as in a story he liked to repeat, he was considered not the nobles' tyrant, but the people's. Openness was the public metaphor of his career, although too often it was only an ostensible openness, indistinguishable from publicity.

Napoleon thus revamps the monarchical relation to the state into terms more acceptable to a new world of mass politics and mass communications. He is the essential step between the absolute monarchs of the seventeenth century and the personality cults of the twentieth century. Strikingly enough, many such modern figures emerge, as did Napoleon, after the collapse of a monarchical system (Russia, Germany, Italy) that is perceived to have been more preoccupied with itself and its international connections than with the country it nominally ruled. In that release of energy appear figures bent on reviving the "true glory" so recently besmirched. Of course, they can be seen as seeking only their own power. Who in public life is not open to such an interpretation? But what is important to note is the terms in which they present that quest. Although such a fame always pretends a large degree of self-sufficiency, it also draws upon and helps create a context of national imagery to support it. The propaganda of the Nazis and the Fascists, for example, spoke a language that was more appealing to Germans and Italians than did politicians from other parties, and their virtuoso use of it is especially heightened by their comparative lack of any party program beyond the effort to say whatever was necessary to be elected.[20]

The difference is instructive. With Napoleon the effort to accomplish a national renovation through an interplay of politics and imagery drawn from the national past is still inclusive of all social groups and shades of opinion. Like many leaders who identify themselves propagandistically with the essence of a nation, Napoleon comes from the outside (Hitler from Austria, Stalin from Georgia) and thus gains the immeasurable advantage of being able to shape its traditions to his own ends without an overwhelming allegiance to one tradition or another. Just as Augustus had created himself from Caesar and Alexander, Cicero and Cato; as Constantine reconciled Christ and Rome; and as Charlemagne embodied both the legacy of Rome and the energy of the European "barbarians," so Napoleon likened himself to both Charlemagne and Constantine, Washington and Joan of Arc. From Napoleon to Hitler, it has been philosophically fashionable to speculate about the extent to which the great man was created by his times (and therefore subordinate to them) or the shaper of them (and thereby superior). The roots of the argument are in Marvell's ambivalent characterization of Cromwell in the "Horatian Ode." Cromwell has ruined "the great Work of Time," but also "cast the Kingdom old / Into another Mold" (33, 34–36). Napoleon still invokes the sanction of the past. But the question becomes more acute with the appearance of Hitler, Lenin, Mussolini, Stalin, and other twentieth-century political "great men" because so often they invoke the past either to reject it out of hand or to summon up its great figures for purposes of exclusion and xenophobia, to purge the nation of "impure" elements. Strength is defined by what you are not. Napoleon had seemed to embody the Rousseauian ideal leader who

---

20. The ruler as performer is a twentieth-century type—witness Stalin, Hitler, Mussolini, both Roosevelts, and Churchill for a range that cuts across political lines. It will later be worth distinguishing between those rulers who felt competitive with artists and those for whom it was not an issue. The first variety are Neronians. Like Nero shamelessly using his power to win music contests, they have such a commitment to the status and reality of art that they consider artists to be politically and personally dangerous people. Stalin calling up Bulgakov both to praise his stories and to announce they couldn't be published is one version of this. Hitler's preoccupation with "decadent" art is another. In both gestures, as in Nero's more obvious way, superiority in all forms belongs only to the state (and to its leader). All other activity must array itself subordinately. Art is a particular problem because even at its most social it asserts both transcendental and historical justification that neither Nero's Rome nor Hitler's Germany could brook.

arose directly from the people rather than from a line of inherited power. By the twentieth century it became clear that such a leader could be as negative and desperate as optimistic and aspiring. Brought into being by the collapse of monarchical systems, the absolute leader of symbolic energy and national renewal could express other moods of the national psyche as well—despair, paranoia, xenophobic defensiveness—a leader to whom the citizen assigned his freedom and liberty rather than the leader whose vitality ensured it.

Both the democratic leader and the totalitarian leader purport to realize the individual through their own actions, to express what the will of the nation wants to express. The difference is that the democratic leader is involved in a constant negotiation about what that will actually is (and thus ought never quite believe in its singlemindedness), while the totalitarian leader identifies it completely with himself (and thus is personally hostile to any deviations). The nineteenth century—by its political enfranchising of more and more groups, by the expansion of its economies into full-scale industrial production, and by its vast increase in the number of ways people and their ideas and beliefs are known to each other—introduces in the history of fame a variety of complex confusions over the line between public and private life, public and private nature, that previously had been an explicit problem, if at all, only for "fictional" characters like Shakespeare's kings. Political philosophers in Rome or Elizabethan England would have recognized a distinction between man as citizen and man as man. But few before Locke would have known what to make of the distinction between man as citizen and man as individual. In democracy and totalitarianism, the political systems we have inherited from the revolutions of the late eighteenth century, the distinctions among man in the abstract, man in the state, and man in himself constitute a crucial parting of the ways. In democracies, which put a premium on individual will, the relation between what is public business and what is private in an individual's nature is a constant argument. In a dictatorship such questions rarely arise. Perhaps, then, a dictatorship is a democracy that can't take the uncertainty of public-private ambivalence, just as a fanatic is someone for whom there is no difference at all, for whom political has swallowed up the personal entirely, to the diminishing of both.

Perhaps modeled on or inspired by the glory spoken of by the American Founding Fathers, Napoleon's *gloire* was his greatest legacy to France, for clearly it needed neither him nor any other individual for its sole support. But Napoleonic leadership, at first so clearly tied to an expansive and exuberant view of the French nation and French pride, became more closed down and self-regarding. Thomas Carlyle and Ralph Waldo Emerson later ascribe the change to the natural bent of the French toward the theatrical. But it might also be seen as the desire of Napoleon, the man of the new imagery, to have the sanction of the old imagery as well, the trappings of monarchy and empire, the festooned faces of the great heroes of the past now dancing attendance on the grandeur of the present. As more and more success became his, Napoleon became increasingly convinced of the power of his self-consciousness, his ability to penetrate the true meaning of men and events. The self-confidence that had buoyed him to his achievements thus became the mechanism of his downfall. As his power was consolidated, a necessary web was created at whose center he sat. Thus contained, he no longer seemed to be the guarantor of personal and political freedom in others, but merely another monarch, enmeshed in hierarchy. Intriguingly enough, then, although national imperialisms spread out across the world in the nineteenth century, Napoleon had a greater personal influence on artists than on politicians, who invoked his name if at all as a kind of individualist megalomania unfit for either republics or monarchies to imitate. But his career had sanctioned and symbolized a personal freedom to aspire to whatever heights one chose. And, if his actual rule had become more and more constricted, and the career open to talents had relied more and more on those whose opinions were subordinate to the emperor's, the bright promise remained. Byron's vacillations between attacking and defending Napoleon (which especially bothered Hazlitt) confirm the doubleness of the Napoleonic image, and the extent to which many believed that Napoleon himself had failed, even while they still yearned for someone like him, who would truly be the sponsor of freedom everywhere. Still convinced of his own importance, Napoleon, during his final exile on the island of St. Helena, remarked to one of his attendants, "The whole world is looking at us, we remain the martyrs of an immortal cause" (Fisher, 115). But he never quite realized the extent to which his political and military defeat was the necessary step to making him an overwhelming success in the psychic life of western Europe. Like Byron's lameness and his melancholy, Napoleon's failure at Waterloo may have reconfirmed his audience's ability to identify with him.

Genius, Originality, and Neglect

Neither aiming at originality of principles or sentiments, nor yet copied from any particular and previous writing, it was intended to be an expression of the American mind.
—THOMAS JEFFERSON on the Declaration of Independence

So far as I am individually concerned, & independent of my pocket, it is my earnest desire to write those sort of books which are said to "fail"—pardon this egotism.
—HERMAN MELVILLE, Letter to his father-in-law, October 1849

Napoleon had brought to life an infinity of eighteenth-century fictional heroes who rose from humble or outcast origins to become great heroes. Byron was the aristocrat for whom aristocratic authority and visibility were not sufficient. Thanks to their intuitive sense of the difference between the gaze from the audience and the gaze toward it, they helped bring a whole armory of the images and gestures of public style onto the stage of modern life. But together with their reach toward larger audiences than public figures had ever known before, they perpetuated as well a mistrust of the new audience for its inability properly to read, interpret, and appreciate the dimensions of their genius. Like Rousseau, whose uniqueness was akin to that of everyone else, the great man of the postrevolutionary period sought to unite the separateness of genius with the politics of general human nature. His uncertain public stance therefore corresponded to the ambiguous nature of his audience: He included reticence in his assertion, just as they could be either the immediate audience of commercial consumption or the transcendental audience of spiritual comradeship. In different ways, the careers of both Napoleon and Byron showed that fame was no longer an inheritance to be assumed by noblesse oblige. But it did have to be either visibly worked for, visibly rejected, or both. Coolness, evasion, and distance were becoming a vital part of the appeal made by the most successful public men, the aura of withdrawal authenticating the burdensome necessity of appealing to an audience that may not understand you.

Like the virtue that may have once been its own reward but now had to be seen (or eavesdropped on) in order to be appreciated, the literary sensibility was beginning to fall from solitary innocence into crowded publicity. An ability that had often been defined by its understanding of the "rules" of literary creation was changing into a personal characteristic, a "genius," that had to be teased out, cultivated, and luxuriantly expressed. The older model of solitary fame, with its withdrawal from the corrupt standards of social renown, was becoming a public position—and one particularly identified with the presumptions of those who entered the world of literature. By the end of the seventeenth century Dryden helped reintroduce genius both as a special characteristic of those engaged in the arts and as an essential element in the continuity of national culture. The genius that Horace said everyone possessed as a direction from heaven had begun to take on the social aspects of a fame Fulke Greville defined almost entirely within the context of the state and the state's reputation. By the latter eighteenth century, men as disparate as James Boswell and David Hume, Oliver Goldsmith and Laurence Sterne, could proudly say that their greatest goal was "literary fame"—a phrase repeated so often that it becomes almost an essential definition of fame itself, or of its least compromised variety. In the decades that followed, the Romantic celebration of "the poet" was complemented by a growing popular preoccupation with the artistic sensibility, not so much for anything it accomplished as for how it generated eccentric behavior and diverting anecdotes. The peculiar habits of Dr. Johnson, Rousseau, or Voltaire were of interest to a small literary world. But gossip about writers, from Byron down to Hemingway and beyond, was immediately the common coin of people who had hardly any interest in reading their books.

The new styles of public assertion were particularly complicated for the writer or artist to assume. They may have shed the name of "maker" along with its artisan implication to assert themselves as "creators." But as yet they were divided in their willingness to be actors, onstage or off. Diderot's vision of the fame in posterity, when true genius could be recognized, was still powerful. This was the fame of private satisfaction, with a small audience of intent readers who exist primarily after the author is safely dead and the work can stand alone, uncompromised by prejudice or envy. But as the new literary fame became more inescapably visible and public, so genius was being forced into postures of social usefulness. In 1719, for example, an anonymous English writer proclaimed the "wide field" open for genius in the world. In his view there is no such thing as a genius with only a private dimension, for "it is certainly the Intention of Providence, that a good *Genius* should be a publick benefit" (24). Everyone may have his own genius, but the harmony of society comes from the interplay of their differences, like the different instruments and notes that create music. The only difficulty the optimistic writer foresees in reaping the social benefits of English genius is that it may be squandered by those who attempt projects too difficult for their powers and create only useless fragments.

Tied as it was to the growing belief in infinite material progress and social betterment, this attitude toward genius had a long life, and is reflected in the American cult of the inventor—from Benjamin Franklin down to Thomas Edison. With enough wit, work, and luck, the individual could go it alone and yet create something that would also benefit mankind. Through individual uniqueness, new systems of understanding would be born. As Wordsworth was to write some hundred years later, "Of genius the only proof is, the act of doing well what is worthy to be done, and what was never done before" (478). But Wordsworth is specifically concerned with genius in the fine arts, particularly poetry, whose "only infallible sign is the widening the sphere of human sensibility, for the delight, honour, and benefit of human nature." Here was a style of genius not so directly connected to social context and material accomplishment, to which the word "popular" could never be appropriately applied. This was not a possession to be bought and sold, but a state of being: You did not *have* a genius; you *were* a genius. The Renaissance had connected artistic genius with the fame of the past. But the genius of the late eighteenth and early nineteenth century, spawned by political upheavals in the name of will and self-determination, was defined almost entirely by individual self-consciousness. Such genius was divine, said Edward Young in *Conjectures on Original Composition* (1759), in which he rhapsodizes about the infinite complexity and untrackable extent of the human mind, along with the need to "reverence" it as much as possible. Young includes scientific advance along with artistic excellence in his definition of originality. But his concerns are less with social usefulness than with awakening the original genius to his own existence. Eve, says Young, peered so intently at her image in the pool not for mere narcissism, but because she glimpsed previously unrecognized personal powers. As there are two varieties of originality, one that goes back to beginnings and one that is beyond anything yet done, so there are two types of genius, one that is an everlasting possibility of human nature and the other a special person. Such a "genius," like the "destiny" of the great man, connected the individual with the patterns of the universe and assured a grand fulfillment in the future. But it was also a defining element of character—like the destiny of Napoleon or the destiny of America—that was yet unspecified, because that would limit its scope.[21]

With originality, in the double sense of unprecedented and a return to roots, becoming a prime criterion of value in art, artistic creators turned against centuries of works that freely admitted their commissioned, collaborative, and externally inspired status. Inspiration, like the muse and the patron, had become aspects of the artist's own being. Both the work and the person were urged to be unique, and the stage was set for a history of stylistic change that would be accompanied by polemics asserting the greater "truth" of each new style instead of the mutations and transformations that had characterized the past. The originality of genius replaced the subordinate relation to the muse. Inspiration would well up from within instead of being imposed from the outside. Assertion would replace receptivity.

"Born *Originals*," Young laments, "how comes it to pass that we die *Copies?*" (20) The reason, he says, is that we imitate, reproducing with only the slightest twist what has already been done. Be original instead, he proclaims, for only then—and here is the central paradox—can we face death with true Christian resignation. Originality assures one of fame, and fame will make one live beyond death in both heaven and posterity. Young himself is seventy-six when he writes the *Conjectures* (he will live to eighty-two), and his great example of the original genius is Joseph Addison, who died forty years before:

> His compositions are but a noble preface; the grand work is his death:
> That is a work which is read in heaven: How has it join'd the final approbation of angels to the previous applause of men? How gloriously
> has he opened a splendid path, thro' fame immortal, into eternal
> peace? (46)

Thus Young sonorously identifies the urge to be a famous original with the urge to die a Christian death. By situating the discussion of genius and fame at the edge of the grave, Young reflects those eighteenth-century theologians who believed the urge to fame on earth to be a proof of the immortality of the soul. Like Petrarch before him and Emily Dickinson later, he manages to present the urge for earthly success in the most appealing pos-

21. Such hints in English as well as French literature are generalized by the Germans, who contribute the distinction between genius and talent—the first the gift of heaven, the second a skill.

sible terms—as a subcategory of the striving for heaven. The venerated Genius of the emperor and the soul of the Christian become one in the originality of the author.

But in a world increasingly conscious of the immediate presence of fame and the famous, such spiritual validation might either ring hollowly or else be confused with more material applause. How could one discern true fame from false? The public that first appeared as a release from the restrictions of patronage, the fellow artists who promised to be a support beyond the applause of a moment, turn out instead to herald a new world of commercialization and competitiveness as the price of freedom. Even when "genius" refers to a quality or a person (rather than to a tutelary spirit like the muse), the concept still reflects a social identity. With genius becoming a state of soul rather than a measurable talent, it might be enough just to announce that one was a poet or a painter in order to be at least self-assured of greatness. Being a hypochondriac, complaining constantly of bodily ailments real or imagined, was an emblem of genius, just as melancholia was in the Elizabethan period, tuberculosis in the nineteenth century, and the paraphernalia of existentialist gloom after World War Two. If one could not demonstrate actual genius, one could at least be a fellow traveler of the disease and its symptoms.

"I don't take no stock in dead people," says Huckleberry Finn, giving an American turn to the energetic commitment only to present and future greatness. But there was a dark side to that freshness as well. An actual work could exhibit the genius of its creator, but more often it brought such an expanded sense of self abruptly down to earth. Underlying the new possibility of fame on earth were the dank reminders of death and failure and the fear that one might not be among the chosen. With a widened scope for individual will arrived the anxiety that it would not be properly or effectively used, or the dread that it would not come for the right things or, upon achievement, would be found to be empty. In fact the number of late eighteenth-century poets and politicians who had bouts of frequent insanity is outstandingly large. It might be too much to ascribe their states of mind to the urge for fame, but its pressures of incitement and frustration surely had a prominent place in their psychological makeup and in the reader's appreciation of their fragile sensibilities. Many had been so before, but no culture had made the relation of genius to madness so expected and so acceptable. "The lunatic, the lover and the poet are of imagination all compact," Shakespeare had written two hundred years before, without concluding that the poet had to be both lunatic and lover to be successful. "Great wits are to madness near allied," wrote Dryden a hundred years before, beginning to identify the madness of frustrated ambition. And, looking back on the poetic generation of the late eighteenth century, Wordsworth in "Resolution and Independence" pushed the analogy even further:

> We Poets in our youth begin in gladness;
> But thereof come in the end despondency and madness (48–49).

The notes of self-pity and braggadocio in Wordsworth's lines are hard to disentangle from his sincere attempt to understand his own confused motives for writing poetry. The survival traits rewarded by a culture can be as responsible for neurosis or mental illness as they are for success. And in the successful one can also trace the lineaments of failure, for often it is circumstance, otherwise known as luck, that makes the difference. Who knows that Catiline in power might not have been able to fashion himself into Caesar or Augustus? What would have happened if Paoli had had the opportunities of George Washington? The psychic kinship of the success and the failure especially becomes a theme in those cultures committed to what we might neutrally call democratic or egalitarian norms for success. When traits that had brought past success become outmoded because of cultural change, those traits are often still clung to in the face of a world that ought to respond to them but does not. When belief in an afterlife is displaced by the hope of posthumous fame, present failure could signify ultimate success. Thus the later eighteenth century also opens a modern era in which genius is often determinately antisocial. To be a true genius seemed to imply necessarily that one was an outsider, and to the extent that such a genius could command a contemporary audience, it would be an audience of those who believed themselves to be outsiders within. Through the medium of the genius, their own self-sufficiency would be guaranteed by heaven, by posterity, or by both.

Wordsworth's lines are preceded by praise of Thomas Chatterton, "the marvellous Boy, / The sleepless Soul that perished in his pride," and the figure of Chatterton helps determine the alternate lineage of neglected greatness that allows Wordsworth to insulate himself from the darker consequences of his own ambitions. The postrevolutionary world of publicity had made it obvious that it was too late to be first, a Robinson Crusoe lording it over an empty island of boundless fame. But the intense awareness of the great who had been neglected might encourage an aspiration otherwise wary of public embrace to define a different mode of fame. Preoccupied with the realization that one could no longer be first, Chatterton himself sought to be the youngest. Delving into the past in order to stage his renown in the present, he had tried to make his literary reputation by pretending to discover the poems of an otherwise unknown fifteenth-century poet named Thomas Rowley. In fact, this was a past, a poet, and poems he himself had created. But even so, despite their guise of antiquity, Rowley's poems received no recognition either for their supposed "author" or for their discoverer, and Chatterton committed suicide at seventeen (in 1770), a cautionary prelude to the youthful generation of Romantic poets and writers to come. For Wordsworth, Chatterton, like Robert Burns, exemplifies the poet rejected by the world, whose fate shows that the possession of genius was always double-edged. In his 'Immortality Ode,' written about the same time as "Resolution and Independence," Wordsworth's image of the child "trailing clouds of glory" had deified an absolute beginning, in which the past was rejected and one took one's lead only from the energies of nature and heaven. But the 'Immortality Ode' also prophesied a world in which life from childhood on was always downhill and the progress of society was a perpetual reproach to the efforts of the individual to recapture the "visionary gleam."

Artists and politicians down to the eighteenth century often associated themselves with the great names of the past to establish a line of personal inheritance. But it was the budding fame culture of the later eighteenth and early nineteenth century that spawned the person, almost always a writer, who actually pretended to be someone from the past. The impersonation was often wholly sincere. Chatterton's guise as Rowley or Macpherson's as the tenth-century Welsh bard Ossian both reflect the impulse of Boswell, Franklin, and Johnson to write either anonymously or under pseudonyms. At the same time that scholars were trying to recapture the authentic texts of Chaucer or the "relics" of English poetry, Chatterton and Macpherson sought to recreate literary history in their own version of "true" poetry. William Henry Ireland, born a few years after Chatterton's death, was one of the most notorious of those who assumed the guise of past reputation to enlarge their own, and his career is an intensified version of the less dramatically tangled aspirations of many other authors. At the age of seventeen, after a visit to Stratford with his father, a printer and occasional author, Ireland became one of the most outstanding Shakespearian scholars in England, specializing in the discovery of manuscripts. In a flurry of antiquarian glory, he found books with dedications to Queen Elizabeth written in Shakespeare's hand, manuscript notes, letters, legal documents, and even two new plays, one (*Vortigern and Rowena*) in Shakespeare's own hand and another (*Henry II*) copied from Shakespeare's original. Literary England was in an uproar. Some of the more scholarly of Shakespeare's editors thought the documents frauds, but their warnings were dismissed as mere envy. Boswell among others came to kiss the precious relics while they were on display at Ireland's house, and Sheridan contracted to produce *Vortigern* at Drury Lane. Meanwhile Ireland plunged ahead and found another group of documents that traced the cache of manuscripts he had already discovered to Shakespeare's own gift to one of Ireland's ancestors as a reward for saving him from drowning.

About a year later, the game was up. Ireland confessed to his sisters that he had forged everything. Still not yet twenty years old, Ireland quickly wrote a book announcing his sole fault in the forgeries and exonerating his father from any blame. Undaunted, he went on a pilgrimage to Chatterton's haunts at Bristol and in 1798 opened a shop where he sold imitations of his forgeries. In 1805 he published a full-scale *Confessions* that recounted his activities in detail. Before his death in 1835 he wrote many other works, among them a poem entitled "Neglected Genius."

If plagiarism can be called the sin of a literary culture preoccupied with imitation, so forgery is the sin of a literary culture infatuated with originality. Plagiarism is a repetition that claims to be authoritative; forgery is a repetition that claims to be original. Both flourish especially when artistic work is considered to be simultaneously a legal possession of the artist and an emanation of his personality. Ireland's "discoveries" are akin to Chatterton's and Macpherson's because they all present literary forgery in the guise of authorial reincarnation. As the preface to *Vortigern* argues, if the play is great drama, why worry about pedantic questions of handwriting or ink: "Forget the prejudice of rigid art, / To read the code of nature in the heart." Ireland, insisted his supporters, was brother in genius to Shakespeare, imbued with the spirit of his past original. That the forgery is revealed and celebrated as self-conscious only enhances his participation in the heritage of originality.[22]

Ireland's later association with William Caulfield, creator of *Blackguardiana: or, a Dictionary of Rogues* (1795) and coeditor of *The Eccentric's Magazine* (1812–1814), indicate how clearly he knew his own goals in the new world of curiosity about the famous that had so recently appeared. Caulfield deserves a small but special niche in the history of fame for the transition his career makes between the engraved portraits of the great that were a staple for printers since the early Renaissance and the tremendously expanded chance for visual notoriety shortly to come with the daguerrotype and photograph. Until *Blackguardiana,* the impulse to memorialize the strange, eccentric, exotic, and merely ostentatious was limited to brief flashes and individual circumstances. But Caulfield, who as a very young man became a collector of old prints and engravings, successfully tapped a market that was interested in portraits and vignettes of all kinds. The overthrow of the aristocracy in France and the Revolution in America had helped create a public for prints and portraits far beyond the old tradition of venerated "noble heads." Just as Ireland did not consider himself a forger but a young genius whose singularity, like Chatterton's, was showing itself in an unfamiliar (and therefore outstanding) way, so Caulfield helped feed the taste for observing and imitating new varieties of personal eccentricity that made Boswell seem decidedly reticent. Through his pages parade famous midwives and famous prostitutes, famous pickpockets and famous ragpickers. Their originality was not in the creation of a work or an achievement so much as in the creation of a self for others to see, admire, and be astounded by.[23]

<hr/>

22. Although discussions of literary plagiarism begin to surface as invective in the seventeenth century, the legal interest in plagiarism is only recent, along with some more precise definitions of the nature of intellectual property. In Furetière's 1727 French dictionary, a plagiarist is defined as someone who takes the work of others in order to get himself glory. With that definition, the kind of glory aspired to in the forgeries of Chatterton and Ireland clearly belongs to a different conception of the relation of writer to writer. See Messina, *Le plagiat littéraire.* In a modern version of the assertion of literary tradition, T. S. Eliot remarks, "Immature poets imitate, mature poets steal; bad poets deface what they take, and good poets make it into something better, or at least different" ("Philip Massinger," 182).

23. A now-forgotten writer of the nineteenth century who made an emblematic attempt to absorb the sanction of neglect into his own ostentatious career was Richard Hengist Horne (1803–1884). Educated at Sandhurst, he became a midshipman in the Mexican navy in the war against Spain, traveled in the United States, and in his mid-twenties started sending poems to English literary magazines. A few years later

Chatterton and Macpherson wrote their poetry under the names of ficti-tious authors; Ireland dressed in the garb of a playwright known primarily in his own profession during his life but who by the mid-eighteenth century had become the object of a virtual cult. Yet all three sought literary fame as the medium of their 'sources'; the disguise allowed them to be more ag-gressive than they might be for themselves. It is appropriate that Ireland, as the most blatantly journalistic and self-promoting should have been the son of a printer-engraver and thus directly involved in the expansion of vi-sual and verbal media that accompanied the late eighteenth-century politi-cal revolutions. But at the same time that mechanisms of publicity and pub-lication were expanding in an unprecedented way, the most self-conscious literary men were fascinated with the question of the anonymous, the ne-glected, and the unfulfilled artist. Wordsworth had both lamented and celebrated the lack of recognition given to Chatterton and Burns. In this system of aesthetic value, the counterpoise to Ireland and Caulfield is the artist-engraver-poet William Blake, one of the few examples of a later cele-brated literary genius who was virtually unknown to his own contempo-raries. Emily Dickinson is another who springs immediately to mind. In both of their careers we see clearly the extent to which writers in the nine-teenth century were beginning to turn neglect into a banner of ultimate value, for themselves as well as for others. As Jerome McGann has pointed out, Blake tried to ensure his artistic freedom by his personal isolation. And it is intriguing that his whole mode of proceeding—the individually pro-duced books, the attack against commercial reproduction—is at some sense at odds with his radical politics. Yet it is much in accord with similar strat-egies of artistic integrity throughout the century—including the miniature, handstitched books in which Emily Dickinson wrote her poems and Char-lotte Brontë wrote her chronicles of imaginary kingdoms.

To be too clearly visible, to be too easily understandable, in short, to be containable by the great and growing public, was beginning to be a mark of shallowness and insignificance. In the context of originality and inspiration, the trope of humbleness that so usually accompanied earlier invocations of the muse—'inspire unworthy me'—virtually vanishes. It is replaced by its typical nineteenth-century version, 'I'm really not interested in fame now or later,' more elegantly phrased by Keats in his epitaph for himself as "Here lies one whose name was writ on water." In both fame and anonym-ity, the Romantic assertion is one of self-sufficiency. Their poetic embrace of being forgotten, and of the "poem nearly anonymous," is supported by

he published "Exposition of the False Medium and Barriers Excluding Men of Genius from the Public" (1833), which argued the need for a literary and artistic academy to prevent mediocrity from conspiring to repress "men of superior ability in all departments of human genius and knowledge." His literary career included the publication in 1877 of letters written to him by Elizabeth Barrett between 1839 and 1846; a history of Napoleon; *Orion,* an epic poem; a life of Van Amburgh, the first widely popular animal tamer; and a final work, supposedly translated from the Arabic, entitled "Sithron, the Star-Stricken."

an appeal to the divided and disguising poets of the previous generation. So Coleridge, still a teenager himself, had invoked the spirit of Chatterton:

> Grant me, like thee, the lyre to sound,
> Like thee with fire divine to glow;—
> But ah! when rage the waves of woe,
> Grant me with firmer breast to meet their hate,
> And soar beyond the storm with upright eye elate!
> ("Monody on the Death of Chatterton," 108–117)

For all the self-dramatizing in such a poem, we should not ignore the usefulness of the figure of Chatterton for early nineteenth-century poets and artists who were trying to resolve their simultaneous desire for fame in both the moment and in eternity. Later in the century, with the elaboration of a theory of the avant-garde, this Romantic gaze toward future justification will be thoroughly merged with Diderot's belief that posterity is the only true arena in which to judge claims to cultural importance.[24]

Thus in the late eighteenth and early nineteenth century an increasingly fame-choked world was beginning to reach out for solace and value to anonymity and neglect as emblems of true worth. Within a world more attuned to visual and verbal statement, the old distinctions between bad fame on earth and good fame in eternity were becoming hard to maintain. Success could easily be confused with visibility, celebrity with fame. The basic predicament, as it winds its way through the century, is how to assert oneself, not only when the social structures of assertion are in flux, but also when their *lack* is considered a virtue, politically as much as aesthetically. The oppressive visibility of careers inspired by the new audience may have caused as much revulsion as imitation. But, often enough, the announcement of exclusive belief in the judgment of the future was made loudly in the present. To support such a seemingly self-contradictory stance, the early nineteenth century developed, perpetuated, and cherished the concept of the neglected genius. Through his idealization, the writer can distance himself from the competitiveness of the present by asserting his solidarity with an unappreciated fellow artist who has been canonized by an untimely death. There is nothing venal or even hypocritical in this stance. It is the natural result of a growing preoccupation with personal fame during one's lifetime, fed by the democratization of political life, the enormous expansion of the publishing industry, the appearance of museums and galleries, and the emergence of a large audience for literature and art—especially in America, France, and England.

Political philosophers as disparate as John Stuart Mill and Karl Marx shared the Romantic notion that the artist is the paradigmatic individual. The concept of neglected genius is thus the era's special turn on the old Horatian paean to posterity. Now it would be not so much the poem as the

---

24. Keats had also early celebrated Chatterton as "Above the ingrate world and human fears" ("Sonnet to Chatterton"). With this in mind, it is enticing to reread Keats's phrase to mean "If your name survives even though written on water, then it has truly lasted,' with an appropriate echo of Jesus walking on water.

poet whose name and fame would outlast the earthly monuments of public men. For the Romantics, Chatterton dying unrecognized in his garret or Mozart squandering his genius in the recital rooms of a succession of unappreciative patrons only confirmed the need to appeal beyond the corrupt present. "Full many a flower is born to blush unseen / And waste its sweetness on the desert air," Gray had written in the *Elegy* (55–56) and politicized the aesthetic point by identifying those flowers with the poor, who, because they could not write and had no money, were doomed to be forgotten. Yet the criticism also contains more than a note of satisfaction. Yes, there may have been a "mute, inglorious Milton" buried in the country churchyard. But there was also a Cromwell, "guiltless of his country's blood" (59–60). It's too bad, in other words, that we have lost potential Miltons because the poor are uneducated. But we should count ourselves lucky that we have lost politicians and military leaders as well. Fame in one's own time, later to be disdainfully called "celebrity," was becoming a hallmark of moral deficiency and, even if merited, might make one into a target for the envious and the venal. In the beginning of his career, Alexander Pope tripped blithely out as the young poet in search of good fame. By his later years, he depicted himself as someone forever hiding from those who were out to make demands on his attention. He had wanted to be noted for his works. But instead he became merely famous.

Thus, through the mediation of a concept like neglected genius, the feeling of abjectness and despair, the sense of absolute alienation from any contemporary audience beyond a few friends could furnish a status of singularity that offered an alternative to the position at the top of the ladder of earthly being that fame represented. Fame was loneliness, and so loneliness might be a variety of fame. Alexander might again admire Diogenes resting himself in the sun and freely discoursing on his contempt for earthly power. The saint in the desert might reappear in small towns and rural parsonages. But the spiritual or philosophical detachment that often marked the solitaries of fame who inhabited previous centuries was distinctly lacking or underplayed in the singular artists of the early modern period. Their isolation was a grand assertion, a glove in the face of conventional standards, a constant and prickly testing of their freedom, even when they were nominally in a subordinate position. As Beethoven said to his patron, Prince Lichnowsky:

> Prince! What you are, you are by circumstance and by birth. What I am, I am through myself. Of princes there have been and will be thousands. Of Beethovens there is only one (Robbins, 210).[25]

* * *

> My revenge, I decided very early, would be to achieve a power which outlasts kingdoms. —JAMES BALDWIN, *Nobody Knows My Name*

25. Lichnowsky's physician, Dr. Anton Weiser, tells the story of the dinner at which Beethoven felt he had been insulted by being asked if he also played the violin.

With the disappearance of a clearly demarcated hierarchy of artistic aspiration, fame in the modern period becomes the equivalent of aristocratic or monarchical inheritance, in which the individual is born again into his or her rightful family. The urge for anonymity emphasized that one sought to speak with the true inner voice of nature and culture rather than merely personally. The praise of the neglected allowed even successful artists to take on some of their sanction, decentering themselves for the immediate culture of the present so that they could center themselves for the future. A crucial element of Romantic art was the effort to make an impression on a public audience, that is, one that was not personally known to the poet but was, in theory, his psychic kindred. The look of destiny, the sanction of neglect, thus made a public assertion that was overheard by an audience rather than forced upon it. Neglect confirmed originality and genius by demonstrating that true art was unappreciated by the new commercial audience. Even as they collectively bought thousands of copies of books, each individual member of the audience could think he or she was doing something daring and unparalleled. Edward Young had argued the connection of originality with Christian (immortal) truth. The generation of Romantic poets generally sheared away the religious implications, but still retained the connection of originality with transcendence—of the standards of society, of history, of even their own fans. Creation, as Victor Frankenstein discovers in Mary Shelley's novel, was an immense and solitary act that the creator did not always have under sufficient control because it was so inseparable from self-creation. The monster wanders "solitary and abhorred" (397), looking for a human companionship denied him by his appearance. Like a good member of an earlier generation, he reads *Paradise Lost,* Plutarch, and *The Sorrows of Young Werther* "to admire and love the heroes of past ages" (395). But he discovers, as did his creator, that the desire to do something grand for posterity more often creates monsters than masterpieces. The crucial question of creation, on both the literary and personal levels, is thrown into greater relief by Mary Shelley's sensitivity as a woman, a daughter (of Mary Wollstonecraft and William Godwin), a wife (of Percy Shelley), and one who herself strongly desired literary celebrity. Her introduction to the 1831 edition of *Frankenstein* emphasizes the fame-engendering atmosphere of both her upbringing and her marriage: "It is not singular that, as the daughter of two persons of distinguished literary celebrity, I should very early have thought of writing. . . . My husband . . . was from the first very anxious that I should prove myself worthy of my parentage and enrol myself on the page of fame. He was forever inciting me to obtain literary reputation, which even on my own part I cared for then, though since I have become infinitely indifferent to it" (259–260). In the summer of 1816, while in Switzerland with Shelley, Byron, and Dr. Polidori, she creates *Frankenstein* in response to Byron's proposal that they each write a ghost story. But the heart of her story contains a crucial ambivalence about the act of creation itself:

Frightful must [the monster] be; for supremely frightful would be the effect of any human endeavour to mock the stupendous mechanism of the Creator of the world. His success would terrify the artist; he would rush away from his odious handiwork, horror-stricken (263).

At the end of the introduction Mary Shelley bids "my hideous progeny go forth and prosper" (264). Her intricate sense of the intensely personal quality of what she has written, along with the need to present it in a way that will entice more readers, mirrors the emblematic modern dilemma of the artist, caught between a dehumanized industrial world and a vastly expanded literary world, whose political and social sympathies make it impossible to aspire either to aristocracy or to popularity. One way out of the dilemma was to make a distinction between the *public,* who wore the detested faces of superficial fashion and aesthetic dullness, and the *people,* who embodied all that was best in the general spirit of nature and art together. Wordsworth, in the essay that first accompanied his collected poems in 1815, makes a crucial formulation of the contrast. After surveying the past and discovering that truly great works and truly great poets are for the most part neglected in their own times, he is led to conclude in contrast that the most celebrated writers must therefore be warped by popular approval:

> Grand thoughts (and Shakespeare must often have sighed over this truth), as they are most naturally and most fitly conceived in solitude, so can they not be brought forth in the midst of plaudits, without some violation of their sanctity (480).

Theater, then, by its immediate appeal is finally incapable of the highest artistic greatness because it cannot accord with the isolation and focus necessary for the poet to produce his best work. But, Wordsworth goes on to say, this does not mean that he does not respect "the judgment of the people" on artistic work, nor that art always refers to itself and can be judged only by its own standards. The difficulty is that there is a public often mistaken for the people, "that Vox Populi which the Deity inspires," and this public must be rejected:

> Foolish must he be who can mistake for this a local acclamation, or a transitory outcry—transitory though it be for years, local though from a Nation. Still more lamentable is his error who can believe that there is any thing of divine infallibility in the clamour of that small though loud portion of the community, ever governed by factitious influence, which, under the name of the PUBLIC, passes itself, upon the unthinking, for the PEOPLE. Towards the Public, the Writer hopes that he feels as much deference as it is entitled to: but to the People, philosophically characterised, and to the embodied spirit of their knowledge, so far as it exists and moves, at the present, faithfully supported by its two wings, the past and the future, his devout respect, his reverence, is due (481).

Whether or not Napoleon's defeat at Waterloo in 1815 shadows Wordsworth's rejection of the fickle and shallow public for the essential and eternal people, the analogy between the writer seeking greatness beyond the moment and the great man following his destiny is strong enough. "The public" is a people fallen, like Wordsworth's glory-trailing child, into history. Since the Renaissance, Roman models of visual being had morally framed a variety of artistic and political aspirations, exonerating the aspirants from mere ambition and empty pride. But, despite the still current classical drapery of public men like Washington and Napoleon, the aspiring man of the new era also sought to gather his authority in his immediate access to the inner life of his audience, speaking to the eternal within the social, the ahistorical within history. As Napoleon can ironically glory in the title of the "people's tyrant," so Wordsworth emphasizes the need for an audience who will feel their affinity with the writer, "a co-operating *power* in the mind of the Reader" (478), without whom the poem is inert and lifeless. To such power, such mutual energy, the momentary fashion and caprice of the new media world of the early nineteenth century is the designated enemy.

Thus, with the greater and greater pressure of a growing "public," the writer began to appeal from one (time-bound and imperceptive) audience to another (eternal and deeply sympathetic) audience, who in the present can foretell as well as the writer the judgment of posterity. In great part, this was an audience that had become more and more skilled in its audience role and therefore had to be appealed to in more and more subtle ways, which registered at once self-consciousness and high purpose, as well as a rejection of the worn-out standards of the past. "I have not the slightest feeling of Humility toward the Public, or to anything in existence—but the eternal Being, the Principle of Beauty, and the Memory of Great Men," writes Keats to J. H. Reynolds in 1818 (Rollins, I, 266). Association with the greats of the past, usually those greats whose true genius was appreciated only later, helped compensate for the scathing attacks that all the Romantics suffered from so many of the newly formed literary magazines of their day. This invocation of this family of true fame was therefore a sentiment much more suited to the times than it was a mere expression of resentment for being badly reviewed. The cult of progress, of growth, of achievement—the image of new dawns, new tomorrows, and a new sense of time so prominent in both the American and the French revolutions—turned all eyes to the future, where perfection and understanding would be achieved on earth. The models of the classical past were still being invoked and would be again, as were the models of Christian retirement and humility. But Shelley, Keats, and Byron, all dying in self-imposed or forced exile, had already prepared the ground for a posterity on earth that would appreciate what they had done. As Raymond Williams among others has pointed out, the Romantic poets more than any other literary generation before or since felt moved to engage in the great social and political issues of their day. And yet the term "Romantic" implies a separation, a willful retreat from the mundane and the political. The paradox goes through to the bone. The pressure for justice and democracy, and the writer's role in achieving it, constantly had to face the abhorrent changes in civilization. Retirement in the old sense of a separation from the world to contemplate eternal things seemed antisocial and hypocritical, not only for a fervent attacker of institutional Christianity as Shelley, but even for the more conventionally pious Byron.

Patronage by the great similarly implied compromises of personal integrity that could no longer be countenanced. Eighteenth-century writers might have been unavoidably forced into patronage, but scorn waited for those who were detected in seeking it too sedulously. In the early 1850s George Eliot ferociously attacks what she believes to be the "self-betrayal" and "radical insincerity" exhibited by Edward Young, just as Herbert Croft, seventy years before, had indicted the "miserable siege of *court* favor" that characterized his early career (Eliot, 24, 33; Croft, 424). Later, to Croft's further disgust, Young was "fond of holding himself out for a man retired from the world," even while he complained of the way the world had neglected him (433). As we look back on the dilemma of the eighteenth-century writer, Young, like Chatterton, seems depressingly caught between the old system of aristocratic patronage, the subscription of the wealthy, and the new reliance on the literary marketplace. But to George Eliot he is a cautionary figure of literary servility, and she lashes out at him with a fury that also seems rooted in the situation of the writer philosophically committed to the people, yet constantly reminded of the public. The new commercial standards of quantitative fame might be deplored, but they would not be totally ignored. There were audiences out there to be reached. Unfortunately, there was no sure way to distinguish them from the ones that were eager to jeer or ignore.

Hostility was therefore in some sense a mark of the kind of success the new writer wanted. Shelley wrote asking his publisher to send him especially the negative reviews; the good reviews of course pleased him, "but it is objection & enmity alone that rouses my *curiosity*" (II, 116). There is bravado in this, but the ambivalence runs all through Shelley's work and that of many of his contemporaries and descendants as well. Poets might be "the unacknowledged legislators of the world," but they should be the famously unacknowledged, and enmity at least recognized their crucial importance. Shelley went back and forth in his own impulses between the people and the public, scorning the latter but sometimes aiming to pay court to it with what he believed to be its kind of material. In 1819, for example, he flatly proclaims that *The Cenci* is "calculated to produce a very popular effect" (II, 116–117), while *Epipsychidion,* he tells his publisher, should appear in an edition of perhaps one hundred copies "simply for the esoteric few" (II, 263). Similarly, in one mood Byron could (not with total mockery) have a character in *Marino Faliero* (1821) refer to "the true touchstone of desert—success." But the whole of his career, from the time of his greatest fame after the publication of the early cantos of *Childe Harold* in 1812, seems to involve a succession of attempts to outrage, through both his life and his poems, whatever audience he had lured along so far, as if to test their adherence, and thereby the substance rather than the fashion of his appeal. Finally, even his loyal publisher, John Murray, refuses to bring out remaining cantos of *Don Juan,* and Byron publishes them himself.

Was it the overpowering experience of his unparalleled fame and what it did to people, what Peter Quennell has called "the paralyzing influence of Byron's celebrity" (73), that impelled him to test his limits? In one aspect he may remind us of Alexander, who saw each new conquest as a further escalating affirmation of himself to himself. But Byron's activity carries with it as well a tinge of the modern anxiety that only rejection is accurate and, for acceptance to have meaning, rejection must be sought and tested. To be rejected so intensely is the insurance of sincerity. It marks a successful evasion of the public's expectations, and therefore an affirmation of the true, unpublic, self. Society, wrote Byron in 1822, is "as now constituted, *fatal* to all great original undertakings of every kind" (*Self-Portrait,* II, 689–690). With appropriate paradox a few months later, Shelley goes a step further: "I detest all society—almost all, at least—and Lord Byron is the nucleus of all that is hateful and tiresome in it" (II, 434). Thus we see the basic bind in which were caught so many uncertainly public figures of the nineteenth century, who in a world of rapidly expanding visual and verbal media—gossip columns, memoirs, caricatures, newspapers—sought a better fame by their dramatic evasiveness. Shelley, who was an avowed recluse and sometimes appeared on his own title pages as "the Hermit of Marlow," perhaps could not appreciate Byron's analogous version of withdrawal in full view of a public. But their kinship is clear. "Self-advertisement" would not appear for a century or more, but "advertisement" had been an English word from the late sixteenth century, at first to denote the declarations of the town crier, then, by the end of the seventeenth century, the posting of placards or the printing of notices. It becomes a verb only in the late eighteenth century, and by the nineteenth century implies any kind of public announcement. So it appears in Byron's letters, and Shelley, who could refuse to allow his publisher to put his name on a book or poem, cited Byron's handling of the publication of his works as precedent for how his own should be treated.[26]

Such self-conscious play between publicity and withdrawal allowed the living artist to stage his own drama of ennobling neglect. Donne or Herbert or Marvell in the seventeenth century could circulate their works in manu-

26. In a typical paradox, Shelley says that he does not want his name on the title page of *Julian and Maddalo,* "though I have no objection to my being known as the author" (II, 246). Compare as well the letter to Leigh Hunt (15 August 1819), where he speaks of *"self,* that burr that will stick to no one. I can't get it off yet" (I, 109). For whatever mixture of practical and psychological reasons, the writers of the Romantic period often published anonymously, while the trend later in the century was to assume another name.

script to a discerning and appreciative audience they could virtually predetermine, at least in class and general outlook. Diderot in the eighteenth century could put some of his greatest works in the drawer with the confidence that posterity would find them and ensure him a reputation free of the animosity of the present. But the writers of the nineteenth century, whether they liked it or not, had to carry on their evasion before a public. Retirement, if allowable at all, would be possible only in the baroque terms of an Emily Brontë or an Emily Dickinson.

Respect for the honored dead, veneration of the neglected and the solitary, eccentricities of dress and behavior, identification with social outsiders—all allow the nineteenth-century artist a variety of ways of either ignoring or staging the paradoxes of being a private person with an increasingly public audience. Shelley dabbled in radical politics, and Byron, as the most famous and successful of the Romantics, was drawn to the delicious lure of unspecified guilt as a way of characterizing his heroes and engaging his audience. Thus, like both Percy and Mary Shelley, he helped add to the modern image of the artist the peculiar social function of representing some lost or repressed part of human grandeur, now warped and distorted but still barely recognizable—compounded of sensibility, sexuality, and violence—and vindicated by its grudging success in the hands of readers. Unlike the past alliances of art and nationalism under the patronage of the great, nineteenth-century artists sought the face of a fame within society that was yet in retreat from everything society ostensibly valued. Their association with hermits and wanderers, eccentrics and criminals, as well as their frequent expatriation, undercut the accusation of pandering to an immediate audience. In the celebration of anonymity, failure, reclusiveness, and even antisocial behavior, they emphasized their separation from the norm even as they appealed to its better nature.

Fame of this sort is therefore a kind of revenge on society for its neglect of "true" values. The artistic strategy of both escaping and competing with the standard of monarchical fame leads, especially in England and France, to the development of a sense of social marginality as a social role itself. In this new role, which would have been unfamiliar even to Rousseau, let alone the more traditional eighteenth-century writers, the artist was both the universal genius of society as well as its victim. In a sense, this was the other side of the Napoleonic coin and along with it came the paranoia that so often accompanies modern fame and glory. No wonder, then, that both Byron and Shelley were so keen to believe that Keats's illness and death were due to an attack on his work in the *Quarterly Review;* it made Keats, like Chatterton, a martyr to the ignorance of the public and its self-appointed critics, even while it confirmed Shelley and Byron in their own more tough-minded resistance to such criticism. Unfortunately, it was untrue, and Keats's own attitudes, as we shall see, are much more in accord with their disdain. Like Shelley and Byron, Keats believed in a new nation where true artistic freedom would be possible—a nation that might exist in France or America, but for their expatriate generation existed even more solidly as a country of the mind, to which no earthly kingdom could ever quite come close. In our own time cultural "neglect" has become much more explicitly politicized. The neglected geniuses now are those whom, critics say, the dominant culture has for its own ideological reasons suppressed. Thus members of a variety of groups are discovered to have been neglected or never to have existed with the force they "deserved." Soon no one will have been "neglected," as the storehouses of the past are turned over and sifted for names and works. The only charge left will be the unanswerable one that many geniuses had never been allowed to develop at all because of their own self-censorship. But in our rush to restore the neglected, the "mute, inglorious Milton," we have lost the Romantic sense that neglect by those whose opinions are empty may in fact be praise, just as we have virtually lost their belief that fame and success are not always in accord. Such beliefs may be self-solacing to the unsuccessful, but they also force some meditation on what is really valuable, the public gaze or those values in whose name that gaze should be avoided as much as possible.

Hazlitt and Keats: The Fame of the Alienated Forerunner

[T]here are none prepared to suffer in obscurity for their country. The motives of our worst Men are interest and of our best Vanity.
—JOHN KEATS, Letter to George and Georgiana Keats

I have some love of fame, of the fame of a Pascal, a Leibnitz, or a Berkeley (none at all of popularity) and would rather that a single inquirer about truth should pronounce my name, after I am dead, with the same feelings that I have thought of theirs, then be puffed in all the newspapers, and praised in all the reviews, while I am living.
—WILLIAM HAZLITT, A Letter to William Gifford

Caught in the conflicting pressures of an unprecedented fame culture, Wordsworth, Shelley, and in particular Byron tack precariously from assertion to withdrawal and back. But it is in the criticism of William Hazlitt and the letters of John Keats that we see the first really concerted efforts toward understanding what the new world of media has done to older ideas of the writer, the artist, the actor and their place in society. On the one side is the ideal—as expressed, say, in the politics of Rousseau, the ethics of Kant, the early promise of Napoleon, the poetry of Wordsworth—that the best achievement of poet or politician is to express a general truth about all humanity. On the other is the daily actuality of an industrial civilization, the rise of a mass reading (and soon voting) public, and the loss of an older, more emotionally cohesive community in the newly intense need to go it alone and achieve greatness for oneself.

William Hazlitt was one of the most popular critics and lecturers of early nineteenth-century England. His works are constantly preoccupied with delving into the nature of the artistic personality, past and present, as a way into understanding how fame works as both personal aspiration and social compulsion. The French and American revolutions had proclaimed a world in which the energies of the present would be released from the shackles of the past and stride abroad like giants. But when Hazlitt views his contemporaries, all that potential has been drained dry and that royal road already narrowed to the point of nonexistence. It would not be too far wrong to call him the first great fame theorist of the modern age, and the presence of Keats and others at his lectures on the English poets is a key to the way he reflected the concerns of a whole generation. Hazlitt treats the sense of fame and genius not as an intellectual, spiritual, or aesthetic category so much as a social and a psychological one. When he writes about the feeling of immortality in childhood or the eccentricity of writers or the egotism of artists, he considers his subjects in a way that any reader could identify with both their aberrations and their grandeur. Artists, writers, and actors in his essays become enlarged metaphors for everyone's sense of self-importance and how to deal with it. These creative individuals are not Renaissance figures whose singularity comes from their special connection with history. Nor are they saints or holy men whose sanction comes from their focus on the single audience of God. They take instead the peculiarly modern form of artistic individuals whose social role is to be antisocial or nonsocial, who look into the past to see only wreckage and into the future to see light.

Hazlitt's brother was a portrait painter and he himself at times tried painting. So perhaps it is natural that he is particularly intrigued with the artistic attitude toward fame. In the special connection of painters to the desire for recognition, Hazlitt sees a crystallization of the malaise of self-importance affecting so many other aspiring public figures of his time. In his most elaborate consideration of the general problem, "On Egotism," Hazlitt attacks pride not as a spiritual sin so much as a social one whereby an individual seeks to reduce all around him to servility. The painters he admires, like Nollekens and Northcote, have a kind of self-containment. They treat everyone alike, from king to commoner, and have no sense of the preordained structures of worldly status. The painters he dislikes, like Benjamin West or Salvator Rosa, turn that self-containment into an oblivious self-will that raises itself totally above anyone else. West, says Hazlitt, believed that the only other person alive who might be his superior was Napoleon. Hazlitt is willing to allow West the excuse of his "natural self-complacency" from being born an American and a Quaker:

> He lived long in the firm persuasion of being one of the elect among the sons of Fame, and went to his final rest in the arms of Immortal-

ity! Happy error! Enviable old man! ("On the Old Age of Artists," XII, 95).

But he has only scorn for artists, like Rosa, in whom personal assertion and willfulness is mistaken for genius. West at least is amiable (and in fact always supported younger painters). But Rosa exemplifies those painters who disdain the "mighty dead" because they are ignorant of how inferior their own work is to that of the past:

> When we forestall the judgment of posterity [by praising ourselves], it is because we are not confident of it ("On Egotism," XII, 157).

This anxiety about posterity, says Hazlitt, is especially a problem of painters, whose work is always fixed on the moment and whose education is so often ahistorical. Thus artists vaunt and self-advertise much more than poets and writers, who are used to their works making their way slowly into public appreciation. Such pride makes a virtue of personal isolation and self-absorption and is the opposite of "manly ambition," which welcomes competition as "the only test of merit." Even when it accomplishes worthy things, it takes no pleasure in them; like Ovid's Erysichthon or Augustine's hungry man empty of God, such people can never be satisfied:

> They go beyond the old motto—*Aut Caesar, aut nihil*—they not only want to be at the head of whatever they undertake, but if they succeed in that, they immediately want to be at the head of something else, no matter how gross or trivial. . . . To them the pursuit is every thing, the possession nothing (XII, 167).

Like royalty, such aspiring egotists can trust no one around them, not even themselves. But royalty at least must pretend to pay attention to others, while Hazlitt's egotists soar away in grand isolation.

As a cultural critic for whom fame was a prime subject, Hazlitt sought to make such self-consciousness suspect. "No really great man ever thought himself so," he begins the essay entitled "Whether genius is conscious of its powers," and goes on to argue that "every man, in judging of himself, is his own contemporary" (XII, 117). Because the "science" of knowing oneself has become more precise, self-consciousness has not only found greater and more varied heights to which to aspire, but it has also become more laden with doubts and the knowledge of its own inadequacies. As Hazlitt says elsewhere, only the young think that posthumous fame is worthwhile because they don't believe in their own deaths, while the aged, with death obviously ahead, would rather have their celebrity on earth ("On Sitting for One's Picture"). Youth is also the time, he notes, when the exuberance of entering into some great project that will make a mark on the imagination of the world carries one over the infinite difficulties of bringing it to completion. No wonder, perhaps, that it seemed to be a specialty of the Romantic poets to propose grand plans and complete only gigantic fragments. In another essay, "On the Feeling of Immortality in

Youth," Hazlitt, like Wordsworth in his "Immortality Ode," celebrates the sense of exuberance felt in childhood and youth, but then despairingly points to its quick end. Once, time was endless for every sort of thought and action and everything was perceived with immense force and clarity, as even the bricks and mailboxes in a foreign country seem unutterably wonderful and new. But soon enough time seems all too short, and the wonderful details of the world only a series of erosions.

In essays such as these, Hazlitt is clearly influenced by the Romantic infatuation with the feeling of personal immortality, the conviction of one's own genius, and the effort to get the world to agree—even as he keenly observes the imperfectly shaped careers of his contemporaries. Napoleon had said that in the modern world politics had replaced fate, laying himself open to Emerson's later high-minded charge that what he called the immortality of his soul was only fame. But Hazlitt is always acutely aware of the need and obligation that even the most reclusive artist has to seek an audience. Whenever he writes about a painter or a writer, he comments on that central awareness that the Napoleonic nature of the new age requires: What is the artist's relation to his audience? In the past perhaps the shy scholar might be the model of the writer. Gray, writes Hazlitt, "was terrified out of his wits at the bare idea of having his portrait prefixed to his works; and probably died from nervous agitation at the publicity into which his name had been forced by his learning, taste, and genius" ("The Shyness of Scholars," XVII, 262). But the age had changed, and now the writer's presence before his audience was becoming a crucial issue. Johnson in the 1780s could write a lengthy comparison of Dryden and Pope with hardly a mention of the public image that in different ways preoccupied both. But for Hazlitt in the 1820s, when he compares Sir Walter Scott and Byron in *The Spirit of the Age* (1825), that issue is closely connected to any analysis of style or meaning. Briefly told, Byron is "the creature of his own will," who stands alone, scorning all comparisons and daring his public to follow him as he tries to escape from the prison of their attention and expectation (XI, 69). Scott, on the other hand, looks only backward, effacing himself to show the reality of his characters, dramatizing "the romance of real life" (XI, 62). At times Hazlitt sees Byron as posturing and assertive, his style full-blown and ostentatious, while Scott is the author as "unknown benefactor," whose transparent style reveals what he wants to show instead of interposing himself. But in another mood, Hazlitt argues that Scott's nostalgia makes him a spiteful supporter of Legitimacy and monarchical rule, while Byron even at his most excessive maintains the connection between liberty and poetic vision and dies "a martyr to his zeal in the cause of freedom, for the last, best hopes of man."[27]

27. Although Scott had been a celebrated poet in his early career, *Waverley* (1814), his first novel, appeared anonymously and subsequent novels were signed by "The Author of Waverley." After a few years the author's identity was generally known, but Scott did not actually acknowledge authorship until 1827. This fascinating example of authorial evasion, to publish without publicity, akin to the pseudonyms of such as Charlotte Brontë (Currer Bell), Marian Evans (George Eliot), and Samuel

It is clear enough that Hazlitt's own nature, what one friend called a "morbid self-consciousness," together with his early artistic aspirations and his later role as critic, contributed much to his sensitivity to varieties of artistic and political self-consciousness that were beginning to appear on the stage of nineteenth-century European history. What he called the "peevish invective" of his comparison between Byron and Scott highlights his own ambiguous attitudes. The "spirit of the age," as nearly as Hazlitt defines it, is an individual ostentation that has created good when it has awakened people to the spirit of liberty, but has too often displayed only the gestures of mere ambition. On such a tightrope, even the most success-ful writers rarely display an ease with their celebrity. As Hazlitt writes of Byron, "he is equally averse to notice or neglect, enraged at censure and scorning praise. . . . He says he will write on, whether he is read or not. He would never write another page, if it were not to court popular ap-plause, or to affect a superiority over it" (XI, 76).

Yet for all of Hazlitt's annoyance at what he considers Byron's postur-ing self-absorption, he nevertheless appreciates the desire for personal and political freedom that this constant commerce between ingratiation and disdain is trying to express. The paradox is embedded in the times. A writer like Scott, who identifies himself with the established order of the past and present, may present his works anonymously, as if they were the direct emanation of truth and history. But for the writer who is a political liberal, like Byron, Hazlitt, Shelley, or Keats, there were more complicated issues. Hazlitt never faltered in his praise of Napoleon because he consid-ered the revolutionary period not only to be the downfall of a system that had repressed individual will and self-determination, but also because it marked the true rebirth of Fame itself, "after having slept a thousand years."[28]

Now unshackled, individual aspiration could soar on its own wings, buoyed by the applause of a new audience, for the first time itself truly free. Since those glorious days, despotism and the divine right of kings had reestablished much of their hold. But, for Hazlitt, to believe in Napoleon was to cherish the memory of that gleaming possibility, not so much as a model of political order and organization but as a model of self, somehow both alone and before an audience, drawing on one's own sensibility at the service of humanity. After a lifetime primarily devoted to writing essays about cultural and personal matters, Hazlitt spent most of his last years working on a massive biography that attempted to vindicate Napoleon from all the charges laid against him by his enemies. Napoleon was the only one of Hazlitt's contemporaries for whom he had unalloyed admiration:

Clemens (Mark Twain), is discussed in 1905 by an aristocratic author who wrote much and signed everything, Bertrand Russell, as an example of an important dis-tinction in the question of personal identity and the difference between what words denote and what they mean. Philosophy was catching up with literature in the play of uncertainty between authority and authorship.

28. It is unclear whether Hazlitt specifically means since Charlemagne or merely a long time.

The only great man of modern times, that is, the only man who rose in deeds and fame to the level of antiquity, who might turn his gaze upon himself and wonder at his height, for on him all eyes were fixed as his majestic stature towered above thrones and monuments of renown, died the other day in exile, and in lingering agony; and we still see fellows strutting about the streets, and fancying they are something! ("On Egotism," XII, 166).

Throughout his work Hazlitt struggles to find a place above the fray of fame from which to criticize such strutting imitators of Byron and Napoleon as well as those moments when Byron and Napoleon too superficially imitate themselves. He is less bothered by Byron's determined singularity than he is by the poet's willingness to serve an audience that seeks sensation rather than the true poetry that "moves best within the circle of nature and received opinion" (XI, 76). Thus Byron's celebrity represents for Hazlitt a problem of democratic art similar to that foreseen by Alexis de Tocqueville, who thought that the new multitudes of readers in America would produce authors who became wealthy and popular without ever being admired: "The ever growing crowd of readers always wanting something new ensures the sale of books that nobody esteems highly."[29] Virtually any presentation of self to the public beyond that in a book (or perhaps in a series of formal lectures) moved Hazlitt to scorn, because its focus on the present implied its capitulation to either fashion or established power. Coleridge, he says, finally sacrifices all his genius as a writer to his talents for talking, with its immediate reception and approval: ". . . he lays down his pen to make sure of an auditor, and mortgages the admiration of posterity for the stare of an idler" (XI, 30). Appropriately enough, *The Spirit of the Age* is published anonymously.

*   *   *

Hazlitt's contrasts between Scott and Byron indicate that the desire for fame, the way one defines it and the way one goes about it, is a continual paradox. *Frankenstein,* published the same year as Hazlitt's lectures, even more elaborately shows how the overwhelming desire to create in solitude a work that will carry your name and fame to future generations—as Victor Frankenstein says, to "pioneer a new way, explore unknown powers, and unfold to the world the deepest mysteries of creation" (308)—too easily can turn into Napoleonic despotism and self-absorption. To the extent that we are now living in the latter days of an originality culture, it is a struggle that still goes on. The artist creates a work in solitude and presents it to an audience. To the extent that it is rejected, he feels both distraught that the world does not share his opinion of its greatness and vindicated in the uniqueness of his conception. Thus, if rejection is bad, acceptance is often

29. Tocqueville's distinction between "the people" and "mankind" in *Democracy in America* (II, 475) bears some strong affinities with Wordsworth's between "public" and "people," as well as Whitman's distinction between "the people" and "democracy" in *Democratic Vistas* (1871). The American context, of course, immediately politicizes the distinction much beyond a matter for speculation about literary audiences.

worse, for it too easily socializes what had gathered strength from its creator's privacy and concentration, diminishing the personal labor poured into creativity by making it a public commodity. The reception of the great work by the world thus can never satisfy the expectations its creator had for its fame and his own. (As Mary Shelley astutely dramatizes in *Frankenstein,* such creators at least in the early ninteenth century are usually male.) Byron's bravado evasion of his audience's approval, his refusal to be frozen by its Medusa gaze, is reminiscent of Rousseau's obsessive alienation of virtually everyone who had taken him in and loved him. The only issue is personal freedom, which publicity simultaneously promises and takes away. Because every fan compromises one's freedom, even the most admiring audience must have its faith constantly tested by greater and greater indignities. Just so, a performer, beloved since a child, might deliberately make herself fatter and more grotesque to see how far that love extended, in order finally to say at the moment of rejection, 'I knew I was never loved for myself.'

Byron was too intrigued by the constant construction and reforming of his public image ever to voice such a sentiment. But it does appear in a letter from Keats to Fanny Brawne:

> . . . and here I must confess, that (since I am on that subject) I love you the more in that I believe you have liked me for my own sake and for nothing else. I have met with women whom I really think would like to be married to a Poem and to be given away by a Novel (618–619).

The contrast Keats makes between the self that is loved more authentically than the work is admired indicates his own constant preoccupation with the intertwined questions of fame and the poetic calling. Virtually at the same time that Hazlitt is delineating the styles of fame and their moral-aesthetic implications, Keats, who attended most of Hazlitt's lectures on the English poets, goes through a fascinating metamorphosis in his own attitudes.[30] During 1817, the year before Hazlitt's lectures, his most ambitious poem so far, *Endymion,* is "inscribed to the memory of Thomas Chatterton." Appropriately enough, then, although Keats generally approves of what Hazlitt says, he is upset at Hazlitt's dismissal of Chatterton as a poet whose works were nothing extraordinary for a boy of sixteen: "He did not show extraordinary powers of genius, but extraordinary precocity." Worse, Hazlitt concludes that Chatterton knew his talents were limited and therefore committed suicide, "to set a seal on his reputation by a tragic catastrophe" but in fact proving his inability to do anything more:

> Great geniuses, like great kings, have too much to think of to kill themselves; for their mind to them also "a kingdom is" (V, 122).

30. Hazlitt's own preference is for the more sociable Burns over the "recluse philosopher" Wordsworth. But, with typical ambivalence, he also recognizes the corroding temptations of celebrity faced by Burns as well as the defensive aspect of Wordsworth's egotism. For further on the somewhat meager information we have about Hazlitt's relation with Keats, see Baker, 247–251, and Bromwich, 362–401.

In the next lecture, Hazlitt, in response to the objections of Keats and others, explained that he was objecting less to the belief in Chatterton's genius "than to the common mode of estimating its magnitude by its prematureness" (123). He then attacks those literary scholars and litterateurs who loudly bemoan the fate of neglected and untimely cropped genius in works that appear, "splendidly bound, in the fourteenth edition, while he is a prey to worms" (125). Aside from the self-deceptive hypocrisy of such celebrations, the idolators of Chatterton are also substituting a preoccupation with the man for a commitment to his works—a species of fan club that has little to do with the qualities of true poetry. Not that Hazlitt believes poems exist apart from those who write them. But true fame should be reserved for those poets who live in the memory because of their work rather than themselves. Only after a poet is dead can this happen properly, not for Diderot's reason that posterity will be more detached in its judgment, but because the real definition of fame is memory, "the spirit of a man surviving himself in the minds and thoughts of other men, undying and imperishable" (V, 144). As Hazlitt later writes about Byron, "the poet's cemetery is the human mind." Death is a "natural canonization" for all: "It makes the meanest of us sacred—it installs the poet in his immortality, and lifts him to the skies" (XI, 78). The desire for popularity is the immediate and gross version of which the desire for fame is the ideal: "The love of nature is the first thing in the mind of the true poet: the admiration of himself is the last." [31] These passages appear in a longer consideration of the nature of fame that prefaces Hazlitt's last lecture, on living poets, in which he again stresses the lack of self-consciousness that characterizes true genius. It is one of his most frequent themes. As he had written elsewhere:

> Most men cease to be of any consequence at all when they are dead; but it is the privilege of genius to survive himself. But he cannot in the nature of things anticipate this privilege ("On the Catalogue Raisonnée," IV, 148).

Here he makes the contrast even stronger: "[H]e who would be great in the eyes of others must first learn to be nothing in his own" (V, 145).

The sentiment seems easy enough to say for Hazlitt, who has taken up the relatively new literary role of the critic: intermediary between artists and the public, chastising one to be better in achievement, the other in understanding. But what of the poets, who—like Wordsworth or Coleridge or Keats—venerated Chatterton as a support against the opinions of a world that could never understand them as they sought to be. During the writing of *Endymion,* a particularly long and ambitious poem, Keats seems especially preoccupied with the implications of making such a claim on

31. Death as the entryway to immortality is a frequent motif during this period and later in epitaphs for the celebrated. Chatterton's suicide encouraged an assumption that the passage from life to immortality through death might be a willful decision.

public attention. His aspiration is to be a poet, a being somehow grander than other men. At times he easily believes that *Endymion* will help confirm that status, "a great task . . . that when done . . . will take me but a dozen steps toward the Temple of Fame" (Thorpe, 82). But at other times his aspirations are so overpoweringly grandiose that he almost feels like giving up. "What a thing to be in the Mouth of Fame," he writes to one correspondent (503), while to others he self-mockingly theorizes on the nature of genius, "a Subject which I am certain I could not do justice to under five years study and 3 vols octavo" (524).

In such passages, we see Keats in a posture exactly like that he objected to so strenuously in Byron, in Wordsworth, and to a certain extent in Coleridge: the poet preoccupied with greatness for himself. Modern poets, says Keats, are petty tyrants strutting around their kingdoms, checking every detail. Wherever he appears, Wordsworth leaves a bad impression "by his egotism, Vanity, and bigotry" (543). Where then is the line between the absolute aspiration Keats holds out for himself ("I think I shall be among the English poets after my death") and the egotism he, like Hazlitt, attacks in Byron and Wordsworth? To a great extent an answer emerges in 1817–1818—the years marked by Keats's composition and publication of *Endymion* and his attendance at Hazlitt's lectures—and the security this answer gives Keats may help to account for the surge of creative energies that in 1819 produces so many of his greatest poems. Through a contemplation of the injunction of the early Romantic poets to follow nature, Hazlitt's effort to formulate the relation between worldly fame and the poetic career, along with his wrestlings with his own work, Keats formulates his belief that the great poet's anonymity is the essential key to his genius and his fame:

> As to the poetical Character itself (I mean that sort of which, if I am anything, I am a Member; that sort distinguished from the Wordsworthian, or egotistical sublime; which is a thing per se, and stands alone), it is not itself—it has no self—it is every thing and nothing— It has no character (576).

As such, it can become any character, much as Shakespeare, with what Keats had earlier called his "negative capability," could dramatize "uncertainties, mysteries, doubts, without any irritable reaching after fact and reason" (528). Thus the genius for Keats is distinguished neither by his strongly marked personal nature nor his ability to impress himself on others and draw others to him, but by his lack of individuality and "any determined character." Yet, even though he identifies such genius with the "negative" nature of Shakespeare, Keats does not aspire to be a dramatist or a novelist, inventing new character and investing them with himself. Instead it is within the poem that all such transformations take place, reflecting the constantly changing nature of the poet. Just as Keats's poet gathers all of human nature into his own, so his ideal poem should escape the twin curses of spurious individuality and empty originality: "Poetry should be great and unobtrusive, a thing which enters into one's soul, and does not startle or amaze it with oneself, but with its subject" (537).

"How beautiful are the retired flowers," Keats continues. "How would they lose their beauty were they to throng into the highway crying out, 'Admire me I am a violet!—Dote upon me I am a primrose!' " (538) The sentiment harkens back to Gray's *Elegy* with its paradoxical celebration of and mourning for the anonymous dead. But Keats's disdain for a poetry of mere personal assertion fully embraces the paradox and sets sail in search of a fame that will come after death to one who rejected superficial egotism in life. The trap is not necessarily publication, but the need to have a public image. Then poets become mere politicians, enslaved to their audiences and their poetic "roles." When he is among others and not thinking about his own work, says Keats, their identities "press upon me, so that I am in a very little time annihilated" (576). Wordsworth and Byron, therefore, in their different ways, are stained with the same theatrical impulse that vitiated the achievements of Napoleon: ". . . [T]here are none prepared to suffer in obscurity for their country. The motives of our worst Men are of interest and of our best Vanity" (584). In the state whose politics are theatrical, complains Keats, people assume titles of office and lose that of man. Thus, Keats's poet is reclusive in character, although shying away as well from the ostentatious solitude of a Wordsworth. Such a life may itself engender the pride and egotism of being a poet, but it also allows him to do better work than he could do otherwise:

> Just so much as I am hu[m]bled by the genius above my grasp, am I exalted and look with hate and contempt upon the literary world. . . . Who would wish to be among the commonplace crowd of the little-famous—who are each individually lost in a throng made up of themselves? (624).

The pose of anonymity, of negative capability, helps Keats distance himself from the threats and lures of the literary world which, if he entered, would swallow him up in "the myriad-aristocracy" of letters. We may not quite believe him when he speaks of "the solitary indifference I feel for applause even from the finest spirits" (527). But the personal utility of his belief is obvious: It allows him to maintain his grand artistic aspirations in some transcendental balance with the need to seek an immediate audience. The pseudonyms of a Charlotte Brontë or the closet-writings of an Emily Dickinson hover in the wings. But Keats publishes freely, exuberantly, and voluminously under his own name.

In these letters of 1817–1819, Keats's effort to allay his desire for personal fame gradually leads him to turn away from even the conception of a general poetic nature as too limiting. The letter to Fanny Brawne that I quoted, with its distinction between himself and his work, implies that he now sees even "the Poet" as a pose, not the greater self to which he had earlier aspired. So too he comes to believe that the lesson of Chatterton's neglect and death is not that such merit ought to be sought out and celebrated, but that it is always a benefit to genius to be opposed by the society around it:

> One of the great reasons that the English have produced the finest writers in the world is, that the English world has ill-treated them during their lives and foster'd them after their deaths (612).

As Keats moves closer to his own early death from tuberculosis at twenty-five, his desire to be "in the Mouth of Fame" mutates into an aspiration to transcend the need for immediate response, whether neglect or praise. All around Keats, both before and after this death, observers like Shelley, Byron, and Hazlitt blamed bad reviews and the harsh criticism of the Tory magazines for his physical disintegration. But Keats in his letters assumes a disdain for earthly censure as well as applause.

Stripped of the language of religion, infused by a new political language of the virtue of individual will and self-determination, Keats's conception of himself as the anonymous poet is reminiscent of the saintly solitude supported by God alone, now reformulated to support the artist's self-esteem against an insensitive commercial society and a crowded urban world. Sociability, the need for interchange with others, is not totally denied, for that would be Wordsworthian egotism. The ideal instead is a self-containment without self-contentment or self-satisfaction, and the line of his aspiration ends less in a mound of great works than in a final effort to go beyond writing itself. "I have been very idle lately, very averse to writing," he says in 1819, "both from the overpowering idea of our dead poets and from abatement of my love of fame" (613). In order to work, the need to work must be redefined, not as a competition with the greats of the past or the present, nor as the desire to have his name on the lips of a vast audience, but in an image of some other self before some other audience, where absolute ostentation and absolute reclusiveness become the same, just as Alexander, if he were not Alexander, would be Diogenes. "I was never afraid of failure," Keats had said in a letter to one of the publishers of *Endymion,* "for I would sooner fail than not be among the greatest" (83). So Keats puts his own more fruitful turn on the *aut Caesar aut nihil* of the early nineteenth century, turning the absolute contrast between success and failure into a talisman against mediocrity, rather than a resignation in front of impossible odds or a mindless thrust to uniqueness.

With such goals, no figure of worldly success can satisfy the need for a model, for the goal itself exists at the intersection of worldliness and unworldliness, where neither private nor public self suffices, because the aim is to transcend such divisions. Thus Keats first reaches for inspiration to Homer and Shakespeare, writers characterized (for the nineteenth century) by their generalized greatness, their anonymous celebrity. But even more than these two great writers, he values the models of Socrates and Jesus. They are the two greatest men, he says, *because they did not write,* and yet their thoughts and ideas and sayings have come down the centuries to us. As such, they represent an ideal world of unpublicized greatness:

I have no doubt that thousands of people never heard of have had hearts completely disinterested: I can remember but two—Socrates and Jesus—their Histories evince it (605).

Jesus in particular, as so often in the past, becomes the way out of earthly concern with personal fame, either during life or after death. By the time of Keats, he has lost any institutionally Christian significance to represent instead fame as a fulfillment of the self, of one's own deepest potentials.

A year or so after *The Spirit of the Age* and five years after the death of Keats, Hazlitt publishes a strange little essay called "Of Persons One Would Wish to Have Seen." It is set twenty years before and recounts an animated discussion among friends, all of them, like Hazlitt, at the beginnings of their literary careers. As each name is proposed by a member of the circle, they discuss whether it would really be worthwhile to see this person. Newton and Locke are dismissed early because there is nothing interesting in them beyond their books. Charles Lamb, who is present, prefers to see more enigmatic writers, like Thomas Browne or Fulke Greville. Chaucer is proposed in company with Petrarch or Boccaccio. The choices then go beyond the literary: Columbus, the Wandering Jew. But the conversation quickly gets back to the literary, for the only statesman from all English history anyone wants to see is Cromwell and the only "enthusiast" is Bunyan. Names and reasons for wanting to see their possessors fly thickly across the room. But finally someone has the last word:

"There is only one other person I can ever think of after this," continued R——; but without mentioning a name that once put on a semblance of mortality. "If Shakespear was to come into the room, we should all rise up to meet him; but if that person was to come into it, we should all fall down and try to kiss the hem of his garment!" (XVII, 134).

The conversation has come to an end, and all leave. "Of Persons One Would Wish to Have Seen" updates a hearty genre, popular in the eighteenth century, that stretches back to Lucian, called the dialogues of the dead, in which men of the present seek to revive the greats of the past, mixing and mingling them from every time and clime. But here, in the age of Napoleon and Byron, the urge for dialogue, in which each great name argues his or her characteristic point of view, is replaced by the desire to see, to observe as in a theater: Chaucer chatting with Boccaccio, Molière reading *Tartuffe* to Ninon de l'Enclos, or Cromwell, warts and all. Appropriately enough for this farewell tour of eternity, the one figure all want to see who lived nearest to their own time is David Garrick, and Hazlitt tells an anecdote of Garrick's total commitment to performance and the immediacy of his audience. Greatness, no matter what its inner nature, appears to the world and to its greatest admirers as a performance that reaches beyond the grave, even in order to deny all that performance seems to assert. And so the discussion itself must conclude by the invocation first of Shakespeare, the playwright who dissolved himself into his characters, and then of the figure whose fame transcends fame, whose name does not even have to be mentioned (and in this context must not be), whose life is both inspiration and reproach to those who desire absolute fame—Jesus.

Carlyle and Emerson:
The Taxonomy of Fame

Our age is retrospective . . . why should not we also [like preceding generations] enjoy an original relation to the universe?
—EMERSON, *Nature* (1836)

The greatest of all Heroes is One—whom we do not name here!
—CARLYLE, *On Heroes and Hero-Worship* (1840)

By the mid-nineteenth century the marketplace of fame had become so crowded that two writers, one in England and one in America, proposed a codification of fame into its eternal human types. Chivalric civilization might be over, along with the exclusive claims of monarchical and aristocratic conceptions of proper behavior and greatness. But just as there was a nostalgia for the trappings of medieval culture in the wake of the novels of Sir Walter Scott, so Thomas Carlyle in *On Heroes and Hero-Worship* (1840) and Ralph Waldo Emerson in *Representative Men* (1850), faced with the tumult of "great men" and the general rush to fame of all kinds, attempted their nineteenth-century versions of the Nine Worthies. In his own way, each tries to reestablish a heroic coherence for cultures that seemed desperately eager to fly apart, as each person, fired by the examples of boldness around him, sought his own destiny, his own star. It was perhaps the last moment such a synthesis could be contemplated and, even as they wrote, the projects of Carlyle and Emerson seemed somewhat anachronistic. Both assumed that the great lived in a common world and that it was through great men that individuals could connect with their own cultures and histories. Meanwhile, in Germany and France, a more scientific history, which demoted the importance of great men in favor of impersonal political and economic causes, was beginning to flourish. But the causal "truths" of general historical movement had little to do with what Carlyle and Emerson were attempting. Their great men were not so much movers and makers in history as they were beacons of being, who, as Emerson said, served to connect every individual with the great forces of time and change: "Such a man was wanted, and such a man was born" (*Representative Men*, 731).

In essence both Carlyle and Emerson attempt to analyze Rousseau's formulation of unique generality into its basic types. Within a museum culture ransacking the past for models and a culture of popular media similarly processing the present, they attempt to synthesize the virtues of anonymity and fame, ostentation and neglect, into the visible saints of the new age, when, because anyone might be potentially Elect, everyone must monitor his (rarely her) Election by keeping his eye on the exemplum. Although Carlyle's rhetoric leads him to call his subjects *heroes,* while for Emerson they are more often *geniuses,* both emphasize their spiritual power. Carlyle's cohort is made up of Odin ("the Hero as Divinity"), Mahomet ("the Hero as Prophet"), Dante and Shakespeare ("Poet"), Luther and John Knox ("Priest"), Samuel Johnson, Rousseau, and Robert Burns ("Man of Letters"), and finally Cromwell and Napoleon ("King"). Emerson's is made up of Plato ("or, the Philosopher"), Swedenborg ("or, the Mystic"), Montaigne ("the Skeptic"), Shakespeare ("the Poet"), Napoleon ("the Man of the World"), and Goethe ("the Writer"). Each group illustrates a style of importance akin to the different political situations of the author's country. Carlyle's figures are often literal leaders of men, while Emerson's are more spiritual and intangible in their sovereignty. Even when Carlyle contemplates an artistic figure, he emphasizes the dominion, the kingship, such a figure has over those who admire him. The hero stands outside of time and therefore is its master, piercing the veil of history that otherwise confines human vision. Shakespeare, for example, constitutes England's real empire and will remain long after the physical empire is gone. In the lapse of three centuries from the Reformation through Puritanism to the French Revolution, Carlyle says, has come the destruction of false sovereignties so that true sovereigns can flourish. His coterie of heroes are, of course, the true sovereigns, and in their lineage they are more connected with each other than with any particular class or country. All heroes are the same, writes Carlyle, with only the particular shape they take and the world's reception of them making any difference between them: "I confess, I have no notion of a truly great man that could not be *all* sorts of men" (93). Protestantism first created the possibility of "a whole World of Heroes" (151). Now the new age of communication will perpetuate the man of letters as the authentic kingly hero—"ruling from his grave, after death, whole nations who would, or would not, give him bread while living" (184)—because he searches out the divine underneath the everyday, gathering into himself the prophetic and priestly offices of the heroes of the past. But, while Carlyle believes that the great man can become anyone, Emerson believes that anyone can become a great man. He speaks more of men than of heroes, and his small group of the great are less monarchs than the prime representatives of other men. While his attitude toward greatness may be similar to that of Hegel contemplating Napoleon at Jena as 'the world-soul on horseback,' his political spirit is more in accord with Whitman's in the preface to *Leaves of Grass:* "Did you suppose there could be only one Supreme? We affirm that there can be unnumbered Supremes" (449).[32]

32. In writing to a friend after the Prussian defeat at Jena (1806), Hegel remarks, "This morning I saw the Emperor Napoleon, that World Soul, riding through the

For all of Carlyle's belief in the importance of great men and the "divine relation" they have with other men, he ends his work with Napoleon, the great man who has willfully corrupted his own promise. Despite his desire to open social status to those with talents rather than only birth or money, Napoleon in his later career began to believe his own star publicity. *"Self* and false ambition had now become his god." This was what had ruined Robert Burns and scarred Rousseau, what Carlyle calls "Lionism," the turning of the hero into a mere celebrity (228–229). This is the ultimate corruption of the hero, because his most vital trait is his sincerity, that is, his truth to himself: his lack of premeditation, his self-restraint, and his self-denial. Not that Carlyle, like some seventeenth-century divine, is against self. But it must be the proper kind of self, the sincere self, the silent and even the reticent self, which believes and therefore can act. The greatest need, he says, is "To unfold your *self,* to work what things you have the faculty for" (266). The hero does this to the utmost. But he is always in danger of being thwarted or warped by society's appeal to his latent lionism. To stay, like Napoleon, in the public eye at all costs, turns heroism into mere sensation and novelty. The great man for Carlyle is the universal man, the monarch beyond nations. But Napoleon, even though "still our last Great Man" (286), had in the later years of his career, been taken over by the French, his native Corsican roughness and sincerity enslaved to pomp and premeditation.[33]

Emerson's disappointment with Napoleon is as strong as Carlyle's, but he approaches his subject differently. By ending with Goethe "the writer," rather than Napoleon, "the hero as King," he establishes a wider scope for the great man in nineteenth-century America, even as a cautionary example to his audience. Throughout Emerson's essays runs the theme of unity in multiplicity, one springing from many. This political contrast with Carlyle extends even to details, for Emerson's great men are even in some sense elected—"As Sir Robert Peel and Mr. Webster vote, so Locke and Rousseau think for thousands" (715)—while Carlyle's are natural rulers. But both emphasize the great man's lack of originality in any innovative sense. It is his sincerity that makes Carlyle's great man an original and a hero, stripping away the encrusted gossip and jargon of human social language to speak directly, "the *original* man, the Seer; whose shaped spoken thought awakes the slumbering capability of all into Thought" (25). Emerson goes even further and denies that the great are original at all. For him they are great *anti*-individualists, whose example liberates everyone else from the burden of ambition, personal egotism, and the sense of "injurious

---

town to a parade. It's a marvelous feeling to see such a personality dominating the entire world from horseback." *Briefe von und an Hegel,* ed. J. Hoffmeister. Hamburg, 1952, I, 120. Quoted by Avineri, "Hegel and Nationalism" (109). Avineri also argues that, when Hegel was looking for a "German Theseus" in 1802, he had Napoleon in mind, "the Great Constitutional Lawyer of Paris."

33. Carlyle says that Napoleon lacks Cromwell's aloneness and his silence because Carlyle's Cromwell is not the Machiavellian of the royalists but the republican Cincinnatus, who wants only to return to his farm once the nation has been saved.

superiority" (625). The great man as monarch has no place in Emerson's system, because each society needs many such great men, so that one alone does not warp the world entirely around himself. The truly great are therefore not so much self-asserters as they are capacious receivers of the works of others:

> Great men are more distinguished by range and extent, than by originality. If we require the originality which consists in weaving, like a spider, their web from their own bowels; in finding clay, and making bricks, and building the house; no great men are original. . . . The greatest genius is the most indebted man . . . all originality is relative. Every thinker is retrospective (710, 715).[34]

The Renaissance rediscovery of the classical past had helped create aspirations for personal fame that were determined and limited by preexisting models—of Alexander or Julius Caesar or Cicero or Virgil. In France particularly, but elsewhere in Europe as well, the state was the way to personal glory, in a monarchy through the king and in a republic through law and the government. The past ratified the present and made it real. Such styles still existed in the nineteenth century and were memorialized in the three-volume biographies of great men that flooded the bookstores. But Carlyle and Emerson mark how much the atmosphere of grand achievement had shifted, even if some of the trappings—the Roman togas and classical tags—remained the same. The audience of the great man—whether political or artistic—was no longer the patron or the classical past or the members of his own class or profession, but the public. And it is on the great man as a promoter of the public good that both Carlyle and Emerson base their pantheon. Carlyle particularly is concerned to distinguish what he considered to be greatness from mere ambition, and his tones echo those of Ovid and Augustine:

> Examine the man who lives in misery because he does not shine above other men; who goes about producing himself, pruriently anxious about his gifts and claims; struggling to force everybody, as it were begging for God's sake, to acknowledge him a great man, and set him above the heads of men! Such a creature is among the wretchedest sights seen under this sun. A *great* man? A poor morbid prurient empty man; fitter for the ward of a hospital, than for a throne among men. I advise you to keep-out of his way. He cannot walk on quiet paths; unless you will look at him, wonder at him, he cannot live. It is the *emptiness* of the man, not his greatness. Because there is nothing in himself, he hungers and thirsts that you will find something in him (263).

---

34. Jonathan Swift had used the spider weaving out of himself as an image of the emptiness of modern originality in *A Tale of a Tub* (1704). His contrast is with the bee who gathers from every flower the pollen to make his honey. Perhaps Ovid's cautionary tale of Minerva and Arachne stands in the background. Emily Dickinson, as we shall see, has much more positive remarks to make about the spider's weaving.

A wretched sight perhaps. But Carlyle's magisterial scorn indicates how common such a figure has become in English public life. The hankering toward performance of such nineteenth-century authors as Byron, Dickens, Tennyson, Whitman, and Mark Twain is the mirror image of the ostentatious withdrawal with which we associate Keats, Shelley, the Brontë sisters, and Emily Dickinson. The light of recognition may ultimately come only from God, but the assertion took place before the eyes of men. Thus policy and personality both required that Napoleon, like Caesar before him and Hitler after, had to publicize his belief in, his subordination to, his star. In some way the devil of purposeful fame-seeking had to be exorcised by a commitment to a transcendent originality ratified by God. As Carlyle indicates, the hero needed to believe in God as his support, and belief itself had to be an integral part of his personality, because otherwise his success and his fame would be merely chance and so subject to the same universal whims that created it from the start. Both Carlyle and Emerson thus record without obvious irony the anecdote of Napoleon in Egypt, that perpetual touchstone of the god-kings, listening to an evening of arguments against the existence of God only to silence everyone by pointing at the sky and saying in effect, "But gentlemen, if there is no God, then who made the stars?"

Democratic Theater and the Natural Performer

America: The Shape of Visible Authority

Players . . . have little reason to complain of their hard-earned, short-lived popularity. The thunder of applause from pits, boxes, and galleries, is equal to whole immortality of posthumous fame. . . . When an author dies, it is no matter, for his works remain. When a great actor dies, there is a void produced in society, a gap which requires to be filled up.

—HAZLITT, "A View of the English Stage"

Carlyle and Emerson had both reacted unfavorably to Byron. The neglected genius, the unsung great original, was more to their taste. But when they cite Napoleon's invocation of the most glittering part of creation, the homes of Roman Genius, as the evidence of God's existence, they insensibly register the impact of a new world of visible public men that can no longer be denied. We must recall that with Byron and Napoleon we are standing on the verge of the invention of photography, with all that it promises for even greater dissemination of the face of fame. Photography appears barely ten years after their deaths, and within ten more it is perfected enough for all the fashionable and aspiring of Europe and America to consider it an unpardonable lapse not to have their pictures taken. By the mid-nineteenth century we have already reached a point in the history of modern fame when the rapid growth of newspapers and magazines, the development of the railroad and the telegraph, along with the rapid sophistication of photography begin the immense changes in the process of communication that still shape our attitudes toward the famous. But, as we have already seen, the fertile groundwork for the extraordinary advance in visible fame had been laid long before the photographic portrait and the *carte de visite* put personal publicity into the hands of anyone who wanted to pay for it. The styles of ostentatious reticence we have just been observing, together with the baroque efforts of writers particularly to add the elements of reclusiveness and otherworldliness to their self-presentation, have a symbiotic relation to the new assertions of face and name, the direct appeal to an immediate audience, made possible by the American and French revolutions.

At first the soldiers and statesmen of the revolution did not immediately realize that a visual image would convey them most vividly to the present as well as to the future. Their lives were filled with the attention of their immediate followers and that seemed to be enough. Yet, because they had conquered in a world where monarchical and aristocratic power had tended to keep the command of visual imagery to itself, many also realized the need for an imagistic continuity between their new world and the old, in order to rival the past while drawing upon its sanction. Thus, for example, both America and France, from the time of their revolutions to the beginning of World War One, witness a revival of civic sculpture to an extent unparalleled since imperial Rome. Here was not the small handful of images of patrons, rulers, and saints that had reappeared with the Renaissance, nor the private galleries of the eighteenth-century English dilettante, but a widely expanded use of civic space to celebrate civic people and civic virtue of all sorts. After 1789 in France, plaster and marble busts appeared almost as regularly as engravings to celebrate the hero of the moment or of the neighborhood. As one jury chosen to award prizes to revolutionary art instructed applicants, the images of liberty should be set up on the pedestals of tyranny (Leith, 126).

That jury did not quite appreciate the irony of its words: The images might be different, but the niches, the pedestals, and the modes of greatness were usually the same. Washington and Napoleon are of course the prime examples of such a discontinuous continuity. Yet typically for the different way such matters work out in America and in Europe, Washington, fully convinced of his own destiny, swiftly became a national symbol, not so much of national power as of national spirit, a unifying image to which all parties could appeal, while Napoleon, "the man of destiny," transformed that self-sufficiency into an imperial rule. The call of the 1780s in France had been for more national themes in painting and sculpture, in response to the surge of feeling set off by the American Revolution. But the American mode, although it drew inspiration and techniques of representation (as well as paper, presses, and other material needs) from France, yet maintained its own uneasy distance from the ideological pressures of past examples of greatness and power. Samuel Johnson in 1759 had argued that the visual image of a private person had little public dimension:

> Every man is always present to himself and has, therefore, little need of his own resemblance, nor can desire it, but for the sake of those whom he loves, and by whom he wishes to be remembered (*Idler*, No. 45, 140).

In essence he argues that the private man's nature and his virtue are purely familial and domestic matters. But the political ferment of revolutionary

America encouraged the search for what might constitute the imagery of just such a private virtue, derived from nature, but now made public. Rousseau, "the citizen of the world," depicted with his fur hat and strange overcoat, is an important example of the connection between the new political philosophy and the new modes of depicting individuals. Along with Ben Franklin, Hume, Boswell, Voltaire, and a few others, his is one of the faces who made the 1760s the seedtime of modern visual celebrity. The engraving and printing trade was expanding enormously, and a major part of their output was the reproduction of portraits of such men. Busts might be ordered by the wealthy, but also in 1774 Josiah Wedgwood inaugurated his portrait-medallions of "illustrious moderns" to bring their images into less prosperous homes. Plates, figurines, earthenware pitchers, flatware—a multitude of household objects featured the faces of the new generation of great men.[1] Franklin in particular is a fascinating representative of this new enfaming process because, as Charles Coleman Sellers points out, he did not look like a traditional "great man" (2). Yet by the early 1760s he was recognizable enough to appear in caricatures without his name being appended. Franklin's first celebrity had come not from his politics or statesmanship but from his experiments with electricity. He was the natural philosopher, who, in the curious iconography of several paintings, calmly watched his harnessed electricity ring a bell in his study, while outside a lightning bolt destroyed a church. By the time of the official Parisian Salon of 1779, his portrait appears in three different artistic modes—engraving, painting, and a bust by Jean-Antoine Houdon, who also contributed busts of Molière, Voltaire, and Rousseau, and would later do John Paul Jones, Washington, Jefferson, and others. Even after he became celebrated as America's diplomatic representative in France (1776–1778), what he meant to those who portrayed him and those who commissioned or purchased his image was something more than vocation or position or heredity. Instead he represented a human possibility so striking that in the Salon of 1779 the painting of Franklin, done by the official painter to the king of France, is merely labeled "Vir" (Man).

In such a portrait, the America of the flesh and the America of the spirit are explicitly united in an image of civic spiritually that represents all humankind. The American Founding Fathers, although preoccupied with a fame and glory that owed a great deal to Roman traditions of civic virtue and national celebrity, nevertheless set the stage as well for the kind of visible but spiritual fame that so characterizes the twentieth century. Franklin, like Washington, Jefferson, and even the more artistically puritanical John Adams, appreciated the propaganda value of such images of an ex-

---

1. Wedgwood had for years searched for a way to make such figures in a Greco-Roman style for a large market. The process was perfected in 1774 and by 1779 the medallions were outselling the tea services through which Wedgwood had first made his fortune. The 1779 catalogue includes an enormous array of heads that can be purchased—classical figures, popes, monarchs, poets, and artists, along with Franklin (under "Philosophers, Physicians, &c.") and Washington (under "Princes and Statesmen").

emplary civic virtue, especially in France, the country to which the most elaborate appeals for support against England were being made. But it was even more effective in America, where the images of the new heroes served to help create a spirit of unity paralleled by the evolution of more abstract national symbols. America was organizing a culture from the ground up, and in that organization the unifying and crystalizing function of faces was of prime importance. As the American "vir" was to replace the monarch as the subject of portraiture, so democratic leaders ought to be visually as well as electorally representative of the entire nation. Dr. John Arbuthnot in 1712 had virtually invented the figure of John Bull and his family as an emblem of middle-class England. But it wasn't until early in the next century, after the appearance of the French Marianne and the American Columbia, Cousin Jonathan, and Uncle Sam that the cartoonists and caricaturists truly elaborated the equation of person and country. Such national figures allowed an individual empathy with public events that superseded the symbolism of king and country. Like the question of democratic leadership or representative men, the personalization of the nation established a language of psychological connection to the country that ran deeply beneath religious or political obligations.

For the historian of fame, the prime factor distinguishing America from England and France is that while England retained its established Church and Napoleon reaffirmed France as a Christian nation in his pursuit of a Charlemagnian victory over the pope (1804), the American Constitution specifically outlawed an established religion. The power of the visible spirit in America, therefore, absorbed a religious sanction instead of competing with it, as was so often the case in both France and England. In the American public man, the solitary sanction of the desert saint and the man of destiny presented itself on the democratic stage. To be seen was to be free, to be heroic, to be American. As Frederick Douglass, the nineteenth-century black journalist, activist, and former slave later wrote of the portrait of Senator Hiram Revels, the first black senator, "Pictures come not with slavery and oppression but with liberty, fair play, leisure, and refinement" (McClinton, 37).

So despite their weariness, the Founding Fathers had their portraits painted. Franklin's words in 1780 could stand for those of Washington, Jefferson, Adams, and others later:

> I have at the request of Friends sat so much and so often to painters and Statuaries, that I am perfectly sick of it. I know of nothing so tedious as sitting hours in one fix'd posture (Sellars, 108).

John Adams, who was at first upset over the French courting of Franklin and deeply distrusted the arts for being part of the apparatus of political and ecclesiastical tyranny, later compromised enough with his distaste to have several portraits done. So long as the favoritism and egoistic ostentation of the old patronage system could be purged, at least portraiture and historical paintings might have a positive social function. Whatever the discomfort, having one's portrait painted could be considered to help the cause and establish the preeminence of civic virtue. Unlike the art of the ancient regime, this new art would be socially useful rather than luxurious and self-indulgent. The sitter was not asserting an ascendancy over the viewer. In some sense, he was putting himself at the viewer's service, as Franklin may have been the first to articulate, in a 1779 letter to his daughter, describing all the objects adorned with his face available for sale in France:

> These, with the pictures, busts and prints (of which copies upon copies are spread everywhere,) have made your father's face as well known as that of the moon, so that he durst not do anything that would oblige him to run away, as his phiz would discover him wherever he should venture to show it.

Franklin's joke about the limitations on his freedom caused by his visual celebrity might ring hollowly in modern ears. But he sounds here perhaps for the first time the paradoxical modern sense of simultaneously being venerated and trivialized:

> It is said by learned etymologists, that the name *doll,* for the images children play with, is derived from the word IDOL. From the number of dolls now made of him, he may be truly said, *in that sense,* to be *i-doll-ized* in this country.

As both printer and patriot, Franklin nevertheless understood the use of such images in drumming up and keeping support for his cause. Even before he wrote, Charles Willson Peale was attempting to set up a portraiture industry in America to compete with the one that already existed in England and France. In 1776 he completed a portrait of Washington that was quickly reproduced and sold as an engraving. Between Franklin and Washington, the citizen-philosopher and the general-statesman, the imagery of the American great man was being established—an accurate depiction of physical detail, plus a certain effort to retailor Renaissance fame motifs for the present: Franklin wearing the lion's skin of Hercules or (in 1785) being led by Columbia to the Temple of Fame; Washington in a military posture that went back to the Charles V of Titian; Thomas Jefferson's portrait being held by the goddess of Liberty while *Fama* toots her trumpet behind (1807). Like the placing of revolutionary heads on tyrannous pedestals, this was less iconoclasm than icon-substitution, adapting old images to new purposes. But in America especially, with its stronger tradition of a distrust of the aristocratic and monarchical associations of visual art, the need to supply a rationale of civic utility and virtue for having one's portrait done was still intense. Thus the American portrait, although presented to a public, transfigured its traditionally aristocratic ostentation and theatricality in order to serve the patriotic cause more explicitly. Although it depicted an individual, its implication went far beyond the person whose features it portrayed into the realm of the spirit. The result was that American visual portraiture took on something of the tinge of sainthood—just as the office of president, like that of pope, was believed to transform a candidate's political self-interest into a disinterested civic spirituality.

In the conflict between Roman fame and Christian fame, the civic and the spiritual were often at odds. In the growing concept of American public fame, the aim was to make them one. As Franklin, Washington, and Jefferson emphasized in their remarks and writings, the democratic public man was *obligated* to do this to establish the dignity of the nation in the face of other nations and to excite support within the nation itself. Public commissioning of the portraits of the new leaders and great men abounded as acts of symbolic unity, just as later, shortly before the end of the Civil War, Congress created the National Statuary Hall, in part to heal the wounds of division by the celebration of great men from every state:

> Statues in marble or bronze, not exceeding two in number each, of . . . citizens thereof, illustrious in their historic renown, or distinguished for their civic or military service, such as each state shall determine are worthy of national remembrance.[2]

But unlike Napoleon, who both fixed himself in relation to an older hierarchy (and finally married into it) as well as tried to generate a new hierarchy in the image of his own career, most of the great figures of the American Revolution, whatever their ambitions and desire for fame, chafed uneasily against the way that history had suddenly made the mass audience, the theatrical celebration, and the visual representation such an important part of that fame. Rousseau with elaborate argument had expressed what John Adams felt less systematically: Theater and traditional portraiture are part of the propaganda of tyranny. In America particularly, both traditional social structure and the theatrical space that mirrored it were at first deeply suspect. As it is today, the foremost theater town in eighteenth-century America was New York, suspiciously enough, a royalist stronghold held by English troops for much of the Revolutionary War. Thus, in the early years of America, public political fame always contained a cautionary element of potential withdrawal. That way those Cincinnatean talents on call when the nation needed them might avoid both the tyrannies of the past and the calumnies of the present.[3] It is impossible to read the letters and sometimes even the public statements of virtually any one of

2. Some distinction ought to be made between those of the Founding Fathers who were willing to have their faces used for propaganda and those for whom the portrait was truly a reminder of past and present greatness. Franklin, for example, had only a few portraits of others in his possession, while Jefferson had images of Newton, Bacon, Locke (his three favorite great men), Columbus, Raleigh, Vespucci, Adams, Washington, Franklin, and Lafayette, among others. The separate cultural traditions of Massachusetts and Virginia obviously play a role in this as well.

3. The public man's pose of reticence and withdrawal is a constant in American politics, where to validate power one must often seem to disdain it. As part of a traditional suspiciousness about power, American democracy seems to encourage its leaders to discount the structural obligations of leadership by asserting an indomitable amateurism. This attitude is clear enough in the last several presidents—virtually all of whom ran as "outsiders" against "Washington" or "the government."

the Founding Fathers without quickly finding an attack on one or several of the others for their ambition, their greed for praise, their vanity, and so on. Such grumblings are not hypocrisy, but the irrepressible manifestation of worries not only about the aspirations of others, but also about their own. They expressed a general uncertainty about the place of personal ambition in the new society the Founding Fathers had created and were (often) finding difficult to keep in order. The communal spirit that had generated and helped sustain the Revolution somehow seemed to ensure, in the great tradition of Roman stoicism, that true fame would come from acts of civic virtue accomplished in the full light of public history. But, with the winning of the war and the efforts to create a peacetime nation, many Americans discovered to their surprise that the purity and communality with which the Revolution had enwrapped their individual ambitions had become threadbare indeed. In early nineteenth-century political discourse, disillusionment is the general tone; and through many of the contemporary remarks about American fame and greatness, deserved and undeserved, there runs an envy of Franklin and Washington both of whom died early enough (1790 and 1799) to be spared the conflicts of party and thus never had to wonder if their achievements would be accurately appreciated, or even if they were worth doing at all. Even though the administrations he presided over were as divided as any that came later, Washington especially became the enthusiastically or grudgingly embraced symbol of a lost national unity of purpose, the image of a more selfless America.

A small but fascinating volume of letters between John Adams and Benjamin Rush, edited by Douglass Adair and John Schutz, allows us to examine this malaise more closely. Entitled *The Spur of Fame,* this selection is drawn from the voluminous correspondence between the two, initiated by Adams in 1805 and lasting until Rush's death in 1813. It focuses on a tenacious central concern that they share with so many of the Revolutionary generation who had the fortune or misfortune to live on into the nineteenth century: Why has there been such a contrast between their original commitment to public life and the way they, their actions, and their ideas have been treated by the new spirit of faction and party? Rush especially is depressed about the time he has spent in public service, not only as a signer of the Declaration of Independence and supporter of the Revolution, but also in his efforts to improve medical practice in Philadelphia. Was it really worth it, he asks, or was it like Catherine the Great's building of an ice palace—an elaborate complex enterprise that ultimately wasted energies that should have been spent in more private and intellectual pursuits. Adams, much more committed to public life in general and the need to stand up for the America he believes in, nevertheless shares Rush's pessimism about the *audience* for public service. One acts for liberty and virtue the best one knows how and instead one becomes the object of mean stories and lying anecdotes. Just as he scorned Franklin's ease among the French, so he attacks Washington's immoderate desire for praise and even more the almost "idolatrous" celebrations of Washington once he died (108). These are mere "aristocratical" shows designed to cover up party interests (113). Even when Washington himself gave a speech, says Adams, he was like Garrick playing Shakespeare: It was all theater. Not that theater doesn't have its political point: The Declaration of Independence, he says, was an effective piece of theater (119). In fact, says Adams, the creators of the Revolution had purposefully decided to make Washington a symbol of national unity to rival any king; therefore they repressed any negative remarks about his military or political stewardship. Echoing Bolingbroke on Louis XIV, Adams concludes, Washington may not have been the greatest president, but he was certainly "the best actor of presidency we have ever had" (132).[4]

So far at least Adams's dislike of the style of visual fame has strong precedents in both Puritan and Stoic views of the corrupt sway magnificence allows. But he also believes that some system of public recognition was appropriate and even necessary. From the beginning of the United States, the Continental Congress had considered it a mark of its dignity to decree "medals to be struck in order to signalize and commemorate certain interesting events and Conspicuous Characters."[5] Adams, along with Franklin, Jefferson, and others conferred on the appropriate designs, and it is worth noting that Adams and Franklin for a time jointly proposed that the Great Seal of the United States should feature Hercules, the archetypal man turned into a god by his own efforts. But such adaptations of the methods and imagery of the past in order to give stature to the aspirations of the new nation have, says Adams, long since been corrupted into mere theater and superficial show. The old enemy was monarchical and aristocratic tyranny; the new is commerce and party self-interest. The political theater of the present, he argues, aims to confuse the emotions of the electorate so that the commercial interests that sponsor it may have their way, for it is in the commercial cities that "the theatrical exhibitions of politics" primarily take place (181). The thirst of recognition of Alexander Hamilton was especially anathema to Adams for its connection to the new monied interests, and he links it metaphorically to Hamilton's support of paper credit—the resting of a great deal of paper money on a small base of gold and silver. "Former ages," writes Adams, "have never discovered any remedy against the universal gangrene of avarice in commercial countries but setting up ambition as a rival to it" (111).

Although Adams himself did not scorn making money, he does profess

---

4. From 1788 to 1800 the Fourth of July was a Federalist party holiday. Then, with the election of Jefferson and a campaign that stressed Jefferson's authorship of the Declaration of Independence, it became a Republican holiday, and the Federalists began to celebrate George Washington's birthday in competition (*Spur of Fame,* 135).

5. During his presidency Jefferson sent hundreds of such medals along with the Lewis and Clark expedition to give to the "most prominent" Indian chiefs they encountered along the way to the Pacific. On the striking of these medals, see *Jefferson Papers, 16,* 54, and Cunningham, 76. Jefferson, like Franklin, was continually interested in the design of coins and medals as a means of presenting the United States symbolically to its citizens and to the outside world.

horror when Rush tells him how much Washington and Franklin left in their wills, and through his letters they swirl as elusive examples, sometimes praised, often condemned, for the mixture of personal aspiration and public service in their careers. What fascinates Adams most about their characters is their silence, for, writes Adams, "silence is most commonly design and intrigue" (64). And the testy Rush responds that therefore Washington particularly could not be called great because the greatest men—Alexander, Julius Caesar, and Jesus—were all sociable rather than silent. Rush's Jesus is clearly not Milton's, who "unobserv'd / Home to his Mother's house private return'd," and the terms of his misunderstanding again indicate the special place of solitude as a characteristic of the new public men in this postmonarchical age. Adams, with his antagonism to theater and to what he calls (he says after Napoleon) "the Scenery of the Business," nevertheless continues to come back to Washington's silence as his most enigmatic and therefore most alluring characteristic, "one of the most precious talents" (42–43, 98). No monarch in Europe, he writes, had Washington's ability, if he didn't want to answer a question, to remain totally silent. And when Adams tries to tote up for Rush the characteristics that made Washington great, they can be readily arrayed into physical presence (height, handsomeness, elegance of movement), social status (a rich man from Virginia), self-control, and silence.

Adams has a greater appreciation than Rush for Washington's silence because he believes that the one element in public action that transforms the desire for fame from a base into a glorious human aspiration is disinterestedness—the passionate commitment to an ideal of human betterment in which one seeks nothing for oneself. Such disinterestedness is not aristocratic superiority but noblesse oblige, and Adams frequently stresses his own long American genealogy as evidence of his disinterested opposition to the money-grubbing new politicians. But in such terms Washington might be considered disinterested as well, and Adams continually returns to the enigma of Washington's character in an attempt to undermine or at least qualify his image. (Here he is clearly writing for posterity, since Rush shared his view of Washington, and was often hostile enough to get a minor chastising from Adams.) Without the social context for aspiration, says Adams, fame is merely self-interest, and so Washington's silence can be understood only as a virtually hypocritical aloofness put on to create an air of mysterious power. How, he wonders, did Washington evolve his curious "system" of public behavior, so reticent and so detached that observers could mistake it for true disinterestedness? With his passion for direct and explicit causes, Adams decides that the answer lies in a passage from Rollin's *Ancient History,* upon which he believes Washington modeled his own career and thereby "our American system of politics and ambition" (94–95). Washington may have been the most sincere practitioner, admits Adams, but the style involves a pretense of being disgusted with public life and retiring from it to domestic affairs in order to demonstrate one's disinterested good faith, and thereby become a ruler.

Thus Adams reveals his own Baconian and Grevillian definition of fame within the state, hedged by public service and civic virtue and capped with an antimonarchical disdain for public display. What he fails to realize is how Washington, Franklin, and Jefferson instinctively appreciated the need for a spiritual sanction of ostentatious reticence to qualify one for rule in the new democratic Republic. He believes instead that he has not received his due as a father of the Revolution because he, like Rush, has neglected to have himself puffed, and "puffers . . . are the only killers of scandal" (217). Franklin and Washington had puffers aplenty, but all Adams can do is to make Rush the confidant of the secret truths of Revolutionary history in the hopes that posterity will make his fame permanent and secure. Temperamentally unable either self-consciously or instinctively to dramatize himself, Adams, like Tocqueville somewhat later, believes that democracy in the new America undermines the disinterested desire for the praise of posterity, substituting immediate success, prosperity, and power for true fame and glory. His position is an honorable one in the annals of fame, and his efforts to distinguish the style of his own ambition from that of his compatriots in revolution poignantly illustrates the mingled strands of personal aspiration and civic duty that characterize all of them. Yet Adams barely appreciates the degree to which America was evolving its native product, and therefore the integral relation between Washington's silence and his theater. In order for Napoleon to be a model for every aspiring young man in nineteenth-century Europe, the Emperor and his policies had to be essentially forgotten. In contrast, the first twenty years of the nineteenth century in America saw the manufacture of myths about the Founding Fathers that, like Parson Weems's tale of George Washington and the cherry tree, made them at once timeless and imitatable, distant yet sympathetic. But Adams in his letters to Rush instead argues the facts, or what he considered to be the facts—who really first thought of independence for America, who wrote this polemic, or who passed that measure—in short, the material of American history, but not of American myth, or of American fame.

In 1824–1825, the American tour of the Marquis de Lafayette lavishly revived these intricately interwoven issues of national purpose and individual fame on the editorial pages of newspapers around the young country. As a young officer, Napoleon had written a brief essay sarcastically contrasting the royalist love of glory with the republican love of country that was expressed in the desire for fame, and Lafayette's joining of the American revolutionary cause showed he fully agreed. As Mirabeau once said of the young Lafayette, *"Il a affiché désintéressement"* (glossed by Adams as "he advertised his disinterestedness" (*Spur,* 92). But he was still unprepared for the fervor with which the Americans of 1824–1825 welcomed the living advertisement of such disinterestedness, just as they had bought edition after edition of the life of Washington by Weems—in search of visible people who acted with such obviously articulated integrity. As an emissary from the purer past, Lafayette focused those issues, glimpsed in the letters of Adams and Rush, that had been the stuff of party polemics since the end of the Revolution: What was the relation between actions undertaken for the good of the country and actions undertaken for personal fame and self-interest? It was a distinction fast becoming anachronistic in America, and perhaps only a foreigner and an aristocrat like Lafayette could still exemplify it. Early on Jefferson had written to Madison of the young Lafayette, "I take him to be of unmeasured ambition but the means he uses are virtuous" (Loveland, 11). Like the ill-fated Chatterton, a virtual contemporary, the teen-age Lafayette had determined to shed his original self to become another, grander person. The schoolmaster's son Chatterton was reborn in the guise of the fifteenth-century poet Thomas Rowley; the French aristocrat Lafayette threw in his lot with the cause of liberty and the American Revolution. The difference, of course, was that Chatterton presented his new self in literature, while Lafayette was a soldier. Yet both embody the revolutionary potential for individuals to change their inherited identities—to become more pure, more essential, to be renewed— that the American and then the French revolutions especially marked and publicized. Both sought recognition essentially for their willingness to be someone else, who yet was in accord with their deepest nature. For Chatterton and the later artistic connoisseurs of neglect, though, the search to become another was often focused on the spiritual and saintly models of Christianity and Jesus himself. But for Lafayette and the Founding Fathers, the other identity that exonerated oneself from the charge of self-interest was that of citizen, defender of civic virtue, champion of liberty everywhere. As Garry Wills concludes in *Cincinnatus,* his study of the image of Washington, "Fame was thus a social glue, a structural element, for the republic in its early days—not only for Washington, but for all those called to service" (129). How could Lafayette's profound ambition be condemned when it, like that of the Founding Fathers themselves, had professedly disinterested goals?[6]

The arts in early America, especially the visual arts, were therefore encouraged by the Founding Fathers and other propagandists of the American vision as a way to supersede the hierarchy of traditional societies by displaying the innate virtues of democratic man. In a world in which the visible display of self was becoming more and more important to the public man, the impression of inner mystery became a prime way to escape the implication that, like the tyrants of the past, one depended entirely on material power. Washington's silence, as the precursor of the solitary emi-

6. Perhaps the most immediate benefactor of the need for a national symbol of unity illustrated by Lafayette's tour was Daniel Webster (1782–1852), whom one historian has called "probably the most often painted, sculptured, and engraved American of his generation" (Voss, 12). Unlike the plain face of Benjamin Franklin that was attractive precisely because it did not resemble the traditional image of greatness, Webster *looked* like a great man and in early portraits often assumed a Byronesque air. Constantly in debt, he was the beneficiary of many loans as well as public subscriptions raised on his behalf as the great orator and unifier for whom the country hungered.

nence of a Byron or a Napoleon, socializes the virtuous isolation of the saint or literary man by making an aura of personal withdrawal part of the new equipment of the public man. And it looks forward to the twentieth-century style of proffering domestic information as the evidence of public accessibility. In earlier times disinterestedness was marked by a willingness to give up or repress private nature and concerns in order to serve the public. Now, of course, the giving up has turned into an exposé, a willingness to make one's private life into an object of public attention as a symbolic submission to the audience that is simultaneously courted and feared. This is the ostentation of equality that has spawned varieties of self-exposure and self-promotion with few precedents in the old world. The Renaissance had revived the classical analogies primarily to justify the existing aristocracy by sanctions other than immediate genealogy or power. But the eighteenth-century revolutions employed such analogies in the service of a new political order and (at least ideally) a new status for all individuals. Fame had ceased to be the possession of particular individuals or classes and had become instead a potential attribute of every human being that needed only to be brought out in the open for all to applaud its presence. The audience was no longer the servant of the visually powerful, but becoming at least their equal partner in the creation of such fame. To the extent that the American Constitution prevented the dictatorship and imperial power that would overtake France under Napoleon, its ideals remain with the Roman Republic rather than the Roman Empire, the marketplace of contending great figures rather than the hierarchy of merit ruled by the unapproachable emperor. Its imperialist time would, of course, come, especially after the Civil War. But at least imagistically the American presidency, despite the quasi-indirect means of election through the Electoral College, detached itself from the class popularity contest it could easily have remained.[7] Washington's silence and Jackson's attack on elitism, seemingly at opposite ends of the political spectrum, are united in their effort to mediate separation with sympathy through an image of the democratic leader.

The restrictive idolization foreseen by Franklin was, however, already becoming a staple of party politics. An incident in the last year of Jefferson's life, just about the time of Lafayette's tour and a few years before Jackson's election, might stand as a cautionary emblem of the dangers for the American public man of being trapped in his image. A sculptor with a new life-mask technique appeared at Monticello to test it on the still artistically inquisitive Jefferson. But the technique was faulty or the atmosphere unsympathetic. The plaster dried too quickly, and the sculptor finally had to hammer the eighty-two-year-old head free with mallet and chisel. But as Tocqueville observed in the early 1830s, hardly anyone yet noticed there was a problem. Aristocratic societies, he wrote, have a fixedness of social position that allows every man to know who he is. But democratic societies, with their freedom of movement, engender the need to be

7. In contrast, senators were elected by their state legislatures until the Seventeenth Amendment (1916) mandated popular elections.

bold and arresting. Democratic man, he said, usually had no lofty ambitions; he just wanted to be first at anything (676). In a world where constant change was possible, the aim was to be singled out of the general equality and made permanent, whatever the cost.[8]

Dickinson and Whitman:
The Audience of Solitude

[I]n democracies writers will be more afraid *of* the people, than afraid *for* them.

—FISHER AMES, "The Future of American Literature"

Nobody is glad in the gladness of another, and our system is one of war, of an injurious superiority. Every child of the Saxon race is educated to wish to be first.

—EMERSON, *Representative Men*

In the face of the increased communications and international awareness that marks the nineteenth century in Europe and America, the ideals of "good fame" often seemed out-of-date, confining, and confusing to artists nurtured on a legacy of retirement and solitude as well as to politicians used to explaining their ambition in terms of civic virtue. Drawing on a traditional distinction, revived in the Renaissance, Hazlitt had separated love of fame, which was based on principle, from love of power, which was always ready to sacrifice principle to immediate gain. But in America, the newly born country with an energetic commercial culture, the contrast between the two was less certain. Here was a nation, with neither an eponymous and ancient founder nor a group of great men collected along the way, that proceeded instead from a pantheon of heroes who had walked the earth only a short while before. In addition it had a government that was not a time-honored or time-encrusted historical monument but the expression of the will of these heroes. Thus in America from the start there was always a premium on the discovery or assertion of emblematic actions and emblematic personalities.

As a sympathetic aristocratic democrat, Tocqueville had no real trouble with the desire to outdo all others. But he did object that firstness in America usually had too much to do with money. Fisher Ames, a professed hater of democracy who believed that man was "the most ferocious of animals" and needed to be controlled by strong laws and strong leaders, was even more severe. Writing just after the turn of the nineteenth century, he surveys the arts and concludes that Americans have not produced "one great original work of genius" (I, 295). The French and the English, he admits,

---

8. "No man's social status is so low but that he has a stage of his own, and no man can, by his obscurity, avoid praise or blame" (Tocqueville, 626).

are equally lacking. But he argues that the political nature of the American democracy ensures that few if any geniuses will be produced there: First, because the present age no longer can boast the immediate audience that animated the writers and warriors of Greece and Rome; and second, because the prime urge in America is not to create what is lasting but what is most profitable:

> Commerce has supplanted war, as the passion of the multitude; and the arts have divided and contracted the objects of pursuit (I, 301).

And commerce is concerned only with the temporary and the transitory:

> [T]he single passion that engrosses us, the only avenue to consideration and importance in our society, is the accumulation of property; our inclinations cling to gold, and are bedded in it, as deeply as that precious ore in the mine. Covered as our genius is in this mineral crust, is it strange that it does not sparkle? . . . At present the nature of our government inclines all men to seek popularity, as the object next in point of value to wealth; but the acquisition of learning and the display of genius are not the ways to obtain it. Intellectual superiority is so far from conciliating confidence, that it is the very spirit of a democracy, as in France, to proscribe the aristocracy of talents (I, 303).

Ames's contrast is between the clear hierarchies of artistic excellence that he believes existed in the past and the obscuring of all distinction that he considers typical of a commercial democracy. But even a convinced supporter of the new America like John Adams could agree about the corrupting effects of money on public life. The money people, wrote Adams, fostered the theatrical, self-displaying politics of the cities in order to appeal to the mob. His answer was to set true fame in opposition to both money and theater, the commercial bankers as well as the pageant-promoting politicians. The noble disinterestedness that Adams and Rush found so lacking in American public life was urged on by a desire for fame specifically opposed to the accumulation of money: It was enthusiastic for state service rather than for material gain, and therefore it furnished a sanction for public presence as spiritual as Augustus's *auctoritas*. For him, as well as for Ames, "rich and famous" would have been a contradiction in terms.

But neither Ames nor Adams understood how concertedly both European and American art in the early nineteenth century was beginning to discover that its mission in a history of culture was to be eternally contrasted with the history of war and politics. Adams's ideal of the disinterested public man was in a sense close kindred to the writers for whom the badge of true success was public neglect, because each served ideals higher than the satisfaction of the multitude. Ames especially, who was much more interested than Adams in an art unconnected to the goals of the state, either minimized or could not foresee the extent to which American artists themselves tried to get out of the trap of popularity and commercial success, even as they courted audiences unbounded by the fashions of the moment.

If the "fit audience" was aristocratic and elitist, while the commercial audience was degraded by its love of show and money, then the quest of the modern poet was toward a self-definition that somehow could manage to encompass both. Not many decades before, Samuel Johnson could mock upper-class dilettante authors by saying that no one but a blockhead wrote for any reason except money. But by the postrevolutionary period, only actually aristocratic seekers of fame, like Byron, could afford to be so open about the desire to make money from their art or politics. Thus in one essay Emerson could satirically indict empty competition and ambition, while in another call ringingly for new great men to appear in the soil of America, which is best suited to nurture them. The paradox winds its way through the century, and Emerson himself at the height of his fame still published some poetry and essays anonymously, as if to keep alive in himself the sense of a literary nature unspoiled by the public gaze, as well as to see if his work might still be judged positively if his notable name were not appended. For the newly emergent aspirants for the fame awarded by a mass society, any visible preoccupation with money automatically labeled them as merely entrepreneurial and self-interested courtiers of what Wordsworth called the public, as opposed to the people. Unlike Johnson, they imitated the aristocratic disdain for money in order to constitute themselves a psychic and democratic aristocracy of human service in whatever realm they entered. As Emily Dickinson wrote, summarizing this distinctive strain in many nineteenth-century literary careers, "To earn it by disdaining it / Is Fame's consummate fee" (No. 1427).

Writers particularly felt the tug of these contradictory urges because, much more than public men or visual artists, their lives and work occupied the margin between private nature and public consumption. The styles of Byron and Keats interweave in many of the artistic, political, and intellectual careers of the nineteenth century. Keats's final striving for a virtually anonymous fame accords with his turning away from the standards of a society in which he had been born the son of a livery stable keeper and trained as a pharmacist. Byron, on the other hand, constantly invokes and plays against his social role and reputation, and his greatest poem, *Don Juan,* gathers much of its energy from an insistent mockery of the already established concept of the "Byronic hero." Byron's style is therefore one of theatricality, Keats's of spiritual transcendence. Until after the American Civil War, the more Byronic figures are European, arrayed around the figure of Napoleon, while the more Keatsian are American, indebted to the Puritan and Quaker distaste for theater and the reluctantly visible patriotism of a figure like George Washington. With the finely tuned coincidences of history, in 1818, in the midst of his period of greatest creativity, Keats's favorite brother George, to whom he writes many of his most revealing letters about the nature of his ambition, sets sail with his wife to start a life in America.[9]

9. Hazlitt also has an intriguing relation to America. His father was a somewhat luckless Unitarian clergyman who moved his family to America when William was

The early nineteenth-century American literary atmosphere into which both Walt Whitman and Emily Dickinson were born emphasized aggression and self-confidence in the shaping of a poetic career, especially for an ambitious young man pressing himself onto the artistic stage of the equally young Republic. Throughout the embryonic literary world of the New England and Atlantic states especially there was a constant talk of genius—where it might flower and what shapes it ought to take. Carlyle had ended *Heroes and Hero-Worship* with Napoleon, although in the previous essay on "The Hero as Man of Letters" he had praised the new priesthood of writers that was the strongest emblem of the new age. But Emerson had gone a step further and ended his *Representative Men* with Goethe, whose genius was to be able to unite in himself an interest in all aspects of modern culture, thus giving solace to those who felt overwhelmed by it. "Society has really no graver interest than the well-being of the literary class," announced Emerson, and concluded that it was the fault of writers themselves if they lost it. By their contact with the eternal springs of human genius, writers could correct and regulate—"monitor" says Emerson—the ills of civil society (750). With no established American church, the bulwark of the nation's purity would be the writer, whose words, like those of the Constitution and the Declaration of Independence, could call America back to the roots of its nature. Authors, implied Thoreau in *Walden,* were the prime democratic aristocrats, able to range over history, freely culling from the vast repositories of the past to create their own work in the present.[10]

Thoreau's worship of language may have been accompanied by a certain diffidence. But for the more aggressive aspirants to literary fame, the result was a race to be in the public eye that was difficult to distinguish from the renown sought by the new nation itself on the stage of the world. Cautionary notes might be sounded about quality, like Horace Greeley's "The Fatality of Self-Seeking in Authors and Editors." But even there the special nature of the author was proclaimed: his genius the mark of his direct connection to ultimate values and his willingness to go public in some sense the warrant of his patriotism. With a critical disdain for such American bumptiousness and not a little pseudoaristocratic hauteur, the young Edgar Allan Poe published a brief sketch called "Lionizing," in which the twenty-five-year-old author commented sardonically and surrealistically on the

---

about five (1783). Four years later, after fruitless efforts to settle down in New York and New England, the family returned to England.

10. Unlike other countries, the United States had begun with self-consciously written documents. With such precedents, it is no wonder Thoreau could write in *Walden:* "A written word is the choicest of relics. It is something at once more intimate with us and more universal than any other work of art" (69). Somewhat less grandiose about practical questions than Thoreau with his belief in the timeless interconnection of all great writing, the Constitution includes as one of its provisions a copyright law. (Literary property had been an early preoccupation of American lawmakers. Connecticut in 1783, for example, had passed "An Act for the Encouragement of Literature and Genius" that mandated a fourteen-year, once renewable, copyright.)

vogue for notoriety of any sort. The word "lionize," to be used later by Carlyle with equal abhorrence, was a comparative newcomer to English. It first meant to visit an extraordinary sight, as did the tourists who went to visit the lions kept at the Tower of London or the visitors to Oxford, whom the undergraduates referred to as lions.[11] Thus the "lion" was not only one who looked but also one who was looked at, and Poe's sketch is primarily a satire on *lionizing* as the creation of celebrity from nothing. His narrator—who begins "I am, that is to say I *was,* a great man"—is declared a genius as a child when he discovers his nose with both hands (212). From then on he devotes himself to Nosology, exhibiting his nose in all the most fashionable venues, where he holds forth on its virtues to admiring crowds. Like Gogol's later story about the man whose nose detaches itself and becomes a greater figure in town than he ever could, Poe's brief, almost inconsequential sketch retains a pre-Freudian innocence.[12] But we should also note how often in the history of the nineteenth century's preoccupation with public fame it is mockingly associated with an ostentatious male sexual swaggering: an aggressive visibility that breaks away from a more retiring nature to sally forth into the world, often in search of what turns out to be self-destruction. Such stories, like the stories of doubles who are released only to attack the "normal" self, can easily be read as fantasies of uncontrollable ambition, the desire for fame in the present with the full understanding of its fragility and insubstantiality, the search for recognition and visibility with the fearful awareness of its emptiness.

Poe himself was of course aiming after literary celebrity as well. But the attitudes toward empty ostentation and mere fashionableness embodied in "Lionizing" indicate the guarded terms under which he wanted it. In the same year he described another self-confessed great man somewhat more realistically, but with the same edge:

> At a very early age, Mr. Willis seems to have arrived at an understanding that, in a republic such as ours, the *mere* man of letters must ever be a cipher, and endeavoured, accordingly, to unite the *éclat* of the *littérateur* with that of the man of fashion or of society. He "pushed himself," went much into the world, made friends with the gentler sex, "delivered" poetical addresses, wrote "scriptural" poems, traveled, sought the intimacy of noted women, and got into quarrels with notorious men ("The Literati of New York City," 1124).

With such premeditated seekers after the public's attention crowding the literary marketplace, the appeal beyond it was inevitable, so that the ultimate heights of fame might be reserved not for the merely ambitious and

11. Interestingly enough for the atmosphere of celebrity self-awareness "lionize" implies, the first citation in the *Oxford English Dictionary* is as a passive verb to denote the celebration of a person (here, himself), made in a letter by the "anonymous" Sir Walter Scott in 1809, who asks not to be lionized in a forthcoming visit.

12. Poe's inspiration is no doubt Sterne's *Tristram Shandy,* which contains a similar play on noses and fame, along with Sterne's efforts to say that noses don't mean anything but noses, the eighteenth-century mock-version of Freud's 'sometimes a cigar is just a cigar.'

the merely talented, but for those geniuses of both politics and art who could best temper their assertion with an ostentatious repugnance for the spotlight.

As perhaps the least politically democratic of all the major writers of the American nineteenth century, Poe directs his satire primarily against the fashionable coteries out to consume the "genius" of the moment. Whitman, on the other hand, echoing the concerns of the Romantic poets, seeks to distinguish between the superficial commercial audience and the broad repository of democratic ideals. As he writes in *Democratic Vistas* (1871), the triumph of the "modern" must be through "the battle, advancing, retreating, between democracy's convictions, aspirations, and the people's crudeness, vice, caprices" (461). Whitman's "democracy" stands in relation to Wordsworth's "people" as Whitman's "people" does to Wordsworth's "public." Similarly, Whitman tries to merge individual self-sufficiency with the greater good of the community: "For it is mainly or altogether to serve independent separation that we form a strong generalization, consolidation" (471). The individual, despite the fears of Tocqueville or Ames, will not be lost in the mass but heightened by it, especially if the government is urged "to develop, to open up to cultivation, to encourage the possibility of all beneficent and manly outcroppage, and of that aspiration for independence, and the pride and self-respect latent in all characters" (475). At the heart of Whitman's argument, as it stands at the heart of that of the democrats of the early nineteenth century, is the analogy between democratic man politically and the figure of Jesus in "the moral-spiritual field." Such singularity comes from wilful separateness that strengthens the individual and the society at once: "the image of completeness in separation, of individual personal dignity, of a single person, either male or female, characterized in the main, not from extrinsic acquirements or position, but in the pride of himself or herself alone . . ." (471). The achievement of such dignity, says Whitman, has been poisoned for Americans by the models of Europe and "that favorite standard of the eminent writer, the rule of the best man, the born heroes and captains of the race (as if such ever, or even one time out of a hundred, get into the big places, elective or dynastic)" (475–476). With writers and artists all pursuing the analogy of the monarchical, the nature of true integrity and singularity is lost:

> The common ambition strains for elevations, to become some privileged exclusive. The master sees greatness and health in being part of the mass; nothing will do as well as common ground (21).

Both Emily Dickinson in her virtual invention of the role of literary recluse and Whitman in his self-presentation as "the Poet" are preoccupied with creating a new poetic language and a new place for the writer in a democratic world. Whitman in both his poetry and prose tries to forge a democratic artistic fame that mediates spiritual generality with personal assertion. Behind his reiteration of the democratic belief in the quality and complexity of every individual is his own effort to evade through poetry the compartmentalized limitation that characterizes nineteenth-century professionalization across the disciplines and vocations. The figure of Jesus (usually not Christianity itself) as well as the context of democratic politics sanctions an evasion of such pigeonholing, a sense of mission and destiny and inner nature beyond official society's ability to understand. Similarly torn, Emerson, Whitman's great sponsor, still periodically tests the waters of anonymity in an uneasiness with Byronic and Napoleonic self-display. But Dickinson, a decade or so their junior, resolutely turns away from even the ambiguous gesture of publication in the service of her literary ambition. Her verse form—with its quick flashes of insight and perception; its compressed, even nongrammatical structure; and its word usage unfound in any dictionary—expresses a search beyond common language into a language that might be truly timeless.

The crucial question was the nature of the audience. As the new, self-consciously created nation (although now becoming a bit shopworn), America was simultaneously a place and a dream, a society of others and a society of the individual spirit. How then to mediate the inspiration to write that America promised with the crowded world of competing writers and new artistic fashions that was the public expression of American openness and freedom? The Renaissance had revived the classical ideal of fame as a reaching for the standards of the past to judge properly the achievements of the present. But the context of America, born without a past, encourages the belief that absolute fame is a turning away from time itself. Writers like Emerson, Thoreau, Dickinson, and Whitman (and for that matter Washington and Jefferson and Paine) helped evolve a democratic spirituality that would equally combat commercialism, technology, and the flatness of constant change. They wrote directly and often explicitly *for* the future and so paid their present readers the compliment of standing with them outside the accidents of time and place. The Renaissance poet and writer took the classical privilege (which defined his calling) of being the mediator and vessel of all human history. But the Americans seem more interested in the spirit beyond history. The true enterprise was posthumous, whether one is successful in his own time or not. No earthly hierarchy, beholding to time, can compensate for the rewards of the spirit.

Instead, the audience for both Whitman and Dickinson is the one sufficient other, whose presence completes the speaker's world by hearing what he or she says. As Dickinson writes to Thomas Wentworth Higginson, the editor of the *Atlantic Monthly,*

> A letter always feels to me like immortality because it is the mind alone without corporeal friend (196).

The search for the actual identities of the "friend" in Whitman's poems or the "master" or "lover" in Dickinson's therefore always runs aground because no one name can suffice. Critics and biographers of Dickinson have often noted that she tended to write differently to different correspondents and, on the rare occasions when she met them socially, would appear dressed in white, carrying flowers or some such parody of the image of herself she had presented already in words. But the creation of such parodies, the projection of such images, indicates again in Dickinson's heightened way how so many artists of the nineteenth century sought to internalize and thereby control the audience that otherwise flooded by in the streets of commerce. Whitman similarly carried on a dialogue within himself between the poet that published and the monitor who thought publicity somehow shameful: "Oppress'd with myself that I have dared to open my mouth" (204). By now, such complaints have the unappealing tinge of self-pity. But we would not be seeing them in terms of the world that helped bring them into being unless we can detect the actual anguish involved in attempting to be the poet who was different. The "real me," says Whitman, stands apart from the poems, "mocking me with mock-congratulatory signs and bows." Nature herself, like God a sponsor of anonymity rather than assertion, attacks him "because I have dared to open my mouth to sing at all."

With such a sentiment we might easily juxtapose any of Dickinson's lines about the loss in meaning that comes from saying something or the silence of the artist that assures the reverberation of the work:

> The Martyr Poets—did not tell—
> But wrought their Pang in syllable—
> That when their mortal name be numb—
> Their mortal fate—encourage Some—
>
> The Martyr Painters—never spoke—
> Bequeathing—rather—to their Work—
> That when their conscious fingers cease—
> Some seek in Art—the Art of Peace— (No. 544).

The aspiration to immortality, the celebration of neglected genius, the loving attention of one friend, the lover who is Christ, and the audience of God—all are ways out of the shackles of the present moment, and they become intensified poetic themes when the most immediate context of creative work is a public world forever compromised by its bland commonality and commercial greed. Whitman worked long and hard over his poems. He published the first versions of *Leaves of Grass* himself, wrote several early reviews anonymously, and sent a copy of the book to Emerson, as if to say in effect 'You have called for an American poet. Here I am.' But increasingly in his later poems he characterized his published self as an illusion—"that Shadow My Likeness"—behind which his real nature lurked—difficult, evasive, a mystery to be plumbed only by those who were his true audience:

> No labor-saving machine,
> Nor discovery have I made,
> Nor will I be able to leave behind me any wealthy
>   bequest to found a hospital or library,
> Nor reminiscence of any deed of courage for America,
> Nor literary success nor intellect, nor book for the book-shelf,

But a few carols vibrating through the air I leave
For comrades and lovers ("Calamus," 106).

The timeless American moment of newness could only be preserved by detaching it from the present and sending it into the future where, wrote Whitman, it would find not the praises of posterity but a reader, "compact, visible, realizing my poems, seeking me" (121). But even though Whitman chose, like Blake, to characterize himself as an artisan intrigued by the new technologies of communication but finally disdainful of the ease with which they reproduced sameness, he nevertheless did publish. Thoreau, carefully writing works for the public often drawn from a private journal housed in an intricate box he made himself, furnishes a more divided interpretation of the writer in a democracy. But it is in the work of Dickinson, popularly considered to be the most private of poets, that the tension between ostentation and reticence, American style, is most clearly marked. In April 1862, Thomas Wentworth Higginson published "A Letter to a Young Contributor" in the *Atlantic Monthly*. A short time later he received the first of many letters from Emily Dickinson, then thirty-one, asking if he would be willing to read and comment on her poems. When he responded positively, she sent four poems, which he declined to pass on to the magazine, but assured her that they were true poetry and encouraged her to write more. After this, they corresponded for many years and Higginson after her death in 1886 became a coeditor of her poems.

Dickinson's experience with Higginson, despite his warmth, seems to have convinced her that publication was not really what she wanted. For all their long correspondence, she never again 'submitted' poems to him, although her letters often included phrases and entire poems. Like many other of her correspondents, he nevertheless considered her a working poet, although one who somewhat eccentrically avoided exposure outside her small circle. In fact it is difficult to understand why Dickinson was so moved by "A Letter to a Young Contributor" to write to Higginson, unless its own paradoxes spoke to hers. In the essay, Higginson continually encourages the need to expose one's work publicly even as he recounts the emptiness of that fame once achieved. He assures his young writers that all editors desire both "to take the lead in bringing forth a new genius" and avoid "premature individualism" (72). To be recognized, they must "write availably" (for which newspaper work is good training) (79). Yet they must also catch the eye of those intelligent readers who alone are "the organ of eternal justice [that] awards posthumous fame," since in "all free governments" it is the public "habit to overrate the *dramatis personae* of the hour" (77, 71). Books do last longer than eloquence, but "earth's evanescent glories" should teach us humility rather than despair, for we will be justified only in heaven. Thus Higginson attempts both to encourage authorship with the laurels of fame and genius, even as he offers the balm of a spiritual view that makes up for the rejection slip and the lack of recognition. (Just because you're neglected, he also warns, leaving no solace unpoisoned, it doesn't mean that you're a genius.) In the end his is the self-satisfied advice of the mediocrely successful, for whom success is not a passion of the self so much as a job well done.

In this sense Higginson and Dickinson represent the two sides of an American pair—the practical and the passionate, the social and the solitary. For all his gentle mockery of her eccentricity (he used to read her letters to dinner parties), this "man of letters" needs her to validate that part of him that believes that afterlife and posterity are the true test of worth. For all her satisfaction with isolation and the occasional theatrics of solitude, she needs his affirmation, as friend and public writer, that she could venture into that arena—if she wanted to. For Higginson the urge to write was part of the new exuberance and pragmatic vitality of America:

> Political freedom makes every man an individual; a vast industrial activity makes every man an inventor, not merely of labor-saving machines, but of labor-saving words; universal schooling popularizes all thought and sharpens the edge of all language. We unconsciously demand of our writers the same dash and the same accuracy that we demand in railroading or dry-goods jobbing (72).

Like the Constitution, he linked the writer with the inventor and he empowered the *Atlantic,* as it empowered the Congress,

> to promote the progress of science and useful arts, by securing for limited times to authors and inventors the exclusive right to their respective writings and discoveries (Article I, viii, 8).

In contrast with this linking of poetry and material progress, Dickinson turns away from worldly honor and rank to associate her own "Barefoot Estate" with the cycles of nature. Like Whitman, trying to contain male and female, high and low, within himself, she exalts common and unheralded things as more glorious than what the world and history value. With such a mission, the true glory is to speak in such a way that the echo will come not from the immediate commercial public but from somewhere else. "I'm Nobody! Who are you?" writes Dickinson.

> Are you—Nobody—Too?
> Then there's a pair of us?
> Don't tell! they'd advertise—you know!
>
> How dreary—to be—Somebody!
> How public—like a Frog—
> To tell one's name—the livelong June—
> To an admiring Bog! (No. 288).

Whitman, with his more intricately balanced position between a present and a future audience, makes a kindred but more public gesture:

> When I read the book, the biography famous,
> And is this then (said I) what the author calls a man's life?

And so will some one when I am dead and gone write my life?
(As if any man really knew aught of my life,
Why even I myself I often think know little or nothing of my real life,
Only a few hints, a few diffused faint clews and indirections
I seek for my own use to trace out here) (8).

Poetry allows both Whitman and Dickinson a directness of personal assertion because only there can Whitman's "real I myself" and Dickinson's "nobody" describe themselves. The mood is not oratorical and collective but direct and personal. The audience is what Dickinson calls "the sole Ear I cared to charm" (No. 26) and Whitman "lover and perfect equal" (109) — a being not identifiable with any particular reader but with each one, ideally and individually. Unlike Whitman, Dickinson limited her immediate audience as much as her ideal one, decisively separating the poet's calling from any aspect that might be called public. As her poems continually assert, the poet's calling is not practical but divine, not in the world but "exterior to time." Since fame is "a fickle food" (No. 1659) and "does not stay" (No. 1475), one must aspire beyond earthly fashions to where the time-bound "Bubble of the Styles" evaporates in the light of heaven (No. 468). Using the kind of paradox she explored in her poems, we might call her the show-off of eternity for the innumerable ways she devised to humble herself in the world even as she asserted herself to posterity and to heaven. The four poems printed by Higginson were the only ones published in her lifetime. In her later years she was so shy that she would talk to visitors only from another room. Yet she continued to write and sewed her poems into book-like packets for readers yet to come. As Jesus defined his mission against the ostentatious grandeur of Rome, so Dickinson had tentatively ventured into print only to retreat into a world of her own creation to become the saint of poetic recluses, whose two prime themes would be fame and death. So too Dickinson would rather not know the new languages of science or law or society that the nineteenth century has devised to talk about the world, even the languages of much nature poetry. Her own sense of what poetry ought to do excludes such daily considerations. Immortality is "the only thing worth larceny" (No. 1365) and the search for immortality finds her, like Petrarch and Young, preoccupied with death, for only on the verge of the grave can she express the fascination with both lover and audience that would otherwise be trivialized into the desire for romance or immediate fame.

In the contemplation of death, "our rapt attention to immortality" (No. 7), Dickinson finds ways both to express and to soothe her obsession with her own survival, not as body so much as poet or name. Since an audience so often distorts the nature of what it hears, it is best to be one's own audience or to trust in the immortal audience that lives beyond death. By itself, says Dickinson, nothing external exists and therefore applause can never justify what has not already been affirmed within. Speak therefore into silence and be unconcerned with the echoes of the world. The public eye and ear that can steal the self away by imposing its own meaning must be replaced by the reader, who truly receives and thereby completes what the poet has said:

> This is my letter to the World
> That never wrote to Me
> The simple News that Nature told—
> With tender Majesty
>
> Her Message is committed
> To Hands I cannot see—
> For love of Her—Sweet—countrymen—
> Judge tenderly—of Me (No. 441).

"Countrymen" strikes almost a Whitmanlike note, for Dickinson rarely makes even a gesture toward any such collective audience. Like the titles of rank that she applies to the birds and flowers, the words of political institution and order are useful only as metaphors for the inner world, to illustrate their own insubstantiality:

> The Heart is the Capital of the Mind—
> The Mind is a single State—
> The Heart and the Mind together make
> A single Continent—
>
> One—is the Population—
> Numerous enough—
> This ecstatic Nation
> Seek—it is Yourself (No. 1354).

Whereas Pope with hopeful self-sufficiency might invoke "one self-approving hour" and distinguish true fame from that of place and position, Dickinson identifies the immortality she seeks with reticence and even social invisibility:

> Publication—is the Auction
> Of the Mind of Man. . . .
> In the Parcel—Be the Merchant
> Of the Heavenly Grace—
> But reduce no Human Spirit
> To Disgrace of Price— (No. 709).

Such an assertion of artistic self-sufficiency is possible because the hierarchies of the world don't count at all and the only necessary audience is God. Dickinson takes these traditional justifications of the saint and merges them with the American myths of God's Commonwealth to establish an artistic fame virtually dependent on neglect and reclusiveness—a fame not only analogous to that explored by Keats and Shelley, but also similarly a forerunner of the late nineteenth-century conception of the avant-garde. Byron had awoken to find himself famous. Dickinson, as she had virtually predicted and insured, would have to die. All exposure in her lifetime would be mere fame, not the immortal "Fame of Myself" that she saw inescapably entangled with death. In an America crowded with men leveraged to equality and greatness by money and books, she, like Keats and Hazlitt, invokes the analogy of a Jesus who was "too intrinsic for Renown" and saw physical life for the triviality it was:

> He gave away his Life—
> To Us—Gigantic Sum—
> A trifle—in his own esteem—
> But magnified—by Fame— (No. 567)

The fame she seeks, writes Dickinson, is in paradise. Yet more often she finds her true home neither on earth nor in paradise but in her own work, a place between the temporal world of noisy fashion and the silence of eternity.

In contrast with Dickinson's focus on the timeless, Whitman celebrates the endless variety of the present, and so his need to distinguish mere reader from true reader is much more intense and his rejection of public praise and recognition just that much more obsessive. "When I heard at the close of day how my name had been receiv'd with plaudits in the capital," "When I peruse the conquer'd fame of heroes," and others of the *Calamus* and *Sea-drift* poems particularly contrast the emptiness of public acclaim with the fulfillment possible with one true friend and lover. Much more than Dickinson, Whitman is poised between the manuscript tradition that he is trying to revive and the world of literary celebrity he simultaneously courts and shuns. Unlike John Donne, George Herbert, and other seventeenth-century lyric and religious poets—for whom manuscript circulation ensured the social class and spiritual orientation of their audience—Whitman explicitly and Dickinson implicitly appeal to a sociologically mysterious but spiritually kindred public that they are trying to awaken into being. The chance of attracting interlopers and mere sightseeing readers is therefore all too possible. Since Whitman must be public in a way Dickinson chooses not to, he also writes poems that even warn away the wrong sort of reader:

> Are you the new person drawn toward me?
> To begin with take warning, I am surely far different from what you
>   suppose;
> Do you suppose you will find in me your ideal?
> Do you think it is so easy to have me become your lover? (101).

"I am not what you supposed, but far different," he says in "Whoever you are holding me now in hand" (95). He does not aspire to be an easily understood or public poet, accessible to all who have heard of him and want to buy. It is dangerous to read him: "The way is suspicious, the result uncertain, perhaps destructive." Thus an older Whitman dramatizes his chafing against the fame he has achieved, with its insidious domestication of everything he believed was new, startling, and transcendent about his message. He has searched for loving readers and he has found instead literal-minded fans who, like a certain Mrs. Criswell, write to tell him that they will be happy to have a child by him, as he 'said' he wanted in such and such a poem.

The badge of honor for Whitman, like every modern artist, is to be loved and appreciated by the stranger—"Passing stranger! you do not know how longingly I look upon you" (103). Such a stranger is the ideal completing reader in whom the work finds its fulfillment and the poet finds love:

> Among the men and women, the multitude,
> I perceive one picking me out by secret and divine signs. . . .
> Some are baffled, but that one is not—that one knows me (108).

But the stranger in the present more often than not mistakes both poet and poem. Only in facing the stranger in the future, the stranger not yet born, who will meet him only in his book, can Whitman relax from the labor of distinguishing his real self from the poet he has created. Then they will have become the same. Dickinson, however, because she chooses not to publish, need not fear the reader who misunderstands. The insistence with which she uses images of public display and audience approval to convey the self-satisfaction that comes from *not* seeking the applause of an audience indicates the powerful hold she maintains over her own ambivalent desires:

> Though None be on our Side—
> Suffice Us—for a Crowd— (No. 789).

And even more explicitly:

> The Soul selects her own Society—
> Then—shuts the Door— (No. 303).

Only in her poetry is she able to hang her head "ostensibly" and be identified by the one gaze that gives real identity: "Her God—Her only Throng" (No. 455). It was a nurturing contradiction that allowed her genius to flourish, a saintly originality not based in daily competition but in democratic eternity. In addition to corresponding with her noneditor and nonpublisher Thomas Wentworth Higginson, Dickinson also wrote occasionally to Higginson's wife and once sent her "a little Granite Book you can lean upon" (*Letters*, 569). Higginson in his essay on Dickinson remembers the book as *Middlemarch*. In fact it was *Representative Men*.

From Dandies to the Avant-garde: Poe, Baudelaire's Poe, and Baudelaire

The highest ambition of every Artist is to be thought a man of Genius.
—SIR JOSHUA REYNOLDS, "Discourses on Art" (1782)

The most beautiful destiny is to have genius and to be obscure.
—BARBEY D'AUREVILLY, *Du dandysme et du Georges Brummell* (1845)

Whitman was searching for a special American brand of heroism to rival the more rigid heroisms of European tradition. Yet even with the example of the well-portrayed heroes of the Revolution, he could feel hampered by the need to be public in what resembled the old way. In Europe, the struggle between assertion and withdrawal rarely took on either Whitman's expansiveness or the renunication favored by Dickinson. There, aspiring women as well as men, still shadowed by a monarchical conception of status, sought more crowded stages for their reticence than a living room in Amherst or the Brooklyn ferry. The expansiveness and expressiveness of the American context always placed a potential premium on visual appearance and appeal to an immediate public, so long as one could appeal to posterity or some higher value at the same time. But in Europe, the artistic mode was marked by both a scorn for public acceptance and a self-announced eccentricity—with both aristocratic and plebeian roots—that opposed the "artist" of all sorts to the society around him. To the extent that it took an American cue, its model, suitably mythologized, was the doomed Poe, dying like a latter-day Chatterton unappreciated and unknown. In the political aesthetic of Whitman, with its effort to embrace the reader as countryman and countrywoman, the poet has a priestly role to play for his society, making up the new democratic religion as he goes along. But in the European evolution from the early nineteenth-century dandy to the avant-garde artist at the end of the century, the audience is not the "people," but (in Stendhal's phrase) the "happy few," for whom the poet or artist becomes a socially alienated saint.

It is easy enough to look back on the fames of the past and expose their connection to the public power of the moment. But it is really with the nineteenth century that the question of fame takes on an explicit political aspect that touches everyone in a society. The great expansion of the reading and viewing public as well as the means of reaching them that marks the nineteenth century ensured that no one aspiring to public recognition, either by inheritance or by assertion, could be unaware of the multitude of ways it had been done in the past and was being done in the present. Stirred by the Revolutionary claims that time had begun again in France and America, inspired by what seemed to be the signs of material progress everywhere, nineteenth-century European man could reasonably assume that the past was important because it had issued in the present. This was progress: The past ends in *me,* the end product of centuries of human development. And to the extent that such model public men as Byron and Napoleon promised their audiences a direct access to some new part of themselves rather than any replay of the subordinate relation to the great men of the past, they too discounted the past as anything but prelude.

But along with the optimism came a revulsion, in those temperamentally and philosophically opposed to the new world as well in those who had at first embraced its promise. As we have seen, even the most public of great men cultivated a soulful solitude and disengagement to protect themselves from the audience who tagged along in their wake. When the message of a progress-oriented society is 'Everything is getting better, what about you?' then anyone might feel that they were left out of the general rush toward success and look for compensation to other standards of status. Actually being a working artist was often the least important qualification. The new heroes of sensibility had legitimized a desire to be great in spirit to which tangible accomplishments might be at best irrelevant and at worst an ugly muck around the ankles of aspiration. The answer instead was a commitment to the style and sometimes the substance of social marginality. The appeal of the outsider, perhaps our most widespread psychological inheritance from nineteenth-century Europe, seems necessarily generated to salve the wounds of a vast number of individuals who, however successful, still felt left out of the triumphal parade of social and scientific progress. One version of the attitude I am beginning to sketch here is what the young Marx in the 1840s called the "alienation" endemic to industrial society, in which the worker in particular but everyone in general experienced the loss of direct connection to the work of his hands and to his place in the social order. Marx excluded the artist from such alienation because his work was his own, and he even described the society of the future as a place where everyone might be an artist in these terms. But so many actual European artists of the nineteenth century (and later) nevertheless gloried in what we might broadly call an alienated status because they considered it to be an emblem of integrity to be so cast out.

The dandy especially took that alienation and turned it into a badge and style of honor. He was an aristocrat whose armor was his self-consciousness. The true dandy, as the figure of Brummell implies, has a self-aware ability, which his imitators lack, to stand outside social convention, extracting from nature its principles of truth and beauty, distilling the people from the public, and even, in a lighter moment, "placing the most ordinary circumstances in a ridiculous point of view"—which Brummell's first biographer tells us was the prime source of his wit (Jesse, I, 106).[13] Detested for its coolness by passionate polemicists like Carlyle, the individual affectations

---

13. Compare Shelley's *Defense of Poetry* (1821, published 1840), where he writes that it is the special role of the poet to make familiar things unfamiliar by his imagination, which "contains within itself the seeds at once of its own and social renovation" (19).

of the dandy nevertheless conveyed a loud personal silence in the midst of the general tumult. Since neither material reward nor popularity was any indication of true greatness, the dandy's assertion of "style" constituted a self-defined marginality to the new middle-class world, and he cultivated a wealth of gestures to designate the ways in which the aspirant to that sort of fame could disdain the horrid alternatives of being either a crowd-pleasing literary politician or a self-made merchant. The Romantic emphasis on inner spiritual creativity and originality sanctioned a style whose basic product was less any piece of artistic work than an artistically composed self, a cultivated sense of being that could be considered a protest against the consumer world of more tangible and reproducible articles that was coming so voluminously into existence. To make up for their lack of place in the society that was building, they would pay an extraordinary amount of attention to themselves, their friends, and to the art that sought to transcend the conventions of public approval. Willfully anonymous as far as the socially approved naming of the present was concerned, they looked instead to justification by their own family of sensibility (harkening back to the Rosicrucian "fame of the brotherhood") or by the unclouded future.

Thus the dandy as spiritual aristocrat, whose style was independent of class or genealogy, might share characteristics with the criminal who disdained normal social standards as well as with the sage and the hero who soared beyond them. Loneliness and neglect would be the sign of a better fame. In a world becoming increasingly specialized, this new fame was decidedly nonprofessional, especially when it touched on the world of art, for nonprofessionalism emphasized the lack of relation between what this kind of artist was doing and the sordid repetitions of vocation or commerce. The attitude had a long life, from Byron in the beginning of the century, whom no one ever managed to see writing at all (he said it was all done in the early hours of the morning after parties) to Aubrey Beardsley at the end of the century, as reported by Max Beerbohm:

> It is a curious thing that none of his visitors ever found him at work, or saw any of his rough sketches, or even so much as his pen, ink, and paper. It was his pose to appear as a man of leisure, living among books (*The Incomparable Max*, 86).

It survives with us still as a modern variation on what Castiglione in *The Courtier* called *sprezzatura,* the ability to make something difficult look easy and offhand, flowing naturally from the personality and nature of the doer, instead of being laboriously worked. "If it does not seem a moment's thought," writes William Butler Yeats, who came to poetic birth in the decade of Beardsley and Oscar Wilde, "our stitching and unstitching has been naught" ("Adam's Curse," 78). To pay too much obvious attention to one's work aligns one with the mere craftsman and artisan, just as to care too much about its success in the world is reminiscent of the commercial hack or tradesman, who must eat by his productions and therefore cooks them for the crowds. Better to be overheard and if a success, an overnight success, like Byron, rather than someone who too obviously worked at it. Only then can the curse of mere craft, commercialism, and, most of all, the demeaning mercantile implications of competition be avoided.

Such a posture was so compelling throughout the nineteenth century because it helped preserve artistic integrity behind a shield of high-minded indifference to the world of commerce and communication that was furnishing more and more outlets for artistic work. Its role in the artistic self-image might even be considered the equivalent of the patron's, mediating between the select few who truly appreciated the artist's work and the general public that was invited only to overhear it. In the canons of originality, the creation of the work and its circulation were absolutely different processes, the second distinctly and, by Byron's time, loudly proclaimed as inferior to the first. Yet both were part of the paradox of nineteenth-century fame—the equivalent of the dandy's pose of publicity through the disdaining of the public. No one may have seen Byron write, but he was as thoroughly up-to-date about the mechanics of publishing as Cicero or Erasmus had been in their own eras. Brummell had said that the dandy had failed if his costume had been noticed as premeditated. But even that austerity cultivated a desire to be noticed for not caring about being noticed. In his immediate inheritors the appeal to a larger crowd to validate one's unconcern and detachment had become de rigueur.

It is always difficult to discuss the metaphysics of a general phenomenon, like dandyism in the nineteenth century or adolescent culture after World War Two, because the great mass of dandies or teenagers of those periods were simply following the fashions of the time. Yet the implications of such trends are profound precisely because fame in the nineteenth century had become so interwoven with fashion. Following the remarkable flurry of new visual forms that began with the American Revolution and ended with the final exile of Napoleon, the nineteenth century in Europe develops a tremendously enlarged armory of techniques for conveying the illusion of human presence, especially in its visual dimension. The varieties of greatness were on the public mind of the nineteenth century. Journals appeared in which readers (now also viewers) who never met an aristocrat or a general or a politician could find out what they looked like, what they wore, where they ate, and what they said—at least in the hearing of a reporter. Reporting itself was on the verge of professionalization. The word "journalist" had been around since the late seventeenth century. But the 1830s saw the introduction of "journalism," taken up in England as a welcome import from France, to denote the newspaper's daily processing of the world. "Gossip column" had to wait until the 1850s, but in the voluminous pages of caricatures, anecdotes, and commentaries on social events, the attitude existed long before the word.

I have been talking here about what could easily be called the birth of modern fashion, and we should note that fashion is a concept nurtured by the nineteenth century, in the general sense of an awareness of dress and style as a form of self-expression available to all those who are interested (and many who were not until they were told it was possible to be). Until the nineteenth century, fashion in clothing was a matter for the upper classes, if at all. But from the moment the stirrings of the Industrial Revolution were first felt in the manufacture of cloth, it became possible to imitate the fashions of the great quickly as well as cheaply. It was only one of the factors marking the general awareness of the impact of fashion on social behavior and social success. We are used to this process now, as ever-quickening waves of superficial change wash over us daily, and new styles are invented or old ones revived to cater to the public's desire to exercise "choice." But we might remember how the media world brought into being by the democratic revolutions first engendered a rapid processing of social phenomena, unparalleled in the past, that cut across class lines and to a great extent stood outside inherited or immediate status.

The new speed with which fashion was being communicated, of course, had an indelible impact on the nature of fame. In Europe especially the standards for seeing and being seen were adapted from the practice of aristocrats and pseudoaristocrats of the early part of the century; and journalists, novelists, and critics—even those of the stature of Balzac or Disraeli—often took their lead from the circles of fashionable wealth. Appropriately, this new conception of the importance of aristocratic style accords closely with a continued attack on aristocratic political power. What cultural credit they did possess was invested more and more exclusively in being seen. Here they were specialists and, if they could no longer unrestrictedly lead as members of a privileged class, they could through their inbred or acquired awareness of what it meant to be onstage. In this competition the so-called "exclusives" of the Regency were one of the last groups to try to maintain the old aristocratic preserve of being the people looked at: the only ones worthy to be seen and the ones who judged the sight of others as well. But Byron, Brummell, and Napoleon, as well as all those who came from outside those standards, used their detachment to establish styles that stimulated the imitation and emulation of large numbers of people. The "exclusives" were fighting a rearguard action against democracy and equality by proclaiming the enclosed perfection of their elite. But by so ostentatiously staging their elitism, they contributed inexorably to both the popularization and merchandising of exclusivity itself. In the 1820s and 1830s a wave of popular English novels called "silverfork novels" allowed readers into these worlds, with an intriguing combination of satire of individuals with homage to the idea of exclusivity—just the thing to solace and entice those who could not be admitted at all. The manners and morals of the more secretive classes were henceforth to be on public view, and the dandy's detachment from social convention was adapted by a new generation of novelists who cast themselves as reporters to the reader from strange and exotic places, often within their own countries. Such elite groups may have been at the top of society financially or socially. But as objects of attention they were merely different and fair game for curiosity as well as emulation. Through the midwifery of fashion, the class-oriented exclusivity of the early nineteenth-century London club spawned the brood of "exclusive" restaurants, boutiques, designer labels, and all the innumerable forms of external status vying for our attention today.

When "society" became another word for "middle class," the outsider might appear anywhere, from the lower depths to the bay windows of exclusive clubs, and even those who by any sociological accounting would be called part of "society" could nevertheless nurture their fragile separateness through gesture, dress, or taste—with a haircut like Byron's or a pair of gloves like Disraeli's, holding a book of poems by Baudelaire. In this sense the generation slightly after that of Byron, Napoleon, and Brummell was the first real generation of *fans*—no longer the rompings of Boswell after Rousseau and Johnson, but fans who came first to imitate, then to supersede. A large audience had begun to appear that sought to imitate the style of ostentation with little care for any actual accomplishment. The aspirant to such intangible but fashionable status could take on the look of some admired public figure and thereby assume some of that figure's aura of publicity as well. The new clothes or rather the new sense of style signified danger, excitement, and mystery—unlike the clothes of the past that merely signified money, vocation, and social status. The urge was a more socially acceptable version of what drove those people who, very early on, began to turn up at insane asylums claiming to be Napoleon. Not that they wanted to rule France or invade Russia; they just wanted to *be* Napoleon. Similarly, by the 1830s and 1840s the hunger for the style of success had created a market filled with aristocratic talismans made from shoddy materials. Those were the signs of "success," or at least the promise that the wearer was someone "on the rise." Ambition fitted itself out with dime-store dandyism and sallied forth: If one wished to be seen, imitate the style of those who are seen and celebrated already. Visual fashion in the nineteenth century, like the artistic urge or the sense of individual worth, had thereby become severed from any necessary relation to social antecedents and had begun to be defined almost solely as a matter of will, signaling to others how one wished to be understood.[14]

We have been noting the merely fashionable and the superficially imitative in popular fiction as well as in popular clothing and merchandise. But every imitation of any quality included the extra membrane of a *learned* aristocracy, a *learned* singularity. Although Ellen Moers in her excellent study *The Dandy* argues that the French version of the English dandy drew its inspiration primarily from books and was therefore always more intellectual than the English, dandyism is by its nature always self-consciously detached and coolly observant. Even at its most flamboyant, it is a con-

14. The word "success" itself begins to mean something different from what it had, not just anything that happened later (like "sequel") or even anything good, but specifically those goods defined by wealth and position. After all, no one can be successful in those terms until there is a society that allows such success, applauds it, and by the end of the nineteenth century is willing to say that a person is "*a* success," both following and fathering himself.

spiracy of observed and observer in the same skin. Like the plays of Byron and Shelley, which were virtually impossible to stage, even though they were aimed at public theater, there was always in the public poses of even the most dandified and ostentatious an irreducible privateness that high-lighted the invisible, unstageable self within. Between the Napoleon complex and the Byron costume falls the dandy. With an elaborateness that would have shocked the plain *citoyen* Rousseau, the dandies and artists of the nineteenth century nevertheless carried out his perception of the necessary antagonism between the public world and the pursuit of individual perfection. They contemplated themselves and, particularly in France, they reformulated what the desire for such singularity meant. As the middle-class society of the nineteenth century became more pervasive, the search for a position beyond its limits became more imperative to every would-be artist or wayward inner aristocrat. Five years after the death of Beau Brummell, Barbey d'Aurevilly, a young Frenchman, wrote in *Du dandysme et du Georges Brummell* (1845) that the dandy was a spiritual being "who carries within him something superior to the visible world." Superior to the visible world, in other words, because so conscious of his own visual impact on it.[15] Thus in one aspect dandyism emphasized an increasing theatricalization of the social self through the signs of exclusivity (which could be merchandised into fashion) and in another it moved toward an almost metaphysical interpretation of the dandy's detachment that led away from the visual panoply into a reclusive and secretive darkness.

To the extent that the artistic dandy had renounced the moral mission dictated for art by a conventional society, the limits of his nature therefore impinged on both the criminal and the saint. At the moment in Hazlitt's essay "Of Persons One Would Wish to Have Seen," just before the figures of Shakespeare and Jesus are invoked, Hazlitt reveals his own choices, Guy Fawkes and Judas Iscariot, the great traitors who stand similarly beyond the normal categories of fame. The English eighteenth century had already witnessed a fascination with the criminal, seen alternately as a kind of bandit-businessman (Mr. Peachum in Gay's *The Beggar's Opera*) by writers still aligned with a cultural upper class and as a kind of individualist artist (Defoe's Moll Flanders) by those with sympathies for figures rising through their own will in a hostile social environment. By the nineteenth century, the socially unreconciled poet could draw on an anti middle-class tradition that included literary forebears stretching back to the chivalry of Robin Hood. The world of crime, ran the myth, was a vital, "original" society, whose antagonism to social conventions and perception of social hypocrisy mirrored those of the writer, the artist, and the dandy. The appeal of the association was obvious to a generation nurtured on the image of grand

15. Compare the English view, wittily summarized by Catherine Gore, that Brummell was "a nobody who had made himself somebody, and gave the law to everybody." Both of these lines are quoted by Ellen Moers (*The Dandy*, 255, 266). Despite my frequent arguments with Moers, her book is the most generally valuable yet written on dandyism in the nineteenth century, and I have relied heavily on her leads into the primary material.

outsiders like Napoleon and Byron. True art could be considered a kind of crime against bourgeois society, a grand rejection of convention, tradition, and every social standard but the fame that should be bestowed on those who so grandly rejected them.

It might be argued that ostentatious costuming in any era always helps foster a distinction between social show and the person within. But until the nineteenth century, the number of sophisticated practitioners was comparatively small and confined to a class that might reasonably believe its outward show a reflection of its inner worth. More important, the interest in using costume as a manipulable set of signals was low or nonexistent. The handful of anecdotes of Antony and Cleopatra slumming in the streets of Alexandria or Peter the Great working as a carpenter in St. Petersburg are striking because they are so few. Typically, they focus on high-status people pretending to be low rather than the (more subversive) other way around. But by the nineteenth century the greater complexity of society and the comparative transience of social status—especially for those artists who occupied a shadow area outside of definite classes—generated innumerable stories preoccupied with psychic doubleness. Most memorable among them is the Jekyll-and-Hyde dramatization of a dark inner nature, solipsistic and antisocial, that could easily be set loose, especially when the socially secure "upper" self sought to prove the heights of its own genius by unprecedented experiments of thought and feeling.

In contrast to social ideals that enforced a uniform of etiquette on everyone who wanted to achieve by the standards of society arose both popular and high-culture writing that praise the unassimilated man, the rebel, the man of feeling, the criminal, whose natural desires cannot be fit into the forms of society, however warped by them they might be. Dickens's characters become eccentrics in order to survive, and the precedent of Byron preserves many despairing psyches in the nineteenth century by being a category for the uncategorizable. Society had inspired the dream of success and simultaneously made it almost impossible to achieve. No wonder the Romantic artist liked to define himself as isolated. And no wonder as well that popular fiction is so concerned with fantasies of power and subjection that both purge and augment the feelings of personal worthlessness society has instilled. Since I am not a prince within, I will be solaced by the criminal, the man outside society, the adventurer, the pirate, the prince of darkness.

When spiritual justification and spiritual fame, traditionally poised in contrast to society and the public world, also begin to have less to do with organized religion than with personal sensibility and the goals of an absolute art, it becomes more difficult to trace clear lines in the history of fame. When each individual potentially has the storehouse of past attitudes and costumes to assemble as he might, then we might think somewhat wistfully about ages past, in which the urge to fame was limited by class, money, and institutional setting—and the task of the historian of fame therefore much simpler. But each era reads the past in its own way, and it is striking how the twentieth century picks out certain aspects of the nineteenth to condemn and others to applaud for the ways we believe we have revolted against or continued its traditions. The horror story was hardly in any quantitative sense a major part of nineteenth-century literature. But the names of Mary Shelley, Edgar Allan Poe, Robert Louis Stevenson, and Bram Stoker loom larger now to us, because the heroic and fatal marginality they dramatized has filtered its way into every realm of our own popular culture and thereby into a recess in virtually every mind that reads or sees. Sherlock Holmes's combination of high-brow aestheticism with a penetrating insight into the criminal mind (because it is so like his own) neatly ties together these elements in one compelling fictional version of unassimilated man. In other tales, the story is couched in the form of a dream or a dimly perceived secondhand tale told by a teller who hardly understands it and is set far from the world of facts and social niceties. There, the tale of horror allows the inner self to flow out, horrible, distended, but somehow grand and inspiring, despite the warped shape the enclosures of society have given it. Horror, whether in Brontë's *Wuthering Heights* or in Poe's stories, is a release from social forms and empirical certainty, so that the mind, the body, the spirit can be explored in all their disorder and irrationality. And still there is the inspiring hope, the Byronic assertion, that an aristocracy of the spirit exists and your inner, truer self is always better than circumstances have made you—that the world and society have never treated you according to your due, whether you are Heathcliff, Jane Eyre, or the Frankenstein monster.

An intriguing distinction here presents itself. In the characteristically American view of psychic horror, for example, Poe's "William Wilson," the hated other constantly arrives just in time to thwart the narrator's effort to get a leg up in the world and exposes him as a cheat or worse. This double is a more moral, a "better self," who mockingly demonstrates how the hero hasn't measured up to his own grand expectations. He is the active version of that other frequent figure in Poe's stories, the true love, who has been inadvertently buried alive, only to rise again in either demonic vengeance or mournful remonstrance. The English double, on the other hand, as in Stevenson's *Dr. Jekyll and Mr. Hyde* or Wilde's *The Picture of Dorian Gray,* implies by his horrid appearance that, while we may have fooled the world, in fact inside we are still squalid and evil. It is fairly common to treat such tales of the double as psychological, often Freudian, expressions of inner darkness and sexual repression. But let us remember that another doubleness every nineteenth-century writer invited each time he put pen to paper was the ambiguous commerce of making public a private act of feeling. In both the American and the English versions of the double story, the most implacable rival for worldly success, undercutting every achievement, is not really another person, but an aspect, higher or lower, of oneself—one's own sense of the compromises and self-warpings that ambition and the urge for recognition entail. Thus we can appreciate the saliency of the writer for understanding the question of fame in the nineteenth century—as crucial as the general-politician for the classical world, the saint for late antiquity, the painter and playwright for the Renaissance, and, as we shall see, the performer for the twentieth century. To use Freud to interpret such themes is somewhat like trying to understand the place of cars in American culture by reading a selection of owners' manuals. For Freud takes his own position in exactly the same evolution—systematizing, generalizing, and speculating upon the seductive shadowland between personal and social nature—a process that might be traced back to Edward Young, whose art, wrote Herbert Croft, consisted primarily "of making the publick a party in his private sorrow" (399).

*   *   *

In the present instance I have no sympathy—at least no pity—for him who descends. He is that *monstrum horrendum*, an unprincipled man of genius.   —EDGAR ALLAN POE, "The Purloined Letter" (1845)

[G]enius is nothing more nor less than *childhood recovered* at will.
          —CHARLES BAUDELAIRE, "The Painter of Modern Life" (1863)

Despite those who would like to believe that our own time is unprecedented in its preoccupation with fame, it is in the European nineteenth century that we can observe the first large-scale effort to supplement or even replace the traditionally tangible sources of fame with a fame of the human spirit struggling against a hostile or indifferent society. In this effort the writer centrally offers himself, an isolated human consciousness, as both sacrifice and guide, so that he as well as his reader might be in some exonerating way delivered from the burden of the search for success. As the Romantics celebrated Chatterton's neglect and Thomas Wentworth Higginson required the ballast of Emily Dickinson's refusal to publish, so Charles Baudelaire seized on Edgar Allan Poe. At the age of twenty-six, a few years after Poe's own death, Baudelaire began what was to be a lifetime of reading and translating Poe's works. From them he extracted, articulated, and passed on to later writers the artistic myth of a lost destiny that the individual could no longer express or know how to fulfill, unless he became "the Poet." Like the philosophic dandy or the later aesthete, the poet set about to make himself worthy of that destiny, which might fall on him as unexpectedly as it did on Napoleon or Byron, by purifying himself and attuning himself to the essential rhythms of the universe. He became exotically learned, he cultivated his sensitivity to everything in the world, and he mocked the emptiness of the public man, as does Poe in a story like "The Man Who Was Used Up." There, a narrator in search of the great political-military hero, Brevet Brigadier General John A. B. C. Smith, at first hears only fashionable gossip about his physical beauty and military courage. Finally, in frustration, he visits the great man's own rooms, where the hero, after being reconstituted by a valet who adds custom-made cork parts to "a bundle of something" on the floor, proceeds to recommend the craftsmanship of those who have supplied his body (314).

But if the public man was an empty suit of clothes, the private man of sensibility was often incapable of anything but suffering, like Roderick Usher in "The Fall of the House of Usher," totally isolated and incapacitated by his own well-cultivated sensitivity. Death kills the body, but success destroys the soul—a paradox dissolvable only if one has the distance and especially the money not to care. No wonder that Poe so often masquerades in his stories as a man of means, a cosmopolitan familiar with the salons and watering spots of the comfortable. No wonder as well that Baudelaire first took him to be that way:

> Aristocrat by nature even more than by birth, the Virginian, the Southerner, the Byron gone astray in a bad world . . . product of a century infatuated with itself, child of a nation more infatuated with itself than all others (Hyslops, 125).

Only later did he discover that Poe was an aristocrat manqué like himself. For most of his adult life Baudelaire was kept on the short financial leash of a small allowance from his mother and stepfather plus whatever he could earn from his writings. Thus, like every other aspiring literary man of the nineteenth century, Baudelaire was materially as well as spiritually caught in the conflict between the need to publish and to purify, to be a success in the eyes of the world and to be a success in the eyes of those he admired (and in his own). In Poe he finds his heightened reflection, the seemingly elegant and well-off young man turning his hand to literature, who is actually virtually starving in a hand-to-mouth existence in commercial literary ventures. By discovering Poe's work, Baudelaire adds "a new saint to the martyrology" of art, "an illustrious failure" (Hyslops, 90).

But the neglected genius of the past, however he may justify the torments of one's nature, is hardly a sufficient guide to fame in the present. To complement Poe, the visionary literary man in search of spiritual fame, Baudelaire, in perhaps his greatest essay, praises Constantin Guys, "the painter of modern life," for being so thoroughly attuned to the immediacies and nuances of his own world that fame is irrelevant. Guys, according to Baudelaire, makes a virtual fetish of anonymity. He refuses to sign his drawings, and he will not let Baudelaire use his name in the essay, where he is referred to as "C.G." or "M. [for Monsieur] G." Guys's originality, says Baudelaire, is "so powerful and so determined that it is sufficient unto itself and does not even seek approval" (328). Unlike the Romantic poet who scorns the cities for the countryside, Guys plunges into the concreteness and variety of city life, seizing on it with an immediacy that becomes transcendent. He has somehow managed to bring together in an artistic and personal synthesis the two personages of Poe's story "The Man of the Crowd": the observing narrator who sits alone in the bow window of a coffeehouse and the old man whom he fascinatedly observes, "the type and genius of deep crime," wandering incessantly through the streets, refusing to be alone. Guys loves equally the crowd and his own anonymity. He is infinitely curious about everything in the world: a "passionate observer" who wants "to see the world, to be at the center of the world, and to remain hidden from the world" (332)—"*un* moi *insatiable de* non-moi" (333)—who "searches everywhere for the passing, fugitive beauty of immediate life" (363). For these reasons, says Baudelaire, Guys does not consider himself an artist, but a man of the world, because artists are too narrow and specialized a breed, like the rest of the nineteenth century, headed only toward greater and greater professionalization, more and more minute preoccupations with their own techniques.

Guys is less artist, then, than dandy, a member of a new aristocracy of the spirit that, argues Baudelaire, appears in the transitional period when democracy is not yet all powerful and aristocracy "only partially tottering and debased." Poised between aristocracy and democracy, such dandies practice an almost spiritual code aimed "to fortify the will and to discipline the soul," cultivating personal qualities that neither money nor work—the two bourgeois beacons of the public nineteenth century—can possibly bestow (351). With his love of light and the things that it shows, and his attraction to personal anonymity, Guys is the consummate contrast both to the public man who seeks the light only that he might shine in it and to the self-advertising artist. Baudelaire himself sits between Poe, his saint of cultural alienation, and C.G., whose ideal might be to vanish entirely and be renowned for his anonymity. As the artist of the immediate, C.G. allows Baudelaire to bring Keats's egotistical sublime and his negative capability together in the same figure, who both stands in the light and helps to create it. The observer of the history of fame might recall the story of the philosopher Diogenes, who told Alexander the Great to stand away because he was blocking and thereby competing with the sun. With nineteenth-century imperialism and the setting forth of innumerable European Alexandroids bent on conquest, the sun that creates the visible world has been once again mistaken for the sun of celebrity and power, and Baudelaire is attempting to restore the balance.

In Baudelaire's virtual mythifying of Constantin Guys, we discover once again the contradictions of the nineteenth-century fascination with the rewards and despairs of public artistic fame. Only a few years after he writes "The Painter of Modern Life," Baudelaire unsuccessfully angles to be elected to the French Academy of forty "immortals." Through the figure of Guys, with his ideal urge toward anonymity, the dandy as self-observer and social-observer can at least momentarily step outside of his own vulnerability to being seen and to being celebrated. "The most beautiful destiny," writes Barbey d'Aurevilly, was " to have genius and to be obscure" (Moers, 274). Only then could one be pure. Now obscurity and evasion of publicity had to be incorporated in order to ensure the innocence of its urge to recognition.

The pose of the observer solidified the righteousness of obscurity by invoking an image not of darkness, but of a power behind the scenes. "The observer," says Baudelaire, "is a *prince* who everywhere enjoys his *incognito*" (333), and whose originality is somehow a function of his shyness.

Two myths help to focus this paradox of the invisible observer. The first was popular in the eighteenth century: the pauper whose virtuous actions will be recognized as those of a prince who must be restored to his inheritance. Richardson's Pamela, Fielding's Joseph Andrews, are among the first versions, and they continue down into the American nineteenth century in the popular figures of Abraham Lincoln, rising to become president from his birth in a log cabin, or the heroes of Horatio Alger, who through acts of courage become visible to an upper-class mentor and thus begin their march to success. The other myth has a more nineteenth-century feel to it: The pauper is still a prince in disguise, but he wishes to remain anonymous, gathering more pleasure *because* his unacknowledged greatness allows him to see and understand all from which his celebrity would otherwise bar him. The pauper revealed as prince is the material version and the prince who stays a pauper the spiritual version of essentially the same story: One chooses to be seen; the other to see—as if that choice can ever be so cleanly made.

With such a revulsion against the standards of success and visibility in the society that surrounded them, there were two prime ways out of the bind, often intertwined: one a cult of failure—a belief that the truly great can never be judged by their own societies and that success and immediate fame virtually ensures that one's work is incompetent—and the other its more aesthetically philosophical Siamese twin, the concept of the avant-garde. The cult of failure in the present to ensure celebration in the future links the later nineteenth-century versions of an unspotted fame with earlier rueful celebrations of the neglect of true genius. The later nineteenth century does still indulge in the old rhetoric—'now he or she belongs with the greats of the ages'—primarily in ceremonies over the coffins of public people. But in the evolution of the image of the outsider, the older Petrarchan and eighteenth-century association of fame and death through the prospect of immortality virtually disappears. The fame that fascinates is the fame on earth, either now or later.

It is striking in this way that the more successful many nineteenth-century novelists become, the more they are preoccupied with characters notable for the grandeur of their expectations and the intricacies of their disappointments. From the 1850s onward, writers in both Europe and America increasingly dramatize the failures of artistic aspiration. It is a theme that not only indicts a society that values only material success, but also reveals a profound ambivalence in those seemingly successful authors for whom it is most compelling. The conditions of modern celebrity have begun to press recognition upon them as a goal—the portrait, the caricature, the photograph, the speech, the interview. But what do such goals have to do with their real work? Their ambition, particularly the spiritual ambition that sets out to make a difference to the moral, intellectual, and aesthetic history of the world, always seems doomed to failure. George Eliot takes up the theme, as do Thomas Hardy, Henry James, and Edith

Wharton, to name a few. Charles Dickens and Mark Twain, with their own penchant for stage performance and self-dramatization, are yet similarly attracted to characters who resolutely turn away from any immediate audience, whether from the motives of a dandiacal detachment or a desire to "light out for the territories." Thus the Romantic paradox of ostentatious neglect, of the acceptance of the people and the rejection of the public, works its way out through the century, as much in the works and attitudes of the well-known and successful writers and artists as among the less familiar and little known. In the climactic scene of Dickens's *A Tale of Two Cities* (1859), for example, Sidney Carton, who had previously been a variety of dandy-observer, gives his life on the guillotine so that Charles Darnay, the active and engaged French aristocrat, can escape: "It is a far, far better thing that I do, than I have ever done." Because of his exact resemblance to Darnay, Carton can impersonate him in a real-life drama before a Parisian mob characterized by Dickens not as a moving group ("mob" originally comes from the Latin *mobile vulgus,* the common people on the move), but as an audience. His greatest role is to submerge his own identity in someone else's so that that other person can escape death.

By the 1890s the Wordsworthian conflict between the people and the public was being restaged in a cultural atmosphere where the classical idea of posterity had been definitely replaced by its modern version—the avant-garde—whose neglected geniuses could claim to be now creating the future history of whatever art they practiced. Theorists of dandiacal detachment and anonymity in the face of a crass society, as well as successful writers and artists who were fearful about the mixture of mere fashion and deserving genius in their vogues, could be relieved from their paradoxes by calling themselves avant-garde. Merit might be neglected in the present, but the future would make amends, for "avant-garde" above all is a term coined by critics whose championing of artists in the present looked to the future for justification of their rarefied taste. The word itself becomes current in English only in the early years of the twentieth century, although it clearly derives from the cultural controversies in the art world of Paris some thirty years before, when it became a habit to establish a *salon des refusés* along with the salon for those painters whose works were accepted by the Academy for showing. Perhaps the gesture to establish the outsiders along with the insiders is typically French. In any case, the term "avant-garde," previously used to apply to purely military matters, the special group of the army in advance of the others, the vanguard (Thoreau's man who steps to a "different drummer"?), became the typical term for artistic pioneers. It embraced the proliferation of established artistic out-groups toward the end of the nineteenth century—the Impressionists in painting, the Symbolists in poetry—who formed the ideological groundwork for the great international movement of the early twentieth century usually known under the collective name of modernism.

In a sense the Romantic assertion of the individual artist's claim to peer into the heart of the world's truth already contains within it the seeds of the avant-garde. The true artist spoke the essential nature of society, while the false reflected only passing fashions—and the true critic discerned the one from the other with an eye unclouded by the prejudices of the present. Such a critic is the artist's fulfilling double, who presents him to the world, just as Baudelaire in *Les Fleurs du Mal* addresses the reader in the often quoted lines "*—Hypocrite lecteur,—mon semblable,—mon frère!*" Like the poet, such a reader is hardly a hypocrite in the trivial moral sense of a dissembler, but in the grand sense of a consummate actor in the farce of life. As kindred spirit and brother, he shares with the poet an understanding that walls out the venal "public" audience, much as Whitman's reader, in poems written at much the same time, is addressed as "friend" or "lover." Any general popularity was in principle suspect, while what was obscure to the "public" could hide more difficult truths. The artist who failed by the standards of his own society had succeeded by the standards of art and the higher society it predicted. For every Victorian Jude the Obscure, ruined by his impossible aspirations, would come a modernist Stephen Dedalus, to be saved because he has chosen art.

But, just as the Byronic or Keatsian or even Napoleonic figure could be easily imitated by those looking only for its gestures and unaware of its substance, so by the end of the century the possibility of being avant-garde was also adaptable into a style of self as well as, or even in place of, a mode of artistic aspiration and achievement. In terms of the nineteenth-century struggle over what kind of recognition was good recognition, the avant-garde was neither a particular style nor a particular attitude toward style, so much as it was a belief in *fame later*. The satisfaction of recognition would be delayed until that moment when the better audience arrived and the true history would be written and the clear eye of posterity made up for the blindness of the present. By our own time, of course, there is no more interest in posterity, and the modern avant-garde has become mere news, as disposable as any other form of self-aggrandizement through public display. In this world of increasingly codified public taste, working artists look to ways of presenting themselves in their own being as much as on the page or canvas. In fact there are and have been many avant-garde styles, all of them essentially self-conscious about the making of art and all very concerned to characterize that making with elaborate formal, thematic, and biographical detail. The late nineteenth and twentieth centuries were witnesses to the most extensive promotion of the importance of art to public and private concerns since Dürer began hobnobbing with humanists. The difference was that in the Renaissance it was primarily painting that promoted itself and its practitioners, while modernism and its immediate forebears were making claims for the arts in general. By the late nineteenth century the marketing of taste was itself a firm part of the artistic scene. "Collector's editions" were advertised as such. Well-trained but impecunious young men hired themselves out to the wealthy to manage the purchase of masterpieces. Museums came into being to lead public taste, exhibit that of their patrons, and formulate the art-historical canons by which artistic greatness would be determined.

The Visible Americans: Abraham Lincoln, Mathew Brady, P. T. Barnum

He had talked, he said, with men who were regarded as great, and he did not see where they differed so much from others. He reasoned, probably, that the secret of their success lay in the fact of original capacity, and untiring industry.
—W. D. HOWELLS, *Life of Abraham Lincoln*

My Splendors, are Menagerie—
But their Completeless Show
Will entertain the Centuries
When I, am long ago,
An Island in dishonored Grass—
Whom none but Beetles—know.
—EMILY DICKINSON

In 1859 Baudelaire denounced photography for the way it gave merely a picture of nature rather than anything from the realm of the imagination, the true place of art. But he was fighting an already lost battle and may have presciently foreseen how his photograph by Étienne Carjat would carry his image as the poet of darkness down to generations who had read few of his actual works. By the later years of the nineteenth century, all the inner Napoleons, neglected geniuses, and spiritual adventurers—let alone the frankly ostentatious public men—had to put on more of a show to catch the attention of both the audience to which they played as well as the one they sought to reject. A turning away from publicity or visual fame in search of a spiritual ideal by both European and American artists could still be a vital protest against the commercialization of art. But the increasing visibility of the avant-garde, for example, indicated how difficult the gesture was to maintain with any purity. Hardy's final novel, *Jude the Obscure,* the tale of one man's futile struggle to be recognized for the immensity of his artistic aspiration, perhaps not too coincidentally appears in 1896, the year after Louis Lumière opens the first motion picture theater. The two events furnish an appropriately Janus-like yoke for the twinned incitement and frustration of the desire for personal recognition that so preoccupies artists in the nineteenth century and so many others in the twentieth.

In the latter nineteenth century the special transcendence promised by the movies still lies ahead. But other engines of fame were gathering momentum. In America *Who's Who* was founded in 1898 and the Hall of Fame at New York University in 1900, while throughout America and Europe photography was already well established as the prime way to bring oneself to the attention of one's relatives, friends, and followers. The silence of the photography allowed a combination of distance and intimacy that was a more domestic version of the Revolutionary portrait of the hero gazing off in the direction of his destiny. By turning human beings into objects of silent contemplation by themselves and others, it embodied the possibility that spiritual virtue might be made visible if properly posed and properly perceived. Unlike the general dressed in military splendor, the new public hero could stand out both spiritually and realistically at the same time, while the photograph froze a moment for eternity.

Photography took hold especially in America, where the insistence on the visibility of all those who aspired to public recognition drew its sanction from the openness with which the country itself was created and its optimistic insistence on an appeal to the suffrage of a democratic audience. Despite the eighteenth-century surge of portraiture for democracy and newly industrialized techniques for producing engravings and mezzotints, it could still be said that the people who voted for Adams or Jefferson or Burr or Madison didn't really know what their candidates looked like. But one of photography's most important effects was to take the art of imaging out of the hands of those skilled enough to paint or engrave as well as those rich enough to buy and place it at the disposal of virtually everyone. In an emblematic event toward the end of the century, Theodore Roosevelt at the age of twenty-seven set out from his ranch in the Dakota Territory to catch some men who had stolen a boat. The weather was wintry and the chase, wrote Roosevelt, took "three days of acute misery" (Sprague, 242). But there was a camera on hand to record the journey and the victorious young rancher standing with his gun over the culprits. The next year Roosevelt returned to New York to reenter a public life he had left behind after the death of his wife and his mother.

There is of course no strict causal connection between Roosevelt's snapshots and his decision to run for mayor of New York or his later public career. But I do want to suggest a causal atmosphere that in the nineteenth century urged the ambitious American public man to include and draw strength from his visual self-consciousness, just as the weak young Roosevelt worked on his body as well as his emotions to strengthen both for his career. Representative democracy and an ever-expanding access to visual publicity went hand in hand. Of course, as Ben Franklin was one of the earliest to remark, the new power of visual media might also involve a new sort of entrapment for both the observer—under the sway of what he is so pleased to see—and the observed—imprisoned by the desire to be seen. One solution had been the gaze of destiny that looked away from the viewer into the fateful future. But the new democratic audience wanted empathy as well as distance. In the aloneness of photography, the public man could be nonsocial but yet theatrical, inheriting the tradition of Washington and

Napoleon but emphasizing as well the aspect of having been come upon, discovered, raised from the log cabin into the public eye. Both politically and imagistically sensitive to his audience, such a public man also continually looked for hints about what details might be considered most independent and appealing. You're a wonderful man, wrote a young admirer to Abraham Lincoln, but you should grow a beard so that the ladies will love you as well. And so Lincoln did. The photograph was the midwife of a moment's meaning. Through it the public man and woman, *any* man and woman, could directly entice the gaze of the viewer. The absent as well as the dead would be present again, and, in a manner only aspired to by writers and artists, the immediate and the eternal promised to be made one.[16]

Photography appeared at just the point that the old generation of the Founding Fathers was dying out and a new heroic commitment was attempting to forge itself. French and English innovations in both the taking and the reproducing of photographs were quickly refined. Not even the nineteenth-century railroad industry seems comparable to the image industry in the rapidity of technological advance. In 1839 L. J. M. Daguerre revealed to the French Academy of Sciences the process he and Nicéphore Niépce had developed. By the mid-1840s Mathew Brady's Daguerrean Miniature Gallery was well established in New York. Hardly twenty years after a sculptor had to hammer the life mask off the head of Jefferson, a photographer (Brady claimed it was himself) had gained entrance to the home of the dying Andrew Jackson to take a less painful image. By 1851 there were approximately one hundred daguerreotype studios in New York City and Americans took three out of the five top medals at the Crystal Palace Photography Exhibition in England, including one for overall excellence awarded to Mathew Brady.

As the enormous number of individual and group portraits that remain to us from the nineteenth century indicates, the individuals who flocked to Brady's gallery stood at the beginning of a great wave still rolling. Their desire to be recorded on film, and the desire of their friends, families, and admirers to retain those images was more than just a personal quirk. It also seems part of an overwhelming cultural need that photography half-discovered and half-stimulated in order to furnish memory with precise visual details of face, dress, posture, and all the ways one appeared to others. There was an immense vogue for individual and group portraits. New processes abounded, and every home inventor experimented with new

16. Grace Bedell wrote to Lincoln with the suggestion on 15 October 1860. On 19 October he writes back wondering somewhat coyly if it would not be considered "a piece of silly affectation" if he began growing whiskers now after never having had them before. The first bearded photograph is dated 26 November and it has been argued that Lincoln began to grow his beard after the election, perhaps because there had been no previous president with a beard. But the thickness of the 26 November beard seems evidence of an earlier growth. His first photograph by Brady at the Washington studio shows a thick beard and head of hair much thinned and shortened in later photographs.

ways of transferring life into something that resembled permanence. Everyone who could afford it (prices ranged from 12.5 cents to $2 in New York at one period) could have a daguerreotype of themselves, and Brady especially began to cater to public interest in possessing the images of the admired greats as well. In 1850 he published *The Gallery of Illustrious Americans,* with lithographs made from his studio's daguerreotypes, including his 1849 White House portrait of James Polk, the first of an incumbent president. In 1860 the *New York Times* celebrated "what manner of men and women we Americans of 1860 are" by printing a selection of his portraits.[17]

Brady and others continued to do individual and celebrity portraiture, but already the unique and unreproducible nature of the daguerreotype was urging inventors on to discover ways of turning the individual image into a multitude. The *carte de visite,* a paper calling card with photograph and signature that could be ordered in whatever quantity the client wanted was introduced in France in 1854 and quickly caught on in America. The *carte de visite* not only added a visual image to the social habit of leaving one's calling card, but, almost from its introduction, it also became a prime means for public figures to strengthen their political or military campaigns with a shower of personalized, pocket-sized portraits. Suitably enough, Napoleon III was an early customer of Disderi, the *carte*'s inventor, while Abraham Lincoln said that he owed his election both to the Cooper Union speech that introduced him to the publishers and politicians of the East and to the *carte de visite* made of him on that occasion by Mathew Brady. The faces and figures of prominent Americans (the *cartes* were usually full figure) could from the 1860s on be included in the albums of their admirers and supporters, as if they were members of the family.

The emotional intimacy that the photograph helped foster between the famous and their audience was also reflected in the movement away from former standards of how prominence was conveyed. The portraits of Washington and other military leaders of the Revolution were still indebted to classical and Renaissance depictions of human glory. To the extent that Franklin's plainness was emphasized or that he and Jefferson were characterized as inventors or natural philosophers, their portraits did depart somewhat from the traditional motifs of public fame. But nothing in artistic portraiture really anticipated the almost total break with the traditional look of a European public face expressed in Brady's photographs of Lincoln. This was a look unadorned by the motifs of fame and glory that even the

17. One of the most intriguing potential celebrities who came to Brady's studio, probably in the late 1840s, was Brigham Young, just after he had succeeded the murdered Joseph Smith as head of the Church of Jesus Christ of Latter-Day Saints and not long before he took his people west to found Salt Lake City and the Mormon state of Deseret. Young also once asked P. T. Barnum how much he could make if exhibited. The answer was $200,000 (Barnum, 403). A religion preoccupied with genealogy and history, Mormon doctrine asserts the special grace brought by Jesus to America, which he visited on the way to heaven after the Crucifixion. The most striking symbol of the religion, the golden statue of the herald angel Moroni that stands atop Mormon temples, strongly resembles a Renaissance fame figure.

French Revolution had only transformed instead of obliterating (and which Napoleon III was spending a good deal of energy from 1852 on trying to revive). It was a look of neither a military man nor an Eastern politician in the Roman patrician style nor a nicely turned out dandy or aristocrat. Here was a homely face on an oversized body wearing rumpled clothes, with perhaps a domestic shawl over his shoulders. It was the plainness of Franklin combined with the stature of Washington—the ordinary man, the representative man, transformed into the extraordinary by both his belief in principle and the demands of history. As Nathaniel Hawthorne described him in print, so he seemed in image, a face and figure that almost magically seemed to take up a preexisting space in the imagination of the viewer, which he had been yearning to fill:

> There is no describing his lengthy awkwardness, nor the uncouthness of his movement; and yet it seemed as if I had been in the habit of seeing him daily, and had shaken hands with him a thousand times in some village street; so true was he to the aspect of the pattern American, though with a certain extravagance which, possibly, I exaggerated still further by the delighted eagerness with which I took it in (310).

Almost as soon as Lincoln took office, the conflict between North and South began. To win the war and keep the country from splitting apart was, he said, "a task before me greater than that which rested on Washington."[18] For the Revolutionary generation Washington represented independence and autonomy from the European yoke, drawing on its imagery to herald a new cause. But Lincoln had the task of keeping the country together, the North and the South, the blacks and the whites, and in his own person convey one palpable image of the integrity of spirit and action to which anyone might rise if summoned by history. In the campaign biography of Lincoln written by William Dean Howells, when he was a twenty-three-year-old reporter, the language of panegyric still reveals the style of greatness Lincoln had hewed out for himself:

> The emigrant, at the head of the slow oxen that drag his household goods toward the setting sun—toward some Illinois yet further west—will take heart and hope when he remembers that Lincoln made no prouder entrance into the State of which he is now the first citizen. . . . Lincoln's future success or unsuccess can affect nothing in the past. The grandeur of his triumph over all the obstacles of fortune,

18. Speech at Springfield, Illinois, 11 February 1861 (*Collected Works*, 4, 190). Lincoln continues: "Without the assistance of that Divine Being, who ever attended him, I cannot succeed." Compare Lincoln's remarks in the fascinating speech made at the Springfield Lyceum almost exactly twenty-five years before (27 January 1838). There he contrasts the motives of the Founding Fathers, who "sought celebrity and fame and distinction" in the success of the Revolution, with a newly ambitious but selfish generation: "Towering genius disdains a beaten path. It seeks regions hitherto unexplored. . . . It *scorns* to tread in the footsteps of *any* predecessor, however illustrious" (1, 113–14). For an intriguing psychological interpretation of Lincoln's conflict between preserving and superseding the past, see Forgie, *Patricide in the House Divided*.

will remain the same. . . . [I]t is the Presidency, not a great man,
that is elevated, if such be chosen chief magistrate (Howells, 50).

Howells's biography was hand corrected by Lincoln, and it is unlikely
that Howells's imagery did not also reflect something of Lincoln's view of
himself.[19] The day after Lincoln arrived in Washington, he made a trip to
Brady's Washington branch, now more grandly called the Gallery of Photographic Art, to have his picture taken. It was to be the first of many trips
to the studios of Brady and others in the area. As Adams and other Founding Fathers had decided to make Washington a visual symbol of American
unity and pride, so Lincoln exploited the new medium to impress his own
image of solemnity and seriousness of purpose on the eyes of the nation.
The pictorial invariableness of his dress—a funereal coat and pants that,
Hawthorne wrote, looked worn so much that they "had grown to be an
outer skin of the man" (310), together with the tall stovepipe hat that
made an extremely tall man look taller—invested him with an air of destiny. Those who knew him complained that his photographs never did
justice to the animation that lighted his otherwise listless features when he
talked or told a story. But perhaps he realized better than they how
the photograph conveyed something of his own direct appeal along with the
magisterial distance of a Washington. Even his insistence on going to the
fateful performance of *Our American Cousin* at Ford's Theater fits into
what seems to be his sense of the need to appear before the people. Lee
had surrendered only a few days before and Grant was to appear before
Lincoln and his cabinet the next morning. The play, which Lincoln had
seen before, celebrated American spirit and energy. A new unity, he hoped,
would be born from the war, and central to the public display of the presidential box was a large engraved portrait of George Washington.

Like Lincoln, Mathew Brady also seemed summoned by history to give
it a new face. Previously a consummate businessman, during the Civil War
Brady paid so little attention to his business that he emerged from it virtually bankrupt and spent most of the remainder of his life trying to persuade the government to buy his photographs. If Lincoln was the face of
America, Brady, with his blithe willingness to take credit for the work of
all his staff photographers and his frequent reprinting of the photographs
of others as his own, was its omnivorous eye.[20] With his wagons filled with
cameras, plates, and developing fluid, Brady plunged headlong into the

19. Lincoln did, however, deny that Howells's biography was "authorized," as the
publishers had advertised—an intriguing bit of hairsplitting. The first campaign
biographies had appeared in the 1824 campaign, when wrangling within the Democrat-
Republicans had ended the "era of good feelings" and votes were divided between
John Quincy Adams (the winner), Andrew Jackson, William H. Crawford, and
Henry Clay. In 1876 Howells's offer to write a campaign biography for Rutherford
B. Hayes was enthusiastically accepted. In the next election, 1880, the year *Ben Hur*
was published, its author, General Lew Wallace, also wrote the biography of suc-
cessful candidate Benjamin Harrison. See Brown, *The People's Choice.*

20. Along with Renaissance artists like Rubens, Rembrandt, and others, Brady
believed that as founder and head of his studio he could sign and thereby take credit
for any work done under his leadership.

Civil War, as if driven by some inarticulate need to preserve on film the apparatus of war, the destruction, and the death. There were generals enough in the photographs of Brady and the many other photographs of the Civil War, although they were usually dwarfed by the figure of Lincoln. But more than generals, more than troop trains, and more even than battles, what remains in memory are the bodies and skeletons and scattered paraphernalia of the dead. Photography had gone to war almost from its earliest days—in the Crimea, in India—although never in such numbers and never before with such fascinated focus on those who had not lived to march in victory celebrations or returned to put a medal on the mantel and reminisce to grandchildren. One wonders what customer would willingly pay for a photograph of black workers shoveling up the bones left after the Battle of Sharpsburg? But Brady took the picture anyway, and many more like it. Not so long after his depictions of "illustrious Americans" had given such a giant shove to the cult of celebrity in the nineteenth century, Brady plunged into photographing those whose only fame came as members of the anonymous dead. Wittingly or not, Brady took the newest means of visual preservation and used it in a devasting critique of those traditions that united fame, glory, and memory with military prowess and military victory. Instead of the tunes of glory, he sounded the Petrarchan theme of the tight embrace of fame and death. Often, he himself appears at the edge of some well-posed photograph of a general's staff. But just as often he looks away from the camera, onto a battlefield that the war has swept across, leaving its debris.

That Brady, the photographer of the famous, should become obsessed with war and death and that Lincoln, whose face and actions stood as a perpetual rebuke to the artifices of aristocratic theater, should be murdered by a second-rate actor, neatly expresses the crisis of national and personal self-consciousness marked by the Civil War, and every American war since then. Franklin's face is the prelude, and Lincoln's face marks a final and radical separation of the image of the American public man from the iconography of the aristocratic and military past. But even directness and plainness and principle needed to exploit the new ways of reaching an ever-widening audience. Few of those who voted for Adams or Jefferson may have known what they really looked like. But by the time of Lincoln, the photograph had made the dissemination of the face even easier than that of the reputation or the ideas.[21] And the pace was ever quickening. Lincoln's funeral train wound through the states for two weeks so that the people might mourn him in person. Even so, it has been estimated, it took months before a majority of the population even knew he had been assassinated. Just under one hundred years later, with the new resources of radio and television, most of the population of a much larger United States

21. Frederick Hill Meserve, the great collector of Lincoln photographs, estimated in 1955 that there were 132 separate depictions of Lincoln taken between 1847 and his death in 1865. Stefan Lorant, examining for duplications, puts the number at 104 (292–93).

had heard of the assassination of John F. Kennedy within twenty-five minutes.

*　　*　　*

Unquestionably, Western man though he be, and Kentuckian by birth, President Lincoln is the essential representative of all Yankees, and the veritable specimen, physically, of what the world seems determined to regard as our characteristic qualities.

—NATHANIEL HAWTHORNE

To the Universal Yankee Nation, of which I am Proud to Be One, I dedicate These Pages.

—Dedication to *The Life of P. T. Barnum, Written by Himself*

The archetypal relation of both Lincoln and Barnum to the idea of being a Yankee illustrates the different ways the American image went after the Civil War. Until then, the American image at home and abroad was spearheaded by Washington, Jefferson, and Lincoln—political men who defined the spirit of their country like European monarchs. But after the Civil War, no president until Theodore Roosevelt could compete in name and face recognition with men such as Barnum, Mark Twain, and Thomas A. Edison. Other figures were crowding onto the public stage—impresarios, writers, inventors—each inspired with the possibility he might be the quintessential American. With them, the theater of public life that before had been so scorned, attacked, or cautiously embraced became an essential part of the equipment of everyone who aspired to popular recognition, just as theater and spectacle itself became a more common part of the new American life of cities and industry and railroads, growing beside and beginning to replace towns and agriculture and horsedrawn transportation. For Mathew Brady the American president was the prime American notable and all other celebrities arrayed themselves in his shadow—a belief that Brady's own movement of his prime activities in photography in 1849 from New York to Washington underlined. But American attention was already shifting away from the exclusive celebrity of the president to styles of fame and aspiration at once more individualistic and more flamboyant.

Just across the street from Brady's New York studio stood the business of the great pioneer of the post–Civil War style of exoticism and profuseness, P. T. Barnum. As Brady had distilled a pre–Civil War visual style of austerity and dignity that was still Roman and stoic in its motifs, P. T. Barnum was the impresario of a newly expansive America, intent on collecting and exhibiting everything that was or claimed to be unique—the best—the only. Writers about Brady are frequently apologetic as they shy around the question of whether Brady was an "artist." After all, he often left the photographing to his cameramen or was not even around when some pictures were taken, and he frequently reprinted pictures taken by others as his own. Torturously, the historians of his work tell us that such "plagiarism" was a common practice in those days. But it is more interesting to align Brady with Barnum, not as an artist but an impresario and a collector, someone intent on exhausting the world of its variety and detail. So many of the prominent figures of the period between the Civil War and the First World War—Brady and Barnum, Rockefeller and Edison, Carnegie and the Wright brothers—were less original artists than men whose great talent was for connecting—putting together things that had never before existed so clearly, so brilliantly, and so effectively. They were self-made men, and their stories were the spur to a thousand lesser careers. But they made themselves from materials ready to hand.

The career of Barnum illustrates the increasingly elaborate sense of being in public that characterized the American performer and the American audience of the later nineteenth century. From 1835, when he made his first show business coup by exhibiting a woman who was supposedly 161 years old and the nurse of George Washington, through his exhibiting of Jenny Lind, Tom Thumb, and thousands of other attractions, until he helped found the tradition of gigantic traveling circuses in the 1880s, Barnum was at the forefront of virtually every important change in the nature of nineteenth-century entertainment, and his genius for the public display of both his attractions and himself highlights a host of related phenomena. Throughout his career, Barnum presented an array of oddities, performers, and theatrical exhibitions that helped shape a new audience for visual display in America. In contrast with the earlier puritanical belief that theatrical display was at its best personally ambitious and at its worst decadently aristocratic and impious, Barnum, the enterprising New Englander, marks the characteristically American shift to a conviction that the stage is the proper display for the democratic, the unique, and the natural rather than the hierarchic and the artificial. Lincoln as perceived by Hawthorne stands between Hawthorne's own literary inclination to praise retirement and obscurity as the test of true value and Barnum's style of necessary self-advertisement, without which that value would never be apparent to the public who wants to know. In such a democratic theater, the old idea that spirituality was possible only without an immediate audience was being superseded by the assertion of American popular culture that there were kinds of spiritual grandeur and uniqueness that flourished best in the eyes of others.

Barnum's career can be handily divided into two periods, with the Civil War roughly in the middle, corresponding to a general shift in the attention of the American audience. From 1835 to his bankruptcy in 1855, it is the individual visual oddity that attracts audiences; from 1860 to his death in 1891, it is the spectacle. Periods of great theater and periods of ostentatious public men do seem to overlap frequently. Greek theater in the fifth century B.C. set the stage for Alexander the Great's search for worlds to conquer and heroes to supersede. Actors and orators learned from each other in the Roman Republic, and there is a strong symbiosis between the rebirth of European theater in the sixteenth and seventeenth centuries and the procession of outstanding monarchs who inspired and learned from its example. The nineteenth century is also such a period, with popular entertainment growing in tandem with the popular revolutions that helped create such political figures as Napoleon, Washington, and Lincoln and such artistic specialists at self-display as Byron, Dickens, and Twain.

Barnum was a prime product of the new age because he became world famous not for anything that he did himself so much as for the way he focused attention on the talents, the peculiarities, and the unique nature of animals, objects, and other people.[22] The typeface now known as "Barnum," with its strange mixture of a grandiose alphabet and its familiar pointing fingers (☞) memorialize Barnum's great genius for drawing mass attention to whatever he chose to exhibit. As many people in Bridgeport or San Francisco later remarked, no one thought much of Tom Thumb or Admiral Dot when they lived around town, until Barnum got a hold of them and turned them into "attractions." As he says in his autobiography, he was never interested in any business that did not depend almost exclusively on speculation—the realm where the material and the imaginative meet—and Barnum's talents were most apparent in that area of speculation where the relation between the object and the profit it brings is least predictable—popular entertainment. He was the impresario, the continuity between all the disparate shows he was presenting, and his audience identified with him more than with his shows because he also invited them to appreciate his knack for knowing what people wanted to see by explicitly asking the basic question of entertainment: Is it worth the price of admission?

Barnum's exhibits were often not worth anything like the prices he was paid to show them. But he brilliantly exploited the desire of a democratic audience to become involved in the show as much as they were involved in their politics. This was not an audience that expected nothing more than to look passively upon aristocratic display, gaping at some grandeur that existed without their intervention. This was an audience, Barnum instinctively realized, that wanted to be "in the know," privy to the backstage, aware of the finances of programs, and up to the minute in matters of con-man sleight of hand and trickery. If Barnum had directed his shows only to the "sucker born every minute," he would never have become the folk hero he was. Instead he just as often revealed his tricks, treating himself as a display like any other in his repertoire. He drew back the curtain most elaborately in the volumes of autobiography that began appearing in 1855, but it was an integral part of his shows as well. As he wrote, "The titles of 'humbug,' and the 'prince of humbugs,' were first applied to me

22. Barnum's only possible competitor for the mid-nineteenth-century prize of most famous American was Paul Morphy (1837–1884), who by 1857 was already recognized as the greatest American chess player and then proceeded to tour Europe defeating all of their greatest as well (that is, all who dared to play). But Morphy, who refused to play for prize money, was upset at all the attention and virtually retired from chess in his early twenties. Some twenty-five years later, in response to published praise of his ability, he wrote a letter to a New Orleans newspaper saying how much greater were the chess achievements of his father and grandfather, who had taught him the game.

by myself" (102). Neil Harris has argued that Barnum let his audience into the act by allowing them to distinguish the humbug from the real. But Harris's analogy between the human puzzles Barnum presented to his audience and Poe's cryptographic detective stories makes the discovery of the real more important than Barnum allowed. Illusion or reality was not a choice Barnum or his audience had to make. They reveled instead in the all-embracing if momentary belief compelled by the show itself. For Barnum to be exposed as a fraud could never undermine, only enhance, his showmanship. Coleridge thought that art required a "willing suspension of disbelief." But nothing so static would satisfy Barnum, who interwove belief and disbelief in an unceasing dialectic. The ordinary con man (a social type that appeared for the first time during Barnum's career) might use the flimflam situation to fleece the unsuspecting rube of his wallet. Barnum not only revealed his tricks, but also made the audience love it and come back for more—because they had been given the privilege of being let in on the processes by which the illusion of reality had been created. He put his audience on their mettle as people of sophistication and insight into what was true and what wasn't—and charged them admission for the chance to prove it.

Barnum's career showed from the start a genius for taking a preexisting situation and making it into an unprecedented attraction. His first exhibit, bought from two other men who had only mediocre success with her, was Joice Heth, the slave who claimed to be 161 years old and George Washington's nurse. Perhaps she was neither; and perhaps the "Feejee Mermaid" was only a monkey cadaver carefully grafted onto a fish. But Tom Thumb and Jenny Lind, the Swedish singer, were certainly everything they claimed to be. To note these four triumphs of the first half of Barnum's career might give the impression that he moved from questionable if not sleazy exhibits to performers of real substance. But that would obscure the similarities between these attractions as well as what they tell us of the audiences that applauded them. Joice Heth, whatever she was in fact, was at least a metaphoric link to the Revolutionary past that in 1835, the year of Tocqueville's visit to America, was slipping away. To sit and listen to someone reminisce about the boyhood of Washington—and Joice Heth was considered to be a wonderful talker and tale-teller—made that past live directly, not as a collection of national icons, but as something more personal and immediate. In her way she was the progenitor of every friend, relative, or employee of the famous who makes a living by bridging the gap between the audience and those otherwise inaccessible figures. Like so many of the objects Barnum was already beginning to collect for the museum he established in 1841, she was a kind of relic, a talisman by which the mystery of the past could be made less mysterious, akin to autographs, photographs, the wooden leg of Santa Anna, the club that killed Captain Cook, or the birthplace of Shakespeare, which Barnum once tried to buy for transportation to America. Writers have often contrasted the European museum—so authentic, well catalogued, and officially sanctioned—from its nineteenth-century American counterpart, also called a "museum," although composed of equal parts theater, sideshow, and storehouse of strange objects. But in cultural implications they were quite similar. As the arguments over Napoleon's artistic booty indicate, the European museum was a rarefied arena for national rivalries. The British accused the French of amassing a collection based on military aggression and seizure (rather than their own supposedly enlightened amateurism and curatorial care). The French accused the British of trying to take away their treasures so that the British Museum would be the most preeminent in the world. Where the Romans might have shown their booty in triumphs, the nineteenth-century English, French, and Germans built museums: to collect the sanction of the past and amass the artifacts of the present in a form that celebrated the aesthetic and historical worth of other countries while underlining their loss of political and military power. History, said the museum, achieves its meaning through my viewing and arraying of it. In such a competition, the entertainment-oriented American museum may be only stating more blatantly the imperial control that the European museums downplayed in their emphasis on the canonization of standards of taste.

Once again, with his American Museum, Barnum picked up something that already existed (it had been Scudder's American Museum). Through his ability to use all the powers of the press—"to which more than any other cause I am indebted for my success in life" (36)—he turned it into a national and then an international success. Unlike the European museum, which exacted a subordination from its visitors even as it assured them that England or France or Germany was the summation of all the world's and history's power, Barnum's American Museum constantly trumpeted its audience's praises by illustrating how everything worth looking at in the world, everything amazing or unique in any way, either originated or wound up in America. In contrast with the academic gentility of the European collection, Barnum's museum celebrated all that America contained. It was a possession of its people rather than that of a particular class or its view of history. On his three-year tour of England and the Continent with Tom Thumb (1844–1847), Barnum taught the world about the fame of America as a nation as well as how fame was being created in America. Cannily enough, he began his campaign for making Thumb an attraction in England by totally ignoring the theater until he had successfully won over the aristocracy. On his arrival in England, English theater managers had told him that a midget was at best a poor draw. But, as Barnum carefully revealed, Tom Thumb was no ordinary midget to be pitied by the crowd as a somewhat sad and peculiar freak of nature. Like Joice Heth, he was an oddity perfectly at home with and proud of his difference from others and exuberantly cheerful about exploiting it in detail. Self-assured and confident, he specialized in gentle mockery of the great and pompous, with his scale-model court dress and carriage and his imitations of Samson in a loin cloth and Napoleon in full regalia. Unlike the midgets of Europe, who recapitulated in the circus their carefully defined role in the Renaissance royal courts, Tom Thumb represented a new democratic midget, thumbing his nose at hierarchy in the friendliest possible way. For a monarch like Victoria, whose underplayed royal style seemed organized as a denial of Napoleonic grandeur, he was an instant success. He was later received with equal pleasure by Louis Philippe, the "bourgeois monarch" of France (who made a point of carrying an umbrella in public) and Polk in the White House. By the time the promotion was well launched, Barnum was discovering that he had become a celebrity himself.

Barnum was no primitive version of modern-day showmen. If anything, they are pale imitations. To appreciate what he accomplished, we must think back to a time when European aristocrats easily welcomed him and his performers into their private salons, and when Abraham Lincoln could interrupt a cabinet meeting to receive and banter with the newly wed General and Mrs. Tom Thumb (otherwise Charles S. Stratton of Bridgeport, Connecticut, and the former Lavinia Warren of Middleboro, Massachusetts). The usual explanation is that Lincoln was looking for comic relief in the midst of the awful pressures of the Civil War. But he was also entertaining American celebrities whose faces and names were beginning to become at least as recognizable as his own. At a time when Lincoln was attempting to hold the country together, here were people, Barnum in particular, who were recognized in Europe not as northerners or southerners, impresarios or midgets, but as Americans. Already in 1850 one English tourist had self-consciously adopted Emerson's phrase and called Barnum a "representative man," *the* American of the nineteenth century as Washington had been of the eighteenth century (Harris, 56). When the Prince of Wales came to America in 1860 for a visit, the highest ranking European ever to see America in person, Barnum proudly announced that his museum was "the only place of amusement the Prince attended in this country" (320). Inevitably, the prince and his party also spent a good deal of time being photographed at Brady's gallery across the street.[23]

Thus Barnum, with his American Museum and his many individual exhibitions and promotions, put his own imprint on the central American question of how to bring together the varying individualities of the American people into something resembling a coherent nation. Each superlative was not at war with every other but pulled together, to the greater glory of Barnum. In particular he pioneered in what might be called the spiritualization of the performer by emphasizing the role of nature and spontaneity in performance. Thus, in the 1850s, Jenny Lind, a European star known primarily to music lovers was turned by Barnum into a phenomenon to be appreciated by millions. As in the American vision of democracy itself, the sanction of nature would validate both the normal multitude and the

---

23. According to Barnum's autobiography, when Ulysses S. Grant returned to the United States after the two-year trip around the world that followed his presidency (1877–1879), he told Barnum that no matter where he went, everyone wanted to know if he knew Barnum (440). Barnum adds that he has received a letter addressed only to "Mr. Barnum, America" (441).

unique individual, the rule and the exception. Only then could the audience not only watch the show but somehow also empathize with it and participate in it. As Neil Harris remarks about Barnum's promotion of Jenny Lind:

> Her performances seemed natural rather than artificial, the spontaneous expressions of a great talent. . . . It was The Spirit of Artlessness presided over by The Spirit of Artifice, and Americans loved it (117, 141).

Thus Barnum concertedly exploited a prime motif of American entertainment, now so familiar: the psychic theater of the natural performer who sings from the heart. In our own time, especially after World War Two, singers such as Judy Garland, Maria Callas, and Janis Joplin similarly exploited the audience's breathless involvement with them. But in the typically raised ante of contemporary fame, unlike Jenny Lind, they also increasingly dramatized their own testing of the edge of physical and psychological disaster—"being themselves" as both idols and victims, constantly pushed by the audiences on which they depended to new feats of psychic and aesthetic cliff-hanging.

But I am getting ahead of the story, for the private lives of Barnum's stars were exhibited primarily to celebrate the unthreatening normality under the surface strangeness. He considered the element of nature in his exhibitions to be the grace, the restorative for the theater, just as his constant efforts to perform ostentatious public service helped undermine the charge of greed and materialism to which he, like so many other nineteenth-century entrepreneurs, were easily open. The 'natural talent' of Jenny Lind, like the feisty directness of Joice Heth and Tom Thumb, redeemed them from any charge that all self-display was the work of the Devil or the European aristocracy. Washington, Adams, and Jefferson could advertise their disinterest primarily through the hierarchic forms of heroic iconography handed down by Renaissance art. But Barnum and Brady made capital of what Lincoln exemplified: An interest turned into disinterest by a straightforward, unbuttoned, demystified presentation of one's public self.

The pre–Civil War half of Barnum's career corresponds to the period of American history in which the individual frontiersman—the pioneer, the scout, and the explorer—embodied a still strong sense of possibility and new beginnings unencumbered by European precedents. Americans of all adventurous sorts spread across the country, giving their names to hills, mountains, rivers, and every conceivable bit of distinguishable landscape. Nature was to be named in American accents, and the naming itself was more a goal than the civilization it seemed to denote. Men like Daniel Boone no sooner named and set up towns and villages than they became disgusted by them and moved on. Barnum's own brand of collecting, naming, and celebrating nature similarly embodied a restless urge to move on. But, with the tremendous push the Civil War gave to the development of industry and the railroad network spanning the country, this frontier entrepreneurship was transformed into a much more elaborate effort to flatter not only the audience's sense of being in the know, but its new awareness of American power as well. In both American entertainment and American civic life, lavish performance was becoming the prime draw, both mirroring and staging an exuberant political and economic expansion. Prizes, contests, and memorial plaques flowered everywhere to mark triumphs large and small; national, local, and personal. Regional and small-town pageants flourished and remained popular until World War One, with their dramatic and picturesque amalgams of past history and future optimism, enthusiastically expressed with the help of a local cast. In 1870 Barnum established "The Greatest Show on Earth," with Don Castello and W. C. Coup, a great innovator who pioneered the use of railroads for circus transportation and introduced the second ring to the show. Here was such a profusion of entertainment that no one could possibly take it in at once, except to say, 'It's all here in America for my benefit.' As Neil Harris remarks, "amplitude had replaced humbug as the vital attraction" (275), and an essential part of amplitude was the explicit advertisement of how much money was being spent to entertain the audience. Julius Caesar and Augustus, like good Roman politicians, affirmed their positions as public benefactors by displaying wealth, armies, and wild animals in public games. Barnum did all that and more. Pageants like Barnum's 1874 "Congress of Monarchs" (purchased from a London circus) were like the old sideshow exhibits in the American Museum, except that instead of prodigies of time and nature, here were lavishly detailed and intricately adorned representations of all the rulers of every country on earth and the most prominent figures from history, dressed in historically authentic costumes and meekly arrayed for Barnum's audience. It was a show, said one eulogizer, unrivaled as "a public spectacle" since the days of the Caesars. Unlike the lavish display of monarchical or imperial power, from which the nation at best received a reflected glory, Barnum's shows emphasized the riches at the beck and call of every American, every individual, who chose to be in the audience. It was spectacle with the illusion of intimacy, as if each viewer were like Ludwig of Bavaria, for whose solitary pleasure full orchestras and companies of performers put on Wagner's new works. When in 1887 Barnum's circus joined forces with those of his greatest rival James Bailey, the banners proclaimed that the new combine constituted the "Centralization of All That Is Great in the Amusement Realm."

Historians have argued that the lavishness of American popular entertainment in the late nineteenth century created a passive audience. But they were passive like potentates, gorging on the profusion and variety that only aristocrats and the very rich could have afforded before. In format and explicit ideology, American popular entertainment, unlike that of other countries, thereby constantly emphasized its basic myth of a classless culture. Barnum, by his canny exploitation of the 'natural' performer before and the overwhelming spectacle after the Civil War, not only articulated but also helped stage and mold those urges into their modern shapes. Although such shapes still exist in other forms, perhaps the frantic publicity surrounding the birth of the Dionne quintuplets in May 1934 was the last time a truly Barnumian event captured the world's imagination. Here was everything that Barnum would have wished for: an act of nature verging on the freakish, yet surrounded by images of innocence both in the babies themselves and their supposedly unaffected doctor Roy Dafoe, who labored for virtue rather than money. Like the audience of Barnum's marvels, the public felt in some way that it owned the Quints and that they were displayed for its benefit. Barnum had encouraged the public to believe it always had a piece of the show and determined its unfolding. He would have appreciated Andy Warhol's notorious remark that in the future everyone will be famous for fifteen minutes. Just wait your turn, he might have added. Your only price of admission is the willingness to be a good audience for everyone else.

Self-made in USA

The church of St. Autonomous (whom I have not the honor to know). . . .
　　　　　　—EDWARD GIBBON, *Decline and Fall of the Roman Empire*

Have I . . . said anything unworthy of Daniel Webster?
　　　　　　—WEBSTER on His Deathbed

By the later half of the nineteenth century, then, even before the tremendous expansion of audience and the media sophistication of our own century, both the resources and the public were available to be exploited and appealed to by those aspiring either to construct greater stages or to appear on them. In France, for example, Napoleon III had followed in the footsteps of his uncle by pressing into service not only the artists and artisans of traditional monarchical display, but also the banner makers and wall painters who were helping found modern advertising. But as usual America pioneered in the implicit democratic and modern assumption that *everyone* could and should be looked at. This it seemed was one of the privileges for which the American Revolution was fought. Napoleon I's career had sent to the men of the nineteenth century, regardless of profession or politics, the message that opportunity for greatness could be seized and molded by oneself. America, a whole nation built on the assumption that God helped those who helped themselves, made that attitude an article of national faith, essentially unquestioned until after World War One. And in that assertion of the will, self-help and self-display were difficult to distinguish. From 1845 on, for example, there was an increasing rivalry between Edwin Forrest, an American Shakespearian actor, and William Macready, the reigning British Shakespearian, over who was the greatest dramatic actor. Although this may seem trivial to us now, it excited great controversy and many prominent citizens took public sides, usually for Macready and "culture." But the partisans of Forrest were so ferociously bent on establishing the superiority of the American performer that finally, in 1849, when both actors were playing in town, the conflict broke out in riots in which some thirty people were killed and more injured. David Grimsted in *Melodrama Unveiled* points out that the Astor Place riot effectively ended a period in which the theater audience, like a kind of popular electorate, exercised a rough control over the activities of managers and performers. But the raucous competition between a homegrown sense of theater and its European forebears was hardly beginning.[24]

In the process older forms of heroism were transformed as well. Up through the eighteenth century, the military and social "honor" of an individual often demanded a duel if that honor had been insulted, for the insult had been made to a sense of integrity that could be defended only by besting the one who had cast doubt on it. The more characteristic assertion of one's honor after the midcentury, in contrast, was to dare something never before attempted, even something foolhardy, like the charge of the Light Brigade in the Crimean War (1854) or the expedition of Gordon to Egypt or Rhodes in Africa, Churchill at Gallipoli or T. E. Lawrence's solo turn in Arabia. As the world became more charted and known, adventurers sought out the remaining unknown and dangerous spots. And always the adventure had to issue in something more than mere victory. There had to be overwhelming odds or some other strange and miraculous detail of setting and situation. In a world without cosmic standards for behavior, the heights of military honor especially demanded godlike scaling. In an increasingly civilized world, the truest glory seemed to come from fearless expeditions into the remaining hearts of "savagery" and "barbarism." Only by fighting with or against the pure and primitive honor of the Indian or Tuareg warrior might the civilized soldier vault outside the perfunctory norms of honor and into some more rarefied place. It is not hard, say, to imagine that Custer brushed aside reports of a massive Indian encampment along the Little Big Horn because that kind of battle was what he sought. The year was the centennial year of 1876; Custer was thirty-seven and thus two years past the minimum age eligible to be president; and a swift, miraculous victory against the Sioux, Cheyenne, and associated tribes could have an enormous effect on a Democratic Nominating Convention scheduled for July. No one can be sure that such thoughts were actually in his mind. But Custer's expeditions always attracted both journalists and freelance photographers looking for sensational material. The flamboyance of his earlier career plus the general atmosphere of military and political glory-hype that characterized the later nineteenth century makes it plausible

24. The theatrical rivalry seemed to exist on the psychic level as well, where personal nature and national character mingled. Grimsted intriguingly contrasts Forrest's public conviction that his performances were always perfect fulfillments of Shakespeare's intention with the self-critical doubt Macready confided to his diary.

that Custer may have been on a quest beyond immediate self-glorification. Photographic equipment was still too cumbersome to take along on an expedition that had to move as swiftly as that against the Sioux "hostiles" in 1876. But one of those killed with Custer at the Little Big Horn was Mark Kellogg, a reporter for the *Bismarck Tribune*.

Crucial to the dissemination of such fame was therefore those new professionals on the American scene—the journalists, who simultaneously said that there were wonderful stories and people in the world but that they were only really appreciated when written about in the pages of the daily newspaper. The newspapers were especially intrigued by expeditions into exotic places and feats of daring, sometimes performed by their own reporters, who adroitly positioned themselves only a hair's breadth away from the central figure. One of the most popular ongoing news stories of the period, for example, was the search of H. M. Stanley for Dr. David Livingstone, the Scottish missionary and African explorer. Livingstone was, of course, not "lost" at all, as far as he and anyone interested in him was concerned. But as far as the *New York Herald,* who hired Stanley, was concerned, he was lost to the public. Like Nelly Bly and other hero-journalists of the period, Stanley was the reporter as explorer, searching out the dark places of the world for mapping and domesticating as information to be presented with a flourish to the readers back home.

When big city dailies expanded after the Civil War, journalists almost immediately nominated themselves as intermediaries between their readers and those they wrote about, familiarizing the already famous and celebrating the previously anonymous, like so many Dantes deciding who should be allocated to hell, purgatory, or heaven. Certainly not all nor most of the varieties of fame they celebrated were entirely new. There was publicity enough for the older forms of honor and status, especially the military and the political. But the newspapers and magazines, by their incessant highlighting of individuals and events to sell papers, and their tendency to translate every situation into the terms of personal will and conflict, were instrumental in creating the signs by which modern fame would be recognized. Mathew Brady had pioneered the focus on visible fame, and the Crimean and Civil wars had introduced the camera as a source for newspaper illustration. By the 1880s the perfection of the halftone print allowed photographs to be printed directly. Henceforth cameras went everywhere, and the pages of the daily newspaper opened an infinite number of windows onto private and public, domestic and exotic experience. The newspaper journalist carried the possibility of seeing more than had ever been seen before into every nook and cranny of his city and the world. While European city planning—say, in Napoleon III's Paris and Franz Joseph's Vienna—reemphasized the power of a newly wealthy middle class, the American city of the late nineteenth century, with its constantly shifting neighborhoods and influxes of population both from abroad and from other parts of the country, emphasized the energy of variety and newfound connections. Social hierarchy was, of course, already embedded in the older American cities, but the dominant impression resembled Barnum's circus of profusion and immediacy—while the European city concentrated its energies on grand boulevards and massive architectural summaries of past traditions. In this civic variety, the newspaper publishers were the new impresarios, and Barnum's perpetual conflict with James Gordon Bennett of the *New York Herald* lightly veils their actual affinity. For the mass reading public, they were akin to more philosophic Victorian sages like Emerson, Carlyle, and Arnold, great comprehenders whose task was to see the world whole.

Like Barnum with a lion-taming act or the dime novelists recounting the adventures of Western heroes, the journalists and other publicists of late nineteenth-century success were selling the public a fascinating blend of empathy and control: empathy with the successful; control through information about them and their world. Here, they said, were people whose integral sense of self, their "character," allowed them to make sense of the world, that is, ensure their success in it. And that success, whether it came from being a famous gunfighter or a money-making industrialist, was affirmed by fame. Even the virtuous had to appear on stage, as Mark Twain parodied in "Story of the Good Little Boy":

> Jacob had a noble ambition to be put in a Sunday school book. He wanted to be put in, with pictures representing him gloriously declining to lie to his mother . . . and pictures representing him standing on the doorstep giving a penny to a poor beggar-woman with six children . . . and pictures of him magnanimously refusing to tell on the bad boy who always lay in wait for him around the corner as he came from school, and welted him over the head with a lath (67).

If virtue was observed, if lights were not hidden under a basket or talents buried in the ground (favorite biblical texts of the period), then the virtuous would surely rise in the world. Virtue, character, and integrity were the hallmarks of being self-made, and the self-made man (there seemed to be few if any self-made women) was the cynosure of every journalist intent on bringing the news of America to itself. In the self-made country, who had not the potential to be self-made himself, with the help of an equally self-made audience? To complement Barnum's celebration of imperial grandeur with another style of national showmanship, Buffalo Bill Cody at the age of twenty-six had ended his Western career to take the part of an Indian scout on the New York stage.[25] In 1883, some eleven years later, his Wild West Show toured throughout the United States and Europe. Like the poor but honest little boys being celebrated by Horatio Alger and others as destined for democratic greatness, the independent frontiersman in the late nineteenth century had to be staged in order to be appreciated. Industrial society was gathering momentum in America. But the stories of self-made busi-

25. The author of the play who had persuaded Buffalo Bill to take the plunge from 'real life' to theater was Edward Z. C. Judson, known as Ned Buntline, a prolific writer of adventure novels and the organizer of the anti-Macready mob at the Astor Place theater riot.

nessmen, intrepid frontier heroes, and reclusive inventors implied that it was still possible, perhaps even now more possible, to do great things on your own, and make a name, especially in America. With its emphasis on the secular meaning of election, in which the audience elects its representative (instead of God electing the special individual), the modern democratic state had implied that the civic hero might be deeply emblematic of all the people rather than an alienated seer or artist—in the aristocratic European model. By the mid-nineteenth century Cinderella was not the otherwise obscure but worthy person picked out by the careful eye of the prince, but, in the form of cabin-to-White-House Abraham Lincoln, she could be the president chosen by the electorate. Thus American popular entertainment had transformed the show of monarchy, whose point was to watch someone who is clearly inimitable and different, into the show whose point was to watch an extension of oneself, in a performance put on for one's special benefit.

The element of theater is central to the concept of the self-made man because it binds together its spiritual and material aspects and allows us to see why financial success could be praised by a whole generation of churchmen and spiritual leaders as divinely ordained. The Civil War had forever destroyed an older concept of unity that had supposedly been embodied in America. But just as Lafayette's visit was seized on by journalists and essayists as an opportunity to reassert the virtues of disinterested social virtue, so the concept of the self-made man, tentatively stated in the 1840s and 1850s but pervasive by the 1870s and 1880s, presented a new way to justify American progress and character. Thrust forward by the popular press's new resources for focus and celebration, it was a style of social being consonant with the aspirations of the age, and both the self-made man and his publicists were intent on transforming the internal sanctions of the old morality into external structures of behavior and self-display. When Robert Burns asked in the late eighteenth century for the power "to see oursels as ithers see us," he wanted that eye as an outside monitor so that, in the subject of his poem, we might not put on airs without realizing there was a louse visibly crawling around on our head. Armed with such self-awareness, Burns could play the self-consciously "original" Scottish peasant for the delectation of the Edinburgh literati, while in America Benjamin Franklin, as he tells it, monitored himself into a career remarkable both for its personal achievement and its contribution to the civic good, despite the negative connotations of such self-regard. But by the 1870s and 1880s the antitheatrical prejudices that most American Protestant sects shared with their European fellows had been replaced by a new willingness to believe in outward signs of election and spiritual transcendence. Popular preachers like Dwight Moody took to the road and put on shows as elaborate as those being mounted by Barnum and Bailey. God's shows, ran the reasoning, should be at least as lavish as the Devil's. In Barnumian terms the passage was like that from the earlier humbug and sideshow to the elaborate circus. After being uplifted by the natural performer in the imperial setting, the audience would go away with an enhanced sense of self for having been present.

Daily life, the Reformation had argued, was a calling as spiritually powerful as any activity more obviously connected with religion. Now, making money (an activity distinctly disapproved by Luther among others) could be even more spiritual—*if* you were a self-made man. Barnum and others referred to "the gland of acquisitiveness" as a basic part of human nature, which extended equally to the accumulation of goods and property as well as to the spiritual self-possession that allowed material success. Thus the money society, in which success meant accumulation, could argue that it was the material realization of the immaterial and spiritual democracy so valued by Adams, Jefferson, and others of the Founding Fathers. In the rough equations of etymology, "fortune" through the seventeenth century had often meant "fate." By the eighteenth century "fortune" took on a more financial meaning, and those innumerable fictional heroes whose adventures were crowned with an unexpected inheritance gave a phrase like "good fortune" the appropriate double meaning. With the great economic expansion of the later eighteenth and early nineteenth centuries, the way was open, or at least much more open than before, to make one's own fortune. It was no longer necessary to bow before fate or even wait for the just reward of virtue from a conveniently rich relative. Fortune was the reward of work, as popular novelists like Horatio Alger would emphasize in a great outpouring of fiction beginning in the late 1860s. Like the open and unlimited field for ambition promised by America itself, "fortune" was less tangible than abstract, a symbol of the new spaces into which the human spirit could move. It was not taken from others, but wrested and molded from nature itself—and there were an infinite number of ways to get it, if one were clever enough. Ideally it came as a by-product of the restless desire for achievement—the adventurous tracking of the pioneers, the daring experiments of the scientists and inventors. The social myths of America in the nineteenth century hardly needed Darwin to validate their assumption that aggression and competition and exploration beyond previous human achievement was an evolutionary trait, a vital need of the human spirit, and a testimony to the nature of America itself. If money came with it, it was the only way society knew to recognize a genius for which money was essentially irrelevant: The best of all worlds, of course, was to be paid for being yourself.

Thus the concept of the self-made man allowed ambition as well as material wealth to profess a spiritual justification. One could strive without guilt for a few more dollars, some battle ribbons, or a grand obituary because God was the true audience; others only eavesdropped. Stultified traditions and creaky hierarchies were all European society had to offer; in America such social fates were overthrown and in their place were set individual morality, industriousness, and perseverance. Journalists set the tone, and soon enough businessmen were blowing their own success horns—Barnum, Carnegie, and John D. Rockefeller among others. From the presses of America and England poured book after book of personal witness to the pursuit of happiness through social mobility and financial accumulation. In an echo of Defoe's view of William III's "personal virtue," inherited wealth and status was a curse; only what was achieved by oneself counted. And each individual who succeeded validated the American promise of success: Whoever you are, wherever you came from, the pursuit is open and free.

Usually such books said very little about the specific talents or methods necessary for success. Success was a spiritual concept. It came entirely from within the self and it built from the ground up, both financially and psychically. The individual's prime resource was "character," which itself was not innate so much as self-controlled and self-created. One of its more obvious manifestations was temperance, which in the nineteenth century meant the refusal to drink alcoholic beverages—a cause ferociously promoted by Barnum among many others. Barnum also proudly retells several anecdotes of his self-control when informed of various personal disasters, including the devastating fires that wrecked his museum. With character and self-control, you could always build again, and, like Diderot's actor, stand back from oneself and admire the social being you had shaped so well.

The success literature typically celebrated the young man from the country who gets to the big city and by character and self-control wins through. The implication was that only in that big city was there a stage adequate for one's talents and that only there would they be truly recognized. Self-made achievement may seem to be defined by its unwillingness to give credit to any force but the dynamic individual. But it was the presses of the city that ground out the publicity for such spiritual solipsism, just as they furnished the dime-novel settings for heroic action on the frontier. Public people, especially those who were rich and successful, were becoming the coin of daily conversation, and their success was something that audiences wanted to read about. It is hard to know to what extent such works were in fact the handbooks to success they professed to be or were instead the first wave of a marketing of vicarious aspiration and success fantasy that has grown infinitely more elaborate in our own time. The young man whose character speeds his rise from poverty to riches and the movie star whose beauty is discovered at a soda fountain have much in common as social fantasies. Even though the self-made young man may actually have to run a company to validate his success, he, like the movie star, is essentially celebrated for his inward, spiritual qualities. In the church of secular achievement, they are both among the saints.

Like so many public aspects of America itself, the concept of the self-made man was an attack against aristocratic privilege. The self-made man owed nothing to influences, especially European ones, and received no help from family connections. Before the Civil War particularly, he was proud of being self-taught. His education was empirical and practical. After the model of Napoleon, he was often especially skilled at mathematics, the pre-eminent gateway to advancement for the new world of business and invention, just as Latin had been for the Renaissance humanist and artist. But now classical studies were often scorned for their "useless" liberal arts, and "genius," with its impractical flashes and unmethodical procedures, was beginning to be the subject of frequent mockery. Like the etiquette literature directed to rising merchants in early seventeenth-century England, nineteenth-century works on self-help concentrated more on manners and morals than on actual methods of business or engineering or invention. But they often dispensed as well with the literary lists earlier books considered necessary cultural baggage. With a world to be constantly remade, there was little time for the past.

Abraham Lincoln had ascribed his winning the presidency to the Cooper Union speech and Brady's photographs. But he was also helped immeasurably by popular tales of the rise from poverty to greatness that allowed his election to affirm some basic belief in American potential and growth.[26] Self-making implied an open-ended world in which there were enough materials for everyone. So long as there were examples of individual success around like Carnegie or Rockefeller or other giants of the late nineteenth century, it was possible to believe that the self-made businessman might be the central model of personal energy and integrity for the entire society— allowing for a few corrupt versions to be read off the moral manifest. Through the economic disasters of 1897 and 1903, publicists and ideologies of self-help still continued to argue that failure was caused primarily by the bad characters of individuals rather than by any flaws, let alone inherent rhythms, in the general system. In 1909 the journalist Elbert Hubbard could still successfully publish a two-volume collection of his interviews entitled *Little Journeys to the Homes of Great Businessmen,* while Julian Ellis in *Fame and Failure: The Story of Certain Celebrities Who Rose Only to Fall* (1919) indicated the inability of a group of now-forgotten nineteenth-century big names "to pass unscathed through the fiery ordeal of success" primarily because they didn't know how to handle money.

World War One, by emphasizing not the openness of opportunity but its limits and, by dramatizing the difficulties of unilateral action by individuals or nations, effectively undermined the myth of endless possibility. Some seventy years after Lincoln, the United States would elect as president a man who embodied the characteristic self-made man of the post–Civil War period, the businessman-engineer Herbert Hoover. But by then the idea of the self-made man had lost most if not all of its cultural centrality. The businessman as an emblem of progress, personal achievement, and the ability of the individual to defeat the great weight of time was becoming hopelessly outdated in a world of more impersonal corporations, where the sights of success tended to be set not at the top but somewhere in middle management. As Laurence Wyllie points out, the self-made man, a concept that in the nineteenth century had been an aid to social progress, be-

26. Horatio Alger also wrote boy-oriented biographies of Lincoln and James A. Garfield (1881).

came in the twentieth century an instrument of social control. As society tightened and became more orderly, the same traits that before might blaze a trail were now in danger of rocking the boat. The vicarious element of success stories, which lulled the audience into passive self-satisfaction, replaced the possibility that they might become inspired and thereby more active. In a tenacious effort to make business the central calling of American life Bruce Barton, in *The Man Nobody Knows* (1925), argued that the businessman was a service-oriented idealist whose ultimate model was "the founder of modern business," Jesus of Nazareth. Rebelling against the ethereal, unworldly Jesus, Barton asked, "To what extent are the principles by which he conducted his business applicable to ours? And if he were among us again, in our highly competitive world, would his business philosophy work?" (163). The answer, of course, was a resounding "Yes!" Jesus, it turned out, was a great businessman and aggressive advertiser of his product. Once again the emphasis in "self-made" had fallen not on the making and the product but on the self, the spiritual achievement. Businessmen might be realists in their methods and operations, but what justified them for Barton, for Theodore Dreiser, and for other literary admirers was spiritual energy. Dreiser's image of that energy, however, unlike Barton's, was more Napoleonic than Christian, or, to turn the analogy another way, perhaps Barton's emphasis on *service,* like that of Andrew Carnegie, John Wanamaker, and other late nineteenth-century successes, aimed to take the curse away from activity that might otherwise seem an insult to the society that had enriched them. The problem of the businessman-hero, like the problem of the self-made man, was the conflict between civic responsibility and individual assertion. Barton's image of Jesus the businessman attempted to provide an inner spiritual armature for a material surface that was often undistinguishable from ordinary greed. In a world of advertising and consumption, he proposed a visionary commerce to reconcile the need to sell the self with the self-disgust that such selling had to be done.[27]

27. *The Man Nobody Knows* was a tremendous best-seller when it first appeared and is still in print more than half a century later. Barton himself was one of the founders of modern advertising, whose small firm became Batten, Barton, Durstine, & Osborn in 1929. He helped the Republican party try to change its upper-class image during the Roosevelt years, created Betty Crocker, and supplied the Salvation Army with its prime slogan: "A man may be down, but he's never out." It is intriguing to speculate about what he would have thought of a businessman-messiah like the Reverend Sun Myung Moon.

Corvo and London: A Status Beyond Money

The motto of a great actor should be *aut Caesar aut nihil.*
—HAZLITT, "Whether Actors Ought to Sit in the Boxes"

The idea instilled in the minds of most boys, from early life, is that
of 'getting on.'
—"Success in Life," *Harper's Magazine* (1853)

Barton's postulation of Christ the businessman is an effort to respond to
the perception that, for many Americans as well as European observers
from Tocqueville on, American materialism bred not a selfless individualism oriented to civic and social good but one preoccupied with personal
gain and power. To disentangle the strains of the spiritual and the material
in the American attitude toward money is not the point here, for the ambivalence toward money is akin to that toward earthly success and fame.
Heroism and celebrity in America has from the first been so tied to the
transcendence of history as a way of making an impression on history (and
one's immediate audience) that the intricate interplay between public assertion and private evasion that characterizes the careers of so many nineteenth-century American public figures is almost a natural growth. The
goal is to attempt to purge achievement of all negative implications—to
strive purely, to win without defeating, to be committed to the life of
achieving—while constantly trying to avoid the compromised surrender to
a sordid public gaze. In the course of the American nineteenth century
Franklin's self-monitoring effort to mediate personal desires and social effect may have metamorphosed into the popular idea of the self-made man
whose success was to the glory of the nation through the grace of God. But
from the first there was a countervoice that equated success with accumulation, greed, and temporality, while failure was a signal of selflessness, morality, and the sanction of eternity. The tendency, as we have seen, had
ample precedent in English and European poetry. In America it was given
an added push by the part of the country most tied to European and aristocratic ways—the South—which had, coincidentally or not, also lost the Civil
War and lost out as well on the postwar industrial expansion that made aggressive self-making a national priority.

In the postwar South failure was connected to a spiritual honor that
could look down on the purely quantitative honor of the North. Robert E.
Lee, the prime Southern hero, believed in a more pervasive self-monitoring
than even Franklin, and his letters to his children are filled with behavorial
admonitions. Like Lincoln's, his ambition was to supersede the Founding
Fathers, and he believed that by heading the Confederate armies his goal
would be accomplished. His armies did not win, but with defeat he ensured that they would remain morally pure. After the war Lee refused to
sell his name to some inquiring companies and became instead the presi-

dent of Washington College. While Grant's presidential administration was involved in numerous scandals, Lee built the school (later Washington and Lee) into one of the best in the country. While Mark Twain was publishing Grant's memoirs, Lee was already dead and on his way to becoming the South's saint of the lost cause, whose moral power came in part from his material failure, adorning the heart of every Southern town with a memorial to the honored dead. Thus was the myth of the noble but tragic South embodied in Lee, exonerated from all blame and heaped with all praise. Unlike the greedy, self-made men of the North, he had a "character" inside and remained the standard of Southern heroism until the premature death of Elvis Presley supplied yet another saint of failure, whose natural talent and moral nature had been usurped and warped once again by the success-hounds of the North.[28]

Thus even in the democratic society of the United States, the nineteenth century witnessed an ambivalence about worldly and especially monetary success that was already well rooted in literary and artistic Europe. Public men had seen the benefit that spiritual sanction gave their politics, and writers especially found it difficult to disentangle the impulses to ostentatious self-staging, on the one hand, and anticommercial reclusiveness, on the other. In the past some were less famous than others. But with the unprecedented expansion of the media of publicity in the nineteenth century, the quest for fame had become much more complicated: in some ways, more a matter of choice, and in others, more a creation of uncontrollable forces. Whether it was expressed in nineteenth-century Europe's imperial expansion or nineteenth-century America's push across the continent, the national assumption of unalienable assertion was often accompanied by a growing anxiety, especially among writers and artists, about one's individual status as a person worthy of recognition, let alone a genius or a member of the artistically elect. In Europe the fervent courtship of commercial artistic success could give rise to feelings of social inauthenticity and personal inadequacy that could be purged only by an embrace of the imagery of failure and wilful isolation, the cultivation of rejection, disguise, and anonymity. In America as well by the later nineteenth century, there was a strong ambivalence about the ability of success to validate achievement, especially in writers like Twain, Jack London, and Frank Norris, who all wanted to believe in the myth at the same time that they dramatized the examples of corrupt status and illegitimate achievement that they saw all around them. When Pope or Rousseau published their letters, confessions, or autobiographies, they sought to supply an inner world of values and

28. According to Thomas Connelly and Barbara Bellows, Presley's death in 1977 set off "an outpouring of grief unmatched since" Lee's funeral in 1870. In their fascinating book, *God and General Longstreet,* Connelly and Bellows persuasively show how the Southern deification of Lee required shifting the blame for his military defeat at Gettysburg to Stephen Longstreet, "the scapegoat of the Lost Cause" (30). Thus Lee could become not merely soldier or Southerner but ideal citizen, the representative of a superior culture tragically lost.

feelings to justify and exonerate their public images. But in the model supplied by American natural performers like Walt Whitman, Mark Twain, or Jack London, we are treated to endless Chinese boxes, each one claiming to be the really personal under the last seemingly personal: This time I'm really going up to the edge, this time I will really tell the truth. Every revelation, however sincere, presupposed a revelation to come. Mark Twain in his notebooks speaks of "my double, my partner in duality, the other and wholly independent personage who resides in me" (348–349) in tones that would not be out of place in Baudelaire or Poe. But Twain's division is even more clearly that between the private writer and the public figure, whose platform performances (of course, under an assumed name) defend him from invasion, just as his fruitless efforts to make money from a new printing technology can be interpreted as yet another effort to maintain control over the lucrative but erosive processes of his own self-exposure.

Two disparate careers of the late nineteenth and early twentieth century, one American and one English, crystalize some of the forces in the air at the dawn of both an immense leap forward in communications, with film and radio, and new and unforeseen modifications in politics, as Napoleonic self-sufficiency mutates into the personality cults of totalitarianism. The two figures I have in mind are Jack London (1876–1916), the American author of immensely popular books about animals and men, and Frederick Rolfe (1860–1913), who called himself (among other things) Baron Corvo, and is remembered less for his books than for his strange life and personality. Two more different writers would be hard to find in the same period: in one corner, the hearty physically assertive American plainspeaker London, a "natural" writer whose literary progeny include Hemingway and Norman Mailer; in the other, the Catholic convert and aesthete Rolfe, whose baroquely mannered style of writing and drawing was preoccupied with the world of the Renaissance and the arcane lore of religion and diabolism. Yet each in his own way constructed a public nature to be the armor of his ambition. Although London more obviously succeeded as the fountainhead of an American tough-guy school of literature and Rolfe more obviously failed as a baroque version of nineteenth-century dandyism, their wrestlings with the impossibility of achieving a truly satisfying and unalloyed recognition are remarkably similar. Corvo's career intricately reflects the tradition of the European neglected genius, constantly searching for the good patron, while London can be cast as the quintessential self-made writer, the American natural genius in search of the good public.

Frederick Rolfe was a painfully self-conscious product of the nineteenth-century contemplation of the nature of artistic genius, with its stress on an eccentricity close to madness and its antagonism to the modern world of business and progress. Impelled by an almost overwhelming sense of his own superiority and importance, he constantly staged a life in which he was playwright, producer, and main character. Perceived as self-contained and self-possessed by those who admired him, he created a myth of himself, at first to make his way in the world, but later to compensate for what he considered to be its ignorance and rejection of his work. Like Oscar Wilde, Rolfe sought to send his bizarre personality forth into the world to clear a path for his literary talent—to act like a genius so that people might pause and conclude he actually was one—in what Frank Harris, another practitioner, called "the personality school of success." But Wilde, until his trial, exile, and subsequent death, was inordinately successful in merchandising himself as the prime "aesthete" to England and America, along with writing a body of work that gave strong foundation to his aspirations. Rolfe in contrast never managed to extend his reputation beyond the very few who read his books and the even fewer who ferociously appreciated them and supported him until, like some late-blooming Rousseau, through petulance or paranoia he would attack them for stifling his genius. Like Joseph Conrad's fictional *Lord Jim* (1900), Rolfe was so intent on realizing only the ideal possibilities he envisioned for himself that he was never satisfied with anything he had actually done. As soon as anyone—patron, publisher, friend—praised Rolfe or sought to help him, an invariable progress began, characterized by his continually escalating demands, that usually ended in contemptuous rejection of the person for not having done enough. In the context of a late nineteenth-century avant-garde that was distilling an aristocracy of the spirit from the heady mixture of dandyism, Catholicism, and diabolism, it seems almost inevitable that Rolfe, the son of several generations of piano makers whose family business had recently failed, first sought validation for his inner sense of uniqueness in the Church where dwelled the Supreme Recognition, Authority, and Audience of God. For years he attempted to join the Church and win its approval not just as convert but as priest. (In later life he sometimes signs himself "Fr. Rolfe," as if to imply he is a priest, and dresses in monastic garb.) But in fact he is rejected by the English Catholic hierarchy for any duties higher than one of the faithful, and thereafter tries alternately to win them over to his cause or to attack them for having fallen from the Church's Truth.

When he takes his case to Rome and again fails to be accepted, he sets up as a painter and takes a job painting religious banners and icons. In the meantime Rolfe had begun to have some success as a writer, publishing several stories in *The Yellow Book,* the greatest commercial success of the 1890s and the flagship of the Decadents. In addition he was writing under several other names for newspapers and magazines as well as completing a historical work entitled *Chronicles of the House of Borgia* (1901). But his most lasting work, although it was hardly successful at the time, is *Hadrian the Seventh* (1904), a novel in which Rolfe's own feelings of uniqueness and isolation are transcendently realized and justified in the story of an English Catholic, alienated and scorned by the conventional Catholic establishment, who becomes the pope. Thus at least in fiction the outsider is discovered to be the prime insider; the Church celebrates and honors what her minions had rejected. In *Hadrian the Seventh,* as in so many of his later works, Rolfe uses his writings as the occasion to stage his revenge on those who had mistreated him and his previous work by refusing to recognize and properly receive his genius and his calling. In *The Quest for Corvo,* published some twenty years after his death, A. J. A. Symons 'explains' Rolfe's combination of megalomania and revenge as a compensation for not having his genius properly recognized, as if it were a rational and wilful, if exaggerated, response to real events. But both Rolfe's desire for spiritual and aesthetic recognition as well as his inability to understand the relative indifference of the marketplace come from the same source. Obsessed simultaneously by his conviction of uniqueness and the need to demonstrate it to a corrupt world, Rolfe can draw on neither the Miltonic solace of the "fit audience" nor the Wordsworthian rejection of the public for the people. Each present praise always implied what might have been or what should be. The actual audience of friends and acquaintances who sincerely admired his talent were under constant threat of denunciation because they prevented him from reaching the ideal, undefinable audience he believed he deserved. Only God's applause could really suffice, and at least on earth his approval had been thwarted by the doltish timeservers of the Church.

An outsized and exaggerated mirror of the late nineteenth-century belief in the otherworldly sanction of artistic aspiration, Rolfe yet constantly sent off manuscripts to a huge variety of publications and publishers. Since both his career and his personality were animated by the world's refusal to celebrate him on his own terms, everything he did might be material for a justifying posterity, and he seized, for example, on the slimmest excuse to write elaborate letters and notes, even to those living nearby or in the same house with him. Similarly, what he considered literature itself to be was in accord with his temperament and ambition. Unlike writers who contemplate the past with either antagonism or embrace, Rolfe was interested neither in literary tradition nor in literary history so much as in his own specially chosen group of cult books with whose contents and authors he could identify himself. Most of them came from the Italian Renaissance, which in the later nineteenth century was enjoying a tremendous revival and celebration. Jacob Burckhardt's *The Civilization of the Renaissance in Italy* (1860), with its exposition of Renaissance individualism and its definition of the Renaissance "state as a work of art," was only one of the most prominent in a flood of books, translations, and editions. Among other results, they gave an immense push forward to the modern interest in Dante, Petrarch, Boccaccio, and other authors of the period, whom we think of as perennially important but who actually had been hardly read for hundreds of years. Rolfe especially steeped himself thoroughly in Cellini's *Memoirs,* with their image of the dynamic artist: ferociously competing and picking fights with everyone around him, yet infused by an almost holy dedication to his art and a belief that its power conveys far greater glory than the merely material status of rulers and soldiers.[29]

Literature for Rolfe was thus a repository of styles of being, to be taken on and put off as he chose. With the great exception of the modern fantasy of *Hadrian the Seventh,* Rolfe's works were often set in the past, and he characterized himself as an emissary from another, better, artistic culture, now virtually wiped out by the new world of mass publishing. Unlike, say, a "modern" American author like Mark Twain, who in 1876, it is said, became with *Tom Sawyer* the first writer to submit a typewritten manuscript to his publisher, Rolfe submitted nothing typed. He wrote his books, like his letters, in a personally devised script, with various colored inks, and, says Symons, "a vast fountain pen." The books were also hand illustrated and then elaborately bound, with Rolfe's own designs on the leather. When they appeared on the publisher's desk, neither their look nor their size corresponded to any familiar format. Inside, as if to distance their eccentricity, Rolfe often chose to present his writings as discovered manuscripts. Like the Gothic novelist using the device of the ancient manuscript or the collection of cryptic notes, Rolfe thus imbedded his own imaginings in the heart of time, costuming his works as he costumed himself. The effect was deliberate, for Rolfe viewed the past not as part of history but as a special place, an alternate world where personal style in the present could be justified by its connection with ancestral heroes. Thus what remains striking in his works is his command of surfaces and the theater of things, while in his personal life and artistic career he characterizes himself as forever trapped in a plot spawned by men—specifically the officials of the Catholic Church, recalcitrant publishers, ignorant patrons, and others, but ultimately by the malevolent Destiny that refused to grant him the ultimate validation he sought. Throughout his life his favorite image for himself was a crab, a figure that appears frequently as a personal monogram, as he himself appears as Nicholas Crabbe in *The One and the Many* and *The Desire and Pursuit of the Whole,* discovered at his death in Venice. After years of staying alive on the charity of a few acquaintances, these last works turn out to be biting satires on all the people who tried to treat him well according to their lights. The titles, with their adaptation of metaphysical concepts to a vision of society, are vintage Rolfe, the Platonic One identified with the irascible but immensely talented outsider searching for integrity, and the Many with the degraded, imperceptive mob determined to thwart him.

29. Rolfe's assumption of the name Frederick, Baron Corvo as his literary pseudonym (or, as he called it, "tekhniknym [trade name]") is usually explained in terms of his relations to the Catholic Church and an early patron, the Duchess of Sforza-Cesarini—most thoroughly so by his most recent biographer Miriam J. Benkowitz. But it seems more suitable that such an idolator of all things of the Italian Renaissance might have taken his title from the monk of Santa Croce del Corvo, who supposedly was given the manuscript of the *Inferno* by Dante himself, because the monk recognized in the seeming vagabond exile a man of genius.

From Tobias Smollett in the eighteenth century down to Rolfe and beyond, one animating modern desire for fame, especially for those who keenly feel their alienation from the realms of glory to which they aspire, has been a revenge on the world for the destiny that somehow caused them to be born in the wrong place. According to the myth of self-assertion and innate genius, their rise should have been effortless, like Napoleon's or Byron's. But society's irrational and corrupt system of determining value forces them into warped shapes and ignoble conniptions to regain their rightful place. So they become misanthropic and crabbed, satirists when they should be idealists. Seventeenth-century revenge, in its Machiavellian and Jacobean versions, usually involves stage managing, personal betrayals, and the manipulations of others in an effort to achieve an undeserved temporal power. But revenge in the modern period takes place in a world where there are many who feel similarly deprived of their rightful place and applaud the revenger as a hero of the spirit striking out against a dreary fate. For the writer particularly it is a revenge against a materialistic world that has ignored the spiritual claims of art and the artist. In *Hadrian the Seventh* Rolfe's often unpleasant real nature is thus turned into benevolent eccentricity, and his paranoia about enemies intent on denying him the accolades his genius deserves is transformed into a triumphant justification as the world acclaims him pope. He reigns for a year and then is assassinated by a Socialist fanatic, his immortality assured.

In Rolfe's almost caricature version of the later nineteenth-century religion of art, career has given way almost entirely to calling. Fame or success should therefore come as it would to a priest with a vocation: Once you have it, you can never lose it, and so will immediately be accepted into the fold. But Rolfe was not accepted, in part, he said, *because* he spent more time on painting and writing than on religion. The wielders of Church authority, he thought, were denying a proper place to one of the most truly spiritual, the preserver of a transcendent ideal, who craved recognition in the name of an absolute aesthetic and spiritual rectitude that yet forever disdained any that he actually received. Accordingly, even in his most destitute state, Rolfe always trusted to fortune. When he did have some money, he rarely thought about using it for future security. His calling would protect him. Through the dense thicket of the letters, denunciations, satires, lawsuits, and incidental writings that poured every day from his pen to publishers, lawyers, friends, intermediaries, and editors about the disposition of his work and the protection of his rights, shines his unquenchable belief in the sanctity of his words and his name, whatever name he chose to take. His recent biographer, Miriam Benkowitz, remarks that, "despite" all the letters (including one denouncing the "unauthorized" thanks for his help in preparing a Venetian hospital report), he finished his more serious literary works. But the energy of revenge argues that it is not *despite* but *because*. The Satanic sense of injured merit fed and was fed by Rolfe's conviction of his artistic calling and mission. Like so many aspirants for fame in the nineteenth century and later, Rolfe was moved by a desire to be popularly recognized and accepted for being out of the ordinary. Nicholas Crabbe, his fictional alter ego, is said to have had a previous life as Odysseus. Thus came together, years before Joyce's *Ulysses,* the outcast modern and the central ancient, the pilgrim-wanderer ennobled by his links to both a past and a posterity that truly appreciate him. In literary modernism's fascination with the theme of reincarnation and transmigration of souls appears once again the artistic effort to establish a sanction and genealogy that can neither be eroded nor effaced by modern society. In the modernist fascination with the difficulty and obscurity of the work of art appears another polemic against too easy acceptance, the mocking of immediate fame for the fame that lies ahead. All of Rolfe's strangeness is therefore for his fans an emblem of uncompromising art and uncompromising selfhood in the face of a hostile world.[30]

Inspired by the dream of an artistic and personal justification outside of bourgeois time, Rolfe sports a lineage from Poe and Baudelaire, and, like Poe, Rolfe alludes to premature burial several times in his works as an image of the indifference the true artist receives from the world. Because his literary accomplishments, even *Hadrian the Seventh,* pale so much next to the repellent magnetism of his personality, Rolfe seems particularly the victim and emblem of a cultural promise that one is special and ought to find out how. In his lifetime admirers were drawn to him because he acted out so lavishly an obsession with recognition on one's own terms that by the 1890s filled many who were either too fearful or too ironic to pursue it themselves. After his death he became a cult figure, and in 1929 a Corvine Society was founded in London. Once safely interred, the eccentric whose fiery presence scorched the ground while he was alive can be transformed into a benevolent deity of sustaining individualism. In Symons's *The Quest for Corvo,* which no doubt sold more than any of Corvo's own books, we can watch the process at work. One of the founders of the Corvine Society, Symons is lured to know more and more about this mysterious and fascinating person, and to become, by his own admission, the only man in the world who has read all that Corvo wrote. Through his quest of the enigmatic Corvo, "a defeated man of genius," Symons, who otherwise wrote little, discovers a shield to brandish against the constant demands of the modern world to sell out. With its structure of mystery and its combination of intuition and scholarly technique, *The Quest for Corvo* is reminiscent of the symbiotic relationship between that great scholar-aesthete of the 1890s, Sherlock Holmes, and his nemesis Dr. Moriarty, or between Dr. Jekyll and Mr. Hyde. Yet here the atmosphere of crime has been transformed into that of a spiritual mission. This is virtually a religious "quest," in which Corvo's own quest for God's validation is replaced by Symons's for Corvo's elusive model of the artistic life. Corvo for

---

30. Unlike Symons's tale of the enigmatic search, Benkowitz's biography turns Corvo's life into the dreary facts of squabbles with landladies, evictions, and so on, thus eroding and even half destroying the fragile edifice of his artistic self-presentation. It is a revenge by recognition that even Corvo could not have foreseen.

Symons, like Poe and Guys for Baudelaire or Chatterton for the Romantics, is a figure of exoneration, a solace for his own sloth about "getting ahead" and a talisman to ward off the pyramiding corruption of the modern world of advertising, popular success, and the obsessive turning of the unique into the repetitious.

*   *   *

The founding of the Corvine Society is only one instance of a widespread canonization of the modern artist as grand victim of a hostile or indifferent world. Yet, with all the contempt for the popular and machine-made reproductions of the individual artistic vision and for all the experiments with obscurity, allusion, and secret reference that make the work an enigma to be actively engaged rather than a trivially immediate experience among all the rest, the embattled artist also sought immediate recognition from the proper audience in the proper terms. In the face of a massive audience with a variety of education levels and degrees of taste, as well as the new expansion of visual media begun in the 1890s with the first movie theaters, this apotheosis of the literary person as prime witness against a corrupt society was one way for the person of artistic ambition to maintain a self-sufficient bravado even as he stormed the heights of recognition. As the example of Rolfe's eccentric grandeur and self-stylization implies, the aspiration to an eternal fame that is yet fully appreciated in the present has by the end of the nineteenth century developed out of its roots in the paradoxical balance of the proudly neglected and into a style of flamboyant assertion. Whereas in the past, we might have to search letters and diaries for the more blatant admissions of artistic ambition, in the 1890s, with taste beginning to be codified by critics, museums, and academic studies, the loudly proclaimed unwillingness to accept no validation other than God or posterity has already become a familiar pose. In the comic mockery of Max Beerbohm, for example, the grand and ghastly battles with the double that image the turmoil of artistic ambition for Poe or Stevenson or even Wilde are represented as by-products of the rage for publicity.

Born in 1872, Beerbohm as a young man was already a contributor to *The Yellow Book,* published his first book in 1896, and in 1898 succeeded George Bernard Shaw as drama critic of the *Saturday Review.* But in an age of remarkable literary figures and baroque forms of artistic ostentation, Beerbohm remains always measured and self-effacing, negotiating through reticence his own peace with the encroaching public world. He was certainly not Wilde with his flamboyant public poses, but neither was he a misanthropic eccentric like Rolfe, creating the cult of his own art, nor a strayed reveler like A. E. Housman, who published *A Shropshire Lad* in 1896 to resounding and continuing critical success and then spent most of the rest of his life completing a massive edition of the *Astronomica,* a Latin astrological poem written by Manilius in the first century A.D.[31] Instead

31. Housman (1859–1936) seems to have divided his writing as well as his life into strictly personal and scholarly spheres. Manilius may be obscure to us and his poem of scant interest either as poetry or learning, but, by editing Manilius, Hous-

Beerbohm chose to stand aside and observe, through cartooning caricature, literary parody, short stories, and essays, the artistic world of his time—declining the grand gesture to work in miniature. Yet, with the exception of Hazlitt's intricate ramblings, Beerbohm probably has more to say about the ontology of fame than any other writer before World War One. Like Hazlitt, Beerbohm was fascinated by the performer who captured the public stage as actor or politician, even while he sympathized most personally with the reclusive and retiring artist. But while Hazlitt took on himself the critic's role of celebrating such unflamboyant recluses, Beerbohm directed the greater part of his energies into wryly contemplating the artist's often confused effort to be a public man, perhaps reflecting his own close relationship to his older half brother Herbert Beerbohm Tree, one of the great actor-managers of the time. Like Hazlitt's, Beerbohm's drama criticism is most illuminating when he talks about actors and actresses—Beerbohm Tree, Henry Irving, Sarah Bernhardt, Eleonora Duse—whose impression of their personalities on their role created the star system of the late nineteenth century, which would later find its way into motion pictures. In such writings he is able to compress wittily the anguish of a century of combat between the demon of publicity and the angel of obscurity. Henry Irving's effectiveness as a performer and public figure, he writes, is comparable to that of Disraeli: "[B]oth men preserved in the glare of fame that quality of mystery which is not essential to genuis, but which is the safest insurance against oblivion" (*The Incomparable Max,* 128). Or, as a young man in one of Beerbohm's stories, who has just taken over the business management of his grandly successful but hermitlike novelist uncle, remarks in tones that might have reassured Charlotte Brontë or Emily Dickinson: "Privacy is the biggest Ad" (*Seven Men,* 201).

Beerbohm's most incisive treatments of the question of literary fame are the stories "Hilary Maltby & Stephen Braxton" and "Enoch Soames," from the collection *Seven Men* (1919). Maltby & Braxton, whose names are linked in the title of the story as if they were a law firm or a store specializing in sophisticated umbrellas, are two young men whose first novels had created an enormous stir in the summer of 1895. "They were both of them gluttons for the fruits and signs of their success" (62), says Beerbohm the narrator, and he follows their careers in the newspapers as their names

---

man was following in the footsteps of Julius Caesar Scaliger and Richard Bentley, two of the greatest classical scholars of the past. Failing his final examinations at Oxford and leaving without a degree, he worked in the Government Patent Office for almost ten years, until a series of articles on classical subjects secured his appointment as Professor of Latin, first at the University of London (1892) and then at Cambridge (1911). Most of his poetry was written between 1886 and 1905, although *A Shropshire Lad* was not published until 1896 and *Last Poems* in 1922. His interest in Manilius began with an essay in 1899 and the edition appeared 1903–1930. Tremendously protective of *A Shropshire Lad,* Housman refused permission for any parts of it to be anthologized and willingly cut his own royalties so that it could be reprinted in cheap editions. With its celebration of the young man as an athlete-soldier doomed to die, it complements his successful effort to redeem his own failure and achieve great renown in the world of classical scholarship.

appear in the lists of more and more fashionable parties. But then both their second novels turn out to be failures and no one talks about them anymore. Beerbohm forgets them until he runs by chance into Maltby in Italy many years later who then tells him the story of their final competition—is not for critical approval or patronage but for invitations to aristocratic parties. At the Annual Soiree of the Inkwoman's Club, Maltby is invited by the Duchess of Hertfordshire to a weekend at her country home. When he is asked if he thinks Braxton would like to come as well, he replies cunningly that Braxton hates to leave town, is very shy, and therefore shouldn't be asked. Although Braxton overhears, he does not actually arrive at the party, yet Maltby constantly seems to see him, like some reproachable double out of Poe's "William Wilson," making his spectral appearances at just the right time to turn Maltby's little social triumphs into utter catastrophe. The greatest indignity occurs at church, when the ghostly Braxton comes down the aisle and sits directly on top of Maltby, eclipsing him as if he were in a bell jar: "You remember what a great hulking fellow Braxton was. I calculate that as we sat there my eyes were just beneath the roof of his mouth. Horrible!" (104). After the service is over, Braxton wordlessly blocks Maltby's way back to the duchess's stately home. Relieved that this is all he must pay, Maltby boards the train back to London, while the silent shade of Braxton watches from the platform. Unable to cope with the specter of Braxton's "envy, hatred, and malice," Maltby's guilt over his small move in the game of social fame propels him out of England with hardly a look behind. He finishes his second novel halfheartedly in France and then comes to Italy where he meets an invalid contessa whose wheelchair he is pushing when Beerbohm sees him again, twenty-four years later. As Maltby finishes his story by talking of his wife, we see that, whatever his withdrawal from celebrity parties, he has not withdrawn from the race for fame, merely translated it to another sphere:

> "She was the Contessa Adriano-Rizzoli, the last of her line. She is the Contessa Adriano-Rizzoli-Maltby. We have been married for fifteen years." Maltby looked at his watch and, rising, took tenderly from the table his great bunch of roses. "She is a lineal descendant," he said, "of the Emperor Hadrian" (111).

If Maltby's Italian apotheosis is reminiscent of the Corvine struggle for some transcendent validation of the sense of inner uniqueness, Beerbohm's Enoch Soames, the "Catholic Diabolist" poet who has published two volumes of his work with no noticeable public or critical impact comes even closer. And in "Enoch Soames" Beerbohm's own ambiguous artistic aspirations are also much more involved. Here he appears not just as an interested observer, but as someone whose success continually galls the artistic rectitude of Soames. As the story begins, Beerbohm, while only an undergraduate litterateur, has had his portrait included in a volume of prominent Oxonians and is quickly introduced to all the most fashionable artistic haunts in London. Along the way he meets the shadowy, almost insubstantial Soames, whose main characteristic is his hunger, "[B]ut—hungry for what? He looked as if he had little appetite for anything" (8). Although Soames wants Beerbohm's friend Will Rothenstein to do a drawing of him for his new book of poems, Rothenstein evades him and tells Beerbohm he can't draw anyone who is nonexistent. Somewhat later, after the publication of Soames's third book (the first two were *Negations* and *Fungoids*), Rothenstein finally does a pastel portrait of Soames and Soames places himself on view next to it in the gallery, although, says Beerbohm, "nobody who didn't know him would have recognized the portrait from its by-stander: it 'existed' so much more than he; it was bound to" (22–23).

So far the story of Soames's career is a light parody of obsessive artistic aspiration. But Soames has a pathetic side as well that indicates Beer-bohm's continuing preoccupation with the question of artistic failure, like a well-tailored working woman crying at the sight of a bag lady whose accumulation of rage underlines the precariousness of her own success and status. On the strength of a small legacy that keeps him alive, Soames has carefully tried to construct for himself the image of a pure literary man, complete with poetic clothes and poetic speech, total belief in his own work and total contempt for the work of others. His style, however, is not flam-boyant but reticent and melancholic. Or at least it tries to be. For in his effort to make his private self into an object of public praise and recogni-tion, he has succeeded only in effacing himself still further. Rothenstein's portrait is the most tangible fame he receives and, like Dorian Gray's por-trait, it is more real than he is. When Beerbohm meets Soames by chance in a restaurant, Beerbohm himself has become successful: "I was a—slight but definite—'personality.' " In the meantime, however, Soames has given up the construction of his own contemporary reputation as a failure, and he makes Beerbohm uneasy: "I was just what Soames wasn't. And he shamed my gloss" (24).

Yet Beerbohm discovers that Soames has still maintained enough self-esteem to want to test his sense of himself and his accomplishment against the judgment of history. At first, Beerbohm tries to console him by saying he hasn't failed; he's only been neglected. Posterity will give his due. But, says Soames with contempt, the hope of posterity isn't enough. If only, says Soames, he could go into the future, enter the reading room of the British Museum, and there look up his name and see what posterity has made of him:

> "Think of the pages and pages in the catalogue: 'SOAMES, ENOCH'
> endlessly—endless editions, commentaries, prolegomena, biographies"—
> but here he was interrupted by a sudden loud creak of the chair at the
> next table (29).

For A. J. A. Symons and the Corvine society, the quest for Corvo was a quest for the sacrificially neglected writer who allows them to live without guilt. For Soames, the quest is for the academic industry of a literary future that will sanction his status and self-respect now. So totally isolated is he in the present from even the smallest audience, and so grand are his expectations, that only his trip into the justification of posterity would be enough. Posterity for Soames has none of the grandeur of Horace or the solace of Emily Dickinson. It is a concept that can free one from the fear of neglect only if it can be actually tested and assured. As Louis XIV commissioned his historians to write of him as if they were in a future age recounting his accomplishments, so Enoch Soames would travel into the reading room of the future to look back and thereby find himself footnoted and edited.

Whereupon, in a gesture well suited to the aspirations of a Catholic Diabolist, the somewhat flashily dressed man sitting at the next table introduces himself as the Devil and offers to transport Soames to 3 June 1997—with the usual conditions. Soames quickly agrees, despite Beerbohm's protests, and thereupon disappears. Five hours later he reappears to submit sourly to Beerbohm's eager questioning about the future and what happened. The trip has been a disaster. Soames can find his name neither in the general catalogue nor in the *Dictionary of National Biography*. Finally, he calls for a new book on twentieth-century literature and copies the only reference to himself he can find—which describes Enoch Soames as an imaginary character in a short story by Max Beerbohm.

The story continues with Beerbohm's weak protests and the Devil's scooping up of his prize. But the essential tale is already complete. Like the narrator of "William Wilson," who discovers that by killing his rival he has killed himself, all of Soames's efforts at recognition and justification bring about only further neglect. Instead of making him more real because more famous, posterity has negated his existence entirely, while Beerbohm has increased his own reputation by the tale of Soames's fruitless effort to be known.[32]

* * *

It may seem like an abrupt step to move from Beerbohm's nonentity genius to Jack London, a tremendously successful American writer noted not for his precious mannerisms and obscurity but for his realism and robustness. But, viewed through the glass of Soames's obsession with recognition, there are acute similarities between London and Frederick Rolfe

32. There is no need to make any direct identification between Beerbohm's avid men in search of the glory of literary celebrity and Corvo, although Soames's affectations and his Catholic diabolism as well as the descent of Maltby's contessa from Hadrian make me wonder. But the general point is that such styles of being were common between the 1890s and the beginning of World War One, with their debt backward to the metaphysical dandies of Baudelaire and their inheritance forward in the sorts of 'literary' role playing that still flower in small colleges and artistic communities everywhere. Corvo's singularity was perhaps in the way he represented that style pushed to the utmost edge of life and death. The war itself also kept alive the concept of neglected genius by the number of promising young writers and artists it killed off. The nostalgia in the 1930s about such might-have-been geniuses is reminiscent of Wordsworth's celebration of Chatterton twenty-five years after his death and across the events of the American and French revolutions. The rift in time created by the great wars is bridged by mourning the glory that has passed unnoticed, and otherwise competitive friends can rally safely around the tomb of the prematurely dead genius.

528 / The Democratization of Fame

that both highlight the question of fame at the end of the nineteenth century and foretell something of the present grotesque celebrity of literary and artistic figures. The Soamesian or Corvine dead end of the effort to behave like an aristocrat without actually being one had ceased to be a major style of the American literary man after the Civil War. Abraham Lincoln, sanctified by assassination, had been a poor child of the raw frontier, not a rich Virginia landowner, and his promise was not that of the good great man Washington or the wise great man Jefferson, but the great man sprung from nowhere, the great man as Cinderella. The European Cinderella, like Napoleon or Rolfe, often proceeded to change into a being wholly different from his lowly roots, perhaps even ennobling his family as well as himself, but still somehow translating the aura of spiritual aristocracy into the furniture of tangible status. But the American Cinderella, like Lincoln or Twain or London, clung for both personal and public reasons to the unsophisticated simplicity and even poverty of his background. As an artist he was not the concealed original or the unacknowledged legislator of the world, but the man of the frontier, taking roads no one else had ever dared, mocking convention from the viewpoint of his indomitable and chosen separateness.

The European sense of avant-garde isolation, as we have seen, has roots back into the eighteenth century. The American is a somewhat more recent growth. But both try to characterize the artist not just as a person who creates words or pictures for entertainment, but someone whose work enlightens and whose character gathers within itself all that is precious about human will in a world increasingly complex and regimented. Thus the special salience of the homosexual perspective for later nineteenth-century European art, with its core feeling of simultaneous alienation from contemporary society and connection with the fellowships of the ancients and the Renaissance: Marginality in the present that was centrality in the past and future. Rolfe's homosexuality, for example, like that of many other artistic and literary figures of the period in England and Europe, further enhances the self-consciousness of an antisocial uniqueness that yet desires the social justification of fame and applause. Oscar Wilde's youthful merchandising of the style of exoticism, after a period of both commercial and critical success, tragically dares the edge between acceptance and rejection with the libel suit against the marquess of Queensberry that leads to his conviction for homosexual offenses (1895). Like Rolfe's, the demand was 'all of me, or none at all.' [33]

In the era of the realistic novelist and the journalistic muckraker, the mission of the American writer bore many ideological similarities to the

33. The connection between fin-de-siècle homosexuality and the styles of modernist fame deserves much more space than I can give it here. Hadrian the Seventh as a doppelgänger for Rolfe has multiple uses in this way: a harkening back to Hadrian IV, the only English pope, as well as to the emperor Hadrian who placed statues of his deified lover Antinous all over the empire. Benkowitz believes that Rolfe's passions were never physically consummated.

European, in their questioning of the values of the visible society and their revolt against a language that distorted reality. But whereas the European attacked bourgeois conventions and Victorian complacency with a mannered, whimsical, allusive, and often wilfully outrageous style, the American was after specificity and clarity: style as a rough, ready, and serviceable medium for experience, the style of no-style. The role of the avant-garde European artist was to reveal what had been ignored or shunted aside, to peer into the labyrinths of the past and present for the strange, the exotic, the difficult to understand. He worshiped an imagination opposed to physical nature, while the American artist played the part of the direct, the unadorned, and the natural. Unlike the European performer, who threw the cloak of elaborate costume and self-consciousness over his bare self, he was the democratic performer, letting bits of bareness show through to announce that there was no play acting going on here.

If the characteristic ambiguities of modern English and European fame focus in the figure of the neglected genius, the ambiguities of American fame appear in the stories of those geniuses whom fame has destroyed. In Europe those conscious of the dangers of fame want to be recognized, but on their own terms, and so they may become eccentrics or polemically avant-garde. In America their colleagues in aspiration are laden instead with the spiritual doubts that any fame on a large scale brings in its wake, and so they seek to nurture a fragile privacy that is their only defense against becoming mere cogs in the fame machine. Both versions spring from something like the Wordsworthian distinction between people and public. But the social situation again helps engender some crucial differences. Beerbohm, for example, writing about Whistler's prose, could say that "an amateur with real innate talent may do, must do, more exquisite work than he could if he were a professional. His very ignorance and tentativeness may be, must be, a means of especial grace" (*The Incomparable Max,* 147). This is very much in accord, say, with Baudelaire's and Guys's assertion of the true artist as a nonprofessional, a nonexpert. Using such language, we might call Jack London just that kind of amateur, who, as Beerbohm says, looks into the "recesses of his own soul" to express himself (*The Incomparable Max,* 147). But in fact London, like Ernest Hemingway, Theodore Dreiser, Sinclair Lewis, Norman Mailer, and so many other American writers call virtually the same traits not amateur but professional. Unlike the Europeans, in flight from a century bent on professionalizing every area of vocation, occupation, and study (including art) and therefore honoring the nonprofessional man of the world, the Americans, coming from a tradition in which the making of art was largely considered not an activity worthy of full-time masculine attention, want to be members of a craft, a profession, along with the rest of their countrymen.

Thus two types of artistic individuality face each other at the end of the nineteenth century, both self-consciously formulated to deal with different but analogous cultural situations. In their most distinctive forms, they cast their shadows on the nature of artistic self-assertion down to the present: the one homosexual and aesthetic, the other macho and "natural." But the seeming contrast between the tough-guy frontiersman and the aesthete-dandy is less important than their kindred place in the history of fame and the self-conscious masculinity of the premeditation and formulation of their codes of self. Intriguingly enough, some of the characteristics of the American author à la London or Hemingway may first appear in the attacks launched by *Fraser's Magazine* in the 1830s and 1840s against the post-Regency dandies. Ellen Moers in her book on *The Dandy* has incisively recounted *Fraser's* general polemic against dandyism, from its publication of Carlyle's *Sartor Resartus* (1833–1834) to Thackeray's frequent attacks against the dandy novelist Bulwer-Lytton. But those attacks may resound more loudly in American literature than they do in England or Europe. Specifically, *Fraser's* attacks a dandiacal (the word is Carlyle's) singularity that it calls essentially antinational. Like the aristocrat he imitates, the dandy asserts links of manners and fashion that transcend national lines. Dandies are therefore foreigners in their own country, and *Fraser's* proceeds to link dandyism with political radicalism of the type seen in England in the union agitations of the previous twenty years. No matter that it is difficult to see the perfumed dandies in company with the Chartist agitators. For *Fraser's* they are equally threats to "England," and therefore equally to be condemned. In their place *Fraser's* postulates as its nationalist code not a new political point of view so much as a new definition of masculinity and of work. Simply stated, it is a cult of manliness, of good comrades together, almost always accompanied by drink and drunkenness; and of work professionally accomplished (the craft of the writer) and professionally paid for (as opposed to the dilettantism of the dandy).[34]

The *Fraser's* polemic has obvious affinities with the pose of the American tough-guy artist, and the more aware writers who contributed to its formulation, like Thackeray and Carlyle, often drop hints that they were attempting to replace one style of self-consciousness with another, rejecting a rarefied, nose-in-the-air dandyism for a rough, hearty, and direct dandyism. Thus may be born the self-conscious polemic of a later style of American male writer, combining what is best in the working classes (good labor) and in the aristocracy (a commitment to national values) without their faults—the one's urge to combine for class interest and the other's disdainful isolation. But if the doom of the European dandy was often a dead-end eccentricity, the doom of the American he-man writer was its obverse, a public acceptance and acclaim that threatened to overcome and smother his preciously guarded "naturalness" and authenticity.

34. Although my emphasis has been on the concept of fame in Western culture, it is intriguing that nineteenth-century Japan also experiences an outpouring of books on self-help and self-making that help transform the samurai code of moral stature and masculinity into precepts more suited for an industrial society. See Kinmouth, *From Samurai to Salary-Man.*

*   *   *

He drove along the path of relentless logic to the conclusion that he was nobody, nothing. Mart Eden, the hoodlum, and Mart Eden, the sailor, had been real, had been he; but Martin Eden! the famous writer, did not exist. Martin Eden, the famous writer, was a vapor that had arisen in the mob-mind and by the mob-mind had been thrust into the corporeal being of Mart Eden, the hoodlum and sailor. But it couldn't fool him. He was not that sun-myth that the mob was worshipping and sacrificing dinners to. He knew better.

Thus muses the hero of Jack London's *Martin Eden* (1909), written when London himself, then in his early thirties, had enjoyed a tremendous popular success for almost ten years as an American writer whose work owed little to the European themes and styles that had dominated the national literature into the end of the nineteenth century. Like Mark Twain before him and Ernest Hemingway after, London was born not on the East Coast, but on the frontier, in his case northern California. Illegitimate and self-educated, his whole personal and social background suited him to be the Cinderella author, rising by his own efforts to the heights of fame and fortune. In the decade of the 1890s—when the Columbian Exposition announced a new vision of a powerful America to the world, when the Alaskan gold rush summoned American adventurers to the Klondike, and when Frederick Jackson Turner tied American character to the idea of an ever-advancing frontier that had now disappeared—Jack London as a teenage writer set forth simultaneously to learn all he could from books and life, ransacking the Oakland library and hitting the road in 1894. At first he traveled with a California army of the unemployed on the march to Washington and later alone in the company of tramps and hoboes. But all the while he observed, he took notes, and he collected facts and anecdotes for his later writings. Experience, especially the experience of situations unfamiliar to a middle-class reading public, was his prime source of literary capital. In contrast to the European plunge into the dark recesses of a dense social world, London's scenes lay outside of cities and towns almost entirely, in the struggles of men and animals both with each other and with the harshness of nature, where something like an "essential" or "natural" rather than a social and self-conscious character might appear and be tested. The 'natural genius' that the Romantic writer sought could be expressed in the figure of the teenage Chatterton, with his escape from the stagnant present into the heroic manners and language of the past. But writing connected the teenage London less with history than with immediate experience. His escape was into the world of nature and the "road."

However antiliterary such themes appear to be, they still had to be expressed in the printed word. London's books may celebrate adventure, travel, and new experiences rather than the refined lives of the sophisticated aesthetes. But he knew full well that they were still books, self-consciously written and pragmatically sent out to be sold. Like Corvo/Rolfe, London was a free-lance writer who responded to the great proliferation of magazines and newspapers in the late nineteenth century by sending out a stream of writings to all of them. Corvo, like the aesthetes of *The Yellow Book,* might still cling to the style of elegant dabbler. But for London vocation and self were one, and writing was a profession, just as the highest accolade on "the road" and one that London gives himself in his stories was to be a "profesh," top of "the primordial aristocracy" of tramps. *Fraser's* and the dandies could debate who best represented English literary tradition because each invoked a different class sanction. But one of the prime assertions of the American writer was his ability to speak for the country as a whole and to define its most cherished ideals. Whatever was natural and unspoiled and direct about him therefore also sought to be validated by popular success. The making of books especially counted; they conveyed the self and its style to a larger audience; and they brought the money that allowed you to do things you couldn't do otherwise, including acts of charity: "I am writing for money," wrote London to a friend in 1900, "if I can procure fame, that means more money. More money means more life to me" (Labor, 82). Thus London makes the goal of fame itself, like the amassing of money through writing, a way to personal freedom. Like Samuel Johnson's sarcastic dismissal of the aristocrat dabbler in literary fame, London's frankness about his desire for money only momentarily stands in for the unquenchable hunger to be *more* through writing that turns Corvo toward the spiritual calling of Church and Art, and London himself toward "the call of the wild." Byron "awoke" to find himself famous; he came out of the dreaming solitude of sleep into a world of admiring glances and applause. But the best metaphor for London's swift fame is the gold strike, the showering down of sudden riches. And one of the first symbols of true financial success for London was that he no longer had to take books out of the library. Now he could buy them for himself.[35]

London's goal as a writer is therefore a synthesis of thought and action, a popularity consistent with greatness. His human heroes possess strength and naturalness, but they often have as well the special sensitivity of the lover of literature. Unlike, say, Joseph Conrad, in whose stories of adventure and its meaning London found models for his own, he rarely celebrates any character for his lack of imagination and his single-minded

---

35. Compare Hadrian's prayer in *Hadrian the Seventh:* "You know why I want freedom, power, and money—just to make a few people happy, just to put a few things right a bit, just to make things easy, just to straighten out tangled lives whose tangles make me rage because I myself am helpless. Is that wrong? No—I swear my aim is single and unselfish. I don't want credit even" (15–16). On the other hand, the urge to put down a preoccupation with either art or money may be a reverse snobbery, as Igor Stravinsky responded to Nadia Boulanger's congratulations on the artistic triumph of his *Firebird* (1910): "That's not very important. What is, is that my name becomes a household word" (Rosenstiel, 91).

ability merely to do his job. His goal is more spiritual and therefore end-less, a quest for nothing more tangible than a better, fuller, more complete, perhaps more unselfish self. "You want to be famous?" asks Ruth, the upper-class young woman to whom Martin Eden has brought some of his early writings.

> "Yes, a little bit," he confessed. "That is part of the adventure. It is not the being famous, but the becoming so, that counts. And after all, to be famous would be, for me, only a means to something else. I want to be famous very much, for that matter, and for that reason" (128).

The "something else" here is the love and approval of this woman, con-ferred upon him with all the power of her emotional and social status. As he says later, "He wanted to be great in the world's eyes; 'to make good,' as he expressed it, in order that the woman he loved should be proud of him and deem him worthy" (192). But the woman sees him less as a lover than as a protégé: ". . . she was too busy in her mind, carving out a career for him that would at least be possible, to ask what the ultimate something was which he had hinted at" (128). When his grander inten-tions become clear, she breaks with him abruptly.

Fired by his own energies and emotions to express himself and a truth about America, Eden is a prime version of the democratic great man, de-manding recognition for the dynamic creative act of fathering himself. As the name Mart Eden implies, Martin is ready and eager to sell the fresh-ness of his vision and the power of his innocence without either apology or hesitance. For a time he thinks that Ruth's approval is satisfaction enough. Identifying the class order with the ladder of spiritual aspiration, Eden gradually discovers as he rises that the person in whom he had lodged all the transcendent ideals for his work is more materialistic than the most mind-deadened laborer and that her love is tainted by its clear dependence on Eden's fame in the world. Neither social success nor the literary fame that brings it satisfies Eden because both show him so blatantly the empti-ness of those desires. Instead of making him more secure, they make him doubt the reality of the person that has achieved them, himself. Both his success and his fame, he says, are "fictions" about his true nature and he watches in despair as that true nature, the root of his talent, slips away. For a time he can regain his old self by visiting the friends of his old life: "Everybody was glad to see Martin back. No book of his had been pub-lished; he carried no fictitious value in their eyes" (357). But as his words begin to appear in print after years of struggle, he finds himself more and more in the company of those for whom "he was the fad of the hour, the adventurer who had stormed Parnassus while the gods nodded" (374). As far as he could tell, he and his work were the same as they had been. The only difference now was that he was celebrated and therefore incessantly being invited to dinner, "because the one blind, automatic thought in the mob-mind just now is to feed me."

The metaphor sends us back to Dante, to Augustine, and to Ovid: The desire to be fed, to be filled, that can never be satisfied with mere food or applause. But for Martin Eden, with his Darwinian individualism and his Nietzschean adulation of the heroism of the artist, there are no other ways to be satisfied. The hunger that started him on the road of literature stays with him to the end. All that he can do is resist the soul-stealing power of the fame machine as much as possible. He thumbs his nose at his new-found celebrity by dredging out every old rejected manuscript in his drawer and selling them off at high prices. Then, in a gesture reminiscent of the Romantic effort to exonerate one's own success by heralding a neglected writer, he helps publish *Ephemera,* a long poem by a friend who had strug-gled with him in obscurity only to commit suicide before any recognition had come to either of them. But nothing can make up for the feeling of nonbeing that fame has brought him. Nothing he reads about himself in the magazines, no portrait or photograph they publish, seems in any way connected with his own sense of identity. It all has to do only with the desire of the reading public to feed its own appetite for sensation:

> It is for the recognition I have received. That recognition is not I. It resides in the minds of others. Then again [it is for] the money I have earned and am earning. But that money is not I. It resides in banks and in the pockets of Tom, Dick, and Harry (392).

Neither the focus on money nor on professional craft helps now. The audi-ence is feeling its power, and Martin has become the glittering focus of eyes that feel continually ennobled by their own brilliance in paying atten-tion to him.

Through Martin Eden, London defines and tries to purge the excess of his own desire for fame and recognition. Eden is like London himself, be-fore he went on the road and discovered that all the Nietzschean strength in the world didn't prevent men from ending up at the "bottom of the Social Pit." Eden marches toward fame, says London, with no sense of any "collective human need." In the essay "How I Became a Socialist" (1903) London describes how he was much the same way—young, strong, and "a rampant individualist" who believed the game of life was "a very popular game for Men. To be a MAN was to write man in large capitals on my heart. To adventure like a man, and fight like a man, and do a man's work (even for a boy's pay)" (*Novels,* 117). But his discovery of the insuffi-ciency of the body turned him to "brain work" instead, and in "What Life Means to Me" (1906) he briefly recounts his own successes as a "brain merchant" and his disillusionment with the sentimental and selfish material-ism of the people he had always looked up to and whose presence he had struggled so to enter (Etulain, 141–42).

Like Corvo, London is the individualist writer in search of a natural comradeship, a community, a code of values outside the degraded relationships of conventional society. At one point in his life, Corvo's ideal retreat takes the form of a proposed new spiritual order, a secular monasticism, suitable both to his frustrated Catholicism and his homosexuality. In London's work the ideal community of socialism in his polemical writings is expressed in his fiction by the moral code of men struggling together in the wild, where individual strength is never enough without mutual trust. Unlike Martin Eden, then, London does have a goal, a "holy Grail" he even calls it, "a spiritual paradise of unselfish adventure and ethical romance," and he says that he will go back among the working classes and try to help build a future where there will be incentives higher than the stomach for achievement and work (Etulain, 145). Eden has no such options. He is London without any resources or even ideals beyond himself. All that he can do to combat his fame is not to write any more and thereby show that his celebrity has come not for what he is but for what he was. Sick of everything, more and more isolated, he takes a ship out to the South Seas. One night, in a final act of will and protest against the fame that clothed him with a self he could not recognize, he slips overboard, dives down deeper and deeper into the water, and then, opening his lungs, exultantly commits suicide.

Suicide and Survival

> I considered life as my property, and therefore at my disposal. Men of great name, I observed, had destroyed themselves; and the world still retained the profoundest respect for their memories.
> —William Cowper

Both Goethe in 1771 and Jack London in 1909 attempt to purge some extreme of their own obsessions by staging the suicide of their fictional surrogates, young Werther and Martin Eden. But while Werther is propelled by his high-strung sentimentality into a doomed romance, Martin Eden's desires are focused almost exclusively on personal recognition and the approval of others for his writing. With the advent of the democratic possibility of fame and glory on earth for anyone who had the genius (and who can be sure they have it unless they try?), success begins to wear as frightening a face as failure. Failure—and its apotheosis in the idea of the avant-garde—at least can appeal to an audience elsewhere. But when, by some quirk of cultural history, success comes to those brought up to believe in the greater glory of earthly failure, fame turns the inner self against the outer self. It has been willfully sought (perhaps without any thought of actually attaining it), won, and discovered to be shallow, un-fulfilling, and empty—a burial above ground, whether celebrated or ig-nored. Such fame is a kind of self-cannibalism: Ovid's Erysichthon eating pieces of his own flesh; Dante's Ugolino eating his children. For his ad-mirers, Chatterton's death had at least symbolically inaugurated the tradi-tion of suicide as an artistic act to shame the world for its lack of atten-tion. But it is really with Martin Eden and the twentieth century that we come on the phenomenon of suicide from despair over fame and seeming success. Just as writing and art for the Renaissance revived the classical ideal of striving for the glory of posterity, so this style of suicide promises to make the self-murderer an envoy to eternity, reasserting the thwarted will and purging the unappeasable ambition by embracing actual death.

Suicide thus takes its place as an important theme in the history of twentieth-century fame, not because it is so characteristic of those who get or fail to get the fame they desire, but because the act and the talk that surrounds it crystalizes conflicts about fame and aspiration that in previous eras might be represented by the saint in the desert, the Renais-sance melancholic, or the nineteenth-century dandy. Artistic suicide, espe-cially the suicide of someone who has tried to achieve recognition for his or her work, is always to some degree a staging of that desire as well as a purgation of it. We feel tender about suicide in the artistic because we inherit the nineteenth-century belief that suicide, like certain forms of madness or crime, indicates a grander spirit, a superiority to the shackles and abrasions of the human condition. In a world without much sainthood, suicide confers a transcendence. It is an assertion of the self, but one that seems not selfish but selfless.

The attitudes expressed by William Cowper as he recounts his own sui-cide attempt are in the process of disentangling themselves from the hos-tility toward suicide expressed since the sixth century by both Church and State. Until the late eighteenth century, both churchmen and legislators in Christian Europe considered suicide to be a sin against God and the king, an act of lèse-majesté for which the soul was subject to excommunication from God's holy communion and its worldly possessions expropriated by the state. But when the sanctions of both Church and State began to have less exclusive rights over the definition of the self, suicide became a more familiar, more justifiable, more arguably reasonable act—an extreme case of the heightened importance of individual will and self-possession. In Cowper's words we hear the echoes of Locke's doctrine of possessive in-dividualism: "I considered life as my property, and therefore at my dis-posal" (Southey, I, 121). Suicide was no longer solely an act against God, no more than artistic creation or philosophic thought was in competition with him. It was instead an act against society, against the present order of things, *in favor of* posterity and eternity. Cowper's suicide attempt oc-curred before Chatterton's ennobled the cult of neglected genius. But his remarks look toward a democratic future in which suicide is a mark of the untrammeled will in a world simultaneously more open to individual desires and more able to thwart them. Many writers remark how happy suicides sometimes are for a time before they commit the act. But the happiness does not seem paradoxical at all. They have decided; they have already died and mourned for themselves; and the suicide will be their resurrection into a better life.[38]

Thus the suicide of the famous or the aspirant for fame in the twentieth century—and after World War Two with a particular intensity—gives a modern turn to the Roman association of fame and death; the moral fame of the Stoics; the Dantesque projection of the Poet into a world beyond life and death; the Triumphs of Chastity, Love, Death, Fame, Immortality, and Eternity sung by Petrarch; the stifled genius celebrated by the Romantics. Suicide of this sort is a willful gesture toward the future, an invocation of the purer attention of eternity or posterity, at the place where death and immortality meet. As suicides are acts of will, they are self-perfecting: You may think you know me or my work, but you don't really. By suicide those who have failed to find proper recognition can make their lives mean what they want them to mean and thereby evade the meaning imposed upon them by either a world that ignores them or a world that blindly and uncritically accepts. "Success" for the potential suicide may therefore be impossible to define. Like fame, it always recedes before you. Once Martin Eden becomes famous, his work has been poisoned for him. He kills himself to cleanse it of the false personality the world has laid upon it.

In the late nineteenth century the question of suicide was given a psychosocial rather than a religious and legal context by the work first of Henry Morselli (1879) and later of Émile Durkheim (1897), whose division of suicide into three categories of altruistic, egoistic, and anomic was a strong influence on the later development of the field. His terms describe different degrees of relation of the individual to the group. In the altruistic suicide there is a submergence into the group, in the egoistic an effort to transcend the group, and in the anomic a feeling of identity loss because of rapid social movement either up or down. Durkheim's categories are therefore efforts to correlate the statistics of suicide with other sorts of social manifestations rather than to construct a theory (and perhaps a treatment) from individual cases. Yet to consider suicide as part of the phenomenon of fame requires a closer attention to individual cases, for we are asking different questions. The social statistician of suicide may be intrigued to

38. As A. Alvarez points out in *The Savage God,* it was not until the sixth century that the Church officially declared suicide to be one of the severest of sins, in a category of its own. Before that, some of the most influential theologians among the Early Fathers (*not* Augustine), perhaps influenced by the importance of martyrdom, considered Jesus himself a suicide, of the sort Émile Durkheim would categorize as altruistic. That suicide through force of will (and without any weapon) exemplifies an admirable self-possession is a major theme in Samuel Richardson's *Clarissa* (1747–1748), where the play upon legal will and personal will becomes quite elaborate. Compare also the legal dictum that "the will speaks only at death."

note that, while the number of suicides in the Los Angeles area rose 40 percent in August 1962, the month of Marilyn Monroe's suicide, the statistics for the year were virtually unchanged. For the historian of fame, however, it is the cultural and personal context of Monroe's suicide that is intriguing, since in suicide, as in the desire for fame, what appears as an individual assertion can also reveal the cultural forces that have helped shape that individuality. The paradox is inevitably modern, and highlighted in the careers of those people whose overwhelming desire for personal fame attempts to mediate the disparity between what they are, what they want to be, and what they are perceived as being. Youthful success especially can mean that one becomes symbolic before one is real, created by others before one can create oneself, especially if the talent for which one is celebrated is considered to be "natural." For the American natural there is a self-destructive glory in not being detached, in not taking on the cloak of European showmanship and premeditation. Samuel Clemens could still assume another name, become Mark Twain, and strut the boards playing the role of himself. But that possibility may have vanished for Jack London, Ernest Hemingway, and their descendants. Vulnerability becomes more and more their stock in trade and, where London could use his Socialist politics as a counterpoise to his aspiration, later American artists, writers, and performers imbibed enough of the European pose to want to be pure, above politics, and thus even less defended.

As the twentieth century wears on, with its vaster and vaster stages, and its more and more crowded press of competitors at the stage door, the conflict of aspirations becomes more acute. London died at the age of forty, almost a decade after the publication of *Martin Eden,* leaving still current controversies over whether or not he committed suicide himself. But, whatever his own actions, his acutely prophetic apprehension of the twentieth-century writer's urge to go public is clearly reflected in one of his last novels, *Michael, Brother of Jerry,* published posthumously in 1917. It is the story of an especially sensitive and talented dog who faces and witnesses interminable pain, humiliation, and even torture when his abilities are discovered and he is put on the vaudeville stage. Michael, says London, is "a natural aristocrat" who learns his tricks, principally the ability to sing, not to show off for anonymous others, but solely for the love and recognition his master gives him. In contrast the animal trainers who exploit his talents after his master's disappearance operate on the assumption that neither love nor food can make animals do the unnatural tricks they require. Only hate and fear are effective in keeping up the invariable level of performance that will consistently astonish and please the public, who want to believe that the animals perform out of a desire only to please their true masters, the audience.

London wrote *Michael, Brother of Jerry* in part to support the work of humane societies. But its energy derives as well from his despairing insight into the destructive incompatibility between natural talent and public performance. By depicting Martin Eden's suicide as the fatal collision of Nietzschean individualism with a suffocating fame, London may have thought that he could preserve the "sincerity" he considered to be his own prime artistic trait as well as the reformer's power to speak out against contemporary social abuses. But in a new century, with an ever-expanding web of ways that information and misinformation could enwrap the minds of millions, there is nevertheless (or necessarily) a complementary urge to seek out and celebrate "natural" talent with a greedy attentiveness, perhaps nurtured by the desire to believe that in this new mechanical and electronic world there were still exemplary figures who did it on their own and with their own resources. Thus in America particularly the Cinderella story of success, perfected by a seventeenth-century monarchist and cultural bureaucrat, continued to gain power. From the log cabin to the White House, from the chorus to center stage, the myth said that the indomitable natural talent drew the spotlight to itself. Yet in darker moments it was also clear that the spotlight moved by its own compulsions and for its own reasons, independent of human aspiration. As London recounts in *Michael,* an animal trainer might have to torment to death a half-dozen dogs before he found one who could balance a silver dollar on the neck of a champagne bottle.

In a history of the nature of public uniqueness, one faces the charge of generalizing the ungeneralizable in every sentence, for uniqueness, its admirers believe, stands outside of time. Critics who have commented on the many suicides of American writers in the period after World War Two often consider the act either as an outgrowth of private torment, a general characteristic of the artistic temperament (with some glances back to seventeenth-century melancholy), or something to do with the terrible fate of being an artist in mass-culture America. But, without minimizing the individual nature of such a gesture (or any other gesture that attempts to bridge private desire and public audience), I must stress the connection of artistic suicide with the general frustrations that are implicit in the aspirations of American artists and the definition of their goals. Such tragic ends are yet connected to something of what is best in the American context—just as Tocqueville linked the grandeur of American possibility with its often warped or mediocre realizations. They particularly correspond to the otherwise vanishing appeal of the verdict of posterity as a sanction for aspiration.

Few of those who aspire to fame in the twentieth century speak of posterity. In its urge to greater stature in the present, modern fame has stripped itself of all but the slightest hints of history. It has as little in common with the classical and Renaissance idea of the justifying future as the "avant-garde" now has to do with the late nineteenth-century division between official, sanctioned art and the many lone explorers who helped shape the modern movement. With our vast increase in communication, virtually every assertion can be publicized, if it is outlandish enough. The European model of ambition always had a top on earth. As such it retained its Roman element: There is nothing above the emperor. But the American model from the start was a kind of secularized saint-hood. When the Roman analogies that preoccupied the Founding Fathers and retained some force until the Civil War effectively disappeared, the potentially unbounded quality of such aspiration became even more apparent. Nothing in the nineteenth century, and little in the twentieth century until the Depression and Pearl Harbor, dented the sense of indomitable possibility that every American could claim as a birthright. The countries of Europe, with their shifting national boundaries, wars, and political and military alliances, set the context for a fame hypersensitive to hierarchy and gradation. But in America, the land many thousand miles from the older civilizations of both East and West, autonomy was built into the national spirit. Poe may have foreseen its pattern 150 years ago when he mock-counseled prospective writers for magazines that if they wanted to get published, "the first thing requisite is to get yourself into such a scrape as no one ever got into before" ("How to Write a Black-wood Article," *Essays and Reviews,* 281). In the world of immediate communication, fame particularly celebrates the fame of the moment, the fame of nature and instinct, of the individual making himself into something unparalleled and unprecedented. While European fame still maintains some connections with the model of the king and the aristocrat, American fame is the unveiling of a self that is its own world, recognizing no other time. It is the fame of Superman, whose "secret identity" bursts forth when called for.

Thus posterity was less an issue than mere survival, for posterity has meaning only when the past does as well. The famous American, or the American aspiring for fame, was thus caught between the immensity of his ambition, its endless urge for more, and the practical question of immediate means and rewards. In the course of the twentieth century, the public's ability to create instant fame and thereby satisfy its own sense of fulfillment becomes more and more powerful, even as the stresses on those so plucked out and ennobled became more severe. The European artist could much more easily distance both patronage and the pressures of the marketplace by invoking a tradition of artistic métier, with organized mysteries to which the public is not invited. But for the more willfully isolated American artist, with not even the vague memory of a guild or supportive group of colleagues, the sense of a calling based on natural genius creates an often destructive interplay between the idea of a career within time and artistic value outside of time.

In the extremes of such a situation, the individual is diverted from the work that should be continued, the career that should be developed, to focus instead on the success that at all costs has to be repeated. In order to believe in one's own self-estimate, one needs to be recognized. But no recognition is sufficient. Each new project has to top the last, because if you don't move upward, you are going straight down. The desire for such an unalloyed success is often more compelling for those who have chosen an "unconventional" personal and social style. If the most absolute, the best fame, is for the self, then when fame lapses its attention, the individual, not the work, is being rejected. Shortly before his own suicide in 1950, the Italian essayist and novelist Cesare Pavese wrote that suicide was "an act of ambition that can be committed only when one has passed beyond ambition" (quoted by Alvarez, 87). In its link between aspiration on earth and a turning against oneself, Pavese's statement has the ring of an essential truth about fame in the period after World War Two. But in its assertion that suicide ensures that one is beyond ambition, it reveals another truth as well—the desire to use self-destruction as the way out of that conflict. If one is self-made, then one ought best to be self-destroyed.

One could trace the motif back a few centuries earlier, to the beginnings of the modern artist: Milton celebrating the Jesus of *Paradise Regained,* who refused all of Satan's lures to show his power and accept his fame; David and other painters of the late eighteenth century fascinated with the figure of the blind Belisarius, once Justinian's greatest general, who doesn't realize he has been recognized by one of his soldiers. Such artists, like the dandies and observers of the nineteenth century, were lured by the reticence of those heroes, their unwillingness to put themselves forward. But how much more poignant does the motif become in Thomas Heggen's *Mister Roberts,* one of the great successes of the immediate post–World War Two period, as both novel and play. To the crew of his Navy supply ship, Roberts is an alternate power to the bombastic and tyrannical captain, the idealization of a high-minded obliviousness to the effect of being watched. Roberts was a leader, the narrator says at one point, "who is followed blindly because he does not look back to see if he is being followed" (3). But in his unconcern for the audience, Roberts also stood in contrast to the needs of his creator, Thomas Heggen, an author swept up in the post–World War Two fascination with any young writer who could make sense of the war and the world it had helped engender. The example of Roberts for Heggen, like the idea of suicide for Pavese, embodies the assurance that self-integrity and self-approval are possible somewhere. But Roberts remains an ideal figure. After the shouting was over, after the novel and play that celebrated one character's selfless lack of interest in an audience, what could Heggen do next to keep that audience's interest in his work, his person, his being? "How do I go on?" he asked Budd Schulberg, who had a precocious success with his novel *What Makes Sammy Run?* at the beginning of World War Two, and Schulberg gives him some pragmatic advice (179). But when the spiritual conflict is so acute, advice is hardly enough. A few weeks later Heggen was dead in his bathtub from an overdose of pills.

For the aspirant whom immediate fame does not satisfy but even depresses, suicide can ensure the purity of self that has been warped and distorted. As John Leggett portrays them in *Ross and Tom*, Heggen and Ross Lockridge, Jr. (the author of *Raintree County*) were immensely successful first novelists in the 1940s whose suicides seem interwoven with their inability to distance themselves from their own celebrity. At first glance, the suicide of the American poet Sylvia Plath in 1963 would seem to be a different sort of artistic self-murder. The very popular novels of Heggen and Lockridge were intensely idealistic and nationalistic about the "real" America, in accord with the national spirit raised by World War Two. Plath's work, on the other hand, which was just beginning to be recognized, was much more in a modernist mode of difficulty aimed at the "fit audience." Its sources of energy were not national identity but her woman's voice, personal history, and fascination with language. Married to the English poet Ted Hughes and residing in England when she died, Plath nevertheless also exemplifies the simultaneous courtship and fear of fame that divided Heggen, Lockridge, and so many others. Obsessed with the desire for literary fame, Plath wrote about her own death until she succeeded in killing herself. She was the stage manager whose will shaped her work until the play got away from her. The performer can leave the leave the stage—but the person who identifies with the performer often cannot. There is no proscenium in life, nor an easily accessible dressing room in which to remove one's makeup and relax. As happens so often, it has been argued that Plath's suicide was inadvertent because she believed that someone was coming who would smell the gas and rescue her. If so, that person, like her suicide itself, would have been the exonerating audience, arriving just in time to relieve Plath of standing without respite on the stage of her own mind. Suicide, which had earlier been an affirmation of the direct relation of an individual to himself and to God outside the standards of the society, in the twentieth century thus takes on more than a touch of theater. Like anorexia nervosa, it might be classified as a response to the modern difficulties in being seen and being properly appreciated that seeks to remove the self from sight, destroying the body to assert one's power over it. In those who praise it for any reasons other than the ending of excruciating pain or terminal illness, it is a death out of love for what is higher than the body, a death that places the suicide beyond envy and competition.

At the beginning of the twentieth century, Martin Eden believed that the only escape possible from the fame that was suffocating his sense of identity and self-worth was through suicide and death. The suicides of Heggen, Lockridge, Plath, and many others in the decades after World War Two indicate how the problem of artistic success had only intensified with the enormous increase in the resources for the distribution of fame the war had brought into being. But it is the suicide of Ernest Hemingway, who wore the most familiar writer's face in the world, that expresses even more clearly the conflicts that enormous fame could bring, even for someone whose energies had long been spent trying to balance his work and his life. After World War One, in the first stages of his career, Hemingway had seemed to carry the burden of early success fairly well. Like other American writers after World War One, Hemingway had chosen another possibility between the twin stupidities of popular acceptance and popular rejection—expatriation. In Europe, especially in Paris, where an artist had status merely for saying he was one, there was a safe place to work, unbothered by the audience of one's native land, free to see that land whole and thereby attempt to express the coherent meaning of an American experience. To an important extent, Hemingway—like many male American writers before and since—tried to separate himself from the prevailing image of culturally approved authorship by emphasizing that what he wrote was subordinate to who he was and what he did. Throughout his life Hemingway was proud of the place of physical daring in what he represented to his audience. But while Jack London, with his self-taught respect for words and books, always praised the reading man who became a man of action and will, Hemingway rarely used writers or anyone of a literary bent as his heroes; instead they were often men of action—who lived in nature or war—with a disdain for the "brain work" that London chose when on the road as a teenager he saw the fatal decay of muscle and blood. Writing for the young Hemingway was a disease or a vice, but also a necessity, a profession, and, he said, the only standard he wanted to be judged by. Like London's preoccupation with his own "sincerity," Hemingway's constant theme was the desire not to be famous, but to write "truly." Scott Fitzgerald may be "crazy about immortality," says Hemingway, but he himself cares little for fame and fortune (701). Those who do, like T. S. Eliot, Henry James, and the Bloomsbury "crowd," don't know anything about real work, only about the nurturing and propagation of reputation (265). In contrast to their obsessive self-promotion and promotion of their friends, Hemingway asserts his own professionalism as a writer trying both to work at his moral best and to confirm his physical courage:

> I am truly, and I say this in all humility, very brave; that is brave enough to sell it as a commodity—and it is the most saleable commodity there is (703).

Embedded in such a statement—written by Hemingway at thirty-seven to his Russian translator—is the awareness that his writing seeks to turn his personal nature into a product that is beyond both reproduction and imitation, the creation of a professionalism—and here is the hidden hope—that has not debased it in the process. As a young author, Hemingway had become acutely sensitive to the process by which the strangers in whose gaze you appear can make of you whatever they like. Yet he also believes he has protected himself enough to publish his stories and novels without injury by carefully separating the spheres of his work and life. Writing to his father in 1927 about the false stories about himself that have already begun to spring up, he says:

> Those sorts of stories spring up about all writers—ball players—popular evangelists or any public performers. But it is through the desire to keep my own private life to myself—to give no explanations to anybody—and not to be a public performer personally that I have unwittingly caused you great anxiety (258).

In 1932 he drafts a statement for his editor Maxwell Perkins to use to disclaim the false publicity about his war record and personal life put out by a film company that had just released its version of one of his stories:

> While Mr. H. appreciates the publicity attempt to build him into a glamorous personality like Floyd Gibbons or Tom Mix's horse Tony he deprecates it and asks the motion picture people to leave his private life alone (379).

These are admirably sarcastic words, although there is something foreboding about Hemingway's comparison of himself first to a man notorious only for being stuck in a deep cave and then (with an echo of Jack London) to the current representative of the great tradition of vaudeville show horses. More ironically, this is the same Hemingway, already hungering for the Nobel Prize, who after World War Two embraces an image of himself as the great American author that includes his picture on the cover of the mass-circulation *Life* magazine and his most recent work, *The Old Man and the Sea,* fully printed inside. Somehow, in the evolution of his career and the continuing American cultural interpenetration of art and show business, Hemingway, like many a movie star, still continued to believe that the frequent appearance of his face in print could be segregated from any effect on his private life. Similarly, he thought that he had no complicity himself in fostering a criticism that gave "inordinate publicity to my personal life" (745) while slighting his work.

Yet that work, in Hemingway's own mind, was bound to the man. How then to separate them? And why do it? By expecting that he could write "truly," and yet feel personally invaded when publicity and journalism sought to show the public more about the "true" writer behind the words, Hemingway was recapitulating his own version of the Rousseauian claim to be unique because his life and thought expressed general truths, along with the Rousseauian paranoia about the disruption of his personal life by people who had never read his books and friends who did not properly appreciate them. Perhaps Thoreau mediated the situation best:

> If I seem to boast more than is becoming, my excuse is that I brag for humanity rather than for myself; and my shortcomings and inconsistencies do not affect the truth of my statement (33).

But, in the tradition of the self-made man, Hemingway saw his rise to the top of his profession and his struggle to remain there in terms of the combat and competition of sports, the prizefight or the baseball game, where the only resource one has is the bare body itself—no past, no tradition, and no aspiration to teach or discover general truths. The great problem for writers, he implies in writing to Arnold Gingrich about Gertrude Stein's increasingly militant lesbianism, occurs when they take accidental aspects of their own nature more seriously than they do their work. Professionalism thus supplied a detachment from the more debilitating aspects of individuality. It served as an armor in which the tender self could sally forth into battle with the world. Like the artistic eccentricity more usual in Europe, professionalism in the Hemingway sense was a species of social isolation and personal purity that linked the American artist with the pioneering spirit of the inventor and the self-reliance of the athlete, just as in Europe it served to link the artist with the aristocrat and the saint. Without professionalism there would be only bare-knuckled competition rather than the fellowship of writers and artists together—to which Hemingway in his letters often wistfully refers. So much of Hemingway's public image emphasizes his role as the egotistically striving top gun of American literature that it comes as a surprise to find him disclaiming competitiveness and trying to reach out to other writers, like William Faulkner or, in the case of someone who at other times seemed to be the special butt of all of Hemingway's rivalry, F. Scott Fitzgerald (in a 1929 letter):

> If you want to have feelings of superiority to me well and good as long as I do not have to have feelings of either superiority or inferiority to you—There can be no such thing between serious writers—They are all in the same boat. Competition within that boat—which is headed toward death—is as silly as deck sports are—The only competition is the original one of making the boat and that all takes place inside yourself (310).

Profession supplies the discipline that allows one to fashion lasting work from the fallible self, purifying all its egotism and competitiveness. True valor, true sainthood, true professionalism required no awards, no canonizations to affirm its conviction of accomplishment. But in a world characterized by the journalistic urge to discover new stars every few seconds and then throw them aside, self-approval was becoming more difficult for anyone whose profession, talent, genius, vocation, or mere occupation had anything to do with the approval of others. Two factors are relevant here: first, the conception of American originality and individuality in which Hemingway generally partakes; second, the special problem of encore for American authors, what F. Scott Fitzgerald in his appropriately theatrical metaphor referred to as the lack of "second acts" in American lives. Augustine invoked the audience of God; John Milton and Alexander Pope asserted their satisfaction with a small but intense group of ideal readers.

But the writers and artists of the twentieth century found such solace more difficult to accept. Within Hemingway's idea of profession there thus resided a longing for a lost Eden of artistic camaraderie, always situated somewhere in the past, perhaps ultimately in the medieval world of guilds and studios, where master and apprentice worked together. But whatever later fantasies about the Impressionists or the American expatriates in Paris or the Algonquin Round Table, each "school" or group was a self-conscious effort to say such connections could still exist. In fact, the modern pressure was entirely in another direction, away from the unrepeatable masterpiece and toward encore and repetition. In Europe it seemed—at least for the expatriates of the 1920s—there was a truly alternate artistic genealogy. Just write something or paint something and you would be a writer or a painter. But in America, if you didn't keep producing, your status as an artist could be taken away. To be onstage is to wonder what to do for an encore. There the professional assertion was met with the audience response: 'What have you done lately?'

Movie stars were only the most obvious examples of the transience of public approval and recognition. Elevated in part through their ability to convey new types of personality and behavior, they often could not believe that, in a few years, their vogue might be over. They had given themselves. That gift had been amply rewarded. What had changed? But public acceptance was not a threshold that, once crossed, meant you were always inside. It was more like a revolving door. Two ways to maintain one's position might be discerned: one, the polishing and honing of a personal style until it gleamed with seamless perfection; the other, the impeccable series of impersonations of as many different styles as versatility allowed. Each had its difficulties, of course. Personal style could be a trap, an encasement of audience love and expectation that, whether in a vaudeville turn or a Hemingway short story, resented any reach toward a new effect. Versatility, on the other hand, threatened to submerge the individual in the various roles unless he managed to keep the audience aware of the puppet master behind the scenes. As Hemingway is a prime example of stylistic perfection and purity, so Picasso embodies the pose of versatility. Like a European repertory performer, able to miraculously inhabit, imitate, and bring to a new intensity all preexisting forms, Picasso defined himself artistically through his ability to parody as much as through his ability to create. Unlike Hemingway, Picasso had no style; or rather, he had many styles, and none of them were the man who wielded them all with sincere impersonation.

The possibility of parody and impersonation, like the pose of eccentricity and marginality, allowed the European artist a freedom from public opinion that the American, obsessed with the expression of natural truth, was denied. *Winner Take Nothing* was the brave title of a collection of Hemingway's short stories. Like so many of his titles, it simultaneously dramatized and undermined the pose of solitary heroism. But even without medals and prizes, there still had to be a winner. The mind that made the work was somehow suspect because it stood apart from the immediate self-reliance of the body. But without the mind there would be no writing. And so the value of writing was at odds with the act of writing, and the time inside the head that writing required was a dismal alternative to what the man—who happened to be a writer—ought to be doing. "People dont write with vitality," wrote Hemingway to Fitzgerald in 1929, "they write with their heads—When I'm in perfect shape dont feel like writing—feel too good!" Hunting, fishing, the immersion in nature, the life in places far away from his reading audience—where he hoped to find hardly anyone who knew he wrote—helped make up for the inescapable vulnerable openness that writing brought:

> I like to shoot a rifle and I like to kill and Africa is where you do that. Like to get very tired too with nothing connected with my head and see the animals without them seeing you (310).

Thus in a letter to Janet Flanner, Hemingway in 1933 mixes some purposefully shocking tell-it-like-it-is bravado with a wistful desire not to be so constantly on stage himself and for once remain the observer. If one's values are those of truth and sincerity expressed through a commitment to professional craft and calling, then popular approval, at first accepted as the due of one's art, can easily metamorphose into the badge of one's actual failure. Unless you make the manipulation of your public image itself part of your themes (Picasso, Mailer, Warhol), the only alternatives seem to be retreat, seclusion, or self-destruction. Jack London sought compensation in his Socialist politics. But Hemingway remains the prime case of someone fatally caught between his genius and its publicity. Craft and the belief in a fellowship of writers were Hemingway's shield against the exposure his vulnerable sincerity invited. But he could not protect himself against the speed with which the disseminated image of "Papa" encouraged every rival son to dispute his position on center stage. Fame coming to the expatriate, the figurehead of the "lost generation," the ex-reporter from Oak Park, Illinois, could be received as a welcome justification for the hard work and integrity. But Hemingway had little insight into the emptiness of public fame and the night raids it makes into that vital sense of personal integrity and autonomy. In twentieth-century America especially, the celebrity of a nonperforming artist always threatens to be the worst self writ large. In the later, internationally famous, years of his life, he seemed to be trying to learn what to do by hanging around with performers—Gary Cooper, Marlene Dietrich—for whom being on stage was second nature or primary vocation. Like an old trouper, he even sends what turns out to be his last letter to a young admirer, his doctor's son, stricken with a fatal disease. Finally, it is only suicide, the blowing away of that burdensome, nagging head, that can restore the integrity and the calm.

Hostages of the Eye:
The Whole World Is Watching

I want people to be able to recognize me by just looking at a caricature of me that has no name on it. You see, I want to be great and
you can recognize great people like Muhammed Ali and Bob Hope by
just looking at a nameless caricature. When everybody can look at
my caricature and say, "That's him, that's Richard Pryor!" then I'll
be great. I know now that I can reach that level. I had doubts before
but I don't have those doubts any more.

—RICHARD PRYOR

It is my ambition to be, as a private individual, abolished and voided
from history, leaving it markless, no refuse save the printed books; I
wish I had had enough sense to see ahead thirty years ago and, like
some of the Elizabethans, not signed them. It is my aim, and every
effort bent, that the sum and history of my life, which in the same
sentence is my obit and epitaph too, shall be them both: He made
the books and he died.

—WILLIAM FAULKNER, Letter to Malcolm Cowley [39]

Without quite planning it, our tracking of the image of fame through the
centuries of Western civilization has returned to Ernest Hemingway, who,
along with Charles Lindbergh, seemed at the beginning of the quest to
represent the essential qualities of twentieth-century aspiration, ideal
models of the spirit. Both Lindbergh and Hemingway were "stars" of the
post–World War One period who lived into the period after World War
Two and, even after their deaths, retained much of their original fascination as self-made men whose careers expressed a self-sufficiency deeply
indebted to professional craft. Crucial to their public images was a publicized aloneness, an exemplary solitude, that yet required an audience to
give it life, which the camera duly supplied.

Compressing complex centuries to moments of pattern, we can note
clear similarities between the ostentatious aloneness of Lindbergh and
Hemingway and that of Alexander twenty-four centuries earlier or Napoleon and Byron at the beginning of the nineteenth century. Such parallels
illustrate the extent to which the mass society of the twentieth century,
seemingly so unprecedented in the technology of its self-expression, yet
fosters with an extraordinary force and intricacy the impulses to a career
of recognition and fame present since antiquity. Until about the mid-
nineteenth century, this final grand movement I have called "the democra-

39. Richard Pryor is quoted from the *Washington Post*, 15 April 1976; Faulkner
from *Letters*, 285. Malcolm Cowley had written an article on Hemingway for *Life*
and Faulkner was reluctant to have a companion piece written about himself: "I
will want to blue pencil everything which even intimates that something breathing
and moving sat behind the typewriter which produced the books" (282). He finally
refused to grant his permission.

tization of fame" could be described as the transformation of certain monarchical and aristocratic customs, habits of mind, and styles of behavior into modes of public assertion for those who had no genealogical sanction and therefore adopted those forms self-consciously—as in their turn did many latter-day kings and aristocrats. Looking back over the history of fame, we can see how by the twentieth century the frames of achievement that had existed before—the audience of citizens, the audience of God, the audience of history—had been superseded by the more palpable and immediate audience for performance. Much more than the famous of any previous century, the famous of the twentieth century, whether in public professions or not, are *onstage.*

In 1802 Wordsworth wrote in praise of Milton, "Thy soul was like a Star, and dwelt apart" (172). Now, however, whatever their praise of the neglected geniuses of the past, it is immediacy of response, contact with an audience, that is more essential to the self-satisfaction of contemporary actors and athletes, politicians and orchestra conductors, than any projection of the grand opinion of posterity. No matter how much by temperament or tradition the aspirants of the present may look to less immediate and therefore, they believe, more permanent standards, they nevertheless take their styles, their gestures, and often their substance as well from that special effort to please an immediate audience. The seeming distinction between performer and writer is preserved in the inscriptions from the opposite sides of the same coin that preface this section: Richard Pryor's desire for immediate visual recognition versus William Faulkner's dream of absolute invisibility except for his books—Falconet's immediacy once again facing Diderot's posterity, Hazlitt's actors facing his authors. And the extremity of both statements, Pryor's with its lineage back to statues of classical heroes and Faulkner's with its literary allegiance to words rather than images, is a reaction to the contemporary emphasis on visibility as the emblem of secular immortality. Pryor's goal is to up the ante to a rarefied realm of instant recognition from only a few sketchy lines, while Faulkner turns his face absolutely against all visual and personal publicity. The traditional goals of artistic and spiritual fame would thus seem to be totally contrary to the roaring cults of personality that characterize so many careers of the twentieth century. But in the century of necessary visibility, no aspiration is exempt from the general definition of what aspiration means, and writers, who from the eighteenth century had tried to uphold the banner of reticence, spiritual transcendence, justification by posterity, and social marginality were often the most strangely torn. So Hemingway both brags and complains to Ezra Pound in 1924, after only two collections of his short stories had been published:

> Having been bitched financially and in a literary way by my friends I take great and unintellectual pleasure in the immediate triumphs of the bull ring with their reward in ovations, Alcoholism, being pointed out on the street, general respect and the other things Literary guys have to wait until they are 89 years old to get (119).

Hemingway's cautionary example is definitely in Faulkner's mind when he refuses the *Life* interview and picture, perhaps along with what John Dos Passos sourly called F. Scott Fitzgerald's "brash enthusiasm for celebrity." [40] But Faulkner also needed to look no further than his own experience in Hollywood and the seesaw between visibility and invisibility that is peculiarly the lot of the artist in the twentieth century. For someone who makes a living from performance—the bullfighter or athlete or actor or politician—accomplishment can always be checked against that audience's immediate response: Is the craft still intact? Are the body and the art one? Hazlitt pointed out how irrelevant the idea of posterity was for actors and with what rightful greed they drank in every laugh, cry, and bit of applause from their immediate audiences. But when workers in the less-tangible arts—where the audience may be far distant and scattered in time and space—try to assume the analogy of the performer, there can be strange and paradoxical divisions within the self and its aspirations. In only a somewhat exaggerated version of the common malady, A. Alvarez in his book on suicide quotes a novelist who had been suicidal in her youth: "When I'm alone, I stop believing I exist" (126). Once the opening is over, the publication day gone, the party cleaned up, and the celebration ended, there remains the need to return to the studio and the typewriter to face alone the old questions: Can I do it better? Can I do it again?

The disparity between the solitude of creative achievement and the social pressure of the public stage on which that achievement must be displayed is, as we have seen, a constant preoccupation of aspirants to any kind of artistic fame since the eighteenth century. In the early decades of the democratic audience and its new great men, older styles of self-presentation still retained their force. But when the visual media in particular became the prime arbiters of celebrity and the bestowers of honor, the armory of public style began to draw more and more of its gestures and attitudes from what the English language with blunt aptness calls "show business." Past aspirants to fame might consciously or unconsciously dissipate the curse of self-assertion by claiming some other, impersonal justification: not me but my country, not me but God, not me but the Church, not me but the people, not me but the genius of art. But the new style of democratic theater cut as close as possible to direct self-assertion by retaining only the frame of the stage. Its claim was 'not me but my performance, my public self,' which was constructed from natural materials for the benefit of the audience. Like some Rousseauian citizen, such a natural performer reminded an audience rusted over with artifice and social order

---

40. *Fourteenth Chronicle,* 134. For writers like Dos Passos who were for their own reasons more sensitive to older styles of artistic assertion, Scott and Zelda Fitzgerald furnished the alternative against which they could define themselves. "They were celebrities in the Sunday supplement sense of the word. . . . It wasn't that I was not as ambitious as the next man; but the idea of being that kind of celebrity set my teeth on edge" (*The Best Times,* 130). Compare John Cheever's response to an interview question by Dick Cavett, "What is fiction?": "The continuous history of our desire to be illustrious" (August 1978).

that inner nature might be brought out and validated in public show. "We are all worms," said the eagerly rising Winston Churchill in 1906. "But I do believe I am a glowworm" (Morgan, 199). In the nineteenth century the promoter-impresario had stressed the moral aspect of his entertainment. By the beginning of the twentieth century it was the entertainer's own natural-spiritual calling that was the drawing card.[41]

As nineteenth-century show business gathered momentum and particular stars and performers began to emerge from the melee on stage, one striking characteristic of the audience's relation to the performer was its awareness of the act of role playing. Advertisements for minstrel shows stressed that whites were *playing* blacks by showing pictures of the actors with and without makeup. Tom Thumb imitated Napoleon and Frederick the Great, and by the 1850s child performers—like Cordelia Howard, Lotta Crabtree, and later Elsie Janis—began to appear whose double talent was to be sentimentally endearing while they mimicked the grownup stars of the day. Thus already by midcentury American show business was making itself and its own star system one of its prime themes. The ironic premeditation of the performers, often wearing the garb of childlike innocence, invited its audience as a co-conspirator into the exploration of a relationship extremely close to that which existed between one's inner nature and the self-made "character" one ought to show to get ahead in the world. The participants in the New York theater riots of the 1840s may have been brawling toughs but, unlike earlier literary characters, who thought stage happenings were real, they were protocritics, clearly supporting the skills of one performer over another. Self-awareness, even of being something that you were not, if well done, would be applauded, especially if everyone was let in on the act. Barnum's early effort to call attention to the possible humbug in his exhibitions thus was complemented by his promotion of the "real" nature and "natural" talents of Tom Thumb or Jenny Lind. Instead of the artificial and the natural being opposed in the centuries-old religious attacks on the stage, the self-conscious enhanced the natural and brought it to perfection.

In both vaudeville and the circus, two of the most popular forms of American entertainment, the audience could thrill to the spectacle of death-defying tauntings of wild animals, fire and explosion, or the law of gravity itself. Death denying it was, as well as death defying, for the drama was again that of human will, ingenuity, and courage asserting itself against powers that could otherwise destroy it. Unlike the magic acts that cast the magician as someone in touch with occult secrets—a more European characterization—these performances of willful daring had the same appeal to American audiences as did the magic of Harry Houdini (1874–

41. Impersonation, either of the worldly great or the greats of show business itself, has been a staple of American entertainment from the mid-nineteenth century on. For both the performers and the audience, it implies that personal style is a costume that, if distinctive enough, can be turned into a commodity. Mae West began her career impersonating Eva Tanguay, just as many have now made careers impersonating Mae West.

1926), whose main theme in all his most celebrated tricks was the successful effort of sharp mind and well-trained body, although faced with suffocation, confinement, and death, to *escape*. At the same time performers like Eva Tanguay on the vaudeville stage and Isadora Duncan for the avant-garde similarly structured their acts on natural movement and rapport with the audience rather than the exhibition of a more statically defined professional skill. In the face of European premeditation, their message was clearly that it all came from the inside. There was no spirit world. Neither the tightest chains nor the most conspiratorial combines could resist the power of an aroused individual nature.

In such a context of performing styles, the political career of Theodore Roosevelt may owe as much to vaudeville as Lincoln's did to photography. Roosevelt was the first American politician since Lincoln to engage the feelings of the electorate so decisively and to place the presidency once again at the center of American culture. He came to prominence when he resigned his post as assistant secretary of the Navy to form the Rough Riders in the Spanish-American War (1898), a group described in the book he published a year later as an amalgam of American society—East and West, rich and poor, educated and illiterate—all fighting in the name of America. Arriving on the national scene at a time of financial collapse, high union-management conflict, and an increased defensiveness on the part of the wealthy, Roosevelt gave the concept of self-help and the self-made man a new resonance by emphasizing the transformation of his own physical weaknesses into the stuff of rough-and-ready military heroism, not for self-interest but for the good of the country. His career showed, as he never tired of pointing out, how someone with ordinary abilities and even more than his share of physical deficiencies could by willpower alone become great. Two years after San Juan Hill, he was elected vice-president on the ticket of William McKinley, assumed the presidency with McKinley's assassination a few months later, and in 1904 was overwhelmingly reelected himself. In a sense he supplied from his own nature a reinvigoration for the *idea* of America similar to that Lafayette had furnished almost one hundred years before: personal success, fame, and honor were not self-interestedly opposed to national glory but intimately connected with it. In Theodore Roosevelt the nature-loving, trust-busting president, as in the backyard tinkerer Henry Ford, or the Lone Eagle Lindbergh, the individual American might glimpse an image of himself or at least of someone whom the expanding world of newspapers, magazines, photography, films, and radio made seem as emotionally close as a friend or a member of the family.

Clearly enough, Teddy Roosevelt was the heir of the post–Civil War self-made man. But he was the fruit of nineteenth-century theater as well, a man as comfortable as Mark Twain or any performer with being on stage, where he played not the part of another so much as a larger-than-life version of himself. By dramatizing his triumphs over tragedy, illness, and "ordinary" talents, Roosevelt sounded for the twentieth century the first notes of a newly pervasive need that achievement and competition (with others or with oneself) had to be accomplished before the public eye to really count. Unlike Martin Eden, Roosevelt battened on the attention. It did not undermine him; it justified him. In contrast with the suicide who destroys his body to show his power over it, Roosevelt restored and perfected his body in front of his audience's validating gaze. Crystalized in his public image was the essential combination of visual assertion and spiritual justification that is at the heart of modern fame: Achievement must be performed before an audience; the best fame is visual. No flowers wasting their fragrance on the desert air need apply.

In what may be still the most popular literary myth of the period, L. Frank Baum in *The Wonderful Wizard of Oz* (1900) reflected the lesson of Roosevelt's career by similarly raising self-help from virtuous practicality into psychological necessity. The Wizard was just an old fraud who did his magic by trickery, and both the original drawings as well as the makeup of Frank Morgan in the 1939 movie version emphasized the analogy with Barnum.[42] But, of course, Barnum would have agreed: The answer was not in the magical Wizard but in oneself. The scarecrow who thought he couldn't think, the woodsman who turned himself into metal because he couldn't love, the lion who roared at people to cover up his fright—all could be cured if they accepted their own role in the curing: The Wizard helps them who help themselves. Belief in the Wizard was irrelevant once he taught you how to become your own audience, believe in yourself, and be what you wanted to be. A glowworm, Churchill might have explained, was a worm that became great by carrying its own spotlight, a worm on stage.

The modern preoccupation with fame is rooted in the paradox that, as every advance in knowledge and every expansion of the world population seems to underline the insignificance of the individual, the ways to achieving personal recognition have grown correspondingly more numerous. Even before the advent of Christianity—and much more so after—fame, however it was defined, promised a way to evade death and deny its ultimate power. We can trace the urge to surmount death by a deathless image back to Egyptian mummies or Roman funeral portraits, and we can note the enthusiasm with which the Renaissance greeted copper engraving as a way of speeding one's image unerringly to posterity. But the intense involvement now possible between seeing and being seen, in both their negative and positive connotations, has far advanced beyond the shadowy self-consciousness fostered by easel painting and the printing press. Through the media of sound, sight, and print individuals can aspire to a dream of ubiquity in which fame seems unbounded by time or space: constantly present, constantly recognizable, and therefore constantly existing. The photograph, with its exaltation of a momentary state of physical being,

42. The Wizard began as a ventriloquist, then did bird and beast imitations, and finally became a balloonist, which brought him to Oz. Dorothy refers to him as "The Great and Terrible Humbug," a title he, like Barnum, dearly loves.

and the motion picture, which further emphasized its subject's immersion in a passing time, helped create the more uneasy relation we now share with those in the spotlight. The Renaissance aristocrats sat on the stage, blurring the distinction between audience and performer. From the 1890s onward, with the development by George Eastman and others of the box camera, the amassing of images and the ability to stand visually outside oneself was made easily available to millions. The professionalization of spectatorship along with the professionalization of leisure had begun in earnest. Through the photograph and the motion picture, images could appear divorced from any historical context—invincible and immortal, ennobled and self-sufficient—yet at the same time performing only for us, the necessary audience.

Of all the new media, it was in the motion picture, silent or sound, that the pure and impure particularly mingled, and the socially marginal character could be focused on with the intensity previously accorded only the central. Through the movies, the spiritual self-sufficiency that had previously been dependent on the relationship with God becomes a more internal possibility of each person in himself or herself, where emotion and matter, spiritual transcendence ("the star") and material success ("the celebrity") mix—the final product of an eighteenth-century belief in the possibility of individuals and nations to become self-made through the exercise of will. Without the movie sense of focus on an isolated figure and the radio tracking of his every position, Lindbergh's solo flight across the Atlantic would not have made the same impression on the world and might not even have been attempted. And Lindbergh's seeming lack of need for an immediate audience, his diffidence, bound him still more tightly to the even vaster audience he actually attracted, until, of course, they decided that the diffidence was disdain and the solitude standoffishness.

Twentieth-century fame is therefore linked to the fame of the past by its element of performance. But the modern media of communication allow that performance to take place in relative isolation. In effect, modern fame becomes a virtually unparalleled *fame without a city,* not just for the clearly distinguished but for anyone who manages to attract its attention. Emphasizing the immediate force of individual will ("I did it my way"), it longs as well for a spiritual fame that rises out of history and becomes part of the permanent language of human images by which individuals measure themselves and their accomplishments. The exemplary famous person here is especially the person famous for being himself or playing himself, like some soon to be great star discovered at a soda fountain or pumping gas. With its echo of Lincoln and the log cabin, it is the modern version of the Cinderella story. But in the story Cinderella is recognized as the princess she always was to begin with; in our own time merely being looked at carries all the necessary ennoblement. The frequent lack of actual accomplishment, which fame moralists find easy to mock ("famous for being famous") is therefore totally functional. It separates the famous less obviously but more absolutely from everyone else. The less you actually had to do or create in order to be famous, the more truly famous you are for yourself, your spirit, your soul, your inner nature.

In the past the crucial influence on personal aspiration might have been the figure of Jesus, the idea of Rome, or the crown of artistic posterity. But now these and every other past standard is inextricably tied to the image of a performer on stage, and even those few who reject that analogy cannot escape the way it shapes their denial. In 1910 an enterprising editor at Harper's persuaded nine prominent Americans, including William Dean Howells, Thomas Wentworth Higginson, and Henry James, to contribute to a volume called *In After Days* that explored the question of an after-life. All of the contributors—the doctor, the lawyer, the scientist, the literary men and women—believed in it in some way or another. "Life," wrote the biographer and popular theologian Elizabeth Stuart Phelps, "is scarcely more than an experiment in vivisection, if death is the end of personality" (33). Some spoke of bereavement, some of memory, and some of the power of love. But each essay was prefaced by a striking photograph of the contributor.

The Politics of Performance

My government must be the foremost [in all Europe]; otherwise it will be destroyed.

—NAPOLEON (1802)

Imagine me going around with a potbelly. It would mean political ruin.

—HITLER (1943)

As visual and verbal communication wraps and rewraps itself around the world, and the rapid dissemination of information implies the creation of an international culture, the ideal of twentieth-century fame has become characterized by an effort to yoke even more firmly than before previously opposed elements of visual, theatrical fame (historically set in civic and political life) with spiritual, intangible fame (with its roots in the Christian conception of the audience not of this world). In the light of such seemingly contradictory goals, it may not be very remarkable that in the twentieth century so many individuals of essentially solitary nature could nevertheless draw vast audiences by both the alluring mystery of their aloneness and their seemingly obliviousness to the audience's attention. Like the characters who inhabit the "fourth-wall" stage of late nineteenth-century realism, they were not heard so much as overheard. Their eyes fixed elsewhere—like the gaze of destiny in the portraits of Washington and Napoleon—they looked toward a more perfect world.

For their immediate audience, in whom the many images created by mass communication can foster a sense of personal fragmentation and insufficiency, the reticence of such figures is part of their fascination. Unlike traditional monarchs and aristocrats, who were imbedded in panoply and show, they project instead an exemplary self-centeredness, which draws others to them. Through the common language of performance, they demonstrate the need of all modern societies in a postmonarchical world for central symbolic figures by which individuals can understand each other and themselves. To admire, to believe in them as quintessences of human nature, is to believe in their fame as the prefiguring of a fame for all—whether in the terms of movie-star transfiguration, heroic isolation, or national glory. Through this secular sainthood, which reduced the number of possible persons to a salient few, the audience's sense of personal unworthiness becomes transmuted by the contemplation of fame on earth, much as religion focused it on hope of heaven. Tangible success and achievement may still be the standard in an actual profession or occupation. But fame of the self, now even on earth, has the chance of being transcendental.

This amalgamation of visual and spiritual fame along with its corollary emphasis on the famous as surrogates for their audiences had a striking effect on the nature of political leadership. In aristocratic societies, the political system to a great extent had determined the system of public fame. In the mass democratic or totalitarian societies of the twentieth century, however, it is fame that primarily determines political power. Through both the totalitarian "cult of the personality" and the democratic appeal to the crowd, the leader (along with lesser politicians) often stresses his symbolic significance more than his actual policies.

Military politicians in the Roman mode had, of course, traded techniques with performers for centuries. War and war leaders had always been crucial factors in the history of public celebrity, with its Roman bias toward rooting personal honor in military and political action. During the American and French revolutions, the basic pattern of public fame was still military; entire countries were mobilized and war, with its attendant horrors and honors, was something that touched everyone in some way. The old Roman imagery could command a new vitality because its emotional cues were no longer the possession of a class but of the entire country. But the total social and economic mobilization that began in World War One, along with the need to appeal to a mass electorate to sanction mass drafting of citizen-soldiers, foretold a quantum leap in the resources for public fame. In America particularly, World War One marked a de facto alliance between the politicians and generals usually in charge of military activities and the stars of the new medium of film to "sell" the war to a strongly isolationist American public uninterested in European problems. Douglas Fairbanks, Jr., Charlie Chaplin, Mary Pickford, and others threw their performing energies into promoting the sale of war bonds. War was a commodity that had to be advertised, and the alliance of performers and politicians is as emblematic as Lincoln's frequent trips to Mathew Brady's photographic gallery in the dark days of the Civil War or Napoleon's lessons from Talma. By the 1920s few could be found who truly believed that the paths of glory lead but to the grave, even if it was only military glory of which they spoke. To a new generation of politicians, who were able to view their constituencies *as audiences* and themselves as necessarily in the spotlight, the rapidly expanding media of communication in the twentieth century presented the opportunity to assert their authority (and thereby power) in unprecedented ways.

What one did with that authority and power depended on a combination of personal temperament and national traditions. In such a company Lindbergh, even though or perhaps because he was never elected to public office, has strong affinities. The popular image of him as the Lone Eagle recalls Washington, Napoleon, and the monarchical eagles they absorbed into their insignia. In her celebration of Hitler in *Triumph of the Will,* Leni Riefenstahl also drew on the popular image of Lindbergh, the bold flier alone in the clouds. Either unmindful or disdainful of such parallels, Lindbergh however always considered himself to be apolitical, "above it all" in the phrase I used at the beginning of this book. In her published diaries, his wife, Anne Morrow Lindbergh, is at pains to insist on his actual lack of any political ambition, even in the years when he was the most visible spokesman for American isolation from the European war against the march of Nazism.

> No one could believe that a man could take his stand out of personal conviction alone, unmoved by political ambition. Implausible as it seems, this was the truth. Throughout his life, Charles Lindbergh consistently turned down all suggestions that he take part in political life. He seemed to know he was unfitted for such a role (xxiii).

As a young girl, she had first met Lindbergh not knowing who he was, because she had just emerged from a long submersion in her college library, writing a paper on Erasmus. There in front of her seemed to be another Erasmian figure who transcended national boundaries not by his learning but by his airplane and his soaring, solitary personality.

For all her insight, Anne Morrow Lindbergh did not see that Lindbergh's sincerely apolitical stance was itself part of a political tradition that would be eager to capitalize on his diffidence. Now it has even become a cliché of American politics that presidential candidates recommend themselves for the highest political office by their detachment from (partisan) politics. But in the period between the two world wars, such an assertion was part of the propaganda of dictatorship (as it had often been of monarchy before). As her diaries make clear, Anne Morrow Lindbergh in a sense saved Lindbergh from the worst consequences of his apolitical stance by becoming his sufficient audience, beyond whom all others were virtually unnecessary. America never lacks for self-styled demagogues. But it is striking how often American styles of public fame have been turned by Europeans into instruments of tyranny and control. British papers in the nineteenth century had glanced nervously at the mania for Jenny Lind stirred up by Barnum and speculated on its dire implications for American politics. But, much more than either the Americans or the British in the past two centuries, it has been the continental Europeans who seem to hanker most after public figures who solve the confusion of events by vesting absolute authority in themselves as surrogates for their followers. In the United States this "civic religion" had a head start, and so American styles of public display have had an inordinate influence. As Napoleon imperialized the imagery of a retiring Washington, so Hitler took "above it all" postures popularized by Lindbergh and turned them into modes of political control. The structure is similar to that set up by Augustus for the Roman Empire: The ruler is absolutely at the apex of ambition and thus allows a bureaucratizing of the ambition of others. But added to this classical solution to the problem of individual striving are the modern elements of (1) a ruler whose career and actions are the emotional realization of the strivings of all and (2) a definition of "all" that gathers its strength from the exclusion of any group considered to be disloyal to the leader and thereby to the "real" nation.

Typically, such figures rise to power after the overthrow of an aristocratic-feudal society and its hierarchic sense of fame. In England, where there was an ironic tradition of royal theater, kingship from George V onward becomes identified with an often antiheroic domesticity: Since the role has been thrust upon you by birth, all you can do is play it as well as you can—like any other citizen and perhaps more purposefully boring than most. But in countries like early twentieth-century Germany and Italy, where the loss of national spiritual direction corresponded to the loss of a war that monarchy had fought, the search for a charismatic leader is more attracted to a theater characterized by myth and simplification. With the crumbling of monarchical authority, the publicity of absolute rule is taken even more seriously, Hitler inspiring more elaborate display than Kaiser Wilhelm, Mussolini than Victor Emmanuel III.[43] Leading countries that had been defeated in World War One and invoking grand images of political and military renewal, their symbolic place in the self-definition of their national audiences often obscured either actual policies or their own personal natures. They replaced the image of hierarchic kingship with a cult of the ruling personality that promised each downtrodden individual he could become more through his identification with the leader. "More" in this sense means less individual: You become better by submitting your own will to the will of history or national destiny and are thus relieved of

43. At least constitutionally, Mussolini shared power with Victor Emmanuel—a situation that Hitler always considered foolish.

the burden of individual striving. Such a leader is someone who answers to the dreams of large numbers of people, symbolically as well as actually achieving for them. Riefenstahl's image of the lone flier, celebrated by the crowd but soaring high above them, was the center of a Hitlerian cult of purity that emphasized the leader's affinities with the godlike and the more than human by a precision of gestures reminiscent of a Roman emperor imitating a statue—an association mocked by Charlie Chaplin's image of the Venus de Milo giving the Nazi salute in *The Great Dictator*. Lindbergh's public image similarly stressed self-containment and purity. But the difference lies in the way the totalitarian leaders translated those individual ideals into the monolith of state imperialism and the cult of the leader. There were some in America who wished to make Lindbergh into such a leader, but he consistently refused. Unlike the dictators, he never seemed to consider himself the archrepresentative of his own country, no matter how well he thought he could articulate its ideals. American to the core, he was still "above it all" and as committed as Erasmus or Franklin Roosevelt to an international order, although Roosevelt's internationalism was pluralistic, embracing, and "social," while Lindbergh's was always intent on analyzing and purifying, in search of the "natural."

With the exorbitant media pressures of the twentieth century, the old Roman profession of soldier-politician had thus been warped into new and often repellent shapes, as political leadership went through periodic stages of what might be called re-spiritualizing—seeking to validate itself in the eyes of an audience-electorate by both invoking heroes from the past and pursuing military action in the present. Similarly adopting Roman precedents, Napoleon, like the Founding Fathers, could still plausibly be considered the emblem of a triumph of individual merit in worlds where political and social power were traditionally the province of those with hereditary claims. But for the twentieth-century dictators particularly, performance and imagery shaped their politics, their economics, and their social policies. Styling themselves descendants of Napoleon and the great Romans, they were in fact more in the line of Caligula, Nero, or Herostratus, the patron saint of notoriety, looking for fame from destruction and caprice, leaders who embodied and thereby excused all the worst potentials of their audiences, stars who led them forward in the name of emptiness, releasing them from the obligation or interest in being better than they might be.

With such leaders, celebrity-visibility in each country is determined if not exhausted by a single image. Hitler, like most imperial and absolutist leaders back to Augustus and the pharaohs, aggrandized all fame into himself. In England or America, where monarchical traditions had been severely modified or pruned away, the relation of the audience to the leader may have been equally intense, but it was much less supine. Albert Speer points out that Hitler actually asked much less personal sacrifice from the Germans than Roosevelt or Churchill did from their countrymen during the war because he was afraid of compromising his popularity. Churchill's career in particular is intriguingly similar to Hitler's. An extreme imperial nationalist with ferocious personal ambition, who believed in the primary significance of personalities in history, Churchill was highly self-conscious about the theatrical in political life and constantly honed his own histrionic ability. As he said at twenty-three,

> I play for high stakes and given an audience there is no act too daring or too noble. Without the gallery, things are different (James, 13n).

Audiences clearly pressed him to greater heights, and yet he was so anxious about his public appearances that he would rehearse for hours to make sure every sentence was properly in place. He was on stage, but he wanted to be there alone. Until he became prime minister in the wake of Hitler's invasion of Poland, he was hated by his political enemies and distrusted by his associates for his ambition, independence, and pugnacity— qualities that became totally appropriate when Britain went to war. Fusing a nation he had previously thought divided and galvanizing an electorate created by a universal suffrage he had ferociously opposed, he led them against an enemy whom he understood in the way Sherlock Holmes understood Dr. Moriarty, as a reflection of himself:

> [I]f our country were defeated I hope we should find a champion as indomitable to restore our courage and lead us back to our place among the nations (James, 318; September 1937).

With each new expansion in the availability and intensity of the media of communication, new images are born and past images reexpressed. Hitler and Mussolini, like Theodore and Franklin Roosevelt, Winston Churchill, and John F. Kennedy, were among the political figures of the twentieth century who instinctively understood how to use the new media not just as a way of disseminating their images and ideas but as a substantially new influence on the processes of thought and politics itself. The voice echoing in the head made possible by radio, as well as the intimacy with the solitary pioneered by film, shapes the nature of their fame and the kind of political power they achieved. As the Vietnamese War illustrates, the deheroicizing technology of modern war, which is inseparable from the technology of its publicity, has by now effectively undermined most of the moral claims of the Roman soldier-politician that his fame is the standard for all others. *Virtus* can no longer be automatically synonymous with virtue when computers guide its aim and television documents its errors. But we might note as well how eagerly and often expertly the new methods of communication were seized upon to sway an audience enormously larger than the legions or courts of old. In that way, without exonerating anyone's actions, we might be better able to understand how unsuited by education, personal experience, or moral background the bulk of that audience was to withstand them. Playing on the power of radio, which burst forth in the 1920s, Hitler took a central place in the revival of a Roman style of impassioned oratory. As the leader of a party without any consistent party program except the desire to be elected, Hitler used the potential of radio to identify even more tightly the isolated audience with his own solitary voice. He was preoccupied as well with the ways in which music could be used to move his audiences and frequently chose what should be played as the introduction to his speeches and the announcements of Nazi victories. Each person, each family, around its radio, could hear his voice and the vocies of those present and wish that he might be there too, to support the Führer and cheer him on, submerging individual weaknesses in his strength.

Such techniques can be ways to intensify and purify a message: a weapon of us against them, the observer versus the observed. Or, in a more democratic context, they can open the way to a more varied and egalitarian relation between the people and its leaders—FDR's fireside chats versus Hitler's inflammatory speeches. The democratic revolutions of the eighteenth century had dethroned tradition and hierarchy and supposedly put reason and merit in their place. But the dictatorships of the twentieth century showed that the change was not inevitable, and that from the downfall of older restrictions could come new tyrannies as well as new freedoms. Many of the early misconceptions about Hitler, like those of Churchill, were caused by comparing him to an old-style "great leader" who, like Augustus, might have gained power through violence, but would "mature" into measured grandeur. In fact Hitler, self-justified by his success, his belief in his star, and his desire to "go down in history as the greatest German," became only worse and worse (Bullock, 232). He had an overwhelming sense of mission to which any ideology but absolute power was basically irrelevant. In his style of totalitarianism, like Mussolini's, all of the paraphernalia of the Roman Empire is revived without any of that empire's effort to include and respect nationalities, religions, and customs alien to its own traditions. Only the Roman *furor dominandi* remained. In wartime the state and the leader would be truly their best selves, armored against their enemies. Thus Hitler especially of all the dictators of Europe and Asia marked both the final apotheosis of the Western tradition of the great man as a military and political leader and the naked revelation of the extent to which those reputations were in fact based on the death of numerous anonymous enemies. Attila and his mound of skulls might be ridiculed as any worthy analogy to the energy of Alexander or the statecraft of Caesar and Augustus. But Hitler, for all the effort to treat him as a demon from outside "normal" history, yet considered himself to be following the example of their power. In an era when absolute authority in many countries was being vested in a single person, he boasted "There will probably never again be a man with more authority than I have" (Bullock, 255). His mission, with its parody of nineteenth-century progress, was to end history with himself as the final hero and Germany as the final state. Bent on outdoing Frederick the Great and Charlemagne, he had all the histrionic self-awareness of his ancestors in the history of fame with none of even the minimal intellect, character, or values they professed. His triumphs, like many of Napoleon's, came for the most part through his ability to divine weakness, insincerity, or irresoluteness in others, especially their inability to understand his total disdain for the traditional modes of politics and diplomacy. Analysis of his policies so often failed then and now because he came into public being animated less by politics, economics, or sociology than by the twisted history of public fame itself; he was the outsider in power, his government the rule of Mr. Hyde.[44]

For those who seek the justification of public exposure, fame is always right; and, until they reach their goal, they have little care for either the malevolent distortions of Virgil's bird-monster *Fama* or the capriciousness with which Chaucer characterized the bored monarch of the House of Fame. Thus, when the keynote of an entire era is that recognition and self-exposure will bring psychic and social fulfillment, it becomes impossible to assert that only "good" fame counts. We might want to make verbal distinctions between fame, renown, honor, recognition, reputation, celebrity, and so on—and have a good deal of moral reason to do so. But we should also be sensitive to the way those lines have become blurred: the Jekyll and Hyde of Fame easily changing faces, Alexander and Herostratus two sides of the same coin. In a world preoccupied with names, faces, and voices, fame promises acceptability, even if one commits the most heinous crime, because thereby people will finally know who you are, and you will be saved from the living death of being unknown. In the familiar paradox, the otherwise antisocial action barely hides a longing for social celebration. Since the Renaissance, assassins have been especially intriguing figures in the history of fame because, whatever their professed motivation, they seek to build themselves and their cause by destroying a prominent public person and thereby absorbing into themselves his or her power of being known. Terrorists in contrast may not necessarily attack well-known

44. Hitler frequently harked back to honored forerunners. Frederick the Great was both a hero to be inspired by and one to supersede. Similarly, the Germanic Charlemagne was raised in opposition to the more French Charlemagne celebrated by Napoleon and Napoleon III. Berchtesgaden, Hitler's mountain retreat, was built so that it had a view of Untersberg, under which legend had it Charlemagne was buried and from which he would arise to restore the German Empire. Frederick Barbarossa had used Charlemagne the same way almost a thousand years before, and was so used in his turn. In 1871, to accompany the Franco-Prussian War, Kaiser Wilhelm I had revived the story of Frederick Barbarossa, who would waken from his sleep of centuries to defend Germany when the time had come. "Barbarossa" was the code name for Hitler's invasion of Russia. I don't want to imply that invocations of the past are always successful. Hitler and his media associates clearly had a talent for such analogies unshared by Kaiser Wilhelm. With the same sense of historical repetition and supersession, after the Nazi defeat of France the surrender was signed in the restaurant railroad car in which France had dictated terms to Germany in 1918.

figures. But, as offspring of modern techniques of publicity, they similarly aim by murder to make themselves and their cause more acceptable and more visible, to dramatize and thereby compensate for their incompleteness, their lack of fame, in the most public manner.

Bent on obliterating whatever he considered to be alien, Hitler represented himself as the spiritual essence of Germany, its reborn inner nature. The assertion is no paradox. Purity and national exclusiveness are as much a hallmark of the dictators of the twentieth century as are their various efforts to utilize the new media to project their seemingly self-sufficient personalities as general political ideals. The belief that the state should be at all levels a place of ideological purity binds together Hitler's Germany, Mussolini's Italy, Mao's China, and Stalin's (as much as Solzhenitsyn's) Russia. It harkens back as well to the absolutist states of the seventeenth century, where Louis XIV's motto *"une foi, une loi, un roi"* (one faith, one law, one king) retrospectively seems an ominous, although more euphonious, prelude to Hitler's *"ein Volk, ein Reich, ein Führer"* (one people, one state, one leader). Politicians in the eighteenth and nineteenth century were still involved in competing for political rights and powers that had previously been the province of nobles and kings. But in the twentieth century the competition was less to be king than to be God. Hitler especially had a knack of making all his actions seem inevitable, necessitated by the fate through which his own destiny and Germany's were aligned. Accordingly, all private life outside state service was potentially subversive. There was no way to aspire but inside the system's own hierarchy, and there was no need to compete with the leader because he continually said he was you already. Anyone who didn't believe that—whether they lived in Hitler's Germany, Mussolini's Italy, or Stalin's Russia—was by definition an alien, outside the nurturing system. Not only were the Jews the source of all world disorder because they owed their allegiance to institutions and ideas that purported to be larger than the state, but they were also the requisite anti-audience. Both their culture and their lives had to be destroyed to signal the purity of what remained.

Hitler's mark was on everything German and anything he thought valuable in the rest of the world he wanted to make German as well. Through art buying and art confiscations more elaborate and wide-ranging than Napoleon's, he sought to decide what the true history and canon of Western art really was and, unlike Napoleon, he frequently caused art to be destroyed that did not suit his standards. Thus, in a strangely appropriate way, the dead end of Roman public heroism represented by Hitler is accompanied by a caricature of the public political man's patronage, in which only one kind of art is allowed to live while all others must perish. Like the Nazi state, all culture approved by the Nazis was assumed to be unitary. In Hitler's master plan the best of it would all finally be on view in the greatest museum in the world, to be built in his hometown of Linz, Austria. In 1945 as his armies were failing everywhere, he was still making selections. The only specific objects mentioned in his will are the Linz museum and the paintings with which he wanted to endow it.[45]

Many have complained about the number of images that overwhelm us everyday. But I would worry much more if, like residents of totalitarian and authoritarian countries, we received only a constantly repeated, limited number of official images, for then it would be easy to accept one man or group as the source of general truth. In America particularly we may be too bound up in the Hit Parade "I'm the bottom, you're the top" view of achievement. But the very sway of fashion also engenders a useful irony about the ferocious purities and rigid absolutisms that dictate a politics that is less democratic, less representative, and less metamorphic. Irony is hardly a quality one would associate with Hitler, for it denies the absoluteness of his claims. Hitler takes his psychic and literal architecture from the Roman Empire, the frozen processional pediments that dictate what ought to be done. In a sense he has no politics but the absolute difference between what he will accept and what he will exclude. Albert Speer remarks on the abrupt shift of emotions that Hitler would stage as he deemed necessary, from violent rage one second to placating sweetness the next. All were sincere because there was nothing inside but some version of Diderot's actor, creating each public feeling with equal emotion. Hitler is thus the consummate public man, with no private life to reveal, looking out of his pictures directly into the eyes of his followers as if to say 'I am you, only more.'[46] Few official pictures of Hitler are in profile, and the contrast with those of Franklin Roosevelt is intriguing. Hitler's theater is one of form, pattern, and symmetry, while Roosevelt's is more like the momentary frames of movies, in which the actor shapes by gestures and intonation what lies around him. The image of Roosevelt that remains is jaunty—cigarette-holder in mouth, head tossed back, cape flowing—a mercurial romantic democratic role-playing, self-mocking performer. Hitler's image in contrast emphasizes the goose-stepping rigidity of the totalitarian with his mania for national purity—the leader of all the people in constant motion versus the leader of the most pure and the tyrant of the rest.

Trapped by his own warped sense of destiny, Hitler believed that the United States could never sustain a military effort because its bourgeois democracy and mixture of races had no central principle of purity and authority to hold it together. In himself he believed Germany had such a

45. Among the intriguing booty that Hitler himself received from Vienna was a set of Gobelin tapestries depicting the life of Alexander. For further on Hitler's art confiscations as well as those of Goering and other Nazi leaders, see Roxan and Wanstall, *The Rape of Art*. On the continuing scandal surrounding Hitler's art confiscations and the hardly half-hearted efforts to return them to their rightful owners, see Decker, "A Legacy of Shame."

46. Hitler's main source of personal funds, from which he built up a great fortune that was used to buy paintings and art work, was his monopoly over German postage stamps. His face appeared on every stamp and on each he received a percentage. The analogy with Augustan coinage hardly needs to be drawn. Here was a negotiable face that not only bought power, but a fixed cut to the one who wore it.

principle. In Hegel's terms, which he often quoted, he was a "world-historical" individual, whose mission was to reshape history according to his own nature. To Albert Speer's disgust, he maintained an antiprofessional and even amateurish pose in whatever he did. But that pose was the badge of his transcendence. An obvious competence and command of detail would undermine his omniscient charisma. He always referred to himself as an artist rather than a politician, because a politician, like any professional, was a compromiser with time, while he sought to be and believed he was above time. It was a collection of attitudes that, as we have seen, are clearly rooted in the nineteenth-century artist's conflicts with the society around him. But Hitler took those attitudes, so radical and fresh in their resistance to convention, and turned them into a political order characterized by its violent hatred of anything that was not a mirror of itself.

Like Corvo's Hadrian the Seventh, Hitler was the outsider who didn't hate the institution so much as he wanted to be its supreme head. He thought he was Germany, and in the end he sought to authenticate his public self by suicide, which, like so many other failed or successful artists, he believed would heighten his posthumous fame and freeze him, like Goethe's young Werther, in "eternity and national immortality" forever (Bullock, 409). After starting the most destructive war in the history of the world and presiding over the attempted eradication of all those individuals and groups he considered to be blemishes on the pure state he embodied, Hitler no doubt thought his suicide was the final act of transcendence, his own self-staged Götterdämmerung. In one final act of control he would fix himself and his image for eternity and become like a Charlemagne, a Barbarossa, or the imperial Christ they imitated, mysteriously gone and so always liable to return. Historians have theorized that Hitler, like Napoleon, was destroyed by his inability to stop. Yet he could not stop because he had no goal on earth. Any substance there was in his policies had long since turned to gesture, which can be authenticated only by repetition. Hitler's career thus embodies, at least for Europe, a final tragic stage in the disintegration of the Roman bond between public fame, political power, and personal authority. In an intriguing echo down the corridors of fame, it turns out that one of the first paintings to be confiscated in Vienna after the *Anschluss* and designated for a prominent place in the Linz museum was Vermeer's *The Art of Painting*. It has been called Hitler's favorite painting, and we might wonder what he saw in its portrayal of an artist standing in front of an easel, beginning to paint a model dressed as some amalgamation of Clio, the muse of history, and *Fama,* complete with trumpet. Perhaps he welcomed its celebration of the power of the artist to elaborate and manipulate the insignia of public fame, for the shape of his own career indicates how decisively he had emptied them of any general moral or political substance beyond mere gesture.

Hostages of the Eye:
The Body as Commodity

> The eye, my dear, the wicked eye, has such a strict alliance with the heart, and both have such an enmity to the understanding. What an unequal union, the mind and body!
>
> —SAMUEL RICHARDSON, *Clarissa* (1747–1748)

> Fame is a mirage and I don't want to fuck it up by looking at its pimples.
>
> —GRACE SLICK (1977)

There is a crucial difference in the quality of fame in hierarchical societies, in which the state in great part defines individual identity, as opposed to contractual societies, in which the state is considered to be a tolerated limitation on individual identity. If one style of Roman-influenced military-political fame reaches a final stage in the totalitarian dictatorships between World War One and World War Two, another, more complex version has issued in the consumer democracies of the postwar world. The Christian challenge to Roman fame had been the challenge of a spiritual definition of human nature to a marketplace definition, fame as a quality of the private self opposed to fame as something for public sale. But in the vast expansion of visual and verbal media after World War Two, such divisions were impossible to maintain. To be a public person, to aspire to recognition of any sort, was to become, willingly or not, a performer, not in the old sense of losing oneself in performance, but in a more modern and self-conscious mode of simultaneously playing oneself and standing back, appreciating the show along with the audience. Similarly, the ancient Roman assertion of the soldier-politician that his fame is the standard for all had to face the test of publicity. In the 1940s, as effectively as FDR, Churchill, or Hitler had used radio before, Charles de Gaulle created a Free French Army for millions of his countrymen who had never seen him—a vision of resistance to the Nazis that his audience helped become real.

De Gaulle may have been one of the last European leaders to maintain the dual role of military-politician. In America the career of John F. Kennedy marks an important shift in the role military service plays in the definition of political fame. Dwight Eisenhower, whom Kennedy replaced as president, was a professional soldier of the sort so celebrated in the past. But war had become so global that he was more administrator than glorious hero and in political practice tended to underplay his military connections in order to present himself as the citizen-soldier.[47] In even greater

47. Even during World War Two, Eisenhower defined his own style of public reticence in contrast to the more obvious glory seeking of Douglas MacArthur and George S. Patton, the quintessential military showoffs of that war. Truman's firing

contrast, Kennedy's own war experience was definitely not that of the professional soldier. The oftentold story of his heroic action after the destruction of PT-109, the subchaser he commanded, emphasized happenstance endurance rather than glorious action or strategic wisdom. Instead of characterizing Kennedy as a military hero, it emphasized the way what he did expressed the potential hero in everyone. For the first time the politician appeared on stage playing himself—the natural actor who might be an extension of his audience. Rather than the powerful war leader, Kennedy, the second son of a self-made father, redoubled the generational equation by schooling himself to be the family hope after the death of his older brother on a suicide mission in World War Two. Unlike Eisenhower, whose visible associates tended to be businessmen, Kennedy, whose wife had been a photographer and whose father had been at one time a movie producer, was a fan who admired the adroit sense of performance possessed by those in show business. They were not just stage or film professionals for him, but wise counselors in having a public self, and he associated with them as Hemingway associated with Gary Cooper or Marlene Dietrich, as if to learn their secrets. The need to perform was becoming a greater necessity for anyone who desired to be president. Richard Nixon may have thought that he had the necessary experience from his virtuoso use of television in the Checkers speech. But, as the debates between Nixon and Kennedy showed, Nixon still believed in the verbal scoring of debating points rather than the effort to convey a sense of intangible assurance about the future. Both Kennedy and Nixon, like most men of their generation, followed Hemingway's motto that "style is grace under pressure." But in style Nixon was like a bad imitation of Kennedy, or rather, Kennedy was a better version of Nixon, in whom anticommunism became heroic rather than mean-spirited, and physical stiffness a stoic endurance of pain rather than an indication of insincerity. Even now, the pattern continues, as Ronald Reagan, the professional actor who can maintain a distance from his part, improves on Jimmy Carter by being able to project a sincerity that in Carter appeared as either sanctimony or nervousness. Carter conveyed only what he seemed to be on the surface. Reagan's experience as an actor, in contrast, far from trivializing his performance as president, allowed him to project a much more complicated character than he may have actually possessed. Little could be read into Carter, while Reagan, like any good performer, suggested a host of possibilities and "personal" messages that could be read as desired by any fan. And, since a strong part of the appeal of any contemporary famous person is to show how being public can be managed with flair and distinction, because of his self-conscious role playing, Reagan clearly indicated he knew much better than Carter how to deal with the burden of celebrity.

It was in the presidential image of Kennedy, however, that Theodore

of MacArthur in 1951 had reasserted civilian control over the more blatant expressions of the military ego. Another cautionary influence may have been the sensation-seeking cold-war patriotism embodied in Joseph McCarthy.

Roosevelt's debt to vaudeville and Franklin Roosevelt's to the stage was decisively transformed into a symbiotic relationship with the displaced star presence of film. Like a true film or television performer, Kennedy combined the desire to be seen and the desire to be desired with an impalpable distance, an abstract immediacy. A child of his era, the first president to have grown up entirely with the movies and the twentieth century, he was steeped in the awareness that being seen on the screen can heighten desire even as the solitude of the image also distances it into something timelessly appealing. The tension involved in that viewing was one of the hallmarks of the era. After World War One, the American artist looked to Europe and frequently to expatriation as the mode of self-assertion. But after World War Two, the focus was at home, and the intensified glare of the American media searched ferociously for the individuals and especially the faces who could become the emblems of America, expressing a new and uneasy complexity through a powerful and somewhat familiar simplicity. Who would be the great American author, politician, or, simply, star? Who could stand for all this diversity and make it comprehensible? In part it seemed to be someone who could be public without seeming ambitious, private without seeming disdainful—a hero with some tinge of the victim, an enigma that the fan believed he alone could understand. Like Thomas Heggen writing *Mister Roberts* about a man whose greatness came in part from his lack of interest in playing to an audience, Kennedy sponsored *Profiles in Courage* to celebrate those politicians of the past whose actions, condemned by their contemporaries, were justified by history. In a world of self-display, the most alluring mysteries were those who acted as if they didn't care. They had somehow tapped into the secret of selling a self whose value was that it was ultimately not for sale.

For those who neither had the instinct nor knew the secret, the growing ostentation of public life in postwar America continued to blur the line between the social sense of a person living in a world of other people and the culturally induced urge to believe that the most important aspect of that "person" was visible. With such an overwhelming need for self-presentation being trumpeted from all areas of national life, it was inevitable that the etiquette of being should be learned from those whose actual business was performance. They were forerunners in self-consciousness. What was their secret? How did they manage the gap between self and role? How did they mediate being onstage, totally immersed in plot, yet aware of the audience watching? Since Rome, politicians had gone to actors to learn oratorical technique. But the analogy of the performer in the twentieth century cuts beneath questions of dress and gesture into the heart of the difficulty so many find living in a mass society: How can I be singled out, be part of my time and yet transcend it, be, in short, a democratic star? What is the difference between my public and private nature? How do I manage their conflicts? And, most important, how do I use each to fuel and speed forward the other?

The explosion of leisure interest in fashion, sports, and entertainment in the 1920s along with the attendant celebration of innumerable new names and faces has by the last quarter of the twentieth century turned into an overwhelming desire by the audience to be looked at as well. Such ostentatious self-making is of course as old as the self-creation of America itself, as is the companion fear that exposure to an audience of others on the stage of the world will never satisfy the "true" need for the audience of posterity or the audience of God. But since the eighteenth century, the performer has become the prime mediator between the fear and the assertion. Released by media exposure from the necessity to appear only in a pre-existing plot, able to move from plot to plot and costume to costume at will, he or she seems separated from social order and has become instead a free agent—mobile, self-possessed, the image of the ideal individual. Ever before our eyes, this officially seen person represents a dynamic version of Locke's definition of the individual freedom to possess and thereby to sell oneself. The audience's belief in the freedom acquired by the performer's fame is therefore crucial to their empathy. Because this freedom is now particularly defined as "being yourself," the performer or his press agents often display emblems of "personal life" and autobiography as a way of gaining audience support, in the same way that an inner sense of being avant-garde (publicized in interviews) may compensate for an excessively commercial exterior. The audience in its turn can then better appreciate the performer's uniqueness along with his popularity, admiring him as a separate being while identifying with him as an extension of themselves.

Since the eighteenth century, acting has gradually ceased to be a mirror of the individual within a structured community and become instead a model for a self that the individual would like to create to insure for social and personal success. This central image of performance is well suited for an industrial world that celebrates a progress toward the best possible product, and the increased awareness of the gaze of others engenders a search for some etiquette of being seen that seems best learned from those whose profession is showing themselves off. One of the marks of the creative consumer of fame is therefore the ability to learn proper behavior from the senior members of the discipline. In an extreme version of the general tendency, Julian Eltinge, the celebrated female impersonator, had a regular column in the 1920s giving makeup hints as well as advertising corsets and other beauty aids. If the tricks made Eltinge look good, went the implied argument, think what they could do for you. Eltinge, after all, despite one obvious drawback, was a professional in the field of self-display. Wrote one admiring reviewer:

> Just as a white man makes the best stage negro, so a man gives a more photographic interpretation of femininity than the average woman is able to give (quoted by Toll, 246).

In these terms, which were becoming widespread, the key to success in the eyes of the world is a self-conscious awareness of the inadequacies of the body and a blithe belief that, no matter how extreme, they can be easily corrected into a "more photographic" and thereby more real image. Charting one's evolving visual self through such images, clipped from magazines or pasted into family albums, promised a control through self-objectification: The body might not be for sale, but it was certainly on display.

How is one justified and made whole in a world without an afterlife, when fame wears the shifting guise of opinion, and everything in time seems meant only to be superseded by what is the latest "new" or "first"— the incessant update? God or posterity no longer suffice. Both must be supplemented by a self validated in recognition but wise to the ways of both inviting and evading performance. So, the self-made turns into the self-styled performer, and every aspect of social life takes on a tinge from the styles of those who are actually in the visible professions. If you don't look like it, you must not be it. And—the Julian Eltinge corollary—only if you're not it, can you see it from the outside and thereby perfect it. The growing permeation of American culture by advertising that begins in the 1920s gave such self-objectification an aura of social glory that corresponded to the nineteenth-century self-help belief that making money signified not the quantity of wealth but the quality of virtue. Together with show business, advertising is a crucial staging ground for the definition of modern fame. In show business the audience watches and thereby possesses the performer as an aspect of itself. In advertising the audience is invited to be part of the performance by buying the product and thereby placing itself on the stage of consumption. The eye appropriates what it sees. Normally, objects remain separate from us, but those images we see on the screen or on the page are continuous with our imagination of what they are 'really' like. Because our imagination participates in their creation, it is difficult to separate who sees from what is seen, whether the image is of human or inanimate objects. In the theater and at the movies we watched others; in advertising we were invited to watch a version of ourselves, made ideal and perfect by the possession of the product. As an aspect of show business rather than of commerce, therefore, advertising sells not objects but the sense of what it is like to be the person who has such objects. In the more baroque phases, mere possession is enough to satisfy. A woman I once knew would shop when she felt depressed, but never wear the often very expensive clothes she bought. Put away in a drawer, they retained the invisible power of command that she wanted to possess; to actually put them on would turn them into mere clothes.

As Bruce Barton's characterization of Jesus the salesman indicates, advertising is predicated on the belief that the most attractive aspect of a product is its least tangible. Augustine answered Ovid by saying that the hunger for praise could be filled only by the audience of God. But advertising exploits that hunger for acceptability by focusing on its audience's feelings of insufficiency and incompleteness without this crucial missing part, the charismatic product that will enhance the self. Like the love that cloys with physical possession, however, no single manifestation can ever suffice, because the longing is for the idea, not for the thing itself. Whatever it is, the product confers beauty, health, status, and social acceptability. Amidst ceaseless competition, it brings calm and ease, since the wisdom of one's choice has already been confirmed. Like the spiritual justification of material success that fueled the idea of the self-made man, the self-enhancement promised by advertising transforms the normal rewards proposed by a society based on consumption and money into something resembling a secular sacrament. The premise is still spiritual and even Augustinian: The true self stands outside ordinary time and can never be complete on earth. But the implication is material: The goal of all consumption and aspiration is self-enhancement.

The Great Depression of the 1930s had decisively eroded the nineteenth-century belief that self-made "character" effortlessly determined economic and social success. But the myth that inner merit is validated by the spiritual benediction of fame continued to flourish. The more uncertain the ways to worldly success became, the more obvious was the decision to imitate the movie stars, who did nothing so well as be themselves. From the mid-nineteenth century onward audiences clamored after performers to learn the secrets of their self-presentation and to buy for themselves their costumes of talismanic power: Julian Eltinge sold mascara just as Jane Fonda now sells exercise lessons. To take lessons in self-performance was to move one step closer to the world where performers mythically dwelled, the world of show business, the world of the famous. Audiences had always come to watch favorite performers. But the vaudeville circuits allowed a degree of career watching that was unprecedented. Beginning in the 1920s, while advertising was creating a world of eager-to-be-satisfied consumers, show business pushed the self-consciousness of Barnum and the vaudeville circuits into a celebration of itself as the place of beauty and harmony, where everyone, with a few nasty exceptions, loves one another. A significant moment comes in 1920, when Florenz Ziegfeld commissions Jerome Kern to write *Sally,* the story of a girl who rises from obscurity to stardom in the Ziegfeld Follies, to be played by Marilyn Miller, who rose. . . . Here was the "star is born" mirror plot that would launch a thousand reflections. A few years later the American musical comedy came to maturity with Kern's *Show Boat,* which allowed the same off-stage/onstage ironies as *Sally* but made them part of the grand plot of show business itself, the community within which you can be yourself even as you impersonate innumerable others to general applause.

By allowing the audience backstage with the actual performers, show business brought them into the community as fans who shared the intangible aura of the famous. The result emphasized the feeling of the fan that performers are deified in large part because the audience pays attention to them. Owning a portrait of Napoleon, for example, was not quite the act of possession that owning a portrait of John F. Kennedy would become. The modern audience of fans, with its elements of both adoration and participation in the life of the star, has intervened. The fan magazine article replaces the theatrical soliloquy and both are superseded by the television interview. To complicate the process, in every one of the visible professions that were getting their start in the years around World War One, there have now grown up several generations of fans who in their turn have become looked at themselves. And so the basic question for a star to answer is always, 'What's it like to be you—famous, recognized, successful in the eyes of others?' Let us in on the "real you," interviewers ask, giving the persons in the spotlight an opportunity to attract the audience to their careers rather than to any individual characters they might play. Nineteenth-century publicity was confined to certain special places and special times. On stage there is an immediate audience and a consequent social support for both performer and role, and, as we have seen, nineteenth-century stage audiences were encouraged to note the differences. But film, with its lack of an immediate audience, forced the performer to project an invisible audience to play to, and star quality, then as now, meant the ability to play to an audience of anonymous others and make them think you meant each one of them alone. As seasoned spectators, we thus look not for style so much as sincerity—actions that don't seem to be performed, from people to whom acres of shining lights and technicians wandering around don't seem to make any difference. That this "sincerity" has little to do with any action or attitude we would consider to be sincere in our families or neighbors hardly crosses our minds, for performers are models of another kind of behavior: 'Under that stress, I wish I could seem so unpretentious and so sincere.' In this prime aspect of modern selfhood, performers are once again ideal versions of ourselves. Through them we can judge our own performances and in their sincerity read how to imply that there is no artifice, only the naked heart. Alexander Pope thought "one self-approving hour" was enough to balance out the need for social praise, but he presented even that hour as a distant ideal. For the fan the star seems to have such ideal approval and, in the first flush of film's monarchy of the visual, the nineteenth-century fascination with national and ethnic types gave way to a fascination with new kinds of individuals. Virtually every memoir of growing up since World War One has its obligatory references to the influence of film stars as silent partners in the creation of the author's personality. Kate Simon, for example, at 13 thought of herself "as desirable as Gloria Swanson, as steely as Nita Naldi, as winsome as Marion Davies . . . like them, invincible and immortal" (179).

"Invincible and immortal." As far as the fan was concerned, such figures were saints of various perfection to which their own "real" natures were footnotes. But the one element still unaccounted for in the mythology was that, while you continued to be natural, you were also being watched. Until fairly recently it was the sports stars who most significantly handled the problem of public exposure because at their best they represented an unself-conscious perfection of the body, displayed for the pleasure of their fans. Here was fame unsullied by the alloy of history, language, or any mediation but the body's own. Public sports in the nineteenth and twentieth centuries, even more than films and certainly more than theater, brought masses of people together in what Gunter Barth has called "that basic form of urban leisure, watching others do things" (25), and the 1896 revival of the Greek Olympic Games explicitly attempted to oppose human physical perfection to the political antagonisms that divided countries. In the 1920s and 1930s especially, sports attracted not only an increasing number of cheering fans, but also a number of painters and writers for whom the physical skill and bodily control represented a model of unpremeditated perfection and closeness to nature like that they sought in their own work. In the context of the baseball or football team or in the more individual sports of boxing and bullfighting existed the ultimate competition—without irony or the self-conscious weight of the past—only the body, the opponent, and the moment. Like Alexander the Great's identification with Hercules, the admiration for an athlete, whoever the fan was, supplied a cleansing of everyday consciousness. Thus scandal in sports was even more heinous than scandal in politics, whose lifeblood was deception. In the eyes of the fan, public sports were played by natural beings civilized enough to follow the rules of the game; like the show business people with whom they often were seen, they were in image at least the latest version of the American natural aristocrat, and many of the anecdotes told about them, celebrated their victories over enemies who had only social status to recommend them.

But radio, films, and television have long since brought a national focus and self-consciousness to what were often local contests, thereby forcing local heroes to try themselves on the national and later international stage. By now, of course, with million-dollar salaries and big-business control of many franchises, it is getting harder and harder to believe in the image of purity that sports once represented. As in so many areas of public life after World War Two, the mechanics of display has itself become a subject of public discussion. In late August of 1980, for example, when George Brett was heading toward a .400 season, Red Smith talked to Ted Williams, who had passed the magic mark in 1941. Williams wished Brett well and warned him about the effect of the cooler weather in the late season. But, as Smith pointed out, Brett also had to deal with something Williams hadn't: "the nation's press at his heels, slick-paper authors hounding him for cover stories, television people constantly on his back, Madison Avenue types hectoring him until his hair fell out in chunks" (*New York Times,* 53).

I have been noting in the self-presentation of public people in the twentieth century the importance of the "natural" that links the athlete pushing his body to the utmost to the movie star "only playing himself." But the example of George Brett, just one among many, indicates the self-conscious frame in which naturalness now has to express itself. The test of performance in sports, as in show business, had become not merely doing your best so much as whether you could take the immense focus on you while you were doing it: Not only can you perform but also can you do it while everybody watches you, hoping that you'll make it but maybe a little happier (or happy in a different way) if you fail? By the 1970s baseball especially had become a theatrical version of its earlier self, not content to be what it was, without also making sure the audience knew it, even to the extent of reviving late nineteenth-century styles in uniforms, a little tighter and more formfitting, to suit the modern fashion. In boxing the trend could be traced from the directness of Joe Louis or Rocky Marciano down through Floyd Patterson and Muhammed Ali. Patterson, caught in between the generations, stayed torn between public performance as the only indicator of success and an anxious feeling of inauthenticity that forced him into false moustaches and noses in order to hide from his fans. Ali, far from hiding when he was out of the ring, made everything, onstage and backstage, into part of the show. Unlike the boxers of the twenties, who seemed to back into celebrity while they did their job, fame was Ali's biggest theme. In the 1920s and 1930s, Babe Ruth, like J. Edgar Hoover and Charles A. Lindbergh, had his own press agent. But by the 1970s the great sports figures, although they may have had press agents as well, created the news themselves. The purity of sincere involvement in the world of physical combat for which their fans used to admire them had, like everything else on the American public stage, taken on the lineaments of a naturalness inextricably linked to self-display.

In a world where most social positions, including professions, are hereditary, ambition can be expressed either in society's narrow terms or else as a dynamic outside force that society must either accommodate or destroy. In the modern world few positions are hereditary, and society is formed instead by the struggle of innumerable personal ambitions, with varying commitments to tradition. Only certain offices, like pope or monarch of England, carry an aura that envelops whoever fills them. At least in theory neither has had to struggle to the top through a morass of competition. They seem to be pure winners, in part because they seem not to have sullied their wills in the search for eminence. They have not forced their way; they have been somehow designated. Such people are the measure of ultimate celebrity because, unlike heroes, they don't have to do anything specific, nor announce any goals. They are celebrated because they occupy a certain position in public life to which attention is directed no matter who is in it. How much better it is when the actual person is vaguely interesting and has amiable personal traits together with some degree of political acumen. Up to a point, the more human they are, the more they will be celebrated, even if their humanity consists primarily in waving to crowds and kissing little children; the most trivial personal gesture will designate them "human." They satisfy a contemporary hunger not for someone at the top, but for an ultimate fame unrelated to the striving in which everyone else is perpetually engaged. Yet, the fact that Pope John Paul II feels the personal need to record songs and allow his plays to be staged merely shows that even such a purely spiritual sanction is not enough in this century of the performer. Like Byron the aristocrat, the pope has to publish as well.

To identify the perfection of performance as a natural talent leads societies into strange waters, and for those below the exalted realms of popes and hereditary monarchs, the conflicts can be acute. The American attitude toward the Olympics, for example, is wonderfully schizophrenic. On the one hand, no matter how much money is spent by television networks and advertisers, the participants must still be considered amateurs, with a pure desire to excel for themselves. In a world where attention is fragmented in a thousand directions and work is rarely rewarding, the Olympic athletes represent a pure focus of individual effort toward the goal of personal and national honor. In these terms, then, to withhold American participation from the 1980 Moscow Olympics was to withhold American purity from a situation corrupted by Russian national self-interest. Yet at the same time that the Olympic audience longs for the purity of intention and motive its athletes represent, it has also experienced the fall. It longs precisely because it has been corrupted, because it has accepted the display and mere show business of an occasion supposed to demonstrate that show is only the outward costume of inner value. Even the athletes who are actually trying to achieve something may be unable to distinguish themselves from their imitators. In the 1980 Winter Olympics a frequently repeated television commercial for the soft drink Tab showed an ice-skating couple practice a spin three times (interspersed with drinks of Tab) before the woman could do the trick without falling. Meanwhile, during the actual competition, a couple awaited their scores sharing a can of Tab. The woman in this pair had in fact fallen during the number they had just performed. Had she seen the commercial and decided that Tab would help her out as well as it had her fictional counterpart? Sometimes, for the famous as much as for the audience, it's hard to tell the difference.

But no conspiracy of television commercials has stolen the authentic American sense of self and replaced it with false images. In the days of Elizabeth I, an antitheatrical satirist could complain that performers who played the role of kings on the stage not only tricked the audience into thinking kings were before them but also might even believe they were kings themselves. Now, in a world of democratic fame, the mere fact of being on stage, of being looked at, was enough to make one feel kingly. Like the natural stage performer, sports stars were therefore attractive not only for their ease of performance but also for the impression they conveyed that, in a consumer society, they weren't selling anything more than themselves. But, as sports became increasingly professionalized big business, the aura of amateurism was required to maintain the ideal. In the 1920s an enormous amount of attention was paid by the press to college sports, on the implicit assumption that amateur athletics were even purer than professional and that young men willing to die metaphorically for

Alma Mater on the ballfield were suitable stand-ins for the military heroes who had done the same literally in the past war. Spectator sports like these were moral entertainments in which spirit and body magically mingled. The fascination with Olympic athletes thus represents the continuing desire to believe that somewhere competition is inspiring rather than mean-spirited and somewhere individual ambition unselfishly contributes to the good of the whole. Such visible fame is the crown of bodily achievement, the transcendent escape from the fray of social competition for the star and, momentarily, for the fan. No wonder that the most storied coach of the 1920s and 1930s, with the most do-or-die teams, was not from one of the Ivy League schools or the military academies but Knute Rockne of Notre Dame.

*   *   *

Throughout the twentieth century the popular feeling has grown that famous people were at once more real than we and less real: More real because of the heightened form of their reality, their images so huge in our eyes and minds; less real because that heightening promised constant availability to us and therefore a willingness to give up their private lives, to be invaded—since, after all, they were on show. For performers who couldn't bridge the gap between what they were selling and what they "really were," the collision was inevitable. John Wayne asking Rich Little the impressionist to read his lines in a John Wayne voice gives the flavor of a successful dissociation. An example from the political realm is Richard Nixon, who, after reading most of the ghost-written manuscript of *Six Crises,* believed he had sufficiently mastered the style of Alvin Moscow, his ghostwriter, to write the final chapter himself. Here are public people totally at home with behavior that we in "normal" life would still consider inauthentic. Both Wayne and Nixon try to stand outside their public natures and accept the necessary fact that fandom caricatures the famous. Nixon's final inability to be as blithe as Wayne is marked by the obsessive taping exposed in Watergate—his effort to get everything about himself collected so that others might search for the coherence in the media-fragmented images.

Especially for the face preserved on film, it had seemed that visible fame might promise to be eternal and show business a world where dreams were realized and identities enhanced. But, true to our national ambivalence about aspiration, there was another version of self-display in which identities were warped and lives emptied of whatever meaning they possessed to begin with. In America the pursuit of self-fulfillment seemed to be an injunction from the Founding Fathers themselves. But many performers as well as more ordinary aspirants attained the place of security in the public eye only to discover that the uncertain sense of self that had driven them cannot be dispensed with so easily. Oddly or appropriately enough, many of the most popular stars of show business could not escape a feeling of inauthenticity about what they were doing. Broadway musicals and Hollywood movies that bemoan the human qualities lost in the push for show business success tell only the social part of the story. But there is a psychological side as well, perhaps memorialized in the many monster films of the early 1930s. For every success story like Jenny Lind, who retired in time, there were stories of psychological breakdowns that success seemed to create more than resolve. There is no question of shedding costumes or makeup after the show, because the show is never over. The performer who hits the top only to disintegrate into a psychic mess has been around in various guises since the middle of the nineteenth century. Having constructed a public self in order to escape from shyness or some more extreme private torment, these aspirants discover themselves entrapped in an audience attention that is intimate but impersonal, embracing without nurturing. But more typically it is the young person thrust into the public spotlight before he or she has been able to build up inner psychic resources who suffers the most. The more obvious wounds are found in the biggest successes. But the scars are visible as well on every high school beauty queen and football star who hasn't quite managed to weather the abrupt drop in audience attention. Heywood Broun's remark in 1925 about college football has a prophetic ring for generations raised on modes of striving then unforeseen:

> To struggle in the spotlight never did anybody any good, and if the man who fails happens to be nineteen years old he may get an ego bruise which will leave him permanently tender. And if he succeeds brilliantly he may be no better off. The American community is cluttered with ineffective young men who gave their souls to dropkicking and then found there was no future in it ("Dying for 'Dear Old—,' " 250).

The loss is the loss of an affirming audience. When the audience withdraws its attention, the transfiguring fame turns into mere ostentation. The early audience hysterias over such stars as Valentino, Garbo, and even the now-forgotten George Bancroft is first a tribute to the power of the disembodied visual presence of those individuals. But it also marks the audience's new-found ability to observe people closely without them knowing it and thereby gain power over them. Voyeurism with its sexual connotation and eavesdropping with its implication of overheard secrets only indicate the most obvious features of the general urge to "know" that the movies cultivated. Here were deities served on a platter, and the convention of not looking directly into the camera enhanced the sense of the audience's privileged view even as it fostered the "destiny gaze" of Napoleonic and Washingtonian portraiture. When the actual audience moved too close, without proper supervision, such a star might become reasonably fearful about injury to the fragile private self that somehow came across so powerfully in film. Like Garbo, explaining her desire for seclusion—"People take energy from me, and I need it for the camera"—the film performer often connected the intensity with which she faced her audience to the extent she was able to keep them at a safe distance. Then the gap between the public image and the private reality need never become an issue.[48]

But for most performers it is difficult to maintain such a distance, and few now are as frank as Garbo or Gable about their ambiguous relation to their audience. "Invasion of privacy" is the more usual cry. Fame is desired because it is the ultimate justification, yet it is hated because it brings with it unwanted focus as well, depersonalizing as much as individualizing. Often the public self is established to buttress a shy and retiring private nature. Then, when the public image threatens to become overpowering, privacy seems to be a retreat, unless that too has been turned into a commodity by the media. Once again, we are verging on the world of show business tragedy—the broken emotional lives that result from the ambition to be justified by the wildly applauding audience. The more dependent on the audience's approval the performer seems to be, the more the audience is monarchical itself, approving or disdaining in part to titillate itself with its own power. Although the fame of the modern performer may be a fame for escaping social constraints by creating a self, exhibited in a body, that is unique, a great part of the attraction for the fan may be likened to the lure of Houdini: Maybe this time he won't escape.[49]

From the mid-nineteenth century on, the performer, particularly the female performer, is celebrated in fiction as the archetypal self-manipulator who shows her superiority to social roles by rising to greatness as an actress. Zola's *Nana* and Dreiser's *Sister Carrie* are only two versions of this theme that show business itself sentimentalizes in works like *Sally* or swallows with a dash of *mea culpa* in ones like *All About Eve*. In great part the attraction of the audience and especially of the fan to the performer thus emerges from the nineteenth century as an attraction to the singular, what is outside normal categories, an attraction to the ideal as well as to the freak. The more natural, the more spiritual, the more sincere such a performer is perceived to be, the more the audience is able to identify with him or her, for actual achievement separates fan and star and turns the relationship from psychic sharing into admiration and subordination. Reversing the situation of the king who licenses the antics of dwarfs and fools, the fan lets the star act for him, claiming affinity by sharing a gesture, a hairstyle, or a piece of clothing. His response is a compound of

48. That this distinction is not generally appreciated even by those who make a living at show business is indicated by those television commercials in which a famous movie star tells us directly that he or she prefers certain brands of cars or coffee. Since the power in film comes from not looking at the audience, such eye contact automatically indicates subordination. Whatever reason we might have to believe them disappears, and they become mere shills.

49. In Houdini's case, in fact, his openness to the audience's idea of him did prove fatal. In 1926, while he was in his dressing room reading his mail, he absentmindedly let a young admirer punch him several times in the stomach and abdomen to test his muscle control. Just over a week later, he was dead of acute appendicitis. It had been diagnosed not long after the punching. But Houdini insisted on completing two more shows. By the time he was operated on, it was too late.

envy for the star's special status and relief to be free of those public pressures, fascinated by the freak and yet reassured of one's seeming normality. No wonder then that failure and discontent and emptiness once again become part of the story of fame, as they had been in the days when the Christian and the Roman view faced each other directly. If the watchword of a culture is progress, when you aren't going up, you must be going down. Since the identification of success with visibility is part of the air our characters breathe, visible fame has therefore become the doctor for all ills and achievement before an audience the compensation for every flaw. No one considered Alexander Pope's twisted spine or Napoleon's short stature or Caesar's baldness or Alexander's mother or Byron's club foot reason for their aspirations until the comparatively recent present. But we invoke them as "explanations" because they reassure us not only that such out-of-scale aspiration is essentially freakish (and not like our own), but also that it is a freakishness that affirms our own grander aspirations—if we would chose to indulge them. For who in a democratic society wants to be excessively different without a good excuse?

As performers have replaced other kinds of public people in an ongoing exhibit of exemplary public behavior, they have become the receptacle for as many terrors as triumphs, the battleground of a collision between the desire for social recognition and the need for some more "private" definition of character, in which the body may promise, but the self holds back. From the early days of film, the audience's curiosity about who the performers were and what might be outside the filmed story spawned fan magazines, whose ersatz constructions put some version of the private lives of the stars on stage as well, until some became the shriveled shells of their own publicity. Only the most self-conscious could use their detachment, their sense of doing a job, to let them off relatively unscathed. But for those who actually used their inner natures as the armature for their public selves, the game was much rougher. In Hollywood during the 1930s there was a famous brothel named Mae's, where all the girls looked like famous actresses and would act just like them, not for tourists so much as for the men who knew and worked with them. Garson Kanin tells the story of taking to bed the one who resembled Carole Lombard and then telling Lombard about it. Lombard laughed and then said she would tell Clark Gable, to whom she was married, but then said she wouldn't, because he would want to go to bed with the girl himself (317). Diderot's actor coldbloodedly stood back and successfully dramatized emotions precisely because he did not really feel them. But such a story as Kanin's represents the more modern possibility that when acting is defined in terms of its "naturalness," the actor is in danger of obliterating the line between self and role, body and identity, being and name.

That an actress even jokingly worries that her actor husband might be intrigued with going to bed with a prostitute who looks and acts like her indicates the unanchored integrity of a whole drifting world. Even for someone in the "business," the body projected on screen was somehow divorced from an actual body and personality, just as the visible fame might seem like an alien imposition rather than a fuller realization. Once that body had been accepted and even praised, there came another level of dissatisfaction: My body is not me; accept now the "real me." But, of course, that "real me" also had to be displayed before it could be noticed, and so in its turn followed the body into the discard pile, corrupted because it had to be visible rather than innately appreciated. Distaste for the body may, in fact, be an occupational hazard of visible fame in the same way that the rest of us diet and worry about our looks. Visible people marry, seeking husbands or wives, and discover they have found only fans, attracted to a self they themselves considered to be unreal and "not me."

In the wake of Eva Tanguay and Isadora Duncan at the beginning of the century, who were able to project from the stage an élan that transcended conventions of form, thus appeared performers, especially in the period from the late 1930s to the early 1970s, who possessed powers to entertain that seemed to inhabit them rather than be in their control. Once onstage or before the cameras, the often shy introverts were transformed into the instruments of their "gift" and, like driving a car at one hundred miles an hour, the best they could do was aim them. Professional training was downplayed in favor of "heart," the true foundation of the spirit pouring over and anointing the audience, who often made them special favorites because of the lavish but subtle way they acknowledged the power of being seen. Unlike their predecessors in stirring up audience emotion, performers like Judy Garland or the young Frank Sinatra, and later Janis Joplin and Jim Morrison, reduced the distance between themselves and the audience. Al Jolson's passions, for example, still wore the nineteenth-century mask of black face. But Garland sat on the edge of the stage, and Joplin roared up to the edge and went right over. Of course, the love song, the intimate aside, and even the possibility of cracking up right there in front of us were gestures that could be easily copied. But it was the pioneers who gave them their emotional status. Unprepared, they had been hit hardest by the movie promise of a world in which you would be totally accepted. Judy Garland's wonderful voice, for example, came out of a barrel-chested body perfectly suited for it. But the demands of movie-star "beauty" forced her to attempt to turn herself into shapes that she was not, until she seemed to see her body as what Aljean Harmetz has called "the undesired repository of her voice" (103). In such a self-selling the "natural gift" has become a curse. Similarly, the life of Marilyn Monroe is a virtual allegory of the performer's alienation from the face and body that are nominally the instrument of her fame. Like the young Elizabeth Taylor, Monroe was both child and woman, to be nurtured and to be desired simultaneously. The sexual lushness she projected went hand-in-hand with the human impression of vulnerability. Wearing a body that was the object of the fantasies of countless others, she felt herself to be empty and so married two sensitive men: first, Joe DiMaggio, the publicly certified athlete and gentleman; and second, Arthur Miller, the publicly certified wise man and writer. But neither could fill the sense of incompleteness she had, which was as responsible for her public appeal as for her personal failure. If stars are saints, Garland and Monroe are clearly among the martyrs.

For performers so drawn to the terrifying edge of what it means to be visible, appreciation is vital, but none is ever enough. Any saving step between offstage and onstage has long since been obliterated, and their faces and their bodies are permanently in fief to their audiences. In the nineteenth century Poe expressed the paradox through his story of the artist who creates the ultimate portrait of his wife without realizing that he is a vampire of the eye who is killing her in the process: "And he *would* not see that the tints which he spread upon the canvas were drawn from the cheeks of her who sate beside him" ("The Oval Portrait," 483). Like the photograph that steals the soul, the portrait of Oscar Wilde's *Dorian Gray* similarly preserves Dorian's beauty only finally to reveal his evil. When he destroys it, he destroys himself. But it is in Wilde's own life, where painter, sitter, and canvas become one, that we see the coming shadow of twentieth-century show business self-destruction written plain in his active agitation for the trial and publicity that lead to his death. So adept at publicity himself, did he think that he could control what would happen but was unprepared for its whirlwind strength? Or did he seek to ensure his fame by ruining himself before anyone else could? "To Oscar Wilde, posing as a somdomite [sic]," the marquess of Queensberry had written, and Wilde chose to dispute the characterization, caught between the reality of posing and the reality of being. The possessive eye of the artist that transforms what it sees has been replaced by the eye of the constant audience that ignores your own reality in order to make you a part of its story.[50]

Wilde's plunge toward a visible publicity inseparable from self-destruction foretells our century's preoccupation with the artist as self-styled (and actual) victim. It unites the artist, otherwise in the heart of the public gaze, with saints, martyrs, and even Jesus himself as a seeker of spiritual truths who desperately tried to shun the Roman spotlight until it sought, captured, and killed him. In the modern world it is rarely preachers or divines who martyr themselves so often as politicians and entertainers. They nominate themselves and the audience chooses to agree that they are scapegoats for the audience's own unsatisfied and ambivalent urge for recognition and public visibility. Scapegoats in general, especially those who are self-appointed, must act their parts visibly and well. By loading our own sinfully Roman desires for exposure upon their frantic efforts to please an audience, we can momentarily be purged.

Scapegoats are crutches, and the more they are leaned on and brought back for encores, the more warped they become. They can never quit

50. In an earlier confrontation with Wilde, the marquess had said "I do not say you are it . . . but you look it, and you pose as it, which is just as bad" (Hyde, 194). This is, of course, the same marquess whose name is associated with the rules for amateur boxing he established.

while they're ahead, because in their own minds they are never ahead. They burn instead with an incandescent flame for which they are their own moths, perpetuating the Romantic myth of flaming genius cut off early because it blazed so high. Such an aspiration to be publicly rewarded for one's inherent, unpremeditated, and unstriven for nature takes its most paradoxical shape in the performers who came to prominence in the 1930s, the first generation to grow up on films. And something of its conflict between the desire to be seen and the desire to disappear, the flaunting of the body and the belief that it was a corrupt shell, is suggested by the strange life of Howard Hughes. Like Lindbergh, he was an aviator, like Edison a tinkerer, but one drawn even more explicitly than they were to the world of entertainment and personal visibility. Producing films, dating and marrying actresses, Hughes was involved in the Hollywood of the 1930s and 1940s in a variety of ways, including his effort to build and fly himself the largest airplane in the world. Only later did he become Howard Hughes the famous recluse. From a world of people who cared about themselves and how they looked all the time, he went into one in which he seemed not to care about himself at all—never seeing anyone, letting his hair and nails grow to grotesque lengths. But in fact his reclusehood was merely the reverse side of his hankering for fame. Like film stars noted for their beauty or leanness who get fatter and fatter, as if to dare the public to love them still—or announce their retirement and therefore their transcendence of Hollywood standards of beauty—Howard Hughes took the film preoccupation with the body several steps down the road. His own body he considered to be a machine and referred to a square-cut left thumbnail as "my screwdriver" (Phelan, 145–46). Driven by a fear of bacteria, he refused to touch anyone or anything without being able to "insulate" his hands before or wipe them afterward. Above all, his body was a precious relic to be preserved from all pollution. His urine was preserved in mason jars. If he could not get the audience who served by choice, he would be satisfied with the audience he paid to serve, and each of his employees had to acquiesce in his elaborate bodily rituals. The image is reminiscent of Caligula slopping around in bathrobe and slippers or Lyndon Johnson holding meetings while on the toilet. In the world where performance is the key to fame and the body its most direct expression, only trivial aspirants aim to be beautiful. The real challenge is to be ugly and grotesque, for then, if you win, you win big. If you're accepted, it must really be for yourself.

As the networks of visual and verbal communication enwrap the world, the older binders of community and the older conferrals of status rely more and more on them for sanction. What has gloomily been called narcissism is thus an individual extension of the curatorial attitude toward the body that performers and sports figures, monarchs and politicians, have had for a long time. It is less to be deplored as some immoral deviation from a visionary model of the integrated and whole self than to be explored as part of the general transformation of individuality and the sense of personal "character" that social and cultural changes have helped bring about. That the orthodoxies of much of twentieth-century psychology have revived the ancient Judeo-Christian assumption of the inferiority of the visible to the invisible self should not blind us to the complexity with which the basic question of personal recognition in a mass society has been engaged. Freud, it is said, refused to let himself be filmed and recorded at the same time because he thought that the combined image would steal his soul, or perhaps make reproducible what he considered to be unique. Film and the visual media display, enhance, and celebrate, but they domesticate and diminish as well. Osa Johnson, the African explorer of the 1920s, once wrote about the way the fear she felt in front of a cannibal chief dissipated after she had seen him on film. Instead of a ferocious, immediate human being, he had become "a screen personality" (132)—intimately accessible, unthreatening, enclosed—turned by film into an ironic version of himself. Her husband, Martin Johnson, had taken the film. But even if the chief had made it himself, the effect might have been more ferocious, but still somehow detached. Freud had no doubt similarly learned the performer's lesson that to be caught in the attention of others is in great part to mean what they want you to mean.

Conclusion:
The Dream of Acceptability

I found it impossible to concentrate. It worried me. I remember staring at my reflection in the mirror on the medicine cabinet. "Here you are, nine years old," I told my image. "And what have you done? You're nothing . . . nothing but a failure."
—VINCENTE MINNELLI, *I Remember It Well*

[I]t was clear to me that no one had looked at me in years. All of the other attentions had been fleeting, partial, obstructed: now, at a moment's notice, now and at last I was seen as I was.
—SCOTT SPENCER, *Endless Love*

Freud's unwillingness to participate in the illusion of human presence that is conveyed by sound film seems now to be an almost archaic gesture of sensitivity. In the last hundred years, the nature of fame changed more decisively and more quickly than it had for the previous two thousand. Visual media became the standard-bearers of international recognition, giving art, religion, and politics shapes they never had before. Napoleon was influencing individual behavior all across Europe long after his armies were defeated and he himself dead. Television stands only latest in the progression from oil painting to copper engraving to photography to movies as an influence on self-presentation and cultural focus. But the reproducibility of the image (and the fame) both widened its appeal and undermined its uniqueness. As fame was more dependent on a mass audience, so it was more closely tied to that audience's gaze toward the famous, just as, when we contemplate the small ignitions or huge novae of past fame, we might wonder to what extent the light comes from them, and to what extent it is conferred by the searchlight of our retrospective attention. The images of fame had become more and more independent of the standards and occasions that had inspired them. With the advent of television, the dominant visual medium emphasized neither the isolation of an individual image (as in painting and photography) nor the self-containment within a series of enclosed stories (as in the movies), but a rapidly shifting group of stories and images that repetitively familiarized the audience with the faces depicted.

There is therefore little significant way in which our invocation of "fame" can be compared to that of the ancients or even of the Renaissance—unless we consider the word and the concept historically. Otherwise we will believe that there is some uniquely modern paradox in the combined vanity and humility of, for example, Robert Frost, or that Marilyn Monroe's urge to self-destruction was either a personal quirk or just another example of an old Hollywood story. In every era and culture of the West since the classical age, fame has been a complex word into which is loaded much that is deeply believed about the nature of the individual, the social world, and whatever exists beyond both. As a way of referring to the ways of recognizing an intensified form of all individual nature, its historical metamorphoses tell us much about how particular ages defined, promulgated, and understood what a person was or could be. The paradoxes that I posed at the beginning of this book—the desire to be different but familiar, famous but the kid next door—thus turn out to be the perennial contradictions of a style of ambition that is the legacy of the past as much as it is the urge of the moment. Without some sense of the historical nature of those vital contradictions, any effort to make a face, a name, or a deed last is merely a trivial and immediate gesture. The urge to fame is therefore not so much a cause as a causal nexus through which more generalized forces—political, theological, artistic, economic, sociological—flow to mediate the shape of individual lives.

Since fifth-century Athens, fame has been a way of expressing either the legitimacy of the individual within society or (in the Christian and spiritual model) the legitimacy of the individual as opposed to the illegitimacy of the social order. Thus the urge for fame mingles one's acceptance of oneself with the desire for others (or the Other) to recognize that one is special. It is the most immediate effort individuals make to reach beyond themselves, their families, and their place in a traditional order to claim a more general approval of their behavior and nature, whether that approval comes from within the world or outside it. The characteristic fame of an era cannot therefore be reduced to the currently available media or to abstract forces often perceivable in retrospect. It is instead a crucial connective between those forces—a much more immediately comprehensible and explicit goal for people living in history as well as a humanly more fruitful way to consider the interplay between individual will and historical movement.

Like many of the fevers, frenzies, and desires of the past, the longing for old standards of "true" fame reflect a feeling of loss and nostalgia for a mythical world where communal support for achievement could flourish. But in such societies that did exist, it was always only certain groups who had an exclusive right to call the tunes of glory, and both visual and verbal media were in the hands of a few. Until the decline of monarchy in the late eighteenth century, the standards of Western fame were generally those of particular classes and groups who had both the social power and the polemical insecurity to want to argue about them. Republican Rome took the fame that Alexander asserted for himself and made it the standard of behavior for an entire oligarchy of politicians and generals. To such formulations Christianity most successfully asserted that the rules of classical fame, with their emphasis on military and political ostentation for the good of state power, were wrong; or, more politely, that they were right only in the most limited, material, and earthbound way. Throughout the medieval reign of Christianity in Europe, and even into the Renaissance revival of Roman styles of aspiration, there is an interplay between the Christian and the Roman views of what constitutes an ideal person, shaped by a debate over what qualities define human character and activity in general.

Until the eighteenth century, these controversies took place within limited sections of society: among rulers, who, for reasons of political, spiritual, or artistic aspiration wanted special sanction for their ambition; and among writers and artists who supplied their patrons and employers with such sanctions, appropriately embroidered with classical and biblical references. In the late Middle Ages and Renaissance, first poets (like Dante and Petrarch) and later painters had redefined a fame competition among the elite to include their own special talents for judging the great of past and present. By the seventeenth century the patron was gradually losing any absolute power to name himself as the only worthy and justifying audience for an artist's worth. Two new audiences were beginning to demand equal consideration: the immediate audience of the theater-going public and the more detached audience for books and prints. Widening the glimpse theater allowed into the lives of the great, printing redefined upper-class preserves like diplomacy and war as worlds that could be entered by anyone talented enough to imitate and thereby to improve. When Falstaff asks "What's honor?" and answers "A word," he marks a shift from a class-oriented definition of honor (and fame) to a self-oriented one that his own success as a theatrical character (and that of Prince Hal) serves to celebrate. In part one might argue that the English monarchy survived, whereas the French vanished, because, thanks to Shakespeare and others, the English had earlier and better training in how to respond to an audience whose gaze increasingly had to be considered as an element of its authority.

The history of fame is inseparable from the history of human self-consciousness, on the part of both the aspirant and the audience. With the eighteenth century, we first discover an urge that seems comparable to our own. The decline in the respect paid to aristocratic military and political fame that is the fruit of the American and French revolutions follows more than a century after Oliver Cromwell's victory over the armies of Charles I had demonstrated that the upper classes had no special monopoly over either military effectiveness or the ability to make England a nation respected throughout Europe. Fame was beginning to be a matter of talent, learning, and personal virtue rather than of birth and inherited rank. With the rise of Washington and later Napoleon, that personal virtue became transformed into the star, the destiny, that singles out the most extreme aspirations. Modern fame, whether ostentatious or evasive, is thus predicated on the Industrial Revolution's promise of increasing progress and the Enlightenment's promise of ever-expanding individual will. Both will and energy, goes the assumption, are boundless, and both are undoubtedly connected to the good of the larger community, because God would not have it otherwise. In the saying popularized by Benjamin Franklin, one of the great exemplars of the new fame, "God helps them that help themselves."

The desire for recognition is a part of human nature especially sensitive both to social structures and to the mode and extent of communications within a society. Achievement and success are therefore generally defined primarily in terms of what other people think is worthy of admiration, and self-help in Franklin's formulation as well as many of its descendants is inseparable from the approval of an audience. Of course, many modern aspirants to fame seek a status opposed to widespread standards of approval and admiration. But whatever their nonsocial or antisocial imagery and aspirations, these urges are still expressed through socially and historically learned behavior, setting one tradition against another. The roots of this counterfame are deep in the challenge of Christianity to the classical idea of what constitutes a person. In their modern and secular form they illustrate the crucial awareness of audience that marks our time. The urge to fame is the urge to play an important, a noticed part in the great human drama, even for turning away. As more sensitivity to the different ways that can be accomplished grows, so do the number of aspirants. In the Middle Ages, no peasant thought he could become Richard the Lion-Heart. Later, others might dream of being members of Robin Hood's band, and later still, every young man struggling with his homework nurtured within a potential Abraham Lincoln.

When daily life is perceived in great part as a constant performance before an audience of others, and the popular media are preoccupied with discussions of the proper and improper way to behave, individual self-consciousness about performance is unavoidable. Our beings have taken on a deep dye from the media romance with the eye. Especially for those whose belief in a personal or a cultural past has been eroded or destroyed, the lives being played out before the cameras and typewriters supply a variety of alternatives to follow and avoid, admire and loathe. From the wardrobe of visual styles and antistyles that the business of showing has developed over the last few hundred years, we each put together our own costume. It is not therefore the separation of fame from achievement that is the crucial moral issue, but the definition of achievement itself as something primarily external. Such is the nature of fame in a media world, where honor becomes less a matter of personal satisfaction and personal values than of an external recognition that makes that inner honor "real." But no such acceptance is final, and it should not seem paradoxical if the famous seem shy and private. For fame implies that one deeply knows the rules for socially significant behavior, not necessarily that one's temperament is in accord with them. In fact the greater one's talent for fame, the greater may be one's temperamental distaste for society, since it is easier to understand and manipulate social expectations if one is somehow outside to begin with. To be entrepreneurial about one's work or one's public self does not mean that one is an entrepreneur; it means that one knows how to survive in an entrepreneurial world, even to the extent of satirizing it by selling what is essentially intangible.

As Tocqueville frequently observed, the rise of the democratic political systems in the late eighteenth century posed important questions about the survival not just of old but of any form of status and striving. Observing the fame world of today, we might add that democracy is also characterized by greater and greater disagreement over what constitutes worthy activity—worth doing, worth knowing about, and worth conveying to others. If fame in a monarchical and absolutist state resembles a pyramid, fame in a representational and democratic society looks more like the silhouette of a mountain range, with a multitude of peaks, none necessarily higher than the others. There the desire for personal fame is a politics of the self, an ideology of personal validation, in which the individual seeks affirmation through a fame defined by the preexisting fame of others. These famous are symptomatic and symbolic, the large-screen projection of those human possibilities a culture believes are the most fascinating and perhaps useful for its survival. Like the Greek dialect that bound together the Hellenistic world or the Latin that linked nations through the Renaissance, the famous are a *koine,* negotiated symbols in a human shorthand by which we process the world. But in the media-swathed world of the present, we can no longer simply compare rulers with Alexander or Julius Caesar or Augustus in the manner that satisfied writers and publicists for centuries. As there are more people in a more complicated world, there is a need for more stereotypes to winnow that complication. The more complex your stereotypes, the better able you are to discern what is relevant to you from what is not. Who can pay attention to everything?

The most striking effect of the democratization of fame has therefore been the transformation of two of its essential aspects: the connection to a world of spiritual value beyond and the connection to a world of human value through the individual. Unlike the ideal Renaissance theater that mirrored the social structure of society, the theater of modern fame is frequently an alternative to the more restrictive roles of the social world. The fame that is spiritually justifying purports to compensate for the social uneasiness of being successful. By now, almost everyone has heard the innumerable stories of the trap of fame and glory. But most still strive, for part of the promise of modern fame is that you and you alone will be able to do it differently, surmounting the past because you have learned from or ignored its examples. Once the spiritual fulfillment promised by modern fame is given, goes its myth, it can never be taken away. In the face of the myriad identities and demands of a more populous world, the spiritual glow conveyed by being recognized means finally not having to say who you are. Touched by the magic wand of this secular religion, the aspirant moves beyond the usual social context of achievement to a place where there is no career, no progress, no advance, no change—only the purity of being celebrated for being oneself.

The aspiration to such purity restates the close relation fame has always had to both death and transfiguration: the desire to find a place where one may live untarnished and uncorrupted throughout the ages. To study the past shapes of fame makes apparent the simultaneous modern desire to be singled out within time and to survive beyond it, that is, beyond death, whether through the Nobel Prize or *The Guinness Book of Records* or a piece of graffiti in the Times Square IRT station. Especially in the present, when more individuals than ever are trying to justify themselves by the approval of the public world, personal fame promises the ultimate means of taking control. In a world of increasing anonymity and powerlessness, where every day on the news life goes on without you, your name in print or your picture in the papers promises at least a moment of respite from despair. For, if an image lasts beyond death, it implies that its possessor is more than human.

But to be more than human is to have become somewhat impersonal; and the desire to be complete and whole through fame seeks a static perfection possible only when life is gone, even if the famous person still in fact seems to breathe. Many seek fame because they believe it confers a reality that they lack. Unfortunately, when they become famous themselves, they usually discover that their sense of unreality has only increased. The audience that awards the famous the ultimate accolade of its attention is less interested in what they think they "really" are than in what role they play in the audience's continuing drama of the meaning of human nature. In such a drama, change is not very welcome, nor is the "real me," unless that role is also fairly fixed. What to the audience is an icon to admire and even worship to the actual person involved can easily become an embalming above ground. Only those willing to act in accord with those expectations—or who can philosophically accept the brief period in which they accord with public taste—will survive the pressure unwarped.

For most of us the final justification of a transcendent social fame is out of reach. Like Sisyphus struggling to push the rock uphill—or the itsy-bitsy spider crawling up the water spout—every time we take one step up, we are in danger of falling two steps back. We are in danger, that is, so long as the model of society is a ladder, on which the myth of absolute individual opportunity is balanced by the companion myth of the precariousness of all uninherited social position. As Elizabeth I and Napoleon and Hitler established their political legitimacy by connecting themselves to past heroic genealogies, so we assume the guise of the famous to organize and legitimize our own uncertain aspirations and ambitions. Especially in America, with its strong self-help and how-to traditions, the selective emulation of public models is part of the national character. If you cannot get fame yourself, then you can become a fan, gathering reflected glory by carefully monitoring the rise and fall of those more avid for the absolute prizes, but allaying the ambition to be personally great by assuming a pose of involved detachment from their triumphs and tragedies.

Fandom mediates the disparity between the aspirations fostered by the culture and the relatively small increments of personal status possible in a mass society. On the one hand appear the gossip columns and "personality" magazines, continually restaging the same drama: The famous may have enormous personal problems, but they prevail because they have completeness to burn. On the other are innumerable gurus whose messages of Eastern spiritualism mingled with Western self-help release their followers from the burden of emptiness by filling it with themselves. But even for the nonfan, there is a larger sense in which the expansion of the possibility for fame and the preoccupation with those who achieve it indicates a deep-seated uncertainty about the survival of individuality itself. Does the increasing complexity and sheer connectedness of the world—the question might run—mean more uniformity or does it mean that self-assertion might be taking on different shapes, unforeseen in the individualities of the past but somehow linked to them? What is the feeling of human presence in a technological world? Can that world be made more intimate by widening the appeal to a communal validation of individual uniqueness? Now that there are more and more people on earth, and social class has become a matter of finer and finer distinctions, in what dictionary do we find self-definitions?

The rarefied atmosphere of absolute fame thus seeps into one's daily life as the desire for acceptability on one's own terms. How can I get ahead and still be loved? How can I compete without envying or being envied? How can I reach the place of fame, where competition is over and I can finally do my own work? In such an urge there are no goals, only the constant ambition to be more, however that state is defined. In America especially there is a psychic underclass in whose ears the need for fame has dinned so long that they have bought Cinderella whole: *aut Caesar aut nihil,* Einstein or shit, "If, baby, I'm the bottom, you're the top." In such an either/or situation, nothing can ever be enough. What appeared at the beginning of the modern era as the frenzy of a few is by now a low-grade fever in millions more. Fevers of the body come and go, killing or tempering. But fevers of the soul need other purgations. A terminal case of this fame malady occurs in those who decided that their incomplete identities have been violated by the famous person to whom they have entrusted them for completion. Such victims of fame overload cannot draw the line between being a fan and being the object of a fan's attention, acting heroically and being known to have acted heroically. In the more extreme versions, they become the star and the star becomes them—and so they seek either to kill or be killed. But for every Oswald or Hinckley, there may be many more like the California policeman who confessed he had fired on and wounded himself so that people would consider him a hero.

The spiritual journey of the past was a journey to restore the innocent soul that had been tarnished by the world. The fame journey of the present is toward that same goal, now garbed in the multiplication of image and name. No wonder that the aspiration to such fantasms of integrity and wholeness also breeds despair. Success needs more success to validate itself, and nothing can finally salve the feeling of incompleteness. It is just this pressure to be whole, to be cured, to be pure, that causes the split in American aspiration between the transcendent fame of ahistorical greatness and the daily world of striving and competition, between absolute fame and professional success. Fed by an atmosphere of general social and cultural progress, the hunger engendered is endless, even though resources, whether material or spiritual, are not. Modern fame thus restates the basic eighteenth-century question of whether creative and socially useful individualism can be separated from mere personal aggrandizement and greed. In a society where success is imaged primarily through possessions, it represents what is still intangible in the urge "to be someone." Fame may bring wealth, but wealth is insufficient cause for fame. The tangible power of the money that runs the world is to a great extent invisible, while everyone clamors for the reputedly greater spiritual power of fame. Only if businessmen are clearly self-made men (in the manner argued by Bruce Barton) or if, like Howard Hughes, their wealth reaches some figure so outlandish that it can no longer be considered "money," can they demand or receive that extra helping of attention that fame rather than mere name recognition entails. Similarly, the transfiguration of fame, or the need for fame to be a form of social purity, makes the old-style fame of civic life more problematic. It is difficult to be elected to fame. Ronald Reagan may have been somewhat famous in the past. But it sounds odd to use the word to refer to him in his public role, as it would sound even stranger if we were referring to less iconographic public officials. John Hinckley implies as much when he is willing to sacrifice Reagan, the actor turned politician, to his love for Jodie Foster, the actress who has preserved her relation to fame untarnished and even enhanced.

*   *   *

How should a history of fame end? Fame is an elusive idea that I have here tried to set to words, one of its older mediums, and it would be easy enough to extract from this book a handful of homilies, maxims, and cautionary cliches. But because the nature of fame is defined by the context, both historical and immediate, in which it appears, no pattern traced here has the force of a determining causality. Fame is metamorphic. It arises from the interplay between the common and the unique in human nature, the past and what we make of it. There can be no single perspective, no secret key by which to unlock what it really is. Instead of seeking to determine its unchanging essence, we have been looking at a less precise history, in which people tell stories about themselves and stories are told about them. Rather than take a pessimistic attitude toward the contemporary preoccupation with fame, which seems to me to depend always on some nostalgia for a past where standards were adhered to because values were fixed, I prefer to wonder what the future of fame will bring. I began writing this book when excess and self-indulgence were being attacked by moralists on all sides. The generation of the 1970s and 1980s was being called a narcissistic "me generation" intent on its own pleasures. I finish it in a time of narrowed expectations and lowered horizons, in which children believe that they can never achieve what their parents have, and many of the same activities attacked before are now viewed as aids to personal health and survival. Is it possible to transmute some of that unpurgeable modern self-consciousness into self-awareness? As Alexander Pope argued at the beginning of the modern period, love of self should lead to love of others. In trying to make a difference, we often lose sight of the difference we do make. In the urge to be separate and distinct, we have forgotten the elements of selflessness in honor and renown as well as the elements of community good in any worthy definition of individualism. The past presses down on every moment and leaves its impressions there. To know the past is to be able to begin to erase those that confine us and to preserve those that liberate. Merely because we may no longer accept certain standards of heroism does not mean that we have to dispense with the idea of heroism itself or cease to remember the aspirations of the past.

At its best, the urge to fame is a desire for recognition and appreciation that is interwoven with the nature of the human community, both socially valuable and personally enriching, beyond the rewards of comfort and status, in a worth inseparable from the good opinion of others. The urge for fame, one recent aspirant has said, is "the dirty secret." But in Western society, it has also been intertwined with ideals of personal freedom that have animated so much political, social, and economic change in the last two hundred years. The difficulty arises when to be free is defined by being known to be free, because then one might be more known than free. When visibility becomes crucial to the way individuals situate themselves in the world, the display of fame, with its Roman progenitors, redirects its selfless aspects to celebrity sponsorship of charity drives and political gestures toward public duty. As the media of communications cover more of the world and take up more time in the day, to be famous means to be talked about. *Fama* flies through the skies once more.

But to be talked about is to be part of a story, and to be part of a story is to be at the mercy of storytellers—the media and their audience. The famous person is thus not so much a person as a story about a person—which might be said about the social character of each one of us. Like some special aspect of ourselves, the famous person also holds out the possibility that there is another self inside, one not totally defined by that social story. In the incessant spotlight the constant tension between those stories—of the talked-of self and the unexpressed self—becomes more acute. Similarly, the basic conflict of modern fame is between the ideal isolation that has been the propaganda of the famous since the eighteenth century and the expanded urge to recognition that has developed in the pressure of democratization and the widening franchise. In one view, the famous exist on a solitary eminence; in the other, they are part of the audience's story about itself. The celebrity goes it alone, even while he praises the audience who has gone along with him.

The talk of fame in our culture has become the prime way of dealing with the ambiguities of such aspirations, especially in defense against psychological explanations that would root the urge to recognition in personal deprivation and private trauma. From one point of view the desire for recognition can easily be considered selfish. But, as I have tried to show, the historical interplay of classical and Christian attitudes has by our own time yielded a paradoxical mingling of the selfish and the selfless in the urge to fame. The more open a society we have, the more professedly equal we are before the law, the greater the urge to personal distinction. The profusion of modern fames obscures the extent to which we are in a world where the individualisms of the past no longer work, and the new individualism has not yet been defined. In the history of Western culture, when certain time-honored fame stories, like the story of monarchy or the story of the avant-garde original genius, can no longer bear the weight of self-justification placed upon them, they collapse and disappear, unless they can change. In the past the famous were figures by which everyone who observed might recall, reinvoke, and support the ideal cohesion of traits they represented. But now they are more often mirrors of a diverse variety, an affirmation of the many differences between us—the atomizations of our past and present. In such a world the famous help answer the question: How do I live?

To the extent that the desire for fame demands a solitary eminence, it too easily becomes a rejection of fellowship, a threat to a just society, a dead end of individualism. Long ago Aristotle worried that the hero may be opposed to the citizen and that heroic assertion may threaten justice. The modern formulation might be that the urge to fame can become a threat when it too consciously replaces any other goal of personal or public good. In past ages audiences were often more interested in what we would call failure than in obvious or immediate success. Secular failure was called sainthood in the Middle Ages. From the Renaissance onward, the voices for fame have tended to be positive, although there have always been questioners. But now especially the questioning of public fame is muted, and few voices are raised against its most obvious and obtrusive demands. When they do appear, they often take the form of essays celebrating someone whose physical courage shows up the general lack of modern heroism. Part of the appeal of such a momentary hero, who might plunge into icy waters to save the victims of a plane crash without a thought for his own safety, is that his action is unpremeditated. For premeditation brings self-consciousness, irony, and all the rusty thoughts that corrode true heroism with thoughts of how it will appear to others. Similarly, the celebration of athletes as heroes, especially those who help the team or those who participate in the sanctified Olympics, enshrines a much simpler and cleaner fame than anyone can manage in normal life—at least until we read about their million-dollar advertising contracts. In their account of the government's effort to create the heroes of the first manned spaceships, both Tom Wolfe's book and Phil Kaufman's film of *The Right Stuff* reveal the satiric potentials in the collision of fame with technology. The crucial moment comes when the other astronauts support John Glenn in his own support of his wife Annie's unwillingness to let President Johnson come into her house. In other words the greatest moment in this saga of heroes is the refusal of publicity.

The old style of fame competition with the greats of the past has been swept away by its innumerable modern manifestations. Is it any longer possible to do one's work, whatever it may be, without periodically opening the most impersonal and high-minded ideal only to discover inside the grinning skull of ambition? The fear that something is done not for itself but for what it may mean to others is implanted in our brains by every glimpse of advertising, publicity, and news trumpeting the constant need to slather product with hype, face with makeup, and event with interpretation. The curse of the democratic availability of "information" is the implication that persons, events, and objects not only cannot be separated from their atmosphere, but that they were also little more than atmosphere to begin with. What can be considered a central or unalloyed fame anymore when news stories and art shows and political stewardships move by us so quickly? When I began this book, I could refer to Jimmy Carter and Farrah Fawcett to exemplify some points about contemporary fame. Now that I am nearing the end of it, I read back over those lines as if they were some ancient text that now needs footnoting. Fame continues, but the famous often vanish as quickly as mayflies or tissues snatched up to soothe a momentary disorder. Only in societies like the Soviet Union—which still maintains a pyramid in which fame is primarily a commodity of rulers and those they deem worthy of society's gaze—does the conflict between the artist and thinker, on the one hand, and the politician, on the other, still continue (although, like Americans, the Russians also celebrate the heroes of the physical, at least until they defect). One Marxist definition of ideology might unveil underlying economic motives to show that an individual's aspiration to fame and honor is a mere mask for more material and class-oriented ends. But the tremendously expanded varieties of fame and honor now available in the non-Communist countries make it seem that the urge to distinction has roots in individual and general history that economic advantage cannot totally explain. Similarly, the internal conflict in Russia between say, the ruling politician and the Nobel-prize-winning scientist, implies that the ideal distribution of economic goods does not compensate for an equivalent redistribution of the possibility of fame, but creates instead a social structure whose fame hungers are more akin to those fostered by the monarchical system of old.

What then is the proper use of the past as a ground for emulation? I would like to be able to stigmatize certain styles of fame and applaud others—and the alert reader will see that I have done so throughout. So often the invocation of the fame of the past has been an evasion of responsibility for one's actions in the present to create a name that will last through the ages: Alexander masquerading as Achilles, Augustus as Apollo, Napoleon as Charlemagne, Hitler as Frederick the Great. Time and personal nature, the propaganda says, have brought us this great man. The assertion of infinitely justifying precedents should warn us of the absoluteness of the aims. The invocation of past models not only allows one to step outside the petty conflicts of the present, but also to avoid a fertile engagement with immediate events and individuals. To know the history of fame is to be able to discern what styles of fame might be relevantly revived—and I don't mean Ronald Reagan invoking Franklin Roosevelt or Marilyn Monroe dressed as Jean Harlow. Where now, for example, are the models of a truly disinterested and principled patriotism like that embodied by Lafayette? The sophistication of image observing that by the twentieth century has become a common heritage has engendered less discussion of what fame ought to be than cynically sentimental comments about the present lack of heroes, while journalists probe into every public life to find the psychological 'truth' that explains away any selfless action.

Since the eighteenth century, the imagery of fame has been more connected with social mobility than with inherited position, and with social transcendence as an assurance of social survival. From Moll Flanders to Ernest Hemingway, success in industrial society seemed to require a self-armoring code to protect the aspiring self. But the nineteenth-century emphasis on self-making and social mobility has disappeared and now it is not the social order so much as an individual's own emotional problems that are conquered, until they can burst forth again under the auspices of *People* magazine. The psychologization of public language (with its assumption of priority over all other sorts of explanation) has made self-monitoring (as Franklin called it), together with the willingness to expose oneself publicly, part of the definition of fame. A "personal" interview these days is therefore more likely to stress a victory over alcoholism or personal tragedy than it is to sketch a Lincolnesque rise from poverty. One wonders how Hemingway's life and death might have been different if he had the resources of the celebrity interview available for insulation and thereby purgation of the pressure of his public image. But some things must happen before others are possible. Hemingway's inability to withstand his own celebrity lies behind Norman Mailer's premeditated effort to create a shielding public persona behind which he can remain free, just as it does behind the ostentatious evasions of publicity carried on by J. D. Salinger and Thomas Pynchon.

The consumer culture and the fame culture are inseparable at the point where anyone of aspiration feels compelled to present himself or herself in the familiar terms by which others are bought or sold by the world. The numerous artistic suicides and quickened dyings in the decades after World War Two may mark the last stand of a belief that artistic value is opposed to popular approval and of an inability to face that celebrity if it arrived. By the 1960s the development of modern personal identity, with its rapid flickering through a variety of public and private roles, was being brought up to date by a sophisticated media awareness of product consumption, dependent on incessant channel switching and an easy acceptance of costume and irony. The last great shift in the history of fame was in the wake of World War Two, and I cannot see that anything very new has happened since, only an increase of the volume, with an added detachment about the process. Of course, individuals still loudly proclaim their desire to be recognized. But there is a decadent flavor to the enterprise now, as if all moves were so well known that no one really cares. The complex interaction of aspiration and achievement that weighed so heavily on Hemingway, Pavese, and Plath could become the cliché response of a thousand interviews of the traveling celebrity.

This book is, of course, itself an effort to step back from what fame has meant in order to show how its pursuit has both inspired and warped individuals and cultures. Does the fact that it could be written help imply that we have reached the end of a fame culture set off in the eighteenth century by the American and French revolutions? Does it imply the end of certain ideas of fame that are inextricably tied to certain ideas of historical progress? May we even be glimpsing through the unavoidable diaspora of modern life the end of fame as all the ages before our own knew it? The glowing possibility is that the present breakup of the fame monopoly of the past into so many separate little shops has created a ferment, a new kind of mass society that potentially can reconcile individuality and community in an unprecedented way. It is altogether possible that the more pluralistic fame standards of today may be a prelude to the political structures of tomorrow. There we might discover a style of multiple aspiration, an ease with the ancient division between the social and the "inner" self, a new integration of one's work life and one's home life, such that the Jekyll/Hyde story might seem to these new people amusingly archaic rather than horribly entrancing. To understand how the urge to fame and recognition mediates our experience of the world can correct the tendency of psychological explanations to undervalue the influence of political and economic systems on consciousness as well as the tendency of economic and political explanations to undervalue the role of fantasy in the engendering of aspiration and action. Instead of the old opposition to public fame, with its roots in the assumed division between public and private self, we might better explore how that public fame could serve as the vehicle of new values of connection and community—a socialist individualism, to name only one possible oxymoron that might subsume the outdated polarities of the past.

In this book I have concentrated on Western culture and, it almost goes without saying, an upper-class and (usually) white male Western culture. St. Augustine may have been black and Cleopatra, Joan of Arc, and Elizabeth I were certainly women. But they made their mark, however wittily, by mimicking or contradicting the dominant definitions of what it meant to be famous. In the past two hundred years those fame paradigms have been captured from the social groups that originally developed them, and gradually spread to other emergent groups, even those whose activities had not been considered famous in great part because their cultural ideals emphasized the group over the individual. But the fame of the past, as we have seen, cannot be unthinkingly replicated in the present, just as the enlightened acquisition of power is useless if it does only what power has always done. The concepts of fame we have inherited began in a low-density world as an effort to centralize political power by centralizing imagery. In this world of diffuse and overlapping authority, the strain of striving for the absolute fames of the past is becoming more and more apparent. In America an important part of the increase in black, ethnic, and feminist self-consciousness in the past twenty years has been the rescue of artists, writers, and other important ancestors who have been "ideologically" neglected by the traditional definers of Western culture. Certainly such figures should both be celebrated for their own sakes and function as models for new generations who otherwise would have to invent themselves without worthy precedents. But this posthumously established fame is little help to the struggling young aspirant who not only wants to know if it is *possible* to be an artist or a politician, but also how to *behave* in that role. Too often the movement toward self-consciousness of groups whose nature and values have been ignored by the mainstream vitiates the force of their new insight by merely elbowing into the same place in the sun occupied by those already there, rather than helping to redefine what achievement and recognition and fame can mean.

Even though these new groups are now, for the most part, still in contention with (and therefore determined by) the older shapes of power, I believe that we are gradually leaving an era in which social role, profession, sexuality, and ethnic origin were the prime determinants of public "character" and entering one in which the commonalty of shared desires is more compelling than their distinctions. This change can be observed on the international level as well, with the growth of orders and institutions that span the previously self-sufficient self-definitions of the long centuries of the growth of nation-states. Glory is a variety of fame particularly connected to the state, a heroic commitment to its continued greatness, just as honor implies a fame defined by the context of a specific social class. When the class and the state are for all practical purposes synonymous, as they were for many centuries in monarchial and aristocratic Europe, then glory and honor often seemed synonymous as well. But as the international order becomes more prominent in the way individuals situate themselves in the world—even at the seemingly trivial level of the constant bombardments of the nightly news—then media fame, with its comparative lack of national specificity and its appeal to what is "common" in human nature, has become the standard of all fame, and saints, sports figures, and movie stars cross national boundaries with equal felicity and ease.

Modern society, with its web of communications and its increasing number of people, is thus on the way to obliterating the old moral distinction between acting and being that has been used to attack theater since the seventeenth century. Individuals still believe that they can become prominent for the purity of their 'real' natures, apart from the way those natures are perceived by others. But often they are then swept up in an ongoing drama that they refuse to understand enabled their self-presentation in the first place. As Orrin Klapp has written in *Symbolic Leaders,* "unless men are masters of their public drama, they cannot be masters of their public characters" (162). Klapp focuses particularly on the problems of the obviously famous. But what he says is relevant to all public life in a world of pervasive media, not only to the desire to be a great leader or a great artist, but also to the urge to achieve some prominence in one's profession or one's locality. Acculturation and socialization have been viewed, especially by outgroups like women or racial and religious ethnics, as the means by which a majority culture represses legitimate minority desires. Without denying any of those charges, I think that the history of fame illustrates how all cultures limit individual desires in the service of general ends that may have once been fruitful but gradually become unrelated to the ends, needs, or desires of anyone. When that disparity becomes intolerable, cultural assumptions change. So they changed in the eighteenth-century England; so they may be changing now. To understand them without either prejudice or defensiveness is the first step to making them irrelevant. The point is not to reject the concept of fame or to demystify it. Why should we reject the part of ourselves that appears most clearly when we are with others?

As we have seen, the desire for fame is a culturally adaptive trait by which the individual retailors traditional standards of distinctive personal nature into a costume by which he can succeed before his chosen audience. In the present profusion of biography and psychohistory, who can doubt that everyone's public personality and private character can be traced back to some precedent or another. Every individual case can be excavated to prove a general cause. But what is unique about every individual is the way those influences have been brought together. They allow us to tell stories to ourselves and to others of who we are. No nature is original except in its creative connecting. What we call character, that which distinguishes us from each other, is less to be found in the stories themselves than in the way we have put them together. To understand the myriad influences on our desire to be recognized and by that understanding to achieve some distance and a useful irony has been the purpose of this book. By understanding the history of fame we will be better able to escape the urges it incites and the sense of emptiness that supposedly only fame can fill. Then perhaps fame might evolve again, and the frenzy of renown be pruned of its excesses so that its energies can cause more vigorous growth.

Afterword to the Vintage Edition:
Fame Without History

The Frenzy of Renown first appeared just over a decade ago. Although I wrote it as a cultural history of the urge to recognition over the last twenty-five hundred years, it is also inescapably a symptom of the history it attempts to describe. Looking back, I can hardly conceive of it being written other than when it was. I began to work on it in the 1970s, when television talk shows were virtually unknown, Oprah Winfrey was still a TV news anchor in Baltimore, and Dr. Toni Grant in Los Angeles was just starting to invite listeners to call in to her radio show to discuss their problems.

Even though fame has been the subject of much writing and visual art for centuries, even millennia—what are the best types of fame? how should fame be achieved?—the peculiarly widespread preoccupation with its shapes and distortions is our own. We didn't invent fame, but we have become almost swallowed up by its insistent presence and by its paraphernalia. Fame in the ancient world used to be a way of honoring what aspired to be permanent in human action and thought, beyond death and all of life's accidents. Now the word is randomly applied to everything from truly significant events and people to the most fleeting blur in the public eye. This lack of discrimination was already well under way in the ten years it took me to research and write *The Frenzy of Renown*. In the book I tried to give fame a history and show how so many of our contemporary tangles about fame and personal identity, striving and ambition, could be understood, if not solved, by a step back and a look at the past. At one point in the middle of my work, a friend who was closely involved in the project kept prodding me to get the book done more quickly. If you don't hurry up, she said, no one's going to be interested in fame anymore.

She probably only wanted me just to get it finished. But if her fear seemed unrealistic then, it seems unthinkable now. There was still a certain amount of obliviousness or diffidence then about the role of communication itself in the act of reporting. These days a great proportion of what the media considers to be news is its own effect on people and events. Since the nineteenth century the experiences of war correspondents have been part of the events they report. Now, reporters standing outside the home of a person in the spotlight interview one another as they wait for the appearance of the nominal center of attention, while their cameramen celebrate the occasion by focusing on all the sound trucks and multiple antennas of their colleagues, and spectators press forward "to be part of history." Only eight years separated the appearance of Theodore H. White's *The Making of the President* (1960) from Joe McGinniss's *The Selling of the President* (1968). A quarter of a century later, the apparatus of media publicity has become the most compelling part of its own subject matter. The media are no longer only what their name implies: intermediaries between events and audiences. Now, a metamedia has come into being, committed to, imprisoned by, and frequently bored to death by its own preoccupation with fame.

To call someone or something famous essentially means "pay attention to this," and in a world overcrowded with people, places, things, and ideas, the problem of what deserves attention is a crucial issue. Fame in modern society has thereby become a common language, the credo of media as well as their basic subject matter: who ought to be famous, who shouldn't, whom we have forgotten, who ought to be remembered.

As the millennium approaches, the incessant media mapping of public celebrations and public burnings seems to signal a desperate search for signposts of authority and direction in a constantly shifting landscape: What does this "famous" event or "famous" person say about who "we"—as a nation and culture—are right *now*? In the years since *The Frenzy of Renown* was published, hardly a week goes by that I'm not called on the phone by a reporter eager for a 'serious' perspective on whether Nadia Comaneci will be able to regain the fame she had as a teenage gymnast, whether the fame of her grandfather pushed Margaux Hemingway to suicide, whether scandals would hurt one movie star's career and help another's, why paparazzi care about taking photos of the famous, why otherwise normal people want to sleep in houses where famous murders occurred or films were made, why some tourists visiting Israel are temporarily swept away by the belief that they are actually Samson or the Virgin Mary ... the list is endless. Always the questions are posed in terms of specific events and individuals. But the real curiosity is about the media's role in the processes of fame: How do you get it? How do you keep it? How do you lose it? Why are we so fascinated by famous people?

Popular culture in democratic societies serves as a form of collective emotional memory, which supports the creation of our social identities, not because we owe allegiance to the state and its institutional occasions, but because we connect the stages of our lives to public people and their doings. Immediate celebrity—open to those who catch what Hamlet calls "the tune of the time"—is due to many factors, including money. But long-lived celebrity and fame have deeper roots. They represent unfinished business in the national psyche, emblems of heroism or villainy, innocence or guilt, that may last for decades, even centuries.

Particularly in the United States, this world of many different groups all calling themselves American, talk of fame and its gradations is one of the few conversations that joins rather than separates us. The media's mission to pay attention feeds its audience's desire that the world make sense and the story hang together. In the nineteenth century, fame in the shape of various Great Men and a handful of Great Women was often the subtext of history. It has now become the overt story. As the world grows more complex, human faces are plastered on every idea and event. Each news story must begin with a personal anecdote, and no political speech is complete without a reference to some otherwise unknown private citizen whose story seems to give the hot air a local habitation and name.

Complex phenomena wear the reduced features of emblematic individuals: Bill Gates stands for the computer revolution, C. Everett Koop stands for health care, and O. J. Simpson—depending on your point of view—stands for spousal abuse, racial prejudice, or the flaws in the criminal justice system. Even though, as a professional military man, Norman Schwarzkopf was more aware than most that much of what he accomplished was the product of an immense supporting group, he still allowed himself to signify the entire American presence in the Gulf War. To his credit, Schwarzkopf in his autobiography had the grace to back away from his exclusive role. Then, in a nice turn, he went on to become a spokesman against prostate cancer—an apt symbol of his jaundiced view of a military masculinity that for a time he seemed to embody.

Of course, none of these changes have occurred unawares or without comment. One mutation, to which *The Frenzy of Renown* may have contributed its small share, has been the increase in self-consciousness among the famous and their audience. Magazines write glibly of the problems facing new names in the fame firmament, stalkers are analyzed in the daily press, and talking heads (including my own) instantly dissect any situation involving the famous for its spine of cultural meaning. Awareness of the element of fame and publicity extends into every kind of subject matter. As I write this in early 1997, I am looking at the February 9 issue of the historically sober *New York Times Week in Review*. More than half of the articles deal with events and issues that have been highlighted—in some cases exaggerated—by the fame of those involved: the relation between criminal trials and civil trials (O. J. Simpson); the Jewish heritage of Madeleine Albright (how common was conversion because of the Holocaust?); the immodesty of various sports stars and politicians (is it a trend?); the effect of television on Serbian politics (the president failed to control it); and the belief that famous people whose star has fallen are dead (they may as well be).

Why is this considered to be valid commentary on the news? One answer is that, for both journalist and audience, to be aware of fame is to be behind the scenes, and to be behind the scenes is to control rather than be controlled. Whether your particular knowledge is gossip about politicians and movie stars, advance reports about the newest fashion trends, secret proof of the existence of aliens, or apocalyptic paranoia about the government, the United Nations, or the New World Order, having such knowledge proves that you're special, that you can't be fooled, and that you understand the heart of things.

Knowing just the story isn't enough without knowing the backstage gossip. When you know both you are no longer an insignificant member of the audience, but somehow an initiate in secret mysteries. To the insider, political candidates are mere front men for their consultants and ideas and policies are less important than meditations on the effectiveness of the spin. Insider phrases like "sound bite" and "photo op" have become part of everyone's vocabulary, and movies arrive complete with other movies about their making. The point is not to demystify the techniques of fame, but to brandish them as the badge of being privy to their expert use.

Some time ago the sociologists Elihu Katz and Tamar Liebes performed a fascinating experiment. By questioning five very different social groups, of roughly the same age and education, who all avidly watched the soap opera *Dallas*, Katz and Liebes tried to find out why they all liked it and what they thought it was about. Four of the groups lived in Israel–Arabs, newly arrived Jewish immigrants from Russia, Jews from Morocco, and Israelis who lived on kibbutzim–and one was from Los Angeles. The Arabs and the Moroccan Jews interpreted *Dallas* as an intricate portrait of the problems of living in extended families. The Russian immigrants interpreted it as a satire of the greed and dehumanization of rampant capitalism. The kibbutzim interpreted it as a wonderful picture of the problems of living in close quarters. But the Americans were particularly fascinated by the backstage gossip. Unlike the other groups, they tended to refer not to the characters but to the actors who portrayed them, and spoke learnedly of the difference between Larry Hagman as J. R. and Larry Hagman as a guest on the *Tonight Show*. Finally, unlike the other groups, who saw *Dallas* as a picture of America, the Americans saw it as a show only foreigners would think was really about America. They knew it was a fiction and were not going to be fooled about its general truth.

Katz and Liebes's study appeared in 1985, but its implications are even clearer today. It was designed as a work of academic sociology. Ten years later, its distinctions between alternate interpretations of an ongoing drama have become a common journalistic way to analyze all public events, especially, of late, the O. J. Simpson trials. Perhaps the contrast between the four groups in Israel and the Americans has also narrowed over the years. I still can't quite get over walking into a hotel room in Budapest in March of 1995 and turning on the television to discover the daily Sky-TV half hour on the Simpson trial. But why be surprised? So many members and ex-members of the British royal family have over the years exchanged a more sedate and ceremonial fame for the more immediate rewards (or punishments) and cheering (or booing) audiences of celebrity. Perhaps that Sky-TV show wasn't merely another example of the world's interest in the continuing circus of American public life, but an indication that they too now wanted to get in on the show.

This desire to be in the know extends not just to the famous but to the idea of fame itself. People become famous in a variety of ways other than by actual achievement. They may dress or sleep or spend their way into fame, or at least into the presence of someone who has it. With enough nerve or sex appeal or money anyone can become famous–for a time. The trick is to stay that way.

The fascination with the famous therefore focuses less on what they did than how they did it. Interviews with even the newest stars and rising politicians usually include an obligatory bow to the pitfalls of fame. It has now become a cliché among the famous to put fame and public recognition down. Politicians regularly leave office "to spend more time with their families," and whole books have been published filled with negative remarks about fame by famous people. The message is always the same: We happy few have escaped the sting. But the mockery of fame invariably uses the same vocabulary as the celebration: I must publicly trumpet my disdain for publicity. It is our puny version of St. Augustine's paradox: After all sins have been purged, only the sin of pride remains. And after the sin of pride has been purged, the last and most difficult sin to purge is the pride in being humble, the desire that an audience witness (and applaud) your contempt for it.

Self-consciousness may make some withdraw from the race. Others just run faster. The desire for fame used to imply that you wanted to do something that was really memorable in the long parade of human nature and history. Perhaps the seekers of the past were deluded that to win a war or write a book or commune with God in the wilderness was really valuable. But at least they aspired to make a mark on time. Now the desire is to be on television, to have your picture in the papers, and to admire those who have done so, not for what they have done, but for how they're seen. In the highest realms of contemporary fame, to call a person famous whose face is unfamiliar seems virtually incomprehensible. Not too long ago there appeared a cartoon by Alain Sempé in *The New Yorker* that summed up the paradox with admirable clarity. In it, a nondescript man on the street is being singled out by a gigantic pointing finger of God emerging from a cloud. The caption reads "You will never be on television."

It took some time for the visual media to gain this power. George Eastman's camera became available for the documenting of private life in 1888. But even though the technology for reproducing halftone photographic engravings was available to newspapers at around the same time, it did not come into general use until the early twentieth century.

Theorists of popular culture have argued that we now live in a world of media images that refer only to themselves, and certainly many artists and writers have indulged in a postmodern playfulness that constantly juxtaposes one thing with another with no particular end in view. But at the same time there exists a secular veneration for the visual image that rivals the fervor of many religions. The singer Sinéad O'Connor neatly brought the two worlds together when in Fall 1992 she ripped up a photograph of Pope John Paul II on stage and was roundly attacked for this impious or impolite act. Similarly, the word "superstar," the 1970s and 1980s designation for a greater-than-ordinary fame, has been replaced by the formerly sacred term "icon," in an effort to indicate a more permanent stature, transcending the celebrity of the moment. Quickly enough it too has become a journalistic cliché, used merely to signify a relatively long-standing model (with a slight tinge of the ideal). To draw a few examples from January 1997: Joan Didion is a literary icon, Albert Einstein is a physics icon, Courtney Love is a modern fashion icon, and breasts, at least female ones, are a cultural icon in U.S. society. Icon status is also not limited to human beings or parts of the human body. Wal-Mart is a retail icon, Van Gogh's sunflowers are icons of expressionism, and the United States is no longer, in the eyes of some jaundiced Russians, an icon of democracy.

The popularity of "icon" may also owe something to its use in computer language as the term for the image which, when selected, reveals a world of new tidings and lore. (I hesitate to say information.) Thus both the computer icon and the holy icon announce that they are potential gateways to a world of greater meaning, while the journalistic use of icon hopes to exploit the atmosphere of transcendence.

By now, when life has become crammed with the paraphernalia of visual immediacy, posterity—which used to be the place where true fame was judged—has become shrunken and attenuated. In early January 1997, the photographer Duane Michals was quoted as saying that the true power of the artist was not to be celebrated in magazines or have work hung in museums, "but that someone you can't even imagine one hundred years later looks at what you've done and it means something to him." It was a startling sentiment, as sweetly old-fashioned as it was rare. More usually, in this world built on the credit card, the future is expected to take care of itself. Politicians talk about the legacy we must leave for our children and then propose short-term solutions to problems that will only burden them further. No past standards of value, no future goals, can compare with attention in the moment. Instead, what thought there is for the future tends to focus on millenarian roundups of how *it* will remember *us*: What were the ten greatest events of the twentieth century? Who were the ten most important persons?

It is obvious enough how the spectacularly famous person whose image appears on every magazine, on the walls of teen-age bedrooms, and on television bears a watered-down resemblance to the saint of old, whose face and figure alone repeatedly invoked his or her divine power of intervention with God. But one intriguing difference between the star and the saint is that the greatest power of the saint tends to come after death. Then the tomb and the fragments of the body, no matter how small, not only powerfully connect the believer to the world of the divine, but also pledge a deliverance from death. In religious terms, this is the numinousness of saints—a quality that in secular terms has been transformed into charisma (also a word with religious roots). But in our culture of immediacy the contemporary saint, like James Dean hidden away in an asylum or Elvis spotted in the supermarket, must still be alive.

The message of early Christianity was the defeat of death by eternal life—for every believer. This was its challenge to the claims of classical fame, which promised that only the great would be eternally remembered. Now, everything of note must happen in the present. At one extreme, death itself becomes a locale of fame. Crimes that used to be relegated to the backpages of newspapers or to the *Police Gazette* become front-page news for months, and reporters are paid enormous sums to write the biographies of murderers. Recently, in a diabolical parody of the veneration of saints, a band of convicts was caught trying to smuggle out bits and pieces of the possessions of Charles Manson to eager fans.

On the more benevolent side of this quasi-religious fame, divine power is frequently invoked—especially in the name of Jesus—in an effort to present the famous accomplishment as not having quite been done by the person who did it. Giving praise to God or Jesus for one's accomplishment helps deflect the egotism implied in the desire for fame. Someone physically caught the pass or ran the race or sang the song. But the fact that the action won the game or the medal or the Grammy—that it became famous—was totally in divine hands. When such humbleness is insincere, it is merely the mean window dressing for pride. But when it is sincere, it may reflect anxieties about self-assertion in a democratic society, anxieties that are the birthright of everyone who simultaneously wants to be different from others and yet much the same. This democratic fame guilt potentially extends toward the neglected and dispossessed in the audience as well. But only fairly recently have large numbers of the famous in America used their fame to further causes of social justice and relieve the suffering of others, rather than treat them all as potential members of the audience.

*   *   *

Although the urge to fame originally was the aspiration for a life after death in the words and thoughts of the community, it has evolved over the centuries into the desire for fame in one's own lifetime, fame not as the crown of earthly achievement but as psychic medicine for a pervasive sense of loss and personal failure. Behind all this obsession with immediacy and satisfaction now is the spreading urge to fame as compensation for whatever faults and fissures there are in the sense of self.

For the ancient Romans, your genius was in the stars. Now, with little thought for either posterity or transcendence, genius is entirely within. This immediate and self-centered fame has become the goal for many who want their characters (or their personalities) appreciated more than their achievements, whose self-centeredness runs ahead of any discernible talent. Stoked on a diet of the names and faces of others, I wonder why I shouldn't be famous too.

In the 1920s Walter Benjamin argued that the mechanical reproduction of art had destroyed its "aura" of separateness and singularity. But now it seems that those early movies and magazines—and the consumer world generally that Benjamin criticized—were actually creating a new kind of aura. In it intimacy and distance became bizarrely mingled. From theater to movies to television, the relationship between the person in the audience and the person on stage alters conspicuously. In theater we have a comparatively direct contact with the performer. Like the athlete, the stage performer is actually doing something in front of us and there is some possibility of reciprocity—in laughs and groans and applause—across the footlights. But in film our relation to performers is both more psychologically immediate and physically separate, and they are usually unaware of our existence, rarely looking directly at the audience, except in musicals, the most theatrical of film forms. While the stage actor is always someone else, the film actor seems to be part of us. Our relation to film actors is therefore a kind of possessiveness, in which they both submit to and evade our goggle-eyed wonder. Perhaps that is the reason why stage actors have few of the problems with fans that film actors do.

Next to television, however, films are a sanctuary of privacy. Television brings the absent performer into every home. Similarly, while everything on television seems to be immediately present, it is actually made up of pieces and snippets from various points in time and space. I realized this with a special acuteness when I appeared on various TV interview shows. So far as a viewer could tell, I was there with the host and the other guests trading remarks. But the host was in New York or Chicago, while I was in Los Angeles, and even when the label at the bottom of the screen made this known to emphasize the immense range of the show, usually I was sitting alone in a studio with a plug in my ear, trying to give the impression that I was having a conversation with people I could barely hear and could not see at all.

Television is hardly unique as a stage for the absurdities of modern fame. But it does provide many striking examples, at the same time allowing moralists the chance to ghettoize the problem and pretend that it is only the craziness of a benighted few. Television's constant commercial litany, along with its weaving together of all its disparate contents into a continuous flow, makes a direct demand on the attention of the audience—to judge, to choose, and to buy—and do it right away. Thus it creates a world of terminal immediacy, where every member of the audience can be both seeker of fame and jaundiced observer, merging the purity of the athlete racing for the Olympic gold with the self-consciousness of the commentator-critic.

In the early twentieth century, the gossip about how movie stars had been renamed by studios or had renamed themselves reflected the immigrant ideal of a new life in America, where the future was wholly open because the past could be forgotten. Now, the story behind celebrity of all sorts has been reconceived as a revelation of shattered family histories and personal psychological damage. But the difference is only superficial. In both, the star's personal history similarly reflects concerns about individual identity and aspiration. In both, the past has been heroically surmounted and the individual can stride shiningly forward.

Among the hopeful, the desire for media attention therefore drifts easily into the belief that it will be healing. Telepathology we might call it, a wound to the self that can be remedied only by being on television. Only by performing, by being seen, can the pain be distanced. Such an overwhelming urge to be validated by a media appearance appears in the way TV talk shows have so sensationalized personal conduct, even while claiming to shed some light on general issues, as well as in the spread of radio talk shows dedicated to opinions that have nothing to recommend them but their sincerity. This vision of fame as therapy is the complement to the pervasive sense of victimization that fuels so much popular psychology and political discussion. Of course, terrible things really happen to people, and others, in the shape of individuals, laws, or policies, are often at fault. But the pervasive fascination with issues such as dysfunctional families, child abuse, sexual molestation, let alone a myriad of lesser faults, encourages the idea that such injuries can be healed only by the public gaze. Similarly, when people appear on television to publicize every fault, sin, or imperfection in hopes of being proved right, they embody the contemporary tendency to believe that the major role of culture is to affirm who we are or what we think we are already—rather than challenge or complicate it.

Yet underneath the grins of pleasure at being on stage runs a fear that this fleeting fame is actually a consolation prize for failing in life. Instead of being a fresher air to breathe, fame becomes something to choke on. Instead of curing problems with the balm of attention, it more often makes them worse. Recently, a young man went on a television talk show, believing that he would meet a secret admirer. He did, although it turned out that the admirer was not the woman he hoped but another man. Three days later, he bought a gun and murdered the unwanted fan, then called 911 and said he had done this because he had been humiliated on television.

It's hard to make up a more perfect epitome of the talk-show experience. You believe you will gain the admiration and the attention of three prized audiences: the person you desire to be desired by, the cheering studio audience looking on, and the even larger but invisible crowd of watchers behind the camera. Instead you discover that being looked at puts you in the possession of those who look. In the dream of fame, we are always rewarded for exactly those traits we think we have. But the reality is rarely so fitting. Fame is a balloon. It allows its possessor to soar over the countryside, to look down on ordinary humanity. But at the same time the famous soon realize that fame has them rather than the other way round. The tornado arrives, the balloon soars off, taking you with it. Even Madonna, who for so long played at dissolving that line between the personal and the public, finally turns out to want her privacy. Without some psychic ballast and a firm hand at the controls, being swept away is as likely to happen to the high school cheerleader as to the aspiring actor or to the newly elected prime minister.

From classical times up until the early modern period there was a strong belief in the virtue of ignoring the immediate audience. The Roman emperor Marcus Aurelius in his *Meditations* wrote that the ideal man acts without observing his acts, or desiring that anyone else observe them—something that as emperor he found hard to do. At the dawn of the modern age, in John Milton's seventeenth-century poem *Paradise Lost*, Satan is preoccupied by his desire for the largest possible audience, and one of his ploys for seducing Eve to eat the apple from the Tree of Knowledge of Good and Evil is to persuade her that Eden is too small a stage for her beauty, with only Adam to admire her. In *Paradise Regained*, by contrast, Jesus rejects all of Satan's temptations, including that of fame. Milton's insight is that the Devil needs an audience whereas the Son, the spiritual hero, can act without the debilitating self-consciousness of worrying about who is watching. Torn in the middle, of course, are Adam and Eve and the rest of us (including Milton), sometimes on stage and sometimes in the audience.

In our world of constant observation and self-observation, how much harder is that effort. Since World War Two, to be watched has been both the dream and the nightmare—by Big Brother, by Candid Camera, and also, as I remember as a child, by Munro Leaf's cartoon character, the Watchbird, who made sure I was minding my manners and helping my mother with the dishes.

In its root sense, "fame" means to be talked about, and the talk of fame has always been widespread. *The Frenzy of Renown* in part set out to explore the self-awareness of the famous of the past and how they used the resources available to them, not only to accomplish what they wanted, but to make sure that others talked of their accomplishments—so that they might do more. What impression would Byron have made if he could have been photographed standing gloomily in the corner of an early nineteenth-century cocktail party? What dimensions would be added or subtracted from Napoleon's power if cameramen were present as he crossed the Alps? In their different ways Byron and Napoleon helped set up models of fame that are still being imitated. Now, at the end of the twentieth century, the volume has certainly gotten louder and the images more outsized, even if more fleeting.

One major difference now is that there is no obvious national consensus about proper behavior, no clear idea of what the Watchbird is really looking for, and any self-monitoring (as Ben Franklin called it) is conspicuously lacking. In that absence, the famous become symptoms by which to read the state of national psychological health, and many look to the approval of an audience instead. The fame lottery constantly casts up potential models, even while the audience keeps a censorious eye on those already there, who have often mounted the national stage expecting only applause—or perhaps their own laugh track.

Although it is beginning to get quite long in the tooth, the United States still likes to think of itself as a Cinderella country, not founded in the dim past like the ancient countries of Europe, but raised up like the ignored and squelched stepdaughter who then blossoms into a princess. Three self-contradictory myths of American character support this validation by fame. The first is that every worthwhile achievement requires hard work. Or, it requires no work, because everything that comes is deserved because you're you—and entitled. The second is that living successfully in the world requires toughness and independence. Or, it requires a deep commitment to tradition and conformity. The third ties the first two together: The truth is inside you and nothing else counts. Or, your truth must be recognized by an audience; otherwise, it is false.

American Protestantism is virtually built on these paradoxes, and its power shapes all American religions and politics. The holy spirit that speaks inside you must nevertheless be exposed and validated before an entire congregation. Harold Bloom in *The American Religion* cites a Gallup poll that concluded that nine out of ten Americans believe that God specifically loves him or her. Bloom points out that in the whole of the Old Testament the only individual so favored was David. But for David, as for the Jesus of the Book of Matthew, God was the ultimate audience. Unlike the Jesus in Matthew, who keeps reminding his disciples not to tell anyone about him, Americans must publicize their chosenness at every opportunity. As Garry Trudeau once remarked, only in America is someone considered arrogant for not giving an interview. Inquiring minds want to know, and there are few hermits and solitaries who can keep them away.

We may now be living in times when many aspects of what some assumed to be the essence of America is changing. It used to be that the American hero was invariably male and white. Now there is a more multicultural America with people of all races and genders expecting and even demanding their share in the national promise. Yet the terms are still the traditional ones of American fame—not just the desire to be different, to have a particular culture or ethnicity or view of the world, but also to be appreciated by the great American audience for that difference, to be known to be different. Like the cowboy hero, who rides off into the sunset by himself but who wants to be known for being solitary and individual, so even the most separatist political or ethnic group wants to be recognized widely for its unwillingness to participate and will often dramatically publicize its disgust for every consensus but the applause of an admiring audience.

Talk of fame is a house of mirrors: the only way we know about such groups is by hearing of them and their lack of interest in our opinions. Like so much about fame and our preoccupation with it, even rejection is acceptance on another level of awareness. To be seen, to be known, to be paid attention to—as a definition of value—is still therefore very much with us and continues to characterize American aspiration as much as it did when Washington, Franklin, Adams, and Jefferson sat down to decide what should be the symbols of America, and how the audience of the world would be told what makes this country unique. The Cold War 1950s were perhaps the last period in which a single-minded definition of Americanism could draw the acceptance of a wide audience. Now fame itself has become the authenticating quality.

But as most performers and people who create for a public audience finally realize, audiences pay at best only partial attention to what the performer wants to happen. Each audience takes the individual desire for recognition and shapes it to fit its own needs. This has happened so often on the talk and exposé shows that waivers of legal rights must be signed, including on one show a box to be checked that says "I acknowledge that in the course of this show I may be accused of a crime." At the same time, without much publicity, psychologists have been hired, to help people who think that being on the show will solve their problems face the depression that sets in when the spotlight moves on and in the ensuing darkness their problems still remain.

Few, however, are discouraged. As the urge to fame increases, so does the power of this audience, not only at talk shows or in polls at election time, but also in the invitation to the viewing public to become a jury who will decide guilt and innocence. Part of the significance of the O. J. Simpson trials was to focus on this newly intense role for the audience in the shaping of American fame. Our legal system is unique in the world for its emphasis on juries. It has been estimated that of all the jury trials that occur in the world, more than 90 percent occur in the United States. As the trial of a famous athlete who became a minor movie star and public figure, the Simpson trial served as the confluence of several audiences: the impaneled audience we call a jury, the audience for sports in particular, and the audience for the famous in general.

The audience's role as observer and judge is hardly new. In both the novel and theater since the nineteenth century, eavesdropping has been a basic condition of narrative art, to watch people when they don't know they're being watched. Like phone tappers and people in movies with tiny video cameras, the audience looks for the secret without knowing what it is. And in our own time, when the secret often purports to be a national if not a worldwide plot, it sometimes becomes hard to know whether the audience wants to expose the conspiracy or join it.

With the televising of the criminal trial, every slip and casual misstatement became grist for an interpretation industry of amateurs and professionals in search of an overall plan or conspiracy. Add to those audiences its involvement in issues that agitate a national audience—race, sexuality, violence—and that trial became perhaps the most emblematic recent event in a time when such events crowded our vision and imagination. But although Simpson's fame was constantly mentioned, there was little awareness among the managers of the trial that fame was a factor—no sense, for example, that having the jury go to Simpson's house was nothing like a normal visit to a defendant's home but more psychologically akin to the celebrity bus tours that wind their way through the Hollywood Hills. Nor was there much awareness of how the national jury, deadened by incessant telecasts of the trial, was unwilling or uninterested in distinguishing between factual guilt, legal guilt, and moral guilt. After all, they were watching a show, and in shows, scripting (and conspiracy) is normal. It's often called art.

Part of the fame of Byron and Napoleon was their inaccessibility—the brief glimpses of them that paintings and prints allowed. But not only has the volume been raised in contemporary fame but its accessibility has seemingly multiplied as well, so that many can cherish the dream of living an outsized life. What they usually forget is that to be famous generally means to be talked about by people who don't know you, and thereby to some degree talked about symbolically. One version of the symbolic person is the intensified god or saint, while a less attractive one is the simplified, flattened-out caricature. Like icons, then, the famous and the heroic are designed to be two-dimensional. Increased accessibility has shrunken the size of the fame. No matter how widespread the image or omnipresent the visual echo, they lack the private mystery that makes the rest of us real—and complex—to each other.

To be famous thus involves both loss and gain to the actual person involved, and the professionally famous person cultivates those aspects of character that—like Jungian archetypes—are often the least personal. That the desire to have such a symbolic self is such a prevalent goal in twentieth-century America underlines how pervasively ritualized our fame culture has become. The famous, the truly famous, are those who bring together previously opposed or contradictory traits. But many people are chosen by fame to speak momentarily for the barely awakened beliefs of thousands or millions beyond them. They may not even know they do this. Like Chaplin's Tramp in *Modern Times*, they may pick up a flag for a purely personal reason and then abruptly discover to their dismay that they are leading a parade.

To be comfortable with the disparity between the you perceived from the inside and the you that is assumed or laid on by an audience is difficult enough for the professional performer. As the actress Molly Ringwald has said, explaining why she had retired for a time from her movie roles as the archetypal teen-age girl to live in Paris for five years, "How long could I have gone on playing Everygirl, when I got so out of the habit of being treated like a normal person?" But what happens to the "normal" people who become momentary symbolic vehicles for the hopes and dreams, hates, fears, or loves of an audience of others and then are dropped? Robert O'Donnell, for instance, was a tall, thin paramedic from Midland, Texas, who, despite claustrophobia, in the fall of 1987 snaked his way down a shaft to rescue an eighteen-month-old girl named Jessica McClure (quickly dubbed "Baby Jessica" by reporters). He was one of several who helped in the rescue. They were all immediately canonized by media attention and proceeded to fight over the movie, book, and TV rights. Talk shows and Hollywood producers flocked in, a television movie was made. As usual, however, nothing lasting came of the media attention. But somehow the spotlight bit more deeply into Robert O'Donnell's soul. While other rescuers gradually moved away from the event and its publicity to restore their normal lives, O'Donnell tenaciously continued to feature it in his image of himself, listing his citations on his resume and identifying himself as Jessica's rescuer whenever possible. But, as time passed, other stories and other rescuers caught the public eye. Six years later, a few days after the Oklahoma City bombing, which seemed to awaken in him the scenes of his triumph, Robert O'Donnell committed suicide.

*   *   *

The structure of fame differs acutely in democratic and authoritarian societies. One kind of fame dead-ends in totalitarianism, a world of uniforms where the leader absorbs and thereby replaces every individual desire for recognition; the other in American capitalist democracy, where the success of each person on stage seems to support the aspiration of the individual in the audience to have his or her own piece of the pie. Although the American and French Revolutions purported to substitute individual achievement for the traditional social hierarchies, new hierarchies grew up in their stead. A world more open to social advancement brought enviousness and competitiveness along with its promised freedoms. Unlike the situation in the monarchical world, where aspiration was strictly limited by class and background, a daunting paradox appeared at the root of democratic fame: There was more freedom to be recognized personally, but greater uncertainty over who would determine what really merited recognition.

In order to ratify "being yourself," you need an audience, for in a democracy there is no king or ruler to be the unquestionable bestower of honor. Even in England, the Queen is only one fame-bestower among many. Fame and honor, usually so united at least in the professed values of hierarchical societies, in democratic societies split asunder. Compared to honor, fame is a far easier category to define, especially fame in the moment. It is also more suitable to a world of diffused populations and overlapping obligations, in which we know many people superficially and few in any depth.

To achieve through innocence is the extreme version of being yourself. As a country founded during the age of sentimentality and romanticism, in a place that presented itself on the world stage as the home of all that was most pure and original in human nature, the United States has particularly been drawn by the lure of innocence. In nineteenth-century America, the Horatio Alger stories tried to harness democratic envy and turn it into a spur to ambition and emulation, while praising the virtues of hard work. But there was always a quotient of pure luck in the success of Alger's hero. The equivalent in the late twentieth century is the Olympic athlete. Both the Alger hero and the athlete share an aura of innocence to which the democratic audience is drawn as the guarantee of the purity of their motives. That innocence bonds the athlete to the unsung hero who plunges into fires or frozen rivers to rescue the hapless victim. They do something physical that cannot be faked, and (at least ideally) they do it without the self-consciousness of wondering what they look like. The Olympics particularly enshrine innocent aspiration, and for all Olympic athletes, the ostensible goal of doing it for the nation—like thanking God—compensates for the undemocratic desire to be different, the foul smell of ego, and the agents waiting in the wings with contracts for product endorsements.

Sometimes audiences want to witness this innocence, as they appreciate the incorruptible physicality of athletes in the midst of a game, and sometimes, as did Robert O'Donnell, they want to rescue it. So Holden Caulfield also dreamed in *The Catcher in the Rye* of rescuing his sister, Phoebe, from the corruptions of the world and himself from a crippling self-consciousness. So too the most perfect embodiment of athletic innocence is the plucky young girl gymnast, overcoming injury or heartache. Death, as usual, adds a special touch. The media fascination with the seven-year-old girl who was killed, along with her father and teacher, as she attempted to fly solo across the country and get into *The Guinness Book of Records*, and with the six-year-old beauty queen, whose murder revealed a world of children pushed into mimicking full-fledged sexual allure, are only two of the many recent examples of the ventriloquizing of innocence for adult prestige and profit. In her book *Hollywood's Children*, the former "Baby Peggy," now Diana Serra Cary, wrote that all the child stars of the 1930s she knew, including herself, were psychologically damaged except Shirley Temple. The reason, she argued, was that Temple's parents had nothing to do with show business and so she did not have to live out their own failed fantasies of fame. In our own time, however, it hardly requires an unrealized career to be a stage mother or father, just the common desire to be in the spotlight and a tractable child to carry that burden forward. As in so many elbowings into the aura of public notice, the two who died realized a far greater fame than they might ever have had in life.

The self-display that feeds talk shows is thus only one of the more egregious examples of a phenomenon that has picked up speed in the last ten years: the assumption that nothing is private anymore. *The Frenzy of Renown* stressed fame as the intersection of our personal and our public senses of character, who we are to ourselves and who we are to other people. But without getting into blaming the present for a self-absorption that in fact has a long past, it does seem that the distinction between public and private life has become decidedly blurred.

Especially in the years since World War Two, the urge to publicity of the private person—mocked by the voice of God declaiming "You will never be on television"—has become a constant of life in the industrial democracies. Originally "private" meant deprived, specifically deprived of public life and identity. A private person in the seventeenth century thus meant a person without rank. As a legal term, it was similar to the Latin *infamis*, not quite equivalent to English "infamous" but meaning—more precisely—without the rights of a citizen. Only very gradually did "private" take on the meanings of secretive and unsociable. With the seventeenth and eighteenth centuries in Europe, there emerged a modern reinvention of the Greek agora that the German philosopher Jürgen Habermas has called "the public sphere": a world of private persons meeting in coffee houses and cafés, talking to each other, reading early newspaper and journals, and thereby shaping a public opinion in opposition to autocratic rule. By the eighteenth century the transformation of those negative meanings into more positive meanings was virtually complete. To be private was a mark of privilege, associated with intimacy and independence. It implied a seclusion that was freely chosen rather than enforced, in contrast to a submission to public orders and institutions.

Not that the relation between public and private was always so neat and high-minded. Feminist political scientists have argued that whatever the political virtues of the public-private distinction, it also served to bar women almost entirely from the public sphere and assign them to the private and domestic. Similarly, the relation between public and private in any individual person was rarely clear. The most common analogy to the strains of public and private in personal identity was in fact the discrepancy between actor and role.

The old religious attack against the theater had stigmatized it as blasphemous to pretend publicly to be another person solely for purposes of entertainment. As Bishop Bossuet, Louis XIV's confessor, said, "Whoever is so mobile that he is prepared to assume any shape, and with no other purpose than to make the world laugh, is unworthy to be called a Christian." It was acceptable in other words for the monarch and his court to make their private natures public and stylized as part of a political ritual. But the line was drawn at acting.

The democratic revolutions in America and France at the end of the eighteenth century toppled monarchical power and sought to create a society in which aspiration was not determined by birth and money but by talent and ability. Democracy, with its assertion of opportunities for all, thus intensified the need to learn new ways of being. New worlds required new selves, and actors, who could play a variety of roles, had a professional expertise in the new etiquettes. Being on stage did not limit or debase who you were. It expanded it. Fame could wear the guise of freedom.

No wonder then that in this new democratic world, the performer should become the model of how to be and how to be seen. When I wrote *The Frenzy of Renown*, I tried to stay as far as possible from discussing anyone still living, not only because I didn't want to turn the book into a compendium of seven-day wonders, but more importantly because I was also acutely aware of how often fame in the past had been defined by its relation to history—Julius Caesar measuring himself against Alexander the Great, Abraham Lincoln striving to imitate George Washington. But now we seem to have succeeded in creating—and celebrating—a fame almost entirely cut off from history. William Hazlitt in the early nineteenth century argued that actors and actresses should always get better seats in the theater and more applause because their art vanished so quickly. But the media of visual representation—photography, movies, television—have enhanced that transience enough to make people believe that the most immediate is also the most desirable. With the loss of any care for the great forerunners or for the standard of posterity, celebrity and fame have run together, questions of lasting value seem irrelevant or precious, and the audience becomes lost in an everlasting now, in which all varieties of fame are reduced to their most immediate form—whose choicest model is the performer.

The anti-theatrical upholders of the soul preached that there should be no difference between actor and role, public and private. But the modern democratic individual realized that there is necessarily a difference and he, and later she, needed to know how to use it. While the urge to monarchical fame arose from a sense of entitlement, the urge to democratic fame often compensated for a sense of insufficiency and a consequent need for legitimacy. As the world became more crowded with the famous, their seeming completeness—they have "made it"—further incited the yearning of those who wanted to be like them. Performers seemed to have the most salient etiquette for democracy because they needed no justification outside themselves. With the nineteenth century, and even more as a result of the media explosion of the twentieth, a third term thus arises between the public and the private world: everyone's mental picture of a public world composed of the faces and names of the famous, a world that more and more wanted to join.

But on the other side of the equation from the preoccupation with private freshness and innocence is the insistence upon guilt. It would be interesting to tote up the actual numbers, but it certainly seems that—with the broad exception of the constant parade of award shows and self-congratulation—most of the stories supercharged by fame have a hint, or much more, of scandal, crime, or death. During a typical week in 1994, from a variety of media sources you could hear Michael Jackson's public statement about the inspection of his penis, buttocks, lower torso, thighs, and "other areas that they wanted" by the Santa Barbara County Sheriff's Department and the Los Angeles Police Department; you could get the details of whatever it was two Arkansas state troopers in search of a book contract claimed they knew about then-Governor Clinton's personal life; and you could top it all off with Court TV's daily summary of the charges and countercharges in the murder trial of the Menendez brothers.

This emphasis on the sexual marks a new eagerness in the knowing audience to rip away the veil of official stories and discover the supposed real truth. Although the preoccupation with sexual scandal has become most pervasive in the last decade, it is a tendency that has been gathering steam since the 1950s, when the general atmosphere of conspiracy encouraged not just the McCarthy and House Un-American Activities Committee investigations, but also the steamy exposés of *Confidential* magazine, and the romans à clef of writers like Harold Robbins, in which the thinly disguised and scantily dressed rich and famous had their supposedly private lives opened for the reader's titillation.

As the audience prides itself more and more on not being taken in, the media has colluded by insisting on turning every public image into a mask that must be torn away. Whereas the fans of the past were content to be fed studio-generated celebratory gossip about the stars, now rumors are a crucial part of the story. And the other major public professions—principally politics and sports—have adopted the movie-star model of publicity. Sports stars who in the past would answer interviews with a few inarticulate words now discuss intricate aspects of the game before the last ball hits the ground. Television cameras have become so commonplace in courtrooms and in Congress that permanent makeup has become a virtual requirement of public office.

Famous people in a democracy may seem like a kind of invincible aristocracy, but they are actually much more vulnerable to opinion. On the surface, the desire for fame seems to be an urge toward autonomy, to be uncaused and uncontrolled. But to have become famous in a democracy is in great part to be spoken by the audience in the audience's language. Although wealth wisely used can lessen the exposure, part of the double urge of the democratic audience is to revere the famous as if they were rarefied and different but, when given the opportunity, to judge them by the lowest common denominator of moral standards, as if to emphasize the actual frailty of the famous, and the obligation they owe those who pay attention to them.

There are two fame stories the public especially likes to hear. In one, the triumph occurs only after the surmounting of overwhelming personal difficulties. Then, after fame is achieved, the second story appears. It is a story of retribution and revenge in which the hero or heroine falls, destroyed by fate, or chance, or just plain arrogance—because they mistakenly took their fame to be their own rather than a gift of the audience. The same audience that celebrated the rise gloats over the fall.

Part of the loss inflicted by the end of the Cold War was that it became more difficult to maintain that darkness loomed only outside the safe confines of America and thereby to minimize or ignore the problems within. As we begin to face whatever changes are going to occur in our society with the loss of the Big Enemy, openness has become a virtue. To speak frankly and directly about social problems, to expose wrongs that festered because they were unspoken, to expose to the air of difficult discussion issues too long ignored—this is the positive side of the new explicitness. It has become harder than ever to hide behind the mask of authority.

But the less attractive consort of that openness is the media personalization of all general questions—its anecdotal inclination to make the conduct of private life into the prime public issue and sexuality the real truth about anyone. Just when colleges, businesses, and governments were drawing up codes of conduct to ensure that no one in the workplace should have to hear language that is insulting or abusive, the code of public discourse—what we hear in the media—seemed to have been lost entirely, all in the name of the public's need to know the facts about the famous. In one area of the national debate, to be treated as a sexual object is the worst thing that could happen to someone. Yet in the explanation of complex events and ideas, everything seems reducible to the personal and the sexual. Not only is all private life fair game, but also its invasion is defended in the name of the public need-to-know—not traits of humanness and vulnerability that might expand and anchor a general issue—but all the dirty little secrets.

In their bland assumption of the virtues of publicity, the media willfully ignore this ferocious, even vengeful, aspect of paying attention: the double life of the audience who applauds and the audience who reviles. Part of the reason may be pure twentieth-century American: Freudianism and Puritanism coming together. Another part goes back to Achilles and his heel. In myth, the hero always has a fault. It is what makes him human—and what ultimately causes his downfall and death. But we have added the wholesale tearing down of cultural figures, the revelation of sordid episodes in their lives as if that undermined their achievement. The weakness of the private self becomes the way to attack the oppressive public image in a virtual parody of the democratic leveling of all distinction, in the name of a rooted and ineradicable similarity beneath the skin—or with the skin's connivance. The story of aspiration has turned into a cautionary tale, and every fan becomes a stalker, bent on showing his worship by breaking down the distance between him and the object of his adoration. Then, of course, we complain that there are no more heroes.

*   *   *

The Industrial Revolution made the relation between worker and machine the central unit of production, changing the nature of manufacture. The Media Revolution, which began with photography in the 1830s, forged a similar bond between machine and audience, changing the nature of perception. With movies, television, and a communication system so large it can absorb anything, human attention must acclimatize to rhythms based on the capabilities of technology.

The introduction of any new technology tends to result in first a situation of overproduction and then an abrupt drop in cost and frequently in value, as the innovation is faced by a crowd of shoddy competitors. At this point in the history of fame, we seem to be facing both—an overproduction that has been on the rise since the end of World War Two, and a spreading depression in which previously valuable attributes and talents have been cheapened by widespread imitation. To continue the industrial analogy, the next step is either the consolidation of individual entrepreneurs or the eradication of them by large combines—which is what is happening with the great entertainment companies, as movies, television, books, and records over the last decade increasingly have shared the same corporate balance sheet. Executives may say all these operations are separate. But they unavoidably rub shoulders and have helped create a web of communication in which the bottom line is to please as many people as possible and constantly to remind us how pleasing they have been by producing self-congratulatory award shows that are pretexts for further performances. Note that the Emmys include a category for best production of an award show.

The media have always been out to convince us that fame is important, and usually we have accepted what they say—at least for a while. Many analysts of culture have criticized the passivity of the popular audience and its supine acceptance of whatever is dished out. The prospect of fame does seem in part to function as a form of social control in democratic societies, to divert the national audience from the difficulties of solving actual problems and living actual lives by presenting the solutions symbolized by famous individuals: If he or she can do it, so can I. One side of the fame equation is thus idealism and aspiration, the other a sleazy vicariousness. In one form it enhances who you are, in another it makes you merely famous.

But when the paradigm of contemporary media fame suffuses all activity, it is difficult to make a clear choice one way or the other, as I learned recently at a professional meeting of people who administer distinguished awards. Here were representatives of many institutions and foundations that yearly honor a wide variety of praiseworthy accomplishments in the sciences, social sciences, arts, and humanities. But they had two dilemmas. The first was the basic one of trying to determine true worth in a world overrun with the insignificant and trivial. That could be solved by mustering a distinguished jury of nominators and judges. The second was more difficult, for it involved a perhaps inescapable paradox: the desire that the media of commercial fame pay more attention, as well as respect, to these prizes, which had been awarded with as little attention to commercial or popular considerations as possible.

An important difference between the democratic media and its audience is that the media must always rely on past paradigms and forms—what has succeeded in the past—while the audience has the potential at least to be ahead, to be unpredictable. Since the Renaissance, one function of fame has been to attack an entrenched social system by showing how a newly enfranchised audience can create new gods. Famous people are often the weapons we use to attack old values. When they break, they are thrown aside, like all useless tools.

Now, in the last decade of the twentieth century, this political aspect of fame has itself been profoundly shaped by an immense daily infusion of information that threatens to render the audience either paranoid or comatose. Eager prophets characterize the new onrush of information as a wonderful new tool to discover truth. But the more usual personal experience is a complex and disordered system filled with entropy, blind alleys, and scams.

What has too often been substituted for a civic and civil sense of contemporary society is a handful of symbols and media celebrities. "Heat-death" is what thermodynamic theory calls that point where all temperatures are the same and there are no sources of heat greater than any other. Is this where we are heading or where we have virtually arrived—at the perfect media democracy where everything is of equally immediate and equally ephemeral value? The success of the Green Bay Packers in winning the 1997 Super Bowl only served to underscore how the glare of the national show has eclipsed everything local and idiosyncratic. The suffocating national moral jury passing judgments is matched by the national bottom line in which highly paid athletes move from team to team solely for money and only a few disgruntled local fans care. After all, it's all on television.

More than ten years ago, at the end of *The Frenzy of Renown*, I expressed some guardedly optimistic hopes for the positive effects of a fascination with fame. Now the optimism is less apparent. Perhaps I should conclude with some trumpeting calls-to-arms, and I certainly do think we wouldn't be so obsessed with celebrities, or tear them down so quickly, if we had a higher opinion of ourselves. It's about time for a rebirth of personal honor and responsibility in which people no longer need to substitute their heroes for themselves. In the long view of history, this isn't fame we see on the current stage. It is soap opera.

Such fame has nothing to do with the memory of significant achievement beyond its use in future trivia quizzes. But it still pretends to wear the crown of the fame of the past. There are two worlds now: the media world and all the grand things that happen in it; and the world of normality, which seems constantly shrinking in significance. Yet a fame without history is a fame without memory as well, and anyone who knows history knows that few famous in the contemporary moment will be remembered.

Perhaps some change is in the air. A recent Roper poll concluded that while three out of four Americans thought that scientific and technological discoveries got too little attention, nine out of ten thought that sports and entertainment figures got too much. At the very least there should be a moratorium on the casual use of the word "famous"—just as Vladimir Nabokov believed "reality" should never be written without quotation marks. Similarly, I often feel a rush of thankfulness when I read the obituaries of people who led exemplary lives and made exemplary contributions to society but were hardly ever in the news. Can we get away from the assumption not only that the public eye authenticates value but also that it ought to? Otherwise the best of democratic fame—the opportunity for each of us to be recognized for what is valuable to all—will become the most petty, and a reason for honor and praise will be turned into just another excuse for a T-shirt.

March 1997

References

I. THE URGE TO BE UNIQUE

Introduction
Above It All: Lindbergh and Hemingway

For reasons mentioned in the Preface, I have, in these lists of sources cited and works I found especially useful, omitted all general histories of the period and biographies of the major figures unless they contained interpretations particularly relevant to my argument. In the bulk of quotations from classical literature, I have generally used the texts established in the volumes of the Loeb Classical Library, published by W. H. Heinemann in London and by the Harvard University Press in Cambridge, Massachusetts. "Loeb" in a citation indicates those publishers and places of publication. Similarly, I have used "Penguin" to stand for the various places in which Penguin Books have been published.

In quoting from prose, I give the page number in parentheses. In quoting from poetry, I have, wherever possible, given the line number(s) so that readers can refer to their own editions. When the nuance of a particular word choice is important and the usual translations not literal enough for my purposes, I have altered them myself and, in the case of older English poets such as Chaucer, sometimes normalized the spelling and substituted the modern word. Otherwise I have used the translation most widely available.

WORKS CITED

Associated Press. In The Baltimore Sun, 12 February 1978, I, 4.

Boorstin, Daniel. *The Image, Or, What Happened to the American Dream.* New York, 1962.

Gibbon, Edward. *The Decline and Fall of the Roman Empire,* 5 vols., ed. H. H. Milman. Philadelphia, n.d.

Green, Fitzhugh. "A Little of What the World Thought of Lindbergh." In Lindbergh, *"We."*

Greville, Fulke. "An Inquisition Upon Fame and Honour" [published 1633]. In *Poems and Dramas,* 2 vols., ed. Geoffrey Bullough. London, 1939.

Hemingway, Ernest. *Across the River and Into the Trees.* New York, 1950.

———. *Selected Letters, 1917–1961,* ed. Carlos Baker. New York, 1981.

Hobbes, Thomas. *Leviathan* [1651], ed. C. B. Macpherson. Penguin, 1968.

Johnson, Samuel. *Selected Writings,* ed. Patrick Cruttwell. Penguin, 1968.

Lewis, Matthew G. *The Monk* [1796], ed. Louis F. Peck; intro. John Berryman. New York, 1952.

Lindbergh, Charles A. *The Spirit of St. Louis.* New York, 1953.

———. *"We."* New York, 1927.

Louis Armstrong—A Self-Portrait, interview by Richard Meryman. New York, 1971.

Mosley, Leonard. *Lindbergh: A Biography.* Garden City, N.Y., 1976.
Niven, David. *Bring on the Empty Horses.* New York, 1975.
Sterne, Laurence. *Letters,* ed. Lewis Perry Curtis. Oxford, 1935.
Time, 19 November 1979, 7.
Walker, Alexander. *Sex in the Movies.* Penguin, 1968.

The Longing of Alexander

Despite the more than twenty contemporaries who wrote about Alexander, our own most direct sources were written in the first and second centuries A.D., some four or five hundred years after he lived, by weaving together the now lost primary sources and adding traditional tales and local details as they came to hand. Hamilton's commentary on Plutarch's biography of Alexander spends a good deal of time construing the text but also conveys a valuable picture of how Plutarch may have sifted his sources and what they were. The two-volume Loeb edition of Arrian's *History of Alexander and Indica* as well as the Penguin volume, *The Campaigns of Alexander,* make the most extensive surviving account of Alexander's career easily available. For an analysis of the sources on which Arrian and other historians drew, see Pearson, *The Lost Histories of Alexander the Great.* Of the recent biographies written about Alexander for a popular audience, Hamilton's reflects the approach of a sceptical historian, intent on pruning the elements of "romance" from the record, while Fox's has a welcome sensitivity to interpretive issues that go beyond the establishment of a narrow accuracy. Fox's notes also give a very full picture of the sources for the reader interested in following the thread of Alexander's career through the labyrinth of controversy. Bamm's biography has many acute remarks, as does Green's, along with some outstanding illustrations.

WORKS CITED

Arrian. *The Campaigns of Alexander,* tr. Aubrey de Sélincourt. Penguin, 1971.
———. *History of Alexander and Indica,* vol. 1, tr. P. A. Brunt; vol. 2, tr. E. Iliff Robinson. Loeb, 1976; 1978.
Bamm, Peter. *Alexander the Great.* New York, 1968.
Fox, Robin Lane. *Alexander the Great.* London, 1973.
Green, Peter. *Alexander the Great.* London, 1970.
Guthrie, W. K. C. *The Greeks and Their Gods.* Boston, 1950.
Hamilton, J. R. *Plutarch: Alexander, a Commentary.* Oxford, 1969.
Hobbes, Thomas. *Leviathan* [1651], ed. C. B. Macpherson. Penguin, 1968.
Homer. *The Iliad,* tr. Robert Fitzgerald. Garden City, N.Y., 1974.
———. *The Odyssey,* tr. Robert Fitzgerald. Garden City, N.Y., 1961.
Pearson, Lionel, *The Lost Histories of Alexander the Great.* American Philological Association Monograph 20, 1960.
Plutarch. *The Age of Alexander,* tr. Ian Scott–Kilvert. Penguin, 1973.
———. *Lives of the Noble Greeks and Romans,* tr. Sir Thomas North. New York, 1941. [Shakespeare's source]
Seneca. *Naturales Quaestiones, The Works of Seneca,* vol. 10, tr. Thomas H. Corcoran. Loeb, 1972.
Snell, Bruno. *The Discovery of Mind,* tr. T. G. Rosenmeyer. Oxford, 1953.
Thoreau, Henry David. *Walden,* ed. J. Lyndon Shanley. Princeton, 1971.
Vermeule, Emily. *Aspects of Death in Early Greek Art and Poetry.* Berkeley, 1976.
Zimmer, Heinrich. *The Art of Asian India,* 2 vols., ed. Joseph Campbell. New York, 1955.

OTHER USEFUL SOURCES

Atkins, A. D. W. *Merit and Responsibility: A Study in Greek Values.* Oxford, 1960.
Badian, E. *Studies in Greek and Roman History.* New York, 1964.

Bell, H. Idris. *Egypt*. Oxford, 1948.
Bieber, Margarete. *Alexander the Great in Greek and Roman Art*. Chicago, 1964.
————. *The History of the Greek and Roman Theater*. Princeton, 1939; 2nd rev. ed. 1961.
Cary, George. *The Medieval Alexander*, ed. D. J. A. Ross. Cambridge, Eng., 1956.
Den Boer, W. *Laconian Studies*. Amsterdam, 1974.
Elgood, P. G. *The Ptolemies of Egypt*. Bristol, Eng., 1938.
Engels, Donald W. *Alexander the Great and the Logistics of the Macedonian Army*. Berkeley, 1978.
Griffith, G. T., ed. *Alexander the Great: The Main Problems*. Cambridge, Eng., 1966.
Hatzopoulos, Miltiades B., and Loukopoulos, Louisa D., eds. *Philip of Macedon*. Athens, 1980.
Heisserer, A. J. *Alexander the Great and the Greeks: The Epigraphic Evidence*. Norman, Okla., 1980.
L'Orange, H. P. *Apotheosis in Ancient Portraiture*. Oslo, 1947.
Quintus Curtius. *Historie of . . . the Actes of the Greate Alexander*, tr. John Brende. London, 1553.
Richter, Gisela M. A. *A Handbook of Greek Art*. London, 1959.
————. *The Portraits of the Greeks*, 3 vols. London, 1965.
Rose, H. J. *A Handbook of Greek Mythology*. New York, 1959.
Ross, D. J. A. *Illustrated Medieval Alexander—Books in Germany and the Netherlands*. Cambridge, Eng., 1971.
Ross, E. Denison, ed. *The Art of Egypt Through the Ages*. London, 1931.
Seckel, Dietrich. *The Art of Buddhism*, tr. Ann E. Keep. London, 1964.
Thompson, Dorothy Burr. *Ptolemaic Oinochoai and Portraits in Faience*. Oxford, 1973.
Woldering, Irmgard. *The Art of Egypt*. New York, 1963.

II. THE DESTINY OF ROME

Public Men and the Fall of the Roman Republic
The Authority of Augustus

In the study of the age of Alexander and throughout this book, general histories were invaluable in determining the large movements of a period as they have been seen across the centuries, as was *The Oxford Classical Dictionary,* 2nd ed. (ed. N. G. L. Hammond and H. H. Scullard. Oxford, 1970) for matters of fact as well as of interpretation. Syme's *The Roman Revolution* is crucial for the period that witnessed the rise of Augustus, with some discounting for having been written in the period that witnessed the rise of Hitler. To aid my understanding of both the Roman Republic and the early Roman Empire, I have drawn extensively on the works of Badian, Brunt, Gruen, Sutherland, and Taylor, along with Gelzer and Weinstock on Caesar's career.

But I must pay a special debt here (and perhaps throughout) to the style and vision of Edward Gibbon and his *Decline and Fall of the Roman Empire* (1776–1788), which has been outdated in detail but remains a monumental effort to understand and thereby to explain both the combat and the interplay of classical and Christian culture.

WORKS CITED

Augustus. *Res gestae Divi Augusti,* tr. and ed. P. A. Brunt and J. M. Moore. Oxford, 1967.
Bailey, D. R. Shackleton. *Cicero*. New York, 1971.
Bowersock, G. W. *Augustus and the Greek World*. Oxford, 1965.
Buchner, Edmund. *Die Sonnenuhr des Augustus*. Mainz, 1982.

Cicero. *Letters to Atticus*, tr. D. R. Shackleton Bailey. Cambridge, Eng., 1965–68.
———. *Letters to His Friends*, vol. 1, tr. D. R. Shackleton Bailey. Penguin, 1978.
———. *Philippics*, tr. Walter C. A. Ker. Loeb, 1926.
———. *Pro Archia Poeta*. In *The Works of Cicero*, vol. 11, tr. N. H. Watts. Loeb, 1979.
———. *Pro Lege Manilia*. In *The Works of Cicero*, vol. 9, tr. H. Grose Hodge. Loeb, 1927.
———. *Tusculan Disputations, The Works of Cicero*, vol. 18, tr. J. E. King. Loeb, 1927.
Dryden, John. Dedication to *Aureng-zebe* [1675]. In *Three Plays of Dryden*, ed. George Saintsbury. New York, 1957.
Green, Peter. "Imperial Caesar." In *Essays in Antiquity*. London, 1960.
Jenkins, G. K. *Ancient Greek Coins*. London, 1972.
Livy. *Works*, tr. B. O. Foster. Loeb, 1926.
Marvell, Andrew. "The First Anniversary of the Government Under His Highness the Lord Protector." In *Complete Poetry*, ed. George deF. Lord. New York, 1968.
McEredy, Colin, and Jones, Richard. *Atlas of World Population History*. New York, 1978.
Nietzsche, Friedrich. *The Birth of Tragedy* and *The Genealogy of Morals*, tr. Francis Golffing. New York, 1956.
Pliny. *Natural History*, Books 33–35, tr. H. Rackham. Loeb, 1952.
Plutarch. "Coriolanus." In *Makers of Rome*, tr. Ian Scott-Kilvert. Penguin, 1965.
Pollini, John. "Studies in Augustan 'Historical' Reliefs." Ph.D. diss., University of California at Berkeley, 1978.
Sallust. "The War with Catiline." In *Sallust*, tr. J. C. Rolfe. Loeb, 1931.
Suetonius. *Suetonius*, 2 vols., tr. J. C. Rolfe. Loeb, 1913.
———. *The Twelve Caesars*, tr. Robert Graves. Penguin, 1957.
Sutherland, C. H. V. *Coinage in Roman Imperial Policy: 31 B.C.–A.D. 68*. London, 1951.
Syme, Ronald. *The Roman Revolution*. Oxford, 1939.
Tacitus. *The Annals of Imperial Rome*, tr. Michael Grant. Penguin, 1956.
Taylor, Lily Ross. *The Divinity of the Roman Emperor*. Middletown, Conn., 1931.
Virgil. *Aeneid*, tr. Allen Mandelbaum. New York, 1972.

OTHER USEFUL SOURCES:
Badian, E. *Foreign Clientelae (264–70 B.C.)*. Oxford, 1958.
———. *Publicans and Sinners*. Ithaca, N.Y., 1972.
———. *Roman Imperialism in the Late Republic*. Oxford, 1967.
Brunt, P. A. *Italian Manpower 225 B.C.–A.D. 14*. Oxford, 1971.
———. *Social Conflicts in the Late Roman Republic*. London, 1971.
Carter, John M. *The Battle of Actium: The Rise and Triumph of Augustus Caesar*. New York, 1970.
Dorey, T. A., ed. *Cicero*. London, 1965.
———. "Honesty in Roman Politics." In *Cicero*, ed. Dorey.
Gelzer, Matthias. *Caesar: Politician and Statesman*, tr. Peter Needham. Cambridge, Mass., 1968.
Grant, Michael. *From Imperium to Auctoritas: A Historical Survey of Aes Coinage in the Roman Empire, 49 B.C.–A.D. 14*. Cambridge, Eng., 1946.
Green, Peter. "Caesar and Alexander: Aemulatio, Imitatio, Comparatio." *Journal of Ancient History*, 3 (1978), 1–26.
Gruen, Erich S. *The Last Generation of the Roman Republic*. Berkeley, 1974.
Jones, A. H. M. *Augustus*. London: Chatto & Windus, 1970.
———. *The Roman Economy: Studies in Ancient Economic and Administrative History*, ed. P. A. Brunt. Oxford, 1974.

Jones, C. P. *Plutarch and Rome.* Oxford, 1971.

Krieger, Leonard. "The Idea of Authority in the West." *American Historical Review,* 82 (1977), 249–70.

Lacey, W. K. *Cicero and the End of the Roman Republic.* London, 1978.

Newby, Jessie D. *A Numismatic Commentary on the Res Gestae of Augustus. Iowa Studies in Classical Philology,* 6 (1938).

Reinhold, Meyer. "Augustus' Conception of Himself." *Thought,* 55 (1980), 36–50.

Scullard, H. H. "The Political Career of a *Novus Homo.*" In *Cicero,* ed. Dorey.

Seager, Robin. *Pompey: A Political Biography.* Berkeley, 1979.

Syme, Ronald. Review of *Divus Julius* by Matthias Gelzer. *Journal of Roman Studies,* 34 (1944), 92–103.

Taylor, Lily Ross. *Party Politics in the Age of Caesar.* Berkeley, 1949.

Toynbee, J. M. C. "Ruler-Apotheosis in Ancient Rome." *Numismatic Chronicle,* 6th series, 7 (1947), 126–149.

Volkmann, Hans. *Cleopatra: A Study in Politics and Propaganda,* tr. T. J. Cadoux. New York, 1958.

Walker, Susan, and Burnett, Andrew. *The Image of Augustus.* London, 1981.

Watson, Alan. *Rome of the XII Tables.* Princeton, 1975.

Weinstock, Stefan. *Divus Julius.* Oxford, 1971.

Williams, Gordon. *The Third Book of Horace's Odes.* Oxford, 1969.

III. THE EMPTINESS OF PUBLIC FAME

The Uneasy Truce: Authority and Authorship

WORKS CITED

Arrian. *The Campaigns of Alexander,* tr. Aubrey de Sélincourt. Penguin, 1971.

Brunt, P. A. "Stoicism and the Principate." *Proceedings of the British School at Rome,* (1975), 7–35.

Chaucer, Geoffrey. *Works,* 2nd ed., ed. F. N. Robinson. Boston, 1961.

Cicero. *Tusculan Disputations, The Works of Cicero,* vol. 18, tr. J. E. King. Loeb, 1927.

Fraser, P. M. *Ptolemaic Alexandria,* 3 vols. Oxford, 1972.

Griffin, Miriam T. *Seneca: A Philosopher in Politics.* Oxford, 1976.

Horace, *Odes and Epodes,* tr. C. E. Bennet. Loeb, 1927.

———. *Satires, Epistles, and Ars Poetica,* tr. H. Rushton Fairclough. Loeb, 1929.

Humphries. See Ovid.

Jonas, Hans. *The Gnostic Religion: The Message of the Alien God and the Beginnings of Christianity,* 2nd ed. Boston, 1963.

Kenyon, Frederic G. *Books and Readers in Ancient Greece and Rome.* Oxford, 1951.

Ovid. *Metamorphoses,* 2 vols., tr. Frank Justus Miller. Loeb, 1916.

———. *Metamorphoses,* tr. Rolfe Humphries. Bloomington, Ind., 1955.

Pausanias. *Guide to Greece,* 2 vols., tr. Peter Levi, S.J. Penguin, 1971.

Pope, Alexander. *The Dunciad.* In *Poetry and Prose,* ed. Aubrey Williams. Boston, 1969.

Putnam, George Haven. *Authors and their Public in Ancient Times,* 3rd rev. ed. New York, 1967.

Suetonius. *Suetonius,* 2 vols., tr. J. C. Rolfe. Loeb, 1913.

———. *The Twelve Caesars,* tr. Robert Graves. Penguin, 1957.

Tacitus. *The Annals of Imperial Rome,* tr. Michael Grant. Penguin, 1956.

Virgil. *Aeneid,* tr. Allen Mandelbaum. New York, 1972.

———. *Aeneid.* In *Virgil,* 2 vols., tr. H. Rushton Fairclough. Loeb, 1932.

———. *Eclogues.* In *Virgil,* 2 vols., tr. H. Rushton Fairclough. Loeb, 1932.

———. *Georgics.* In *Virgil,* 2 vols., tr. H. Rushton Fairclough. Loeb, 1932.

Warmington, B. H. *Nero: Reality and Legend.* London, 1969.

Zumwalt, Nancy. *"Fama subversa:* Theme and Structure in Ovid's *Metamorphoses* 12."* In *California Studies in Classical Antiquity,* ed. Ronald S. Stroud and Philip Levine, vol. 10. Berkeley, 1978.

Christianity and the Fame of the Spirit

As the *Oxford Classical Dictionary* was an important resource for classical material, so the *Oxford Dictionary of the Christian Church* was especially useful for material in this section. For the text of the New Testament, I have generally used the separate volumes devoted to the Gospels in the Pelican Gospel Commentaries series: *Saint Matthew* (J. C. Fenton, 1963), *Saint Mark* (D. E. Nineham, 1963), *Saint Luke* (G. B. Caird, 1963), and *Saint John* (John Marsh, 1968), along with the *New English Bible,* supplementing them with the Greek New Testament for specific readings when necessary, and *The Interpreter's Bible.*

The most fruitful writings on the life and times of Augustine as well as the entire context of late antiquity are those of Peter Brown. For the cultural context of late antiquity, with its mingled world of pagans and Christians, see also Frend, *Martyrdom and Persecution in the Early Church,* Dodds, *Pagan and Christian in an Age of Anxiety,* and the essays in Momigliano, ed., *The Conflict Between Paganism and Christianity.* Lantenari in *Religions of the Oppressed* makes some interesting implications about the shape of Christianity before it triumphed politically. Victor Turner and Edith Turner consider the important Christian practice of pilgrimage as a way of weaving together a far-flung community in *Image and Pilgrimage.*

WORKS CITED

Augustine. *The City of God Against the Pagans,* 7 vols. Loeb: 1–3 (tr. George E. McCracken, 1957); 4–7 (tr. William M. Green, 1963); 8–11 (tr. David S. Wiesen, 1968); 12–15 (tr. Philip Levine, 1966); 16–18, 35 (tr. Eva M. Sanford and William M. Green, 1965); 18, 36–20 (tr. William C. Greene, 1969); 21–22 (tr. William M. Green, 1972).

———. *Confessions,* tr. R. S. Pine-Coffin. Penguin, 1961.

———. *Confessions,* tr. William Watts. Loeb, 1912.

———. *On the Psalms,* vol. 1, tr. Dame Scholastica Hebgin and Dame Felicitas Corrigan. Westminster, Md., 1960.

Barnes, Timothy D. *Constantine and Eusebius.* Cambridge, Mass., 1981.

Bloch, Herbert. "The Pagan Revival in the West at the End of the Fourth Century." In Momigliano, ed., *Paganism and Christianity,* 193–218.

Brown, Peter. *Augustine of Hippo.* Berkeley, 1967.

———. *The Cult of Saints: Its Rise and Function in Latin Christianity.* Chicago, 1981.

———. "The Rise and Function of the Holy Man in Late Antiquity," *Journal of Roman Studies,* 61 (1971), 80–101.

———. "The Saint as Exemplar in Late Antiquity." *Representations* 2 (Spring 1983), 1–28.

———. *Society and the Holy in Late Antiquity.* Berkeley, 1981.

Cavafy, Constantine. *Collected Poems,* tr. Edmund Keeley and Philip Sherrad; ed. George Savidis. Princeton, 1975.

Chadwick, Henry. *The Early Church.* Penguin, 1967.

Cochrane, Charles Norris. *Christianity and Classical Culture.* Oxford, 1944.

Delaney, John J. *Dictionary of Saints.* Garden City, N.Y., 1980.

Dodds, E. R. *Pagan and Christian in an Age of Anxiety: Some Aspects of Religious Experience from Marcus Aurelius to Constantine.* Cambridge, Eng., 1965.

———. "Tradition and Personal Achievement in the Philosophy of Plotinus." *Journal of Roman Studies,* 50 (1960), 1–8.

Dorey, T. A. "Honesty in Roman Politics." In *Cicero,* ed. T. A. Dorey. London, 1965.

Frend, W. H. C. *Martyrdom and Persecution in the Early Church.* Oxford, 1965.

Gage, Nicholas. "Greek Ritualists Invoking Saints Walk on Coals." *New York Times,* June 1, 1980, I, 11.

Grabar, André. *Early Christian Art: From the Rise of Christianity to the Death of Theodosius,* tr. Stuart Gilbert and James Emmons. New York, 1968.

Henry, Paul, S.J. *Saint Augustine on Personality.* New York, 1960.

Jerome. *Selected Letters,* tr. F. A. Wright. Loeb, 1933.

Julian. *The Caesars.* In *Works,* 3 vols., tr. F. A. Wright. Loeb, 1953–54.

Lantenari, Vittorio. *Religions of the Oppressed: A Study of Modern Messianic Cults,* tr. Lisa Sergio. New York, 1963.

MacKail, J. W. *The Lesson of Imperial Rome.* London, 1929.

Marcus Aurelius, *Meditations,* tr. C. R. Haines. Loeb, 1930.

van der Meer, F. *Augustine the Bishop,* tr. Brian Battershaw and G. R. Lamb. New York, 1961.

Momigliano, A. D., ed. *The Conflict Between Paganism and Christianity in the Fourth Century.* Oxford, 1963.

Montaigne, Michel de. "Apology for Raymond Sebond." In *Complete Essays,* tr. Donald M. Frame. Stanford, 1958.

Nitzsche, Jane Chance. *The Genius Figure in Antiquity and the Middle Ages.* New York, 1975.

O'Connell, Robert J. *St. Augustine's Confessions: The Odyssey of Soul.* Cambridge, Mass., 1969.

Plato. *Republic,* tr. Francis M. Cornford. London, 1941.

Turner, Victor, and Turner, Edith. *Image and Pilgrimage in Christian Culture: Anthropological Perspectives.* New York, 1978.

Vogt, Joseph. "Pagans and Christians in the Family of Constantine the Great." In Momigliano, ed., *Paganism and Christianity.*

Wills, Garry. "Radical Creativity," *MLN,* 89 (1974), 1019–28.

OTHER USEFUL WORKS

Attwater, Donald. *The Penguin Dictionary of Saints.* Penguin, 1965.

Bainton, Roland. *The Penguin History of Christianity,* 2 vols. Penguin, 1967.

Bowersock, G. W. *Julian the Apostate.* Cambridge, Mass., 1978.

Brandon, S. G. F. *History, Time, and Deity.* Manchester, Eng., 1965.

Dudden, F. Homes. *The Life and Times of St. Ambrose,* 2 vols. Oxford, 1935.

Farmer, David Hugh. *The Oxford Dictionary of Saints.* Oxford, 1978.

Preus, James S. *From Shadow to Promise: Old Testament Interpretation from Augustine to the Young Luther.* Cambridge, Mass., 1969.

St. Prosper of Aquitaine. *Defense of Saint Augustine,* tr. P. DeLetter, S.J. London, 1963.

Sambursky, S., and Pines, S. *The Concept of Time in Late Neoplatonism.* Jerusalem, 1971.

Walbrook, F. W. *The Awful Revolution: The Decline of the Roman Empire in the West.* Liverpool, Eng., 1969.

IV. THE INTERCESSION OF ART

The Imagery of Invisible Power

For my discussion of Christian art and portraiture, especially the image of Jesus, I am especially indebted to these works of both André Grabar and Ernst Kitzinger in addition to those cited:

Grabar, André. *Byzantium: Byzantine Art in the Middle Ages,* tr. Betty Forster. London, 1966.

———. *Christian Iconography: A Study of Its Origins,* tr. Terry Grabar. Princeton, 1968.

———. *The Golden Age of Justinian: From the Death of Theodosius to the Rise of Islam,* tr. Stuart Gilbert and James Emmons. New York, 1967.

———. *L'Empereur dans l'art byzantin.* London, 1971.

Kitzinger, Ernst, and Senior, Elizabeth. *Portraits of Christ.* Penguin, 1940.

Two virtually contemporary lives of Charlemagne by Einhard and Nottker the Stammerer are handily available in *Two Lives of Charlemagne.* For more scholarly treatments see Jacques Broussard, *Charlemage et son temps* (Paris, 1968); Robert Folz, *Le Souvenir et la légende de Charlemagne dans l'empire germanique médiéval* (Paris, 1950) and *The Coronation of Charlemagne, 25 December 800,* tr. J. E. Anderson (London, 1974); Arthur Kleinclausz, *Charlemagne* (Paris, 1977); and Peter Munz, *The Origin of the Carolingian Empire* (Universities of Otago and Leicester, 1960).

The special issues of the depictions and ceremonies surrounding medieval kingship are discussed most trenchantly in Kantorowicz, *The King's Two Bodies.* See also his *Laudes Regiae: A Study in Liturgical Acclamations and Mediaeval Ruler Worship* (Berkeley, 1946), as well as Ernst Benkard, *Undying Faces,* tr. Margaret M. Green (London, 1929), and Ralph E. Giesey, *The Royal Funeral Ceremony in Renaissance France* (Geneva, 1960).

WORKS CITED

Barnes, Timothy D. *Constantine and Eusebius.* Cambridge, Mass., 1981.

Cary, George. *The Medieval Alexander,* ed. D. J. A. Ross. Cambridge, Eng., 1956.

Einhard and Nottker the Stammerer. *Two Lives of Charlemagne,* tr. Lewis Thorpe. London, 1969.

Grabar, André. *Early Christian Art: From the Rise of Christianity to the Death of Theodosius,* tr. Stuart Gilbert and James Emmons. New York, 1968.

Hennecke, Edgar, *New Testament Apocrypha,* ed. Wilhelm Schneemelcher; tr. R. McL. Wilson. Philadelphia, 1964.

Iskandarnamah: A Persian Medieval Alexander-Romance, tr. Minoo S. Southgate. New York, 1978.

Kantorowicz, Ernst H. *The King's Two Bodies: A Study in Mediaeval Political Theology.* Princeton, 1957.

Kitzinger, Ernst. *The Art of Byzantium and the Medieval West: Selected Studies,* ed. W. Eugene Leinbauer. Bloomington, Ind., 1976.

———. "The Cult of Images in the Age before Iconoclasm." *Dumbarton Oaks Papers,* 8 (1954), 83–150.

Nottker the Stammerer. *See* Einhard.

The Romance of Alexander the Great by Pseudo-Callisthenes, tr. from the Armenian by Albert M. Wolohojian. New York, 1969.

Speer, Albert. *Inside the Third Reich,* tr. Richard and Clara Winston. New York, 1970.

Tacitus. *Histories,* tr. Kenneth Wellesley. Penguin, 1964.

OTHER USEFUL WORKS

Bainton, Roland. *The Medieval Church.* New York, 1962.

Bloch, Marc. *Feudal Society,* tr. L. A. Manyon. Chicago, 1961.

Brandon, S. G. F. "The Portrait of Christ: Its Origin and Evolution." *History Today,* 21 (1971), 473–81.

Brooke, Christopher. *Medieval Church and Society.* New York, 1972.

Gerhard, H. P. *The World of Icons.* New York, 1971.

Kantorowicz, Hermann. *Studies in the Glossators of the Roman Law.* Cambridge, Eng., 1938.

Ladner, C. B. "The Concept of the Image in the Greek Fathers and the Byzantine Iconoclastic Controversy." *Dumbarton Oaks Papers,* 7 (1953), 1–34.

Painter, Sidney. *A History of the Middle Ages.* New York, 1953.

Ragsdale, William Cannon. *History of Christianity in the Middles Ages: From the Fall of Rome to the Fall of Constantinople.* New York, 1960.

Southern, Richard. *The Medieval Church.* Penguin, 1970.

Ullmann, Walter. *A History of Political Thought in the Middle Ages.* Penguin, 1965.

Weitzmann, Kurt, ed. *Age of Spirituality: Late Antique and Early Christian Art, Third to Seventh Century.* Princeton, 1979.

The Intermediary and His Audience

The life of Francis of Assisi has been told many times, although not often enough in terms of the way he tried to define what he believed to be his mission in relation to the traditional structures of piety and sociability in his world. As so often in these pages, what was believed and told about him has as much importance for the nature of his fame as what he actually did.

Among other works, I have consulted E. M. Almedingen, *St. Francis of Assisi: A Great Life in Brief* (New York, 1967); T. S. R. Boase, *St. Francis of Assisi* (Bloomington, Ind., 1968); and Lawrence Cunningham, *St. Francis of Assisi* (Boston, 1976). John Baldwin's *The Scholastic Culture of the Middle Ages* focuses on the universities as a particular seedbed for the assertion of mind against authority. Also, for Dante, Petrarch, and Boccaccio see especially Francis Fergusson, *Dante* (New York, 1966); *Dante: His Life, His Times, His Works,* tr. Giuseppina T. Salvadori and Bernice L. Lewis, anthology by Thomas G. Bergin (New York, 1970); Paget Toynbee, *Dante Alighieri,* ed. and intro. Charles S. Singleton (New York, 1965); Mark Musa, tr. and intro., *Dante's Vita Nuova* (Bloomington, Ind., 1973); Ernest Hatch Wilkins, *Life of Petrarch* (Chicago, 1961); and Vittore Branca, *Boccaccio: The Man and His Works,* tr. Richard Monges and Dennis J. McAuliffe; ed. Dennis J. McAuliffe (New York, 1976).

For Chaucer, I have used Robinson's edition and then normalized the spelling and translated a few less familiar words to make the text more readable. *The House of Fame* has attracted a large share of commentary in recent times that essentially attempts to situate it in relation to other works and to general conceptions of fortune. See, for example, Koonce, *Chaucer and the Tradition of Fame;* Patch, *The Goddess Fortuna;* and Ann C. Watts, " 'Amor Gloriae in Chaucer's *House of Fame.*" Watts is especially attuned to parallels with classical authors such as Ovid and Boethius as well as with Petrarch.

WORKS CITED

Baldwin, John. *The Scholastic Culture of the Middle Ages, 1000–1300.* Lexington, Ky., 1971.

Boccaccio, Giovanni. *Concerning Famous Women,* tr. Guido Guarino. New Brunswick, N.J., 1963.

———. *The Fates of Illustrious Men,* tr. and abr. Louis Brewer Hall. New York, 1965.

———. *Life of Dante.* In *The Early Lives of Dante,* tr. Philip H. Wicksteed. London, 1904.

Carandente, Giovanni. *I Trionfi nel primo rinascimento.* Rome, 1963.

Chaucer, Geoffrey. "The House of Fame." In *Works,* 2nd ed., ed. F. N. Robinson. Boston, 1961, 280–302.

Curtius, Ernst Robert. *European Literature and the Latin Middle Ages,* tr. Willard Trask. New York, 1953.

Dante Alighieri. *Inferno,* tr. Mark Musa. Penguin, 1971.

————. *Paradiso,* tr. P. H. Wicksteed. London, 1956.

————. *Purgatory,* tr. Mark Musa. Bloomington, Ind., 1981.

————. *Rima petrosa. See* Petrarch, *Lyric Poems.*

Goldthwaite, Richard A. *The Building of Renaissance Florence: An Economic and Social History.* Baltimore, 1980.

Hemingway, Ernest. *Across the River and into the Trees.* New York, 1950.

————. *Islands in the Stream.* New York, 1970.

————. *Selected Letters, 1917–1961,* ed. Carlos Baker. New York, 1981.

Koonce, B. G. *Chaucer and the Tradition of Fame: Symbolism in the "House of Fame."* Princeton, 1966.

Lydgate, John. *The Fall of Princes,* 4 vols., ed. Henry Berger. London, 1967.

Mattingly, Garrett. *Renaissance Diplomacy.* Boston, 1955.

Mommsen, Theodor E. "Petrarch and the Decoration of the *Sala Virorum Illustrium* in Padua." *Art Bulletin,* 34 (1952), 95–116.

Patch, Howard Rollins. *The Goddess Fortuna in Medieval Literature.* Cambridge, Mass., 1927.

Petrarch, Francesco. *Letters from Petrarch,* tr. and ed. Morris Bishop. Bloomington, Ind., 1966.

————. *Lyric Poems: The "Rime sparse" and Other Lyrics,* tr. and ed. Robert M. Durling. Cambridge, Mass., 1976.

————. *Rerum familiarium libri I–VIII,* tr. and ed. Aldo S. Bernardo. Albany, 1975.

————. *The Triumphs of Petrarch,* tr. Ernest Hatch Wilkins. Chicago, 1962.

————. *Tryumphes of Fraunces Petrarcke,* tr. Henry Parker; ed. D. D. Carnicelli. Cambridge, Mass., 1971.

Pope, Alexander. *Poetry and Prose,* ed. Aubrey Williams. Boston, 1969.

Schroeder, Horst. *Der Topos der Nine Worthies in Literatur und bildender Kunst.* Göttingen, 1971.

Sherman, Claire Richter. *The Portraits of Charles V of France (1338–1380).* New York, 1969.

Smart, Alastair. *The Assisi Problem and the Art of Giotto: A Study of the Legend of St. Francis in the Upper Church of San Francisco, Assisi.* Oxford, 1971.

Watts, Ann C. " 'Amor Gloriae' in Chaucer's *House of Fame.*" *Journal of Medieval and Renaissance Studies,* 3 (1973), 87–113.

OTHER USEFUL WORKS

Baldwin, John, and Goldthwaite, Richard, eds. *Universities in Politics, Case Studies from the Late Middle Ages and Early Modern Period.* Baltimore, 1972.

Coolidge, John C. "Boethius and 'That Last Infirmity of Noble Mind,' " *Philological Quarterly,* 42 (1963), 176–82.

Gilbert, Alan H. "Notes on the Influence of the *Secretum Secretorum.*" *Speculum,* 3 (January 1928), 84–98.

Morris, Colin M. *The Discovery of the Individual, 1050–1200.* New York, 1972.

Petrarch, Francesco. *Letters on Familiar Matters, Rerum familiarium libri IX–XVI.* Baltimore, 1982.

Wilkins, Ernest Hatch. "The Coronation of Petrarch." *Speculum,* 18 (1943), 155–97.

Printing and Portraiture: The Dissemination of the Unique

A wide-ranging account of European portraiture in its first great age of reflowering is John Pope-Hennessy, *The Portrait in the Renaissance* (Princeton, 1966). Much of our view of the Italian Renaissance has been conditioned by accepting or varying the argument of Jacob Burckhardt in *The Civilization of the Renaissance in Italy* (1860), tr. S. G. C. Middlemore (1878). A reprinting is the Modern Library edition

(New York, 1954). The concept of a Golden Age under Lorenzo the Magnificent has been criticized by a few recent writers, but what he attempted to do or what at least occurred around him is unmistakable. The issue of patronage is approached in a variety of settings in *Patronage in the Renaissance* (ed. Guy Fitch Lytle and Stephen Orgel. Princeton, 1981). Giorgio Vasari's sixteenth-century biographies of painters, sculptors, architects, and so on, have appeared in a variety of editions. For a recent account of his career, see T. S. R. Boase, *Giorgio Vasari: The Man and the Book* (Princeton, 1979). On British portraiture Roy Strong's works have been particularly valuable to me, while the basic source for engraved works is Arthur M. Hind, *Engraving in England in the Sixteenth and Seventeenth Centuries. A Descriptive Catalogue with Introductions*, 3 vols. (Cambridge, Eng., 1952–1964; third volume edited by M. Corbett and M. Norton). See also the extensive collection of Renaissance emblem-books reprinted by Garland Publishing (New York, 1976) under the editorship of Stephen Orgel.

For a detailed view of the impact of printing on medieval book-making methods, see Sandra Hindman and James Douglas Farquhar, *From Pen to Press: Illustrated Manuscripts and Printed Books in the First Century of Printing* (Baltimore, 1977). The many implications for the shape and spread of knowledge inherent in the invention of printing are brilliantly surveyed in Elizabeth L. Eisenstein, *The Printing Press as an Agent of Change: Communications and Cultural Transformations in Early-Modern Europe*, 2 vols. (New York, 1979), which includes a running argument against Burckhardt's assumption that fourteenth-century Italy is the seedbed of the modern world.

The European response to America is covered in a variety of essays included in Fredi Chiappelli, ed., *First Images of America*, 2 vols. (Berkeley, 1976). Martin Waldseemüller's *Cosmographiae Introductio*, where the name "America" was popularized, has been recently reprinted with an English translation by Joseph Fischer and Franz von Wieser (U.S. Catholic Historical Society, Monograph 4, 1966).

WORKS CITED

Adams, Robert M. *The Roman Stamp: Frame and Facade in Some Forms of Neo-Classicism*. Berkeley, 1974.

Alberti, Leon Battista. *On Painting* [Written 1435–36; published 1540], tr. John R. Spencer. New Haven, 1966.

Bainton, Roland. *Erasmus of Christendom*. New York, 1969.

Baron, Hans. "Franciscan Poverty and Civic Wealth in the Fourteenth Century." *Speculum*, 13 (1938), 1–37.

Barrett, W. P., ed. *The Trial of Jeanne d'Arc*. London, 1931.

Bellamy, John. *The Tudor Law of Treason: An Introduction*. London, 1979.

Berger, John. *Success and Failure of Picasso*. Penguin, 1965.

Brooke, George C. *English Coins from the Seventh Century to the Present Day*. London, 1932.

Cahn, Walter. *Masterpieces: Chapters on the History of an Idea*. Princeton, 1979.

Cast, David. *The Calumny of Apelles: A Study in the Humanist Tradition*. New Haven, 1981.

Davis, R. H. C. *The Normans and Their Myths*. London, 1976.

Elton, G. R. *Reform and Reformation: England, 1509–1558*. Cambridge, Mass., 1977.

Gerhard, H. P. *The World of Icons*. New York, 1971.

Gies, Francis. *Joan of Arc: The Legend and the Reality*. New York, 1981.

Greville, Fulke. *Life of Sidney* [published 1652]. Oxford, 1907.

———. *Poems and Dramas*, 2 vols., ed. Geoffrey Bullough. London, 1939.

Guinti, Jacopo. *The Divine Michelangelo: The Florentine Academy's Homage on His Death in 1564*, ed. and tr. Rudolf Wittkower and Margot Wittkower. London, 1964.

Hager, Alan. "The Exemplary Mirage: Fabrications of Sir Philip Sidney's Biographical Image and the Sidney Reader." *ELH*, 48 (1981), 1–16.

Hirsch, Rudolf. "Printed Reports on the Early Discoveries and Their Reception." In *First Images of America*, vol. 2, ed. Chiappelli.

Jantz, Harold. "Images of America in the German Renaissance." In *First Images of America*, vol. 1, ed. Chiapelli.

Liebert, Robert S. *Michelangelo: A Psychoanalytic Study of His Life and Images*. New Haven, 1983.

Lightbody, Charles Wayland. *The Judgements of Joan: Joan of Arc, A Study in Cultural History*. Cambridge, Mass., 1961.

Murray, Linda. *Michelangelo*. London, 1980.

Neale, J. E. *Queen Elizabeth I*. London, 1934.

Painter, Sidney. *French Chivalry: Chivalric Ideas and Practices in Mediaeval France*. Baltimore, 1940.

Panofsky, Erwin. *Albrecht Dürer*. Princeton, 1955.

Phillips, John. *The Reformation of Images: Destruction of Art in England, 1535–1660*. Berkeley, 1973.

Phillips, Margaret Mann. *The 'Adages' of Erasmus: A Study with Translations*. Cambridge, Eng., 1964.

Quinn, David B. "New Geographic Horizons: Literature." In *First Images of America*, vol. 2, ed. Chiappelli.

Raleigh, Sir Walter. "An Epitaph upon the Right Honorable Sir Philip Sidney, Knight, Lord Governor of Flushing." *In Poetry of the English Renaissance, 1509–1660*, ed. J. William Hebel and Hoyt H. Hudson. New York, 1929.

Sidney, Sir Philip. *Selected Poems*, ed. Katherine Duncan-Jones. Oxford, 1973.

Strong, Roy. *The Elizabethan Image: Painting in England, 1540–1620*. London, 1969.

———. *The English Icon: Elizabethan and Jacobean Portraiture*. London, 1969.

———. *Portraits of Queen Elizabeth I*. Oxford, 1963.

———. *Tudor and Jacobean Portraits*, 2 vols. London, 1969.

Thevet, André. *Les Vrais Pourtraits et vies des hommes illustres grecz, latins, et payens, recueilliz de leur tableaux, livres, medalles antiques et modernes*, intro. Rouben C. Cholakian. Delmar, N.Y., 1973.

Vergil, Polydore. *English History*, vol. 1, ed. Sir Henry Ellis, *Camden Society*, o.s. 36 (1846).

Vertue, George. *Anecdotes of Painting in England* [1762–71], published by Horace Walpole, 3 vols., ed. Ralph N. Wornum. London, 1849.

Voet, Leon. *Antwerp, the Golden Age: The Rise and Glory of the Metropolis in the Sixteenth Century*. Antwerp, 1973.

Warner, Marina. *Joan of Arc: The Image of Female Heroism*. New York, 1981.

Wind, Edgar. *Pagan Mysteries in the Renaissance*, rev. ed. New York, 1968.

Wittkower, Rudolf, and Wittkower, Margot. *Born Under Saturn, the Character and Conduct of Artists: A Documented History from Antiquity to the French Revolution*. New York, 1969.

OTHER USEFUL WORKS

Alberti, Leon Battista. *On Painting and Sculpture*, ed. and tr. Cecil Grayson. London, 1972.

Alciati, Andrea. *Emblematum flumen abundans*. Manchester, Eng., 1871.

Arciniegas, German. *Amerigo and the New World: The Life and Times of Amerigo Vespucci*, tr. Harriet de Onis. New York, 1955.

Barber, Richard. *King Arthur in Legend and History*. Totowa, N.J., 1974.

Blunt, Anthony. *Andrea Mantegna: The Triumph of Caesar*. London, 1975.

Brown, Mary Milbank. *The Secret History of Jeanne D'Arc, Princess, Maid of Orleans*. New York, 1962.

Burke, Peter. *Culture and Society in Renaissance Italy, 1420–1540.* New York, 1972.

Chambers, E. K. *Arthur of Britain.* London, 1927.

Dorey, T. A., ed. *Erasmus.* Albuquerque, N.M., 1970.

Elton, G. R. *Policy and Police: The Enforcement of the Reformation in the Age of Thomas Cromwell.* Cambridge, Eng., 1972.

Ferguson, Arthur B. *The Articulate Citizen and the English Renaissance.* Durham, N.C., 1965.

———. *Clio Unbound: Perceptions of the Social and Cultural Past in Renaissance England.* Durham, N.C., 1979.

———. *The Indian Summer of English Chivalry.* Chapel Hill, N.C., 1960.

Guy, J. A. *The Public Career of Sir Thomas More.* New Haven, 1980.

Henkel, Arthur, and Schöne, Albrecht. *Emblemata. Handbuch zur Sinnbildkunst des XVI und XVII Jahrhunderts.* Stuttgart, 1967.

Hind, Arthur M. *A History of Engraving and Etching, from the Fifteenth Century to the Year 1914,* 3rd ed. Boston, 1925; New York, 1963.

Holt, Elizabeth Gilmore, ed. *A Documentary History of Art,* vol. 1. Princeton, 1981.

Huizinga, Johann. *Erasmus of Rotterdam.* New York, 1952. (Unlike the 1924 edition by Scribner's, this includes a selection of letters.)

Huppert, George. *The Idea of History: Historical Erudition and Historical Philosophy in Renaissance France.* Urbana, Ill., 1970.

Ivins, W. M. *Prints and Visual Communication.* New York, 1969.

Judson, Alexander C. *Sidney's Appearance: A Study in Elizabethan Portraiture.* Indiana University Publications, Humanities Series 41, Bloomington, Ind., 1958.

Kelley, Donald R. *Foundation of Modern Historical Scholarship.* New York, 1970.

Kingsford, Charles Lethbridge, ed. *The First English Life of King Henry the Fifth, Written in 1513 by an Anonymous Author Known Commonly as the Translator of Livius.* Oxford, 1911.

Kipling, Gordon. "Henry VII and the Origins of Tudor Patronage." In Lytle and Orgel, *Patronage in the Renaissance.*

Koebner, R. " 'The Imperial Crown of this Realm': Henry VIII, Constantine the Great, and Polydore Vergil." *Bulletin of the Institute of Historical Research,* 26 (1963), 29–52.

Lee, Rensselaer W. "Ariosto's *Roger and Angelica* in Sixteenth-Century Art: Some Facts and Hypotheses." In *Studies in Late Medieval and Renaissance Painting in Honor of Millard Meiss,* vol. 1, ed. Irving Lavin and John Plummer. New York, 1977.

Levis, H. C. *Baziliωlogia: A Book of Kings.* New York, 1913.

Lewi, Angela. *The Thomas More Family Group.* London, 1974.

van Marle, R. *Iconographie de l'art profane au Moyen-Âge et à la Renaissance. II: Allégories et symboles.* The Hague, 1932.

Martindale, Andrew, introd. *The Complete Paintings of Mantegna,* notes and catalogue Niny Garavaglia. New York, 1967.

———. *The Triumphs of Caesar in the Collection of Her Majesty the Queen at Hampton Court.* London, 1979.

Mayor, A. Hyatt. *Prints & People: A Social History of Printed Pictures.* Princeton, 1971.

More, Thomas. *A Dyalogue Wheryn Be Treated Dyvers Maters as of the Veneracyon & Worship of Ymages. . . .* London, 1530.

Morison, Samuel Eliot. *Admiral of the Ocean Sea: A Life of Christopher Columbus,* 2 vols. Boston, 1942.

Morison, Stanley. *The Likeness of Thomas More: An Iconographical Survey of Three Centuries,* ed. and suppl. Nicolas Barker. New York, 1963.

Orgel, Stephen. "The Renaissance Artist as Plagiarist." *ELH,* 48 (1981), 476–95.

Panofsky, Erwin. "Erasmus and the Visual Arts." *Journal of the Warburg and Courtauld Institutes,* 32 (1969), 200–227.

———. *Problems in Titian, Mostly Iconographic.* New York, 1969.

Reid, George William. *Works of the Italian Engravers of the Fifteenth Century Reproduced in Facsimile by Photo-Intaglio.* London, 1884.

Reinach, Salomon. "Pégase, l'Hippogriffe et les Poètes." *Revue Archéologique,* 5th series, 9 (1920), 207–35.

Steadman, John M. "Perseus upon Pegasus and *Ovid Moralized.*" *Review of English Studies,* 9 (1958), 407–10.

Steinberg, S. H. *Five Hundred Years of Printing.* Penguin, 1961.

Strong, Roy. *The National Portrait Gallery, A Brief History.* London, 1969.

Taylor, Frank, and Roskell, John S., eds. *Gesta Henrici Quinti: The Deeds of Henry the Fifth.* Oxford, 1975.

Williamson, Hugh Ross. *Lorenzo the Magnificent.* London, 1974.

V. THE DEMOCRATIZATION OF FAME

From Monarchs to Individualists

There are numerous books available in which to observe the careers of the artists of this period and to notice the change in self-consciousness of themselves, their work, and their social positions. Those I have found most useful are listed below.

The lavish displays of sixteenth- and seventeenth-century kingship in the shape both of court festivities and "progresses" around the countryside and cities, including the designs for triumphal arches done by such as Dürer as well as Thomas Dekker, have become an important part of the discussion of the reigns of Charles V, Francis I, Elizabeth I, and others. See Stephen Orgel, *The Illusion of Power* (Berkeley, 1975); Roy Strong, *Splendor at Court: Renaissance Spectacle and the Theater of Power* (Boston, 1973); and Francis A. Yates, *Astraea: The Imperial Theme in the Sixteenth Century* (Boston, 1975). For Dürer's patron, whose celebrations or efforts at celebration are perhaps the most interesting aspect of his rule, see William C. McDonald, "Maximilian I of Hapsburg and the Veneration of Hercules: On the Revival of Myth and the German Renaissance," *Journal of Medieval and Renaissance Studies,* 6 (1976), 139–54.

Throughout its history, nationalism, whatever its political basis, is inseparable from a self-conscious manipulation of the images of the past and their meaning. On the beginnings of such an explicit sense of national culture in seventeenth-century Europe, see Orest Ranum, ed., *National Consciousness, History, and Political Culture in Early-Modern Europe* (Baltimore, 1975); and, specifically on the organization of French literary and artistic culture to the greater glory of Louis XIV, Ranum's *Artisans of Glory: Writers and Historical Thought in Seventeenth-Century France* (Chapel Hill, N.C., 1980).

On the Elizabethan and Jacobean literary man, see Gerald Eades Bentley, *The Profession of Dramatist in Shakespear's Time* (Princeton, 1971); Stephen J. Greenblatt, *Sir Walter Raleigh: The Renaissance Man and His Roles* (New Haven, 1973), and his *Renaissance Self-Fashioning: From More to Shakespeare* (Chicago, 1980); Jonathan Goldberg, *James I and the Politics of Literature* (Baltimore, 1983); Richard Helgerson, *Self-Crowned Laureates: Spenser, Johnson, and the Literary System* (Berkeley, 1983).

WORKS CITED

Alpers, Svetlana. "Interpretation Without Representation, or the Viewing of *Las Meninas.*" *Representations,* 1 (1982), 31–42.

Arbuthnot, John. *Life and Works,* ed. George A. Aitken. Oxford, 1892.

Bacon, Francis. *Selected Writings,* ed. Hugh G. Dick. New York, 1955.

Bercovitch, Sacvan. *The Puritan Origins of the American Self.* New Haven, 1975.

Blake, William. *Selected Poetry and Prose,* ed. Northrop Frye. New York, 1953.

Bolingbroke, Henry St. John. *Letters on the Study and Use of History,* 2 vols. London, 1752.

Boswell, James. *Life of Johnson* [1791]. London, 1953.

————. "A Poetical Espistle to Doctor Sterne, Parson Yorick, and Tristram Shandy." In *Sterne: The Critical Heritage,* ed. Alan B. Howes. London, 1974.

Brooks, Van Wyck. *The Dream of Arcadia: American Writers and Artists in Italy, 1760–1915.* New York, 1958.

Browne, Sir Thomas. *Prose Works,* ed. Norman J. Endicott. Garden City, N.Y., 1967.

Butler, Samuel. *Hudibras* [1663–1678], ed. John Wilders. Oxford, 1967.

Butterfield, L. H. "B. Franklin's Epitaph." *New Colophone,* 3 (1950), 9–39.

Carew, Thomas. *Poems, with His Masque Coelum Britannicum,* ed. Rhodes Dunlap. Oxford, 1949. [The masque was originally published in 1633.]

Charles I. *Eikon Basilike* [1649], ed. Philip A. Knachel. Ithaca, N.Y., 1966.

Churchill, Charles. *Poems,* 2 vols., ed. James Laver. London, 1933.

Defoe, Daniel. "The True-Born Englishman." In *Anthology of Poems on Affairs of State: Augustan Satirical Verse, 1660–1714,* ed. George deF. Lord. New Haven, 1975.

Descartes, René. *Discourse on Method* [1637] *and Other Writings,* tr. F. E. Sutcliffe, Penguin, 1968.

Diderot, Denis, and Falconet, Étienne. *Le Pour et le contre: Correspondance polémique sur le respect de la postérité, Pline, et les anciens auteurs qui ont parlé de peinture et de sculpture,* intro. Yves Benot. Paris, 1958.

Donne, John. *Letters,* ed. Edmund Gosse, 2 vols. London, 1899.

Dryden, John. *The Dramatic Works,* 6 vols., ed. Montague Summers. London, 1932.

————. *Poems and Fables,* ed. James Kinsley. Oxford, 1970.

Falconet, Étienne. *See* Diderot.

Foucault, Michel. *The Order of Things: An Archaeology of the Human Sciences.* New York, 1970.

Franklin, Benjamin. *Autobiography,* intro. Dixon Wechter; *Selected Writings,* ed. Larzer Ziff. New York, 1959.

Fraser, Antonia. *Cromwell, the Lord Protector.* New York, 1973.

Freud, Sigmund. *Introductory Lectures on Psychoanalysis,* tr. and ed. James Strachey. New York, 1966.

Fuller, Thomas. *The Worthies of England,* ed. John Freeman. London, 1952.

Gordon, D. J. "Poet and Architect: The Intellectual Setting of the Quarrel Between Ben Jonson and Inigo Jones." In *The Renaissance Imagination,* ed. Stephen Orgel. Berkeley, 1975.

Gray, Thomas. *See* Lonsdale.

Greene, Graham. *Lord Rochester's Monkey.* New York, 1974.

Grieg, J. Y. T. *See* Hume.

Grossman, Allen. "Milton's Sonnet 'On the late massacre in Piemont': A Note on the Vulnerability of Persons in a Revolutionary Situation," *Tri-Quarterly,* 23–24 (1972), 283–301.

Hall, Joseph. *Virgidemiarum* [(*The Book of Blows*]. In *English Poetic Satire,* ed. George S. Rousseau and Neil L. Rudenstine. New York, 1972.

Harvey, William. *Anatomical Exercitations, Concerning the Generation of Living Creatures.* London, 1653.

Heywood, Thomas. *An Apology for Actors in Three Books* [1614]. London, 1841.

Hobbes, Thomas. "The Answer of Mr. Hobbes to Sir Will. D'Avenant's Preface before Gondibert." In *Seventeenth-Century Verse and Drama,* vol. 1, ed.

Helen C. White, Ruth C. Wallerstein, and Ricardo Quintana. New York, 1967, 224–30.

——. *Leviathan,* ed. C. B. Macpherson, Penguin, 1968.

Hume, David. *Letters,* 2 vols., ed. J. Y. T. Greig. Oxford, 1932.

Jonson, Ben. *Complete Masques,* ed. Stephen Orgel. New Haven, 1969.

——. *Complete Poetry,* ed. William B. Hunter, Jr. Garden City, N.Y., 1963.

Kahr, Madlyn Millner. *Velázquez: The Art of Painting.* New York, 1976.

Locke, John. *An Essay Concerning Human Understanding,* ed. Peter H. Nidditch. Oxford, 1975.

Lonsdale, Roger, ed. *The Poems of Gray, Collins, and Goldsmith.* London, 1976.

Lukes, Steven. *Individualism.* New York, 1973.

Macpherson, C. B. *The Political Theory of Possessive Individualism: Hobbes to Locke.* New York, 1962.

Marvell, Andrew. "The First Anniversary of the Government Under His Highness the Lord Protector." In *Complete Poetry,* ed. George deF. Lord. New York, 1968, 93–104.

——. "An Horatian Ode upon Cromwell's Return from Ireland." In *Complete Poetry,* ed. Lord, 55–58.

Mattingly, Garrett. *Renaissance Diplomacy.* Boston, 1955.

Milton, John. *Complete Poems and Major Prose,* ed. Merritt Y. Hughes. New York, 1957.

Neale, J. E. *Queen Elizabeth I.* London, 1934.

Orgel, Stephen, and Strong, Roy. *Inigo Jones: The Theater of the Stuart Court.* Berkeley, 1973.

Perrault, Charles. *Contes de ma mère l'Oie.* Paris, 1932.

Pope, Alexander. *Poetry and Prose,* ed. Aubrey Williams. Boston, 1969.

Pottle, Frederick A. *James Boswell: The Earlier Years, 1740–1769.* New York, 1966.

Rochester, John Wilmot, Earl of. *Complete Poems,* ed. David M. Vieth. New Haven, 1968.

Rousseau, Jean-Jacques. *Confessions,* tr. J. M. Cohen, Penguin, 1954. [completed 1765, published 1781]

Shakespeare, William. *The Complete Works,* gen. ed., Alfred Harbage. Penguin, 1969.

Shelley, Percy Bysshe. *Shelley's Critical Prose,* ed. Bruce L. McElderry, Jr. Lincoln, Nebr., 1967.

Silverman, Kenneth. *The Life and Times of Cotton Mather.* New York, 1984.

Snyder, Joel. "*Las Meninas* and the Mirror of the Prince." *Critical Inquiry,* 11 (1985), 539–72.

Soriano, Marc. *Le Dossier Charles Perrault.* Paris, 1972.

Stone, Lawrence. *The Crisis of the Aristocracy, 1558–1641.* Oxford, 1965.

Tiffin, Walter F. *Gossip About Portraits.* London, 1866.

Vaughan, Benjamin. *See* Franklin.

Williams, Raymond. *Keywords: A Vocabulary of Culture and Society.* New York, 1976.

Wilmot, John, Earl of Rochester. *Complete Poems,* ed. David M. Vieth. New Haven, 1968.

OTHER USEFUL WORKS

Alpers, Svetlana. *The Art of Describing: Dutch Art in the Seventeenth Century.* Chicago, 1983.

Alsop, Joseph. *The Rare Art Traditions.* New York, 1982.

Barish, Jonas. *The Anti-theatrical Prejudice.* Berkeley, 1981.

Buffenoir, Hippolyte. *Les Portraits de Jean-Jacques Rousseau,* 2 vols. Paris, 1913.

Burtt, E. A. *The Metaphysical Foundations of Modern Science.* New York, 1952.

Fussell, Paul. *Samuel Johnson and the Life of Writing.* New York, 1971.

Goldscheider, Ludwig. *Johannes Vermeer.* London, 1958.

Halewood, William H. *Six Subjects of Reformation Art: A Preface to Rembrandt.* Toronto, 1982.

Harré, R., ed. *Early Seventeenth-Century Scientists.* London, 1965.

Holt, Elizabeth Gilmore. *A Documentary History of Art,* vol. 2. Princeton, 1958.

Lemay, J. A. Leo, ed. *The Oldest Revolutionary: Essays on Benjamin Franklin.* Philadelphia, 1976.

Magurn, Ruth Saunders, tr. and ed. *The Letters of Peter–Paul Rubens.* Cambridge, 1971.

Merton, Robert K. *Science, Technology, and Society in Seventeenth-Century England.* New York, 1970.

Millar, Oliver. *The Age of Charles I: Painting in England, 1620–1649* [Rubens and Van Dyck]. London, 1972.

Strong, Roy. *Van Dyck: Charles I on Horseback.* Penguin, 1972.

Volk, Mary Crawford. "On Velázquez and the Liberal Arts." *Art Bulletin,* 60 (1978), 69–86.

Wallace, Robert. *The World of Rembrandt, 1606–1669.* New York, 1968.

Woodfill, Walter L. *Musicians in English Society from Elizabeth to Charles I.* Princeton, 1953.

Yates, Francis. *The Rosicrucian Enlightenment.* London, 1972.

The Posture of Reticence and the Sanction of Neglect

WORKS CITED

Adair, Douglass. *Fame and the Founding Fathers,* ed. Trevor Colbourn. New York, 1974. (The title essay was originally written in 1967.)

———, and Schutz, John. *The Spur of Fame: Dialogues of John Adams and Benjamin Rush, 1805–1813.* San Marino, Calif., 1966.

Addison, Joseph. *Spectator,* no. 562 [July 2, 1714]. In *Works,* vol. 4. London, 1884.

Anonymous. "Of Genius." *The Occasional Paper,* 3, 10 (1719); repr. in *Augustan Reprint Society,* 4, 2 (1949), ed. Gretchen Graf Pahl.

Avineri, Shlomo. "Hegel and Nationalism." In *Hegel's Political Philosophy,* ed. Walter Kaufman. New York, 1970.

Baker, Herschel. *William Hazlitt.* Cambridge, Mass., 1962.

Baldwin, James. *Nobody Knows My Name.* New York, 1961.

Beethoven, Ludwig van. *Beethoven: A Documentary Study,* ed. H. C. Robbins. London, 1970.

Boyer, Abel. *The English Theophrastus: Or, The Manners of the Age.* London, 1702.

Bromwich, David. *Hazlitt: The Mind of a Critic.* New York, 1983.

Byron, George Gordon. *Byron: A Self-Portrait, Letters and Diaries, 1789–1824,* 2 vols., ed. Peter Quennell. London, 1950.

———. *"Famous in my time": Byron's Letters and Journals,* vol. 2 [1810–12], ed. Leslie A. Marchand. Cambridge, Mass., 1973.

———. *Selected Letters and Journals,* ed. Leslie A. Marchand. Cambridge, Mass., 1982.

Carlyle, Thomas. *On Heroes, Hero-Worship, and The Heroic in History* [1840]. London, 1870.

Coleridge, Samuel Taylor. *Selected Poetry and Prose,* ed. Elisabeth Schneider. New York, 1951.

Crèvecoeur, J. Hector St. John. *Letters from an American Farmer* [1781], ed. Warren Baxter Blake. London, 1958.

[Croft, Herbert]. "Young." In Samuel Johnson, *Lives of the English Poets*, 2 vols. [1779–81]. London, 1952.

Dickinson, Emily. *The Complete Poems*, ed. Thomas H. Johnson. Boston, 1960.

Diderot, Denis. *Paradoxe sur le comédien*, ed. Raymond Laubreaux. Paris, 1967.

Dircks, Richard J. *Richard Cumberland*. Boston, 1976.

Eliot, George, "Worldiness and Other Worldliness: The Poet Young." In *Essays and Leaves from a Note-Book*. New York, 1883.

Eliot, T. S. "Philip Massinger." In *Selected Essays, 1917–1932*. New York, 1932.

Emerson, Ralph Waldo. *Nature*. In *Essays and Lectures*, ed. Joel Porte. New York, 1983.

―――. *Representative Men*. In *Essays and Lectures*, ed. Porte.

Fisher, H. A. L. *Bonapartism*. Oxford, 1961.

Fleming, E. McClung. "From Indian Princess to Greek Goddess: The American Image, 1783–1815," *Winterthur Portfolio*, 3 (1967), 37–66.

Goldsmith, Oliver. *See* Lonsdale.

Grieg, J. Y. T. *See* Hume.

Hazlitt, William. *The Complete Works*, 21 vols., ed. P. P. Howe. London, 1930–34.

Hemingway, Ernest. *Selected Letters, 1917–1961*, ed. Carlos Baker. New York, 1981.

Hofstadter, Richard, ed. *Great Issues in American History*, 2 vols. New York, 1958.

Howe, Alan B., ed. *Sterne: The Critical Heritage*. London, 1974.

Hume, David. *Letters*, 2 vols., ed. J. Y. T. Greig. Oxford, 1932.

Hutt, Maurice, ed. *Napoleon*. Englewood Cliffs, N.J., 1972.

Jefferson, Thomas. *See* Hofstadter.

Jesse, William. *The Life of Beau Brummell by Captain Jesse* [1844], 2 vols. London, 1927.

Johnson, Samuel. *See* Croft.

Keats, John. *Complete Poems and Selected Letters*, ed. Clarence Dewitt Thorpe. New York, 1935.

―――. *The Letters of John Keats*, 2 vols., ed. Hyder Edward Rollins. Cambridge, Mass., 1958.

Leith, James A. *The Idea of Art as Propaganda in France, 1750–1799*. Toronto, 1965.

Leyda, Jay. *See* Melville.

Lonsdale, Roger, ed. *The Poems of Gray, Collins, and Goldsmith*. London, 1976.

Marvell, Andrew. *Complete Poetry*, ed. George deF. Lord. New York, 1968.

McGann, Jerome. "The Text, the Poem, and the Problem of History Method." In his *The Beauty of Inflections: Literary Investigations in Historical Method and Theory*. Oxford, 1985.

Medwin, Thomas. *Conversations of Lord Byron*, ed. Ernest J. Lovell, Jr. Princeton, 1966.

Melville, Herman. *The Portable Melville*, ed. Jay Leyda. New York, 1952.

Moers, Ellen. *The Dandy: Brummell to Beerbohm*. London, 1960.

Pope, Alexander. "Epistle IV, to Richard Boyle, Earl of Burlington." In *Poetry and Prose*, ed. Aubrey Williams. Boston, 1969.

Quennell, Peter. *Byron: The Years of Fame*. Hamden, Conn., 1967.

Quinn, Dorothy Mackey. "The Art Confiscations of the Napoleonic Wars," *American Historical Review*, 50 (1945), 437–60.

Robbins, H. C. *See* Beethoven.

Rollins, Hyder Edward. *See* Keats.

Russell, Bertrand. "On Denoting." In *Reading in Philosophical Analysis*, ed. Herbert Feigl and Wilfred Sellars. New York, 1949.

Schorsch, Anita. *Mourning Becomes America: Mourning Art in the New Nation*. Clinton, N.J., 1976.

Shelley, Mary. *Frankenstein* [1818]. In *Three Gothic Novels*, ed. Peter Fairclough; intro. Mario Praz. Penguin, 1968.

Shelley, Percy Bysshe. *Letters*, 2 vols., ed. Frederick L. Jones. Oxford, 1964.

Silverman, Kenneth. *A Cultural History of the American Revolution*. New York, 1976.

Thorpe, Clarence Dewitt. *See* Keats.

Tocqueville, Alexis de. *Democracy in America* [1835–39], tr. George Lawrence; ed. J. P. Mayer. New York, 1969.

Whitman, Walt. *Leaves of Grass and Selected Prose*, ed. John Kouwenhoven. New York, 1950.

Williams, Raymond. *Culture and Society, 1780–1950*. New York, 1958.

Wordsworth, William. *Selected Poems and Prefaces*, ed. Jack Stillinger. Boston, 1965.

Young, Edward. *Conjectures on Original Composition* [1759], ed. Edith J. Morley. Manchester, Eng., 1918.

OTHER USEFUL WORKS

Bate, Walter Jackson. *The English Poet and the Burden of the Past*. Cambridge, Mass., 1970.

Berman, Marshall. *The Politics of Authenticity*. New York, 1970.

Birley, Robert. *Sunk Without Trace*. New York, 1962.

Bloom, Harold. *The Anxiety of Influence*. New York, 1970.

Buonaparte, Napoleon. "Sur l'amour de la patrie." In *Napoléon inconnu*, ed. F. Masson and Guido Biagi. Paris, 1895.

Colton, Judith. *The "Parnasse françoise": Titon du Tillet and the Origins of the Monument to Genius*. New Haven, 1979.

Cummings, Frederick J.; Schnapper, Antoine; and Rosenblum, Robert. *French Painting, 1774–1830: The Age of Revolution*. Detroit, 1975.

Disraeli, Isaac. *The Literary Character* [1840], ed. B. Disraeli. London, 1859.

Dowd, David L. "The French Revolution and the Painters," *French Historical Studies*, 1 (1958), 127–48.

Einstein, Alfred. *Music in the Romantic Era*. New York, 1947.

Fleming, E. McClung. "The American Image as Indian Princess, 1765–1783." *Winterthur Portfolio*, 2 (1965), 65–81.

Fried, Michael. *Theatricality and Absorption*. Berkeley, 1980.

Goode, J. M. *Outdoor Sculpture in Washington, D.C.* Washington, D.C., 1974.

Gross, John. *The Rise and Fall of the Man of Letters*. London, 1969.

Harris, Neil. *The Artist in American Society: The Formative Years, 1790–1860*. New York, 1966.

Herold, J. Christopher. *The Age of Napoleon*. New York, 1963.

Hutt, Maurice, ed. *Napoleon*. Englewood Cliffs, N.J., 1972.

Janson, H. W. "Originality as a Ground for Judgment of Excellence." In *16 Studies*. New York, 1973.

Keynes, Geoffrey. *Bibliography of William Hazlitt*. London, 1931.

Laver, James. *Dandies*. London, 1968.

Lefebvre, Georges. *Napoleon: From 18 Brumaire to Tilsit, 1799–1807*. New York, 1969.

Maurois, André. *Napoleon: A Pictorial Biography*. London, 1963.

McFarland, Thomas. "The Originality Paradox." *New Literary History*, 5 (1973–74), 447–76.

Meisel, Martin. *Realizations: Narrative, Pictorial, and Theatrical Arts in Nineteenth-Century England*. Princeton, 1983.

Messina, Salvatore. *Le Plagiat littéraire et artistique dans la doctrine, le législation comparée et le jurisprudence internationale*, Académie de Droit International, 52 (1935), 443–582.

Neumeyer, Alfred. "Monuments to Genius in German Classicism." *Journal of the Warburg and Courtauld Institutes*, 2 (1938–39), 159–63.

Park, Roy. *Hazlitt and the Spirit of the Age: Abstraction and Critical Theory.* Oxford, 1971.

Parker, Harold T. "The Formation of Napoleon's Personality: An Exploratory Essay." *French Historical Studies,* 7 (1971–72), 6–26.

Poe, Edgar Allan. *A Chapter of Autography* [1836], ed. Don C. Seitz. New York, 1926.

Trilling, Lionel. *Sincerity and Authenticity.* Cambridge, Mass., 1972.

Wilson, Arthur M. *Diderot.* New York, 1972.

Democratic Theater and the Natural Performer

WORKS CITED

Adair, Douglass, and Schutz, John. *The Spur of Fame: Dialogues of John Adams and Benjamin Rush, 1805–1813.* San Marino, Calif., 1966.

Alvarez, A. *The Savage God: A Study of Suicide.* New York, 1972.

Ames, Fisher. "The Future of American Literature." In *American Thought and Writing,* 2 vols., ed. Russel B. Nye and Norman S. Grabo. Boston, 1965.

Barbey d'Aurevilly, J. A. *Anatomy of Dandyism* [*Du Dandysme et du Georges Brummell*], tr. D. B. Wyndham-Lewis. New York, 1928.

Barnum, P. T. *Barnum's Own Story,* ed. Waldo P. Browne. New York, 1927.

Barth, Gunter. *City People.* New York, 1980.

Barton, Bruce. *The Man Nobody Knows: A Discovery of the Real Jesus.* Indianapolis, 1925.

Baudelaire, Charles. "Le Peintre de la vie moderne" [1863]. In *Oeuvres,* vol. 2, ed. Y.-G. Le Dantec. Paris, 1932.

Baudelaire on Poe: Critical papers, tr. and ed. Lois Hyslop and Francis E. Hyslop, Jr. State College, Pennsylvania, 1952.

Baxter, Maurice G. *One and Inseparable: Daniel Webster and the Union.* Cambridge, Mass., 1984.

Beerbohm, Max. *The Incomparable Max.* New York, 1962.

———. *Seven Men and Two Others.* London, 1950.

Benkovitz, Miriam J. *Frederick Rolfe: Baron Corvo.* London, 1977.

Broun, Heywood. "Dying for 'Dear Old–': A Study in Sportsmanship." In Odell Shepard, ed. *Essays of 1925.* Hartford, Conn., 1926.

Brown, William Burlie. *The People's Choice: The Presidential Image in Campaign Biographies.* Baton Rouge, La., 1960.

Bullock, Alan. *Hitler: A Study in Tyranny,* rev. ed. New York, 1958.

Buonaparte, Napoleon. *See* Herold.

Carlyle, Thomas. *Sartor Resartus* [1834], ed. Charles Frederick Harrold. New York, 1937.

Connelly, Thomas L., and Bellows, Barbara L. *God and General Longstreet: The Lost Cause and the Southern Mind.* Baton Rouge, La., 1982.

Cowper, William. *Works,* ed. and with life by Robert Southey, 15 vols. London, 1836.

[Croft, Herbert]. "Young." In Samuel Johnson, *Lives of the English Poets,* 2 vols. [1779–81]. London, 1952.

Cunningham, Noble E., Jr. *The Image of Thomas Jefferson in the Public Eye: Portraits for the People, 1800–1809.* Charlottesville, Va., 1981.

Decker, Andrew. "A Legacy of Shame: Nazi Art Loot in Austria." *Art News,* 83 (December 1984), 54–76.

Dickinson, Emily. *The Complete Poems,* ed. Thomas H. Johnson. Boston, 1960.

———. *Selected Letters,* ed. Thomas H. Johnson. Cambridge, Mass., 1971.

Dos Passos, John. *The Best Times.* New York, 1966.

———. *The Fourteenth Chronicle.* Boston, 1973.

Douglass, Frederic. *See* McClinton.

Ellis, Julian. *Fame and Failure: The Story of Certain Celebrities Who Rose Only to Fall*. Philadelphia, 1919.

Emerson, Ralph Waldo. *Representative Men*. In *Essays and Lectures*, ed. Joel Porte. New York, 1983.

Etulain, Richard W., ed. *Jack London on the Road: The Tramp Diary and Other Hobo Writings*. Logan, Utah, 1979.

Faulkner, William. *Selected Letters*, ed. Joseph Blotner. New York, 1977.

Forgie, George B. *Patricide in the House Divided: A Psychological Interpretation of Lincoln and His Age*. New York, 1976.

Gibbon, Edward. *The Decline and Fall of the Roman Empire*, 5 vols., ed. H. H. Milman. Philadelphia, n.d.

Grimsted, David. *Melodrama Unveiled: American Theater and Culture, 1800–1850*. Chicago, 1968.

Harmetz, Aljean. *The Making of the Wizard of Oz*. New York, 1977.

Harris, Neil. *Humbug: The Art of P. T. Barnum*. Boston, 1973.

Hawthorne, Nathaniel. "Chiefly About War Matters." In *Collected Works*, vol. 12. Boston, 1893.

Hazlitt, William. *The Complete Works*, 21 vols., ed. P. P. Howe. London, 1930–34.

Heggen, Thomas. *Mister Roberts*. Boston, 1946.

Hemingway, Ernest. *Selected Letters, 1917–1961*, ed. Carlos Baker. New York, 1981.

Herold, J. Christopher, ed. *The Mind of Napoleon*. New York, 1955.

Higgins, David. *Portrait of Emily Dickinson: The Poet and Her Prose*. New Brunswick, N.J., 1967.

Higginson, Thomas Wentworth. "A Letter to a Young Contributor" [April, 1862]. In *Atlantic Essays*. Boston, 1871.

Howells, William Dean. *Life of Abraham Lincoln*, intro. Clyde C. Walton. Bloomington, Ind., 1960.

Hubbard, Elbert. *Little Journeys to the Homes of Great Businessmen*. Aurora, N.Y., 1909.

Hyde, H. Montgomery. *Oscar Wilde*. New York, 1975.

Hyslop, Lois and Francis E. *See* Baudelaire.

In After Days: Thoughts on the Future Life by W. D. Howells, Elizabeth Stuart Phelps, John Bigelow, Julia Ward Howe, Henry M. Alden, Thomas Wentworth Higginson, William Hanna Thomson, Guglielmo Ferrero, and Henry James; with portraits. New York, 1910.

James, Robert Rhodes. *Churchill: A Study in Failure, 1900–1939*. London, 1970.

Jefferson, Thomas. *Papers*, ed. Julian Boyd, vol. 16 (30 November 1789 to 4 July 1790). Princeton, 1961.

Jesse, William. *The Life of Beau Brummell by Captain Jesse* [1844], 2 vols. London, 1927.

Johnson, Osa. *I Married Adventure*. Garden City, N.Y., 1940.

Johnson, Samuel. *The Idler and the Adventurer*, ed. W. J. Bate, John M. Bullitt, and L. F. Powell. New Haven, 1963.

Kanin, Garson. *Hollywood*. New York, 1974.

Kinmouth, Earl H. *The Self-made Man in Meiji Japanese Thought: From Samurai to Salary-Man*. Berkeley, 1981.

Klapp, Orrin. *Symbolic Leaders*. New York, 1964.

Kunhardt, Dorothy Meserve, and Kunhardt, Philip B., Jr. *Mathew Brady and His World*. Alexandria, Va., 1971.

Labor, Earle. *Jack London*. New York, 1974.

Leggett, John. *Ross and Tom: Two American Tragedies*. New York, 1974.

Leith, James A. *The Idea of Art as Propaganda in France, 1750–1799*. Toronto, 1965.

Lincoln, Abraham. *Collected Works*, 9 vols., ed. Roy P. Basler. New Brunswick, N.J., 1953–55.

Lindbergh, Anne Morrow. *War Within and War Without. Diaries and Letters, 1939–44*. New York, 1980.

London, Jack. *Martin Eden*. New York, 1909.

———. *Michael, Brother of Jerry*. New York, 1917.

———. *Novels and Social Writings*, ed. Donald Pizer. New York, 1982.

Lorant, Stefan. *Lincoln: A Picture Story of His Life*, rev. ed. New York, 1969.

Loveland, Anne C. *Emblem of Liberty: The Image of Lafayette in the American Mind*. Baton Rouge, La., 1971.

McClinton, Katharine Morrison. *The Chromolithographs of Louis Prang*. New York, 1973.

Mellon, James, comp. and ed. *The Face of Lincoln*. New York, 1979.

Meserve, Frederick Hill. *See* Kunhardt.

Minnelli, Vincente. *I Remember It Well*. Garden City, N.Y., 1974.

Moers, Ellen. *The Dandy: Brummell to Beerbohm*. London, 1960.

Morgan, Ted. *Churchill: Young Man in a Hurry, 1874–1915*. New York, 1982.

Phelan, James. *Howard Hughes: The Hidden Years*. New York, 1976.

Phelps, Elizabeth Stuart. See *In After Days*.

Poe, Edgar Allan. *Essays and Reviews*, ed. G. R. Thompson. New York, 1984.

———. *Poems and Tales*, ed. Patrick F. Quinn. New York, 1984.

Reynolds, Sir Joshua. *Discourses on Art*. New York, 1961.

Richardson, Samuel. *Clarissa* [1747–48], 4 vols. London, 1932.

Rolfe, Frederick [Baron Corvo]. *Hadrian the Seventh*. London, 1904.

Roosevelt, Theodore. *See* Sprague.

Rosenstiel, Léonie. *Nadia Boulanger: A Life in Music*. New York, 1982.

Roxan, David, and Wanstall, Ken. *The Rape of Art: The Story of Hitler's Plunder of the Great Masterpieces of Europe*. New York, 1964.

Schulberg, Budd. *The Four Seasons of Success*. Garden City, N.Y., 1972.

Sellars, Charles Coleman. *Benjamin Franklin in Portraiture*. New Haven, 1962.

Sennett, Richard. *The Fall of Public Man*. New York, 1977.

Shelley, Percy Bysshe. *Shelley's Critical Prose*, ed. Bruce L. McElderry, Jr. Lincoln, Nebr., 1967.

Shepard, Odell. *See* Broun.

Simon, Kate. *Bronx Primitive: Portraits in a Childhood*. New York, 1982.

Slick, Grace. Interview. *Oui* (February 1977).

Smith, Red, "George Brett's Public." The *New York Times*, 24 August 1980, S3.

Southey, Robert. *See* Cowper.

Speer, Albert. *Inside the Third Reich*, tr. Richard Winston and Clara Winston. New York, 1970.

Spencer, Scott. *Endless Love*. New York, 1980.

Sprague, Marshall. *A Gallery of Dudes*. Boston, 1967.

Symons, A. J. A. *The Quest for Corvo* [1934]. Preface by Julian Symons. London, 1966.

Thoreau, Henry David. *Walden*, ed. J. Lyndon Shanley. Princeton, 1971.

Tocqueville, Alexis de. *Democracy in America* [1835–39], tr. George Lawrence; ed. J. P. Mayer. New York, 1969.

Toll, Robert C. *On with the Show*. New York, 1976, 246.

Twain, Mark. *The Complete Short Stories*, ed. Charles Neider. New York, 1958.

———. *Mark Twain's Notebook*, ed. Albert Bigelow Paine. New York, 1935.

———. *Pudd'nhead Wilson* and *Those Extraordinary Twins*, ed. Sidney E. Berger. New York, 1980.

Voss, Frederick, and Barber, James. *Daniel Webster*, Washington, D.C., 1982.

Webster, Daniel. *See* Baxter.

Weems, Mason Locke. *The Life of Washington*, ed. Marcus Cunliffe. Cambridge, Mass., 1962.

Whitman, Walt. *Leaves of Grass and Selected Prose*, ed. John Kouwenhoven. New York, 1950.
Wills, Garry. *Cincinnatus: George Washington and the Enlightenment*. Garden City, N.Y., 1984.
Wordsworth, William. *Selected Poems and Prefaces*, ed. Jack Stillinger. Boston, 1965.
Wyllie, Lawrence. *The Self-Made Man in America*. 1954.
Yeats, William Butler. *Collected Poems*. New York, 1959.

OTHER USEFUL WORKS

Adams, Henry. *The Education of Henry Adams*. Boston, 1918.
Adams, William Howard. *Jefferson and the Arts: An Extended View*. Washington, D.C., 1976.
Anderson, Quentin. "John Dewey's American Democrat." *Daedalus*, vol. 108, no. 3 (Summer 1979), 145–59.
———. "Practical and Visionary Americans." *American Scholar*, vol. 45, no. 3 (Summer 1976), 405–18.
———. "Property and Vision in 19th-Century America." *Virginia Quarterly Review*, vol. 54, no. 3 (Summer 1978), 385–410.
Banta, Martha. *Failure and Success in America: A Literary Debate*. Princeton, 1978.
Baudelaire, Charles. *Selected Critical Studies*, ed. D. Parmée. Cambridge, Eng., 1949.
Becker, Ernest. *The Denial of Death*. New York, 1973.
Berman, Eleanor Davidson. *Thomas Jefferson Among the Arts: An Essay in Early American Esthetics*. New York, 1947.
Bulwer-Lytton, Edward George. *Pelham, or, The Adventures of a Gentleman*, ed. Jerome J. McGann. Lincoln, Neb., 1972.
Bush, Alfred L. *The Life Portraits of Thomas Jefferson*. Charlottesville, Va., 1962.
Cameron, Sharon. *Lyric Time: Emily Dickinson and the Limits of Genre*. Baltimore, 1979.
Cary, Diana Serra. *Hollywood's Children*. Boston, 1979.
Cawelti, John. *Apostles of the Self-Made Man*. Chicago, 1965.
Christopher, Milbourne. *Houdini: The Untold Story*. New York, 1969.
Connolly, Cyril. *Enemies of Promise*, rev. ed. London, 1948.
DiMeglio, John. *Vaudeville, U.S.A.* Bowling Green, Ky., 1973.
Epstein, Joseph. *Ambition*. New York, 1980.
Ewen, Stuart. *Captains of Consciousness: Advertising and the Social Roots of the Consumer Culture*. New York, 1976.
Farmer, Richard, and Hirsch, Steven. *The Suicide Syndrome*. London, 1980.
Fest, Joachim C. *Hitler*, tr. Richard and Clara Winston. New York, 1974.
Fiedler, Leslie. *Freaks: Myths and Images of the Secret Self*. New York, 1978.
Fitzgerald, F. Scott. *The Crack Up*, ed. Edmund Wilson. New York, 1945.
Forster, E. M. "Anonymity: An Inquiry." In *Two Cheers for Democracy*. Penguin, 1951.
Fox, Richard Wightman, and Lears, T. J. Jackson, eds. *The Culture of Consumption*. New York, 1983.
Giacometti, Georges. *La Vie et l'oeuvre de Houdon*, 2 vols. Paris, 1929.
Giddings, Anthony. *The Sociology of Suicide: A Selection of Readings*. London, 1971.
Goode, William J. *The Celebration of Heroes: Prestige as a Social Control System*. Berkeley, 1978.
Haber, Tom Burns. *A. E. Housman*. New York, 1967.
Halsey, T. H. "Benjamin Franklin: His Interest in the Arts." In *Benjamin Franklin and His Circle: A Catalogue of an Exhibition*. New York, 1936.
Harris, Neil. *The Artist in American Society: The Formative Years, 1790–1860*. New York, 1966.

Higginson, Thomas Wentworth. "Emily Dickinson." In *Carlyle's Laugh and Other Surprises*. Boston, 1909.

Hobsbawm, Eric, and Ranger, Terence, eds. *The Invention of Tradition*. New York, 1983.

Holt, Elizabeth Gilmore, ed. *The Triumph of Art for the Public: The Emerging Role of Exhibitions and Critics*. Garden City, N.Y., 1979.

Howells, William Dean. "The Man of Letters as a Man of Business." In *Literature and Life*. New York, 1902.

Idzerda, Stanley. "When and Why Lafayette Became a Revolutionary." In *The Consortium on Revolutionary Europe*. Athens, Ga., 1978.

Lahr, John. *Automatic Vaudeville*. New York, 1984.

Lasch, Christopher. *The Culture of Narcissism*. New York, 1979.

Lifton, Robert J. *Revolutionary Immortality: Mao Tse-tung and the Chinese Cultural Revolution*. New York, 1968.

Lynn, Kenneth S. *The Dream of Success: A Study of the Modern American Imagination*. Boston, 1955.

Maehr, Martin L. *Sociocultural Origins of Achievement*. Monterey, Calif., 1974.

McKendrick, Neil. "Josiah Wedgwood and the Commercialization of the Potteries." In *The Birth of a Consumer Society*, ed. Neil McKendrick, John Brewer, and J. H. Plumb. Bloomington, Ind., 1982.

McLean, Albert F., Jr. *American Vaudeville as Ritual*. Lexington, Ky., 1965.

Meredith, Roy. *Mr. Lincoln's Camera Man: Mathew B. Brady*. New York, 1946.

Misruchi, Ephraim. *Success and Opportunity: A Study of Anomie*. Glencoe, Ill., 1964.

Monaco, James, ed. *Celebrity*. New York, 1978.

Moody, Richard. *The Astor Place Riots*. Bloomington, Ind., 1958.

Newhall, Beaumont. *The History of Photography*. New York, 1964.

Oliva, Achille Bonito. *Europe/America: The Different Avant-gardes*. Milan, 1976.

Oliver, Andrew. *Portraits of John and Abigail Adams*. Cambridge, Mass., 1967.

O'Neal, William Bainter. *Jefferson's Fine Arts Library: His Selections for the University of Virginia Together with His Own Architectural Books*. Charlottesville, Va., 1976.

Poggioli, Renato. *The Theory of the Avant-Garde*, tr. Gerald Fitzgerald. Cambridge, Mass., 1968.

Poirier, Richard. *The Performing Self*. New York, 1971.

Quick, Michael, et al. *American Portraiture in the Grand Manner: 1720–1920*. Los Angeles, 1981.

Rank, Otto. "The Artist's Fight with Art" and "Success and Fame." In *The Myth of the Birth of the Hero and Other Writings*, ed. Philip Freund. New York, 1959.

Rosnow, Ralph, and Fine, Gary Alan. *Rumor and Gossip: The Social Psychology of Hearsay*. New York, 1976.

Rourke, Constance. *Trumpets of Jubilee*. New York, 1927.

Sainsbury, Peter. *Suicide in London: An Ecological Study*. London, 1955.

Schickel, Richard. *His Picture in the Papers*. New York, 1973.

———. *Intimate Strangers: The Culture of Celebrity*. New York, 1985.

Schoeck, Helmut. *Envy: A Theory of Social Behavior*, tr. Michael Glemry and Betty Ross. New York, 1969.

Sennett, Richard. *Authority*. New York, 1980.

Shapiro, Theda. *Painters and Politics: The European Avant-Garde and Society, 1900–1925*. New York, 1976.

Shaw, Peter. *The Character of John Adams*. Chapel Hill, N.C., 1976.

Silverman, Kenneth. *A Cultural History of the American Revolution*. New York, 1976.

Simpson, Eileen. *Poets in Their Youth: A Memoir*. New York, 1982.

Sobel, Bernard. *A Pictorial History of Vaudeville*. New York, 1961.

Somkin, Fred. *Unquiet Eagle: Memory and Desire in the Idea of American Freedom, 1815–1860*. Ithaca, N.Y., 1967.

Sprott, S. E. *The English Debate on Suicide from Donne to Hume*. LaSalle, Ill., 1961.

Stein, Jean, with Plimpton, George. *Edie*. New York, 1982.

Talese, Gay. *The Overreachers*. New York, 1965.

Ulmer, Gregory L. *The Legend of Herostratus: Existential Envy in Rousseau and Unamuno*. Gainsville, Fla., 1977.

Weber, Max. *The Theory of Social and Economic Development*, tr. A. M. Henderson and Talcott Parsons; ed. and intro. Talcott Parsons. New York, 1947.

Wecter, Dixon. *The Hero in America: A Chronicle of Hero-Worship*. New York, 1941.

Wick, Wendy C. *George Washington: An American Icon: The Eighteenth-Century Graphic Portraits*, intro. Lillian B. Miller. Charlottesville, Va., 1982.

Woolf, Cecil. *A Bibliography of Frederick Rolfe, Baron Corvo*. London, 1957.

Index